The Tiananmen Papers

THE TIANANMEN PAPERS

COMPILED BY

Zhang Liang

EDITED BY

Andrew J. Nathan and Perry Link

WITH AN AFTERWORD BY ORVILLE SCHELL

PublicAffairs

NEW YORK

Library of Congress Cataloging-in-Publication Data

The Tiananmen papers / edited by Andrew J. Nathan and Perry Link; with an afterword by Orville Schell.—1st ed.

p.   cm.

Includes index.

ISBN 1–58648–012-X

1. China—History—Tiananmen Square Incident, 1989.

2. China—Politics and government—1976–

I. Nathan, Andrew J. (Andrew James), 1943– II. Link, E. Perry (Eugene Perry), 1944–

DS779.32.T537 2001

951.058—dc21   00–045823

10 9 8 7 6 5 4 3 2

Contents

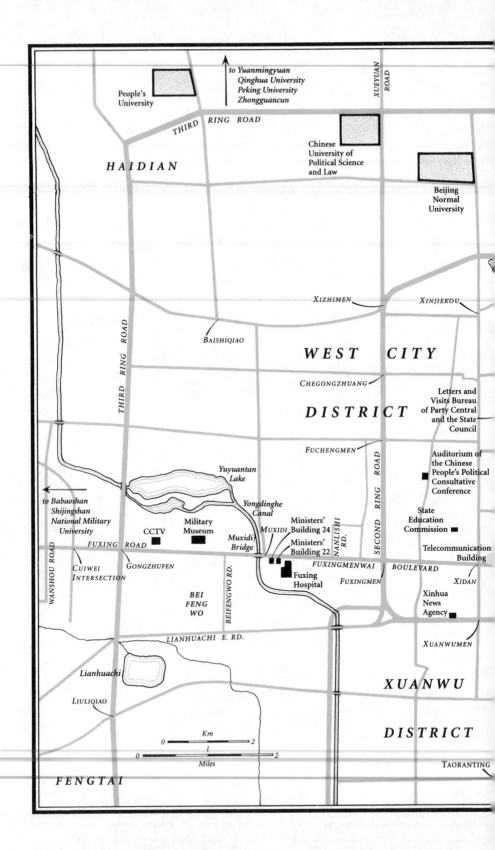

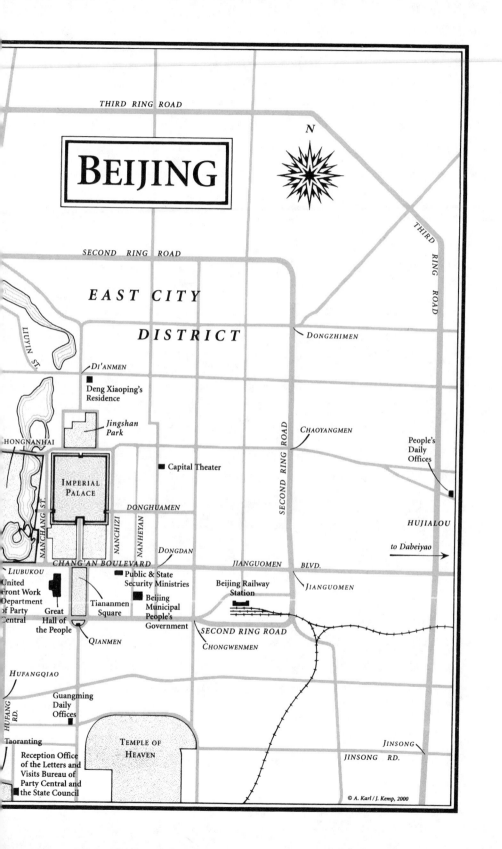

THIRD RING ROAD

BEIJING

N

SECOND RING ROAD

EAST CITY

DISTRICT

DONGZHIMEN

LIUYIN ST.

DI'ANMEN

Deng Xiaoping's
Residence

Jingshan
Park

CHAOYANGMEN

People's
Daily
Offices

ZHONGNANHAI

Capital Theater

IMPERIAL
PALACE

SECOND RING ROAD

DONGHUAMEN

HUJIALOU

NANCHANG ST.

NANCHIZI

NANHEYAN

to Dabeiyao

DONGDAN

CHANG'AN BOULEVARD

JIANGUOMEN   BLVD.

LIUBUKOU

United
Front Work
Department
of Party
Central

Public & State
Security Ministries

Beijing Railway
Station

JIANGUOMEN

Great
Hall of
the People

Tiananmen
Square

Beijing
Municipal
People's
Government

SECOND RING ROAD

QIANMEN

CHONGWENMEN

HUFANGQIAO

Guangming
Daily
Offices

HUFANG
RD.

Taoranting

JINSONG

Reception Office
of the Letters and
Visits Bureau of
Party Central and
the State Council

TEMPLE OF
HEAVEN

JINSONG   RD.

© A. Karl / J. Kemp, 2000

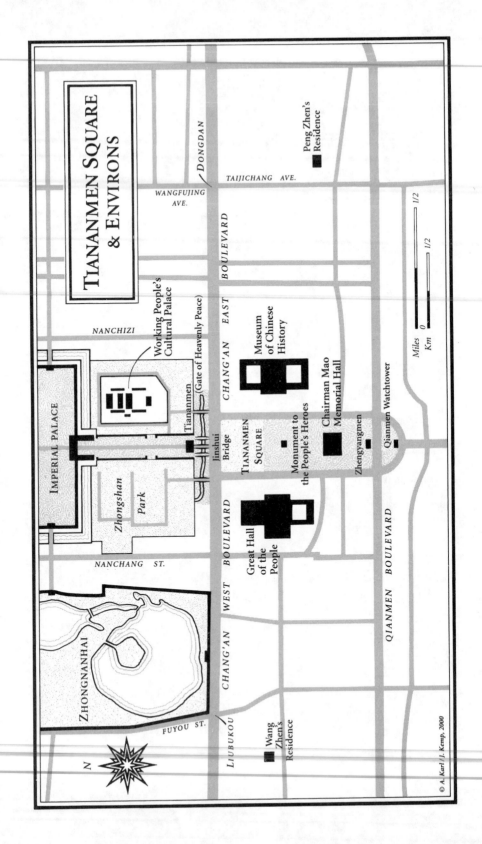

TIANANMEN SQUARE & ENVIRONS

DONGDAN

Peng Zhen's Residence

TAIJICHANG AVE.

WANGFUJING AVE.

NANCHIZI

Working People's Cultural Palace

(Gate of Heavenly Peace)

Tiananmen

Jinshui Bridge

CHANG'AN EAST BOULEVARD

Museum of Chinese History

IMPERIAL PALACE

Zhongshan Park

TIANANMEN SQUARE

Monument to the People's Heroes

Chairman Mao Memorial Hall

Zhengyangmen

Qianmen Watchtower

NANCHANG ST.

WEST BOULEVARD

Great Hall of the People

QIANMEN BOULEVARD

ZHONGNANHAI

CHANG'AN

LIUBUKOU

Wang Zhen's Residence

FUYOU ST.

N

© A.Karl / J. Kemp, 2000

Miles 0   1/2

Km   0   1/2

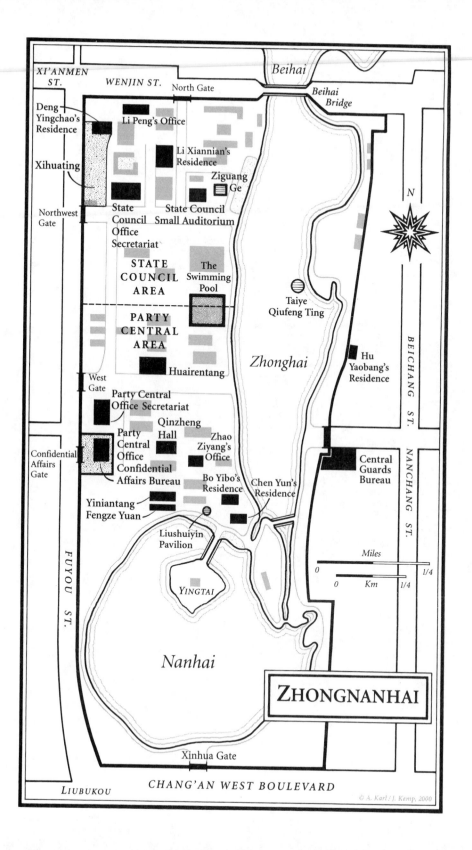

Reflections on June Fourth

ZHANG LIANG

Twelve years is an instant in history but a long time in a person's life. For one who experienced it, June 4, 1989, weighs heavily in the memory. History seems frozen there. To write about June Fourth is to recall the blood of thousands of young people spilled on the streets around Chang'an Boulevard in Beijing. Time may wash away the bloodstains, but not their memory. History and the people will ultimately judge June Fourth as one of the most dramatic and significant episodes in the worldwide pursuit of democracy in the twentieth century. Certainly it was the greatest event of that kind in China.

June Fourth was not merely a student protest or a patriotic democracy movement. It was the culmination of the biggest, broadest, longest-lasting, and most influential pro-democracy demonstrations anywhere in the world in the twentieth century. It also came to a tragic and painful end, in blood and in victory for dictatorship.

The failure of the June Fourth movement was inevitable, as we must acknowledge when we draw lessons from the painful experience. It did achieve significant effects: The movement encompassed all media and reached to almost every major Chinese city; to virtually all institutions of higher learning; to nearly half of the professional and technical high schools; to many mines, factories, and offices; and into some rural areas. Altogether, nearly a hundred million people participated in one form or another. The movement was autonomous, spontaneous, and disorderly—in some ways a pressure valve for popular dissatisfaction and anger with the government. But it failed because of the weakness of the reform faction at highest levels of Party leadership, because of divisions among the demonstrators

and their lack of a tight organization or program, and because of the gulf that separated the intellectuals from the workers and farmers. The movement's very failure constitutes one proof that it was not—as its enemies charged—an organized,
plotted "counterrevolutionary riot" or outbreak of "turmoil."

This patriotic democracy movement ended in tragedy, but it left an important
legacy. Those who worked for the collapse of the Eastern European Communist
systems and the dissolution of the Soviet Union doubtless drew some lessons
from its failures.

Remembering June Fourth evokes strong emotions. China has undergone
great changes in the subsequent years, but those who wish to serve the country
must still reflect deeply on the lessons it offers. Such reflection, because it is
banned, has yet to appear in public inside China. My own view is that in thinking
about the trends and possibilities in China today, we should try to be cool and
rational and not allow emotion to prevent us from looking squarely at China's
actual conditions. I see four lessons.

First, the arrival of democracy in China will have to depend on people in
China. Even though the Chinese Communist regime has become thoroughly corrupt, it has also strengthened itself through economic growth and the improvement in people's lives, and these achievements have enabled it to intensify its
organizational penetration into almost every corner of society. There is no political force in China that can stand up to it. People who do not like what the Party
does must realize that they have nowhere else to turn; they can rely only on themselves. Even though the end of communism in China seems a foregone conclusion, the fall of the Chinese Communist Party will be accomplished not by an
outside force but only by its own members.

Second, reversal of the verdict on June Fourth is another historical inevitabil-
ity, as well as the wish of most of the Chinese people. June Fourth weighs on the
spirits of every Chinese patriot, and almost every Chinese knows that official
reevaluation is just a matter of time. The Party's top leadership has been divided
about the event ever since it occurred. By now many of those responsible for the
decision to crack down—notably Deng Xiaoping and others of the Party
Elders—have passed away. Calls to reverse the verdict have grown stronger both
inside and outside the Party. These calls will eventually form the mainstream, and
the liberal forces in the Party will undoubtedly respond by seizing a historic
opportunity not only to reverse the verdict but to move toward discarding the
Communist system.

Third, the pro-democracy faction in the Party is the key force for pushing political change in China. The Chinese Communist Party has long since ceased to be a traditional Communist party. It is now a mélange of factions with diverse goals and differing ideologies. The differences between radicals and conservatives in the Party are now sharper than those between the Party and its traditional rival, the Kuomintang. The Chinese Communist Party resembles the Communist Party of the Soviet Union around 1989. What looks on the outside like a solid structure can break into pieces overnight. What will replace the Chinese Communist Party will probably be a new force that emerges from within it, a group that regrets the errors of the Communist system more deeply than anyone else, a group deeply committed to establishing a healthy democratic system. This group will unite with democratic forces at home and abroad to establish a truly democratic system.

Fourth, the building of democracy in China has to depend on forces rooted inside China. Those who have worked overseas for democracy, freedom, and rule of law and who have sought the support of the international community have done necessary work. But the basic solutions to China's problems must be sought at home. People committed to democracy and freedom must imitate Zhao Ziyang's spirit of "If I don't walk into the flames, who will?" and risk the sometimes inevitable price of self-sacrifice. If people studying overseas really want to devote their lives to the motherland, they should return home and join with the liberals inside the Party to stand unambiguously with the masses of workers and farmers. The mentality of one-quarter of the people in China's rural areas is still mired in the 1930s. Chinese democracy still has a long, hard road before it; we need as many well-educated activists as we can get.

June Fourth happened over a decade ago but has hardly faded in people's memories. Far too many questions about it have never been answered. The first step in achieving an accurate, complete, and objective evaluation is to publish the facts that restore the true face of history. As a witness to the events as well as a participant, I feel it is my duty to the Chinese people and to history to publish a complete and faithful record of the decisions that lay behind what happened. These materials are authentic; the documents, both those that are translated and those that are summarized in this book, speak for themselves.

The material is arranged in day-by-day chronology beginning with the death of Hu Yaobang on April 15, 1989, and ending with the Fourth Plenum of the Thirteenth Central Committee on June 24. Each day's records include, in this order, high-level central Party decisions, accounts of the situation around the country, and international responses and media reports. The materials are presented with a minimum of commentary so that the reader can make independent judgments.

The book reveals the entire course of events—and especially the decisions of the top leaders—that led to June Fourth. Some of the material published here is unknown to top Party people even today. But this book will withstand the test of history, and I hope it will also make a fundamental contribution to building democratic government in China.

As Lu Xun said, "A true warrior dares to stare the sadness of life in the face and to see the blood that drips there."[1] In memorializing June Fourth, this is the historic choice we too must make.

---

[1] Lu Xun (1881–1936) is widely regarded as China's greatest modern writer. The quotation is the first sentence of the second section of a famous 1926 essay, "Jinian Liu Hezhen jun" (In memory of Ms. Liu Hezhen).—Eds.

The Documents and Their Significance

ANDREW J. NATHAN

Obtaining information from the highest levels of the People's Republic of China is unusual but not unheard of. During the Cultural Revolution, Red Guards mimeographed two volumes of Mao Zedong's unpublished speeches and conversations that they had taken from Party archives, and they circulated them to promote loyalty to his every word. In 1972 Mao's wife, Jiang Qing, gave a series of personal interviews to an American historian, apparently seeking to consolidate her reputation as a partner in her husband's revolution. Less spectacular examples can also be cited of documents and eyewitness reports that have cracked open the shutters on one of the most secretive political systems in the world.[1]

But the present volume is unprecedented in the drama of the story it tells, the fullness of the record it reveals, and the potential explosiveness of its contents. It

---

[1] *Mao Zedong sixiang wansui* (Long live the thought of Mao Zedong), 1967 and 1969, mimeographed volumes that have been reproduced in various forms; Roxane Witke, *Comrade Chiang Ch'ing* (Boston: Little, Brown, 1977). (Chiang Ch'ing is Jiang Qing.) Also Roderick MacFarquhar, Timothy Cheek, and Eugene Wu, eds., *The Secret Speeches of Chairman Mao: From the Hundred Flowers to the Great Leap Forward* (Cambridge, Mass.: Council on East Asian Studies, Harvard University, 1989); John Byron and Robert Pack, *The Claws of the Dragon: Kang Sheng, the Evil Genius Behind Mao—and His Legacy of Terror in People's China* (New York: Simon and Schuster, 1992); Ruan Ming, *Deng Xiaoping: Chronology of an Empire*, trans. Nancy Liu, Peter Rand, and Lawrence R. Sullivan (Boulder: Westview, 1994); and Wu Guoguang, *Zhao Ziyang yu zhengzhi gaige* (Zhao Ziyang and political reform) (Hong Kong: Taipingyang shiji yanjiusuo, 1997). Through the 1990s documents surfaced in Hong Kong allegedly emanating from Zhao Ziyang and Bao Tong on the one side and the Party's ideological conservatives on the other; specialists believed many of these documents were authentic.

consists of full or partial transcripts from hundreds of documents detailing the highest-level processes of decisionmaking during the fateful events in Beijing in spring 1989. Not only was this one of the most important events in the history of Communist China, but the world—and the Chinese people—have no other such intimate account of top-level politics from any period in Chinese history.

Tiananmen began as an effort on the part of Beijing students to encourage continued economic reform and liberalization, but it quickly evolved into a demand for far-reaching change. The student hunger strikers in Tiananmen Square gained the support of tens of millions of other citizens, who took to the streets in scores of cities over the course of several weeks to demand a response from the government. The government at first tried to wait out the hunger strikers, then engaged them in limited dialogue, and finally issued orders to force them from the Square. In the course of reaching that decision, the Party suffered its worst high-level split since the Cultural Revolution.

Several noteworthy books and an important documentary film have told the story of the Tiananmen events from the viewpoint of students and citizens in Beijing.[2] What we have here for the first time is the view from Zhongnanhai—the former Imperial park at the center of Beijing that houses the Party Central Office, the State Council Office, and the residences of some top leaders. Although the leaders occupied distinct official posts in a triad of organizations—the ruling Chinese Communist Party, the State Council (government cabinet), and the Central Military Commission—behind those red walls they acted as a small and often informal community of perhaps ten decisionmakers and their staffs. They were joined in their deliberations at crucial moments by the eight "Elders," China's powerful extraconstitutional final court of appeal. Three of the Elders were most influential, and among these the final say belonged to Deng Xiaoping, who was retired from all government posts except one and lived outside Zhongnanhai in

[2]The best narrative works in a sizable literature include Timothy Brook, *Quelling the People: The Military Suppression of the Beijing Democracy Movement* (New York: Oxford University Press, 1992; rev. ed., Stanford: Stanford University Press, 1998); Craig Calhoun, *Neither Gods nor Emperors: Students and the Struggle for Democracy in China* (Berkeley and Los Angeles: University of California Press, 1994); and Orville Schell, *Mandate of Heaven: A New Generation of Entrepreneurs, Dissidents, Bohemians, and Technocrats Lays Claim to China's Future* (New York: Simon and Schuster, 1994), part 1. Throughout the book we cite three important documentary collections, edited by Han Minzhu; by Michel Oksenberg, Lawrence R. Sullivan, and Marc Lambert; and by Suzanne Ogden, Kathleen Hartford, Lawrence Sullivan, and David Zweig. The only substantial work on the democracy movement in the provinces is Jonathan Unger, ed., *The Pro-Democracy Protests in China: Reports from the Provinces* (Armonk, N.Y.: M. E. Sharpe, Inc., 1991). The documentary film is *The Gate of Heavenly Peace*, produced by Long Bow Productions in 1995.

a private mansion with his own office staff. Here the most crucial meetings of these tormented months took place.

Into Zhongnanhai flowed a river of documentation from the agencies charged with surveilling and controlling the capital city of Beijing and the vast nation beyond it. On a daily and hourly basis, Party Central received classified reports from the Beijing, Shanghai, and other provincial and municipal authorities; from the two security ministries (Public Security, charged with internal police work, and State Security, charged with foreign intelligence and counterintelligence, among other tasks) and the domestic and foreign bureaus of the Xinhua News Agency, whose work included intelligence gathering in addition to news reporting; from the military hierarchy, the Party's Propaganda and United Front Work Departments,[3] the State Education Commission, the Railway Ministry, the Agriculture Ministry, the industrial ministries, the Posts and Telecommunications Ministry, and other cabinet-level agencies; and from diplomatic missions abroad. The material included reports on the states of mind of students, professors, Party officials, military officers and troops, workers, farmers, shop clerks, street peddlers, and others around the country; the thinking of provincial and Central leaders on policy issues; press, academic, and political opinion abroad; the traffic on railways; the discussions in private meetings; man-in-the-street interviews; and much more.

Often such materials were distributed only to the top forty or so leaders, and many were limited even more sharply to the five-man Politburo Standing Committee plus the eight Elders. (The Communist Party's Politburo Standing Committee is the highest organ of formal political power in China, despite constitutional provisions that legally give that role to the National People's Congress [NPC], which only recently has been emerging from history as a rubber stamp for Party decisions.) Certain documents went to only one or a few leaders. Taken as a whole, these reports tell us in extraordinary detail what the central decisionmakers saw as they looked out from their compound on the events unfolding around them and how they evaluated the threat to their rule.

Added to these are minutes of the leaders' formal and informal meetings and accounts of some of their private conversations. In these we observe the desperate conflict among a handful of strong-willed leaders, whose personalities emerge with unprecedented vividness. We learn what the ultimate decisionmakers said among themselves as they discussed the unfolding events: how they debated the

---

[3]United front work is work to win over and find common ground with non-Party people in service of major Party goals.

motives of the students, whom they identified as their main enemies, which considerations dominated their search for a solution, why they waited as long as they did and no longer before ordering the troops to move on the Square, and what they ordered the troops to do. Perhaps most dramatic of all, we have definitive evidence of who voted how on key issues and their reasons for those votes, in their own words.

The documents reveal that if left to their own preferences, the three-man majority of the Politburo Standing Committee would have voted to persist in dialogue with the students instead of declaring martial law. Had they done so, China's recent history and its relations with the West would have been very different. Dialogue with the students would have tipped the balance toward political reform, and China today might well be an open society or even an electoral democracy, possibly under the rule of a reformed Communist Party. Instead, the divided Politburo Standing Committee honored a secret commitment to refer serious disagreements to the Elders. The Elders in turn decided for stability over reform, dismissed Party leader Zhao Ziyang, deployed force, "saved the revolution," and elevated the man who rules China today, in 2000, Jiang Zemin. The result has been more than a decade of political stasis at home and strained relations with the West.

Now a few who are in a position to do so have decided to rejoin the struggle for democracy by the strongest means available to them: revealing the true story of June Fourth.

.   .   .

But who are they? Why have they done this, and how? I must tell what I can of this story, but my account is circumscribed by the need to protect the compiler of the documents.[4]

Documents of the sort included in this book are available to only a tiny handful of people in China. The compiler has been able to obtain them and has been entrusted by fellow reformers with the task of getting the papers into the public domain in order to challenge the official story that Tiananmen was a legitimate suppression of a violent antigovernment riot.

He sought me out in a place outside China, explained this much, and asked for my help. Why me? I am a professor of political science at Columbia University,

---

[4]The name on the title page, Zhang Liang, is a pseudonym.

specializing in Chinese politics and foreign policy. I have written and spoken on Chinese domestic politics and foreign policy in a variety of academic and nonacademic contexts. I am on the boards of two human rights organizations that pursue issues relating to China[5] and serve on the editorial advisory committees of some publications associated with the Chinese pro-democracy movement in exile. I was involved in the publication both of Dr. Li Zhisui's memoirs of his service as Chairman Mao's personal physician and of the prison letters of the dissident Wei Jingsheng.[6] Some of my words and actions have been viewed as friendly to China, some as critical. The compiler said he and his friends did not approve of all my views and actions but that they had followed my views over the years, considered me fair-minded, thought I would be willing to get involved in a project as controversial as this one, and believed I would respect the integrity of the materials. He said he thought we shared a common purpose: loyalty to the truth of history—words he chose for the epigraph of the Chinese edition of the book.

I did not relish getting involved in such a difficult project. Since I am not a politician, the prospect of getting involved in Chinese politics was more alarming than attractive. Since editing the documents is not a work of creative scholarship, I stood to gain little academic credit. But if I agreed to help, I would have to bear the heavy responsibility of evaluating whether the documents were genuine. Nonetheless, I did not feel I could refuse my help if I believed they were.

Over the course of several years, through a variety of channels and methods, I have satisfied myself that the materials in this book are genuine. I did so partly by working with the text itself, corroborating a number of details that could not have been fabricated. And I did it partly by working with the compiler on both the text and the publication process.

Americans may find it hard to understand why the compiler is willing to reveal the contents of the documents but nothing about himself or how he brought the material out of China. He has some of the same motives that whistle-blowers everywhere have, especially the need to protect himself, his family, and his colleagues from retribution. But the deeper reason for his reticence lies in the conviction that the Chinese Communist Party is the only force powerful enough to change the system that it has itself created.

Those who have broken with the Party to try to change it have been silenced at

---

[5]Human Rights Watch and Human Rights in China.
[6]Li Zhisui, *The Private Life of Chairman Mao* (New York: Random House, 1994); Wei Jingsheng, *The Courage to Stand Alone: Letters from Prison and Other Writings* (New York: Viking Penguin, 1997).

home or sent into exile and have lost all influence. The compiler is trying to act in a way that the majority of the Chinese Communist Party leaders can identify with. Over recent decades, revealing policy disagreements through Hong Kong or overseas media has become an acceptable—if still rare and risky—practice. But revealing physical documents or signature features of the documentary system remains out of bounds. In fact, such seemingly arcane distinctions are not foreign to our own political culture, which tacitly accepts the leaking of content but tends to prosecute the act of compromising sources or physical documents. In refusing to disclose his identity or the processes involved in bringing his material to the West, the compiler has stayed, by his own lights at least, on the right side of the line that separates patriotism from betrayal, constructive conflict from all-out opposition.

Despite this, I have deciphered enough of the story behind his approach to me to find myself not only able but obligated to help get the truth out. Others involved in the project know some of what I know, but the final responsibility for authentication rests with me. Unfortunately, since I cannot share my grounds for certainty with readers for the time being at least, I can only ask them to consider the evidence of authenticity that lies within the documents themselves.

As readers will see, *The Tiananmen Papers* possess an internal coherence, richness, and human believability that would be almost impossible to fake. They cover events in Beijing, the provinces, and the military; reveal what happened in open and secret meetings among the demonstrating students and the groups of intellectuals who supported them; quote at length from foreign news reports; describe intelligence findings from conversations by Chinese journalists with American China specialists; and give the names of diplomats calling on Chinese leaders during the crisis. Some of this was in the public record, as readers will see by following the references in the footnotes to the three main documentary collections in English. Some of the material might have been discoverable by arduous research. But much of it would appear to be virtually impossible to reconstruct by any conceivable research effort. In short, it is hard to imagine a means of creating a plausible forgery at such a deep level of detail.

The papers include accounts, from the state security apparatus and other intelligence sources, of the activities of many named individuals who are now in the West. In a number of instances known to those of us involved with this project and in other cases where we were able to check with the people involved, we have found the accounts to be corroborated. Because of the need to maintain total secrecy as we prepared this book, however, we were not able to check most of the accounts with the people they describe.

In claiming that the documents are genuine I do not assert that every fact in them is correct. The same would be the case with the documents of any government. State Security Ministry accounts of the activities of intellectuals backing the students seem biased. We believe accusations of manipulation of the movement by the United States and Taiwan were unfounded. State Security Ministry charges that George Soros was an agent of the Central Intelligence Agency (Chapter 9) are not credible. The death toll given in the internal report quoted in the Epilogue is no different from the death toll officially published at the time and is not necessarily the last word on the subject. Contrary to a State Security Ministry report of May 21 (see Chapter 6), we do not believe it was Wang Juntao who came up with the idea of a hunger strike for the students. Such examples warn us to use the documents with caution.

A number of knowledgeable people have read the manuscript in whole or in part, and all share my impression of its authenticity. This includes those of us involved in the project (two of whom, Perry Link and Orville Schell, were in Beijing at the time of the events described here), as well as two Chinese journalists who followed the Tiananmen events closely, one in Beijing and one from outside China.

The compiler at first wanted the documents published in Chinese, with foreign language editions coming out when they were ready. Because of the sensitivity of the project, early publication in Chinese proved difficult. Eventually I found it easier to work first with a Western publisher to create an English-language text, from which several foreign-language translations have been made, and to seek out a Chinese publisher second. To meet the needs of the Western publishing system, the book had to be shortened, explanatory material had to be added, and sources needed to be identified. The result is two separate books. The one in Chinese contains about three times as much documentary material but little of the explanatory and source-citation apparatus of the present work. The Chinese volume is scheduled to be published in spring 2001. More detail on editorial and translation issues is offered below.

.   .   .

Although the compiler and I were both motivated, as he said, by the truth of history, it was clear from the beginning that he also had political goals that I, as a scholar, could not share. As he implies in his Preface, he hopes that *The Tiananmen Papers* will show that the student movement was legal and well-intentioned, that the government mishandled it, and that the students' and citizens' demands for openness and dialogue should have been honored. He believes that a series of political reforms should be revived and broadened to allow a free press, autonomous student organizations, free labor unions, and the like. Of course, such reforms would spell a radical change in the nature of Communist Party rule, but the compiler believes that this is the only way for the Party to realize its nation-saving mission.

Such a drastic change would obviously have to involve an intense political struggle, as wrenching as the one in 1989 that set China on its current hard-line course. Top leaders' careers would again be on the line. As I worked on the translation and editing, I tried to figure out whom this project was likely to help and whom it would hurt. My conclusions are my own, and the compiler bears no responsibility for them.

In my view, the publication of this book is likely to damage the careers of the two most powerful leaders in China, Jiang Zemin and Li Peng, and to boost the authority of several of their high-ranking rivals. Since the fault lines in China's leadership run deeply throughout the Party at all levels, the fates of millions of officials throughout the political system will also be affected.

Jiang Zemin is China's supreme leader, occupying the triple posts of Party general secretary, state president, and chairman of the Central Military Commission. (These are the three legs of China's political structure. The "state" is equivalent to the Western idea of a government and includes a cabinet called the State Council and a legislature called the National People's Congress. The ruling Chinese Communist Party is the real source of authority. It makes the most-important decisions and conveys them to the state apparatus for implementation. The military is a largely independent power structure answerable to the top leadership only through the Central Military Commission.) Jiang's term of office as general secretary is scheduled to end in October 2002, and his term as state president ends in March 2003. Some commentators expect him to try to retain his post as chairman of the Central Military Commission after these expirations, in order to continue to exert influence as a Party elder from behind the scenes, as Deng Xiaoping did in the period described in this book.

In 1989 Jiang was Party secretary in Shanghai. He committed no heinous act at that time, although his closing of the *World Economic Herald* newspaper (Chapter 2) is still widely resented by intellectuals. What the Tiananmen papers reveal is that his accession to supreme power came about through a constitutionally irregular procedure, the vote of the Elders on May 27, and that the Elders chose him because he was a pliable and cautious figure who was outside the paralyzing factional fray that had created the crisis in the first place. This was widely suspected, but the details have never been known before. Release of these details will undercut Jiang's authority. Although Jiang is not necessarily a committed political conservative, he has deferred to the concerns of conservatives as a way of balancing contending forces and maintaining his own power. Weakening him will diminish an obstacle to political reform.

Even more seriously damaged by the documents' revelations will be the second-ranking member of the Party hierarchy, Li Peng. Besides his position in the Politburo Standing Committee, Li as of this writing is chairman of the Standing Committee (that is, top officer) of the National People's Congress.[7] His Party and state terms in office end at the same times as Jiang's (2002 and 2003, respectively). Li was premier in 1989, and he committed acts that I believe most Chinese readers will feel can only be expiated by his fall from power. Not only did he advocate a hard line against the students and go on television to declare martial law, as is already known, but the documents show that he manipulated information to lead Deng Xiaoping and the other Elders to see the demonstrations as an attack on them personally and on the political structure they had devoted their careers to constructing. The Tiananmen papers also reveal his use of the intelligence and police agencies to collect information that was employed to persecute liberal officials and intellectuals after the crackdown.

Western readers may respond to the documentary record of Li's behavior more favorably than Chinese readers. Li was perhaps the most capable, certainly the most resolute, politician on the scene in 1989. He showed toughness and energy under pressure and responded to confusing events with coolness and clarity. If Li saw the student movement as a mortal challenge to the regime as constructed, history suggests that his judgment was not far from the mark. To be sure, Li emerges from the documents as vengeful, judgmental, and politically rigid. But he was no opportunist. He was committed to Party dictatorship as a principle, and he was not afraid to uphold that principle no matter how unpopular it was. Nor was he responsible in any direct way for the shedding of blood, according to the documents. The killings occurred, despite orders to the contrary, when inadequately trained troops went out of control.

But it is only in a pluralistic culture that one can admire a politician for performing ably in a bad cause. What will matter more to Chinese readers is that Li

[7]The Standing Committee of the National People's Congress exercises the NPC's authority when the NPC is not in session.

was on the wrong side of history. As this book goes to press, he is the highest-ranking standard bearer of conservative forces who believe that China can get through its current crises only by maintaining strict political and ideological discipline and sticking to state socialism. In the years since Tiananmen, this group has enjoyed great influence, reflected in recurrent political crackdowns, arrests of dissidents, closings of liberal newspapers and magazines, the tightening of laws against free association, and a hard international line on human rights. The political undermining of Li would remove a major obstacle to liberal reforms and closer ties with the West.

Three of Li Peng's allies from 1989 sit in the Politburo. Li Tieying, who served as Politburo member and minister of the State Education Commission in 1989, worked tirelessly to bottle up student activists on their campuses. Luo Gan, a protégé of Li Peng, served as State Council secretary general, thus handling the details of Li's hard-line maneuvers in 1989, including issuing instructions to the Public Security and State Security Ministries and the People's Armed Police. In 2000, as a Politburo member, he supervises the country's foreign intelligence and counterintelligence work and the internal police and justice systems. Jiang Chunyun, who served as Party secretary of Shandong province in 1989, managed the crisis locally without bloodshed, but because of his close political relations with Li Peng, he spoke more loudly in favor of the hard line than did most provincial leaders. After 1989 he enjoyed a series of promotions, including appointment to the Politburo. All three men are likely to be damaged by the appearance of this book, and the net effect may be to open further leeway for reform.

In total, then, five members of the twenty-two-man Politburo stand to be damaged by the revelations of *The Tiananmen Papers*, including the two most senior leaders and the three directly beneath them. The others who would be most subject to criticism for their roles in 1989 are deceased or out of power. Deng Xiaoping, who bore ultimate responsibility for the Party's response to the students, died in February 1997. In any case, he emerges from the documents as perhaps a more sympathetic figure than he appeared at the time. He was drawn reluctantly into the decisionmaking—bemoaning to his confidant Yang Shangkun the fact that he had to bear such responsibility at his advanced age—and was willing to support Zhao Ziyang's conciliatory line until that line demonstrably failed. Persuaded by Li Peng and his allies that the demonstrators were hostile to him personally and to the Party, Deng authorized the use of force but also insisted that no blood be spilled. He ordered the new leaders to continue on the path of economic reform and opening to the West. The Tiananmen papers thus make it possible for Deng's successors to reverse the verdict on Tiananmen, if they are so inclined, without destroying his reputation and his legacy, on which their own legitimacy still partly relies.

Along with Deng, one other deceased Elder plays a central role in the book: Deng's comrade-in-arms Yang Shangkun. Some of the material has been supplied by one of Yang's friends, leading to the supposition that people close to Yang hope to benefit if his reputation is enhanced. But Yang Shangkun and his cousin, Yang Baibing, both lost power at the Fourteenth Party Congress in 1992, and in subsequent years Jiang Zemin transferred most of their military followers out of power, so it is not clear that there remains much of a Yang group among today's contenders for influence.

Of the other six Elders who took part in the crucial decisions of April–June 1989, five are deceased. The one former Elder who is alive at the time of this writing, Bo Yibo, is not politically active. Yao Yilin, the fifth-ranking member of the five-man Politburo Standing Committee in 1989, whose antagonism to the students was even shriller than Li Peng's, died in 1996. The two leaders of Beijing Municipality at that time, Party secretary Li Ximing and Mayor Chen Xitong, who joined Li Peng to manipulate information given to the Elders and who helped him prepare the political conditions for a military crackdown, are out of power. Li Ximing is retired, and Chen Xitong lives under medical house arrest after having been convicted in a corruption scandal. Thus the papers' political target is narrow.

By contrast, eight members of the senior leadership are likely to benefit from the revelation of their roles in 1989. Not surprisingly, they are all pro-reform (although this does not necessarily mean that they share the views of the compiler; we have no way to know). Zhu Rongji, China's premier, was Shanghai mayor in 1989. He argued against the dispatch of troops to his city and arranged for a bloodless end to the demonstrations. Li Ruihuan was Party secretary and mayor of Tianjin. He maintained dialogue with student demonstrators and, like Zhu, avoided bloodshed. If Jiang Zemin's and Li Peng's careers suffer setbacks, Zhu and Li are potential beneficiaries.

There are others in the Politburo who might benefit as well. Tian Jiyun, in 1989 vice premier in charge of agriculture and foreign trade, sided with Zhao Ziyang in advocating dialogue with the students. Wei Jianxing, minister of supervision in 1989, participated in dialogues with the students and actively investigated corruption charges leveled by the student demonstrators. Wen Jiabao, a follower of

Zhao Ziyang who was director of the Central Party Office and was in charge of handling paperwork for the Politburo and the Central Committee, favored a moderate line, was sidelined from decisionmaking when Zhao lost power, and bears no responsibility for the military crackdown. Li Changchun, then governor in Liaoning, and Wu Guanzheng, then governor in Jiangxi, were both moderates and personally conducted dialogue with the students in their provinces. One of the two military men in the Politburo, Chi Haotian, then chief of general staff, took a moderate position on how to handle the demonstrators and had no voice in the ultimate decision to use force, although his job required him to follow orders in administering the crackdown. The publication of *The Tiananmen Papers* is likely to enhance these men's ability to pursue reform.

There are also powerful figures outside today's Politburo with a stake in the publication of *The Tiananmen Papers*. Zhao Ziyang himself, purged as Party secretary because of his refusal to participate in the crackdown, lives under semi–house arrest. As in the case of Li Peng, Western readers' response to Zhao's recorded behavior may differ somewhat from that of Chinese readers. He was a liberal and a democrat whose vision of change Westerners are likely to applaud, but the documents also show that he made some serious mistakes. He underestimated the student challenge, left town at the start of the crisis, and wasted the support of his key patron, Deng Xiaoping. Most difficult for Westerners to comprehend may be his decision to put personal loyalty to Deng above principle and to resign rather than resist when he knew that the crackdown was coming.

But Chinese readers are likely to see this story differently. Zhao's refusal either to participate in or to resist the crackdown can be seen as the response of a principled official in the Confucian tradition, who chooses retirement when he faces a conflict between his obligations to the people and his loyalty to his patron. Moreover, *The Tiananmen Papers* reveal that the Politburo Standing Committee was obligated by a secret intra-Party resolution to refer any stalemate to Deng and the Elders. The documents further show that Deng Xiaoping exercised absolute control over the military through Yang Shangkun. Had the Standing Committee refused to honor its obligation to refer the crisis to the Elders, Deng had ample means to exert his authority. All this will temper Chinese readers' judgment of Zhao's seeming weakness.

Zhao is too old to return to the political stage. Nonetheless, any information that burnishes his reputation strengthens the prospects of his former subordinates, who occupy positions throughout the central and local Party and government apparatuses. Of these, the most influential is probably Wen Jiabao, mentioned above, who as a Politburo member and vice premier is one of the most powerful moderates in the government and a potential future premier.

The third-ranking member of the Politburo Standing Committee in 1989 after Zhao and Li Peng was Qiao Shi, whose portfolio included the sensitive areas of personnel and security work. We can see from his remarks at crucial meetings of the Politburo Standing Committee that he was not in favor of using force (against the background of the whole record, I interpret his abstention on the issue of martial law at the crucial meeting of May 17 as the expression of his preference not to impose martial law). But also like Zhao, he deferred to Deng Xiaoping by refraining from casting what would have been the deciding vote to block martial law.[8] Qiao's indecisiveness was no doubt explained by his knowledge that resistance to Deng would have been futile. But his wavering led to the sacrifice of his political ambitions, because when the Elders selected a successor to Zhao they decided that Qiao was too weak. In 1997 Qiao retired from his Party posts at the prodding of Jiang Zemin. Like Zhao, he is too old to be a power contender, but he also has followers in the liberal wing of the Party who have a stake in his reputation.

The third Standing Committee member who supported Zhao in 1989 was Hu Qili. He was then the fourth-ranking member of the Politburo Standing Committee. His career had been patronized by Hu Yaobang, whose death sparked the student movement, and he endorsed much of what the students stood for and favored resolution of their demands through dialogue. At a crucial point in the documents, we see Hu Qili using his control of the press to authorize full reporting of events, thus providing the first and so far only episode of press freedom in Communist China's history. With Zhao and Qiao, Hu completed the potential three-man majority in the Politburo Standing Committee against the use of force. His political career essentially ended with the purge of Zhao Ziyang, although he remains on stage in the honorific position of a vice chairman of the Chinese People's Political Consultative Conference.

The remaining nine members of the Politburo as of 2000 have relatively little either to gain or to fear from the revelation of their behavior in 1989. They were either too far from Beijing or too low in the hierarchy to bear responsibility one way or the other for the events recounted in this book. The highest-ranking of this group is the vice president and heir apparent to Jiang Zemin, Hu Jintao. In

---

[8]The difference between Zhao and Qiao was that Zhao voted against martial law but then did nothing to resist it. Qiao abstained from voting. Zhao refused to participate in the enforcement of martial law. Qiao continued in government, arguing consistently for measures to prevent bloodshed. Zhao was fired for breaking with Deng. Qiao stayed in office but was denied further advancement because he was perceived as weak. (Hu Qili behaved in the same way as Zhao.)

1989 he was serving as Party secretary in Tibet. Although he was often in Beijing trying to recover from altitude sickness, he had no direct role in the events there. Li Lanqing, who is now a Politburo Standing Committee member, was then only vice minister of foreign trade. The second military Politburo member, Zhang Wannian, in 1989 was commander of the Jinan Military District, one of the military regions not involved in events in Beijing. Many of today's Politburo members were provincial governors or Party secretaries[9] in 1989, serving away from Beijing. Such people can afford to view the publication of *The Tiananmen Papers* with equanimity, and their attitudes will probably pivot on whether or not they want the Party to pursue political reform in the coming period.

Although the Politburo appears to contain a pro-reform majority, the influence of number-two leader Li Peng and his three supporters, plus the caution of Jiang Zemin, make it impossible to reengage the project of political reform. The compiler and his colleagues apparently expect the publication of *The Tiananmen Papers* to break this paralysis.

But why doesn't the majority simply vote to examine the Tiananmen archives on its own? Part of the answer probably lies in the search for consensus that—to judge by the meetings reported in this book—characterizes Chinese decision-making processes. As long as a substantial group do not want to reopen the subject, the others may not want to start a fight about it. In addition, we have to assume that almost nobody in high office today knows all the details of the events or has ever seen any significant portion of the material that *The Tiananmen Papers* contains. Li Peng is the sole exception; only he was in high office in Beijing at the time. People in lower posts in 1989 would have certain knowledge only of reports they participated in writing and of specific meetings they attended. I assume that even a leader as powerful as Jiang Zemin cannot surreptitiously examine the archives, since access to such sensitive records must require a Politburo vote or would at least become known to other members of the top leadership. Reopening the issue without knowing in advance what the records say would precipitate a complicated political struggle with unpredictable consequences. Seeking to remain in power by balancing various factions, Jiang might reasonably be reluctant to take that risk for uncertain gain.

What the compiler has done is to cut the Gordian knot by placing the documents in the public domain. By forcing the Politburo to confront Tiananmen and by showing that the damage of reversing the verdict will be borne largely by Li

---

[9]Each province has a Party secretary who runs Party affairs and a governor who runs government affairs. The Party secretary is the more important of the two.

Peng and a small group of those close to him, he hopes to jump-start the interrupted march toward what he says will be a more democratic future for China.

. . .

As a foreigner, I do not presume to intervene in Chinese affairs, and as a scholar, I place my priority on authenticity and accuracy rather than political consequences. What is important to me about *The Tiananmen Papers* is that they contain the richest record I have ever seen of political life in China at the top and offer fundamental insights into China's trajectory since 1989 and into the future. The following analysis is again my own, for which the compiler bears no responsibility.

Perhaps the most striking revelations concern the role of Deng Xiaoping and the eight Elders. Part of this story was placed on the public record by Zhao Ziyang in his meeting with Mikhail Gorbachev on May 16 (see Chapter 5): Deng's guidance was sought on important matters. What Zhao did not reveal was that the Politburo resolution of October 1987, to which he referred in his meeting with Gorbachev, actually gave Deng the formal power to approve or overturn decisions of the working leadership. Moreover, a second resolution adopted at the same time gave Yang Shangkun and Bo Yibo the right to attend Politburo and Politburo Standing Committee meetings as observers on behalf of Deng and the other two senior elders, Chen Yun and Li Xiannian.

To some extent, these resolutions may have been adopted to show respect to the three senior comrades who at that time had just retired from their posts in the Politburo Standing Committee. But perhaps they were also a way to deal with the emerging breakdown in the Deng Xiaoping–Chen Yun consensus that had enabled the older comrades to guide China through two decades of spectacularly successful economic reform. In the mid–1980s, reform had become more difficult and policy debates sharper just as a new generation of leaders was stepping to the helm. In this increasingly contentious atmosphere, the 1987 resolutions may have been aimed at preventing the factional disagreement from creating a stalemate. Whether or not this supposition is correct, this was precisely the function the resolutions came to perform in 1989.

The Tiananmen papers show that during the crisis Deng participated intimately in every important decision. His personal aide, Yang Shangkun (whose formal position was head of state but whose real job was Deng's business manager within the leadership), attended all important Politburo meetings. The most important decisions were made at Deng's house. It was Deng's idea to label the demonstrations "turmoil." He made the decision to declare martial law, he accepted the resignation of Zhao Ziyang, he engineered the selection of Jiang Zemin, he gave the order for the military to move on the Square, and after the crackdown he set the policy direction of trying to continue the ten-year project of economic reform and opening to the West despite the setback dealt to those projects by the events of the spring.

Deng did not play this role happily. On May 19 he complained to Yang about the burdens of power: "You know that I've taken a lot of heat inside the Party since this whole thing broke out . . . ," Deng lamented. "I have to give the nod on every important decision. I carry too much weight, and that's not good for the Party or the state. I should think about retiring—but how can I, right now? . . . Stepping down is not all that easy."

Nor was Deng's power absolute. Before his word was final, Deng needed agreement among the Elders. This is a group that as far as I know had no fixed boundaries and no history of meeting together either before or after the Tiananmen events. The six men and one woman whom Deng summoned to join him in this caucus were not the oldest surviving members of the Party, nor were they necessarily those who had served in the highest posts, nor the most physically vigorous. They appear to have been a mixture of some with the longest Party careers (Deng himself and his most powerful colleagues Chen Yun and Li Xiannian, along with Yang Shangkun), some who were especially close to Mao (Li Xiannian, Yang Shangkun, Wang Zhen), some who fell out with Mao but were proved by history to be right (Chen Yun, Peng Zhen, Bo Yibo), and one—the sole female member, Deng Yingchao—who had no great political distinction of her own but who was the widow of the revered late premier, Zhou Enlai. Notably excluded, or self-excluded, from this group were the two surviving marshals of the Chinese military, Xu Xiangqian and Nie Rongzhen, whose reasons for opting out of politics are explained in Chapter 6.

This group met four times and made four big decisions: to declare martial law, to fire Zhao, to appoint Jiang, and to send in the troops. Lesser decisions and implementation were handled by the Politburo Standing Committee and the Central Military Commission—the former supervised by Yang Shangkun on behalf of Deng and the Elders, the latter directly managed by Yang.

The dynamics of the Elders' meetings are interesting. Deng convenes them at his home and has the privilege of summing up the final decision. But we observe his deference to Chen Yun and Li Xiannian. When the time comes to nominate possible replacements for Zhao Ziyang, it is Li and Chen who raise Jiang's name, and it is clear that the two of them and Deng have consulted before the meeting. The lesser Elders show that they know their places. Wang Zhen speaks infrequently, if intemperately, and defers to Deng. Deng Yingchao speaks briefly, once per meeting. Yang Shangkun provides balanced information but has no discernible views separate from Deng's.

Although the Elders functioned only briefly as a government body, their existence reflected an underlying and continuing principle that had been invoked previously and may be invoked again as long as the Chinese Communist Party continues to see itself as a revolutionary rather than a constitutionalist party: the tradition of supreme rulership forged by Mao Zedong. The role of the supreme leader in Communist China is extraconstitutional but not illegitimate. China's much-bruited transition to rule of law will thus involve more than setting up legal codes and courts. If the transition is to be real, the Party will have to abandon the idea that whatever it feels it has to do is legal, no matter what the procedures involved.

What makes it necessary to have such an extraconstitutional organ? *The Tiananmen Papers* helps us to see how a supreme leader like Deng Xiaoping is created by factionalism within the system, even against his own will. What we have here is only a snapshot in time, and of course, at a moment of crisis. But it is our closest look ever at Chinese Communist Party factionalism in action.

In *The Tiananmen Papers* we see how the dynamics of factionalism in China combine personal ties and power interests with real issues of policy and ideology. Zhao Ziyang and Li Peng both have their patrons among the Elders and their close followers and brain trusters among their own and the next generations of leaders. What crystallizes these personal links into politically meaningful factions are policy dilemmas intrinsic to China's transition from the failed Maoist system to an unclearly charted future. The clash we see here is an agonized battle over hard choices that produce valid differences of opinion. Zhao Ziyang's instincts were to loosen up politically in order to invigorate the economy, accepting a consequent loss of control but maintaining authority through a more consultative style of leadership. Li Peng's instinct was to focus on stability, keep political control, and deal with the consequent economic shortfall by more energetic planning and exhortation. Both were legitimate visions of how to steer this vast nation through the shoals of reform. The compiler shows in the Prologue that the underlying issues go back to the mid–1980s, and he could have taken it further back.

In any political system, somebody who can decide, whether rightly or wrongly, is indispensable. But in the Chinese system there are no horizontal organs—courts or legislatures—with institutionalized powers to resolve deadlocks. The big issues are extruded upward and create the pressure, of which Deng Xiaoping complained to Yang Shangkun, for somebody to take ultimate responsibility. Even those, like Zhao, who fundamentally disagreed with Deng's decisions found it more honorable to accept them than to stand up for what they believed in, so necessary did they feel it was for the system to have somebody to decide.

A further and related feature of Beijing's political processes in 1989 was the ultimate importance of military force. A major part of Yang Shangkun's portfolio on Deng Xiaoping's behalf was managing the coercive apparatus of the regime. The one official post Deng Xiaoping had not yet relinquished in 1989 was also the one that Mao Zedong relied upon to maintain ultimate authority when many of the other top leaders turned against him and the Party and state apparatuses crumbled during the Cultural Revolution, and the one that Jiang Zemin is thought likely to try to retain after he retires from his Party and state offices in 2002–2003: the chairmanship of the Central Military Commission. The chairman of the Central Military Commission commands the armed forces, not the Party chairman, the premier, or the minister of defense. These forces include not only the People's Liberation Army and its numerous garrisons throughout the country but also the People's Armed Police, who, as we will see throughout this book, guarded government offices and other important installations.

In 1989 Yang Shangkun was serving as standing vice chair of the Central Military Commission, running it on Deng's behalf. When the decision for martial law was made, when the purge of Zhao Ziyang had to be explained to a doubting military, when the order was given for the troops to move on the Square, in every instance it was Yang Shangkun, not any member of the State Council or Politburo, who stepped to the podium. In addition, Yang supervised the Central Guards Bureau through its director, an old subordinate of his. Just as Mao had in his time, therefore, Deng controlled the personal security of all his comrades-in-arms, including the nominal Party and state leaders and the other Elders. And just as in Mao's day, considerations of personal safety were a powerful obstacle to any attempt to dislodge the supreme leader from power.

Despite the personalism of power, one is struck by the formality and ceremony of the decisionmaking processes. In Politburo Standing Committee meetings, for example, intense struggles are muted by respect for procedures that call for full discussion and, if possible, consensus decisions. Meetings of the full Politburo, attended by important leaders from the provinces, are so stately that it almost seems as if the imperial traditions of Zhongnanhai still weigh on their socialist inheritors. There are few signs of the kind of underhanded moves one associates with palace politics: mutual spying, denunciations, planted documents, personal scandals, attempted coups d'état. The disagreements are brought into the open, the issues are debated on the merits, the deadlocks are duly reported to Deng, and nobody acts without his imprimatur. Perhaps it was precisely because of Deng's dominating personal power that no one dared to behave otherwise.

Although the political process in Beijing was sometimes time-consuming, it was ruthlessly decisive once Deng had spoken. Against this backdrop, it is surprising to notice the degree of independence often exercised by the provinces. This independence can be discerned only through careful reading of their reports, because signs of disagreement are buried beneath layers of formulaic endorsement of Party Central's policies. (The same is true of documents from the ministries and commissions and from units of the military.) But the fact is that each province is as large in size and population as a European country, and each had to handle its own situation. Their different ways of doing so were not merely adaptations to local circumstances but reflections of local leaders' different styles of governance and even different values.

Yet in the end the center held. No province broke away, and except for a single senior officer, the military also held firm. Despite endlessly voiced misgivings, the bureaucracy was solid. The split was only at the top, an important, maybe the worst possible, weak link to be sure, and yet not a fissure that extended all the way through the system. Bureaucratically, the Chinese system proved to be a strong one.

Following a tradition that goes back at least to the Ming emperors, the central leaders displayed a voracious appetite for raw information. The Party's intelligence flow was impressive for its quantity, less so for its analysis. The two security ministries provided a flow of reports throughout the day on events in various parts of Beijing and in the provinces. The Xinhua News Agency provided extensive and timely surveillance of events within China and foreign reactions to Chinese events. (Despite its designation, Xinhua is as much an intelligence service as a media service. It does release news to subscribers for publication, but a large, perhaps the larger, part of its work is to serve as a channel for classified reports compiled by the staff of the State Security Ministry and the first and second intelligence departments of the People's Liberation Army General Staff.)

Through *The Tiananmen Papers*, we can see that police agents circulated freely among the students and intellectuals involved in the demonstrations. (On the evidence of the documents collected here, they do not seem to have penetrated deeply into the dissident community abroad or into the circles in Hong Kong, Taiwan, and elsewhere that offered aid to the students.) Domestic intelligence from the security ministries and Xinhua appears quite frank and informative concerning the mood of the people. This has certainly not always been the case in the history of the People's Republic of China (PRC). Mao Zedong's regime was famous for being willing to hear only good news and then misleading itself with it. Under Deng this practice had evidently changed, and the reports we see here are merciless in their honesty about ideological doubts in various sectors of the population. But good information only goes so far: Many of the leaders were still able to believe that the mass uprising resulted from manipulation by "a tiny minority."[10]

Perhaps this is partly because the police reports were seldom very useful. They were long on incident and short on analysis. The most instructive items in the leaders' intelligence flow were the reports from the foreign press. These reports may seem unremarkable to readers in the West, but the compiler has included examples because they were among the most thematic and predictive of the materials the leaders had available as they attempted to decipher events in the streets. It is possible that, as scholars have long suspected, the intelligence agencies preferred to let foreigners speak for them when it came to calling attention to unpleasant trends and voicing awkward possibilities.

It is striking that in an authoritarian police state, the leaders should keep such close tabs on public opinion. The best explanation is Machiavelli's, that it is easier to rule by consent than coercion. And indeed, the story here shows how sharp a battle the students and the regime fought for public support and how much greater a price the government had to pay for suppressing the students because of the public support they had gained. As we read the reports of the students' activities, we become aware of a subtle rhetorical game. At the beginning the students shout slogans that fall within or barely stretch the bounds of regime-approved patriotism and reform. The police note signs of more radical ideas on campus, but when the students go into the streets they use more acceptable language. This makes it hard in the initial period for the regime to figure out what is at stake in the student challenge. On the government side, Zhao and his colleagues struggle to find the right note to strike. They too must occupy the rhetorical high ground. In some cases the formulas involved are subtle: Chapter 3 tells

---

[10] *Jishaoshu*, "a tiny minority," is a stock phrase used to belittle and isolate one's enemy. Our translation will be consistent throughout.

about a struggle over whether to include a single phrase in Zhao Ziyang's May 4 speech.

In an authoritarian system public opinion does not have to be followed, but it cannot be ignored. Reports from all sorts of agencies to Zhongnanhai made clear that the state of the public mind was parlous in 1988–1989. The death of Hu Yaobang set a spark to a pile of tinder that had grown very deep.

.　　.　　.

The students did not set out to pose a mortal challenge to what they knew was a dangerous regime. Nor did the regime relish the use of force against the students. The two sides shared many goals and much common language. Through miscommunication and misjudgment, they pushed one another into positions in which options for compromise became less and less available. Several times a solution seemed just within reach, only to dissolve at the last moment. The slide to calamity seemed slow at first but then accelerated as divisions deepened on both sides. Knowing the outcome, we read the story with the sense of horror that we receive from true tragedy.

The student movement started with a desire to commemorate the reformer Hu Yaobang, who had died on April 15. To be sure, there was a provocative edge to the students' behavior, attributable to the relatively freewheeling atmosphere the government had tolerated during the strong reform push of the previous few years. By bringing their slogans off the campuses into Tiananmen Square, the center of the capital city, the students further thumbed their noses at Party control. Still, most of them stayed within the bounds of certain pieties, acknowledging Party leadership and positioning themselves as respectful, if disappointed, supporters of the Party's long-term reform project.

The first small misstep occurred when government officials refused to receive student petitioners at the Great Hall of the People. Overnight on April 19–20 demonstrators and police clashed at the Xinhua Gate of Zhongnanhai. On April 20–21 a variety of autonomous student organizations formed, which in the leaders' eyes was a dangerous development whose only precedent in the Communist period was the chaos of the Cultural Revolution. A huge demonstration greeted Hu Yaobang's memorial service on April 22.

Despite these developments, Zhao Ziyang—who as Party secretary held ultimate responsibility for managing the problem—believed that once Hu's funeral was over, the students would feel they had made their point and would disperse.

On the contrary, the lack of a clear response from the Party emboldened the demonstrators. While Zhao was away for a week-long state visit to North Korea, the other leaders, headed by Li Peng, brought the problem to Deng Xiaoping. In the exaggerated version they told him, the students were aiming to overthrow the regime. Deng labeled the movement "turmoil" *(dongluan)* and said it had to be decisively denounced. His words were reflected in an editorial published in the April 26 edition of the *People's Daily.*

This was a second and larger mistake. The editorial was aimed at setting boundaries, warning the majority of loyal students not to be misled by a small group of radicals. But the label "turmoil" proved inflammatory. We have used this standard PRC translation throughout the book despite its awkwardness in English because of its iconic importance. But a better translation might be "riot," with its implications of intentionality and violence. The word had especially strong negative connotations in China because it had often been used to refer to the upheavals of the years of the Cultural Revolution between 1966 and 1969.

The students believed that if they ended the demonstrations while the protests were still officially considered turmoil, they would be exposed to harsh punishment. Only if their movement was labeled "patriotic" and "democratic," they felt, could they safely withdraw from the Square. So the paradoxical effect of Deng Xiaoping's verdict was to raise the stakes so high that the students were trapped in the Square. There they served as a magnet for others who joined them as the stalemate continued.

But Deng's involvement raised the stakes for the Party as well. On the one side, Zhao Ziyang felt that the crowds were not challenging the ultimate leadership of the Communist Party, that their central demands were for dialogue and for the Party itself to solve the problems the students had raised, and that to get to work on these goals, which the Party shared, the Party should withdraw the April 26 turmoil verdict. Deng was willing to consider his advice. But Li Peng argued, also with good reason, that the editorial had already made a clear distinction between an innocent majority and a guilty minority and that those who insisted on overturning the editorial were precisely the guilty ones whom the Party needed firmly to confront. Any concession would fatally undermine the prestige of the government and Deng's authority.

At a deeper level, the Zhao-Li confrontation centered on two basic issues about the Party's relations to the citizens: Were good-hearted citizens smart enough to avoid manipulation; that is, could the Party trust citizens' good sense? Even more fundamental, was a peaceful resolution worth having, given that it would require creating precedents of consultation and citizen power that would hamper the Party's established style of rule? Or was the cost of a peaceful outcome to government authority and political stability too high to pay?

The constant injection of new actors made the situation ever harder to handle. New groups of students came into the Square and were reluctant to see the movement end before they had a chance to participate. Groups of liberal intellectuals came out in support of the students' goals. Some of the provincial leaders shipped their problems to Beijing by letting the radical students board the railways; Li Peng tried to put a stop to this by ordering local authorities to stop the students from traveling. So divided were the students that when government negotiators asked their leaders whether they could speak for their constituents, they responded that they could not.

The students, however, faced a parallel confusion on the government's side. Amid the mix of soft and hard voices, they could not be sure whether they were making progress or facing a stone wall. With such a constantly shifting negotiation agenda, closure was impossible. The momentum of protest grew. Although some students returned to classes, others joined the strike. New leaders emerged, new issues were added to old ones, and demonstrations burgeoned in the provinces.

Final defeat befell Zhao's strategy on May 13, when the students announced a hunger strike. Besides some provocations by the government, the main catalyst seemed to have been the impending visit of Soviet leader Mikhail Gorbachev, whom the students treated as a symbol of reform. The summit that the authorities had envisioned as a triumphant climax to years of diplomacy was thrown into the shadows. The huge foreign press contingent that had come to Beijing for the summit turned its attention to the student movement.

At a Standing Committee meeting on May 16, Zhao nonetheless continued to argue that the way to end the hunger strike was to accept the students' demand to change the verdict of the April 26 editorial. The break in the leadership was now critical and had to be taken to Deng. On the morning of May 17, Deng made the decision to side with Li. Moreover, he drew the logical conclusion: the need for martial law. In a Standing Committee meeting later that day, Zhao and Li continued to clash, and the Standing Committee split on martial law, 2–2–1, with Qiao Shi abstaining. The Elders then stepped in, firing Zhao, using Li Peng to implement their plans for repression, and selecting Jiang Zemin to succeed Zhao Ziyang once peace was restored.

Now the descent into disaster accelerated. We observe a process of demonization unfold, both between the regime and the students and between the two Party factions. The surviving leaders placed all the blame for events on Zhao. Intellectuals in the Square declared a Manichaean battle between light and darkness. Student demonstrators swore an oath to die rather than retreat. Ominously for the leaders, reports from some cities showed signs of a linkup between students and workers. The firestorm of opposition at home and abroad heightened the regime's sense of being under siege.

In the last days of May there was one final, unexpected flash of hope. Demonstrations wound down nationwide, and students from the provinces began to leave Beijing. It seemed as if the mere threat of force had been enough to solve the problem. But some campuses generated calls for a nationwide movement of peaceful resistance, and a hard core of students newly arrived in Beijing from the provinces insisted that the sit-in should continue until a meeting of the National People's Congress scheduled for June 20. Again the time horizon for solving the situation had shifted, and the Elders decided to act. They met in fateful conclave with the three remaining members of the Politburo Standing Committee on June 2 to consolidate their decision to clear the Square by force.

What happened next was one of the most common yet preventable kinds of tragedy in the world: demonstrators and troops getting out of control. China paid dearly for a lack of democratic openness, which could have made demonstrations a more routine matter and could have acclimated the government and the police to handling them.

In the months and years after the bloodshed, Deng Xiaoping labored to prevent the catastrophe from derailing economic reform. No matter what, he insisted reform and opening to the West must continue, and even intensify, or China would regress. Political reform, however, was a different matter. The leaders drew the lesson that China must freeze political reform to avoid instability and should avoid changing its political system to resemble those of the West.

Yet the Party remained divided on this issue. Zhao Ziyang's rebuttal of Li Peng's charges against him at the Fourth Plenum of the Thirteenth Central Committee in June criticized the Deng line from the liberal direction. He argued that the Party could not survive without bolder political reform. Zhao's view remains widely popular, especially among younger officials within the Party.

Throughout the subsequent years, the issue of how to label the student movement has remained alive. Just before ordering the troops to move, the leadership made an official determination that the incident was a *fan'geming baoluan* (counterrevolutionary riot), an even more severe label than "turmoil," implying (falsely) that the demonstrators were armed and had shed blood. Neither designation has ever been officially withdrawn. But in deference to opinion at home and abroad, informal official usage has gravitated to the softer term "political storm" (*zhengzhi fengbo,* equivalent to "political flap"), a term first introduced by Deng a few days after the crackdown.[11]

Since 1989 there has been a constant stream of appeals for formal reconsideration. Ding Zilin, the mother of a student who died on June 4, has led a movement to demand an accounting. In 1999 Bao Tong, a former high-ranking Zhao Ziyang aide, circulated a letter urging the party leaders to acknowledge the mistakes made ten years earlier, calling the opportunity to reverse the verdict the current regime's "greatest political resource" for reviving its legitimacy.[12] On a broader canvas, the Party has faced constant demands for political reform. It has responded with arrests and purges of dissidents outside the Party. But a sharp debate over reform has also developed within the Party. In the course of this debate, participants on both sides started to use a technique that had previously been rare in the history of the People's Republic of China: leaking documents to the outside world—a technique of which the present book is a spectacular extension.

So long as these demands for acknowledging the Party's mistakes during Tiananmen continue to be rejected, the Chinese regime is not the liberalizing, corporatist, consultative, or "soft-authoritarian" system that many in the West make it out to be. To be sure, it has diminished the range of social activities it purports to control in comparison to the totalitarian ambitions of its Maoist years. It has fitted its goals of control more to its means and no longer aspires to change human nature. It has learned that many arenas of freedom are unthreatening to the monopoly of political power.

But the Party also believes it has learned from Tiananmen that democratization is not an irresistible force. There is a widespread view in the West that where globalization and modernization occur, fundamental changes in the Party-state system are inevitable, leading to the rise of civil society and some form of democracy. Whether this is right or wrong, the leaders in power in China do not believe it. For them, the lesson of Tiananmen is that at its core, politics is about force.

The events of 1989 left the regime positioned for its responses to later chal-

---

[11]In his talk to the martial law troops on June 9 (see the Epilogue), Deng used the phrase "this storm," but later references added the word "political." In his June 9 address Deng also defended the use of the term "turmoil."

[12]Bao Tong letter, released March 25, 1999; Chinese text obtained from Human Rights in China.

lenges, such as those of the Chinese Democratic Party in 1998–1999 and the Falungong religious movement in 1999–2000. In both of these incidents and others, the key to the Party's behavior was its fear of independent organizations, whether of religious people or students, workers or farmers, with or without a broad social base, and with or without Party members as constituents. The core political issue has remained what it was in 1989, even if the sociology has been different: The Party believes that as soon as it gives in to any demand from any group it does not control, the power monopoly it views as the indispensable organizational principle of the political system will be destroyed.

Many others in China, however, share the view held widely overseas that this kind of political rigidity cannot persist in the face of rapid social and ideological change. Can the regime muddle through and survive, or will it implode? The backers of this book are trying to avoid the latter outcome. By reopening the issues that were closed in 1989, they want to open a breach in the power monopoly without causing a collapse.

.   .   .

To help readers understand and evaluate what they are about to read, I want to describe in more detail the genre and format of the documents; how they have been selected, translated, and annotated; and how this volume relates to the Chinese book that is to be published separately.

Most of the documents excerpted here are reports from subordinate agencies to Party Central, the State Council, or both. Bureaus filing such reports include the two security ministries, other ministries, ministry-level commissions (such as the State Education Commission), provincial-level Party committees and governments, military regions and districts, and local agencies of central bureaucracies. There are reports on media coverage of events in Western, Hong Kong, and Taiwan media. We do not know exactly how each of these kinds of documents was compiled or processed, but it is clear that they arrived in Zhongnanhai frequently and, depending on their provenance and content, were circulated promptly to different sets of high-ranking leaders. The chapters of this book are arranged chronologically, from mid-April to late June 1989, and each day's document traffic contains materials of these types, arranged in approximately the order in which I have just described them.

In addition, *The Tiananmen Papers* contain records of high-level meetings and conversations, which also appear in nearly every day's set of documents. These include formal meetings, such as those of the Politburo or its Standing Committee; informal meetings, for example, of the Elders; and conversations among two or more people, face-to-face and on the telephone. The most common kind of formal meeting record is referred to as *jilu* (minutes). Such minutes were prepared by specialized staff relying on notes taken at the meeting, sometimes supplemented by tape recordings. They preserve the order of speakers and much of their natural language, but not the hems and haws that might be revealed in a simple transcript, and as necessary they rearrange speakers' grammar and the structure of their remarks so that they read more smoothly, focus more consistently, and are clearer than would be the case in pure oral discourse. We present these passages in quotation marks, because this is the way they are presented in the minutes themselves. Other meeting records are called *jiyao*, which we translate as "summaries." ("We" refers to Perry Link and me. Perry is Professor of Chinese at Princeton. We worked so closely together on the manuscript that it is impossible to separate our contributions.) These are records of decisions reached at each meeting.

For informal conversations among the leaders, the compiler relies chiefly on four sources. The first are recollections that were provided to the Party leadership by the people involved as part of the post-crackdown investigation of Zhao Ziyang's wrongdoings. These recollections were printed for distribution at the Fourth Plenum of the CCP Thirteenth Central Committee, which took place on June 23–24, 1989. (This meeting is described in the Epilogue.) Zhao Ziyang also gave his version of events at this time. The second and third are briefings that Li Peng and Yang Shangkun gave to groups of their subordinates; during these briefings, they extensively rehearsed their involvement in events. Finally, the compiler uses a series of memoranda of conversations supplied by a friend of Yang Shangkun. All of these sources are identified where they are used in the book. Since a given conversation is often described in several such sources, the compiler has combined information to reconstruct most of the accounts of conversations throughout the book. Here, as in minutes, we use quotation marks, reflecting the fact that even though these are not direct transcripts, they were presented by immediate participants as authentic records and are often mutually corroborated.

The book in your hands is the result of three stages of selection, which reduced a large original set of documents to book length. The compiler first selected several thousand documents that he considered to be the most significant amid the flow of hundreds going in and out of Zhongnanhai each day. I advised him that to serve a broad readership he must be even more selective. The documents chosen should focus on the crucial considerations that went into the decisionmaking in Zhongnanhai. Moreover, to save space, the documents selected for inclusion should in most cases be excerpted rather than reproduced complete.

The compiler then undertook a second stage of selecting and excerpting, producing a computer-printed Chinese-language manuscript of 516 pages, or about 570,000 Chinese characters. That manuscript, containing roughly three times as much material as is included in this volume, will be published in Chinese.

The compiler's central interest has been to elucidate the sources and dynamics of the division among the elite over how to respond to the crisis. Thus for both the onset of the crisis and its outcome, in his view the crucial documents are those that expose the decisionmaking process in Zhongnanhai. These are also the documents that add the most to the historical record, since the student side of the struggle is already relatively well covered in available sources. Furthermore, the compiler believes that the leaders were heavily influenced by events unfolding around the country as reported by local party committees, the two security ministries, the Xinhua News Agency, and other channels, so he has given considerable space to those local reports. The local reports are also important because the full nationwide scale of the protests has never been known until now. He has selected those foreign media reports that he believes drew close attention from the leaders, shaping their understanding of the challenges they faced and their view that domestic turmoil was connected to foreign antagonism to their regime. To link the documents together, the compiler added some explanatory and interpretive material aimed at Chinese readers. He did his best in these passages not to editorialize. There are also places where he departs from the documentary mode and integrates several sources into a story.

To produce a book of manageable size, we had to make a third round of cuts, which the compiler authorized us to do. To enable foreign readers to keep track of the narrative even after cutting, we have condensed some of the material into summaries. These summaries are set off from direct translations of documentary material by being set in a sans serif, bold typeface. The summary sections attempt to preserve the sense and substance of both the compiler's interpretive transitions and the original documents he quotes from, while also incorporating elucidations that we deemed necessary for Western readers. Scholars can review whether we have summarized the original material fairly by comparing these condensed sections to the Chinese edition.

Passages of direct translation are set in standard, serif typeface. In making selections of what to translate from what was already a selection of documents, we tried to follow the same principles we urged on the compiler: to highlight the central narrative line of Zhongnanhai decisionmaking, to keep in view events in the provinces, and so on. Since much of what the leaders learned through police reports and similar sources—especially about the demonstrations in Beijing—is already known to us in the West, we opted in favor of documents that present new material. This meant selecting in favor of minutes of top-level meetings and reports about the pro-democracy movement in the provinces. The book thus serves as a self-sufficient narrative, but with a focus where other accounts have not been able to look.

The compiler also authorized us to add explanatory material that we believed would be necessary for non-Chinese readers. This includes interpretive cues embedded in the summaries (for example, identifying locations or persons or explaining the implications of somebody's statement), an editors' note at the start of each chapter, and explanatory footnotes. (All footnotes are ours except for those few marked as having been supplied by the compiler.) In addition, for the foreign-language editions, the compiler has provided a source citation for each document from which we translate directly. These are not found in the Chinese-language edition. To save space, in sections where we summarize documents, we merely indicate the type and source of the document and the date—for example, a report from the State Security Ministry on such and such a date.

For the passages of direct translation, our goal as translators was accuracy both of content and of style. Within the bounds of accuracy, we also aimed at readability. This meant not only getting the meaning right but also using the type of diction in English that the document used in Chinese—formal if it was formal, for example, and conversational if it was conversational—and making the diction as natural in English as it was in Chinese. We made a series of decisions familiar to all translators. Sometimes we reversed the order of elements in a sentence to produce the sense of action that a Chinese sentence conveyed; we left out words if they were redundant in English; we made certain choices about number, gender, and tense that English requires but Chinese does not. We translated familiar Chinese idioms using familiar English idioms, except when we preserved exotic-sounding terms that have become standard, such as "turmoil" for *dongluan*.

A few additional points for those who compare the English and Chinese texts: To provide easier access for foreign readers, we have changed some chapter titles and section headings, combined some sections, added dated running heads, and occasionally rearranged the order of some elements in the text for clarity. We have inserted some caesuras into passages of direct translation where the Chinese text breaks a direct quotation with a transitional sentence of some sort, if this seemed to indicate an abridgment of the original text. Our summaries of foreign sources, even English-language ones, are translations from the Chinese, not transcriptions of the originals. We often refer to the regime or the authorities as "the government" in the generic English-language sense, even though Chinese discourse differentiates between "Party" and "state" authorities. The Chinese language does not distinguish between colleges and universities, so when we use either term it stands for both.

The work of summary and translation involved several people and went through several stages. I selected the passages to summarize and translate. Five translators, who have chosen to remain anonymous, helped us with first drafts of much of the translation and summary. Perry Link and I reviewed and corrected the entire manuscript several times.

It has been a privilege to work with Perry, one of the eminent China specialists of my generation. The experience of working alongside him for long hours has been a happy one. We thank Orville Schell, whose professional judgment and moral support have been invaluable. He made important editorial suggestions and raised questions that pushed us forward in the complex process of confirming that our intuitions about the documents' veracity were correct. I salute the courage and scholarly commitment of all who took part in a project that is going to be unwelcome to some powerful people in China and that may be controversial abroad.

At a point when I was overwhelmed by the difficulties of clarifying legal issues, getting financial support to start the translation, and finding a publisher, I turned to Robert L. Bernstein, a pioneer in the fields of publishing and human rights. Without Bob's help, enthusiasm, interest, and insight, my colleagues and I could not have finished this project. I am grateful to Fiona Druckenmiller for funds to start the translation while the search for a publisher was still under way. No one but Peter Osnos of PublicAffairs would have had the political sensitivity, courage, and marketing genius to handle the challenges of this project. We received invaluable assistance from Geoff Shandler and Robert Kimzey in shaping the book for better reading and Kathy Delfosse gave the manuscript an editorial scrubbing that left it much improved.

I wish to thank two lawyers who provided pro bono advice at times when it was sorely needed, Jerome A. Cohen and R. Scott Greathead.

It was crucial to keep this project secret until it was published, yet I needed to seek help from a number of people in order to get the job done. Besides those already listed, I would like to thank, without naming, several friends in academia, journalism, and publishing in various places around the world who helped me and kept confidence.

This project intruded itself on busy lives already committed to worthy projects and imposed great demands on the time of each participant. During the protracted course of this project, all the people involved stood in solidarity on the issue of publishing the work and contributed in substantial ways to its quality. I wish in particular to salute the compiler, who placed the most at risk in this project and who displayed good judgment and personal integrity during difficult times.

The Tiananmen Papers

1986–Spring 1989
Seeds of Crisis

EDITORS' NOTE: The pro-democracy movement of spring 1989 gave vent to deep social dissatisfactions. But it would never have grown as large or lasted as long as it did had the leaders not been divided over how to respond to it.

These disagreements at the top were long standing, but they intensified from late 1986 onward as the Party faced new challenges of reform. In the earlier stage of reform, starting in the late 1970s, the Party had dissolved the agricultural communes and unleashed rapid growth in the rural economy. In the mid–1980s the Party had turned its attention to the more intransigent problem of reforming urban industrial enterprises. But the industrial reforms had foundered on the conservative managerial culture of state ownership. Attempts to decontrol prices, increase competition, and expand market mechanisms brought inflation in the economy, corruption in the political system, and a "crisis of faith" among intellectuals.

The national mood reflected a profound questioning of China's leaders, political system, and direction. But it was hard to tell whether the social contract was breaking down as a result of inflation and corruption, or a normal civil society was emerging as a result of prosperity and liberalization. In any case, Deng Xiaoping remained the indispensable man of Chinese politics. But his impulsive decisionmaking style was becoming less suitable for an increasingly complex political economy and turbulent society.[1]

---

[1]For more background on these themes, see Andrew J. Nathan, "Reform at the Crossroad: Chinese Politics in 1988," in Nathan, *China's Crisis: Dilemmas of Reform and Prospects for Democracy* (New York: Columbia University Press, 1990), 97–115; and Perry Link, *Evening Chats in Beijing* (New York: W. W. Norton, 1992), 51–118.

1986–Spring 1989

A divided Party leadership

In the mid–1980s the leaders faced a difficult choice between political liberalization and ideological tightening, a dilemma framed for them by the needs of economic reform. One group, headed by Party General Secretary Hu Yaobang and Premier Zhao Ziyang, considered what they called political reform to be essential to removing the obstacles to economic reform. Other members of this group included Lu Dingyi (a former Party propaganda chief), Wan Li (a vice premier, after March 1988 chair of the National People's Congress Standing Committee), and Xi Zhongxun (a member of the Central Secretariat and after March 1988 deputy chair of the NPC Standing Committee). As of late 1988, this group still enjoyed the support of Deng Xiaoping.

A second group of leaders, headed by Party Elders Chen Yun (a retired economic policy-maker), Li Xiannian (head of state until March 1988), and Peng Zhen (until March 1988 head of the NPC), feared that weakening Party control would encourage ideological and social disorder. They stressed the dangers of "bourgeois liberalization," by which they meant strains of thought tending toward capitalism. They demanded that the Party take steps to restore organization and ideological discipline, especially the obligation of Party members, including intellectuals,[2] to support the ideas and policies of Party Central.[3] Other members of this group included Zhou Enlai's widow, Deng Yingchao, and ideologues Hu Qiaomu and Deng Liqun. In deference to their concerns, in 1986 Deng Xiaoping authorized the Party to step up ideological propaganda under the rubric of "building socialist spiritual civilization."[4]

[2] The term "intellectuals" (in Chinese, *zhishifenzi*) refers variously, depending on context, to anyone with a high school education, to college students and college graduates, or, as here, to higher intellectuals including writers, college faculty, media personnel, propagandists, and other "thought workers" of various kinds. The intended referent is usually clear from context but seldom precise. In the context of events in Beijing in spring 1989, "intellectuals" usually means the writers and thinkers who advised the students.

[3] "Party Central" or "the Center" refers to the top decisionmaking organs of the Chinese Communist Party (CCP). The referent is vague and depends on context. Formally, the Center means the Central Committee, constitutionally the Party's ruling body. The Central Committee meets in plenary session only once a year. Making daily decisions on behalf of the Central Committee are the Politburo (in 1989 consisting of seventeen persons) and above that, the Politburo Standing Committee (in 1989, five persons). Serving the needs of these organs are such bodies as the Central Office (*Zhongyang bangongting*) and others whose functions are explained as the story unfolds. Important decisions could also emanate from various working conferences of top leaders or from speeches given by influential leaders to groups of working-level officials. Behind the Politburo and its Standing Committee, and becoming involved in its crucial decisions in 1989, was a loosely defined body of retired leaders of whom the eight most influential became known as the "Elders." None of these sat on the Politburo or the Standing Committee. The most powerful among them was Deng Xiaoping. In any case the CCP, as the ruling party, made all important decisions both for itself and for governmental, or "state," organs, and for the military via a Party organ called the Central Military Commission.

[4] That is, correct ideological and moral thinking among the populace.

The struggle between the two factions intensified when student demonstrations broke out in Beijing and some other cities in December 1986. Although the students returned to classes in January 1987, on January 16 the Politburo, with Deng's acquiescence, forced Hu Yaobang to resign from his post of Party general secretary and to take responsibility for what was seen as his weak leadership in combating ideological deterioration. This was a blow to Deng's plans for his succession, since Hu Yaobang and Zhao Ziyang were the two men he had been grooming to take power. Deng moved Zhao, the remaining successor, into Hu's vacant position as Party chief and in 1988 chose former vice premier Li Peng to replace Zhao as premier.

Despite his concessions to the concerns of his conservative colleagues, Deng instructed Zhao not to let the antiliberalization campaign interfere with either economic or political reform. Deng's vision of political reform was limited. It involved "separating Party and government," by which he meant changing administrative procedures so that Communist Party organs interfered less directly in government, leaving the latter to function more independently and with greater expertise, especially in managing the economy. To work out the details, on September 16, 1986, the Politburo had appointed a Small Group for Research on Reform of the Central Political System. Zhao Ziyang headed the committee, and his chief aide in its work was Bao Tong, who was to play an important role in the events of spring 1989.[5] It was this group's ideas that Zhao relied on in presenting a modest blueprint for diminishing and routinizing the Party's role at the Thirteenth Party Congress in October 1987.[6] In a move designed to prepare the way ideologically for intensifying economic reform, the Congress also declared that China was in the "preliminary stage of socialism," meaning a stage at which it was appropriate to use such capitalist methods as markets and profit-seeking management to achieve economic growth.

On the advice of reform economists, in spring 1988 Zhao proposed and Deng approved an attempt to abolish rapidly the existing system of state-set prices for major industrial inputs and products and allow prices to float to market values. This would potentially remove much of the slack for state-owned enterprises while also abolishing some of the most lucrative opportunities for corruption. But even before the plan was formally decided, rumors about it precipitated widespread panic buying. First the more conservative Elders Chen Yun and Li Xiannian and then Deng himself called for abandoning the price reform plan, and Zhao complied. As a result of this experience, Deng's confidence in Zhao was shaken, Zhao's political reform plans were shelved, and his economic reforms were also put on hold.

---

[5]Wu Guoguang tells the story of this political reform research group in *Zhao Ziyang yu zhengzhi gaige* (Zhao Ziyang and political reform) (Hong Kong: Taipingyang shiji yanjiusuo, 1997).
[6]Excerpts from the report appear in Michel Oksenberg, Lawrence R. Sullivan, and Marc Lambert, eds., *Beijing Spring, 1989, Confrontation and Conflict: The Basic Documents* (Armonk, New York: M. E. Sharpe, 1990), 95–101.

Crime on the rise

The March 1989 work report submitted by the Supreme People's Court to the Second Session of the Seventh National People's Congress showed that in 1988 the nation's courts had dealt with a record-breaking 55,710 cases of economic crime: 8,428 people were tried for corruption, 1,584 for accepting bribes, 1,699 for profiteering, and 198 for smuggling. Another 15,787 cases of economic crime reached the courts in the first quarter of 1989. People were found guilty of corruption and bribery in 6,433 of these cases, which was an increase of 27 percent from the previous year. Corruption cases that involved ten thousand yuan[7] or more and were committed by leaders at the county (or for the military, regiment) level or higher reached 1,338 for the quarter, an increase of 107 percent from a year earlier.

Serious cases of economic crime involving government officials had a pernicious ripple effect throughout society. The Public Security Ministry reported 560,000 criminal cases in 1989 for the first quarter alone, compared to 540,000 such cases for the entire year of 1985. The situation in Hunan was representative.

> Excerpt from Hunan Provincial Party Committee, "Move actively to fight all-out war for comprehensive management of social order," report to Party Central, April 13

Hunan Public Security has launched a relatively successful all-out war against criminal activities this year, but prospects for the future remain grim. The situation has drawn strong criticism and palpable discontent from the people.

Since the beginning of the year, many people have written to the Party Committee to point out social problems, to inform on criminals, or simply to vent their feelings. The letters are accusatory and angry and betray a sense of anxiety. Some complain that bandits, robbers, and pickpockets are now so common that lawlessness reigns. It used to be that battery was a serious crime, but now, these letters say, even murder seems no more serious than slaughtering a chicken. It used to be that bandits dared only to operate deep in the mountains or in remote areas, but now they are down in the cities committing crimes on trains, buses, and ferry boats. Prostitution, out of sight for years, has returned. Gambling, fights over water and land, and organized battles between clans have all reached levels of frequency, size, and destructiveness that are unprecedented since Liberation.

A study by Hunan Public Security has revealed severe criminal activity in five

[7]The yuan is the Chinese unit of currency. In 1988–1989, one U.S. dollar traded for 3.71 yuan at the official exchange rate and for about 8.1 yuan on the black market in Beijing.

areas: (1) Major crime, including robbery and burglary, has increased sharply. Last quarter we had 14,040 criminal cases in the province, of which 2,739 were classified as "serious" and 125 as "major." These figures represent increases, respectively, of 51 percent, 96 percent, and 52 percent over the same period last year. (2) Organized banditry is rampant. In January and February 2,182 members of 615 gangs were tracked down. . . . (3) Grave robbing has become widespread. Since 1987 more than 2,700 grave sites have been ransacked in Changsha, a thousand or more of which were ancient burial sites dating from Ming and Qing times.[8] . . . (4) Prostitution and gambling are increasing. More than 25,000 cases were reported in the province in the last quarter, which is an increase of 17 percent over last year; fines for these crimes exceeded 1.75 million yuan, and property valued at more than 290,000 yuan was confiscated. Cases of prostitution are up 62 percent over last year and cases of dissemination of pornography up 80 percent. Gambling, formerly a covert practice, is more widespread and is now out in the open. (5) There are more cases of demonstrations, public petitioning, and other disruptions of public order. Armed battles between villages or counties over land and grave sites are a regular occurrence. Some combatants build their own firearms, and others attack military units to seize weapons.

What has caused the sharp increase in criminal behavior and disruption of public order? Comrades in Public Security believe that mercenary motives are the main cause of the crime frenzy. Statistics show that 82 percent of major crimes are traceable to money. Specific contributing factors to the focus on money are (1) loss of financial control as well as rampant inflation; (2) desire for an extravagant lifestyle; (3) weakened security in units that have been slow to implement preventive measures; and (4) slow response by authorities and low success rates in solving crimes. In the last quarter, the success rate in solving serious and major crimes was 73 percent, a 6 percent decrease from a year ago; the rate for major theft and robbery was only 68 percent and in some counties and cities was as low as 40 percent or 50 percent.

The Standing Committee of the Provincial Party Committee scrutinized the causes of these problems and concluded that one immediate cause was a common view that social order is the business only of public security agencies. Certain Party and government organizations maintained a hands-off policy, which in turn led to failures in public security. . . . Criminals found loopholes in a system in which public security personnel take percentages of the fees for cases and

[8]A.D. 1368–1912.

in which offenders can pay fines to get their cases reduced or dismissed. The quantity and quality of prosecution and law enforcement personnel do not meet evolving needs. Not only are rates of crime solution low, but many law enforcement personnel even participate in crime and thus exert a baleful influence on society. Good Samaritans often get no support or protection, and this allows bad behavior to spread while the righteous are suppressed. Some comrades feel that the underlying cause of this situation is that we have been lax in ideological education. People value only money and think only of money, and hence all segments of society become saturated with corrupt practices and such antisocial behavior as idleness, greed, illicit sexual transactions, theft, pickpocketing, robbery, bribery, and fraud. Some comrades note that lax ideological education has undercut the traditional virtues of the Party and the nation and see this as a great blunder. It is time to face these problems and to solve them.

Problems of public order reached even into the prisons. A Justice Ministry report of February 8, 1989 described a riot that broke out in a labor reform farm in the southwestern corner of the Taklimakan Desert in Xinjiang. More than eighty prisoners wielding hammers and knives killed prison guards, seized an area of the prison, took hostages, and torched buildings. Ten people died.

A report from the Xinjiang Labor Reform Bureau described eleven major prison riots that had broken out in twenty-three labor reform camps over the past year. Ninety-six prisoners escaped, and three guards were killed. In the first quarter of 1989, an additional seven serious disturbances involved theft of weapons and led to the murder of three guards and the escape of thirteen prisoners. The report cited four serious problems in the province's labor reform system. First, supervisors ignored laws and sometimes broke them. Prison staff beat, insulted, and abused prisoners; prisoners, in response, resisted reform and sought revenge. Second, lax management gave informal "cell bosses" and "prison tyrants" a free hand. Dominant prisoners beat up other prisoners, and the most savage became "prison overlords." Third, because labor camps were located in the most remote and desolate places, prison staff and their families complained that they too served life sentences, and young people had begun to shun careers at labor reform farms. Recently, seventy-two young male guards in Yutian County had reached marriageable age at a time when there were only four eligible females within forty kilometers. Such hardship only increases their tendency to vent frustrations on prisoners. Fourth, the quality of prison food had declined, and prisons were overcrowded, conditions that were a breeding ground for strife among prisoners.

Ideological conditions in the military

A January 1989 report to Party Central from the General Political Department of the People's Liberation Army (PLA) said that although there were all kinds of ideological problems in the military, most of them were related to the troops' material interests. First, the military budget had not increased in years. If inflation was taken into account, this meant the budget had shrunk. Weapons stockpiles were deteriorating. Combat readiness could be affected. Second, military property and facilities were inadequately protected. Military installations had been vandalized. The growth of a market economy had led to economic disputes between local communities and the military, which wanted to expand into various lines of business that competed with local agriculture and industries. Third, military families saw their living standards falling behind those of civilians. Fourth, the government lacked an effective policy for helping military personnel transfer to civilian jobs. And fifth, civilians had little understanding of the military, and the once fervent popular concern for the welfare of soldiers was a thing of the past.

A March 1989 Central Military Commission (CMC) report described problems that had arisen since mid-decade as military officers brought their families to live with them near their posts, a phenomenon called localization.[9]

> Excerpt from Central Military Commission Office, "Investigative report on the phenomenon of 'localization' in the officer corps," March 18

Since 1985 nearly all regional force officers have set down roots in the communities where they serve, and many officers of the field armies stationed in places where conditions are relatively good have done the same.[10] One group army has reported that 30 percent of its officers have families living within fifty kilometers of its camp and that nearly two-thirds of its officers below battalion rank are married. Such localization has obvious advantages for families, but it creates the following new problems for the strength of the armed forces.

1. Localized officers tend to leave camp to be with their families on Sundays and holidays. . . .
2. Localization leads to lax discipline. . . .
3. Localization makes normal rotation of officers difficult. Some officers

---

[9]The Chinese term is *jiamenhua.*

[10]The Chinese army is divided into more lightly equipped regional forces, whose mission is to defend the region, and more heavily equipped and mobile main force or field armies, which are assigned to move around within or beyond Chinese territory in case of war.

regard any base more than fifty kilometers from their homes as a "remote unit" and resist transfer. . . .

4. Localization invites pilfering of military provisions. Officers' dependents sometimes show up at a base and "use their own pots to cook military rice." . . . Some officers even set up arrangements with supply personnel to send nonstaple food directly to their own quarters. This sets an extremely bad example for the soldiers.

On March 31, after nearly two months of inspecting his units, Commander Liu Jingsong of the Shenyang Military Region reported that soldiers' low political consciousness was related to outmoded teaching styles among their political instructors. He offered three suggestions for raising consciousness within the armed forces: (1) Instructors should stop proclaiming that "everything is wonderful." For example, an increase in the price of pearl rice should not be presented as an increase in living standards. (2) Instructors should stop using cut-and-dried written study materials and focus on actual problems that reflect officers' and soldiers' daily lives. (3) Leaders should practice what they preach. If a leader campaigns against corruption while taking gifts and bribes, the masses are going to say that "onstage he describes the problem, offstage he demonstrates it."

Calls for reform from local leaders

Local Party and government leaders pressured the Center to crack down harder on corruption and to provide firmer leadership in reform. A December 1988 speech by pro-reform Tianjin Party secretary and mayor Li Ruihuan stressed the need to start fighting corruption by giving heavy sentences to some family members of top leaders. He also called on the Central leaders to provide a stronger ideological rationale for reform, to use the safety valve functions of the media by allowing them greater latitude to reflect popular grievances, to pay more attention to the growing gap between rich and poor, and to build popular support by arousing nationalist sentiment in support of the reform program. In March 1989 the popular reformist mayor of Shenyang, Wu Disheng, filed a report with Party Central and the State Council blaming some problems of reform on a lack of balance, firmness, and focus in the policies emanating from the top. Li's and Wu's views were similar to those of many local officials.

The angst of youth

In March 1989 two agencies reported to Party Central and the State Council on a nationwide survey of youth, conducted from October to December 1988.[11]

> Excerpt from Joint Committee on Women and Youth of the Chinese People's Political Consultative Conference and the Central Office of the Communist Youth League, "Report on a survey of the current state of ideology among youth," March 28, chapter 3, sec. 1

The main trends in the thinking of our nation's youth are good. But in the current social environment, which has not been put fully in order, the question of young people's thinking harbors some sharp challenges. Lack of understanding or poor handling of these problems could bring serious consequences. Several factors could generate instability among our youth, especially the highly educated. If we do not deal with them properly and allow conflict to intensify, there could be an impact on reform and on national stability.

1. On the attitude toward the Four Basic Principles:[12] The majority of our young people uphold the Four Principles, but these are mainly farmers and soldiers. Only 3.35 percent of youth believe there is no need for the Four Principles, but these doubters are concentrated among college graduates. They are mostly teachers, students, and technical personnel. Those who unambiguously state that Marxist-Leninist ideology is ill suited to our country's reform and opening comprise 9.75 percent, a percentage that must not be ignored. Here too, college graduates form the large majority. Our questionnaire showed that 20.2 percent believe "reform" combines socialism and capitalism, and most of these, again, were college students or college graduates. This is proof of ideological confusion at the higher educational levels.

---

[11]"Youth" *(qingnian)* officially refers to persons aged eighteen through thirty-five. We do not know the methodology employed in this survey, but sophisticated sampling techniques were not widely used in China at this time. The percentages given are probably biased by unknown sampling errors.

[12]The Four Basic Principles, or Four Principles, were minimum standards for ideological rectitude laid down by Deng Xiaoping in a speech on March 30, 1979. They were adherence to Marxism-Leninism-Mao Zedong thought, to socialism, to the dictatorship of the proletariat, and to Communist Party leadership. In the struggles between reformers and conservatives, everyone agreed that these four principles must be upheld; the question often debated, however, was what they meant.

2. On the reputation of the Chinese Communist Party: Among respondents, 31.5 percent believed that the panic buying in summer 1988 showed the people's lack of confidence in the government. Most of the people holding that opinion were people engaged in business or, again, those with advanced educational backgrounds. Only 22.8 percent of respondents believed that the reputation of the Communist Party will improve. There were two different opinions on the Party's current reputation: 24.5 percent saw it as being about the same this year as last, while 20.3 percent saw it as having fallen this year; 29.7 percent felt that trust in the Party and government had increased after the Thirteenth Party Congress,[13] but about the same number, 29.1 percent, felt it had decreased.

3. On the value of student protests:[14] The views of young people about how to handle student protests differ widely from those of Party Central. Favorable views on student protest—which coincide with the views of adults, according to surveys—are especially worth noting; they are evidence of an unstable ideological foundation in our society. For example: Are student protests a legitimate way for youth to voice opinions? Yes, 59.2 percent; no, only 8.2 percent. Are student protests a legitimate way for youth to oppose corrupt practices? Yes, 57.0 percent; no, 13.3 percent. Is it wrong to say that students protest because they like to make trouble? Yes, it is wrong, 49.3 percent; no, this is correct, 7.8 percent. Is it wrong to say that student protests hinder the government's reform efforts? Yes, it is wrong, 37.7 percent; no, this is correct, 9.2 percent. Do student protests show that young people are patriotic? Yes, 38.9 percent; no, 17.1 percent. It is obvious that the great majority of young people approve of student protests. The same questions posed to the adult population yielded the following results: Are student protests one way for students to oppose corrupt practices? Yes, 60.1 percent; no, 12.3 percent. Are student protests a legitimate way for youth to voice their opinions? Yes, 51.8 percent; no, 12.2 percent. Is it wrong to say that students protest because they like to make trouble? Yes, it is wrong, 42.5 percent; no, this is correct, 8.3 percent. The similarity of attitudes between young people and adults should be a major concern.

4. On confidence in reform: Young people are extremely sensitive to many aspects of reform and are anxious about the rising cost of living; 63.8 percent of respondents consider the unchecked rise of prices to be their greatest worry. Their views on reforms in housing policy are essentially as follows: Reform must

[13] In September 1987.
[14] Here "student protests" is a general reference; actual student protests had last occurred in the fall of 1986 in Hefei, Shanghai, and elsewhere.

be evenhanded, and no one should get special privileges; if rents are to be raised and houses to be sold, then workers' wages must rise and housing subsidies must be available. This approach varies markedly from the policies and plans of the Center. The survey shows that young people's enthusiasm for reform, and their willingness to work for it, have fallen off since the Third Plenum of the Thirteenth Central Committee.[15] They have misgivings about the direction and prospects of reform as well as about its goals and benefits. Because channels of communication are not good, the views and ideas of many young people who are worried about the future of reform do not receive the attention they deserve.

5. On public ethics: Corruption brings serious harm to the environment in which young people grow up, and if our struggle against corruption makes no progress, the young will naturally feel resentful. Our survey finds that young people believe that in the real world, job promotions are based not on the fruits of hard work or pursuit of learning but on one's parents' connections and on the favor of leaders. The majority of young people estimate that social ethics are worse this year than last and that the overall picture is now much worse than it was before the Thirteenth Party Congress. The gradual decline in social ethics, combined with the percentage of youth (20.5 percent) who believe that the self is the be-all and end-all for any endeavor, could produce narrow pursuit of personal gain and lead to aberrant political behavior.

Faculty disaffection and amnesty appeals

A report of March 17, 1989, from the State Education Commission to Party Central and the State Council reported on preparations for an academic conference to commemorate the seventieth anniversary of the May Fourth Movement.[16] According to the report, views among the nearly two hundred young and middle-aged faculty[17] contacted for opinions about the conference deviated from the official line. Some were critical of the Communist revolution and felt that moderate reform would have been a better path for China in the twentieth century. Many felt that the May

---

[15]In November 1988.

[16]The May Fourth Movement in favor of "science and democracy" was initiated by the May Fourth Incident of 1919, when students in Beijing, protesting international approval of Japan's claims to Shandong Province after World War I, marched to the house of a cabinet minister and burned it down. The movement is viewed both as the high tide of Chinese liberalism and as the starting point of the Chinese Communist revolution. Intellectuals expected the seventieth anniversary in 1989 to provide an opportunity for advocates of political reform and democratization to stress the historical pedigree and respectability of these goals.

[17]"Middle-aged" in Chinese refers to people from age thirty-six to their middle fifties.

Fourth Movement had introduced an incomplete version of Marxism into China, teaching only how to seize power but not how to build the economy or construct a fair society. Others argued that Marxism had become distorted by its encounter with Oriental peasant culture. In any case, the critics implied that Marxism had become an obstacle to rather than a force for China's development. Even those affirming the spirit of May Fourth held views contrary to the official interpretation, saying that May Fourth stood for complete adoption of Western values and above all for individual freedom.

The General Office of the Central Committee received an urgent report, dated December 3, 1988, from the Sichuan Provincial Party Committee on a series of protest posters[18] that had appeared on the campus of Southwest Jiaotong University. The posters emotionally attacked the Party for inflation, inequality, and worsening living conditions and called on intellectuals to rise up and demonstrate against the government. Party Central instructed provincial authorities to be sure these demonstrations did not occur. The Shanghai Municipal Party Committee also filed a report in March 1989 detailing the deteriorating living conditions and morale of young instructors at fifty-one institutions of higher learning in that city.

In addition, the Party faced challenges from liberal intellectuals inside and outside the establishment. Three leading liberal intellectuals—Fang Lizhi, Liu Binyan, and Wang Ruowang—had been expelled from the Party in early 1987 in connection with the dismissal of Hu Yaobang. On January 6, 1989, Fang, a professor of astrophysics and former academic administrator, wrote an open letter to Deng Xiaoping recommending amnesty for Wei Jingsheng, China's most famous dissident, who had already served nearly ten years in prison, and for other political prisoners. A letter supporting this idea and signed by thirty-three prominent intellectuals was sent to the NPC and Party Central on February 13. A letter urging faster and more radical political reform was issued on February 26 by forty-two prominent intellectuals. And on March 14 a group of forty-three intellectuals signed a letter to the NPC supporting the call for release of political prisoners.[19]

Protest potential on the campuses

The authorities kept a close watch on campus sentiment in the two years after Hu Yaobang's dismissal. In this period Party Central and the State Council received at least fifty reports on student attitudes from the State Education Commission, the Xinhua News Agency, and the govern-

---

[18]*Dazibao,* literally "big-character posters," are handwritten and often anonymous posters, usually containing criticisms, complaints, or dissident ideas, that are pasted up in public places. In this book we translate *dazibao* as "protest poster" or "wall poster."

[19]Three of these letters are reprinted in Oksenberg, Sullivan, and Lambert, *Beijing Spring,* 166–168, 169–171.

ments of the provinces, autonomous regions, and province-level municipalities.[20] Among the problems they mentioned were student dissatisfaction with ideological constraints, low wages for intellectuals, the rising cost of living, dissatisfaction with policies on study abroad, and laxness by the people in charge of political thought work[21] on college campuses. Additional factors are analyzed in the following report.

> Excerpt from State Education Commission, "Report to Party Central and the State Council on student protests in the 1980s and the current ideological state of college students," July 19, 1988

1. A summary of student protests. . . . As of this spring, the relevant personnel are predicting that a third nationwide student protest [after those of 1985 and 1986–1987] could occur in September and October [1988], owing to the fact that the reform program has entered its most difficult and critical phase and students are looking mostly at its negative side. Based upon preliminary statistics, from January through June of this year, student unrest, major and minor, has surfaced in forty-six institutions of higher learning in thirteen provinces and municipalities. Following the murder of Chai Qingfeng, a graduate student at Peking University,[22] student protests were averted by the Center's timely and decisive actions. A graduate student at Peking University said, "This protest took place without sufficient theoretical or organizational preparation. It was organized by freshmen and sophomores who had high-flying ideas but produced low-level results. It was premature, and it failed." This protest did not relieve much of the students' frustration.

2. Basic causes of student protests. . . .

A. Corruption in the Party and society easily stimulate extremist sentiments in youth. Although these unhealthy trends undeniably exist, students are easily misled by rumors and exaggerated claims. Student discussions often focus on such issues as "children of high-ranking officials getting leadership posts" and "children of high-ranking officials setting up companies."

---

[20]China's thirty province-level administrative units in 1989 included twenty-two provinces, five autonomous regions (like provinces, but nominally ruled "autonomously" by national minority peoples), and three cities (Beijing, Tianjin, and Shanghai) directly administered by the Center. In this book we use "province-level" as an abbreviation for all three.
[21]Political thought work *(zhengzhi sixiang gongzuo)* is the work of conducting ideological propaganda on campuses, in the military, and in other settings. It is conducted in various forms, including formal meetings and individual conversations.
[22]We follow this university's practice in translating its name as Peking University rather than Beijing University.

B. Students are frustrated by shifts in the official media's propaganda line. Prior to the first student protest in 1985, newspapers held the students in high regard, as if they were favored by heaven. But after the protest, the students were angry when newspapers accused them of extravagant lifestyles. They were especially upset by phrases like "the working class does not agree [to support you in such a style]" and "[you are only] a small handful."[23]

C. Students complain that they have no access to leaders. Channels are seldom open, and even when they are, no response comes back. School leaders are reluctant to meet with students because they fear that sentiments will become even more polarized if they cannot respond adequately to student concerns.

D. A small number of bad elements have infiltrated colleges to stir up trouble. Every student protest has been joined by a few bad elements with murky backgrounds from society at large. Some were active in the 1978 Democracy Wall movement,[24] such as the fiancée of Wei Jingsheng, who is currently serving a prison sentence, and Wei's other followers. Some are members of such underground groups as the Guizhou Enlightenment Society.[25] Such groups were also active in the 1986 student movement. There are followers of the Gang of Four ideology, and there are others who are critical of the government. Take, for instance, Liu Gang, a graduate in physics from Peking University who was responsible for the Peking University magazine *Free Talk* and who is currently unemployed. He participated in the 1986 protests and in this most recent one. From June 6 to June 9 [1988], every evening he espoused his political agenda at rallies at the Peking University Triangle.[26] He takes a consistent viewpoint and is protected by certain people. People like Fang Lizhi and his wife Li Shuxian have also been extremely active.

It appears that a tiny minority of people wrote the reactionary posters during this latest protest at Peking University. They used pseudonyms such as The Poor Monk of Yan Garden, The Hunanese, and The Blue Sail of Peking University.

[23] *Yixiaocuo,* which we translate as "a small handful," is (like *jishaoshu,* "a tiny minority") a familiar term of political abuse in Chinese Communist rhetoric. It refers to a small group of wrongheaded people who are responsible for misleading a large group of good-hearted people. In practice the term is used to try to split a movement by suggesting that only a few leaders will be punished. Later in this book we will see the government using *yixiaocuo* against the demonstrators and the demonstrators using it against Li Peng and his allies in the government. We have translated the term identically throughout so that readers can note its use.
[24] The Democracy Wall movement was a pro-democracy and pro-reform popular movement that partly took the form of hanging protest posters on a wall, which became known as Democracy Wall, in central Beijing in 1978–1979. In 1979 Wei Jingsheng was sentenced to fourteen years in jail for his participation.
[25] A group of Guizhou-based dissident poets who also participated in the Democracy Wall movement.
[26] The Triangle *(sanjiaodi)* in the heart of the Peking University campus was its students' favored location for their posters, discussions, and rallies.

Infiltration by hostile foreign powers has also been a factor. Because Premier Li Peng studied in the USSR, some in the West have marshaled international public opinion to attack him. Posters at Peking University show this.

The report summed up the lessons of dealing with the most recent student protest by urging (1) solid leadership by university Party organizations and presidents, who should move firmly against expressions of reactionary views; (2) mobilization of progressive graduate students and key teachers to do thought work on students; (3) establishment of security stations at key schools; (4) strengthening of the ranks of people conducting political thought work on campuses.

In mid-June 1988, officials responsible for political thought work at more than thirty universities nationwide gathered at the Chinese University of Science and Technology in Hefei, Anhui Province, to discuss the results of a vast questionnaire-based survey that had been conducted under the title "Current University Students' Ideology and Choices." The meeting reported to Party Central and the State Council that there was an increasing tendency for students to be politically confused or even to hold wrong views. For example, 39.7 percent of students believed that the concept of a Communist society is utopian and will never be realized. Students were described as increasingly concerned with personal interests and as advocating fighting for oneself and putting personal needs above all. Among students, 53.4 percent did not want to become Party members, 46.7 percent thought that Party behavior was getting worse, and 15.9 percent blamed negative trends in the Party on corruption in the leadership.

Moreover, 53.6 percent attributed the nationwide student protest of late 1986 to corruption in the state system; 14.3 percent said that participants in the 1986 student protest had done nothing wrong; and 42.3 percent said that, should a similar protest occur in the future, their decision to participate would depend on circumstances. Only 41.7 percent believed that modernization should follow the socialist path; 46.7 percent did not care what "ism" it followed so long as the country gets wealthy; and 8.8 percent agreed to the proposition that we "should add capitalism to the curriculum and implement total Westernization."

In March 1989 the Central Committee of the Communist Youth League[27] sent a report to Party Central and the State Council describing a survey of student attitudes at twenty-three Beijing institutions of higher learning. The report discerned a sort of "substable state" on the campuses. Some students said that the ideology articulated at the Thirteenth Party Congress did not make sense. They described China as a rudderless ship, pitching in the ocean and making passengers sick. Some said that the ten years of the Cultural Revolution (1966–1976) constituted a state of anarchy and that the ten years of reform (1978–1988) constituted a state of government with no doctrine; the former was a decade of turmoil, the latter a decade of aimless change. Some said

---

[27]The Communist Youth League is a nationwide organization for teenagers who hope eventually to join the Communist Party. Youth League membership is virtually automatic for those who apply; Party membership is not.

that Marxism is outdated, others that China has the worst record of democracy even among socialist countries.

The report said that some students are pessimistic about their own futures and have given up studying. The Tuo [TOEFL–Test of English as a Foreign Language] faction only studies English in hopes of getting admitted to school overseas, while the Ma [mahjong] and Qiao [bridge] factions spend all their time gambling. Fewer and fewer register to take the graduate school entrance exam. According to some students, people seem to be waiting for something, as if a major incident is on the horizon. The report argued that such attitudes, if left unchecked, could lead to destabilizing incidents. Large-scale protests might occur given sufficient stimulus from without, and smaller-scale incidents over matters relating to students' direct interests seem unavoidable. The authorities should be alert to the possibility that some people will spread negative views during the coming May Fourth anniversary.

Foreigners see economic challenges but not a political crisis

In late 1988 and early 1989 the Center received numerous foreign press reports that emphasized China's economic problems, but the reports did not anticipate political disorder. Three reports got considerable attention in Zhongnanhai. In the *Daily Telegraph* for November 17, 1988, China specialist Graham Harkins[28] argued that political change had not kept up with changes in the economic system and that China did not seem to have a leader capable of meeting this challenge. In the *Los Angeles Times* on March 19, 1989, Edward A. Gargan said that the Chinese economic planning system had collapsed. The government was unable to afford the political price it would have to pay to reverse the loss of control over prices, and part of the leadership wanted to reverse course on reform. The system was drifting, its direction unclear.

A reporter from the Xinhua News Agency spoke with American China specialist Harry Harding Jr. in March 1989, at a conference in Washington, D.C., and reported his views to Beijing in an intelligence serial for top leaders entitled *Reference Proofs.*[29] Harding was cautiously optimistic about China's prospects so long as there was no major change in the pro-reform top leadership. To better manage strains in the U.S.-China relationship over the issues of Taiwan and human rights,[30] Harding urged the Chinese government to seek closer contacts with its critics.

---

[28]Name guessed from the Chinese transcription.

[29]*Cankao qingyang. Qingyang* literally means "proofs," but these proofs are not put into public print.

[30]The Taiwan issue refers to U.S. insistence that China's claim to Taiwan be settled peacefully and Chinese demands that the United States cease interfering in China's internal affairs by maintaining its guarantee for the security of Taiwan. The human rights issue involved criticisms of Chinese human rights violations by U.S.-based nongovernmental organizations, media, members of Congress, and the administration.

CHAPTER ONE

April 8–23

The Student Movement Begins

EDITORS' NOTE: The death by heart attack of the popular pro-reform leader Hu Yaobang on April 15 fell like a spark into the highly flammable atmosphere of elite division and popular disaffection. For the Party leadership, Hu was a "loyal Communist fighter" and "great proletarian revolutionary," but for students he was a symbol of liberal reform and clean government. They launched spontaneous mourning activities, using Hu's death as an opportunity to express their dissatisfaction with the pace of political change. These activities spread rapidly, surprising the leaders and eliciting much foreign attention.

At first, most of the students were careful to remain on the right side of the regime's ambiguous ground rules for action and speech. They marched to mourn rather than to protest, and they focused their attention on Hu Yaobang's contributions to the Party, the need to accelerate political reform, and opposition to corruption. But a minority raised more dangerous issues, such as democracy and press freedom, or voiced slogans with a hostile edge against the Party or certain leaders. The leaders were divided in their evaluations of the student movement's threat.

Because officials refused to meet student petitioners at the Great Hall of the People, a sit-in developed in front of Zhongnanhai's Xinhua Gate starting the night of April 19. The security ministries and local governments provided almost hour-by-hour and campus-by-campus reports on student activities in Beijing and throughout the country. Two reports from Beijing municipal authorities to Party Central depicted the student movement as dangerous. The emergence of autonomous student organizations sharpened the challenge to the regime. Opinion hardened among the Elders.

When the leaders gathered for Hu's memorial service on April 22, they encountered a peaceful but vast demonstration outside the Great Hall of the People. Although the demonstration was extremely worrying, Zhao Ziyang nonetheless won the approval of the supreme leader, Deng Xiaoping, and prevailed on his Politburo colleagues to take a relatively soft line with the students. The leadership seemed to assume that the students had made their point and would now be willing to go back to classes. It was a wildly inaccurate assumption, but Zhao was confident that all would be well as he departed for a week-long state visit to North Korea. His absence from China was to prove crucial in the decisions to come.

April 8–15

The death of Hu Yaobang

At 9 A.M. on April 8, in Qinzheng Hall at Zhongnanhai, Zhao Ziyang chaired a Politburo meeting to discuss views on a document called "Central Committee Decision on Certain Questions in Educational Development and Reform (Draft)." Hu Yaobang, although relieved of his position as Party general secretary in January 1987, remained as a member of the Politburo and attended this meeting. Commissioner of Education Li Tieying briefed the members.

> Based on participants' notes of an oral report[1] given by Wen Jiabao, in his role as secretary of Party Committees of units under Party Central and director of the Party Central Office, to the senior working staff of those offices, and of an oral report given by Luo Gan in his capacity as secretary general of the State Council and secretary of Party Committees in ministry-level state organizations, to senior staff of those offices

During this briefing, Hu Yaobang sat with a pinched look. Minister of Defense Qin Jiwei later recalled, "I sensed something wrong about Comrade Yaobang from the time the meeting opened. His face was ashen. But he was straining to keep up appearances." About three quarters of an hour into the meeting, as Li Tieying was reviewing the education budgets of recent years, Hu appeared to be fading. He rose to request permission to leave. But as soon as he rose to his feet, he collapsed back into his chair.

"Comrade Ziyang . . ." His voice broke off as his hand faltered in the air,

---

[1]This kind of oral report by a leader to staff is called a *tongbao*.

describing a semicircle. Everyone present, caught by surprise, stood up and stared at the ashen-faced Hu.

"It's probably a heart attack. . . . Don't move him!" someone said.

"Anyone have nitroglycerin?" Zhao Ziyang asked urgently.

"I do!" It was Qin Jiwei, who also had a heart condition. He took two pills from his briefcase and put them into Hu Yaobang's mouth. Then to Hu Qili, who came rushing over, he said, "Hurry and lay Comrade Yaobang on the floor."

Hu slowly opened his eyes as staff members telephoned Liberation Army Hospital 305, which was only a block from Zhongnanhai. Paramedics were on the scene in about ten minutes. That afternoon, after Hu's condition had improved slightly, he was transferred to Beijing Hospital for observation.

Everyone was alarmed about Hu's condition, but no one expected him to die. Beijing Hospital sent daily reports to the General Office of the Central Committee, and these were relayed to Zhao Ziyang and other members of the Politburo. All reports indicated that Hu was on the road to recovery.

Thus the news of his death on April 15 was that much greater a shock. Zhao Ziyang immediately summoned all Politburo members who were currently in Beijing to attend a meeting to plan arrangements for a funeral and obituary. He also instructed the General Office to "notify elder comrades such as Xiaoping, Chen Yun, Xiannian, Peng Zhen, Yingchao, Marshal Xu, and Marshal Nie."[2] The meeting was somber and yet rushed.

"We're deeply saddened and shocked at Comrade Yaobang's passing," said Zhao Ziyang.

"Really a pity," added Yang Shangkun. "Who'd think he'd go so soon?"

Then Zhao turned the discussion to practical issues, including the formation of a funeral committee. He began with his own brief assessment of Hu's life: "Comrade Hu Yaobang was a loyal, tried, and tested Communist fighter, a great proletarian revolutionary and politician, an outstanding political worker for our army and a prominent leader who held many important Party posts over a long period of time. His funeral should accord with the norm for standing members of the Politburo."

"I entirely agree with Comrade Ziyang's suggestion," Yang Shangkun offered.

"Comrades," Zhao then asked, "are there any objections to the assessment or the funeral recommendation?"

[2]The style used here of expressing names in two syllables implies affection and respect. The full names of Chen Yun and Peng Zhen are two syllables to begin with. The full names of the others are Deng Xiaoping, Li Xiannian, Deng Yingchao, Xu Xiangqian, and Nie Rongzhen. For the last two, the word *shuai* (marshal) provides one syllable.

When no one objected Zhao went on, "The assessment of Comrade Yaobang must 'seek truth from facts.'[3] Let's ask the General Office to forward the obituary draft to the older comrades Xiaoping, Chen Yun, and Xiannian for comment. Comrades [Hu] Qili and [Wen] Jiabao, can you please consult with Comrade Li Zhao[4] about funeral arrangements?"

Zhao Ziyang also raised the matter of social stability at the meeting. "Comrade Qiao Shi," he said, "please keep a close watch on how Comrade Yaobang's death might impact society."

"At the moment, society's in pretty good shape," Qiao replied. "Things are fairly stable. There are no signs of any large or organized disturbances. Personnel at all levels of the security and legal systems will keep close tabs on responses in society to Comrade Yaobang's death."

"Consumer prices are rising fast," Yao Yilin commented. "And the gap between rich and poor is getting bigger. We'd better watch that some people don't use the mourning for Comrade Yaobang as an excuse to make their complaints."

"Comrade Tieying," interjected Li Peng, "we should keep a close eye on the universities, especially ones like Peking University. College students are always the most sensitive."

"Things are good at the universities," Li Tieying replied. "It's not very likely there'll be any trouble."

Li Ximing, Party secretary for the Municipality of Beijing, pronounced, "We absolutely must protect social order in the capital and guarantee social stability during the mourning period."

"Comrade Qili," said Zhao Ziyang, "can you ask the news agency to prepare an announcement, and also watch for overseas reactions to Comrade Yaobang's death?" Then, to Secretary Rui Xingwen of the Central Committee Secretariat, who was in charge of propaganda and public opinion, Zhao said, "Comrade Xingwen, tonight Party Central is going to release an announcement on Comrade Yaobang's funeral for joint broadcast by Central People's Broadcasting and China Central Television (CCTV). Can you ask the Broadcast Ministry[5] to notify the stations to be ready?"

Deng Xiaoping's secretary, Wang Ruilin, observed the senior leader's reaction when he heard

[3] *Shishiqiushi*, a classical phrase that Deng Xiaoping, beginning in the late 1970s, made into a national slogan to promote his "practical" approach to problem solving, as opposed to Mao Zedong's ideological approach. The phrase is a code for pragmatism.
[4] Hu Yaobang's widow.
[5] The Radio, Film, and Television Ministry.

the news of Hu Yaobang's death on the morning of April 15: "He immediately ground out his cig-arette and crossed his hands weakly across his chest. Then, a moment later, he lit up another cig-arette and puffed at it fiercely." That afternoon, when Zhao Ziyang went to Deng's home at Miliang Lane, Di'anmen District, to report Hu's death in person, Deng had recovered from his shock and had already asked his wife Zhuo Lin to telephone Hu's widow Li Zhao to express condolences. He told Zhao Ziyang that he agreed with the Politburo's statement on Hu, approved of the funeral arrangements, and would attend the memorial.

The news of the death elicited various reactions from other senior leaders, according to mem-bers of their staffs. Chen Yun, who was ill at the time, had little to say.

Li Xiannian's reaction was to say over and over, "How could that be? How could it be? I called him only a few days ago, and he sounded fine." His tone of voice seemed to reflect his sadness at Hu's death and remorse over his earlier insistence that Hu resign.

Wang Zhen, known for his strong "peasant ideology," let out a long sigh at the news of Hu's death. Wang and Hu were from the same county, Liuyang in Hunan Province, and the two had been close until the younger Hu became Party general secretary. After this promotion, Hu did not listen to Wang as he had before, and Wang seemed envious of Hu as the new "number-one citi-zen of Liuyang County." Wang waited for his chance, which came in 1987, to topple Hu Yaobang.

The top leader most deeply affected by the news of Hu's death was Marshal Nie Rongzhen. He sent Comrade Li Zhao a letter of condolence that said, "It is extremely painful to me that Comrade Yaobang has left us before I have! I am old and frail and must rest my hopes on younger genera-tions. I mourn Comrade Yaobang's death deeply. The Central Committee's obituary is a good assessment of Comrade Yaobang, so I will add only this note on his performance during the War of Liberation: When he was successively a military column commissar and corps political director,[6] he was very good at political work. . . . Officials and ordinary people who met him had only good things to say about him. He made outstanding contributions to the liberation of North China."

April 15–17

Initial reaction at home and abroad

From the time of Hu's death to the morning of April 17, some fifty reports flowed into Party Central and the State Council from local governments, the two security ministries (State Security and Public Security), and the Xinhua News Agency describing responses to the death among offi-

---

[6]In the Shanxi-Suiyuan Fourth Corps.

cials and ordinary people. Throughout the 1980s Hu had earned a reputation as the top leadership's strongest advocate of leading China out of the stifling constrictions of the Mao years. Although most Chinese were satisfied with the Center's evaluation of Hu, some complained that he had not been given enough respect in the years after his forced retirement. Spontaneous mourning activities occurred on campuses. People gathered at the Monument to the People's Heroes[7] in Tiananmen Square with wreaths, flowers, and couplets praising Hu as a reformer and a democrat. In Shanghai large and small protest posters appeared on university campuses. In Xi'an young people brought wreaths to the square in front of the Posts and Telecommunications Building. The police reports made clear that the spontaneous mourning reflected Hu's popularity as a voice for values that young people believed in.

Over the same period, Xinhua and other agencies provided top officials with more than one hundred reports on foreign reactions. The story of Hu Yaobang's death and the way the government was dealing with it received worldwide coverage, most of it favorable. The foreign press praised Hu for his pragmatism and honesty and commended the government for announcing his death promptly. Most foreign media anticipated that the loss of Hu would have no impact on Chinese politics. But the Japanese Kyodo and Jiji news agencies both raised the possibility that against a background of widespread feelings against inflation and corruption and student demands for more democracy, popular mourning activities could develop into a challenge to the government, especially if the government tried to brush them off too lightly.

April 17–18

The student movement begins to spread

On April 17 student mourning activities began to spread from the Beijing campuses into the nation's symbolic central space, Tiananmen Square. The Square lies at the geographic center of the capital city and just southeast of Zhongnanhai, where the last dynasty's emperors had their hunting park and where the top Communist leaders now work. Beginning with the May Fourth Movement in 1919, Tiananmen has also become a traditional site for popular protests. These protests have often been led by university students, who are especially numerous here because Beijing is the country's preeminent center of higher education.

Party Central and the State Council had ordered the Public Security and State Security Ministries to keep close watch on the students, which they did. According to their reports, on the after-

---

[7]A stela in Tiananmen Square where many activities took place.

noon of April 17 some six hundred students and young faculty from the Chinese University of Political Science and Law (CUPSL) entered the Square with mourning banners and wreaths. They shouted slogans in favor of freedom, democracy, and the rule of law. Police officers were unable to disperse the crowd. More than ten thousand student marchers and onlookers gathered, staying until 4 P.M.; six students from CUPSL placed a flower wreath at the foot of the Monument to the People's Heroes.

Foreign reporters made recordings, took pictures, and tried to find out whether the students harbored antigovernment feelings. In one such interview overheard and recorded by a security official, a demonstrator insisted that the students' only purpose was to express their respect for Hu Yaobang in a law-abiding way. Questioned further by the foreign reporter, the student added that the demonstrators favored reform and that opposing dictatorship did not mean opposing the government.

Groups of students from other Beijing universities also conducted mourning activities, and by 5 P.M. some nine wreaths marked with the names of institutions of higher education had been placed near the monument. In the early evening a crowd of two to three thousand gathered in front of the monument and heard spontaneous speeches and readings of poems praising Hu. The group included Beijing residents, people from out of town, and foreigners. At 9:10 P.M. a foreign TV reporter recorded an interview with a citizen from outside Beijing who said that students from his town would follow the example of Beijing's students in taking to the streets. By dawn the next morning there were still two or three hundred people at the monument, and they showed no signs of dispersing.

Meanwhile, a column of about a thousand marchers had set out from Peking University. They were joined by an additional two thousand or so from other universities along the route. Significantly, the column included nine cars registered to foreign embassies, with embassy officials and foreign reporters mixing with and talking to the marchers. About 4:30 A.M. the column entered the Square, unfurling a banner of mourning for Hu on the monument and setting wreaths. A student speaking from the monument said the students were self-organized, had nothing to do with the officially sponsored student organization, and had elected representatives to negotiate with the government. He said the students were demanding, among other things, that the government resign to apologize for having made mistakes in policy. Prompted by other students, he added that the students demanded freedom of the press and of speech, democratic elections, and greater transparency[8] in government. All this was recorded by foreign reporters.

According to another report, students from the Beijing Institute of Aeronautics marched to the gates of Beijing Normal University to try to get its students to join them but were turned back by staff and guards.

---

[8]Transparency *(toumingdu)*, a translation of *glasnost* in Soviet usage, was a popular idea among Chinese students in 1988.

At dawn on April 18 several hundred students from Peking University and People's University started a sit-in in front of the Great Hall of the People and demanded to be received by a leader of the rank of NPC Standing Committee member or higher. They announced seven demands of the government: (1) affirm as correct Hu Yaobang's views on democracy and freedom; (2) admit that the campaigns against spiritual pollution and bourgeois liberalization[9] had been wrong; (3) publish information on the income of state leaders and their family members; (4) end the ban on privately run newspapers and permit freedom of speech; (5) increase funding for education and raise intellectuals' pay; (6) end restrictions on demonstrations in Beijing; and (7) hold democratic elections to replace government officials who made bad policy decisions. In addition, they demanded that the government-controlled media print and broadcast their demands and that the government respond to them publicly.

A standoff prevailed throughout the day. At 8 A.M. and again at 5:30 P.M. lower-ranking officials met with student representatives Guo Haifeng and Wang Dan, both from Peking University. But the students were not satisfied. Meanwhile, students from many campuses continued to converge on Tiananmen Square; they were joined at the end of the day by others who had been sitting in before the Great Hall of the People, where the NPC had its offices, at the edge of the Square. Students praised Hu Yaobang as the "soul of democracy" and sang the worldwide Communist anthem, the "Internationale."

By 10:50 P.M. about two thousand students and onlookers had moved from Tiananmen to the Xinhua Gate of Zhongnanhai.[10] The crowd was disorderly, and transport along Chang'an Boulevard was obstructed.

The leaders' vigilance

On the morning of April 17 the Politburo continued work on the draft decision on education, which they had been discussing on April 8 when Hu Yaobang had his heart attack. That afternoon, Li Tieying reported separately to Zhao Ziyang and Li Peng on some of the campus memorial activities for Hu Yaobang around the country. He said that He Dongchang had alerted him to some worrisome trends and that the State Education Commission (SEC) would immediately issue an instruction on how to deal with them.

Zhao Ziyang said that the students' patriotism should be affirmed, although any inappropriate

---

[9]"Spiritual pollution" was Party jargon for Western cultural influences. In fall 1983 a nationwide campaign to "eliminate spiritual pollution" petered out after a few months, but the goal, as well as the phrase, remained active among a portion of the leadership. The national campaign against "bourgeois liberalization" occurred in 1987.

[10]One of the main gates to Zhongnanhai, located on the broad central thoroughfare, Chang'an Boulevard, not far to the west of Tiananmen Square.

methods of action should pointed out to them, and that they should be instructed to take the broad view and let reason be their watchword. Li Peng said that problems should be nipped in the bud. The same day Yao Yilin warned Li Peng that there were advocates of bourgeois liberalization who had been waiting for just such an opportunity as Hu Yaobang's death. He said that they would try to take advantage of the students' patriotism to promote their ideology and that their activities must be blocked.

That evening Li Peng telephoned the mayor of Beijing, Chen Xitong. The premier had just read a batch of materials that had been sent over, from which he understood that there was a large gathering of students in Tiananmen Square. He wanted to know what was going on. Chen gave Li a simple report and the next morning sent over a fuller report.

> Excerpts from Beijing Municipal Government, "Report on mourning activities for Comrade Hu Yaobang at Beijing institutions of higher education," April 18

Mourning activities for Comrade Hu Yaobang by Beijing university students began to show signs of heating up on April 17.

According to data compiled this morning by the Municipal Education Bureau, since Comrade Hu Yaobang's death, students from twenty-six Beijing universities have held spontaneous memorials. More than seven hundred eulogies, memorial couplets, and posters have appeared on campuses.

On the morning of April 17 the situation at Peking University remained fairly normal. At noon a few people began shouting outside the student dormitories, which brought many students downstairs. Within twenty minutes, one thousand to two thousand students, mostly freshmen and sophomores, had congregated in the Triangle area. They were shouting and highly emotional. After making wreaths and banners, they left for Tiananmen. At People's University a "Democracy Wall" appeared on the evening of April 17. Spontaneous memorial activities took place on other campuses that until now had been quiet. In addition to pasting up eulogies, memorial couplets, and posters, students made speeches, set up symbolic biers, and delivered wreaths to the Square. Some even demanded to attend the funeral. In a single day, ninety-three handwritten memorial couplets[11] appeared at the Beijing University of Science and Engineering.

Analysis of more than seven hundred posters, memorial couplets, and eulogies shows that their contents seem to fall into three categories: (1) normal expres-

---

[11] *Wanlian* (elegiac couplets).

sions of mourning (most are this), (2) protests against injustices that Comrade Yaobang suffered during his life, and (3) inflammatory attacks on the current state of society.

According to some students, activities of this sort had been talked about for quite a while, and Comrade Hu Yaobang's death only provided the occasion for them to emerge. Accordingly, we will watch developments closely, will warn potential manipulators against distorting the direction and purposes of the mourning activities, and will take steps to block the activities of certain key persons.

The SEC issued its promised notice on April 18. It ordered provincial education departments and officials of those universities it administers[12] to "carry out painstaking thought work to strengthen guidance of students . . . [and to] keep a clear head in dealing with certain people with ulterior motives who would use this occasion to attack the Party and government."

Student mourning in the provinces

On April 17 and 18 province-level Party Committees sent reports to Party Central describing the mourning activities for Hu that were occurring in their jurisdictions and reporting how they were handling them. In Shanghai, groups of up to several thousand students conducted spontaneous demonstrations, with one group unsuccessfully demanding to be received by officials of the Municipal Government. After holding an urgent meeting, the Municipal Party Committee, headed by Jiang Zemin, issued a notice ordering that mourning activities be carried out within work units and not beyond, in order to avoid effects on public order.

In Tianjin the police managed for the most part to confine student demonstrators to the campus of Nankai University. In Nanjing students applied to the police for permission for a march by an estimated ten thousand students from several campuses. The police attempted to dissuade them, citing the difficulties of keeping order, and the students relented, but comrades in the provincial Public Security Department expected them to carry out a large-scale mourning activity of some kind anyhow.

Student mourning activities for Hu were also reported in Xi'an. In Hunan the Provincial Party Committee warned that the apparent calm on some campuses was deceptive. An uneasy mood prevailed among students and faculty. Mourning activities might peak during the official meetings to memorialize Hu. Some were even saying that mourning activities for Hu should be combined

---

[12]The SEC administers the majority of China's universities. A few specialized schools fall under other government ministries.

with the activities to commemorate the upcoming seventieth anniversary of May Fourth. To deal with this possibility, the committee had ordered all relevant departments to step up their work guiding students and to provide round-the-clock staffing to keep watch on the situation.

Foreign reports see a confrontation emerging

Foreign reports forwarded to Zhongnanhai on April 17 and 18 all concentrated on events in Beijing, with the exception of one Associated Press story that mentioned student activities in Shanghai. The reports stressed the confrontational nature of student demands. Reuters quoted some diplomats and China analysts as predicting that the authorities could not prevent the spread of the student movement and might eventually have to use force to suppress it. The *Hong Kong Standard* noted that the student movement followed upon earlier demands for amnesty for political prisoners and for a broadening of democratization and that it occurred at a time of anticipation created by the impending seventieth anniversary of May Fourth. Hence it was likely to increase in size and to develop into a broader pro-democracy movement.

April 19–22

Laying siege to Xinhua Gate

> Combined excerpts from State Security Ministry, "The situation on the scene at Xinhua Gate," report to Party Central and State Council duty offices, 11:51 P.M., April 19; and State Security Ministry, "The situation on the scene at Xinhua Gate," report to Party Central and State Council duty offices, 6:08 A.M., April 20

After 11 A.M. on April 19 students from Qinghua University, Beijing Normal University, Beijing University of Science and Technology, and other institutions carried wreaths to Tiananmen Square. Along the way more than a thousand students from Beijing Normal carried banners and shouted slogans such as "Yaobang will not die!" "Down with dictatorship!" "Down with autocracy!" "The

people loved the people's secretary, and the people's secretary loved the people!"
"Keep the May Fourth tradition alive!" "Long live democracy and science! Long
live education! Long live teachers!"

Many people gave speeches in front of the Monument to the People's Heroes.

Students from the Central Academy of Fine Arts carried a gigantic portrait of
Comrade Hu Yaobang and rested it against the carved relief on the monument. A
sign next to it read, "How can we revive his spirit?"

By nightfall roughly twenty thousand people, including three thousand to
four thousand students, had congregated in the Square and placed fifty-five
wreaths and twelve funeral banners in front of the monument. Beijing Public
Security summoned one thousand policemen from precinct stations to maintain
order in the Square.

In the evening the Beijing Government broadcast a "public notice" directing
that starting at 5 A.M. on the twentieth, Public Security would cordon the monument off and require that people approach it and lay their wreaths in a civilized
manner. The Youth League was to organize three hundred university students to
receive people presenting wreaths.

By 9 P.M. more than one thousand students from eight departments at the
Central Institute of Finance had left the Square to return to their campus.

Public Security announced at the Square that wreaths should be placed in
front of the monument and not sent to Zhongnanhai.

Around 10 P.M. students from the Central Academy of Drama entered the
Square carrying helium balloons bearing the message "Yaobang will never die."
Police ordered the balloons removed. At 11:10 P.M. more than eight hundred
Qinghua University students left their campus to show support for the students
at Xinhua Gate, but police blocked them.

That night two thousand or three thousand students from Peking University,
People's University, Beijing Normal University, and the University of Political Science and Law gathered at Xinhua Gate, where they were surrounded by six thousand or seven thousand onlookers. The students shouted, "Li Peng come out! Li
Peng come out!" and made six failed attempts to break through the police lines.

At 11:40 P.M. a Beijing Public Security vehicle arrived to broadcast proclamations from the city government. At 1 A.M. on the twentieth the People's Armed
Police (PAP)[13] and Public Security separated students from onlookers and

---

[13]The People's Armed Police *(wujing)* are a separate force from the regular police *(jingcha)*. The
former are under the command of the People's Liberation Army, the latter are part of the Public
Security Ministry. One of the jobs of the PAP is to guard government and Party offices.

removed the onlookers to a location several hundred meters distant. Fewer than three hundred students remained in front of Xinhua Gate.

From 1 A.M. to 5 A.M. these students maintained a confrontational position before the police cordon, but no major conflict occurred. In order to ensure normal operations in the capital, the Beijing Government decided to declare temporary martial law and to bus the students back to their campuses after persuading them that this was best. More than a hundred students were unwilling to board the buses, and this led to scuffles with police. One student, after being forced onto a bus, shouted, "Down with the Communist Party!"

Because forcible measures were used, it is possible that students may undertake larger-scale actions in response.

The siege of Xinhua Gate heightened the leaders' alarm.

> Account drawn from *Materials for the Fourth Plenum of the Thirteenth Central Committee*, "Remarks of Comrade Yang Shangkun," Secretariat of the Fourth Plenum of the CCP Thirteenth Central Committee, June 23–24, 1989; and Central Military Commission Office, "Yang Shangkun's talk to a small-group meeting at the Enlarged Meeting of the Central Military Commission," May 23[14]

Yang Shangkun telephoned Zhao Ziyang on April 18.[15]

Yang Shangkun: "What do you think, Comrade Ziyang, about the students' mourning of Comrade Yaobang in the past few days?"

Zhao Ziyang: "Comrades Qiao Shi and Qili have briefed me, and I've been on the phone with Comrade Li Ximing to ask that the city government keep a close watch on the students' activities to ensure stability during the mourning period. On the whole I think we should affirm the students' patriotism."

---

[14]Yang Shangkun gave an important speech at an enlarged meeting of the Central Military Commission on May 24 (see Chapter 7). On the preceding evening he spoke at a small-group meeting *(xiaofanwei huiyi)* attended mainly by CMC commissioners and senior officers of the Martial Law Command.—Comp. An enlarged meeting occurs when an organ like the Politburo, its Standing Committee, or the Central Military Commission invites nonmembers to attend. A "small group" in this context is an ad hoc working group of ranking officials.—Eds.

[15]This account of a private conversation and others later in the book are reconstructions from the documents cited, in which participants gave their retrospective accounts of what was said. For details, see the Introduction.

Account drawn from *Materials for the Fourth Plenum of the Thirteenth Central Committee,* "Remarks of Comrade Wen Jiabao," Secretariat of the Fourth Plenum of the CCP Thirteenth Central Committee, June 23–24, 1989

Later the night of April 18, after receiving a report from Wen Jiabao about the students who had gathered outside Xinhua Gate and about their attempts to break through police lines, Zhao said:

"Have Comrade [Yang] Dezhong call in the Central Guard. The security of Zhongnanhai and Xinhua Gate must be absolutely guaranteed. Be sure all the police at Xinhua Gate remove their bayonets and avoid physical contact with the students. Get word to the Municipal Government as well."

Wen Jiabao telephoned the duty officer at the Beijing Party Committee and ordered him to ensure both the security of Xinhua Gate and the safety of the students. Wen Jiabao then went to Xinhua Gate with Yang Dezhong to participate personally in the operation.

On April 19 Party Central announced that a memorial service for Hu Yaobang would be held at the Great Hall of the People at 10 A.M. on April 22 and that mourners could pay their respects at this time. Late at night on the nineteenth Zhao Ziyang telephoned Beijing Party secretary Li Ximing for an update on Xinhua Gate and the situation at Beijing universities. After Li briefed Zhao, the following exchange took place:

Account drawn from Beijing Municipal Party Committee Office, "Speech of Comrade Li Ximing at the meeting of university Party secretaries and presidents in the capital," April 23

Li Ximing: "It is clear that the student protests in Beijing began moving in a new direction on the eighteenth. Certain people with ulterior motives are exploiting the students, and we're drafting a report to Party Central about this. Don't you think the Politburo should meet to discuss the student protests, Comrade Ziyang?"

Zhao Ziyang: "The first thing we have to do is handle the situation at Xinhua Gate. You have to get your job there done first."

Account drawn from Party Central Office Secretariat, "Oral report by Shangkun, Li Peng, Qiao Shi, and Yilin on the cur-

> rent situation, May 22, evening," section containing Li Peng's remarks

When the news that students were massing at Xinhua Gate reached Li Xiannian on the evening of April 19, Li telephoned Li Peng and said:

"These students have been acting up for several days now, Comrade Li Peng. How did this thing spread to Xinhua Gate? They were out there last night, and they're back out there again tonight! What's going on, anyway? Is somebody orchestrating this from behind the scenes?"

After two nights of unrest at Xinhua Gate, Li Peng told Luo Gan, State Council secretary general, and later Politburo Standing Committee member Yao Yilin that the unrest was getting out of hand. After hearing a second briefing from SEC head Li Tieying, Li Peng instructed the SEC to insist that every university steadfastly follow the spirit of Party Central and the State Council. He then spoke with Li Ximing and Chen Xitong, demanding that the Municipal Government take decisive action; in consequence, the municipal authorities declared temporary martial law in the vicinity of Xinhua Gate.

> Beijing Municipal Party Committee and Beijing Municipal People's Government, "Trends worth close attention during the mourning for Comrade Hu Yaobang at Beijing institutions of higher education," report to Party Central and the State Council, April 20

In the early morning of April 18 the mourning activities of students in Tiananmen Square changed direction because of the destructive acts of certain people with ulterior motives. During the first few days, the vast majority of students who came to Tiananmen Square were sincere in their grief and displayed deep feelings for Comrade Yaobang. But on the morning of April 18, as the following facts show, a new direction emerged:

1. Slipping political ideas into mourning activities: At 4 A.M. on April 18, after more than three thousand students from Peking University and People's University had hung a white banner that read "The Soul of China" on the Monument to the People's Heroes, several hundred students went to sit in at the entrance to the Great Hall of the People and delivered seven political demands to the Standing Committee of the National People's Congress. These demands, which echoed the

speeches, slogans, wall posters, and leaflets of the previous two days, called in various ways for:

> Freedom and democracy.
>
> Completely repudiate efforts to "eliminate spiritual pollution."
>
> Lift all bans on newspapers and implement freedom of the press.
>
> Require officials to resign for serious mistakes.
>
> Make the Central Government subject to popular votes of confidence.
>
> Publicize the incomes of leaders and their children.
>
> Release political prisoners unconditionally.

2. The appearance of reactionary language: Between April 15 and the evening of the nineteenth, 1,654 wall posters appeared at thirty-one Beijing universities. On the eighteenth students began to post and to shout reactionary slogans directed at senior leading comrades such as Xiaoping, Ziyang, and Li Peng. "Down with corrupt government!" "Down with the Communist Party!" and "Down with autocracy and dictatorship!" are examples.

3. Troublemakers working hard on inciting the masses: People have been spreading rumors that Comrade Yaobang was "hounded to death" or "died of apoplexy." Instigators mill among students in the Square saying, "Why demonstrate here? Go to Zhongnanhai, go to the Great Hall of the People." Wall posters call for students to get organized and form a unified committee to coordinate activities. They also urge students to go into factories, shops, and the countryside to mobilize the masses against corrupt government. Some posters at Peking University even incite students to "Attack Zhongnanhai! Torch Zhongnanhai!"

4. Laying siege to Zhongnanhai: In the early morning and evening of the nineteenth, several hundred students, shouting slogans and singing the "Internationale," laid siege to Xinhua Gate and beat policemen while nearly ten thousand people looked on.

5. Programmatic slogans and organizational activities: At some schools, wall posters call for the formation of a committee to revise the Constitution and of autonomous student associations[16] to operate under their own bylaws; they also call for provincial federalism,[17] freedom of the press, and freedom of speech. During the first few days of mourning activities, concerned citizens talked some

---

[16]Student associations organized and controlled by the government had been in place for a decade or more. When students tried to organize autonomous student associations, the government regarded them as illegal. In translation we will distinguish "official" from "autonomous" associations.

[17]*Difang zizhi*, literally "local autonomy" but usually referring to a province-based federal system.

of the extremist students into ending their activities voluntarily and leaving the scene. But beginning on the eighteenth, exhortation no longer worked. The students congregated, sat in, gave speeches, and then laid siege to Zhongnanhai. Student sentiments came more into harmony as their actions became more concerted. These were clear signs of organization within their ranks.

The Municipal Party Committee and the Municipal Government have taken the following steps to deal with this situation:

First: Launching a political offensive in which reason will be the watchword. Through public broadcasts and personal persuasion, we are reasoning with the students in order to expose the evil intentions of the minority and to persuade the students to return to their campuses and to their books, to join the organized activities for mourning Comrade Yaobang, and to transform their sorrow into action by concentrating on their studies.

Second: Publishing proclamations and banning illegal activities. On April 19 the Municipal Government published three proclamations to ensure social stability and the normal progress of mourning activities and took strict precautions against subversion and instigation by the minority.

Third: Using martial law measures[18] to keep the situation from escalating. In the early mornings of April 18 and 19, in order to stop the student siege at Zhongnanhai and to alleviate traffic jams on Chang'an Boulevard, the Municipal Government took the decisive step of employing temporary martial law methods as a way of dispersing the student troublemakers at Xinhua Gate; it also dispatched buses to return students to their campuses.

Fourth: Calling an emergency meeting to enlist the cooperation of people in charge of districts, counties, bureaus, universities, corporate headquarters, and enterprises. Beijing Mayor Chen Xitong chaired the meeting, and Party Secretary Li Ximing and Deputy Secretary Li Qiyan both spoke. They asked all unit heads to give faithful accounts of the situation, to expose the minority of troublemakers, to carry out their duties actively, to guide the masses effectively, to reinforce organizational discipline, and to work hard to stabilize the overall situation in order to facilitate the normal process of mourning for Comrade Yaobang and to focus on the regulation, consolidation, and deepening of reform and opening.

On the same day, at the behest of Li Peng, Li Tieying directed the SEC to send a second notice to provincial and municipal education departments and the universities under the commission.

---

[18]*Caiqu jieyan cuoshi*, which implies short-term, limited use of martial law measures, as distinct from a declaration of martial law.

Excerpts from State Education Commission, "Notice on doing a good job of organizing mourning activities for Comrade Hu Yaobang," April 20

Party secretaries at the various schools must strengthen organizational leadership of the mourning activities for Comrade Hu Yaobang, . . . must give timely guidance to expressions of student opinion and complaint, and must make strong and clear refutations of incorrect opinion. School authorities should meet with persons who are causing trouble or inciting others and point out their mistakes in no uncertain terms. . . .

With regard to the small group that has laid siege to Xinhua Gate, the Beijing Municipal Government has adopted necessary and legal dispersion tactics to regulate traffic and ensure the normal operation of government offices. The police do not carry batons or wear leather belts. It should be anticipated that some persons will exploit this situation to spread rumors, so special attention must be paid to getting the students to study Xinhua News Agency commentaries[19] and instructing them not to be misled by rumors. In the meantime, students from outside Beijing should be discouraged from entering the city.

Birth of the Autonomous Federation of Students (AFS) in Beijing

Security agencies and Beijing municipal authorities kept close track of the intensifying student movement on April 20–21.[20]

Excerpt from Beijing Municipal Party Committee and Beijing Municipal People's Government, "Bulletin: Peking University students prepare to establish a 'united student association,'" bulletin to Party Central and State Council duty offices, April 20

[19]Editorials issued by Xinhua, to be published in newspapers around the country, containing the official view of the demonstrations.

[20]There are a series of documents from this period in Suzanne Ogden, Kathleen Hartford, Lawrence Sullivan, and David Zweig, eds., *China's Search for Democracy: The Student and the Mass Movement of 1989* (Armonk, New York: M. E. Sharpe, 1992), 83–92, and in Han Minzhu, ed., *Cries for Democracy: Writings and Speeches from the 1989 Chinese Democracy Movement* (Princeton: Princeton University Press, 1990), ch. 1.

The democracy salon[21] at Peking University reconvened from 11 P.M. yesterday until 1 A.M. this morning to discuss setting up a "united student association." The meeting reviewed past student protests that had failed owing to a lack of leadership and unified action, and it determined that the task at hand was to build effective leadership for the campus democracy movement. Around midnight, Wang Dan announced the abolition of the current official student association at Peking University and the creation of a "Planning Committee of the United Students' Association of Peking University." Seven students, including Ding Xiaoping, Wang Dan, Yang Tao, and Feng Congde, were chosen as a leadership committee under which eight departments were formed—propaganda, workers and farmers, public order, communications, theory, logistics, and others. The Planning Committee announced that it will lead all student movements between April 20 and May 4 and that, later on, new graduate and undergraduate student associations will be created to lead spontaneous democracy movements on campus while a "United Association" will unify similar groups at universities across the nation.

A "program" of eleven items was announced at the meeting. The items repeated the demands in the petition presented to the Standing Committee of the NPC on April 18 but added, significantly, "release Wei Jingsheng" and "insist that Deng Xiaoping be specific about what he meant by the failure of education during the ten years of reform."[22]

A "Letter to All Beijing Universities" circulated at the meeting. It proposed that "the various schools use representatives of their democratic student organizations to choose delegates to a joint 'Mediating Committee for the Democratic Petitioning Activities of Universities in Beijing' that would unify and lead the spontaneous activities that have already grown strong on university campuses in Beijing." Someone relayed Jin Guantao's[23] opinion that the time to act had come and that the students should begin with concerted passive resistance. Around 1 A.M. more than two thousand students from Qinghua University showed up outside the Peking University library to meet with the Peking University students, who agreed to send representatives to Qinghua that day at noon to discuss united action. Early in the morning, the Planning Committee sent representatives to

[21]A series of informal meetings on the Peking University campus, beginning in spring 1988, where students discussed topics related to democracy.
[22]Students were eager to acknowledge that general education had been slighted, but they worried that Deng's true meaning had been that political education—meaning ideological control—had not been strong enough.
[23]A researcher at the Chinese Academy of Sciences.

establish contact with various institutions and to organize people to make armbands, wreaths, and so on. We believe that the students will use strikes as one form
of protracted struggle.

During the day on April 20 the State Security Ministry filed a series of reports from the Square. The 2:40 P.M. report said that a crowd had begun to gather at the Monument to the People's Heroes around 2 P.M. and had by now swelled to four thousand or five thousand. At 2:35 more than two hundred students from the Institute of Printing carried three wreaths into the Square; then more than two hundred students from the Chinese University of Geology arrived holding aloft a banner that read "Eternal glory to Secretary General Yaobang."

Police detained more than four hundred Peking University students at Zhongguancun, a residential area near the campus. More than two hundred students from the Beijing Institute of Aeronautics walked from the university district to Tiananmen; more than two hundred students from the Central Institute of Finance left their campus; and students from Beijing Normal University and People's University were milling around outside People's University.

According to the 4 P.M. report, more than one thousand students from the Beijing Institute of Aeronautics had set out for Tiananmen wearing white flowers and carrying banners that read, "Summon the spirit of democracy and freedom," "Heroic spirit of the nation," "Heroic spirit of China," and "Root out corrupt officials." Students from the Beijing Institute of Economics pasted wall posters on the Monument to the People's Heroes that claimed students had been arrested and beaten. In the afternoon it rained. Most of the students stayed out in the rain, but most onlookers headed for cover in underground passages.

This report continued:

> Excerpt from State Security Ministry, "Situation in Tianan-
> men Square on the twentieth," 4 P.M., April 20

Tiananmen is bustling; all sorts of ideas are floating around. An elderly female
intellectual said, "Why doesn't someone take charge? Wall posters on the monument say students have been beaten and arrested, and we have no way of knowing the truth of the matter. This same kind of thing happened during the April
Fifth Movement in 1976."[24]

A middle-aged man who appeared to be an official analyzed the reasons why
the students had taken to the streets: "First, they think Comrade Hu Yaobang was
dismissed unfairly in 1987. The problems in society last year were much worse, so
why, they ask, weren't Zhao Ziyang and Li Peng removed from their posts? Sec-

---

[24]Demonstrations in Tiananmen Square on April 5, 1976, mourning the passing of Premier
Zhou Enlai and criticizing Mao Zedong and his radical supporters. Hundreds were arrested.

ond, they want to take the opportunity to push for democracy and for reform in the political system. Third, they don't like the infighting in Party Central; they want to know what's going on. Fourth, Hu Yaobang's style was popular; he was honest, open and straightforward—not like some of the corrupt leaders who are now on top." Another person commented, "Tiananmen Square is a complete mess. People are out there making speeches attacking Party and state leaders, which hardly seems consistent with mourning activities."

The 6:30 P.M. report said one thousand students from Peking University, the Chinese University of Political Science and Law, Beijing Medical University, and Beijing University of Science and Technology were on their way to Tiananmen. At 10 P.M. another report said more than eight hundred students had entered the Square with banners bearing messages such as "Education saves the nation," "Peaceful petitioning," and "Oppose violence."

The 8:35 P.M. report said students at the monument were shouting, "Down with dictatorship," "Demand freedom," and "Down with the police." The students had a discussion and decided to go home until 8 A.M. on the twenty-second. According to reports, students at a few universities in Beijing were preparing to form a "united student association."

The 10 P.M. report said that as many as eight hundred students were returning to their campuses, leaving the Square virtually deserted.

The Beijing Municipal Public Security Bureau reported that more than fifty students from Tianjin showed up at the Square but then left along with the Beijing students. Another hundred Tianjin students who are planning to demonstrate in Beijing have bought tickets for the 2 P.M. train to Beijing on April 21.

The student sit-ins at Xinhua Gate were an unprecedented embarrassment to the top leadership of the Party. In response, on April 21 *People's Daily* published an editorial entitled "Maintenance of Social Stability Is the Prime Concern," a signed commentary called "How We Should Mourn Comrade Yaobang," and a news report called "Several Hundred People Create Disturbances at Xinhua Gate." But to the students these articles seemed ill informed and unconvincing, and the protesters grew even angrier during the day on the twenty-first.

> Excerpt from State Security Ministry, "April 21 student trends at the Chinese University of Political Science and Law," "Important intelligence bulletin" (*Yaoqing kuaixun*), no. 173, April 21

School authorities reported that three students went to Tiananmen Square on the evening of April 19 to take part in memorial activities. Shortly after 11:30 P.M. they decided to take a number 22 bus back to school, but because of crowding on

Chang'an Boulevard they opted for the subway instead. When they reached the street south of the Great Hall of the People, they were met and driven apart by two columns of PAP. One student, Wang Zhiyong, was surrounded by PAP officers and beaten unconscious with leather belts. Two students from the Lu Xun Institute of Literature helped him get back to campus, where he was treated at the school clinic and then sent to the Third Affiliated Hospital of the Beijing Medical University. The hospital's report said he had suffered "scalp wounds, a minor concussion, and external eye injuries."

Today Wang's bloody clothes were displayed on the campus of CUPSL, and enraged students called for a strike. School authorities objected strenuously to the strike while agreeing to report the incident to Beijing authorities through proper channels. Yesterday a group of student representatives and school authorities met with leaders of Beijing's government to go over what had happened, and afterwards authorities posted a notice discouraging students from striking. But students tore down these notices and during the overnight hours posted renewed calls for a strike, attaching four demands: "(1) students and teachers should stay away from classes April 21 and 22 to protest the illegal police behavior; (2) the government must punish the perpetrators severely; (3) the police must publish an apology in the open press and report the details of the incident accurately; (4) a response to the second and third demands must be received by 5 P.M. on April 23 or further action will be taken."

Around noon students on campus burned copies of the newspaper that had carried the editorial "Maintenance of Social Stability Is the Prime Concern" and the accompanying piece by the *People's Daily* commentator. They also smashed bottles for about half an hour.[25] At 1 P.M. some of the students went to Xizhimen and handed out leaflets that asked, "Where is principle? Where is conscience? Where is justice? Where is law?" The leaflets told the story of Wang Zhiyong and then said, "We must ask what led the police to abandon the most fundamental standards of decency and humanity. Are we to believe that the laws of the People's Republic permit them to behave this way? Have they no brothers and sisters of their own? Do Party and military discipline allow such behavior? We insist that the perpetrators be punished!"

Student emotion is now concentrated on the beating of Wang Zhiyong. We hope the incident will be clarified as soon as possible in order to prevent the situation from getting any worse.

[25]Bottles (*xiaoping* in Chinese) were effigies for Deng Xiaoping.

Excerpt from State Security Ministry, "April 21 student trends at Peking University," "Important intelligence bulletin" *(Yao-qing kuaixun)*, no. 174, April 21

Some of the students at Peking University began a class boycott this morning, and announcements of a boycott appeared on campus. Students outside classroom buildings and at the doors of classrooms were persuading other students to stay away from classes. "Strike today" was scribbled on blackboards.

During the morning, posters reading "Boycott" and "Protest the violence of police beating of students" appeared in the Triangle area on campus. The poster titled "Boycott" read, "Our Planning Committee, on behalf of all students, is calling a campuswide boycott to begin at 8 A.M. on April 21 to protest the savage beating of students by police[26] and the ensuing distorted reports of these events. We demand: (1) public newspaper coverage and (2) severe punishment of those responsible. We call upon all ardent and decent students and teachers at Peking University to join the boycott and not to return to class until the demands are met."

Around noon someone with a bullhorn told listeners at the Triangle about the "April 20" student beating, calling it an inhuman act and urging students to march in protest.

In the afternoon a fifty-member "petitioner delegation" of students from Nankai University [in Tianjin] arrived at Peking University.

Excerpt from State Security Ministry, "April 21 student trends at Beijing Normal University," "Important intelligence bulletin" *(Yaoqing kuaixun)*, no. 175, April 21

Today a "communiqué" signed "Wuerkaixi"[27] appeared at Beijing Normal listing these demands: (1) Strip the official student association and graduate-student association of all their powers. (2) Join the provisional Student Federation of Beijing Universities. (3) Begin a campuswide boycott of all classes and examinations beginning April 22. (4) Come to an oath-taking rally for all universities that will be held on campus at 10 P.M. Everyone from our school should attend

---

[26]A reference to the forcible removal of students from the area in front of Xinhua Gate on April 20.
[27]This first-year student from Xinjiang at Beijing Normal University would soon be famous, but at this point he was still unknown. "Wuerkaixi" is the Chinese version of his Uighur name.

and help to provide bread and soft drinks for our fellow students from other campuses.

Reports identified the following illegal organizations as having surfaced in Beijing: Planning Committee of the United Students' Association of Peking University, the Leadership Group for Progress in Socialist Democracy (Qinghua University), the Support Committee (Beijing Foreign Languages Institute), the Association of Chinese Intellectuals, the Autonomous Student Association of Chinese People's University, and the Autonomous Student Association of Beijing Normal University.

Excerpt from Beijing Municipal Party Committee and Beijing
Municipal Government, "Situation in Tiananmen Square on
the twenty-first," fax, 11 P.M., April 21

Today Tiananmen Square was relatively calm during the daytime, but after nightfall the number of people suddenly increased and the atmosphere grew tense.

1. The number of students bringing wreaths to the Square in the daytime hours fell off noticeably; the great majority of people milling in the Square were gawkers. Between 8 A.M. and 7 P.M. eight universities and one research institute, each represented by as few as forty students and as many as two hundred, sent wreaths and funeral banners. After delivering the wreaths to the Monument to the People's Heroes and conducting a brief ceremony, the students left the area, except for a few who stayed behind to copy poems and elegies. Three institutions helped maintain order by bringing their mourners to the Square by school bus and truck.

2. Although few students came to the Square during the day, there were, nonetheless, frequent disruptions. Between 1 P.M. and 7 P.M. there were four major disturbances, the most serious of which occurred from 2:50 P.M. to 3:05 P.M. when several thousand onlookers rushed at the east side of the Great Hall of the People, breaking through the police cordon and surrounding three policemen. Eventually the crowd reached the top of the stairs and stood before the columns of the Great Hall. A detachment of police emerged from the Great Hall and drove the crowd back onto the Square. Our analysis shows that the cause of today's disturbances was that a large crowd of nearly ten thousand onlookers blindly rushed after foreign correspondents or followed students who were leaving the Square.

3. Out-of-town students began arriving in the Square in groups. At 2:35 P.M. more than fifty students from Nankai University poured out of the Beijing Railway Station. They walked down Chang'an East Boulevard and entered the Square at 3:25 P.M., attracting several thousand onlookers along the way. They carried a huge portrait of Comrade Hu Yaobang and four banners that read, "Delegation of petitioners to the capital from Nankai University," "Support the righteous actions of students in Beijing and across the nation," "Democracy, freedom, and science," and "Long live the spirit of Yaobang." After delivering wreaths to the monument, they paraded around the Square with their school flags and banners. Twice they passed out copies of a petition to the Standing Committee of the NPC. It demanded reform in the way NPC delegates are chosen, a reduction in the number of delegates, elevation of the job of NPC delegate to a full-time position, a clear separation of the respective rights and functions of the Party and the NPC, competitive elections, higher educational standards for delegates (to the high-school level), and freedom of the press. These activities of the Nankai students raised emotions in the Square to a fever pitch and attracted forty thousand to fifty thousand onlookers.

4. Rumors flooded the Square, and the masses began debating all kinds of things. Many people were saying, "Students were beaten by police" and "The students are going to repay a blood debt." Ren Wanding, a reactionary from the Democracy Wall days of 1978, incited the masses by saying, "The people are praying for the country to wake up to the rule of law, which is bound to come sooner or later in any case. Today Democracy Wall has new life." The police tried to arrest him, but students blocked the way, and eventually Ren left the Square on his own.

Reliable sources report that students at fifteen universities in Beijing have formed a student association that has its own department of public order, department of liaison, department of information, and so on. They plan to rendezvous at Beijing Normal and to enter the Square around 10 P.M. in order to occupy a good position for tomorrow's memorial service.

5. At 10 P.M. nearly ten thousand students from Qinghua and nine other universities came from Xueyuan Road and moved along Xidan North Avenue toward Tiananmen.

The participating schools were Qinghua University, Beijing University of Science and Technology, Beijing Institute of Aeronautics, Beijing Agricultural University, Beijing Normal University, Beijing Institute of Posts and Telecommunications, Beijing Engineering University, North China Jiaotong University, the Central Institute for Nationalities, and Peking University. As the students walked, they shouted "Down with official profiteering!"[28] "Down with corrupt officials!" "Freedom of the press!" "The press must tell the truth!" "Long live democracy!" "Violence is shameful!" "Oppose dictatorship!" "Down with authoritarianism!" and "Patriotism is no crime!"

The masses lining the roads often applauded the students, stimulating them further and causing them to shout "Long live the people!" "Long live understanding!" and "What are we doing? We're telling the truth!" Onlookers placed hot water and cups along the road for the students to drink.

The movement intensifies in the provinces

In the days leading up to the official memorial service, Zhongnanhai received a series of alarming reports on the situations in certain major cities, especially on the campuses. Protests seemed to have been spurred to a new level by the April 20 *People's Daily* commentator's article on the Xinhua Gate incident. Crowds were larger and more turbulent, the social base of participation broader, and slogans and posters more radical.

In Xi'an, for example, according to a series of reports from the Shaanxi Party Committee, crowds exceeding ten thousand gathered daily; they consisted not only of students but also of workers, officials, and other residents. Their discussions were not limited to Hu's death but also included inflation, salaries, and housing problems. Many campuses had wall posters carrying the latest news from Beijing, often drawn from reports broadcast by the Voice of America. On April 20 a huge crowd of about ten thousand students and onlookers broke into the provincial government office building and parking lot, demanding dialogue with the provincial governor. They were held off by members of the People's Armed Police. The students were incited toward violence by some unemployed young people, but they did not respond and eventually returned to their campuses in buses sent by school authorities. Subsequently the rest of the crowd diminished and was eventually dispersed by rain.

At approximately hourly intervals on the night of April 20, the Jiangsu Party Committee filed a series of reports describing a student demonstration in Nanjing. This demonstration interfered with traffic and included such radical slogans as "Shedding blood doesn't matter; freedom is the most valuable thing," "In Beijing they attacked Zhongnanhai; what shall we do here?" and "Welcome May Fourth by carrying out a struggle." Students shouted slogans at the gates of the provincial government building but resisted attempts by unemployed youth to incite them to break in. They returned to Bell Tower Square, and the crowd grew to more than ten thousand, interfering

---

[28] *Guandao*, "official profiteering," refers specifically to selling at higher free-market prices goods or raw materials procured at the lower fixed rates in the planned sector of the economy.

with traffic. A student who identified himself as coming from Hehai University read a proclamation demanding that the day's demonstration be recognized as patriotic and law-abiding and that the authorities take measures to fight corruption and increase transparency.

The Hubei Party Committee reported on student demonstrations in Wuhan, noting four differences between these demonstrations and those that had occurred in early 1986: First, the 1986 demonstrators had been undergraduates, and mostly first- and second-year students at that; this time graduate students were in the lead. Second, slogans and demands in 1986 were vague and abstract; now they were clear and highly political, with a definite anti-Party and antigovernment slant, including explicit attacks on Deng Xiaoping, Zhao Ziyang, Yang Shangkun, and Li Peng. Third, the movement was more complicated ideologically. The students had broadened their concerns to include politics, economics, culture, education, ideological theory, social mores, and social order, and in contrast to the situation in 1986, they were eliciting widespread sympathy from faculty members and officials. Fourth, the demonstrations were larger in scale and duration and were having greater impact on social order.

The Party Committee reported that educators in the province suggested the following causes for these differences: First, there was a widespread feeling that reform had been mishandled: Policy directions had changed too often, younger officials had not been promoted, and old leaders were still exercising too much power. Second, intellectuals resented the fact that their champion, Hu Yaobang, had been forced to resign in 1987. Third, many students and intellectuals had lost faith in the theory of Party leadership because of the Party's apparent inability to reverse the deterioration of social mores and social order.

Politically radical slogans turned up among students in Hunan and Anhui as well. Local authorities reported they were taking measures to prevent violent incidents.

Leaders' views harden

The sit-in of large numbers of students at Xinhua Gate on April 18–19 stimulated some of the retired Party leaders to express their opinions and the active leaders to take new measures.

Account based on *Materials for the Fourth Plenum of the Thirteenth Central Committee,* "Remarks of Comrade Chen Xitong," "Remarks of Comrade Wang Zhen," "Remarks of Comrade Wang Renzhong," "Remarks of Comrade Yao Yilin," "Remarks of Comrade Song Ping," and "Remarks of Comrade Tian Jiyun," Secretariat of the Fourth Plenum of the CCP Thirteenth Central Committee, June 23–24, 1989; and from

> Li Peng, "Report on mistakes committed by Comrade Zhao Ziyang during the anti-Party antisocialist turmoil," report to the Fourth Plenum of the Thirteenth Central Committee, June 23[29]

Peng Zhen telephoned Chen Xitong on April 20.

"With Beijing in chaos like this we've got to guard against a 'second Cultural Revolution.' There must be some black hands behind these students, so we'd better get to the bottom of things."

Wang Zhen telephoned Deng Xiaoping.

"These students are in rebellion, Comrade Xiaoping. They've attacked Xinhua Gate. We've got to do something right away!"

The same day Li Peng went to see Deng Yingchao, who said:

"We should approve of the students' patriotism but must expose the people with ulterior motives who are prodding the students to cause trouble."

Wang Renzhong telephoned Li Xiannian.

"Chairman Li, the Hubei Party Committee tells me that college students in Wuhan are also stirring up a big ruckus. If we don't take action soon the whole country could fall into anarchy."

Song Ping met with Yao Yilin and the following exchange took place:

Song Ping: "I think it's obvious, Comrade Yilin, that the Beijing students are bent on causing trouble. People like Fang Lizhi have been extremely active. There must be people with ulterior motives manipulating the students, and Party Central had better take quick action before things get out of control."

Yao Yilin: "The students are hiding behind the mourning for Yaobang to demand so-called democracy and freedom. But a lot of them are in the dark; they don't realize what's really going on. The truth is that bourgeois liberal elements

---

[29]An English translation of Li Peng's report has been published in *The China Quarterly* 128 (December 1991): 888–901.

have been waiting a long time for a chance like this. They're exploiting the students' patriotism. We have to get the truth out as soon as possible. The events of these last few days show that this student unrest could turn into real turmoil."

On the morning April 20, Tian Jiyun went to see Zhao Ziyang, hoping to get Zhao to change the date of his scheduled visit to North Korea on April 23. Tian was one of Zhao's most trusted friends and lieutenants, and Zhao always took his views seriously.

Tian Jiyun: "Comrade Ziyang, the situation in Beijing and other cities is extremely tense. Can't you put off your visit to Korea?"

Zhao Ziyang: "I've thought about that, too; but to postpone a state visit would lead foreigners to speculate that our political situation is shaky, so I'm going to stick to the schedule."

That morning, after consulting with Yao Yilin, Li Peng decided to form a standing group to keep a close eye on the student protests. Li then telephoned Zhao Ziyang.

Li Peng: "The protests in Beijing and other cities around the country are getting worse, Comrade Ziyang. Don't you think we need a Politburo meeting?"

Zhao Ziyang: "The protests were triggered by the death of Comrade Yaobang. To judge from the slogans, the majority of the students love the Party and the country. The student mainstream is good. I've already told Comrades Tieying and Ximing several times that they should give better guidance to the students. Our main task right now is to be sure the memorial ceremony for Comrade Yaobang goes off smoothly."

In the afternoon an urgent document from Yang Shangkun's office at the Central Military Commission reached Zhao Ziyang. Deng Xiaoping, in order to ensure the security of Beijing and of the Tiananmen area, had directed that two divisions and two regiments from the Thirty-Eighth Army of the Beijing Military District, about nine thousand soldiers, be dispatched to reinforce the police in maintaining order in the capital and in escorting Comrade Hu Yaobang's hearse to Babaoshan Cemetery. The document was signed by Yang Shangkun, and Zhao Ziyang approved it.

At 4 P.M. Li Peng met with Li Tieying, Luo Gan, Yuan Mu, He Dongchang, Zeng Jianhui, and Liu Zhongde and ordered them to keep a close watch on developments and to provide copies of all State Council General Office reports on the student movement to Yuan Mu. Li gave the same order to Wen Jiabao in a written note. From then on, Yuan Mu became Li Peng's eyes and ears in the matter.

Zhao Ziyang consulted with Hu Qili and Rui Xingwen on the topic of news reporting.

Zhao Ziyang: "Published news and opinion should be more positive. We should affirm the students' enthusiastic patriotism but should also try to soften the conflict and point out that social stability is crucial to reform and opening."

After reading the State Security Ministry's "Report on the Appearance of Illegal Organizations at Universities," Li Peng forwarded the document to Li Tieying with the following instruction:

"Comrade Tieying, notify universities to curb these organizations in accordance with the law."

On the basis of instructions from Zhao Ziyang and Li Peng, Li Tieying ordered the SEC to issue a third notice to educational authorities around the country.

> Excerpt from State Education Commission, "Notice on doing a good job of political thought work among the students and guaranteeing stability at the schools and in society," April 22

On the evening of April 19, at a democracy salon session at Peking University attended by two hundred or three hundred students, seven students from Peking University organized a Planning Committee of the United Students' Association that would "lead all student activities" from that day forward. . . . In the meantime, at Nankai University, Tianjin University, and elsewhere, students have met and announced the creation of a "provisional student association," also called a "New Awakening Society."

There are indications that there are people manipulating the leaders of these organizations and planning to set up organizations that will network with workers and farmers and win them over. . . . These intra- and intercollegiate organizations have not gained the required approval of school or government authorities, nor have their leaders been democratically elected by the student bodies. Hence they are illegal organizations. They will polarize student populations and seriously disrupt and undermine the stability of campuses and the stability and unity of society in general. They must be curtailed according to law.

The foreign press sees a serious challenge

Between April 19 and April 22 agencies provided Central leaders with thirty-seven foreign media reports. Reports on the Xinhua Gate incident and the mourning demonstrations cast these events as the greatest challenge to the government in ten years, noted the government's inability to stop the demonstrations, and awarded victory in the first round to the students. Reports on the establishment of the spontaneous student organizations described them as a rebellion against the principle of Party control and noted that in response to discouragement in the official press the organizations had only expanded. The Japanese newspaper *Asahi shimbun* predicted that unless the government responded seriously to students' demands, the movement would be difficult to stop. A report in the April 22 *South China Morning Post* received much attention from the leaders. It reported growing support for the students among intellectuals, who were emboldened by the Party's earlier failure to crack down on challengers such as Fang Lizhi, and it suggested that an alliance between students and intellectuals would present an unprecedented challenge to the CCP.

April 22

Hu Yaobang's memorial service and Zhao's three principles

Shortly before 10 A.M. on April 22 (one week after Hu's death), Deng Xiaoping arrived at the Great Hall of the People, where he was greeted by Zhao Ziyang, Li Peng, Wan Li, and Qiao Shi. Except for Chen Yun, who was too ill to come, the other Elders were also in attendance. Wang Zhen complained to Deng that the student demonstrations near the Hall had made it difficult for some senior leaders to get to the service, and he urged Deng to send police to drive the students away. But Deng told him the matter was not so simple and that this was not the time to discuss it.

The memorial address, delivered by Zhao Ziyang, praised Hu Yaobang along the lines already presented in the April 15 death announcement. This meant, however, that the leadership had not accepted a suggestion made by Hu's family, the Hunan Provincial Party Committee, and some senior pro-reform intellectuals that Hu be labeled a "great Marxist," a label that would have affirmed the value of his liberal ideas.

After the ceremony the Elders went home. Qiao Shi and Hu Qili accompanied the coffin to the Babaoshan Cemetery. On the way to the door, Zhao Ziyang reminded Deng Xiaoping that he was leaving the next day for North Korea and said that he had suggested to his colleagues in the Politburo three principles for resolving the student movement.

Accounts drawn from *Materials for the Fourth Plenum of the Thirteenth Central Committee*, "Remarks of Comrade Zhao

Ziyang," Secretariat of the Fourth Plenum of the CCP Thirteenth Central Committee, June 23–24, 1989

Zhao Ziyang: "First, now that the memorial service is over, we should firmly prevent the students from demonstrating and should get them to return to classes immediately. Second, we should use legal procedures to punish severely all who engage in beating, smashing, and robbing.[30] Third, the main approach to the students should be one of persuasion,[31] and to do this we can hold multilevel dialogues."[32]

Deng Xiaoping: "Good."

Zhao Ziyang: "While I'm away, Comrade Li Peng will be responsible for managing the work of Party Central. If anything happens, he will report to you."

Other members of the Politburo urged Zhao to hold a meeting to discuss how to handle the demonstrations. Zhao said there was no time for a meeting, but he repeated his three points to Yang Shangkun, Li Peng, Yao Yilin, Li Ximing, and others.

Zhao Ziyang: "I just discussed three suggestions for handling the student movement with Comrade Xiaoping, and he agreed with them. Let me explain them again to you comrades.

"First, now that the memorial service is over, social life should be brought back to normal. We should firmly prevent the students from going into the streets and demonstrating, and we should get them to return to classes as soon as possible.

"Second, we must at all costs avoid any incident of bloodshed, because if such an incident should occur it would give some people the pretext they are looking for. But we should use legal procedures to punish severely all who engage in beating, smashing, and robbing.

"Third, we should actively adopt a policy of persuasion toward the students and hold multilevel, multichannel, multiformat dialogues with them."

Yang Shangkun: "I support Ziyang's opinion."

Zhao Ziyang (to Li Peng): "While I am away, you will be in charge of the daily work of Party Central."

[30] *Da za qiang* (beat, smash, and rob) was a set phrase used to describe Red Guard violence during the Cultural Revolution. It still had strong negative connotations in 1989.

[31] *Shudao*, literally, "dredging," hence, "guidance by persuasion, clearing away obstacles to consensus in people's minds," as distinct from *yindao*, "guidance by instruction or by leading the way." These are two methods of political thought work.

[32] *Duocengci de duihua*, dialogues at many levels, implying that the students' demand for dialogue with top leaders could probably be turned aside by offering them dialogue with lower-level leaders, who were supposed to be in close touch with their constituents in any case.

Li Peng: "I agree with the three-point opinion that Comrade Ziyang has just expressed. If there is any major event, we will quickly inform you."

Zhao thus gave clear instructions on handling the student movement before his departure, even though he did not call a Politburo Standing Committee meeting.

While these events were taking place inside the Great Hall, a peaceful but vast, self-organized gathering involving several tens of thousands of students was taking place outside in the Square and along both sides of Chang'an West Boulevard, where Hu's cortege was to pass. The details were reported to Party Central by the Public Security Ministry.

During the official ceremony the students observed a solemn silence. Afterward they presented a petition demanding (1) that the coffin be driven once around the Square so the students could pay their respects one last time; (2) that Li Peng hold a dialogue with the students; and (3) that the news of the day's student activities be published in the newspapers. Otherwise, they threatened, they would storm the Great Hall. At 12:50 P.M., three student representatives knelt on the steps to the Great Hall, the one in the middle holding up a large paper containing seven demands. As their wait for someone to emerge to accept the petition lengthened, the onlookers began to talk among themselves in sympathy. Some shouting and shoving broke out between civilians and the military and PAP troops guarding the Great Hall. Some onlookers threw shoes, but student monitors got control of the crowd and kept the peace. Some staff members from inside the hall came out and spoke with the kneeling students. About 1:30 P.M. the three students, still holding up the scroll listing their demands, came down the steps and rejoined the crowd. Shortly afterward the student ranks started to move back to their respective campuses, with the intention, according to some, of starting a boycott of classes.

Meanwhile, on the campus of Peking University, according to a report from the State Security Ministry, only five hundred students and faculty showed up to watch the broadcast of the official memorial service in an auditorium with a capacity of two thousand, while outside, in the Triangle, protest posters containing strong language appeared. Interviews with students revealed much anger at official corruption and a sense that only by demonstrating and putting up protest posters could students draw the leadership's attention to this issue.

Fifty-six reports to Zhongnanhai from provincial authorities and the two security ministries showed that mourning activities took place normally around the country except for two locations. In Xi'an a student demonstration led to a violent incident in which cars and apartments were torched and eighteen people were arrested. In Changsha violence broke out during a student demonstration. Some twenty shops were looted, and ninety-six people were detained.

April 23

Zhao Ziyang departs; the student movement spreads

On the morning of April 23 Zhao Ziyang again instructed Hu Qili and Rui Xingwen to have the positive side of the student demonstrations emphasized in press reports. That afternoon he left for North Korea, seen off at the Beijing Railway Station by Li Peng, Qiao Shi, and Tian Jiyun. Zhao told the three that he stood by his three-point opinion for handling the student movement.

At the suggestion of He Dongchang, Li Tieying sent a fourth notice from the State Education Commission to all provincial-level departments of education and institutions of higher education under SEC control. These notices mentioned the violent incidents in Xi'an and Changsha and gave orders to discourage similar incidents elsewhere.

> Excerpts from State Education Commission, "Notice on maintaining normal order for teaching and studying and normal order for working," April 23

All areas should discourage students from demonstrating in the streets and should warn students that illegal elements can seize such opportunities to cause trouble.... The memorial service for Comrade Hu Yaobang is now over. We must return directly to work if we are to maintain normal order in study and work. ... Instructors must persist in performing their duties no matter what; they must mobilize students to come to class on time. Midterm exams must go ahead as scheduled; no requirements can be relaxed. ... Emotions are high in some districts and schools, especially around some issues created by rumors. In such cases we should use dialogue, calmly seek truth from facts, and get to the bottom of things in order to win over the majority. ... Protest posters—especially those containing obvious errors—should be promptly taken down.

That day there were fifteen separate reports that plans for students to boycott classes were brewing on key campuses in Beijing. A State Security Ministry report on People's University was typical. It reported that a flyer circulated saying that the Thirty-Eighth Army had been ordered to enter Beijing.[33] Another flyer announced that students at Peking University, Beijing Normal University, and other campuses had decided to boycott classes. Around 2 P.M. a poster titled "Procla-

---

[33] As the text has already noted, this rumor was correct.

mation by Ph.D. Students at People's University" appeared on campus, announcing a doctoral candidates' boycott of classes and stating seven demands.[34] These included the resignation of all leaders over the age of seventy-five, an end to the financing of CCP activities by the state treasury, an end to press censorship, and the establishment of a Committee for Clean Government comprising people from all levels of society to investigate corruption at all levels of government. When this report arrived at Zhongnanhai at 3:30 P.M., Yuan Mu immediately showed it to Li Peng, who pronounced the doctoral students' demands "a naked declaration of war against the Party."

That evening Li Ximing and Chen Xitong held a meeting with the Party secretaries and the presidents of seventy universities in the capital.

Excerpt from Beijing Municipal Party Committee and Beijing Municipal Government, "Comrades Li Ximing and Chen Xitong held a meeting this evening with seventy Party secretaries and school presidents from institutions of higher learning in the capital," fax to Party Central and State Council duty offices, April 23

Li Ximing: "When Comrade Hu Yaobang's memorial service was over, the students were supposed to return to their classes. This was our sincere wish, but our sincere wish did not come to pass."

Chen Xitong: "There are reports of new developments on the campuses today. First, some students want to boycott classes at seventeen schools, including Peking University, Qinghua University, People's University, and Beijing Normal University. Some of them want to abolish the official student and graduate student organizations and form autonomous student associations. Second, there were student demonstrations at eight institutions, including Beijing Normal University, the National Minorities Institute, and the University of Science and Technology. Some students shouted 'Down with bureaucrats!' Third, on some campuses students have taken control of the campus public-address systems. Some students at People's University today occupied the broadcast station, but the station learned of the action in advance and managed to remove the equipment first. At Peking University students are setting up a news center. At Qinghua some students are preparing to set up a broadcast station. This shows that this student movement is a planned, organized turmoil.[35] Those of us called upon to

---

[34] A portion of this poster, containing only five items, is included in Ogden et al., *China's Search*, 107.

[35] *You zuzhi, you jihua de dongluan.* This is the first occurrence in the documents of the stock phrase that appeared in the April 26 editorial and became for a while the nub of controversy between the regime and the students.

act should take decisive measures against the minority of activists who are encouraging boycotts and demonstrations; we must not go easy on them."

Li Ximing: "The Municipal Committee has ordered all Party and government personnel on the campuses to go among the students tomorrow morning to urge them back to class and to listen to their views. Tomorrow afternoon the committee will hold a meeting with Youth League secretaries and chairs of student associations to gather reports and plan the next steps."

At 10:30 P.M. the State Security Ministry sent an urgent report to Zhongnanhai.

> State Security Ministry, "This evening student delegates from twenty-one Beijing institutions of higher learning meeting at Yuanmingyuan announced the establishment of an illegal student organization," fax to Party Central and State Council duty offices, April 23

Between 6 and 10 P.M. on the twenty-third, representatives of students from twenty-one universities met in Yuanmingyuan[36] to establish a provisional student planning committee. They elected Zhou Yongjun of the CUPSL as their chair. (Zhou, who was chair of the autonomous student group on the CUPSL campus, was one of the three students who presented the list of student demands on April 22 in Tiananmen Square.) The students also set up three teams, in charge of public speeches, soliciting donations, and maintaining order, and named a temporary leader for each. Headquarters for the three teams were set up on CUPSL's campus. This morning students ordered the official CUPSL Student Association to hand over its office space to this new committee, which announced that from now on all university students would be under its unified command.

Sixteen reports sent from the provinces to Zhongnanhai on April 23 showed that in most places the situation was relatively calm, without large student demonstrations or acts of resistance. But this was not so everywhere.

> State Security Ministry, "Situation among Tianjin college students," fax to Party Central and State Council duty offices, midnight, April 24

---

[36]The Summer Palace of imperial times, now a park near Peking University.

At 6 P.M., more than ten thousand students from Nankai University, Tianjin University, and other schools in Tianjin carried out the largest demonstration the city has seen in ten years. We have determined that the direct causes of this outbreak were the return to Tianjin of students who had gone to the memorial service in Beijing and their use of protest posters to expose what had happened at dawn on April 20, outside Xinhua Gate on April 22, and in Tiananmen Square. These reports excited some of the students, and they decided to take to the streets again. The demonstration was orderly throughout. Students marched four abreast, in a column stretching a mile or more. Student monitors linked arms at the edges of the column to prevent outsiders from mixing in. The students marched to the municipal government office building but did not remain there long. During the demonstration police cars drove ahead of the marchers to clear the way, and several thousand police were placed along the streets to maintain order and to disperse traffic. As a result there was no disorder or confrontation. The demonstration ended by 11:50 P.M.

Foreign media report that the students are determined

Twelve reports came into Zhongnanhai on April 23, all emphasizing the new direction taken by the student movement. The Associated Press reported that Chai Ling, spokesperson for the newly formed United Students' Association, said the Peking University students had decided to oppose the original plan to end the boycott on May 4 and now suggested that their activities should have no fixed end date. According to Reuters, "Activists at Peking University said today that they were determined not to let their demands for freedom and democracy end in defeat because of a lack of organization, as had happened with student movements earlier in the 1980s." Reuters noted that students had established a news center aimed at countering official propaganda. The Japanese newspaper *Sankei shimbun* likened the student movement to antisystem uprisings in Czechoslovakia and Hungary. Perhaps most ominously, the Kyodo News Agency reported that student leaders had urged workers to strike. The agency predicted that if the workers did indeed join the movement, it would shake the Communist Party to its roots.

CHAPTER TWO

April 24–30

The April 26 Editorial

EDITORS' NOTE: In Zhao Ziyang's absence, Li Peng called a Politburo meeting on April 24 to hear reports about the spread of the student movement in Beijing and around the country.

The next day some members of the Politburo met informally with senior Elder Deng Xiaoping at his home. The briefing was dominated by those most antagonistic to the students. They persuaded Deng that hostile forces had become involved and that the students were getting more radical, their ultimate target being to overthrow him and the Chinese Communist Party. Deng denounced the movement. His views were reflected in an April 26 editorial in the *People's Daily,* the main Party newspaper.

Because of its harsh judgment of the student movement, the editorial became a new focus of dissatisfaction not only among students but among citizens as well. The rapidly expanding support for the movement became too broad to allow for a quick, repressive solution. After a divided Politburo Standing Committee meeting, the leaders turned their efforts to winning people back, partly through softer-sounding public statements and partly through organizational work, especially on campuses, via administrators, professors, officials of the Youth League, and the official student associations. But reports showed that many of these people were themselves wavering and critical of the Party's attitude.

Meanwhile, from Shanghai, Party Secretary Jiang Zemin filed a report on measures taken to close a pro-reform newspaper, the *World Economic Herald,* which had promoted activities to mourn Hu Yaobang. On April 30 Party General Secretary Zhao returned from North Korea amid mixed signs that the student movement might be calming down.

April 24

Politburo meeting called by Li Peng

In the afternoon of April 24, when Chen Xitong learned that students from twenty-one local schools had already formed a "planning committee," he realized that the previous day's plans about working through responsible officials at the various campuses would probably be useless. At 3 P.M. that day he and Li Ximing arrived at Wan Li's office in the Great Hall of the People.

> Account drawn from *Materials for the Fourth Plenum of the Thirteenth Central Committee*, "Remarks of Comrade Wan Li" and "Remarks of Comrade Li Ximing," Secretariat of the Fourth Plenum of the CCP Thirteenth Central Committee, June 23–24, 1989

Chen Xitong: "The student movement in Beijing is getting bigger every day; reactionary organizations are out in the open; they are inciting students to boycott classes and teachers to go on strike. Today nearly fifty thousand students in thirty-nine schools are not in class. Moreover, the turmoil on the campuses has already started to spread to the rest of society. Even some of the reactionary elements from Democracy Wall have come back to life. The outlook is grim."

Li Ximing: "The students themselves would not be able to come up with this kind of power. Black hands and provocateurs are behind them. Investigation has shown that the most eager of the Peking University students are operating under the direction of Fang Lizhi's wife Li Shuxian.[1] Fang himself has not entered directly into the student movement, but he has been the students' main avenue to the foreign media. And there are some others with ill intentions as well."

Wan Li: "The conditions you report are important, and the situation in Beijing is indeed worrisome. I see Tiananmen Square every day.[2] But I still believe that the great majority of the students are patriotic and side with the Party. They mean well. We have to distinguish the bad apples from the rest."

---

[1]Fang Lizhi, an astrophysicist at the National Observatory in Beijing, had been an inspiration to students in the 1986 pro-democracy demonstrations in Hefei, Anhui Province, where Fang was then vice president of the Chinese University of Science and Technology. Li Shuxian, Fang's wife, was an associate professor of physics at Peking University. Both Fang and Li had participated in democracy salon meetings on the Peking University campus in spring 1988.

[2]The Great Hall of the People, seat of the National People's Congress, is on the edge of Tiananmen Square.

Li Ximing: "What should we do now?"

Wan Li: "The Politburo Standing Committee should meet as soon as possible to study the situation in Beijing and elsewhere and then come up with a policy."

Chen Xitong: "Can you suggest a meeting?"

Wan Li: "Okay, let's call Li Peng right now."[3]

Li Peng agreed that the situation was serious and said he would call a meeting for that evening. Chen Xitong attended for the Beijing Municipal Committee, He Dongchang represented the SEC, and Yuan Mu and Zeng Jianhui participated as department heads. Others who attended were Yang Shangkun, Qiao Shi, Hu Qili, Yao Yilin, Wan Li, Tian Jiyun, Li Tieying, and Li Ximing.

> Excerpts from Party Central Office Secretariat, "Minutes of
> the April 24 Politburo Standing Committee meeting"

Li Peng: "Our main item of business today is to hear reports from the Beijing Municipal Committee and the State Education Commission on developments at the universities in the capital and their possible expansion into the rest of society. Everyone knows that following Hu Yaobang's death students from several dozen schools in the capital began to write wall posters and then marched in the streets, boycotted classes, and openly proclaimed illegal student organizations. A small minority is manipulating the students, and the situation has become grim."

Li Ximing: "From the beginning of the student movement the Municipal Committee and the Municipal Government have held twelve meetings of various sizes. Last night we held a meeting for the Party secretaries and school heads of more than seventy universities in the city. Each school was required to post notices calling on Party members, officials, and activists to mingle with students and do political work on their thinking. This morning Party and government leaders at the various schools went to work among the students, but the results were negligible. Students basically ignored what school officials said and told them that dialogue with them will not solve the problem. In the afternoon the Municipal Committee held a meeting of all Youth League secretaries and all chairs of the official student associations in the capital. These people reported almost unanimously that they were isolated on their campuses. Some of the official student associations had been smeared as 'illegitimate.' By contrast the ille-

---

[3]In the absence of Party Secretary Zhao, Li Peng as second-ranking member of the Politburo had the power to call a meeting.

gally established 'autonomous student associations' were full of vim and confidence. In sum, evil is winning over good."

Chen Xitong: "In breadth, size, and intensity, this student movement is unprecedented in the reform era. . . . At present, about sixty thousand students at thirty-nine universities are boycotting classes. Some continue to put up protest posters, distribute handbills, fabricate rumors, and harm people's minds. Others have formed illegal organizations, taken over campus public-address systems, and forced the dissolution of official student associations. Still others are taking to the streets, making speeches, soliciting donations, and sending envoys into factories, high schools, elementary schools, and even to other provinces in efforts to stir the entire nation to boycott classes and go on strike. We can say that the student movement in the capital has already evolved from its origins as spontaneous expression of grief for Hu Yaobang into agitation and turmoil."

He Dongchang from the SEC gave a detailed survey of the student movement in Beijing and across the country over the preceding ten days. Then he commented on the current student movement.

"[This student movement] has already reached institutions of higher education in more than twenty large and medium-sized cities. Be it through protest posters, slogans, demonstrations, boycotts, or the formation of illegal organizations, the goal throughout has been to shake things up, cause trouble, create turmoil, attack the Party, and attack socialism. . . . Students in Wuhan openly chanted 'Down with the corrupt government' and 'Down with the bureaucratic government.' A poster titled 'Beijing Normal University Journalism Department Protest Poster' bewailed 'Xiaoping controlling the country, gripping the reins of power'; it even called for 'catching the murderers.' At Fudan University in Shanghai, a couplet read 'The Four Principles[4] are the source of the nation's misfortune; freedom and democracy are the root of the nation's revival.' At Nankai University in Tianjin, a poster entitled 'Guidelines for a New May Fourth' openly attacked Comrade Li Peng. . . . A small minority with ulterior motives took the opportunity of the Hu Yaobang memorial to spread rumors and create disorder. Riffraff used the occasion to 'beat, smash, and rob.' The incidents in Changsha and Xi'an and at Xinhua Gate were all of this basic kind, and we can't say that these are just simple cases of looting. An even more worrisome fact is that posters and meet-

4See footnote 12 in the Prologue.

ings devoted to plotting strategy have begun to appear. For example, at a joint conference of the *World Economic Herald* newspaper and *New Observations* magazine on April 19, people openly clamored for a reassessment of the campaigns against 'spiritual pollution' and '[bourgeois] liberalization.' The conference emphasized its support for the student demonstrations, even saying that in them 'we see China's future and China's hope.' On the campus at Peking University, a 'Declaration to Our Compatriots' from 'professors at Peking University, People's University, and Qinghua University' said, 'The most urgent task now is propaganda, not mourning' and 'We must have clear goals, not just random action.' The illegal United Students' Association was set up on instigation from people like Fang Lizhi's wife Li Shuxian."

Li Tieying: "The Education Commission has already sent out four general notices aimed at stabilizing the situation on university campuses across the country. But it seems this will be difficult. We could even be headed toward nationwide turmoil."

Hu Qili: "The circumstances of this student movement are extremely complex. Many things are mixed together, and it's not easy to separate them out. The bad people among the students may be a tiny minority, but the power of this tiny minority must not be underestimated."

Qiao Shi: "We certainly don't want to see any harm done to the growing democratic atmosphere in society, but no country can permit unruly freedom or irresponsible freedom. The patriotism of the majority of the students must be affirmed, but their readiness to follow others blindly must be rooted out. We need to point out that their tendency to follow blindly allows others to take advantage of their good intentions. . . . In Changsha, Xi'an, and elsewhere we have seen examples of riffraff beating, smashing, robbing, and burning. Although the situation in Beijing, Tianjin, and Shanghai looks all right on the surface, the possibility of such explosions cannot be excluded. We need contingency plans for emergencies."

Yao Yilin: "Bourgeois liberal elements with ulterior motives have already exploited this student movement, and it already has grown into what we call turmoil. We must publicize these facts as soon as possible. We must express the attitude of Party Central clearly and make the whole nation, especially the students, aware of the movement's true character. It is hard to imagine what the consequences will be if we fail."

Li Peng: "The declaration by doctoral candidates at People's University that I read yesterday was a naked and overt challenge to the Party. In my view we are deep into a struggle with bourgeois liberalism."

Yang Shangkun: "Calm and stability in the capital are of the utmost importance: If the capital is calm, the whole nation will stay at peace. As for the student movement, we must unite the great majority of the students while exposing those who exploit the situation. Above all we must not let this question of the student movement harm our hard-won stability and unity."

Yao Yilin: "In view of the present situation, I propose that the Center form a Small Group to Halt the Turmoil."[5]

Standing Committee members Li Peng, Qiao Shi, and Hu Qili supported Yao Yilin's proposal, and the Small Group to Halt the Turmoil was duly formed. Li Peng was named its head, and Li Tieying, Li Ximing, Chen Xitong, He Dongchang, and Yuan Mu were members.

The Standing Committee decided to (1) issue an urgent notice to all areas in the name of Party Central and the State Council reporting the situation and recommending countermeasures; (2) charge the Beijing Municipal Committee with mobilizing the masses throughout the city, beginning on April 25, in order to expose the plotters and to conduct a resolute struggle against the enemy forces ranged against the Party and against socialism; and (3) try, in light of the seriousness of the situation, to present a report to Deng Xiaoping in person the next morning.

Later that evening, Party Central and the State Council issued a notice across all of China. It bore the following instructions to provincial leaders:

> Excerpts from Party Central and the State Council, "Urgent notice on doing current work well and carefully preventing the situation from getting worse," April 24

Begin immediately to defend resolutely stability and unity in the political situation. The effort to stop current trends should focus on preventing the boycotting of classes, intercity travel by students, the formation of autonomous student associations, and similar activities. Institutions of higher education must be vigilant in preserving security and pursuing political work. Local institutions must quickly identify and control students who have arrived from somewhere else. Public security should provide appropriate safeguards. . . . You must apprise all Party organs and all Party leaders in large factories and mines of the situation, and you must make sure that they understand the facts clearly and further that they effectively make sure all the workers in their units achieve clear understanding. They must strictly forbid students from coming into factories to make contacts. . . . There remains a possibility that unanticipated incidents will continue

---

[5] A "small group" in this context is an ad hoc working group of ranking officials.

to occur; if this happens, you must handle matters in strict accordance with the Center's policies for dealing with such incidents. You must take care not to allow the problem to spread or conflicts to intensify. At the same time, you must take decisive measures against the minority of lawless elements and move quickly to halt their activity and to punish them. Under no circumstances be soft. . . . Public Security departments should have contingency plans set, including plans for traffic control, in order to be prepared to take decisive measures no matter what might happen.

The day after this notice was sent, Party standing committees at the provincial level across China held meetings to study it and to determine concrete methods for implementing it.

Meeting to form an autonomous student association at Peking University

On April 24 Zhongnanhai received seventeen communications from across China about the nascent student movement. Students at Nankai University in Tianjin had begun a boycott of classes under the leadership of the newly formed Autonomous Federation of Students (AFS), and in Hunan posters reading "Down with Deng Xiaoping" had appeared on the campuses of Hunan Normal University, Zhongnan Industrial University, and elsewhere. A report from the State Security Ministry recorded what went on at Peking University.

> Excerpts from State Security Ministry, "On the process of establishing the Planning Committee for the Autonomous Federation of Students at Peking University," report to Party Central and the State Council, in "Extracts of important news" (*Yaoqing zhaibao*), no. 71, April 24

A meeting to form an autonomous student association began at 2:47 P.M. on April 24 and ended at 4 P.M. The meeting was announced from Building 28, located near the Triangle. The broadcast facility, which the students had set up themselves, also carried recorded speeches and messages of support for the students from their parents.

Beginning around 2 P.M., about 80 percent of all Peking University students trickled into what they called "May Fourth Square." About two hundred students wearing red armbands on which "Beida" [Peking University] was written in ink formed a "monitoring team" to help keep order. Everyone who entered "May

Fourth Square" had to wear a school badge or show other positive identification as a student, worker, or reporter.

The students represented nearly every department in the university. Some carried banners identifying their department, and some carried placards bearing messages. They formed orderly ranks in the square.

Several dozen foreign journalists were very active on the scene interviewing and making video- and audiotapes.

A student representative of the planning meeting mounted the rostrum, took a microphone, and delivered an "opening statement" whose main message was, "We have come together today for the common goals of democracy and science. Seventy years ago our predecessors on this sacred ground spoke of Mr. Democracy and Mr. Science; today, seventy years later, it is still hard going here for democracy and science. Devastation is still everywhere in our land. But today we have finally stood up and are determined to keep going, relying on our quickened blood to keep going and never look back."

Next a student described the preparatory work that had gone into the meeting. This included effectively pulling together student wishes for democracy and work on implementing an indefinite boycott of classes, an effort that had seen initial success. The student went on to describe the next steps, which were these:

1. to continue with petitions and persist with the boycott;
2. to prepare to form a "Planning Committee for a United National Students' Association";
3. to produce an autonomous student organization through democratic elections;
4. to form speakers' bureaus and fund-raising teams.

Then there were announcements of "principles," "organizational structure," and the like.

Next, ten members of the Planning Committee introduced themselves one by one. The tenth introduced himself as "Zhang Zhiyong, sophomore in the International Politics Department." He said that the student movement had entered its second phase. Phase one had required bravery; now what was needed was wisdom. He wanted to continue, but some of the others grabbed the microphone and forced him off the stage. A member of the Planning Committee shouted into the microphone that someone had exposed Zhang Zhiyong as an emissary of the Graduate Student Association[6] and a Party stooge. The organizers later announced that Zhang Zhiyong had been expelled from the Planning Committee.

---

[6] A Party-organized association.

Then a student got up on stage and announced "the repudiation of all the powers of the existing undergraduate and graduate student associations and the formal establishment of the Planning Committee for the Autonomous Association of Peking University Students."

Another student mounted the stage: "I am Wang Dan, a freshman in the History Department.[7] A senior Party member who was in many student movements during the Nationalist period told me this student movement of ours is the greatest one in the seven decades since May Fourth. We can be proud of our place in history. Our continuing sit-in at Tiananmen demonstrates the power of the people. We're going to take back the powers of democracy and freedom from the hands of that gang of old men who've grabbed those powers away from us."

Next, a crane operator from the Xuanwu District Construction Company, who said he represented the "working class," proclaimed support for the students by shaking his fist in the air and telling the students to "found a new China." This person's name was reported to be Wang Chengyue.

A student who called himself a representative from Qinghua University said he hoped the Peking University students would unite and be rational.

A student who said he represented Beijing Engineering University said he hoped people at Peking University would get into action soon.

The last student to speak said, "I've come here full of hope; I am an older graduate student in the Department of Law, and I'd like to offer myself as a legal adviser to the Planning Committee and help it get united."

The following is from a conversation State Security personnel had with a student who asked to remain anonymous:

The student said there were five reasons for the rise of this student movement: (1) Many students had been determined to pursue a democracy movement for quite some time, and Yaobang's death was only a catalyst. (2) Students these days feel that Marxist-Leninist theory no longer makes sense. (3) Students are extremely negative about corruption and the general social ethos and have no confidence that the problems can be solved. (4) Students are highly pessimistic about their prospects for job assignment. (5) Students feel strong urges to participate and to make themselves heard.

This student said that few students opposed the movement and that opinions differed only on how it should be done. One side favors "keeping things at an appropriate level." This group holds that a student movement should make soci-

---

[7]In Chinese universities students enter a major department in their first year of study.

ety and the top leadership aware of student concerns and pleas but should stop there lest it become counterproductive. On the other side are the radicals. A few of the extremely radical students have told their parents that "even if I go down, the movement will go forward." Some students have already prepared for bloodshed. A lot of the students are swayed by their youth and their emotions, and quite a few are just out to have a good time. When they get into a scene, they get carried away and join in with everybody else.

This student felt that the government has made several mistakes in handling the student movement. When the students first went to Xinhua Gate to present demands, someone should have come out to receive them or to invite some representatives inside for a chat. This could have avoided the siege at Xinhua Gate that happened the second time around. When the students did lay siege to Xinhua Gate, the police should not have beaten them. But these two mistakes were not the most serious. The worst one was the failure to respond at noon on April 22 when three student representatives, with other students weeping behind them, knelt outside the Great Hall of the People asking to see Premier Li Peng. The government's imperious attitude in this incident hurt the students deeply, led to extreme disappointment with the leadership, and handed the extremist elements an issue. It probably also sowed the seeds of larger demonstrations to come.

This student believes there will probably be more demonstrations on May 4. He offered the following opinions on how to deal with future demonstrations:

1. On the process and structure of decisionmaking about the student movement: He felt that the government had fallen into a fixed pattern in which the students took initiatives while the government only reacted. By now most of the students can predict that a certain move on their side will bring a certain countermove from the government. When students laid siege to Xinhua Gate, this student himself was able to predict that the government would respond with a "general announcement," and he could also guess almost exactly what it would say. So the government has slipped into a reactive role and is being led around by the nose. The concerned government organs need to increase their capacity for rapid response so that someone can make decisions immediately whenever an unforeseen situation arises. They could even consult privately with selected students before making decisions. He said there are students willing to cooperate with the government in handling the student movement; they would ask only that the government promise absolute secrecy in order to avoid pulling out the rug from beneath them.

2. On the question of dialogue: The government should consider this question

seriously. The government should seize opportunities for dialogue before students opt for action. In order to avoid bloodshed and extreme acts, the government should find ways to dispel the students' oppositional mood and make some investments in their goodwill. In dialogue with the students, substantive issues can be sidestepped but one point has to be absolutely clear: that the government affirms the democratic aspirations and patriotism of the students. It is all right to reject their methods or decisions, but not their motivations.

3. On the question of reporting on the student movement: News reports should be as objective as possible and should use labels carefully, distinguishing clearly between students and lawless elements in society and equally clearly between the majority of students and the minority of student troublemakers.

4. On wall posters: There have always been a lot of different opinions on college campuses, and this is true of attitudes toward this student movement as well. But because wall posters are officially forbidden these days, the only ones who put them up are the rabble-rousers—at the Triangle at Peking University, for example. If authorities stopped tearing down or covering over the posters, a variety of voices would emerge. Students would have a better chance to judge things for themselves and to move from emotion toward reason.

Foreign commentary

On April 24 Zhongnanhai received twenty-eight foreign news reports focusing on the activities of the students. Foreign agencies reported that the students were determined to continue their strike until their demands were met yet worried that the government could easily move troops into Beijing and arrest their leaders. Foreign media reported that the Chinese news media wanted independence from Party control and that there was broad support for the students among intellectuals. Several papers noted the unprecedented scale of the students' challenge but did not expect the government to remain tolerant indefinitely. In the long run, the London *Sunday Telegraph* opined, the students would be no match for a tightly disciplined Party organization that controlled the forces of public order.

April 24–25

Incident in Xi'an

The following report arrived at Zhongnanhai on April 25:

> Excerpt from Shaanxi Provincial Party Committee and Shaanxi People's Government, "Report on the situation surrounding the April 22 incident," report to Party Central and State Council, April 25

According to preliminary figures at the Xi'an Public Security Bureau, 270 people had been taken into custody by 1 P.M. on April 24 for "beating, smashing, robbing, and burning." Of those, 72 were students from colleges, high schools, or grade schools. Sun Dianqi of the Xi'an Municipal Committee has reported that there have been no deaths and that, to judge from the condition of the injured, no one, whether military police, Public Security officers, or arrestees, is likely to die.

Sun Dianqi, who was primarily responsible for handling this unexpected incident, said even though some of the offenders who set fires, looted, and so on had been caught, others were able to escape because of confusion at the scene and ineffective coordination among the police. But Public Security made videotapes at the scene and gathered a large amount of evidence; the chief perpetrator, who had set fire to many automobiles, Wang Jun, had been tracked down and arrested.

Sun Dianqi also reported that leaders at provincial and municipal levels, as well as those in charge at the scene, repeatedly stressed there should be no beatings. Still, many of the arrested were severely beaten with sticks, belts, and fists. Sun said under the circumstances some of the poorly educated military police and Public Security officers were overcome with rage, making such breeches of regulation hard to avoid.

Those arrested are now at various precinct offices (Weiyang, Xincheng, Yanta, Lianhu, and others) of the Xi'an Public Security Bureau undergoing intensive interrogation. Initial interrogation has already been completed on 164. Of these, 32 (or 18.9 percent) are college students; the rest include 54 workers, 24 farmers, 18 unemployed, and 37 others (high school and grade school students, individual entrepreneurs, and drifters). After preliminary interrogation, 106 were released.

Fifty-five cases are currently in interrogation: one person is being held in criminal detention, thirty-nine have been held for trial, fifteen are in administrative detention, two are awaiting interrogation, and one is severely injured and in the hospital.

Sun Dianqi believes some riffraff escaped the police this time. The number of freed convicts in Xi'an now stands at fifteen thousand, and there are ten thousand or twenty thousand others under Public Security surveillance and control. Given the chance, any of these people might seek revenge. May 4 is approaching, so we must be fully prepared for what might happen.

The Municipal Committee has already settled on the following measures:

First and most important, do political thought work among university students.

Second, organize forces to respond to unexpected incidents. The Xi'an Military Command has already begun to mold fifteen hundred workers into fifteen militia units under a unified command structure. The main responsibility of these militias is to guarantee security in their own work units.

Third, work urgently to root out all the criminal elements who were involved in the April 22 incident. To this end we will intensify interrogation of detainees in order to get leads and at the same time encourage the masses to expose criminals.

Fourth, prepare for potential developments on May 4; in addition to working within the schools, we will broaden the scope of control and pay particular attention to the basic levels.

On April 25 Public Security provided materials—including the following excerpts—on the situation in Xi'an universities:

> Excerpt from State Security Ministry, "Recent situation in Xi'an universities," report to Party Central and the State Council, April 25

Over the past couple of days the situation at the colleges in Xi'an has, on the surface, calmed down. Class attendance has returned to normal, but students are still buzzing over how the April 22 incident was handled.

At Xi'an Jiaotong University, the responsible person on the Standing Committee said that beginning April 23 the school has used "Patriotism and Hygiene Month" as a pretext to clean almost one thousand protest posters off campus walls. Even though students had learned from Voice of America that Beijing students were boycotting classes, the news did not have much of an impact. Most students continued going to class.

On April 23 Northwest University issued an urgent notice asking students to observe stability and unity, to keep the big picture in mind, to make their opinions known through proper channels, and to be clearheaded and distinguish between right and wrong. Furthermore, they must not go out on the streets to demonstrate without authorization; violators will bear all the consequences. To all this the students submitted on the surface but remained unconvinced inside.

We have reports that some of the arrested students from Xi'an Jiaotong University, Northwest University, Northwest Polytechnic University, and other institutions have returned to their schools. Some students, with bloody bandages on their heads or even with severe injuries, are being treated at hospitals. Some students have disappeared, and there is much talk about this fact. Students are saying things like, "This is too cruel! Who'd have guessed the police could be this harsh, beating innocent students? . . . And not just students, but old people, women, and children, too!" or "People under arrest have no power to resist. . . . The Communist Party has always emphasized sticking to their own rules of conduct; so why do they have to beat people with sticks and leather belts?"

The leadership at these schools is worried about what might happen next. They think the calm that currently pervades Xi'an campuses is only temporary and that actually things are far from calm. Students at all the schools are forming secret liaisons, probably to plot more activity. Something even bigger may be in store for May 4.

A violent incident also occurred on April 22 in Changsha. The Hunan Provincial Party Committee reported on April 25 that the police had arrested 138 people for "beating, smashing, and robbing," including workers, farmers, self-employed and unemployed persons, and students.

April 25

"Networking"

A State Security Ministry report from Wuhan on April 25 carried the first news of a developing trend. A week after the start of the student movement, some Beijing students were leaving the city to "network" *(chuanlian)*[8] with students in other provinces. For example, a person identifying

[8]The term *chuanlian*, also translated as "linking up," arose during the Cultural Revolution to describe the movement of young people into factories, offices, schools, farms, and elsewhere, eventually reaching all corners of the country and especially Beijing, to organize and to spread and absorb the revolutionary word. The usage invokes, either positively or negatively, the image of Cultural Revolution–style activism or chaos.

himself as a nineteen-year-old Youth League secretary from the Automation Department at Qinghua University showed up at a number of campuses in Wuhan and told students that the Beijing student movement was unified around seven demands. Students in Beijing did not plan to demonstrate any more, he said, but would concentrate on boycotting classes and on arousing support among the capital's citizenry. He claimed that Youth League committees and official student organizations sided with the student movement and were providing various forms of support. Wuhan students should do the same. No victory could be achieved without the support of the working class. Students from other cities had sent delegates to Beijing to support the capital student movement, and they were in the process of creating a national organization to replace the official All-China Students' Federation and to make preparations for May 4.

A report from the Zhejiang Provincial Party Committee to Zhongnanhai reflected attitudes held by school officials in many institutions of higher education around the country. They perceived policies emanating from Beijing as oscillating between tough and soft and wanted more-consistent guidance from the Center on how to impose discipline on the students and what to do if they failed. The schools were willing to hold dialogue with the students, but the students' demands went far beyond topics that school officials were qualified to discuss.

An abortive dialogue

At 6 P.M. on April 25 the State Security Ministry reported to Zhongnanhai on an abortive attempt by officials of the All-China Students' Federation and its Beijing branch to arrange a meeting between student representatives from Qinghua University and some high-ranking national officials. The Qinghua-based Peaceful Petition Organization Committee first demanded such a meeting. But when it was granted, they set new conditions and in the end failed to send delegates to meet with the waiting officials, who included Liu Zhongde, deputy secretary general of the State Council, and He Dongchang, vice minister of the State Education Commission. The report suggested four possible reasons for the students' behavior: internal divisions, lack of preparation for the dialogue, possible manipulation by figures behind the scenes, and possible concern that if Qinghua students alone engaged in such dialogue, students from other schools would accuse them of selling out the student movement.

A Xinhua News Agency report on this incident, published in the April 26 *People's Daily*, created great irritation among Qinghua students, who regarded the report as biased and as aimed at splitting the students.

Deng Xiaoping and the April 26 editorial

At 9 A.M. on April 25 Li Peng, Yang Shangkun, Qiao Shi, Hu Qili, Yao Yilin, Li Ximing, Chen Xitong, and others went to Deng Xiaoping's home to report. Li Peng sketched the evolving situation for Deng, aided by interjections from other members of the group. Chen Xitong then spoke about the situation in Beijing. What Deng said when he had heard the reports was to form the basis of the April 26 editorial and would become the Party's verdict on the nature of the student movement.

> Excerpt from Party Central Office Secretariat, "Important meeting minutes," April 25

Li Peng: "Comrade Xiaoping, with things developing so rapidly, those of us on the Standing Committee who were in town met last night to hear reports from the Beijing Municipal Committee and the State Education Commission on the situation in the universities and the tendencies in society more generally. We all feel that the situation in Beijing now is extremely grim."

Hu Qili: "This is the largest student movement in ten years, and there have already been student demonstrations in more than twenty large and medium-sized cities across the country."

Li Peng: "Some of the protest posters and the slogans that students shout during the marches are anti-Party and antisocialist. They're clamoring for a reversal of the verdicts on spiritual pollution and bourgeois liberalization. The spear is now pointed directly at you and the others of the elder generation of proletarian revolutionaries."

Deng Xiaoping: "Saying I'm the mastermind behind the scenes, are they?"

Li Peng: "There are open calls for the government to step down, appeals for nonsense like 'open investigations into and discussions of the question of China's governance and power,' and calls to institute broader elections and revise the Constitution, to lift restrictions on political parties and newspapers, and to get rid of the category of 'counterrevolutionary' crimes. Illegal student organizations have already sprung up in Beijing and Tianjin."

Deng Xiaoping: "What?"

Chen Xitong: "Illegal student organizations. At Peking University some students have imitated Poland's Solidarity to form their own Solidarity Student Union."

Li Peng: "The small number of leaders of these illegal organizations have other people behind them calling the shots."

Li Ximing: "They say the person behind the illegal student organization at Peking University is Fang Lizhi's wife."

Chen Xitong: "We've already asked the relevant departments to find out the status and background of the leaders of these illegal student organizations as soon as possible."

Li Peng: "In Beijing there have been two attacks on Xinhua Gate in quick succession; in Changsha and Xi'an there was looting and arson on April 22; and in Wuhan students have demonstrated on the Yangtze River Bridge, blocking the vital artery between Beijing and Guangzhou. These actions seriously harm social stability and unity, and they disrupt social order. Those of us on the Standing Committee all believe that this is turmoil and that we must rely on law to bring a halt to it as soon as possible."

Chen Xitong: "I will report to Comrade Xiaoping on the situation in the universities in Beijing over the last few days. Since the twenty-third, more than sixty thousand students have boycotted classes at forty-eight universities. These boycotts have four special characteristics.

"First, they incite public opinion and seek to build popular support. On forty-two campuses since April 23 there have been speeches and demonstrations aiming to pull support from centrist students and from faculty. Students at Peking University, Qinghua University, Beijing Normal University, People's University, and other schools have gathered in classroom buildings and on exercise fields to demonstrate and give speeches, primarily appealing to students to boycott class and to professors not to teach. At Beijing Normal, they openly chanted 'Down with Deng Xiaoping.' Students are putting up all kinds of protest posters in the streets and are distributing handbills to expand their influence within the larger society. Illegal student organizations have taken over the public-address systems at Peking University, Qinghua University, People's University, and the Central Institute for Nationalities.

"Second, the student boycotts bring pressure for dialogue with the Center. At Peking University, Qinghua University, Beijing Normal University, People's University, Chinese University of Political Science and Law, and other schools, illegal teams of student monitors have formed. Members of these teams are stationed at the entrances to classrooms or classroom buildings, preventing students from attending classes. At the Beijing Institute of Posts and Telecommunications, these students simply padlocked some classroom doors.

"Third, the boycotts aid in soliciting donations and accumulating funds. Beginning on April 24 students campaigned for contributions at Sidaokou, the zoo, the exhibition hall, the art museum, Xidan, Fuxingmen, Tiananmen, and other locations. One student from Peking University said that on the afternoon of the twenty-fourth they received more than five thousand yuan in donations.

"Fourth, the strikes give rise to all kinds of rumors. One particularly widespread rumor on the campuses says the famous president of Qinghua University, Liu Da, recently went to visit Comrade Xiaoping at home to report on the situation on his campus. Comrade Xiaoping listened and then, according to the rumor, said the army should be sent in to crush the student movement."

Yao Yilin: "The nature of this student movement has changed. It began as a natural expression of grief and has turned into social turmoil."

Yang Shangkun: "It's crucial that we maintain social order throughout the country, especially in the capital. We certainly can't allow a few people with ulterior motives to make use of this movement to manufacture turmoil. We've got to expose them as quickly as possible."

Deng Xiaoping: "I completely agree with the Standing Committee's decision. This is no ordinary student movement. The students have been raising a ruckus for ten days now, and we've been tolerant and restrained. But things haven't gone our way. A tiny minority is exploiting the students; they want to confuse the people and throw the country into chaos. This is a well-planned plot whose real aim is to reject the Chinese Communist Party and the socialist system at the most fundamental level. We must explain to the whole Party and nation that we are facing a most serious political struggle. We've got to be explicit and clear in opposing this turmoil."

Hu Qili: "Comrade Xiaoping's comments are extremely important. We must spread them as quickly as possible."

Li Peng: "Comrade Qili, shouldn't we organize an editorial in the *People's Daily* right away, in order to get the word out on what Comrade Xiaoping has said?"

The meeting came to a close shortly before 11 A.M. Yang lingered to speak with Deng Xiaoping.

> Dialogue described in the same way in three sources: memoranda of conversations supplied by a friend of Yang Shangkun who cannot be further identified; Central Military Commission Office, "Yang Shangkun's talk to a small-group meeting at the Enlarged Meeting of the Central Military Commission," May 23; and *Materials for the Fourth Plenum of the Thirteenth Central Committee*, "Remarks of Comrade Yang

Shangkun," Secretariat of the Fourth Plenum of the CCP
Thirteenth Central Committee, June 23–24, 1989

Deng Xiaoping: "This student movement shows that we haven't been thorough enough in our political thought work. We've talked about the Four Principles, and we've talked about political thought work and about opposing bourgeois liberalization and spiritual pollution, but we haven't followed through. We haven't carried these things out."

Yang Shangkun: "With political thought work frail and the legal system flawed, we've got to expect that there's going to be illegality, misbehavior, and corruption. This student movement didn't just pop up by chance; it grew out of certain social conditions."

Deng Xiaoping: "The student movement happened because our campaign against liberalization didn't go far enough and because we didn't root out spiritual pollution. If our work against bourgeois liberalization had been finished right, this kind of thing couldn't have happened. And our work against spiritual pollution was even worse—it petered out after only twenty days!"

Although Deng's remarks indirectly show he was dissatisfied with Zhao Ziyang's conduct of the antiliberalization campaign, it is noteworthy that he made the comments to Yang Shangkun alone instead of at the full meeting. He continued to maintain confidence in Zhao Ziyang on the reform-and-opening front.

That afternoon the CCP Central Committee General Office sent a telegram to Zhao Ziyang in North Korea telling him about the Standing Committee's decision and relaying Deng Xiaoping's remarks. Individual reports were also sent to Chen Yun, Li Xiannian, Peng Zhen, Deng Yingchao, and other Party Elders. Later that day Zhao Ziyang replied by telegram.

Telegram, Zhao Ziyang to Standing Committee, April 25

To the Standing Committee and Comrade Xiaoping:
I completely agree with the policy decision of Comrade Xiaoping with regard to the present problem of turmoil.

The same day, the State Education Commission held a meeting for the Party secretaries of the major universities in Beijing as well as some in Tianjin and Shanghai. At the meeting, Commissioner Li Tieying relayed the spirit of the Standing Committee's brief meeting on ending the turmoil and then said:

> Excerpt from State Education Commission, "Comrade Li Tie-
> ying's Speech at the April 25 Forum of Party Secretaries of
> Some Universities," April 25

The Center has decided that major news programs tonight will broadcast an important *People's Daily* editorial. All education officials and school Party secretaries must conscientiously study and comprehend the spirit of this editorial and at the same time direct all Party branches to organize officials, Party members, teachers, and student activists to unify their thinking and unify their understanding of the facts. . . . At each school Party and Youth League organizations, officials, and teachers must go deeply among the students to carry out patient and thorough thought work and education. You must master situations as soon as possible and use the right political thought work to address every kind of confusion and misunderstanding the students may exhibit.

He Dongchang, vice minister of the SEC, added this:

> Excerpt from State Education Commission, "Summary of a
> forum of Party secretaries of some universities," April 25

There are signs that some of the students boycotting classes have begun to contact high school students. This deserves close attention. We have to remember the lessons of the Cultural Revolution: We can't let them get the kids excited; we have to take measures to anticipate and stop this before it starts.

On the suggestion of Li Peng, the deputy chief of propaganda, Zeng Jianhui, then composed a draft for an editorial in the *People's Daily* called "The Necessity for a Clear Stand Against Turmoil." After Li Peng and Hu Qili edited the draft, it was broadcast the evening of April 25 on national radio and television news programs. It appeared in the *People's Daily* the next day.[9] Key parts of the finished copy followed Deng Xiaoping's remarks closely.

> Excerpt from editorial, "The necessity for a clear stand against
> turmoil," *People's Daily*, April 26, p. 1

---

[9]The text is translated in Michel Oksenberg, Lawrence R. Sullivan, and Marc Lambert, eds., *Beijing Spring, 1989, Confrontation and Conflict: The Basic Documents* (Armonk, New York: M. E. Sharpe, 1990), 206–208.

This is a well-planned plot . . . to confuse the people and throw the country into turmoil. . . . Its real aim is to reject the Chinese Communist Party and the socialist system at the most fundamental level. . . . This is a most serious political struggle that concerns the whole Party and nation.

At 9 P.M. Li Tieying directed that "Notice Number 5," summarizing the correct attitude toward the April 26 editorial, go out to all province-level offices of the Education Commission and affiliated schools.

Student response to the editorial

Before the April 25 evening broadcast of the April 26 editorial, there were reports from around the country that the students were growing tired after ten days of demonstrations and that organizers were seeking ways to keep the movement alive. But the editorial created an explosive reaction that pushed the student movement to a new high.

A 7:30 P.M. State Security Ministry report from Peking University said the editorial had been broadcast repeatedly throughout the campus from 6:30 P.M. on. Students debated its meaning, some fearing that the government would soon start arresting people, others insisting that the movement should be carried on until at least May 4. A 10:40 P.M. report said that students from People's University marched through the university district to other campuses calling for support to continue the boycott of classes, then returned to their own campus to avoid a clash with a group of eight hundred police. A 10:50 P.M. report noted that student leaders were meeting to decide how to respond to the editorial. Youth League leaders and professors were quoted as saying the government line was too harsh, the label "turmoil" was unfair, the reversal from the previously tolerant policy was too sharp, and matters would not have come to this extreme if the government had agreed to enter into some form of dialogue with the students.

Demonstrations against the April 26 editorial occurred the night of April 25 in Changchun (the largest), Shanghai, Tianjin, Hangzhou, Nanjing, Xi'an, Changsha, and Hefei. According to the report of the Jilin Provincial Party Committee, about three thousand students from Jilin University and other campuses held a sit-in before the office of the Provincial Party Committee and demanded that the Party secretary come out to meet with them. The demonstrators were eventually dispersed peacefully through the efforts of three hundred policemen and Party and education officials.

April 26

Responses from the provinces

Each provincial-level Party Committee responded to the April 26 editorial and the telegram from the Central Committee and the State Council by holding an urgent meeting of its own standing committee and reporting back to the Center. These reports expressed support for Deng's position and described how the Center's decision was to be applied in each locality.

Shanghai's Party Committee reacted most quickly, reporting that no turmoil had occurred there. In order to assure that the situation remained calm, officials would carefully study the April 26 editorial and continue to pay close attention to production and other routine work. Party secretary Jiang Zemin met with fourteen thousand Party officials from basic-level work units at 3 P.M. on April 26 and warned them to be on the alert against illegal organizations or unusual protest posters. He announced that the Party was firing Qin Benli from his post as editor-in-chief of the *World Economic Herald* for violating Party discipline. The paper would be reorganized.

Beijing, Jilin, Shaanxi, Hubei, and Zhejiang reported that they held meetings with work unit–level officials to study the editorial and that they had made preparations to mobilize officialdom and the masses to block the formation of illegal organizations and to isolate anyone who attempted to damage public order.

Several provinces struck less alarmist notes. Without directly contradicting the April 26 editorial, Heilongjiang, Liaoning, Henan, Fujian, Jiangxi, and Xinjiang reported that there was nothing as serious as turmoil going on in their localities.[10] The local situations were calm, although in some places students had come from Beijing to try to get the support of local students. These provinces promised to remain alert and to oppose firmly any activity that might lead to turmoil.

April 26–29

The response in the military

After the April 26 editorial was published, the General Political Department of the People's Liberation Army distributed an urgent notice requiring all officers and soldiers to study the editorial

---

[10]Three of the leaders of these provinces would be promoted to the Politburo in 1997: Li Changchun (then governor of Liaoning), Wu Guanzheng (then governor of Jiangxi), and Jia Qinglin (then deputy Party secretary of Fujian).

carefully and instructing high-ranking officers conscientiously to "grasp the spirit" of Deng Xiao-ping's remarks. Furthermore, it said:

> Excerpt from General Political Department, "Urgent notice on firmly and thoroughly carrying out Party Central's policy on upholding stability and unity and taking a clear-cut stand against the turmoil," April 26

All units in the military must resolutely carry out the directives issued by Party Central and the Central Military Commission to guarantee the stability and unity of the armed forces and must resolutely follow orders from Party Central and the CMC. They must grasp trends in society and the trends in thinking within the armed forces in order to ensure in a targeted way[11] that officers and soldiers do not believe or circulate statements not beneficial to stability and unity, that they do not participate in any activities not beneficial to stability and unity, and that in their thinking they preserve the high degree of stability and centralized unity expected in military personnel. . . . No matter what the circumstances, all units should resolutely trust Party Central and the CMC, adhere closely to them, and act in strict accordance with orders from Party Central and the CMC. . . . All units in the military must be prepared in their thinking, organization, and readiness for action.

The notice also stipulated that "any unit's deployment of military personnel, however minor, must be reported to and approved by the CMC."

Although they backed Party Central in their responses, some units noted that officers hoped the Center would stick to the path of reform and resolve some of the problems the students were highlighting.

> Excerpts from Beijing Military District, "Situation summary on seriously studying the April 26 editorial and firmly maintaining unanimity with Party Central," April 29

After the April 26 *People's Daily* editorial was published, more than two hundred commanders in the Beijing Military District immediately formed a reading group to carry out study and discussion. There was unanimous agreement that it is imperative to stand united with Party Central and to preserve a political situation of stability and unity.

---

[11]The phrase "in a targeted way" means "with regard to the specific issue at hand," in this case, the student turmoil.

1. The editorial is timely, correct, and powerful. In discussion, the small group[12] from the Twenty-Seventh Army felt that the *People's Daily* editorial had been published in timely fashion, was correct, and served as a powerful blow against a tiny band of bad people who had attacked the Communist Party and carried out "beating, smashing, and robbing." . . . The small group from the Thirty-Eighth Army reported that "on April 22, while our troops were maintaining order in the Babaoshan area, a few people with ulterior motives started to stir up trouble with some of our soldiers,[13] and some officers were influenced by this. The *People's Daily* editorial has given us good teaching materials for the education of our soldiers."

2. We hope the Center will deepen the reforms, building strength by banishing flaws. The small group from the military logistics department of the Beijing Military District said although turmoil had appeared, it had occurred in only part of the country. The future of the reforms is bright, and the only problems are problems that grow out of progress. We must not swear off food for fear of choking, and we must not lose faith in reform. . . .

The small group from the Twenty-Seventh Army pointed out that, viewed from another angle, this turmoil tells us that in order to deepen the reforms it will be necessary as soon as possible to solve the problems of corruption in government, the Party, and society in general, as well as unfairness in job assignments, excessive inflation, and so on.

The small group from the Hebei Province Military District felt that the turmoil shows that while the Center increases funding for education it must also strengthen political thought work among students. Otherwise we will have a situation of "the Communist Party bringing forth students who oppose the Communist Party."

The small group from the Military District of Inner Mongolia felt that only the methods of education and guidance should be used on the students. The Center's restrained and tolerant attitude toward some of the inflammatory words and actions of the students was entirely laudable. But the riffraff who have infiltrated the students' ranks must be harshly attacked and resolutely suppressed.

3. We should take concrete action to maintain political stability and unity at the Center. . . . All the officers who took part in the study groups said it was imperative to identify with the Party and embrace the Party's worries as their own. Some

---

[12]Unlike the leadership-level "small group" discussed in footnote 5 in this chapter, the small group referred to here is a discussion section into which members of an organization are divided in order to carry out the process of "political study."

[13]A reference to efforts by Beijing citizens to persuade soldiers not to move against them.

~~had already been sending letters and telegrams to relatives and friends at schools~~ in the capital, telling them to obey the words of the Party and government.

> Excerpts from Shenyang Military District, "Situation report on study of the April 26 editorial," April 28

On the afternoon of April 27 the Party Standing Committee of the Shenyang Military District collectively studied the *People's Daily* editorial and Comrade Deng Xiaoping's remarks on how to deal with the chaos facing the nation. There was unanimous agreement to resolutely uphold the Center's decision to halt the current turmoil and, through the concrete actions of a steady military, to make contributions to the maintenance of stability and unity. . . .

. . . The Party Standing Committee of the Shenyang Military District also pointed out that since the present turmoil may continue, the leadership and units stationed in the city must be prepared in thought and organization and must be ready for action so that we will not be immobilized by lack of preparation should the problem grow larger and should use of the military become necessary. But we must be clear that this case is not the same as disaster relief: We cannot dispatch troops at will. Before deploying a single soldier from any unit in any area, we must request permission and await approval from the CMC and the PLA Headquarters. . . .

Any person sent out on business or a mission must be educated well and strictly instructed not to become a looker-on, not to join any debates, and not to participate in any trouble. No officers or soldiers are permitted to go among the students to network, and still less should they ever allow students to come among them to network.

Response of higher education officials

In the three days after the publication of the editorial the State Security Ministry and Xinhua News Agency sent thirty-six reports to Zhongnanhai on the reactions of various social strata. Many citizens felt that the editorial was too harsh—that it "defined the nature of the incident at too high a level of seriousness"[14]—and that it was not helpful to resolving the problem.

The reports described widespread sympathy and protective feelings for the students among university presidents and other high-ranking Party and administrative officials. Some of these

---

[14]*Dingxing tai gao.*

officials were cited by name as stating that the April 26 editorial had exaggerated the danger of the demonstrations, widened the gap between the students and the government, and removed the basis for dialogue that might have led to a smooth resolution of the student's grievances. One official revealed that on his campus, two-thirds of faculty members were refusing to attend meetings to study the editorial. Others pointed out that the blame for the demonstrations ultimately lay in the failings of the Party itself, without which the students would have no need to protest.

April 27

April 27 demonstrations

On April 27 huge student demonstrations in opposition to the editorial swept major cities. They occurred not only in cities where demonstrations had already taken place, such as Shanghai, Tianjin, Changchun, Xi'an, Wuhan, Nanjing, Hangzhou, Hefei, Changsha, Chengdu, and Chongqing, but also in cities where demonstrations now broke out for the first time: Shenyang, Dalian, Shijiazhuang, Jinan, Nanning, Kunming, Shenzhen, Yinchuan, and Guilin.

Yang Shangkun had sought and received Deng Xiaoping's permission to move about five hundred troops of the Beijing Military Region's Thirty-Eighth Group Army into Beijing for the period from April 27 to May 5 to protect the Great Hall of the People and to serve as a reserve force in case of need. Yang gave strict orders that weapons were not to be used if any clash should break out with students or citizens.

A State Security Ministry report to Zhongnanhai described the April 27 Beijing demonstration. It said fifty thousand students from many campuses had marched through the city, maintaining good order throughout and creating a favorable impression among bystanders. Students carried banners, including one that bore quotations from Deng Xiaoping and Lenin in favor of democracy. They sang the song "Without the Chinese Communist Party There Would Be No New China"[15] and elicited tears from bystanders when they shouted, "Mama, we haven't done anything wrong." In high spirits and under tight discipline, they avoided clashes with police and troops, and to minimize provocation, they returned to their campuses by way of the Second Ring Road instead of passing through Tiananmen Square. Public security officials analyzed all this as part of a student

[15]The song was a favorite of students, even after the June 4 killings, because of its ambiguity. It said only that the Communist Party was responsible for China as it currently existed, and whether one took this as praise or blame was up to the listener. But because it was an officially approved song, no one could object to their singing it.

strategy to seize the high ground and avoid charges of counterrevolution, which could land a person quickly in prison.

The same report included student comments on the demonstration. Some students felt they had gained a victory by carrying out the demonstration despite police warnings not to do so. Others noted that support from the citizenry had been essential because it made it impossible for the troops to use force. Students also sensed that the police sympathized with them. There was a feeling of elation that no violence had broken out. Students felt that their strategies were working.

Coping with the reaction

On the morning of April 27 Hu Qili, the Politburo member in charge of ideology and newspaper editorials, and Rui Xingwen, the secretary of the Central Secretariat, had summoned the heads of the Xinhua News Agency, the *People's Daily,* the *Guangming Daily,*[16] and other newspapers. These officials expressed frustration at censorship of stories on the student movement. Everyone, they said, was denouncing them—even their own reporters. Reporters would interview the students and write stories, but the stories could not be printed. Reporters complained that the students, eventually realizing that these stories never went anywhere, wouldn't do interviews any more. They preferred to talk to foreign journalists, who published what they said. The media heads said that they now didn't know what to do about covering the student movement, and they hoped Party Central could give them some clear guidelines.

> The following is based on internal publications by several of
> the news agencies whose members participated in the meeting

Hu Qili: "I'd say the chief editor at a newspaper has the right, on something like this, to decide what should or should not be reported. You shouldn't have to ask permission about everything."

Rui Xingwen: "There are, actually, a lot of reforms we should make on the news front. We can't just stay the same decade after decade. The big forces of change in society are forcing reforms in the news—and those reforms are exactly what the people want. While we change, though, we've got to stick with the principles of being positive and being dependable. News reports have to tell the truth; we absolutely mustn't put out fake news, and we can't be off the mark in what we say."

[16]The official newspaper for intellectuals.

Later in the meeting Hu Qili and Rui Xingwen made it known that they would welcome dialogue with reporters on the question of reform in the news media. Their general tone in this discussion seemed to do much to bring fresh air to the repressed world of the media. Chief editors could now be a bit bolder than they had been.

The student demonstration in Beijing on April 27 was the largest since the protests began, and it was echoed in other cities around the country. It put Li Peng in an awkward position. He had expected the April 26 editorial to pacify the students, but obviously it had only added fuel to the fire. Party Elders Li Xiannian, Deng Yingchao, Wang Zhen, and Bo Yibo and Song Renqiong, the vice chair of the Central Advisory Commission, peppered Li Peng and his people about what was going on and asked him to try something else.

On the afternoon of April 27 Li Peng asked Yuan Mu to draft another *People's Daily* editorial. "The main point of the editorial," Li said, "should be stability. The overriding issue right now is to preserve social stability." Yuan Mu complied.

> Excerpt from editorial, "Defend the big picture, defend stability," *People's Daily*, April 28, p. 1

All innocent and well-meaning young students should understand that in any large mass event dragons mingle with the fish. People with hidden intentions are just waiting for you to get too excited and for your actions to go too far so that they can exploit you for their own profit. . . . If you believe the insult, slander, and attack on Party and state leaders in all the protest posters that appear everywhere, if you buy all the rumors about "seizing power" and "taking over," if you skip classes and go networking, our country could well fall into total chaos again.

Next, Li Peng telephoned Li Tieying to ask about the State Education Commission's plans for another notice to the education bureaucracy.

> Account drawn from *Materials for the Fourth Plenum of the Thirteenth Central Committee*, "Remarks of Comrade Li Tieying," Secretariat of the Fourth Plenum of the CCP Thirteenth Central Committee, June 23–24, 1989; and Party Central Office Secretariat, "Oral report by Shangkun, Li Peng, Qiao Shi, and Yilin on the situation, evening, May 22," section containing Li Peng's remarks

Li Tieying: "I've already told Comrade He Dongchang to put out another notice requiring all education offices and schools to propagandize broadly and deeply[17] the *People's Daily* editorial and the relevant spirit of Party Central; to carry out dialogue with officials and teachers and to look for appropriate opportunities to dialogue with students; and to take strong and resolute measures to stop student networking, especially any networking, agitating, or troublemaking among high school or grade school students.

Li Peng: "When you put out the notice you have to emphasize the complexity and long-term nature of this struggle."

Accordingly, on April 28 the SEC distributed a sixth notice throughout the state education system. It was entitled "Urgent Notice on Doing a Better Job of Stabilization of the Situation on the Campuses and Unification of Thinking and Understanding"; it urged school authorities to step up efforts to help students and staff correctly understand the struggle in Beijing.

Li Ximing and Chen Xitong held a meeting of capital university presidents and Party secretaries on the morning of April 28. It opened with reports from major campuses. Officials reported that when they learned on the evening of the twenty-sixth of student plans to march in the streets the next day, they mobilized Party and Youth League officials to go to the dormitories to dissuade the students. This proved difficult. Leaders of the autonomous student organization at Peking University claimed that "we could stop organizing student demonstrations, but students are going to demonstrate anyway, so we might as well organize them." Officials at the Chinese University of Political Science and Law met with Zhou Yongjun, the student leader on that campus and chair of the AFS in Beijing, until 3 A.M. Zhou finally agreed not to organize a demonstration, and then the school provided him with a car so that he could go to inform students at Peking University, People's University, and other schools of his decision. But the next day Zhou had "broken his promise," officials said. He was out in the streets. At Qinghua University the student group called the Peaceful Petitioners announced it would dissolve on the evening of the twenty-sixth, but at 11 P.M. news came that it had formed a "liaison group." In sum, these officials said, the students seemed to be flip-flopping but probably would not give up until they reached their goal of a dialogue with Party Central.

The school officials made these suggestions:

1. In order to pacify the popular mood, the Center should dramatically crack down on a few instances of corruption within the Party.

2. In order not to lose a large portion of the populace, the Center should distinguish between turmoil and students' deep patriotic feelings.

3. In order to calm the students, members of the Central Committee should meet with students, let them air their complaints, and listen to them patiently.

---

[17]To "propagandize broadly and deeply" is to spread to every part of China and instill distinctly into everyone's thinking.

4. Party authorities should establish clear policies on whether and when to punish student leaders by expelling them from school or from the Youth League. School officials noted that these dire threats were currently being made but that it was unclear whether they could or should be carried out. To do so could produce side effects.

After hearing the reports of the school authorities, Chen Xitong announced the following measures for pacifying the student movement:

> Excerpt from Beijing Municipal Party Committee, "Summary of a meeting of responsible persons from institutions of higher education throughout the city," April 28

1. On returning to campus, take stock of the particular situation and identify where it falls short of the spirit of the April 26 editorial.
2. Do everything possible to win over the people in the middle; patiently work on people's thinking; engage students in theoretical debate; use reason to persuade them.
3. If more student demonstrations develop, continue with a policy of restraint; try to dissuade students from taking to the streets, and do what you can to divide and weaken them. The rationale for this approach is not government weakness but a concern for stability in the overall situation. If a student were to get injured in a demonstration, that could become a rallying point that would be harmful to the larger situation.
4. Disband illegal student organizations. If students form new ones, disband them again; keep doing this as if it were a tug-of-war.
5. Progressive elements should put up wall posters to cover up the posters of the illegal organizations.

As the meeting closed Li Ximing emphasized that school authorities "must look upon this as a political struggle; there are still some comrades whose thinking has not come around, and it must come around as soon as possible. It's especially important that comrades inside the Party keep clear heads and not let the students confuse them."

Li Peng chairs a Politburo Standing Committee meeting

After talking with Yang Shangkun and others, Li Peng decided to hold an enlarged meeting of the Standing Committee of the Politburo on the afternoon of April 28 to revisit the question of how to put down the student movement. There were no differences on fundamental principle at the meeting, but the speakers revealed different opinions on how to deal with the student movement. Without contradicting one another directly, some members stressed the good intentions of the students and their popular support, others their links with dissidents and hostile foreign forces. When Zhao Ziyang returned from North Korea, he would walk into a situation in which the rest of the leadership was already polarized.

Excerpt from Party Central Office Secretariat, "Minutes of Politburo Standing Committee Enlarged Meeting," April 28

Li Peng: "The whole country responded vigorously when the *People's Daily* editorial was published. It sounded an alarm bell against turmoil in the minds of all the people, and it struck fear into the hearts of the bourgeois liberal elements. It alerted province-level governments to take preventive measures. Stability in the nation, and especially in Beijing, benefited greatly. Of course there were a few professors, students, and members of society who did not completely understand the editorial, and even some officials who did not unite their thought with the spirit of the editorial. This only shows how important it is that we be clear about what's going on here: This turmoil is the result of long-term preparation by a tiny minority of bourgeois liberal elements hooked up with anti-China forces outside the country. For this reason, we must fully realize the complex and protracted nature of this political struggle."

Chen Xitong then reported on the meeting with Beijing university authorities that had taken place earlier in the day, and He Dongchang reported on the national situation. Several Politburo members were eager to speak.

Yang Shangkun: "I've seen reports that a lot of people felt the editorial's use of the terms 'turmoil' and 'serious political struggle' went too far. I think these people didn't read these terms properly in context and wouldn't have been so offended if they had. 'Turmoil,' for example, appears only in connection with some abnormal and unhealthy incidents that appeared around the country. We should explain this when we have the chance. I think that most students have good intentions and that our emphasis should be on shaping and guiding their actions, not on repressing them. So far we've shown them a very tolerant attitude; the fact that we used no force against such a large demonstration yesterday shows how restrained and tolerant we've been. But we also have to let the students know that stable and unified situations do not come easily. Single-minded demonstrations and boycotts of classes don't solve any problems and can even make things worse."

Qiao Shi: "If we look at this carefully, we can see that the students' shift from mourning Comrade Hu Yaobang to more recent organizing activities was in large part motivated by idealism and concern for the nation. Many of the student slogans agree with such Party Central policies as rooting out corruption, strengthening clean government, emphasizing education, promoting rule of law, and so on. But the students' behavior is short on reason and careful consideration: Many just follow the crowd and don't use their own heads. That's why it's so easy for a few people with ulterior motives to exploit them. So I think we need to open up different levels of dialogue with the students as soon as possible. We need more transparency."

Yang Shangkun: "Comrade Qiao Shi has a good point. We should require all departments in all areas to begin dialogue in various forms with students, faculty, workers, and people at all levels. Beijing can lead the way."

Tian Jiyun: "The reason why the masses support this student movement so much is that the students have articulated attractive slogans that the masses identify with. So the Center needs to reflect on why this student movement could lead to such large turmoil. No one's denying that certain bad people exploit the students to their own advantage, but the Center's own problems are what give these people a foothold. A lot of stories circulate these days about cabals of the 'princes,' the 'secretaries,' and the 'sons-in-law,' and it makes people sick. The Party's fallen very low; if we can't get the Party in order we'll never get rid of corruption, and turmoil will always be with us."

Bo Yibo: "In the days since the student movement began, foreign speculation on our politics has had another field day. I just saw an article in yesterday's *Far Eastern Economic Review* called 'The Future of China's Reforms.' It described ten scenarios for China a decade from now, and nine of them were terrible. Only the scenario entitled 'Accelerated Reform' was rosy, and it assumed abandonment of the socialist system and establishment of multiparty politics. The implication was that China's present reforms are a dead end. Why are foreigners trumpeting this kind of stuff? Because they want to encourage the students and to throw our Party and our national spirit into confusion."

Song Ping: "It's really true that there are a few people who want to exploit the student movement in order to oppose the Party and socialism. On the twenty-fifth, Fang Lizhi told the *Asian Wall Street Journal* that if China's human rights situation doesn't improve, foreign companies should pull out their capital. This is nothing but brazen, naked treason."

Chen Xitong: "Fang Lizhi and his wife were the backstage directors of the democracy salon at Peking University. Now they've openly pointed their spears at Comrade Xiaoping, slandering him as 'manipulating things from behind a curtain.'[18] They've had a big influence on the student movement. At the meeting for university authorities a few days ago I explained to everyone about Comrade Xiaoping: how he enjoys great prestige both inside and outside the Party, both here and abroad, and how at the Thirteenth Party Congress a clear rule was established that although Comrade Xiaoping no longer holds a leadership position in the Party, on all questions of critical importance the Politburo is to ask him for guidance.[19] Xiaoping, Chen Yun, Xiannian, Peng Zhen, and the senior comrades are treasures of our Party. After everybody heard my explanation they felt it had helped to set the record straight."

Yao Yilin: "Some people are saying that students join this movement voluntarily, out of a sense of historic mission, with nobody prompting them from behind the scenes. That's utter nonsense."

Li Peng: "Besides Fang Lizhi and his wife, there are some leaders of illegal organizations from the Democracy Wall period, and also some people who have hurried back from the United States to start petitions. There are some intellectuals helping the students make plans, and some reporters encouraging the student movement. Every day foreigners of unclear status go in and out of the college campuses in Beijing, making appointments with the leaders of the illegal student organizations to plot strategy. And two days ago a meeting of the central standing members of the Kuomintang in Taiwan decided to openly support the student movement. This shows that the background of this student movement is getting more and more complex."

Li Ximing: "These leaders of the illegal student organizations are openly meet-

[18]A cliché that traditionally referred to a mother or other female relative who controlled a young emperor from behind the scenes. It refers most recently to the Empress Dowager Cixi, who ruled China from "behind a curtain" for many years in the late nineteenth century.
[19]Zhao Ziyang would later be criticized for publicly revealing this secret decision of the Thirteenth Party Congress to Mikhail Gorbachev.

ing with foreign reporters and giving them interviews. They've snatched power from the Youth League and the legal student organizations, and they're getting support from reactionary forces. A few days ago a reporter from L'Agence France-Presse interviewed a student from Beijing Normal called Wuerkaixi. This illegal organization leader is only twenty years old and is a Uighur.[20] Reports say he gets the worst grades in his class at Beijing Normal. How can somebody like this understand strategy? There must be people behind him telling him what to do. This Wuerkaixi's way out of control, and that's why we've got to expose these people, we've got to let others know the truth about them."

Yang Shangkun: "The Foreign Affairs Ministry reports that people overseas have been paying more and more attention to this student movement over the past week. First it was some Chinese students abroad expressing their concern. In Boston, Chinese students demonstrated in front of the consulate on the twenty-fourth and have already set up a North American Branch of the United Association of Chinese Students;[21] Chen Jun, Hu Ping,[22] and others have published an 'Open Letter to All University Students in China.' On the twenty-sixth a press secretary for the U.S. State Department referred to the student movement for the first time. . . . Government officials and national assembly members in some countries have asked our embassies about the political situation and have expressed hope that we won't take harsh measures. People in Hong Kong are also paying close attention to this student movement, and in their minds they are connecting our treatment of the movement with the return of Hong Kong. Xu Simin, Liao Yaozhu,[23] and other patriotic individuals[24] have been calling publicly for the government to begin dialogue with the students soon and to refrain from taking military action against them. The international reaction to our tolerant handling of the April 27 demonstrations has been quite favorable."

Hu Qili: "The student movement is putting more and more pressure on our media. Reporters have been writing articles about the movement only to have their editors quash them. This angers the reporters; they say the students yell at them for

---

[20]Uighurs are a Chinese minority ethnicity who are concentrated in the Xinjiang Autonomous Region in central Asia.

[21]In Chinese, *Zhongguo xuesheng tuanjie lianmeng Bei Mei fenhui.* So far as we know, there was no group in the United States with this name; it may be a partial confusion for the Chinese Alliance for Democracy *(Zhongguo minzhu tuanjie lianmeng),* founded by Hu Ping and others in 1983.

[22]Dissidents residing in the United States.

[23]Xu Simin was a member of the People's Political Consultative Conference, Liao Yaozhu a representative to the National People's Congress.—Comp.

[24]Patriotic individuals are influential persons who are not members of the Chinese Communist Party but who express support for it.

somebody else's decisions. Authorities at many newspapers have reported this problem; they say they themselves feel the heat. Reporters at *Science and Technology Daily, Farmers' Daily, Workers' Daily,* and *China Youth Daily* are all asking for reform in news reporting, and they ask it more and more heatedly all the time."

Li Tieying: "This student movement is still growing. College students in Beijing have already gone into fourteen high schools and grade schools to network. They're asking the younger students to take to the streets, and this is truly frightening. The State Education Commission has already put out a notice requiring all education offices to intensify their work on high school and grade school students and forbidding outsiders from entering the schools to organize.

"Three things set this student movement apart from earlier ones. First, this one isn't limited to Beijing; there have been demonstrations at large and medium-sized cities across the country. Second, the illegal student organizations in Beijing are planning to expand, with the ultimate aim of becoming a national organization to replace the existing legal national student organizations. And third, this student movement has support not only from reactionary forces but from a portion of the masses as well. So this student movement will not be easy to deal with. Just as Comrade Li Peng said, we must prepare for a long battle."

The meeting concluded that dialogue with the students should be pursued. It was decided that the official All-China Students Federation and Beijing Municipal Students Federation would arrange for a roundtable dialogue between representatives of Beijing students and State Council spokesman Yuan Mu; He Dongchang, vice minister of the SEC; Yuan Liben, general secretary of the Municipal Committee; and Lu Yucheng, deputy mayor of Beijing, among others, on the afternoon of April 29. On the afternoon of the thirtieth, Li Ximing, Chen Xitong, and others would also have a dialogue with official student representatives. At the same time, officials in all departments of the State Council as well as Party and government leaders at the province level were to begin multilevel, multichannel dialogue with students.

"How great will the impact of the student demonstrations be?"

On April 27 the Xinhua News Agency, the Defense Ministry, and the State Security Ministry all forwarded to Zhongnanhai an article by American China specialist Andrew J. Nathan. It had been published in the Chinese-language *World Journal* newspaper in New York. The article argued that although the demonstrations indicated a severe legitimacy crisis, the student movement was unlikely to overthrow the government. Among other reasons, the students lacked strong ties with other social groups, and the Party still had ample reserves of military force to deal with any threat to its rule.

April 29

Jiang Zemin rectifies the *World Economic Herald*

Jiang Zemin's purge of the Shanghai newspaper *World Economic Herald* was a seminal event in the 1989 democracy movement. It led to extensive protests by journalists across China and strengthened Zhao Ziyang's determination to pursue press reform. On the other hand, it also became political capital for Jiang Zemin, whose credit in the eyes of Deng Xiaoping and the other Elders for quashing the *Herald* was a factor propelling him into position as the new general secretary of the Party.[25]

> Excerpts from Shanghai Municipal Party Committee, "Report on the situation in rectifying the *World Economic Herald*," report to the CCP Central Committee, April 29

On April 20 the Propaganda Department of the Shanghai Party Committee learned from the April 17 issue of the Hong Kong newspaper *Overseas Chinese Daily* that the *World Economic Herald* (henceforth *Herald*) was planning to establish a column to memorialize Comrade Hu Yaobang. On the afternoon of April 21 Zeng Qinghong, deputy secretary of the Shanghai Party Committee, and Chen Zhili, director of the Propaganda Department, met with Qin Benli, editor-in-chief of the *Herald*, in order to understand recent currents of thought and how they related to the *Herald*. Comrade Qin Benli said that the *Herald* did indeed intend to devote several pages in a coming issue to a memorial symposium that the *Herald* and the magazine *New Observations* had convened in Beijing on April 19. Comrades Zeng and Chen asked to see the proofs as soon as possible, and Comrade Qin at that point agreed to have them delivered early the next morning.

---

[25]For an account of how protesters saw the *World Economic Herald* incident, see Han Minzhu, ed., *Cries for Democracy: Writings and Speeches from the 1989 Chinese Democracy Movement* (Princeton University Press, 1990), 104–105, 187–190.

By noon on the April 22 the proofs still had not arrived, so the Propaganda Department telephoned in the afternoon to press the *Herald* for delivery. Qin Benli could not be located. At 4 P.M. he was found at the offices of *Liberation Daily*,[26] and he said the proofs had just been sent. Zeng Qinghong and Chen Zhili received the proofs at 4:30, and after reading them had their office call Qin Benli to arrange a meeting.

At 8:30 that evening, Zeng and other comrades met with Qin to discuss issue 439 of the *Herald*. They patiently pointed out that Shanghai newspapers were all publicizing Comrade Hu Yaobang's superior qualities, expressing their sorrow, and stimulating passion in the masses to promote the Four Modernizations[27] and to revitalize the nation. All of this was the proper responsibility of the print media. But in the long *Herald* article, which ran to about twenty thousand Chinese characters, some sensitive parts seemed unfit for publication. At the time, students were still on the streets and holding meetings, and some extremist individuals were shouting improper, even reactionary, slogans. Teachers and officials at universities had been working hard, day and night, to keep the students in check and to ensure that mourning activities for Comrade Yaobang moved ahead properly. At such a time, one must consider the social effects[28] of propaganda work. Therefore, given their esteem for the *Herald* and their desire that it maintain a healthy publishing record, they suggested the deletion of remarks by Yan Jiaqi, Dai Qing,[29] and others blaming Comrade Deng Xiaoping, urging that Comrade Hu Yaobang's "mistakes" be reconsidered, and demanding that the verdict on bourgeois liberalization be "reversed." . . .

Comrade Qin replied, "I'll take full responsibility if anything goes wrong. Since Comrade Jiang Zemin hasn't seen the proofs yet, the Party Committee and Propaganda Department are free of any responsibility." Comrade Zeng Qinghong said, "This isn't about who takes responsibility; it's about the overall effects on society. Besides, it is inappropriate to publish any comments without letting the persons who made the comments read and approve the proofs, especially where sensitive issues are involved." (It was later determined that some of the quoted persons, after learning of the planned publication, explicitly withheld permission to publish their words.) Qin continued to insist that he would take

[26]Where issues of the *Herald* were printed.
[27]A plan to achieve modernization of China's industry, agriculture, national defense, and science and technology by the year 2000. First enunciated by Zhou Enlai in 1975, it became a major policy of the Deng Xiaoping regime in the late 1970s.
[28]"Social effects" is a standard term that means "effects on the thinking of readers."
[29]Yan Jiaqi was a liberal-minded political scientist; Dai Qing an outspoken journalist.

full responsibility and refused to agree to the revisions. Zeng Qinghong reported the incident to Jiang Zemin.

Comrade Jiang Zemin told Comrade Wang Daohan[30] about the situation, and then he and Wang went to the *Herald* editorial offices, where Jiang Zemin sternly reprimanded Qin Benli. Comrade Daohan, having read the proofs, said, "It's not appropriate to publish these sensitive materials in the current situation. We have to be responsible to the Party. Some of the issues can be brought to the attention of Party Central through proper internal channels. It's also incautious to publish references from the symposium to things Comrade Yaobang has said over the past couple of years, since they haven't been verified by the Party or his family."

Wang continued, "As Party members, you and I are expected to follow the spirit and principles of the Party, especially in circumstances like this. Deleting a few paragraphs won't affect the overall layout of the paper. Besides, you haven't devoted any space to the April 22 memorial for Comrade Yaobang or to Comrade Zhao Ziyang's eulogy, and this doesn't accord with practical political or journalistic standards."

In the end Comrade Qin agreed to the deletions. . . .

On April 23 Comrade Wang Daohan was surprised to see a copy of the unrevised newspaper delivered to his home. He immediately called Comrade Cai Beihua, deputy publisher of the *Herald*, who said his own copy had arrived at 8 P.M. the night before. Comrade Wang then phoned Comrade Qin Benli to accuse him of going back on his word.

Investigation reveals that Qin had decided to move up publication of issue 439 in order to get copies to Beijing by April 22, prior to the memorial for Comrade Yaobang. Around 10 A.M. on April 21, the *Herald* had already notified the printing department of the *Liberation Daily* that this issue of the *Herald* would be published ahead of schedule. The issue went to press around 6 P.M. on the twenty-second, and shortly thereafter copies were distributed to the usual offices and individual recipients. About four hundred copies were sent to privately managed newspaper vendors. Quite a few were also sent directly to Beijing.

Meanwhile, on the morning of the twenty-third, foreign newspapers ran stories about how the *Herald* had been "seized" and "closed down." It was later determined that this had happened because the Beijing office of the *Herald* had contacted foreign reporters in person and by telephone, hoping to enlist international opinion in its cause.

---

[30]Honorary chairman of the *Herald* board of directors.—Comp.

That afternoon the Party Committee again demanded that the *Herald* redo its editing and layout of this issue and get it to press in a timely fashion. Comrade Qin Benli offered an alternate layout and promised the Party Committee a speedy printing. But that very evening Comrade Qin held an editorial meeting at his home at which he said, "I don't think we ever did anything wrong. Those deleted parts are exactly what we wanted to say." He also attacked Comrade Xiaoping, saying, "Getting Deng Xiaoping to do a self-criticism [on the matter of dismissing Comrade Hu Yaobang from office] was exactly my aim. The sooner Deng does that, the sooner he takes an initiative, the sooner he will regain the people's trust. If he does a self-criticism, we'll support him." . . .

On the evening of the twenty-fifth the *Herald* sent the Shanghai Party Committee an "urgent message" saying that in order not to "intensify the conflict" and "enlarge the issue," the paper had decided to go forward with distribution of the uncorrected, already printed copies of issue 439. The message was marked "FYI," suggesting the paper felt there was no need to get agreement from the Party Committee before distributing the issue.

On the twenty-sixth the Party Committee convened a meeting of its Secretariat at 1 A.M. and a meeting of the Party Standing Committee at 10 A.M. to discuss the *Herald* problem. These meetings reaffirmed that the uncorrected version of issue 439 could not be distributed. Since Comrade Qin Benli was in serious violation of discipline, he would be dismissed as editor-in-chief and as a member of the Party group in Shanghai, and the *Herald* would be "rectified."

That afternoon the Party Committee organized a rally for all officials in the city to "stand firm against turmoil." Comrade Jiang Zemin announced the Party Committee's decision and warned sternly that "some people are trying to enlist international opinion to lessen our resolve, but they will never succeed; they cannot shake our determination to maintain stability and unity."

On April 27 the Leading Group for Discipline of the Shanghai Party Committee entered the *Herald* offices and set to work. Since the comrades in charge at the *Herald* remained recalcitrant and would not sign off on the revised version of issue 439, the deputy publisher, Comrade Cai Beihua (who had no actual duties at the publishing house), signed the proofs for the Group for Discipline.

The Shanghai student movement had not been very active before the *Herald* incident. Jiang Zemin knew, though, that rectifying the *Herald* would elicit a strong reaction from students as well as journalists. Moving quickly, he met on April 27 with the heads of all institutions of higher learning in Shanghai to study and analyze recent trends on the campuses. Speaking for the Party Committee, Jiang presented the educators with six demands.

> Excerpt from "Comrade Jiang Zemin's speech at a meeting of responsible persons from institutions of higher learning in the entire city," Shanghai Party Municipal Committee, April 27

1. Promptly convey the latest spirit of Party Central to Party committees on the campuses and use that spirit, in addition to the April 26 *People's Daily* editorial, to unify the understanding of officials and Party members.

2. Now that the activist work of the recent past is over and the campuses are relatively calm, seize this opportune moment to work on the thinking, education, and guidance of students and faculty, paying special attention to winning over the masses in the middle.

3. Push for deep and broad education about the importance of stability and unity; adopt strong measures that will absolutely prevent the formation of illegal organizations; ban illegal demonstrations and marches; prohibit all forms of networking by college students in factories, villages, schools, and government offices; be especially vigilant to prevent college students from networking with high school students.

4. Distinguish clearly between conflicts "among the people" and those "between us and the enemy";[31] remember that there is a difference between the domestic and the foreign; keep foreigners from meddling in campus affairs.

5. Strengthen control on the campuses and tighten up school policies and rules. Take disciplinary action against troublemakers who refuse to listen to reason.

6. Be prepared for a long struggle. Each campus should have two working groups: one to focus on the daily work of education and the other to deal with unforeseen incidents and to concentrate on keeping things stable.

As Jiang Zemin was spelling out these countermeasures, a storm of protest over the Shanghai Party Committee's rectification of the *Herald* was brewing in the news media in Shanghai. Eventually it spread to the whole country.

Yuan Mu's dialogue

Li Peng assigned Yuan Mu, State Council spokesman, and He Dongchang, vice minister of the

---

[31]A reference to a famous essay by Mao Zedong, "On the Correct Handling of Contradictions Among the People" (1957), in which Mao distinguished between conflicts "among the people," which are benign and should be resolved peaceably, and conflicts "between us and the enemy," in which all-out struggle is appropriate.

SEC, to conduct a dialogue with the students. When the two met with Premier Li on the morning of April 29 to prepare, he instructed them to make a strong defense of the April 26 editorial in order to protect the prestige of the Party and the state. They were to make clear to the students that the issue addressed in the April 26 editorial was the political struggle over whether to negate Communist Party leadership and the socialist system. The editorial was targeted against the illegal behavior of a small minority of people, not against the students in general. But the students must be aware of the their responsibility.

At 2:30 P.M. Yuan, He, and two other government representatives received forty-five students. Yuan took a hard line throughout.[32] There was no serious problem of corruption inside the Party, Yuan said, and Party leaders were reducing expenditures by canceling the annual Beidaihe meeting at the beach and banning the import of expensive cars. He also denied the existence of a censorship system even though the editor-in-chief of the *World Economic Herald* had just been fired. Demonstrators in Beijing, Yuan claimed, were manipulated by persons behind the scenes who presented a serious threat. He and his colleagues evaded many of the students' questions by changing the subject.

Li Peng and other leaders were pleased with Yuan's performance. Tian Jiyun commented sarcastically that he was an excellent practitioner of shadow boxing.

Student reaction

The tape of the Yuan Mu dialogue, broadcast on China Central Television on the evening of April 29, was not well received. Students took to the streets in protest or demonstrated on their campuses in twenty-three cities, including Shanghai, Tianjin, Wuhan, Lanzhou, Changchun, Shenyang, Hangzhou, Changsha, Chongqing, Chengdu, and Xi'an.

The State Security Ministry reported that two-thirds of the students on five major Beijing campuses were upset with the dialogue. They complained that the participating students were primarily from the official student groups rather than real representatives of student interests, that the dialogue was not equal, and that Yuan Mu and his colleagues avoided some substantive issues. At a press conference Wang Dan and Wuerkaixi announced on behalf of the Autonomous Federation of Students in the Capital (which had just dropped the word "Temporary" from its title) that they rejected the dialogue as phony. Wall posters on campuses criticized and ridiculed the participants.

---

[32]Excerpts from the dialogue are in Oksenberg et al., *Beijing Spring*, 218–244.

April 30

Mixed signals in the student movement

Zhao Ziyang returned from North Korea on the morning of April 30. Li Peng, Qiao Shi, Tian Jiyun, and Wen Jiabao met him at the Beijing Railway Station, and Zhao told them he would like to hold a meeting of the Politburo Standing Committee the next day to analyze the student movement and discuss strategy. Zhao then went home to read documents on the movement so that he could form his own understanding and analysis.

Meanwhile, Li Tieying, after studying Yuan Mu's and He Dongchang's dialogue with the students, told his deputies at the State Education Commission that "artful dialogue can be useful in getting the majority of teachers and students to raise their consciousness and unify their thinking." Later that day the State Education Commission issued "Notice Number 9" to province-level education offices and their affiliated universities. Students were to read copies of the student dialogues with Yuan Mu and He Dongchang, and all officials, teachers, and students were to study the April 26 editorial with care. "Notice Number 9" further stated that "our most important task is to guide the masses of students in recognizing the nature of this struggle and to unify their understanding of it, while at the same time delegitimizing and suppressing all illegal organizations."

That afternoon, in the second-floor conference room of the Beijing Party Committee building, Li Ximing, Chen Xitong, and others engaged in a dialogue with twenty-nine students from seventeen universities in Beijing. In response to a question about official profiteering, Chen said, "We're well aware that if we can't clean up the economic environment and get a grip on the chaotic barter of materials and commodities, then there's no way we can deepen the economic reforms. We're calling on everybody in society to help in exposing and punishing the profiteers. We especially welcome the assistance of students in economics and law."

When one student asked about Chen's own family income, the mayor seemed happy to reply. "My salary and allowances come to about three hundred yuan a month. The combined salaries of my wife and two children total less than five hundred yuan. My wife and children haven't been involved in the profiteering at all." Then he continued, pointedly, to say that "some people say my son embezzles and takes bribes, but that's false. Rumors like that remind me of the Cultural Revolution."[33]

On April 29 and 30 universities in Beijing were calmer than elsewhere in the country. Students

---

[33]Later records, which came to light when Chen was charged with corruption in 1996, showed that Chen's corruption began the day he assumed office as mayor and grew to massive proportions. Yuan Mu, another major player in the dialogues with students, also abused his official position for personal gain in the years following June Fourth.—Comp.

at most schools were still boycotting classes, and student leaders had turned their attention to planning their next moves. Many students were eagerly anticipating the upcoming anniversary of May Fourth.

> Excerpt from Beijing Municipal Party Committee, "Situation of students returning to classes at institutions of higher education throughout the municipality," report to Party Central and the State Council, April 30

On April 29 the Beijing Municipal Department of Education filed statistics on forty institutions of higher learning. Students at ten universities—Dance, Fine Arts, Physical Education, and others—are attending class as usual. At six institutions—including Broadcasting, Light Industry, and Tourism—80 percent of students are attending class. Attendance rates at certain others schools—Nationalities, Forestry, Chinese Medical Science, Beijing Aeronautics, and others—are gradually recovering. But at more than twenty institutions—including Peking University, Qinghua University, People's University, and Beijing Normal—students are still boycotting classes. Virtually no students at the University of Political Science and Law are going to class.

A similar report for April 30 showed little change from the day before, even though authorities from several ministries—including Public Security—had visited campuses in an effort to persuade students to return to class. With Peking University, Qinghua University, People's University, and Beijing Normal University setting the pace, students at forty-five schools were now boycotting class. There were about ninety thousand boycotters, about 70 percent of all college students in the city.

Party leaders at Zhongnanhai received a total of twenty-seven reports on student activity in the provinces for that same day, April 30, and all these reports showed that student unrest was steady or increasing. The reports from Shijiazhuang (Hebei Province), Taiyuan (Shanxi Province), and Tianjin—three of the closest cities to Beijing—told of extraordinary rebelliousness. The report from Tianjin warned that "four days after the publication of the *People's Daily* editorial, the number of wall posters has increased on the campuses of Nankai University and Tianjin University. Between one-third and one-half of the students remain out on strike."

Overseas coverage

On April 30 the State Security Ministry filed a report with Zhongnanhai summarizing three main themes in foreign reporting on the events of late April:

1. The student movement had become the international issue of greatest concern to the Western media. From April 16 to 30 the *New York Times* carried eighteen articles or editorials on China; the *Washington Post,* sixteen; the *Baltimore Sun,* thirteen. The three major television networks in the United States each gave the April 27 demonstrations two minutes of air time. The press in other Western countries behaved similarly. The slant of coverage was pro-student, and the media noted the Party's "loss of control." Images of smiling policemen, students climbing on military vehicles to explain democracy to the soldiers, and citizens donating cash to the demonstrators created a favorable impression. The foreign press portrayed the government's acceptance of dialogue as a student victory.

2. The Western media exaggerated the significance of the movement, treating it as a result of deep popular dissatisfaction with the government.

3. Westerners urged the government to avoid repression, to accept the students' criticisms, and to undertake democratic reforms. ABC television called the Chinese government a paper tiger. The negative Western press response to the April 26 editorial helped mobilize Chinese students abroad to go to Chinese embassies to protest the editorial. A *Washington Post* editorial expressed hope for the collapse of communism in China.

CHAPTER THREE

May 1–6

Signs of Compromise

EDITORS' NOTE: As student activities continued nationwide, Zhao Ziyang and Li Peng clashed at a Politburo Standing Committee meeting on May 1. Zhao stressed the need to respond to the students' legitimate concerns with accelerated political reform, and Li argued that restoration of order had to come before any further reforms could be considered.

In any case, the leaders agreed that quick measures needed to be taken to bring the demonstrations under control by May 4. Otherwise that anniversary might inflame the students further. May 4 was also the date that Beijing was scheduled to host an internationally watched meeting of the board of governors of the Asian Development Bank (ADB).

A conciliatory speech by Zhao Ziyang on May 3 got a good response from the students, but a dismissive press conference by State Council spokesman Yuan Mu fueled their anger. A large-scale demonstration was held May 4, but the students' declaration showed room for compromise by emphasizing values they held in common with the government, and they declared their intention to return to classes May 5. Meanwhile Zhao, whose authority in handling the protests was diminished by his failure to get quick results, nonetheless persisted in his moderate line. He told the ADB board that the students were raising respectable issues and argued privately with Li Peng over whether the line of the April 26 editorial should be modified. Reactions from the provinces suggested that the Center was being seen as indecisive. Provincial leaders filled the breach with their own recommendations, which were sometimes mutually contradictory.

May 1

Student activities continue

May 1 was International Labor Day, a national holiday, but neither the students nor the government took the day off. More than three hundred journalists working for *People's Daily* and other official publications sent telegrams of support to the Shanghai *World Economic Herald.* At noon the State Security Ministry sent Zhongnanhai a report on a press conference that the Autonomous Federation of Students had held that morning at Peking University. About sixty domestic and foreign reporters had attended, and some had made recordings. There were three TV cameras, a sign of strong foreign interest. Wang Dan ran the meeting, during which students announced seven demands, read a proclamation criticizing the government for failing to enter into equal dialogue, issued a letter they had composed for Hong Kong compatriots, read aloud letters of support received from Beijing intellectuals and from Chinese students studying in the United States, and so on.

Twelve additional reports on campus activities in Beijing pointed out that students were in the process of electing delegates to a planning committee to establish a national association of the new autonomous student organizations. The planning committee was gathering evidence on corruption in high places, such as special work arrangements for the children of the top leaders, so that its members could cite these cases in future dialogues with the leaders. The reports also suggested that the students were moving to establish a national coordinating committee to lead the nationwide demonstrations and that they would demand the government recognize this committee's legality.

In the provinces Shanghai students were most active. The Shanghai Municipal Party Committee's report said students held a secret meeting to make plans for a citywide demonstration to be held the next day. The demonstration was to demand, among other things, protection for freedoms of association, demonstration, press, and publication and restoration of Qin Benli's position as editor-in-chief of the *World Economic Herald.* The students also planned to demand that the government explain why it had leased large tracts of land on Hainan Island (off the coast of Guangdong, in the South China Sea) to foreign businessmen. On learning of these plans, the Shanghai Municipal Party Committee ordered school authorities to use all possible measures to prevent the demonstrators from leaving the campuses.

The Politburo Standing Committee meets

On the afternoon of May 1 Zhao Ziyang chaired a meeting of the Politburo Standing Committee, which was attended by Li Peng, Qiao Shi, Hu Qili, and Yao Yilin. It was his first meeting with this group since his return from North Korea. In addition, Yang Shangkun and Bo Yibo exercised their rights to attend as representatives of the Elders.[1] Li Tieying, Li Ximing, and Chen Xitong provided briefings. The mood was fairly relaxed.

> Excerpts from Party Central Office Secretariat, "Minutes of Politburo Standing Committee meeting," May 1

Zhao Ziyang: "You've worked hard, comrades. On the student movement, I support Comrade Xiaoping's major speech and the Standing Committee's decision of the twenty-fourth. Thanks to your fine work, the initial handling of the protests has produced good results. Our main task today is to analyze the situation and discuss specific strategies."

Chen Xitong: "The protests were greatest during the two days after the publication of the April 26 editorial, but now they are at low ebb. Over the past couple of days we've had several productive sessions with the students, and many of them have desisted. Leaders of some of the illegal student organizations are afraid of being arrested. At Qinghua, for example, some of them have resigned and announced they will no longer participate in demonstrations. The parents of one of the leaders of an illegal organization at Peking University took him home and forbade him to take part in any more demonstrations. Wuerkaixi, the troublemaker at Beijing Normal University, is so afraid of arrest that he told the Associated Press he is going to stay close to his dormitory and stop organizing. It seems our tactics of dialogue and divide-and-conquer are working. The students are becoming afraid of leading, and even of being led. The leaders in some of the illegal organizations have begun accusing each other of careerism or of working for the Youth League or an official student association. Some of the older and more respected students are fearful of standing in the front line of the protests,[2] and this also works to our advantage."

---

[1] At the First Plenum of the Thirteenth Central Committee in 1987, the Politburo passed a resolution that on major issues the Politburo would seek the guidance of Deng Xiaoping and the other Elders and that final control *(baguan)* over major Politburo decisions would rest with Deng. The resolution also gave Yang Shangkun and Bo Yibo the right to attend Politburo Standing Committee meetings, although not to vote. This was a separate resolution from the one about Deng Xiaoping that Zhao Ziyang revealed to Gorbachev on May 16, which resulted in the charge that Zhao had divulged an important Party secret.—Comp.

[2] Student marchers sometimes arranged to place freshmen and sophomores in the front lines of

Yang Shangkun: "How likely is it that we'll see a big demonstration on May 4, and how many students do you think might come out?"

Chen Xitong: "It's still possible there could be a big demonstration—maybe thirty thousand to forty thousand—but probably not any bigger than the April 27 demonstration. One sign of this possibility came this morning when the Autonomous Federation of Students held a press conference for Chinese and foreign correspondents and made a nine-point announcement that yammered about a nationwide boycott of classes by college students. But the vast majority of students have begun distancing themselves from the leaders of these illegal organizations. These leaders will gradually be isolated."

Li Ximing: "The Beijing Municipal Party Committee has come up with a seven-point 'antiturmoil' plan to head off any major upheavals on May 4 or thereafter. Tomorrow morning the Party Committee and the Municipal Government will convene two meetings: Li Qiyan[3] and I will meet with university leaders, and Xitong and Yuan Liben[4] will meet with business leaders and district, county, and bureau officials. Our tasks will be to further raise their consciousness about the difficulty, complexity, and long-term nature of this political struggle.

"Personally I doubt that the troublemakers are just going to throw up their hands in defeat. This problem's not going to go away easily. The key to winning the struggle is to bring the majority of people over to our side. At the universities, we have to win over the masses in the middle. And the same goes for factories, villages, and businesses. If we can do good thought work with these groups, it'll be easier to isolate the troublemaking minority. And the key to winning over the masses lies in our own determination and unity. Without it, we'll never win over the masses in the middle. We also have to expose the methods of the troublemakers—like their spreading rumors to deceive the masses. We also need to remain absolutely resolute against illegal networking. We've proposed that work units write down the affiliations and purposes of any group that comes to network, as well as the group's size and the names of its members. The Self-Employed Workers' Association must instruct its members that they should not give money to the students. If they wish to make donations, they should support education, not illegal activities. To ensure that the Asian Development Bank meeting proceeds smoothly we have instituted security measures to prevent the sort of beating, smashing, and robbing that occurred in Changsha and Xi'an.

---

marches, where arrest was more likely, in order to protect juniors and seniors who were closer to graduation and job assignments. Party officials made such job assignments and could easily use them to punish targeted students.

[3] Deputy secretary of the Beijing Municipal Party Committee.

[4] A member of the Standing Committee of the Beijing Municipal Party Committee.

We've clearly instructed every unit, right down to the neighborhood committees, to persuade citizens not to be spectators at demonstrations on May 4 or to mingle with the students if they go out on the streets."

Li Tieying: "Nationwide the size of student protests seems to be growing, not shrinking. But the prohibitions on students' intercity networking are having an effect.... [Reading from an SEC report] 'Out-of-town students have been found at universities in eighteen cities, including Shanghai, Tianjin, Hangzhou, Wuhan, Xi'an, Harbin, Changchun, Nanjing, Changsha, and Hefei.' The universal procedure for dealing with this problem is to have school security agencies expel out-of-town students from campuses as soon as they are identified. This has proven very effective. The student movement's been going on for half a month now and for many students the novelty is wearing off. Our goal of splitting the students has borne fruit, particularly since the dialogues. I think that a large-scale, nationwide demonstration on May 4 is inevitable but that the movement will fizzle out after that."

Chen Xitong: "Let me add two points on the student networking: First, about Beijing students going out of town: On the same day that students formed illegal organizations at Peking University they threatened to send people all over the country. A wall poster at Beijing Normal University on April 23 said, "Let's go nationwide!" and urged the Autonomous Federation of Students to send propaganda teams across the country to foment a national protest movement. Later Beijing students became active in Shanghai, Nanjing, Hangzhou, Wuhan, Xi'an, Changsha, Harbin, Changchun, Shenyang, Hefei, and elsewhere. According to a report by the Beijing Youth League Committee, about a third of Qinghua students are currently away from campus, and at other campuses the figure is one in four.

"My second point is about out-of-town students coming to Beijing: On the twenty-first and twenty-second, more than one hundred students from Nankai University in Tianjin arrived in Beijing to participate in activities at Tiananmen Square. A week later, on the twenty-ninth, more than one thousand students from Tianjin University, Nankai University, and the Hebei Institute of Technology arrived in Beijing at 5:15 P.M. on train number 78; they were already distributing leaflets on the train before their arrival. On April 30 more than four hundred students from Hebei University arrived in Beijing. There were also some students from the North China Institute of Electrical Power and the Tangshan Institute of Coal Mines. Some brought along their school flags, and they were reported to be preparing for a huge gathering at Beijing Normal University on the morning of May 4. Unless there's some kind of dramatic reversal, it looks like student networking will only get worse."

Qiao Shi: "My view is that students are in a holding pattern these days, conserving their energy for a long, drawn-out fight. I've taken a look at the materials, and I can't imagine that the students are calming down. Quite a few have participated in demonstrations and boycotts and in putting up wall posters. They don't observe a distinction between themselves and the tiny minority of troublemakers with ulterior motives, and they've already been implicated in turmoil, so why not—from their point of view—just keep going and see what the government's going to do about it? Some of their teachers, who have been stung during earlier protests,[5] avoid taking a stand and just keep quiet. On the other hand, some of the officials in charge of politics and student life also lie low because they want to leave themselves a way out in case the official view of this movement reverses at some point down the line and leaves them out on a limb. So we need to be even clearer about the political borderlines in this matter, and we need to get the students out from under the cloud of participating in turmoil."

Hu Qili: "The longer the strike drags on, the more people will join it. Right now the press is somewhat confused. When the students first took to the streets they pointed a finger at journalists, accusing them of lying. That raised hackles among some journalists. Then when the *World Economic Herald* incident came along, journalists and some intellectuals just couldn't take it any more. So far, about four hundred or five hundred journalists nationwide have in one way or another pledged support for the *Herald* and Qin Benli. Some have lodged a protest with the Shanghai Municipal Party Committee, demanding that the wrong be righted. The situation on Shanghai campuses has gotten pretty tense in recent days."

Zhao Ziyang: "We should think about this *World Economic Herald* problem very carefully before we jump to any conclusions. I feel that the Shanghai Municipal Party Committee moved too hastily and bungled the matter. Their simplistic approach to the problem only made it worse, and they wound up trapping themselves in a bad position. We need to support their decision anyway, of course."

Yao Yilin: "We need to buckle down and get these student protests settled. The sooner we get to work, the sooner we'll get things back on track. The state's got so much important work to attend to, and look how these protests are tying up the energies of so many people. Letting things drag on like this is no good for the

---

[5]Qiao is probably referring to the student movement of 1986. Professors who supported that movement suffered for it later.

Party, the state, or the people. We can't expect the students' thinking to turn on a dime, so we just might have to be tough with them when toughness is called for. In any case, we can't let the student movement get in the way of the normal functioning of government organs or interfere with the normal life and work routine of the masses."

Bo Yibo: "We absolutely have to stop the student movement from getting any bigger! Students are networking all over the country. This is serious! We can't let the tragedy of the Cultural Revolution happen again! We've got to take consistent steps nationwide, from top to bottom, or we're headed for big trouble. Don't underestimate these students. If they get carried away, there'll be a big threat to political stability and unity, and that in turn will affect the progress of our reform and opening. In the last few days foreign newspapers have begun to speculate again about a struggle raging among China's leaders. One British newspaper even reported that our slowness in reprimanding the students reflects ideological chaos inside the Party. It went on to say that there appear to be serious internal conflicts over how to handle the crisis and that the student movement might well grow into a far-reaching power struggle. So the deeper we get into sensitive matters like this, the more decisive and clear our actions will probably have to be. But dialogue with the students might still be the best strategy for undermining and suppressing the protests. We'll score big if we can handle it this way."

Yang Shangkun: "Two important international events are scheduled for Beijing in May. The annual meeting of the board of governors of the Asian Development Bank opens on the fourth, and then we have the visit of Comrade Gorbachev, who is coming to normalize relations between China and the Soviet Union. How we handle these protests will be a test of our abilities and an indication of our international influence. As things stand now, persuasive dialogue seems to be the best strategy for avoiding further escalation. We must unite the majority and isolate the tiny minority. We can utilize these two international activities to show that the Chinese Communist Party has the ability and confidence to put down student protests through peaceful means."

Zhao Ziyang: "We must continue to focus on guidance and should pursue multilevel, multichannel dialogue in many ways, even while putting pressure on the students to return to their classes without delay. The day after tomorrow I'll be speaking on the seventieth anniversary of May Fourth, and I plan to focus on two issues. One will be that we must continue to 'grasp with two hands,' meaning to take just as much care with political work as with economic work. The other is the need to accelerate the reform of our political system, especially the building of a system of socialist democracy based on law. Times have changed, and so have people's ideological views. Democracy is a worldwide trend, and there is an international countercurrent against communism and socialism that flies under the banners of democracy and human rights. If the Party doesn't hold up the banner of democracy in our country, someone else will, and we will lose out. I think we should grab the lead on this, not be pushed along grudgingly. We must, of course, insist on Communist Party leadership and not play around with any Western multiparty systems. This basic principle can allow no compromise."

Yang Shangkun: "One-party rule has to be able to solve the question of democracy as well as the problem of supervisory mechanisms to guard against negative, unhealthful, and even corrupt phenomena within Party and state organs. This is the only way our Party can achieve long-lasting strength."

Zhao Ziyang: "Our Party must adapt to new times and new situations and learn how to use democracy and law to solve new problems. For instance, we must increase transparency in political life, bring the NPC into full play, reinforce and perfect multiparty cooperation and political consultation under Communist leadership, perfect and reform the electoral system, increase the masses' supervision of the Party and the government, guarantee and regulate freedom of speech by law, allow legal demonstrations, and so on. In sum, we must make the people feel that under the leadership of the Communist Party and the socialist system they can truly and fully enjoy democracy and freedom. The socialist system can demonstrate its superiority only by increasing the power of its appeal to the people. Leaders at every level need to adapt to working and living under a system of democracy and law. We cannot allow people to promote bourgeois liberalization under the banner of democracy, but at the same time, our opposition to bourgeois liberalization must not interfere with the promotion of democracy. From now on, the important function of Party leadership should be to guide people in building a system of democracy and law and to turn our socialist country into one truly governed by law."

Li Peng: "Some socialist countries launch political reforms only when conflicts in society are severe and the Party is crippled. This makes control of the process nearly impossible. So our first order of business should be stability. Once that is achieved, we can talk about reforming the political system."

Hu Qili: "Building a democratic system should go hand in hand with growing the economy. Democracy mustn't get out ahead, but neither should it lag behind. Right now the problem of stability has to take precedence over everything else. Stability doesn't mean people can't voice their opinions, of course. True stability will come only when socialist democracy is fully in place. On the other hand, if politics are unstable, then even what we've achieved so far will be lost."

Bo Yibo: "That's exactly right. The two must complement each other. If we don't put political reform at the top of our agenda, problems arising from economic reform will be hard to solve, and social and political conflicts will only get worse. We should grab the initiative by launching democratization now, while the leadership role of the Party is relatively strong. But the most urgent task facing us right now, of course, is to end the student movement and stop the turmoil as soon as possible."

Li Peng: "The seriousness of this protest movement is unprecedented, and the range of its impact is also serious. Leaders of illegal student organizations are plotting even bigger activities. They openly promote slogans that reject our opposition to bourgeois liberalization, because what they want is the kind of absolute freedom that tramples on the Four Basic Principles. They spread all kinds of rumors. They attack, slander, and insult Comrade Xiaoping and other Party and state leaders. They call for the establishment of illegal organizations, for which they demand Party and government recognition. If they get their way, then everything—reform and opening, democracy and law, building socialist modernization, you name it— will vanish into thin air and China will take a huge step backward."

Zhao Ziyang: "It's quite true that the protests are very serious and have far-reaching effects. And no one is denying that a tiny minority of people are in there fishing in troubled waters and pushing bourgeois liberalization. But the student slogans that uphold the Constitution, promote democracy, and oppose corruption all echo positions of the Party and the government. I share everyone's views that we must move quickly to defuse a situation that has nearly gotten out of hand. Reform of any kind has to be based in social stability. A great country like ours cannot put up with any more provocation, so I am going to put great stress on the importance of national stability. Our young people, especially the college students, must understand its critical importance. If stability is lost, then we lose everything. All we get is turmoil."

Zhao reminded everyone that they had received copies of the advance draft of his May 4 speech to the ADB and asked them for suggestions for revision. The meeting ended with decisions aimed at maintaining public support for the government line and resisting student networking. The Standing Committee decided that all campuses nationwide should organize activities to commemorate May Fourth, so there would be no interference with the ADB meeting scheduled to take place that day in the Great Hall of the People.

May 2

Twelve demands for dialogue

On May 2 the students at Peking University who were planning a national association of autonomous student organizations announced over their campus public-address system that five students, led by Wang Dan and Feng Congde, were now in charge of plans for activities to commemorate May Fourth. At 2:30 P.M. a group of more than seventy students from more than forty institutions presented a petition at the combined Letters and Visits Bureau[6] of Party Central and the State Council.[7] The petition made twelve demands for a series of dialogues between students, selected by the students themselves without interference from official student organizations or the government, and government officials, to be publicly broadcast and conducted on an equal basis. The students stated that if these demands were not answered by noon on May 3, they would continue to exercise their right to petition on May 4. The petition was immediately forwarded to the members of the Politburo Standing Committee and to Yang Shangkun. The Politburo Standing Committee decided to have Yuan Mu hold a press conference on the morning of May 3 to counter the students' demands.

That evening the State Security Ministry reported on some noteworthy developments on Beijing campuses, particularly Peking University's campus. An announcement was posted there that Chinese students from sixteen California campuses had raised U.S.$8,477 to contribute to the student movement. A broadcast over the university's public-address system listed a series of political demands, called Deng Xiaoping's Four Basic Principles the main obstacle to the democracy movement, and urged students to carry out a nationwide demonstration later in the month when Soviet leader Mikhail Gorbachev arrived in China for the Sino-Soviet summit. Students also demanded that the top leaders should move out of Zhongnanhai and turn it into a park, Mao's body should be removed from its Tiananmen Square mausoleum and buried in the Babaoshan Cemetery, and Tiananmen Square should be turned into a place for free speech like London's Hyde Park.

---

[6]Letters and visits bureaus throughout the bureaucracy handle appeals from citizens.
[7]Text of the petition in Suzanne Ogden, Kathleen Hartford, Lawrence Sullivan, and David Zweig, eds., *China's Search for Democracy: The Student and the Mass Movement of 1989* (Armonk, New York: M. E. Sharpe, 1992), 158–160.

Student demonstrations in Shanghai

A series of reports from the State Security Ministry described the May 2 Shanghai demonstrations to Zhongnanhai as they were taking place. The students gathered on their campuses and marched toward Shanghai's People's Square, where they conducted a sit-in, heard speeches, and presented petitions, whose demands were similar to those of other student petitions, to the city's People's Congress. About seven thousand students came to the square, which police prevented bystanders from entering. In the evening the students left the square and went to the Bund,[8] where they conducted a sit-in in front of the offices of the People's Municipal Government. A maximum of about eight thousand people demonstrated. Security personnel recorded a number of pro-student comments by onlookers. The students started to disperse around 10:05 P.M. but planned to return the next evening at 6.

May 3

Zhao's speech commemorating May Fourth

On the morning of May 3 Zhao Ziyang delivered a speech at a conference to celebrate the seventieth anniversary of May Fourth, which was attended by many high Party and government leaders.[9] The speech focused on preserving stability and opposing turmoil, but it also praised the role of youth and contained a crucial passage that affirmed the patriotism of the student demonstrators and the legitimacy of their desire for democracy and opposition to corruption. It had been drafted by Bao Tong and reviewed by the Politburo and the Central Committee Secretariat. In this process several members, including Yang Shangkun, Li Peng, Qiao Shi, Yao Yilin, and Li Ximing, had suggested that the phrase "oppose bourgeois liberalization" be added. At the urging of Li Peng, Yang Shangkun sought out Zhao before the meeting to ask whether this phrase had been added. Zhao smiled and said, "Comrade Shangkun, I think in the present atmosphere it's better for the time being not to emphasize it." Yang did not press the matter. Later, when the Party took stock of Zhao's mistakes at the Fourth Plenum of the Thirteenth Central Committee in June 1989, Yang would refer to this incident when criticizing Zhao for refusing to accept other people's suggestions after his return from North Korea.

---

[8]Shanghai's riverfront avenue where, at that time, major government offices were located.
[9]Text of the speech in Michel Oksenberg, Lawrence R. Sullivan, and Marc Lambert, eds., *Beijing Spring, 1989, Confrontation and Conflict: The Basic Documents* (Armonk, New York: M. E. Sharpe, 1990), 244–251.

Yuan Mu's press conference

In a press conference also on the morning of May 3, State Council spokesman Yuan Mu rejected the Peking University students' twelve preconditions for dialogue.[10] His remarks emphasized six points: First, it would be unreasonable to exclude the official student organizations from the dialogue, as the petition demanded. To hold a dialogue only with certain groups and not others would not be conducive to unity among the students. Second, dialogue should be without preconditions. Third, the petition took the form of an ultimatum and was threatening to the government. Fourth, although the government was not planning to punish students for extremist words and actions, those who violated the criminal law would be punished accordingly. This would involve mainly nonstudent elements who had wormed their way in among the students and were inciting them. Fifth, the government would continue to deal calmly and carefully with the students. Sixth, there were some evil people hidden deeply behind the scenes and manipulating the students. For the time being the government was not going to do anything about them because they were too intimately mixed in among the students. Yuan also pointed out that he had followed foreign reporting on the incident, and most reports praised the government's correct policies, although a few reports aimed at inciting the turmoil to even greater heights.

Unfavorable student reactions

On the afternoon of May 3 the State Security Ministry reported that students everywhere were dissatisfied with Yuan Mu's remarks. They believed that Yuan expressed a hard-line attitude and that he failed to understand the students' motives. Students especially resented Yuan's claim that they were being manipulated by elements behind the scenes and insisted their actions were spontaneous and their motives were good: to help the Party and government correct their errors. The students were busy preparing banners and homemade loudspeakers, and some teachers feared that if the government reacted too strongly the students' attitudes would harden. A group of students went to the Letters and Visits Bureau of Party Central and the State Council to ask for an answer to their petition. The spokesman there told them there would be no further answer beyond what had been said at the press conference.

The State Security Ministry also reported that student representatives from forty-seven Beijing campuses voted to hold a demonstration in Tiananmen on May 4. The students planned to march on the Square and distribute handbills calling, among other things, for democracy, dialogue, protection of constitutional freedoms, support for the *World Economic Herald,* and opposition to corruption.

[10]Report on the press conference, Oksenberg et al., *Beijing Spring,* 253–254.

On the same day the Beijing Municipal Party Committee submitted a report that alarmed Li Peng, Yao Yilin, and Yuan Mu. It said that students from twenty-eight Beijing campuses had elected a sixty-five-person "dialogue delegation" under the aegis of the Beijing AFS, despite the fact that this group had already been declared illegal. Moreover, as soon as it was established, this dialogue delegation declared itself separate from the AFS, thus creating yet another independent student organization.

The delegation's initial agenda for dialogue had three items: (1) the government's official view of the student movement; (2) questions of reform of the political structure that were raised by the problem of corruption; and (3) the legalization of the AFS in keeping with constitutional guarantees of freedoms of the press, publication, and association. Work on these three issues was divided up among the campuses, and each issue had a series of demands. For example, the second item included a seven-point set of demands involving such issues as democratization within the Party, freedom of the press, and changes in government decisionmaking processes in order to remove opportunities for corruption.

Reports from around the country on May 3 showed there were student demonstrations only in Nanchang and Xining. In other large and medium-sized cities students prepared for demonstrations on May 4. The Shanghai Municipal Party Committee reported that two-thirds of the students in the three main campuses in that city were boycotting classes.

Journalists decide to join the demonstrations

On May 3 the State Security Ministry reported on a May 2–3 meeting of Beijing journalists convened by the Beijing correspondent of Guangzhou's *Asia-Pacific Economic Times,* ostensibly as a seminar in honor of May Fourth. The meeting took place in the northeast quarter of Beijing at the Lu Xun Museum, which happened to be the location of this correspondent's temporary office. Several dozen journalists in Beijing, including the Beijing staff of the *World Economic Herald,* attended. The topic soon moved from memorializing May Fourth to the closing of the *Herald* in Shanghai and from there to the issue of freedom of the press. The discussion was so heated that it had to be extended into a second day and so loud that on the second day the museum staff asked the participants to move the meeting out onto the lawn. On the second day, foreign, Hong Kong, and Taiwan reporters attended with tape recorders and video cameras.

The group decided to circulate a petition among Beijing journalists for signature, demanding a dialogue with Central leaders on the question of press freedom. They also decided reporters and editors could join the demonstrators on May 4 either as petitioners or as participants in a collective journalistic effort to observe and report the demonstration.

May 4

The "May Fourth Declaration"

Tens of thousands of students from fifty-one campuses marched on Chang'an Boulevard and in Tiananmen Square on May 4 and then issued a declaration that they would return to classes May 5. The security ministries made timely reports as these activities unfolded. The students set out from their campuses about 8 A.M. and converged on Tiananmen from three directions. About 11 A.M. they broke through the police cordons that had been set up around the city center. About noon the first column entered the Square, and the other two arrived about 2 P.M. Drums, banners, slogans, and singing kept the crowd excited. About 3 P.M. a student leader under the banner of the AFS read a "May Fourth Declaration."[11]

The Declaration stated that the current student movement was a continuation and development[12] of the great patriotic student movement of seventy years earlier. It shared an ultimate goal with the government: China's modernization. Like the government, the Declaration continued, the students stood for the traditional May Fourth values of democracy, science, freedom, human rights, and rule of law. It called on the government to accelerate political and economic reform, guarantee constitutional freedoms, fight corruption, adopt a press law, and allow the establishment of privately run newspapers. Important first steps would include institutionalizing the democratic practices that the students themselves had begun to initiate on the campuses, conducting student-government dialogue, promoting democratic reforms of the government system, opposing corruption, and accelerating the adoption of a press law. With the help of hundreds of thousands of citizens, the Declaration claimed, the students had so far achieved a series of unprecedented victories for the cause of democracy and the May Fourth spirit, but it noted that the victories were fragile and that it was necessary to continue the struggle.

The students then read out a four-point AFS decision: The students (1) would return to classes; (2) would continue to negotiate with the government over their demand for dialogue; (3) depending on the outcome of those talks, might take further actions; and (4) would go forth among the citizens of Beijing to give speeches explaining the May Fourth petitioning movement.

The students left the Square about 3 P.M. There had been about as many demonstrators as at the April 27 demonstration, but, importantly, participants came from a larger number of schools, including some from as far away as Guangzhou, Shenzhen, Hainan, and Hong Kong—each group

---

[11]Excerpted in Han Minzhu, ed., *Cries for Democracy: Writings and Speeches from the 1989 Chinese Democracy Movement* (Princeton: Princeton University Press, 1990), 135–137.

[12]*Jixu yu fazhan*; Mao had claimed to "continue and develop" the thought of Marx and Lenin, and Deng the thought of Mao.

with a flag identifying itself. There were also about two hundred reporters and editors carrying banners with such slogans as "Making news public is good for stability and unity" and expressing support for the *World Economic Herald* and Qin Benli. Banners and slogans among the students emphasized the May Fourth spirit, dialogue, opposition to corruption, and the ongoing struggle for freedom and democracy and against rule by a handful of Elders. There were fewer observers this time than on April 27, but the citizens along the route expressed support for the students. The Beijing Municipal Public Security Bureau reported some incidents between police and demonstrators or observers in the course of the day.

Large-scale demonstrations around the country

Protests were not restricted to Beijing. On May 4 Zhongnanhai received reports on student demonstrations in fifty-one cities around the country, all marking the seventieth anniversary of May Fourth in similar ways and making similar demands. In Shanghai, up to eight thousand students conducted sit-ins in front of the Municipal Government and Party headquarters to promote the demand for dialogue. They also distributed handbills calling attention to inflation and corruption, which drew a strong reaction from citizens. In Xi'an some twelve thousand students demonstrated, demanding that charges published in the newspapers against the April 22 demonstration be retracted and that the government conduct dialogue with the students. Demonstrators posted charts exposing connections among the offspring of high officials.[13] The students were received by a Shaanxi Province vice governor, Sun Daren.

In both Wuhan and Hangzhou about ten thousand students marched, sat-in, and demanded control of inflation, liberalization of the press, and opposition to corruption. Seven thousand marchers in Chongqing staged a sit-in at the municipal government buildings, demanding that the government declare their movement legitimate and guarantee that it would be reported fairly in the local media and that municipal officials would enter into dialogue with them. In Changsha six thousand student demonstrators handed out a "Letter to Our Countrymen" that called on workers, farmers, and individual entrepreneurs to support the students. In other cities demonstrators numbered from one thousand to six thousand. There was no violence, both because the students preserved order and because local authorities forbade the police to use force.

---

[13] *Guanxi tu*, charts of who is connected to whom, implying networks of corruption.

Zhao Ziyang presses conciliation in public and private

While the students were reading their declaration in Tiananmen Square, Zhao Ziyang was meeting with delegation leaders and other high officials of the Asian Development Bank at the twenty-second annual meeting of its board of governors. There he gave a speech that some later famously criticized as "expressing a second voice" of the leadership because it was so much more moderate than Deng Xiaoping's line.[14]

> Excerpts from Party Central Office, "Comrade Zhao Ziyang's speech at the meeting of the board of governors of the Asian Development Bank," May 4

I believe the basic attitude of the great majority of the student demonstrators is one of both satisfaction and dissatisfaction with the Communist Party and the government. These students do not oppose our underlying system, but they do demand that we eliminate the flaws in our work. They are satisfied with our achievements in reform and construction over the past decade, as well as with the nation's general development. But they are irritated by mistakes we have made along the way. They are calling on us to correct those mistakes and to improve our work style, and these calls in fact correspond nicely with positions of the Party and the government, which are also to affirm our accomplishments and to correct our mistakes.

Are there attempts to exploit the student movement, and is such exploitation going on now? China is so huge that there are always going to be at least some people who want to see us in turmoil. There will always be people ready to exploit our students, and they will miss no opportunity to do so. Such people are very few, but we must always be on guard against them. I am confident that the great majority of the students will see this point. Demonstrations are continuing in Beijing and elsewhere, but I have no doubt that the situation is going to calm down gradually and that China will be spared any major turmoil.

We should meet the students' reasonable demands through democracy and law, should be willing to reform, and should use rational and orderly methods. Let us put this more concretely: What most bothers the students right now is the scourge of corruption. But the Party and government have been working on this problem in recent years, so why are there so many voices of complaint, and why

[14]Xinhua News Agency's summary of the speech appears in Oksenberg et al., *Beijing Spring*, 254–256, and excerpts appear in Han, *Cries for Democracy*, 132–134.

are they so loud? There are two reasons, I believe. One is that our flawed legal system and our lack of democratic supervision allow corruption to rage out of control. The other is that our lack of openness and transparency leads to rumors, inaccurate accusations, wild exaggerations, and outright fabrications about what the Party and government are doing. Most Party and government workers in fact live on low wages and have no income beyond their fixed salaries, let alone any legally sanctioned privileges. Yes, there are people who skirt the law, who grab special privileges; but there are fewer of them, and they do less harm, than people think. Of course the problem of corruption has to be solved, but that has to happen—can only happen—through reforms such as perfecting the legal system, improving democratic supervision, and increasing transparency.

And these same principles apply to how we should deal with the student demonstrations themselves. We need to use democracy and law and to reason in an atmosphere of order. We need to use dialogue to consult broadly with students, workers, intellectuals, members of the democratic parties, and citizens from all parts of society. We must exchange ideas and promote mutual understanding through democracy and law in an atmosphere of reason and order, working together to solve problems that concern everyone.

What we need most right now is calm, reason, self-restraint, and order as we move to solve problems through democracy and law. If the Party and government are willing to proceed in this way, I am confident that students and other segments of society will also find this to be the best way.

Zhao's speech before the board of the ADB had been drafted by Bao Tong but, unlike his speech commemorating May Fourth, had not been discussed by the Politburo Standing Committee or sanctioned by the Central Secretariat. Zhao felt good about the speech before he delivered it, and nearly everything he heard afterward was positive.

Later in the day Li Peng had a private conversation with Zhao about the speech:

> Account drawn from *Materials for the Fourth Plenum of the Thirteenth Central Committee*, "Remarks of Comrade Zhao Ziyang," Secretariat of the Fourth Plenum of the CCP Thirteenth Central Committee, June 23–24, 1989; and from Li Peng, "Report on mistakes committed by Comrade Zhao Ziyang during the anti-Party antisocialist turmoil," report to the Fourth Plenum of the Thirteenth Central Committee, June 23

Li Peng: "That was an excellent speech, Comrade Ziyang, and the response has been very positive. I'll echo you when I meet with the Asian Development Bank delegates tomorrow."

Zhao Ziyang: "I tried to set a mild tone. I hope it'll do some good in quieting the student movement down and in strengthening foreign investors' confidence in China's stability. . . . Comrade Li Peng, when I got back from North Korea I heard about the strong reactions to the April 26 editorial in the *People's Daily*. It seems to have turned into a real sore point that has the students all stirred up. Do you see any way to turn things around and calm them down?"

Li Peng: "Comrade Ziyang, as you know, the editorial reflected the spirit of the April 24 Politburo meeting, particularly the views of Comrade Xiaoping. There may be problems of tone here and there, but we can't possibly change the core message."

Zhao Ziyang: "Let me tell you how I see all this. I think the student movement has two important characteristics. First, the students' slogans call for things like supporting the Constitution, promoting democracy, and fighting corruption. These demands all echo positions of the Party and the government. Second, a great many people from all parts of society are out there joining the demonstrations and backing the students. And it's not just Beijing that's flooded with protesters; it's the same story in Shanghai, Tianjin, and other major cities. This has grown into a nationwide protest. I think the best way to bring the thing to a quick end is to focus on the mainstream views of the majority. My problem with the April 26 editorial is that it sets the mainstream aside and makes a general, all-encompassing pronouncement that the majority just can't accept; it generates an us-versus-them mentality. I have no quarrel with the view that a handful of people oppose the Four Basic Principles and are fishing in troubled waters. I said that in my speech today. But it's hard to explain, and also hard to believe, how hundreds of thousands of people all over the country could be manipulated by a tiny minority. The students feel stigmatized by the April 26 editorial, and that's the main thing that's set them off. I think we should revise the editorial, soften its tone a bit."

Li Peng: "The origins of this protest are complex, Comrade Ziyang. The editorial did not accuse the vast majority of students of creating turmoil. When Yuan Mu had his dialogue with the students, and again when he spoke with journalists, he explained the government's position several times over. The students should be quite clear about this by now. The trouble is, there's no sign the protests are subsiding. In fact, quite the opposite: Now we have illegal student organizations that are openly pressuring the government. You've read the petition from that

'AFS,' so you know they're trying to squeeze out the legal student organizations. And not just that: They want to negotiate with the Party and government as equals. They even add a lot of conditions, as if they're above the government. That petition of theirs was itself a threat. The elder comrades like Xiaoping, Chen Yun, and Xiannian are all convinced that a tiny minority of people are manipulating this protest from behind the scenes. Their purpose is quite clear: They want to negate the leadership of the CCP and negate the entire socialist system. I agree with our Elder comrades. And that's why I hold to the view that the April 26 editorial is accurate and cannot be changed."

Zhao Ziyang: "I'm not opposed to the term 'turmoil' in the editorial. But I believe that this refers only to the scale of the protest and to the degree to which it has affected social order and that it does not foreclose the question of the political nature of the protest—I mean whether it's spontaneous or antagonistic.[15] I think we should publish another editorial distinguishing the majority of students and sympathizers from the tiny minority who are using the movement to fish in troubled waters, to create conflicts, and to attack the Party and socialism. That way we can avoid a sweeping characterization of the protests as an antagonistic conflict. We can concentrate on policies of persuasion and guidance and avoid the sharpening of conflict. This kind of approach is the best way to help calm the situation."

Li Peng: "I disagree, Comrade Ziyang."

And so the discussion ended. Neither man could persuade the other, and the two parted holding to divergent views on the April 26 editorial.

---

[15] *Didui de;* antagonistic in the sense of Mao's theory of antagonistic conflicts ("between us and the enemy") and nonantagonistic conflicts ("among the people"). If the demonstrations constituted an antagonistic conflict, the students' activities would constitute political crimes, to be punished severely. See footnote 31 in Chapter 2.

May 5

Mixed reactions to Zhao's speech

On May 5 the provincial-level units filed reports on local responses to Zhao's talk. All the provinces started by endorsing Zhao's fair, balanced, calm appraisal and acknowledging that his strategy would help calm things down. A few reports went on to discuss doubts and questions. The reports from Beijing and Liaoning, for example, both raised the point that some comrades were troubled that Zhao had not called the student movement turmoil and had even said that large-scale turmoil could not break out. This, they felt, seemed to contradict the statement in the April 26 editorial that the movement already was turmoil. Zhao's position on agitators—that some instigation by agitators was inevitable—seemed far different from the concern expressed about outside manipulators both in the editorial and in Yuan Mu's press conference. Some comrades in Shanghai were confused over whether street demonstrations were considered acceptable or not and whether the students' demands were considered to be in line with government policy or not. Since Zhao had not come out clearly against the students' demands or methods, local officials felt that his talk undermined the efforts they had been asked to make in urging students not to go into the streets to demonstrate.

But most provincial reports implied that Zhao had not gone far enough in his sympathetic response to the movement. Heilongjiang stated that Zhao's analysis of the causes of the movement was fair as far as it went but that some comrades believed it was necessary to establish effective mechanisms to place government officials under popular supervision. Jiangsu called for the Center to take concrete steps to satisfy some of the students' demands. Zhejiang said that small-scale disturbances should be considered normal in the course of constructing more democratic political institutions and that the authorities should not overreact. Guangdong argued that more open channels of communication between citizens and government would have prevented the students from resorting to demonstrations and petitions in the first place. Shaanxi reported that some personnel wished the April 26 editorial had taken a tone more like Zhao's; they also warned that local workers had been so upset by the hard line of the April 26 editorial that if the government were to take that kind of line, they might be easily organized to rise up. Gansu suggested that if the Center wanted to establish stability, the way to do it was not to suppress criticism of corruption but to suppress corruption itself. According to Sichuan, Zhao's speech pointed the right direction for resolving the crisis but still did not take the corruption problem as seriously as necessary. And Yunnan's report urged that the Party make both immediate concessions and long-term progress on the key problems that the students had raised.

May 1–6

The focus overseas: What is the next step?

Between May 1 and May 6 sixty-two reports reached Zhongnanhai on foreign reactions to the events of recent days. Press analyses of Zhao's Asian Development Bank talk portrayed Zhao as taking control of events after his return from North Korea and as laying down a new, softer, and more effective government strategy for dealing with the demonstrations—a strategy that would strengthen Zhao's hand in leading the Party toward deeper political reform.

In the United States, President George Bush said that it was not for him to tell the Chinese government what to do but that some of the student demands were worthy of support and China should continue on the road to democracy. In testimony before a congressional committee reported to Zhongnanhai by the Xinhua News Agency, a State Department official stated that nonpeaceful repression of the students would have a deleterious impact on U.S.-China relations. Brookings Institution scholar Harry Harding Jr. stated that the United States should express its support for political reform without intervening in any particular incident. The committee also heard testimony from a Chinese Ph.D. student in political science at Harvard, Pei Minxin, who, Xinhua noted, had visited Taiwan in the past. Pei urged the U.S. government to warn the Chinese government not to use force against the students and suggested a list of sanctions the U.S. government should impose if force were used. Xinhua also submitted a series of reports on demonstrations and other activities in support of the student protesters by Chinese students in several U.S. cities and in England, West Germany, and France.

The foreign press portrayed the student movement as passionate, sincere, and spontaneous. The London *Independent* quoted Harvard political science professor Roderick MacFarquhar as warning the Chinese government not to make the mistake of creating a student martyr around whom a nationwide movement similar to Poland's Solidarity might coalesce. Several Hong Kong papers praised the students, but the *Hong Kong Standard* pointed out that they could not push forward political reform without allying with pro-reform leaders within the Party, something that might be difficult since they had directed criticisms at almost all the top leaders, pro-reform or otherwise. Other reports highlighted a fact that must have seemed threatening to Zhongnanhai: Longtime dissidents at home and abroad were participating in the movement.

CHAPTER FOUR

May 6–16

Hunger Strike

EDITORS' NOTE: Zhao struggled to consolidate consensus within the leadership around his conciliatory line toward the students. On May 6 he enlisted Yang Shangkun to tell Deng Xiaoping why he thought it was necessary to soften the verdict of the April 26 editorial. Yang passed this word along, and Zhao followed up in a conversation with Deng on May 13. Deng was willing to consider anything, so long as the students were somehow cleared from the Square in time for Gorbachev's visit.

Meanwhile, at a May 8 Standing Committee meeting, Zhao got his colleagues started on the arduous task of framing plans for a serious attack on corruption in the Party. Zhao wanted to start at the top, abolishing the leaders' privileges and investigating their families and closely connected companies. He also proposed stepped-up efforts toward greater press autonomy, easier approvals for public demonstrations, and other liberalizing reforms.

On May 10 the full Politburo clashed over how to handle the student movement. Members agreed on the danger of the situation but disagreed over Zhao's line on how it should be handled. Zhao criticized Jiang Zemin for mishandling the *World Economic Herald* incident, and Jiang stoutly defended himself. (In a private conversation a day later, Yang Shangkun and Deng Xiaoping agreed that Jiang's handling of this incident struck just the right balance between discipline and reform-mindedness.) In any case, the Politburo decided to make further efforts at dialogue with the students.

The student movement was also conflicted. Although some students returned to classes, others advocated continuing the strike. New leaders emerged, and various groups presented various demands. Journalists and intellectuals spoke out, new issues were added to old ones, and demonstrations burgeoned in the provinces.

Disaster struck for Zhao's moderate strategy on May 13, when the students announced a hunger strike. Over the course of the next few days the intellectuals joined in, there were incidents in the provinces, and the summit that the authorities envisioned as a triumphant climax to years of diplomacy with the Soviet Union was thrown into the shadows. The huge foreign press contingent that had come to Beijing for the summit turned its main attention to the student movement.

May 6

Zhao Ziyang discusses press reform

On the morning of May 6 Zhao Ziyang met with Hu Qili and Rui Xingwen to talk about their jobs in supervising the news media. Hu Qili pointed out that one of the students' major complaints was that reports on their activities in the Chinese press were biased. This issue had also caused widespread dissatisfaction among the reporters themselves. Rui added that the press needed credibility to serve as an effective voice for the Party, but at the moment even the press workers themselves didn't believe what they read, heard on the radio, or saw on television. Aside from the short-term impact of the student movement in press circles, Rui said, a long-term issue was to speed up reform of the entire press system.

Zhao agreed. Recent reporting on the students had been more open than before, and no harm had resulted. Press reform was a trend of the times, which the Party should turn to its benefit. A truthful, objective, and credible press was part of the democratic politics that the Party wanted to build. Hu told Zhao that journalists were organizing a petition campaign to demand dialogue with the leaders. Zhao replied that such dialogues would be useful. At the same time, the Party should continue to guide press work by warning against excessively radical views. The Party should be cautious in dealing with any sensitive incidents in journalism and should not put itself in a position to be criticized again as it had in the case of the *World Economic Herald*.

That afternoon Hu and Rui reported Zhao's remarks to the leaders of major Beijing press units.

A conversation between Zhao Ziyang and Yang Shangkun

On the afternoon of May 6 Zhao Ziyang paid a visit to Yang Shangkun.

Excerpts from memoranda of conversations supplied by a friend of Yang Shangkun who cannot be further identified

Zhao Ziyang: "Since I got back from North Korea I've been reading to try to get caught up on this situation. I've spoken with Comrades Qiao Shi, [Hu] Qili, [Tian] Jiyun, and Xu Jiatun,[1] and two days ago I had an exchange with Comrade Li Peng. I'm trying to get an overview. I've felt all along that the main currents are positive: pro-Party and pro-reform. Many of the young students want to see the reforms go more quickly and the country reach a higher level of democracy. But although their intentions are good, they can get carried away in what they say and do; they sometimes don't stay cool and reasonable. In my speech to the Asian Development Bank delegates, I stressed the importance of calm, reason, self-restraint, and order. I think we can settle these protests through democracy and law."

Yang Shangkun: "Your speech went over well within the Party. Qiao Shi, Wan Li, Manager Rong,[2] and Xu Jiatun all said it was a good speech. It also went over well with the students and with society in general. Most of the universities in Beijing have resumed classes, which shows the effect you've had. You're quite right that this movement is different from earlier ones, because this time the students have really broad support, including officials from all levels in the Party and government. The students' slogans are also prudently put: They endorse the Communist Party and support 'reform and opening.' In these respects they represent the views of the vast majority. It's also clear that outsiders—diehard liberals, certain foreign forces, and anticommunist elements from Hong Kong and Taiwan—are putting ideas into the students' heads. But the mainstream of the movement is positive."

Zhao Ziyang: "I think if we can handle this movement well, it'll help us advance the reforms."

Yang Shangkun: "So we should not suppress this movement but guide and divide it:[3] win over the majority of the students and isolate the handful of anti-communists who are intent upon our destruction. . . . The students are demanding honest and clean leadership. They oppose embezzlement, official profiteering, and special privilege. These are the same issues our Party has raised. So we should view the support of the students and the masses as a good thing. We should use dialogue to identify the reasonable demands of the masses and then accept those

---

[1] Director of the Xinhua News Agency in Hong Kong. The agency served as the key outpost of the Beijing government in Hong Kong before June 1997.

[2] Rong Yiren, chair of the All-China Federation of Industry and Commerce and China's leading state-sponsored businessman.

[3] *Shudao fenhua*, "guide and divide," is a long-standing CCP leadership technique connected with the technique of political thought work and the united front tactic of "uniting with the majority and isolating the minority." It means to guide the understanding of most people along lines that comport with Party policy.

demands. I think we should implement practical measures to end these corrupt practices."

Zhao Ziyang: "I've been thinking about this problem, too. On the corruption issue, for instance, especially when it involves the children of high-ranking officials, I plan to take the lead. I'm going to write to the Central Government and ask for an investigation of my own children's activities. If they've been corrupt, they should be punished in accordance with the law. The same goes for me personally. In the matter of 'special provisions,'[4] we should ask members of the Standing Committee to begin by giving up their own privileges, although we could keep them for the elder comrades such as Xiaoping, Xiannian, and Chen Yun. And we need to reform the system of providing airplanes, trains, and bodyguards for members of the Standing Committee when they travel abroad. We can keep these for the elder comrades, but we need to reduce the transportation costs and the entourages for new members. And the most basic need is to get the Standing Committee of the NPC, as soon as it can, to debate and enact laws against embezzlement, official profiteering, and special privilege."

Yang Shangkun: "Xu Jiatun has already told me what you said about this."

Zhao Ziyang: "What I most want to discuss with you today is this idea I have about the April 26 editorial. I think it's intensified the conflict by calling the protest turmoil. That description may be ill considered. I hear that it shocked a great many officials and citizens when they read it. They disagreed with the content of the editorial and have blamed Comrade Xiaoping. There's even talk that somebody's been trying to push Comrade Xiaoping out front on this problem. We must protect Comrade Xiaoping's image and prevent it from being sullied."

Yang Shangkun: "I agree. . . . We must protect Comrade Xiaoping's prestige."

Zhao Ziyang: "There are two main tasks before us. One is to persuade Comrade Xiaoping to change his characterization of the student movement; the other is to ask the Standing Committee to reconsider its resolution. What do you think? You and Comrade Xiaoping are old comrades-in-arms. What if you raise the issue with him? I'll work on the Standing Committee."

Yang Shangkun: "Let me think about it. You might have some trouble with the Standing Committee."

Zhao Ziyang: "There shouldn't be any problem with Qiao Shi and Hu Qili, but Yao Yilin and Li Peng might not be receptive."

Yang Shangkun: "I'll talk to Comrade Xiaoping. You know how he is: He might listen, but he might not. Anyway I'll try."

---

[4] *Tegong*, a system that provides low-cost food and other provisions to officials at the rank of vice premier and above.—Comp.

May 5–7

Students debate what to do

In response to the May 4 declaration of the AFS and Zhao's soft-line speech to the Asian Development Bank, students around the country returned to classes during the period May 5–7. The exceptions were students in Xining, who continued to boycott classes to protest a local news report, and students in Taiyuan, who were protesting a statement by a city official.

During that period the State Security Ministry filed reports on the situations on specific campuses in Beijing. On May 5 class attendance on some campuses was as high as 80 percent. At Peking University it was only 50 percent because students were involved in a debate over whether to continue the strike or to try to obtain dialogue with the government through official student organizations with the help of the school's Party Committee. At Beijing Normal University attendance was low because of the influence of Wuerkaixi, who had announced that the boycott of classes would continue.

On May 6 a rough voting procedure at Peking University showed that most students supported continuing to boycott classes. That afternoon the AFS held a meeting at Beijing Normal University and decided that the boycott would first continue at Peking University and Beijing Normal University and would then extend throughout the city but that for the time being, protest activities would be carried out only within the campuses. The group decided to approach the Stone Company[5] for assistance with printing costs. That afternoon four students delivered a "petition from the Dialogue Delegation of Beijing College Students" to the Letters and Visits Bureau of the General Offices of Party Central and the State Council, asking for a response by May 8. The petition asked for a public dialogue with Party and government officials on the student movement and on how to deepen economic and political reform.

On May 7 Wang Dan called for a continuation of the boycott of classes, arguing that this was necessary in order to support a petition that a group of reporters planned to deliver to the All-China Journalists' Association on May 9.

Foreign opinion continued to reflect sympathy for the students' effort to maintain pressure on the government. An example was a commendatory May 7 *Washington Post* portrait of Wang Dan and Wuerkaixi.

---

[5]Stone was a computer company located in the university district of Haidian and run by executives sympathetic to the students. Its chief executive officer, Wan Runnan, fled China after June 4 and became a leader of the Chinese democracy movement overseas. Activities by the director of its research institute, Cao Siyuan, are recounted in Chapter 7.

May 8

Politburo Standing Committee meets

On the morning of May 8 Zhao Ziyang chaired a meeting of the Politburo Standing Committee to hear reports on the student movement, to formulate strategies, and to begin a discussion of cleaning up government and building democracy. The meeting opened with reports on the status of the student movement by Li Ximing and Chen Xitong.

> Excerpts from Party Central Office Secretariat, "Minutes of the Politburo Standing Committee meeting," May 8

Li Ximing: "This clearly is a planned, organized conspiracy. Why is the situation at Peking University so explosive? Because Fang Lizhi and his wife, Li Shuxian, are orchestrating it from behind the scenes. The so-called Peking University democracy salon was organized with their support. Now the reactionary group Chinese Alliance for Democracy[6] has openly admitted that it has had a part in the movement. The U.S. Congress has even held hearings on student protests in China. Therefore, our most urgent tasks must be unity of thought and coordination of action. In the face of this political struggle, the Beijing Party Committee and the Beijing Municipal Government are determined to walk stride-for-stride with the Central government, and we hope the Center will provide guiding principles so that we can move quickly to keep the situation from getting out of hand."

Chen Xitong: "Over the past few days, the Beijing Party Committee and the Beijing Municipal Government have been put in a very awkward position. The people's reaction to Comrade Ziyang's speech to the Asian Development Bank was quite positive. But some comrades have expressed concern. Those at institutions of higher education, in particular, are at a loss about what to do. They say, 'The secretary's speech did not label student movement as 'turmoil,' nor did it confirm that evil elements are manipulating it from behind the scenes. The tone of the speech differed from that of the April 26 editorial, and this is confusing. Who are we supposed to follow?'"

Zhao Ziyang: "I take full responsibility for any mistakes in my Asian Development Bank speech.... This protest is the culmination of several evolving factors,

---

[6]The Chinese Alliance for Democracy (CAD) is an émigré pro-democracy organization founded in 1983 and based in the United States.

foreign and domestic. Its social causes are many and complex, but they include the following:

1. An unequal distribution of wealth in recent years has led to social polarization and to the emergence of a small group of very rich people that includes government officials and their sons and daughters. This has created doubts in many people's minds about the nature of our socialist system.

2. Mistakes in our work have led to a sharp decline in the trust the masses once had in our Party.

3. Inflation has lowered the living standards of the masses and led to widespread malaise. This is a main reason why these protests have exerted such a powerful mass influence. If we want to bring the protests to an end in a timely fashion and to solve some of the problems that concern the masses, we should show the people that we are hard at work on the issues of cleaning up government and building democracy."

Bo Yibo: "This movement is not an isolated incident involving just students. It has affected the normal life of society. The Beijing populace sympathizes with the students, and this tells us that the student slogans express feelings that the masses have. I think that what Ziyang proposes will win people's hearts. As the ancients said, 'Lead with virtue, awe with law,' and 'Those who rule with virtue will prosper; those who rule by force will perish.' I remember in the early years of our People's Republic how the Communist Party built its prestige on the foundation of clean, honest government. This had tremendous popular appeal. The Party really did 'seek happiness for the people'[7] back then. But over the past twenty years that glorious image of the Party has been tarnished by corrupt elements. They use their power for personal gain, wallow in corruption, and are obsessed with greed. It pains me just to think about it. If we're going to restore the Party's image, then I think we've got to start with clean government, and we *must* begin with the Center. This is the way to eliminate political turmoil from the ground up, to quiet the voices of discontent among the masses, and to achieve our goal of long and peaceful rule."

Qiao Shi: "We mustn't underestimate the dangerous conflicting interests that exist in society today, nor should we underestimate the complaints of the masses. This student movement shows us that if problems that concern large numbers of people are not properly resolved, social stability will be at risk. Now is the time to take concrete steps to clean up the government and to build democratic politics.

---

[7]A phrase describing Mao Zedong from the Cultural Revolution anthem "The East Is Red."

If we move boldly and can guide the masses skillfully, then the students' demands for reform, their support for the Communist Party (even if it is only perfunctory), and their underlying patriotism can all be channeled toward political reform, more vigorous democracy, clean politics, and the elimination of corruption. All this, in turn, will invigorate our young people's patriotism and fighting spirit."

Li Peng: "The State Council has decided to send a report on cleaning up and rectifying businesses to the Standing Committee of the NPC as soon as possible. We must resolve to rectify some of the large, influential companies that are linked to the children of high-ranking officials, and we should publicize the results of this rectification, punishing those who are guilty of misdeeds and clearing the names of those who are not. We have to do this if we're going to clean up government, and it will be a big step in restoring Party prestige in the eyes of the people."

Hu Qili: "I'm afraid some of the methods of leadership and political agitation that worked so well for our Party in the '50s, '60s, and '70s are no longer so effective. Take public opinion, for example. We really do have to increase transparency and openness in our press; if we don't, then never mind the common folk; the journalists themselves will have lots of complaints: that their articles can't express their true feelings or that they can't get published if they go too far in what they write. So we need to move quickly on press reform by discussing and presenting some press laws. And we should reform the political system, advancing concrete proposals that will show the people the Party is serious about promoting democracy. Beyond that, we should make an explicit announcement that we have established a system for high-ranking Party and government officials to publicize their personal wealth. These, too, are critical steps in cleaning up the government and restoring the image of the Party and the government."

Yang Shangkun: "Out there on the streets the students have been showing everyone something they call the 'official family chart' or sometimes the 'revolutionary connection chart.' It lists the children of officials who hold positions at the ministerial level and above. This chart has become infamous and is costing the government a lot in popular trust. Comrade Xiaoping was incensed when he heard about it. I've seen it, and it's partly correct, partly not. But it can do great damage to the prestige of the Party and government. I think we need to choose an appropriate moment to deal with this issue openly. But I also believe that the talented and honest children of high-ranking officials have as much right as anyone else with similar qualifications to serve in high positions. The rub is that we've got to guarantee the 'similar qualifications' part, because a lot of the people doubt we can do that. In our political reform we should set up a kind of systematic process for choosing and promoting officials assuring that the most able and the most honest are identified regardless of whether their parents are high officials or ordinary people. Currently we have no such system, and this, in fact, only holds the children of high-ranking officials up to popular ridicule and dishonor. Even if they accomplish a great deal in office, the masses will still believe they got their positions only because of their parents. So we also need to move quickly to set up a system for the open selection and appointment of officials."

Yao Yilin: "I have nothing to add except that I think this protest is far from over. Things may seem relatively quiet these days, but the students are busy planning their next moves and the people with ulterior motives are busy filling the students' heads with ideas. We're the ruling party, so it's our prerogative to accept opinion when it's good and reject it out of hand when it's bad. This movement has already consumed too much of our energies. The students are now using delaying tactics, but we can't delay with them. We can't afford to. If force is necessary, we should use it. We can't let these protests keep us from our regular work."

Zhao Ziyang: "I think we all agree with Comrade Yilin. We absolutely can't let the protests keep us from our regular work. Of course, in dealing with the movement we must still insist on a strict distinction between the majority of fervently patriotic students and the handful of people who are intent on exploiting the situation to fish in troubled waters, create conflict, and attack the Party and socialism. My preference is that we identify the concept of clean government as our primary reform of the political system and then link it intimately with democracy, law, openness, transparency, supervision by the masses, and popular participation. On clean government, my tentative suggestions are that the State Council report as soon as possible to the Standing Committee of the NPC on the matter of systematizing and rectifying businesses; that we make public the income and background of officials at the deputy minister rank and higher; that we cancel the special provisions privilege for members of the Politburo under the age of seventy-five or eighty; that we have the Standing Committee of the NPC set up a special committee to conduct independent investigations into the accusations against officials and their families; and, after broad-based discussions, that we formulate press laws, laws governing marches and demonstrations, and so on. I also propose that we place the contents of today's meeting on the agenda for a meeting of the full Politburo for further discussion so that we can come up with an even more comprehensive and effective program."

May 8–9

Conditions for returning to class

The State Security Ministry reported on May 8 that the Peking University student planning committee decided to continue the boycott of classes and announced five conditions for ending it: The government must withdraw the April 26 *People's Daily* editorial, recognize the legitimacy of the AFS, take measures against corruption, restore the position of cashiered *World Economic Herald* editor-in-chief Qin Benli, and reconsider Beijing's ten articles of regulation restricting marches and demonstrations.

When a group of four students representing the Dialogue Delegation went to the Letters and Visits Bureau of Party Central and the State Council to get a response to their petition for dialogue, a spokesman told them that the government was already conducting multilevel, multichannel dialogue with students and would continue to do so through school authorities and official student organizations.

On May 9 the State Security Ministry reported that students at several Beijing universities planned a bicycle demonstration to increase pressure on the government. The AFS expelled Zhou Yongjun, the student leader at the Chinese University of Political Science and Law, because he had made an unauthorized announcement that the boycott of classes was ending. In the wake of the controversy among student leaders over this action, Wang Dan gave a speech over the Peking University public-address system announcing that he was withdrawing from the student planning committee but would return if needed. Students should exercise the rights guaranteed by China's Constitution whether the government liked it or not, Wang said, and students should exercise their own democracy without interference from the university Party branch or administration.

Petition of 1,013 reporters

On May 9 two reporters delivered to the All-China Journalists' Association a petition from 1,013 journalists working for more than thirty official news organizations in Beijing.[8] The journalists wanted to discuss the *World Economic Herald* incident, their right to report the student movement accurately, and what they considered the false claim by government spokesman Yuan Mu that Chinese journalists already enjoyed freedom of the press. Nearly one thousand Beijing college students were present to support the petition.

[8]Text in Han Minzhu, ed., *Cries for Democracy: Writings and Speeches from the 1989 Chinese Democracy Movement* (Princeton: Princeton University Press, 1990), 190–192.

Also on May 9, Zhongnanhai received a report originally published in the New York *Asian-American Times* stating that Chinese journalist Liu Binyan, currently living in the United States, had announced plans to launch an independent magazine in the United States, to be called *China! China!*, which would report on developments in China without favoring any party.[9] Liu saw the current struggle as complicated but said he was optimistic for the long run because the student movement had exploded the myth that the Chinese people were incapable of rising up. Freedom of publication, said Liu, was something the Chinese had enjoyed before 1949, and the CCP had been wrong for forty years to deprive the people of it.

May 10

Opinions divide in the Politburo

On the morning of May 10 Zhao Ziyang chaired a Politburo meeting to discuss the student protests nationwide and the problems of building democracy and rooting out government corruption.

> Excerpts from Party Central Office Secretariat, "Minutes of the Politburo meeting," May 10

Zhao Ziyang: "Thanks to the extremely restrained and tolerant attitude of the Party and government, and thanks to the increasingly rational behavior of the students, who have become more orderly, we have avoided escalation so far. Most of the students are back in class, and things are better than we thought they would be. The protests are not yet over, of course, and there's still much we need to do. But maybe we can turn a bad situation to our advantage by leading the patriotic students and people into a new order that is both socialist and democratic."

Li Tieying: "As of yesterday, the protests around the country were still fairly muted. Students in Beijing, Tianjin, and Shanghai have for the most part confined their gatherings and marches to their campuses, doing so-called 'campus democratic construction.' This afternoon the AFS is going to hit the streets with a big student demonstration-by-bicycle."

Yang Shangkun: "How many students will do that?"

---

[9]The magazine was never published.

Li Ximing: "At least several thousands, we think. The police have been deployed."

Li Tieying: "It's worth noting that the cities that recently were most raucous have now calmed down, while some of the quieter cities—like Taiyuan, Lanzhou, Xining, and Haikou—are now getting stirred up. Yesterday five thousand students in Taiyuan sat in at the provincial government offices and demanded a dialogue with Wang Senhao."[10]

Li Peng: "I read a report on that. The demonstration was caused by dissatisfaction over a May 8 dialogue between provincial leaders and students. The students raised a ruckus from 10 P.M. the day before yesterday until 6 P.M. yesterday—twenty hours straight. They threatened that if their demands for more dialogue were not met, they would create an international incident by disrupting today's opening of the 'Two Conferences and One Festival.'[11] The General Office of the State Council has ordered the Shanxi Provincial Government to resist resolutely any expansion of the problem."

Li Tieying: "Yesterday in Lanzhou, three thousand students from five universities took to the streets to show their dissatisfaction with the five dialogues that students from each campus had had with provincial Party and government leaders. They demanded a unified dialogue with representatives from all the campuses together. Yesterday, when a deputy Party secretary and a vice governor went to Lanzhou University to talk with students, they responded with a sit-in in front of the Gansu provincial government offices. Lanzhou University closed its gate, but the students pulled the gate down and more came streaming out. About one thousand tried to storm the provincial building, but five rows of armed police blocked them and secured the gate. The students then began throwing bricks and bottles at the armed police. Four policemen were injured, and three were sent to the hospital; one received seven or eight stitches for a head wound. It is fortunate that the encounter did not get out of control. The ban against gatherings in front of the Gansu provincial building was lifted this morning. In Haikou a march by five hundred students at Hainan University, which lasted from yesterday evening until this morning, was touched off by bad food in the campus cafeteria. This shows that even a trivial matter can trigger a major incident."

Li Ximing: "Everyone here is aware of the situation in Beijing. Comrade Li

---

[10]Governor of Shanxi Province.
[11]Referring to the Shanxi International Trade Technology Conference, the Shanxi Cultural and Arts Festival, and the Shanxi Import and Export Merchandise Exhibition.—Comp.

Peng is better informed than I, so I'll just add two points: First, a number of intellectuals, as well as a smattering of foreigners, have gotten involved in the Beijing protests. The universities are strictly limiting entry by foreigners, but still lots of them turn up every day. Gorbachev will be here in a few days, and the movement's masterminds see this as a golden opportunity. Today's bicycle demonstration is just one of their gambits. We've got to stay very much on our toes."

Zhao Ziyang [looking at Li Ximing]: "Take care of your health."

Li Peng: "Ximing and other Beijing leaders haven't had a decent night's sleep in three weeks."

Li Ximing: "My second point is that we have to keep a close eye on the workers in Beijing. There are signs that they're getting involved in the disturbances. The most serious examples have come from the Beijing Mining Bureau, which reports that it has received ten petitions as of yesterday, including one delivered by 280 people. One-third of the six thousand members of mining families have participated so far."

Wan Li: "Who are these people?"

Li Ximing: "Mainly farmers turned miners, farmers living near the mines, and their family members. They're demanding higher wages, a resolution of their status as urban residents, and insurance programs for retirees. In the past few days three phone lines at the Beijing Mining Bureau have been cut, and local farmers blocked the south gate of the Fangshan Mine by building a wall of stones more than a meter high in front of it. On several occasions farmers working for the mines have broken into the dining hall and stolen grain. We're studying carefully and working hard on the problems of pay for family members and urban residency status for farmers who have taken up urban jobs."

Yang Shangkun: "We must make absolutely sure that this doesn't affect social stability. If the workers rise up, we're in big trouble. Especially while Gorbachev is here, we must be careful to let the people know that the Party and government are taking all of their reasonable demands seriously. We can't let the students and citizens get in the way of the Sino-Soviet summit."

Zhao Ziyang: "In addition to talking with students and journalists, we need to sit down with workers and listen attentively to what they say."

Li Ruihuan: "Let me say something about the situation in Tianjin. The students there always follow the students in Beijing, usually about half a step behind. Our stance toward them has been clear: You can have dialogue with us so long as you abide by the Constitution; we won't stop you from marching, but you can't disrupt social order. I've told them we will solve individual problems as they come up—seeking truth from facts. So the overall situation in Tianjin is normal; workers go to work as usual and citizens live normal lives. The point I'd like to make, though, is that we can't just attribute these protests to the death of Comrade Yaobang or to a tiny minority of instigators. In the forty years since the founding of our People's Republic, our Party has learned some painful lessons—in the Anti-Rightist Campaign,[12] the Cultural Revolution, and so on. From the looks of things now, another major political mistake might cost us all of our remaining popular support."

Bo Yibo: "Could you be more specific?"

Li Ruihuan: "I see several causes of these protests: First is a growing sense of dissatisfaction among students, combined with an increasing tendency to favor the notions of democracy, freedom, and human rights. Second is influence by Western thinking—radical reformism, liberalism, and nihilism. Third is the behind-the-scenes support they get from a tiny minority of liberal elements in China. Fourth is covert instigation by hostile foreign forces. For all these reasons, we very much need dialogue. We can't confront the students with inflammatory or antagonistic propaganda any more, and we mustn't use the 'anti-Party, antisocialist' label. Intellectuals and students have grown extremely sensitive to this label, and now, ironically, whoever gets it pinned on him immediately gains a lot of sympathy. We should take a sober look at what has caused the strong rebellious streak in the popular mood in recent times. We said there would be no inflation, then in fact inflation came—how could people *not* feel rebellious? After the last student protests[13] we expelled Liu Binyan and others from the Party, and it only enhanced their prestige; they suddenly became famous 'dissidents.' We shouldn't handle these people this way any more. It makes no sense just to arrest dissidents and hold them in prison. Instead, we should send them abroad and not let them come back for a certain amount of time."

Bo Yibo: "I agree with Comrade Ruihuan. Given China's great size, large population, and complex problems, only the Communist Party can marshal the nation's spirit for reform and opening. This fact should give us full confidence, as well as the ability, to put down the protests through peaceful means. We should

---

[12]In 1957 Mao Zedong launched a purge of about five hundred thousand officials and intellectuals as "rightists." Because work units (publishing houses, universities, hospitals, and so on) were obliged to uncover certain quotas of these "rightists" within their ranks, many persecutions and arrests were arbitrary. For more, see Mu Fu-sheng, *The Wilting of the Hundred Flowers* (London: Heinemann, 1962); and Merle Goldman, *Literary Dissent in Communist China* (Cambridge: Harvard University Press, 1967), ch. 9.

[13]In late 1986.

reaffirm the policy of the Third Plenum of the Eleventh Central Committee against holding any more political campaigns."[14]

Jiang Zemin: "The situation in Shanghai falls somewhere between those of Beijing and Tianjin. Things have calmed down in the past few days. We tried to estimate the probable fallout over the rectification of the *World Economic Herald,* but it turned out to be worse than our estimate."

Hu Qili: "The day after the *Herald* was rectified there was a big demonstration in Shanghai. Marchers were chanting 'Return our *Herald,*' calling for the reinstatement of Qin Benli, and demanding free speech. Wang Ruowang, Bai Hua,[15] and Qin Benli were marching in the front row."

Jiang Zemin: "It's not a totally bad thing when some of these liberal elements jump out in the public eye. The problem arises when students and some other intellectuals get drawn in. Mixing fish eyes and pearls makes our work harder."[16]

Zhao Ziyang: "The Shanghai Party Committee was hasty and careless in dealing with the *Herald;* it painted itself into a corner and turned a simple issue into a mess."

Jiang Zemin: "We followed Party principles scrupulously in the *Herald* matter. We focused on the big picture and drew a clear distinction between Party members and the general public. Qin Benli tried to deceive the Party Committee by feigning compliance. He violated the most fundamental Party regulations and deserved his punishment. The problem was that the press blew everything out of proportion. The Party Committee's position on the student movement has been absolutely clear: We will never allow protests to disrupt Shanghai's production routine or social order, will never permit the rise of illegal organizations, will ban all illegal demonstrations and marches, will forbid all forms of networking, and will dutifully carry out thought work and guidance among teachers and students. In particular, we will strive to win over the masses in the middle, to defuse confrontations, and to get things settled down as quickly as possible."

Zhao Ziyang: "In a huge country like ours it's impossible to expect that no problems will crop up. We'll always be facing one problem or another, but for the most part they won't be too serious."

---

[14]Society-wide campaigns against such things as corruption, waste, rightist thinking, and animal pests and in favor of land reform, farm collectivization, steel production, and other goals were an almost constant feature of China's Maoist years from 1949 to 1976. In 1978 the Third Plenum of the Eleventh Central Committee called for an end to such campaigns.

[15]Wang Ruowang and Bai Hua were liberal-leaning writers located in Shanghai.

[16]The Party would want to punish diehard liberal elements but not ordinary people drawn in spontaneously.

Yang Shangkun: "Ziyang's notion of pacifying the student movement through democracy and law is good and seems quite workable right now."

Li Peng: "I think the first step in pacifying the movement is to get students back into their classrooms. The sooner they go back, the better off society will be. Some colleges around the country are nearly in anarchy right now; wall posters that insult and slander Party and government leaders have appeared everywhere. There have been attempts to seize local power. Demonstrations, student strikes, and networking have cropped up all over the place. Students have stopped obeying campus rules and are thumbing their noses at local regulations about marches and demonstrations. And they call this democracy? This is freedom? How is this different from the Cultural Revolution? If we let it go this could pull our whole country into a morass of chaos. That's why the State Council has sent the Standing Committee of the NPC a draft proposal for a 'Statute on Assembly, Marches, and Demonstrations.'"

Wan Li: "It's already on our agenda."

Li Peng: "So although dialogue is important, we must never give the students the impression that we are encouraging their protests. We must take a clear stand and make not the slightest concession on matters of principle. Student demands for democracy should be accommodated only within the constraints of our national realities; we can only go slowly and methodically in accordance with our sanctioned procedures. We must not fall victim to emotion or lose perspective."

Yao Yilin: "I've always felt that we must take a clear stand on these protests. They are turmoil, pure and simple. We can't let the protests influence normal social order, we can't grant a dialogue every time the students demand one, and we can't agree with everything they say just because they point out mistakes in our work. We are the Communist Party, and the Communist Party serves the people. Our government is the people's government. We've got nothing to be ashamed of, and the whole world can see our tolerance and restraint."

Wu Xueqian: "Our embassies are reporting that many countries, particularly Western capitalist countries like the United States, England, and France, find our tolerance and restraint surprising, to say the least. Officials in some countries have told our embassy personnel privately that they think the students have gone too far."

Yao Yilin: "We must deal with the students as parents to children, being strict when necessary. We listen to them when they're right and rebuke them when they're wrong. I support the Standing Committee's opinion that this protest has consumed too much of our energy. The students have started to use delaying tactics, but we can't afford delay. When a forceful stand is called for, we must be forceful. These protests must not disrupt our normal routine."

Yang Rudai, Sichuan Party secretary, gave a brief account of the protests in Sichuan and then said:

Yang Rudai: "One reason why so many people cheer the marchers is that they are fed up with government corruption. They're pleading for the Center to adopt concrete and forceful measures to punish anyone involved in corruption."

Tian Jiyun: "The demand to punish corrupt officials has been a common cry throughout the protests, and it's a signal that we haven't done enough in this regard. All kinds of obstacles to economic reform that we have been encountering recently are rooted in our lack of progress with political reform. Inequitable distribution, rampant profiteering, and corruption have led to a serious decline in our Party's prestige. We need to take effective measures to clean up government and to accelerate our steps toward democracy."

Hu Qili: "Reform of the news media can play an important part in speeding up democratization. A critical press will help maintain the vitality and longevity of our Party and government. We must enact press laws that our journalists can rely upon and that will make it possible for them really to inform people of major events, to reflect public opinion about those events, and thus to help the public play a supervisory role."

Song Ping: "We really need to take some strong measures to halt corruption. The issue invariably arises in dialogues between officials and students. One student slogan in Shanxi, for example, said 'The Party Committee's office tower is the best in the nation, while the common people's average income is second to worst.' In yesterday's dialogue with officials from the Gansu Party Committee, a student raised the issue of 'Party secretary specialized households.'"[17]

Yao Yilin: "What's that mean?"

Song Ping: "He was referring to Li Ziqi, the Gansu Party secretary. According to the Central Organization Department, Li's wife is deputy director of Gansu Light Industry, and one of his sons just became mayor of Wuwei."

Qin Jiwei: "How common is this among province-level officials?"

Song Ping: "The Organization Department says that quite a few family mem-

---

[17] *Zhuanyehu,* or specialized households, were rural families who, under the reform policies, were allowed to go into business for themselves, often using former collective assets such as fish ponds, pigs, or orchards.

~~bers of the powerful are either in politics or in business. Li Ziqi's case is not~~ unique."

Qiao Shi: "Corruption could indeed have grave consequences for the Party and the nation. The corruption cases the Central Discipline Commission hears have been increasing in both number and severity every year, and they are clearly responsible for the rising tide of popular dissatisfaction. Comrade Ren Jianxin[18] tells me that the number of criminal cases nationwide has now reached eighty-two thousand per quarter, which is an increase of 15 percent over a year ago, and that many of those are corruption cases. If we don't tackle this problem head-on, the Party and the country are in real trouble."

Zhao Ziyang: "We must get to work punishing corruption immediately. My preliminary thoughts are that the Standing Committee of the NPC should hear reports on the cleanup and rectification of businesses and should also form a special committee to conduct independent investigations of high-ranking officials and their families who may be involved in corruption."

Wan Li: "I propose that the NPC Standing Committee form its own clean government committee."

Zhao Ziyang: "That's a wonderful suggestion, and the campaign against corruption should begin with me. My children should be the first to be investigated. If they're guilty, they should be punished, and the same goes for me if I am found to have any involvement. Then the Politburo should also lead by example and should publish the incomes and backgrounds of officials at the rank of deputy minister and higher and should cancel the special provisions for members of the Politburo under the age of seventy-five or eighty. We need to move on this now."

The meeting decided that Central leaders should hold discussions with various groups: Zhao Ziyang and Li Peng with workers; Hu Qili, Rui Xingwen, and Yan Mingfu (director of the Party's United Front Work Department) with journalists; and Li Tieying, Li Ximing, and Chen Xitong with students. Wan Li's visit to the United States and Canada should proceed as planned, and it was emphasized that detailed measures must be taken to ensure the safety of Gorbachev and the success of the Sino-Soviet summit.

---

[18]President of the Supreme People's Court.

Beijing bicycle demonstration

About ten thousand students from eleven Beijing universities, responding to calls from the AFS and the autonomous student organizations on the campuses, rode around Beijing on bicycles on the afternoon of May 10 distributing copies of their petition for dialogue and other printed materials. The students stopped at several major news organizations to shout slogans, ending up at the *People's Daily* before returning to their campuses. Reportedly some writers, including novelist Zheng Yi,[19] participated in this demonstration.

That evening some eight hundred students at People's University heard rousing speeches from *Guangming Daily* reporter Dai Qing and Chinese Academy of Social Sciences researcher Bao Zunxin, who welcomed the student movement as marking a new stage in China's search for democracy. Bao denounced the April 26 editorial for its Cultural Revolution–style thought and language.

The Beijing Party Committee reported that Muslim students at the Nationalities Academy were planning to demonstrate in Tiananmen Square on May 12 to protest publication of a book called *Xing fengsu* (Sexual customs). Published in March 1989 by the Shanghai Cultural Publishing House, it contained a discussion of Muslim sexual customs that many Chinese Muslims found objectionable.

An international event in Taiyuan is broken up

Student demonstrators in Taiyuan broke up a ceremony inaugurating an international economic technology conference, an import-export fair, and an art and culture festival. Their banners and slogans attacked the Provincial Party Committee for putting up a large office building that was out of keeping with Shanxi's poverty and the poor provincial funding for education. In the afternoon demonstrators broke into the conference site grounds; they were followed by onlookers. The total crowd was estimated to be about twenty thousand. The demonstrators shouted for dialogue with Governor Wang Senhao but were told he had already left.

Reports claimed that foreigners attending the two meetings were frightened. Many vacated their hotel rooms and demanded immediate airplane reservations out of town.

In the afternoon students demonstrating at the conference site joined students already sitting in at the provincial Party and government offices, where they shouted slogans against official cor-

---

[19]Zheng Yi, best known for his novel *Old Well* and his exposé of Cultural Revolution atrocities *Scarlet Memorial: Tales of Cannibalism in Modern China* (Boulder: Westview, 1996), was put on the wanted list after June 4. He escaped to Hong Kong and now lives in the United States.

ruption. Three attempts to break into the grounds were repulsed by the People's Armed Police. In the evening provincial government officials negotiated with student representatives and reached an agreement promising that the governor would meet with the students. Then the students returned to their campuses.

May 11

Deng Xiaoping and Yang Shangkun have a talk

Yang Shangkun and Deng Xiaoping, both from Sichuan, had a close relationship that dated to the 1930s, when they worked in the central Soviet area.[20] Their friendship deepened in the 1950s when they were confidants and allies while each held high Party posts in Beijing. Both were purged during the Cultural Revolution: Deng was exiled to Jiangxi, and Yang was labeled (along with Peng Zhen; Luo Ruiqing, former public security minister; and Lu Dingyi, former propaganda minister) part of "a four-shop anti-Party enterprise." Yang's fate was worse than Deng's. He was incarcerated much of the time, was repeatedly "struggled,"[21] and got little reprieve until Deng reemerged politically in 1978.

Deng accorded Yang full confidence immediately. He first sent him to be vice governor of Guangdong Province and then, in September 1980, brought him back to Beijing to fill a number of high posts in the government and military, eventually including that of deputy chairman and secretary general of the Central Military Commission, where he managed the routine affairs of the commission for Deng. In 1982 he joined the Politburo, and in 1988, with Deng's strong support, he became president of the People's Republic of China at age eighty-two. Deng was a comrade to his other peers—such as Chen Yun, Li Xiannian, and Peng Zhen—but to Yang he was a close friend. Even Wang Zhen, who was immaculately loyal to Deng, was never as close to him personally. And Hu Yaobang, Zhao Ziyang, and Wan Li, who were Deng's primary disciples in the 1980s, regarded him more as a mentor than a friend. Because of the special relationship between Yang and Deng, Yang could come and go from Deng's home at will, and he naturally became the intermediary whenever the Politburo needed instructions from the nominally retired senior leader.

Yang was also closer to Zhao Ziyang than to any of the other four members of the Politburo

---

[20]*Zhongyang Suqu*, meaning the Jiangxi Soviet, an area where the Chinese Communist forces under Mao established their rule.

[21]In "struggle" *(douzheng)*, the victim was usually placed alone at the center of animated crowd who began with hostile questions and taunts; often proceeded to spitting, slapping, and beating; and sometimes went as far as causing serious injury or death.

Standing Committee. Both had worked in Guangdong, and many of their views were similar. On the sensitive issue of the student protests, therefore, Yang's intermediary role was crucial.

On the afternoon of May 11 Yang Shangkun went to Deng Xiaoping's residence.

> Excerpt from memoranda of conversations supplied by a friend of Yang Shangkun who cannot be further identified

Yang Shangkun: "This student movement's a lot different from the one two years ago. This time the students have broad support—among teachers, journalists, even some officials. Their slogans say what a lot of ordinary people would like to say but don't, and that's where the broad appeal comes from. Recently universities across the nation have formed so-called autonomous student organizations, and an AFS in Beijing is now openly engineering the movement. On the whole, up till now, it seems the movement has broad popular support even while bourgeois-liberal extremists are actively exploiting it. It also seems infected with anti-Chinese Western forces and some counterrevolutionary organizations from Hong Kong and Taiwan."

Deng Xiaoping: "We've never run into this before—a small handful of bad people infiltrating the student population and the masses and stirring them up with their slogans against corruption. We're left fumbling over what to do. The students are forcing our hand, I'm afraid."

Yang Shangkun: "The reason the protest escalates is that people with ulterior motives are taking advantage of the strong popular distaste for corruption."

Deng Xiaoping: "When the people oppose corruption, of course we agree. Now, with operatives who have ulterior motives out there also opposing corruption, we still have to say that we agree, but of course we know that for them this is only a smoke screen. Their real aim is to topple the Communist Party and overthrow the socialist system."

Yang Shangkun: "The Standing Committee has already held some meetings about the student movement. Zhao Ziyang suggested that we settle things by democratic and legal means. The Politburo has also recommended that the NPC Standing Committee meet in June to study the major issues that the students have raised and that people are concerned about."

Deng Xiaoping: "What'd you think of Zhao Ziyang's Asian Development Bank speech?"

Yang Shangkun: "His tone was moderate, different from the basic tone of the April 26 *People's Daily* editorial. The response across the country was favorable.

In Beijing some of the students who had been boycotting went back to class. But reaction from other provinces and cities has been mixed. Beijing and Shanghai officials, for instance, have complained that by not stressing the turmoil issue—saying only that 'major turmoil will not appear in China'—Zhao set a different tone from that of the April 26 editorial. The editorial stressed the existence of black hands operating behind the scenes, and Ziyang only said this was 'of course hard to avoid'—a comment that puzzled a lot of people. Wang Zhen commented to me that 'Zhao Ziyang can do just about anything, but is one speech by him going to quell the protests?' I think Ziyang's speech has done something to cool the movement down, but it's hardly ended; it's just catching its breath."

Deng Xiaoping: "After Zhao's Asia Bank speech, Comrade Xiannian phoned to tell me that the Central Committee is speaking with two voices. Comrade Chen Yun also sent a message asking me to read Ziyang's speech. Some people, of course, found the speech persuasive and moving. I've been thinking about this question constantly the past few days: What's the best way to settle this thing?"

Yang Shangkun: "I met with Zhao Ziyang a few days ago, and he asked me to report some of his ideas to you. He thinks the April 26 editorial's choice of words about the student movement was unfortunate; it was too severe. He also said, 'There's a rumor going round about how someone is using Comrade Xiaoping as a shield in all this, and about how we should protect Comrade Xiaoping's image.' Zhao's feeling is that we should provide guidance for the movement and divide the great majority of students from the tiny minority of anticommunist trouble-makers, whom we should isolate. He hoped we would look for a chance to alter some of the judgments of the April 26 editorial."

Deng Xiaoping: "What'd the others on the Standing Committee think?"

Yang Shangkun: "He told me these things in private. He still hasn't mentioned them at Standing Committee or Politburo meetings. He thinks Qiao Shi and Hu Qili might agree with him, Li Peng and Yao Yilin probably not."

Deng Xiaoping: "I think Yao Yilin has the most clear-cut opinions and most determined attitude on the Standing Committee. The Politburo and the Standing Committee have to be firm when we're faced with major political issues. But we should, of course, do everything possible to settle this movement peacefully."

Yang Shangkun: "Gorbachev will be here in a few days. The leading group of the Central Foreign Affairs Committee wants a smooth visit, so they've made a detailed plan for it. The plan's been circulated to the Standing Committee. I've also given special orders to Wu Xueqian[22] to be sure your summit meeting with Gorbachev comes off without a hitch."

[22]Because he was the vice premier in charge of foreign affairs.

Deng Xiaoping: "When Gorbachev's here, we have to have order at Tiananmen. Our international image depends on it. What do we look like if the Square's a mess?"

Yang Shangkun: "Tiananmen is our national face. Especially when Gorbachev's here, we just can't let it turn into a stinking mess. I'll make sure they[23] are clear on this."

Deng Xiaoping: "What do you think of the different ways Shanghai, Tianjin, and Beijing are handling their protests?"

Yang Shangkun: "Beijing has taken the firmest stand. Li Ximing and Chen Xitong devote nearly every waking hour to the protests. They're terrified that they'll be held responsible if something disastrous happens. I heard Chen Xitong heave a sigh and say, 'Now I know how hard it is to be mayor of the capital.' I think their nerves have been stretched dangerously thin. It's no wonder some of their opinions are too harsh."

Deng Xiaoping: "It's not easy to stay cool under pressure."

Yang Shangkun: "Tianjin's done best at controlling the situation. Li Ruihuan's stance is clear: He says yes to dialogue, no to breaking the law. He allows student marches but not disruption of social order. He tells people to solve problems as they arise, seeking truth from facts. That's why Tianjin's in good shape. Li Ruihuan's pretty thoughtful."

Deng Xiaoping: "He knows philosophy and can think dialectically."

Yang Shangkun: "Shanghai's stance has been most clear-cut. Jiang Zemin was very direct in the *World Economic Herald* matter. I saw the report on how Shanghai dealt with the *Herald*. I know the Party Committee's decision was unanimous, but the whole thing stirred up a lot of strong reactions around the country and overseas, especially among journalists. Shanghai's taken a lot of heat. Personally I think Shanghai could have handled the matter more tactfully."

Deng Xiaoping: "Comrade Chen Yun told me after Jiang Zemin shook up the *Herald*, 'We should handle the student demonstrations the way Jiang Zemin would.' And Xiannian said, 'Jiang Zemin insists on the Four Principles but sticks with reform and opening up at the same time. He's got it just right politically, has strong Party loyalty, and can see the big picture.' Xiannian completely approves of Jiang's methods."

Yang Shangkun: "Jiang Zemin knows how to handle protests. I remember last time,[24] when Jiang Zemin spoke with students at Jiaotong University, he recited passages from Marx in English. Xiannian was so impressed that he ordered Party

[23]The leaders in charge.
[24]Meaning late 1986.—Comp.

work committees to arrange for all major units of the Central Government to watch videotapes of Jiang's talk. This really struck me."

Deng Xiaoping: "How's thought work going among the troops?"

Yang Shangkun: "Since the student movement began the General Political Department has put out four notices directing major military districts to work hard on the political thinking of both officers and soldiers, but without getting in any way involved with local governments' handling of the protests. If local governments need the help of the military in restoring order after any beating, smashing, and robbing, they have to get permission directly from the Central Military Commission. The military is taking political education very seriously. Some military districts have even arranged dialogues between officers and soldiers, and these are well targeted and very effective. The thinking of the leading groups at the seven military regions and three headquarters departments is all in line; there are no signs of disunity."

Deng Xiaoping: "The three of us—you, me, Zhao Ziyang—need to have a good talk."

May 11–12

The idea of a hunger strike is born

State Security Ministry reports on May 11 and 12 drew attention to some alarming trends among students in Beijing. On May 11 a group of graduate students at Peking University posted a notice proposing that students conduct a hunger strike, time and place to be determined, and occupy Tiananmen Square to greet Gorbachev when he arrived in Beijing on May 15. At a meeting attended by about four hundred students and some thirty foreign reporters, the student planning committee at Peking University announced that the headquarters of AFS was moving to Peking University and that it would launch a campaign to gather signatures for an invitation to Gorbachev to come to the university to speak.

On the public-address system, students debated how to use Gorbachev's visit to promote their cause, in view of the fact that he had led Soviet political reform so much further than the Chinese leaders had taken their own political reform. The campus public-address system broadcast word that student delegations from Tianjin and Shanghai were coming to Beijing—the former group to welcome Gorbachev and demand government dialogue, the latter to press the issue of Qin Benli, the *World Economic Herald,* and press freedom. The AFS posted sign-up sheets on several major campuses for students willing to start a hunger strike at noon on May 13 on behalf of freedom of the press, student-government dialogue, and democratization. Evidently, the AFS intended to use Gorbachev's visit to reinvigorate the pro-democracy movement and intensify pressure on the government.

On May 12 about two hundred students on bicycles showed up at the Journalists' Association to express support for journalists they believed were holding a dialogue with government spokesman Yuan Mu. In fact, Yuan had held a press conference and had already left by the time the students arrived.

In the afternoon Bao Zunxin spoke to an audience of about four hundred students at Peking University. He praised the students' discipline and the clarity of their goals, called for the reversal of the April 26 editorial, and said the only way to avoid reprisals was to persist until full victory was achieved. The students and intellectuals should cooperate to this end.

Nationwide Muslim protests

On May 12 Muslim students and citizens demonstrated in Beijing, Hohhot, Lanzhou, and Xining against *Sexual Customs*. The Public Security Ministry issued an urgent notice telling the authorities in the four localities to deal with the demonstrations on a combat-ready basis and to keep the Muslim movement strictly separate from the student movement.

In Lanzhou, more than twenty thousand excited demonstrators overturned a truck, beat a driver, burned copies of the book, and demanded the death sentence for the authors. Three hundred Muslims clashed with PAP soldiers guarding the provincial government complex. They injured 115 of the troops and broke into the courtyard, where they damaged the reception room but were prevented from entering the main building. Thirty-two demonstrators were arrested and found to be heavily armed.[25] The city had never in memory seen such a large demonstration, or an event uniting so many parts of the Muslim community.

In Xining about ten thousand Muslims marched on the provincial government building. The crowd was orderly and did not clash with the PAP troops. Government officials met with some representatives of the crowd, who then reported back that the government sympathized with the demonstrators, considered *Sexual Customs* a bad book, would report the demonstrators' opinions to the Center, and would give a further response within three days.

In Hohhot municipal Party and government officials held dialogue with representatives of some five hundred demonstrators who were sitting in at the intersection in front of their offices. The demonstrators could not understand how the government allowed the publication of a work

---

[25]In a Chinese context this refers to weapons like knives and bricks rather than guns.

that was so damaging to relations among the country's ethnic groups. They asked not only that the authors and the responsible editor be sentenced to death but that the publisher be made to apologize to the Muslim community through the official media.

In Beijing about a thousand Muslim students demonstrated, with a permit from the Public Security Bureau. They demanded that the Party protect their constitutional right of religious belief by punishing the authors of what they considered to be an insulting book. Joined by several hundred more students, they delivered petitions to the Chinese Islamic Association and to government religious affairs offices. Finally, they approached the Great Hall of the People via Tiananmen, where, surrounded by some thirty thousand to forty thousand onlookers, they handed a petition to the director general of the NPC's Letters and Visits Bureau. He promised that it would be promptly delivered to the relevant leaders.

"A turning point"

Of twenty-seven reports on foreign media sent to Zhongnanhai on May 11 and 12, most celebrated the students' idealism and anticipated that their actions would accelerate the decline of old-fashioned authoritarianism. Robert Delfs in the *Far Eastern Economic Review* called the events a turning point in Chinese history. Zhao Ziyang now had an opportunity to push forward peaceful reform with the support of students and intellectuals. The risk was that the soft response to the students would encourage other dissatisfied groups, such as workers and farmers, to adopt confrontational tactics.

Authorizing a liberal press policy

On the afternoon of May 12 Wan Li, the chairman of the Standing Committee of the National People's Congress, departed for a planned twenty-one-day state visit to Canada and the United States. He considered shortening the trip, but Zhao Ziyang told him it was not necessary.

Over the course of three days—from May 11 through May 13—top Party officials in charge of propaganda held a series of dialogues with journalists at news organs throughout the capital and at the Party's United Front Work Department. A consensus emerged on several points: The students' motives were good even if their methods were immature, and the Center should undertake dialogue with them. The safety-valve role of the press should be developed by allowing it to report more fully on problems in society. Coercive methods such as those suggested by the April 26 editorial would not resolve the student movement; instead, the government should deal with the issues that caused the movement. The press system should be pluralized so that the Party and government controlled its own newspapers directly and other major papers indirectly but allowed private papers to operate on a commercial basis under their own boards of directors. This system should be embodied in a Press Law that should first be subjected to public discussion and then be adopted by the National People's Congress.

In the course of these meetings Hu Qili and Rui Xingwen informed the news workers that Zhao Ziyang favored far-reaching press reforms to achieve the goals of objective, truthful reporting. The two of them and Yan Mingfu expressed their support for this goal, believing that the present crisis offered an opportunity to move decisively toward fuller, more truthful reporting. Both stressed that from now on questions of layout—showing which stories are most important—should be decided by editors, not Party officials.[26]

May 13

A three-way conversation: Deng, Zhao, and Yang

On the morning of May 13 Zhao Ziyang and Yang Shangkun went to Deng Xiaoping's home and reported on their recent work. This was the first time Zhao had seen Deng since the Hu Yaobang memorial. Deng's conversation two days earlier with Yang had given Deng a clearer understanding of Zhao's position. Zhao was still unclear about Deng's view of the April 26 editorial.

After some pleasantries about Deng's health and some comments on the situation in North Korea, they came to the point. Taking up where the conversation between Deng and Yang had left off, Zhao explained the positions he had taken at several Politburo meetings.

> Excerpt from memoranda of conversations supplied by a
> friend of Yang Shangkun who cannot be further identified

Zhao Ziyang: "Comrade Xiaoping, first I'd like to report to you on some of my thinking since the student movement and turmoil began. The student movement has mushroomed since mid-April; what all of us, including me, have been trying to do is to settle it down as quickly as possible. But I've noticed that this movement has two particular features we need to pay attention to: First, the student

---

[26]Until that time, editors had to ask permission and approval from Party organs before determining which stories to run as "lead" and "second lead" in the layout of newspapers and in order of presentation on television.

slogans all support the Constitution; they favor democracy and oppose corruption. These demands are basically in line with what the Party and government advocate, so we cannot reject them out of hand. Second, the number of demonstrators and supporters is enormous, and they include people from all parts of society. So I think we have to keep an eye on the majority and give approval to the mainstream view of the majority if we want to calm this thing down."

Deng Xiaoping: "It was obvious from the start that a tiny minority was stirring up the majority, fanning the emotions of the great majority."

Zhao Ziyang: "That's why I think we have to separate the broad masses of students and their supporters from the tiny minority who're using the movement to fish in troubled waters, stir up trouble, and attack the Party and socialism. We have to rely on guidance. We have to pursue multilevel, multichannel dialogue, get in touch with people, and build understanding. We mustn't let the conflicts get nasty if we expect things to settle down quickly."

Deng Xiaoping: "Dialogue is fine, but the point is to solve the problem. We can't be led around by the nose. This movement's dragged on too long, almost a month now. The senior comrades are getting worried. Chen Yun, Peng Zhen, Xiannian, Wang Zhen, and Sister Deng[27]—and me too—are all worried. We have to be decisive. I've said over and over that we need stability if we're going to develop. How can we progress when things are in an utter mess?"

Yang Shangkun: "Gorbachev will be here in two days, and today I hear that the students are going to announce a hunger strike. They obviously want to turn up the heat and get a lot of international attention."

Deng Xiaoping: "Tiananmen is the symbol of the People's Republic of China. The Square has to be in order when Gorbachev comes. We have to maintain our international image. What do we look like if the Square's a mess?"

Yang Shangkun: "The protests keep going, and now the students are starting a hunger strike. I'm afraid this major state event is going to get disrupted. Visits by heads of state are big events; all countries take them seriously. And the two sides have gone over every detail of Gorbachev's visit in advance. We must ask the students and the residents of Beijing to help us be sure everything goes forward as planned. That's something anybody with the slightest amount of patriotism should be able to accept. But I do wonder if it's going to be possible to have this welcoming ceremony as we planned it—there in the open Square, at the east entrance of the Great Hall of the People."

---

[27] *Deng Dajie*, that is, Deng Yingchao.

Zhao Ziyang: "To welcome Gorbachev in the right place and the right way involves the country's honor. I think the vast majority of students will realize this, see the big picture, and not disrupt the welcoming ceremony. I think these young students can understand this. The Beijing government and the SEC have already explained its importance to them."

Deng Xiaoping: "But if the students get carried away with extremism, they won't think of all this."

Yang Shangkun: "Still, we'll proceed as planned."

Zhao Ziyang: "I'll stress the importance of the Gorbachev visit one more time in the media this afternoon."

Deng Xiaoping: "As I've said before, the origins of this incident are not so simple. The opposition is not just some students but a bunch of rebels and a lot of riffraff, and a tiny minority who are utterly against opposing bourgeois liberalization. These people want to overthrow our Party and state. With this small handful mixed in with so many students and masses our work becomes much harder. We have to understand the complexities here; this is not just between the students and the government."

Zhao Ziyang: "The consensus in the Politburo has been to use the policies of guiding and dividing, winning over the great majority of students and intellectuals while isolating the tiny minority of anticommunist troublemakers, thereby stilling the movement through democratic and legal means. In order to get things going, Politburo members have already begun dialogues with various groups. This morning Li Peng is going to Capital Iron and Steel,[28] and this afternoon I'm meeting with representatives of Beijing workers. In the next few days Hu Qili's people will be talking with journalists, and—"

Deng Xiaoping: "What do the ordinary people in society think?"

Zhao Ziyang: "The protests are widespread but limited to cities that have universities. The rural areas aren't affected, and the farmers are docile. So are urban workers, basically. The workers are unhappy about certain social conditions and like to let off steam from time to time, so they sympathize with the protesters. But they go to work as usual and they aren't striking, demonstrating, or traveling around like the students."

Yang Shangkun: "The thinking in the army is fully in line with the Central Committee and the Central Military Commission. These protests are not going to spread to officers or soldiers in the military."

[28]A large, state-owned model enterprise with a strong Communist Party organization.

Deng Xiaoping: "This whole outbreak should lead us to think about things, to take a hard look at the past. I've told foreigners that our biggest mistakes of the past ten years have been in education. What I meant, mainly, was political education—not just in schools or for the young but for society in general. We haven't done enough in this area, and that was a huge oversight. These last few days I've been thinking. We've been right all along that the Four Basic Principles and the policies of reform and opening are mutually beneficial. If there's been a mistake, it's that we've been lax about the Four Basic Principles. We haven't used them as the foundation in educating the people, the students, and all the Party members and officials. We have to insist on both things at once; we can't ignore the political side. We must not give an inch on the basic principle of upholding Communist Party rule and rejecting a Western multiparty system. At the same time, the Party must resolve the issue of democracy and address the problems that arise when corruption pops up in the Party or government."

Zhao Ziyang: "The Party has to adjust to new times and situations. We have to do a good job with political education but then use the methods of democracy and law to solve actual problems. You have always emphasized the need for more transparency in political life, for a full use of the NPC's supervisory role, for more and better use of the system of political consultation and Communist-led cooperation with the democratic parties,[29] for more popular oversight of the Party and the government, and so on. These principles are extremely important, especially now. When we allow some democracy, things might look 'chaotic' on the surface; but these little 'troubles' are normal inside a democratic and legal framework. They prevent major upheavals and actually make for stability and peace in the long run."

Yang Shangkun: "We have to separate legitimate demands for democracy, including proper exercise of democratic rights, from bourgeois liberalization. We can't let people promote bourgeois liberalization under the banner of democracy; and on the other hand, when we crack down on bourgeois liberalization, we have to be sure we don't squash democracy."

Zhao Ziyang: "When you raise the banner of democracy and law, you win the hearts of the people. It has great appeal to the masses and brings them together. I remember Comrade Xiaoping saying in 1984 that it's an important task of Party leadership to lead the people in building democracy and a legal system, so that our socialist country can be justified in calling itself a nation of laws. I think we

---

[29]Here, "democratic parties" refers to eight small noncommunist parties that remained in China after 1949 but that have been entirely subservient to Communist Party rule.

should grab the chance to build a socialist democratic system that suits China's unique circumstances. We should do it in a planned, paced, and orderly fashion, under Party leadership and based on the Four Principles."

Yang Shangkun: "We're just going to have to do everything we possibly can to beat corruption, to get rid of it. The people are gnashing their teeth at the very mention of corruption these days. They can't wait to see another embezzler get exposed."

Zhao Ziyang: "No doubt about it, getting rid of corruption is the most urgent task before us. The people are watching us, waiting to see if we really mean what we say. The Politburo's been considering whether to make clean government a major goal in the political reform plans—tying it in with democracy, a legal system, openness, transparency, supervision by the masses, and mass participation—and adopting some specific measures and procedures that really will solve the problem once and for all. The fight for clean government and against corruption has to start with the Politburo, and I've already asked the Politburo to kick things off by investigating my children. If they've been corrupt, then they must submit to the laws of the state. Wan Li has also proposed that the Standing Committee of the National People's Congress set up a special 'clean government committee.'"

Deng Xiaoping: "We need to tackle the corruption issue head-on, take on at least ten or twenty major cases, and handle them with a high degree of transparency. We must seize this chance to solve the corruption problem. Recently I've been thinking about why we've had such a hard time solving this problem so far, and I've concluded that it's probably because so many high-ranking officials and their families are involved. This may well be the reason why so little has been accomplished, even though we've been talking about it for years. We can't put this off any longer. In this movement, there haven't been any slogans opposing reform or opening up. Most have homed in on corruption. Of course, this could be a smoke screen for inciting the people to other things. But that doesn't change the fact that we need to rectify the Party and achieve our strategic goals. If we don't punish corruption, especially when it's in the Party, we're really courting disaster. . . . The Standing Committee has got to be decisive, and it has to stick with principle, when we're faced with a political crisis like this. And of course we must do everything possible to resolve this student movement peacefully."

This three-way talk produced little of substance, but at least it showed that Deng Xiaoping trusted Zhao Ziyang. This evidence of trust contradicts claims at the Fourth Plenum of the Thir-

teenth Central Committee in June 1989, when Zhao Ziyang was formally stripped of power, that Zhao's and Deng's views had been directly opposed from the start. Deng did not mention the April 26 editorial in this conversation, nor did he specifically point out what to do next. He seemed to hope only that Zhao would come up with a solution—almost any solution—that could end the movement quickly and effectively.

Zhao Ziyang and Li Peng meet with workers

While Deng, Yang, and Zhao were meeting at Deng's house, Li Peng went to Capital Iron and Steel and spoke with workers there. Many of the workers expressed sympathy for the students' goals in opposing corruption and inflation, one suggesting that the government should hold regular discussions with various sectors of society. Li Peng responded that the government was researching methods to institutionalize dialogue through appropriate channels. It had initiated a temporary economic slowdown in order to get economic and associated social problems under control. And it would soon announce concrete measures against corruption, including action on specific cases.

That afternoon Zhao Ziyang, together with Qiao Shi, Hu Qili, and Yan Mingfu, met with representatives of Beijing workers in the Great Hall of the People. Zhao had already learned that the students had started their hunger strike in Tiananmen Square. Realizing that his promise to Deng Xiaoping that this would not happen had been too optimistic, he was under great pressure to resolve the situation before Gorbachev's visit. So his remarks to the workers dwelt almost exclusively on the importance of the summit and the need for all patriotic Chinese to help guarantee its success and do nothing to damage China's national image. He stated that the legitimate demands of the students were of concern to the leaders as well and that concrete measures would be introduced at the scheduled June meeting of the NPC Standing Committee to resolve some of these problems. In response to one worker's question, Zhao said the leaders still relied on Deng Xiaoping and the other Elders for key decisionmaking.

After this meeting, Zhao met with Yang Shangkun, Li Peng, Qiao Shi, and other officials in Zhongnanhai to review the situation of the demonstrations. The student hunger strike and invitation to Gorbachev incensed the leaders, who decided to send Yan Mingfu, and if necessary, Li Tieying, Li Ximing, and Chen Xitong, to urge the students to call off the strike. Meanwhile, they resolved to move Gorbachev's welcoming ceremony from the East Gate of the Great Hall of the People, on Tiananmen Square, to the Beijing airport.

The hunger strike begins

Letters and Visits Bureau of Party Central and the State Council, "Reception report" (*Jiedai jianbao*), May 13

At 2 A.M. on May 13 the Letters and Visits Bureau of Party Central and the State Council received another demand from the Beijing AFS for dialogue with Party and government leaders, and at 8 A.M. that day a functionary named Zheng Youmei conveyed the agreement of Party Central and the State Council. The students wanted the number of students in the dialogue to be increased from twenty to two hundred. Zheng resisted, pointing out, "Dialogue is serious business; we cannot just change its terms on whim." The students said government refusal to increase the size of the student delegation would be a sign of bad faith. After the students left, Zheng informed the Xinhua News Agency that government representatives would meet with the students on May 15.

Later that morning the AFS posted a "Declaration of a Hunger Strike" and a "Manifesto for a Hunger Strike" at Peking University, Beijing Normal University, and the Chinese University of Political Science and Law.[30]

Original handbills provided by the Public Security Ministry to Party Central and the State Council, May 13

DECLARATION OF A HUNGER STRIKE

In this bright, sunny month of May, we have begun a hunger strike. During the glorious days of our youth, we have no choice but to abandon the beauty of life. Yet how reluctant, how unwilling we are!

The nation is in crisis—beset by rampant inflation, illegal dealings by profiteering officials, abuses of power, corrupt bureaucrats, the flight of good people to other countries, and deterioration of law and order. Compatriots, fellow countrymen who cherish morality, please hear our voices!

[30]Translated in Michel Oksenberg, Lawrence R. Sullivan, and Marc Lambert, eds., *Beijing Spring, 1989, Confrontation and Conflict: The Basic Documents* (Armonk, New York: M. E. Sharpe, 1990), 258–260; Han, *Cries for Democracy*, 199–202; and in part in Suzanne Ogden, Kathleen Hartford, Lawrence Sullivan, and David Zweig, eds., *China's Search for Democracy: The Student and the Mass Movement of 1989* (Armonk, New York: M. E. Sharpe, 1992), 213–214.

The country is our country.

The people are our people.

The government is our government.

Who will shout if not us?

Who will act if not us?

Though our shoulders may be frail, though we are too young to die, we must leave, we have no choice. History demands this of us.

Our genuine patriotic fervor and peerless loyalty are dismissed as "turmoil." We have been accused of harboring "ulterior motives," and of "being exploited by a small handful of people."

We ask all honorable Chinese—workers, farmers, soldiers, ordinary citizens, intellectuals, celebrities, government officials, police, and the people who have fabricated the charges against us—to put your hands over your hearts and examine your consciences. Of what crime are we guilty? Are we really causing turmoil? We leave our classrooms, we march, we go on a hunger strike, we sacrifice our very lives. Yet our feelings are trifled with time after time. We endure hunger in our pursuit of the truth—for which we are beaten by the police. When our representatives kneel down to plead for democracy, they are ignored. Our demands for dialogue on equal terms are met with interminable delays. The safety of our student leaders is at risk.

What are we to do?

Democracy is the noblest human aspiration; freedom is a sacred human right, granted at birth. Today both must be bought with our lives. Is this fact something the Chinese people can be proud of?

This hunger strike has been forced upon us. We have no choice.

It is by a readiness to die that we struggle for life.

But we are children, still children! Mother China, look at your children. Hunger is destroying our youth. Can you not be moved when you see death approach us?

We do not want to die. We want to live, and live fully, because we are in the prime of our lives. We do not want to die; we want to learn all we can. Our nation is wretchedly poor. We don't have the heart to abandon our homeland through death. That is not what we seek. But if the death of a single person or of several people will enable a greater number of people to live better, or if these deaths can make our homeland stronger and more prosperous, then we have no right to live on in ignominy.

Do not feel sorry for us, mothers and fathers, as we suffer from hunger. Do not feel sad, uncles and aunts, when we bid farewell to life. Our only desire is that the

Chinese people enjoy better lives. We have but one request: Please do not forget that we did not seek death. Democracy is not the concern of only a few, and the building of democracy cannot be accomplished in a single generation.

It is through death that we await a sweeping and eternal echo.

When a person is about to die, he speaks from his heart. When a bird is about to die, its cry is most plaintive.

Farewell, friends, take care. Loyalty binds the living to the dead.

Farewell, loved ones, take care. We don't want to leave you, but we must.

Farewell, mothers and fathers, please forgive us. Your children cannot be loyal citizens and worthy children at the same time.

Farewell, countrymen, let us repay our country in the only way left to us.

May the pledge that we write with our lives clear the skies in our republic.

MANIFESTO FOR A HUNGER STRIKE

Dear countrymen, following up on our momentous demonstrations, today we resolve to begin a hunger strike in Tiananmen Square.

Our reasons are:

1. To protest the government's indifference toward our boycott of classes;
2. To protest the government's labeling our patriotic, democratic student movement as "turmoil," and many distorted press reports.[31]

We demand of the government:

1. Immediate dialogue—concrete, substantive, and on equal terms—with the Dialogue Delegation of Beijing College Students.
2. A fair and unbiased acknowledgment of the legitimacy of the student movement, labeling it "patriotic" and "democratic."

Time for commencement of the hunger strike: 2 P.M., May 13.

Location: Tiananmen Square.

Battle cries:

"This is not turmoil. We demand redress!"

"Immediate dialogue! No more delays!"

"Fasting for the people—we have no choice!"

"International public opinion, please come to our aid!"

"World press, please support us!"

"Democratic forces, please stand by us!"

---

[31]The text translated by Han, *Cries for Democracy*, lists this as reason 3, while 2 is "to protest the government's foot-dragging in arranging dialogue." Apparently different versions of the document circulated.

At 9:30 A.M. the student planning committee at Peking University announced a plan for a hunger strike.

HUNGER STRIKE PLAN

1. At 11:30 A.M., monitors will muster at the south gate.
2. At noon, the hunger strikers will proceed to Beijing Normal University. At 1 P.M. they will take oaths at a rally and place telephone calls to Chinese and foreign correspondents, Chinese and international Red Cross organizations, and foreign governments.
3. Discipline: No intake of food is permitted except for water and soft drinks. Chocolate and other foods shall not be consumed by any participant.

> State Security Ministry, "On May 13 Peking University students swear an oath to go on hunger strike," report to Party Central and the State Council, May 13

A plea for emergency donations was posted on the bulletin board at the south gate of Peking University. Donations were sought from teachers and students for a "departure lunch" for striking students at Yanchun Garden.

At 10:30 A.M. about 160 students wearing white headbands gathered outside Peking University's Building 29 to take an oath as the Peking University Hunger Strike Group. The oath read:

> I solemnly swear that, in order to promote democracy in the motherland and to bring prosperity to the country, I will go on a hunger strike. I resolve to obey the rules of the hunger strike group and will not break my fast until we have achieved our goals.

The striking students then enjoyed a "departure meal" that young teachers from Peking University hosted at Yanchun Garden. A banner from the Peking University Writers' Group that read "Heroes are departing, we await their return" hung inside the restaurant. The striking students took group photos in front of the banner.

At 12:20 P.M. about four hundred members of the Peking University Hunger Strike Group (including monitors, first-aid personnel, propaganda workers, and logistics staff in addition to the 160 who had signed the oath) set out for Beijing Normal University, where striking groups from other universities were to assemble before leaving for Tiananmen Square.

At 3:25 P.M. roughly two hundred striking students entered Tiananmen Square from Chang'an West Boulevard carrying banners that read "Uphold the Constitution. Give us back justice!" "Respect education. Give us back our campuses," "The *Herald* is blameless. Benli is innocent," while shouting the slogans "We demand dialogue!" "Freedom to march!" and "Down with government corruption!" After circling the Square, they formed a circle north of the Monument to the People's Heroes, with monitors keeping outsiders away.

Official reports said that when onlookers asked the students, "Didn't you already have a dialogue with the government?" the students answered, "Yuan Mu and his group just beat around the bush, refusing to answer our questions. They were not sincere." Other students said, "Those delegates didn't represent us. If we'd been there, they'd have been hard put to answer our questions!"

At 4:10 P.M. another group of two hundred to three hundred students wearing white headbands entered the Square on bicycles shouting slogans: "Dialogue now, no more delays!" "Down with corruption, starting with the Central Government, and starting now!" "Down with policies that keep the people ignorant!" and "Freedom of the press!" About fifteen minutes later, another thousand or so students entered the Square carrying banners that read, "Hunger strike—we have no choice!" "We won't eat fried democracy!"[32] "Hunger strike—demand dialogue!" "Hunger is bearable; lack of democracy is not!" "Weep for democracy; grieve for the hunger strike," and so on. The Square filled with banners from twenty to thirty schools, including Peking University, Qinghua University, Beijing Normal University, and the Shanghai Hunger Strike Petition Group.

Demonstrators raised a banner reading "Hunger Strike" in front of the Monument to the People's Heroes. A student with a bullhorn read a brief declaration from the AFS:

> The primary goal of this action is to oppose corruption and nepotism[33] in the Party and in society at large. The government has consistently procrastinated on dialogue with students, so we have decided on our own to come to Tiananmen Square for a hunger strike as a means of appeal and protest.

The student announced that signatures were being gathered at universities to demand a meeting with Gorbachev. Next a student leader read the "Declaration

---

[32]The meaning of the phrase is obscure. A leader of the Tiananmen demonstrations told us it meant that students were so determined not to eat that they would not break their hunger strike even for something as delicious as fried democracy. But another participant thought it meant they would not tolerate fake democracy.

[33]Specifically *qundai guanxi*, "connections through female relatives."

of a Hunger Strike," and at 5:40 P.M. the strike began. Some students handed out photocopies of photographs and shouted, "Here is the true picture of the April 20 atrocity when police beat students! See with your own eyes what the government calls tolerance and restraint." Crowds reached greedily for the handouts.

At 6 P.M. three student leaders from the AFS—Wang Dan, Wang Chaohua, and Ma Shaofang[34]—held a press conference for foreign and domestic journalists on the steps of the west entrance to the Museum of Chinese History. They announced that "the students are determined not to quit this hunger strike until their goals are reached."

At 8 P.M. Yan Mingfu, chief of the Party's United Front Work Department, met with Liu Xiaobo, Zhou Duo,[35] Wang Chaohua, Wang Dan, Wuerkaixi, Chai Ling, Ma Shaofang, and other college teachers and AFS delegates, all of whom sat at the session separately from each other.

> Excerpts from Party Central United Front Work Department, "Director Yan Mingfu meets with a group of college teachers and student representatives from AFS and other groups," in "Important intelligence report" (*Yaoqing baogao*), May 14

Yan Mingfu: "Party Central affirms the mainstream of this movement. We are reviewing all reasonable student demands in order to form workable strategies and measures for resolving the issues. Naturally, you must not expect results overnight. You students should know that the Standing Committee of the NPC has put many of your most pressing issues on the agenda for its meeting in late June. This shows how determined we are to solve these problems according to democracy and law. It is perfectly understandable that you have various opinions and complaints. This is normal."

The following exchange took place between Yan Mingfu and a student who represented the hunger strikers:

Student: "The government must accept the forty students whom the AFS has named to participate in the dialogues and must broadcast the dialogue live."

[34]Wang Chaohua was a Ph.D. student in Chinese literature at the Chinese Academy of Social Sciences. Ma Shaofang was a student the Beijing Film Academy.
[35]Zhou Duo is head of the General Planning Department of the Stone Company and formerly a lecturer in the Institute of Sociology at Peking University.

Yan Mingfu: "I'll pass your request on."

Student: "If the government does not agree, it will be very hard for all the hunger strikers to end the strike and return to school."

Yan Mingfu: "The situation has developed into something more than what originated in your good intentions at the beginning, and you are no longer in control of what is happening. A hunger strike accomplishes nothing, either for the country or for your own health. If you present your demands and suggestions through proper channels, I can responsibly tell you the door to dialogue is always open. It is essential that you remain rational, keep the big picture in view, and uphold the dignity and interests of the nation."

Yan Mingfu closed the meeting by saying:

Yan Mingfu: "At a time when the leaders of China and the Soviet Union are about to hold a summit meeting, you should be particularly concerned about upholding the dignity of the nation and should cease all disruptive activities. If you do not, you will lose the sympathy and support of the people. Please try to talk some sense into the students who are hunger striking in the Square."

But Yan Mingfu's exhortation fell on deaf ears. After the meeting Yan briefed Zhao Ziyang:

> Account drawn from *Materials for the Fourth Plenum of the Thirteenth Central Committee,* "Remarks of Comrade Yan Mingfu," Secretariat of the Fourth Plenum of the CCP Thirteenth Central Committee, June 23–24, 1989

The situation is complicated. The participants at the meeting—the AFS, the Dialogue Delegation, and representatives of the hunger strikers—are in disagreement among themselves. They didn't even sit together. I'm not sure any of them truly represents the hunger strikers or can exert any influence on them.

The government's first effort having failed, it turned to its backup plan. At 9 P.M. the Beijing Government sent paramedics from the Beijing Municipal Red Cross and two ambulances from the city's Emergency Center to prepare for first-aid duties at the Square. Then at 2:30 A.M. on May 14, Li Tieying, Li Ximing, Chen Xitong, and four other prominent officials[36] went to the Square to urge

[36]Deputy secretary general of the State Council An Chengxin, deputy secretaries of the Beijing Municipal Committee Li Qiyan and Wang Jiaqiu, and vice mayor of Beijing Zhang Jianmin.

the students to return to their campuses. Some of the outraged students shouted, "Too late, too late!" "You should have known it would come to this; why do you come only now?" Other students complained, "We've been sold out. Someone's been negotiating with the government!" But most students simply ignored the Li Tieying entourage, which split into groups to talk with the frustrated student strikers. The following exchange took place in Li Tieying's group:

> Excerpt from State Council Office, "Leaders' activities," in "Yesterday's situation" (*Zuori qingkuang*), May 15

Li Tieying: "Why do you want to hunger strike?"

Student A: "Because the government is dragging its feet. Today's broadcast said that a dialogue will be held on the fifteenth, but we have no confidence that it will actually take place."

Li Tieying: "What's the real purpose of your strike?"

Student B: "We're not trying to bring down the government. We just want to help it clean things up. Take official profiteering, for instance: What's stopping the government from rooting out a few big embezzlers? We want a clean, honest government."

Chen Xitong: "How far do you plan to take this hunger strike?"

Student C: "Until we lose consciousness, right until they carry us out on stretchers."

Student D: "We're making news in order to wake up the people."

Li and his colleagues left, having failed to change any student minds.

May 14

Reactions to the hunger strike

> Account drawn from *Materials for the Fourth Plenum of the Thirteenth Central Committee*, "Remarks of Comrade Wang Renzhong,"[37] Secretariat of the Fourth Plenum of the CCP Thirteenth Central Committee, June 23–24, 1989

---

[37]Wang Renzhong was Li Xiannian's most trusted subordinate.

On May 14 a series of conversations took place among the Elders. Li Xiannian telephoned Deng Xiaoping.

Li Xiannian: "Things are going too far, Comrade Xiaoping, and we're getting backed into a corner. We have to meet to decide on a strategy. What's our Party going to do?"

Deng Xiaoping: "I agree with you that the situation is extremely grim."

Li Xiannian and Chen Yun, who were out of town resting, cut short their convalescences and returned to Beijing the same day.

> Account drawn from *Materials for the Fourth Plenum of the Thirteenth Central Committee*, "Remarks of Comrade Bo Yibo," Secretariat of the Fourth Plenum of the CCP Thirteenth Central Committee, June 23–24, 1989

When Chen met former vice premier Bo Yibo, he said:

The students have moved steadily from sticking up posters to demonstrating to occupying radio stations to forming illegal organizations—and now they defy us with a hunger strike. If we don't call this turmoil, how can we face the memory of the tens of thousands of martyrs who shed their blood for China's revolution?

> Excerpt from National People's Congress Office Secretariat, "Comrade Peng Zhen holds a meeting, gives an oral report on the situation to Zhu Xuefan and six other deputy standing committee chairs," May 26

Peng Zhen, former mayor of Beijing, placed a rare phone call to Deng Xiaoping to say:

Your line against bourgeois liberalization is correct, but it's been neglected for a long time, and now we're now seeing the results in the form of great ideological confusion. It is ideological confusion inside the Party that has produced this student movement. We cannot but worry about this confusion. I'd like to see us do something to turn the tide.

> Account drawn from *Materials for the Fourth Plenum of the Thirteenth Central Committee*, "Remarks of Comrade Wang

Zhen," Secretariat of the Fourth Plenum of the CCP Thirteenth Central Committee, June 23–24, 1989

Wang Zhen visited Deng Xiaoping at Deng's home.

Wang Zhen: "There are two voices inside the Party, Comrade Xiaoping. If we don't come down hard on these students right now, there'll be no peace for the Party, no peace for the country, and heads will roll."

The majority of Beijing residents, unlike the top leaders, offered sympathy and support to the striking students. Beijing intellectuals were especially vocal. As news of the hunger strike spread, Chinese and foreign journalists turned their attention away from the Sino-Soviet summit and toward the striking students in the Square.

On the evening of May 13 the State Security Ministry delivered to Party Central, the NPC, and the State Council a poster titled "We Can No Longer Remain Silent" that had appeared at Peking University, People's University, Beijing Normal University, and Qinghua University and that was signed by a number of well-known intellectuals. It said:

A march by Beijing intellectuals in support of students striking in the Square will begin at 2 P.M. on the fifteenth at the Fuxingmen Overpass. . . . Intellectuals must no longer remain silent! We must show the world our conscience, our courage, and our social responsibility! Let us write history!

The State Security Ministry also provided Zhongnanhai with an open letter addressed to Party Central, the Standing Committee of the NPC, and the State Council from about three hundred professors and young teachers at Peking University:

On May 13 students from Peking University and Beijing Normal University began a hunger strike. This was a clear escalation of their movement; it created a sense of crisis and captured the attention of local citizens and foreign observers. The attitude and actions of the Central Government and the Beijing Government will now be critically important and will have a decisive influence on what happens from here on. In order to promote reform and maintain social stability, and also to protect the physical and psychological well-being of the students, we teachers propose the following:

1. People in top positions in the Party and government should immediately hold meaningful dialogue with students to bring the situation to a speedy and satisfactory conclusion.

2. An objective and fair evaluation of the student movement should be made at once in order to reassure the public as well as Party members. There should no more delaying tactics.

3. The hunger strike should be taken very seriously and treated with genuine concern, caution, and humanitarianism. Every possible means should be used to ensure the mental and physical well-being of the students.

On May 14 Beijing college students again walked out of classes to show their support for the students on hunger strike in the Square. Teachers at Peking University, Beijing Normal University, and other institutions put up posters proposing that teachers join students in a strike "beginning on the fifteenth if the government does not respond to student demands by 11 P.M. tonight."

> State Security Ministry, "Trends in Tiananmen Square on the fourteenth," fax to Party Central and State Council duty offices, 11:58 P.M., May 14

Today more than one thousand students began a hunger strike in the Square. About twenty thousand students and citizens looked on during the day, and this number grew to one hundred thousand in the evening. The students who were hunger striking and sitting in were well behaved. Student monitors maintained order and prevented outsiders, who were not so well behaved, from entering the area. The protesters gave speeches and sang patriotic songs like "September Eighteenth,"[38] the "Internationale," "Bloody but Unbeaten,"[39] and the national anthem. In the morning, when the Chinese flag was raised, students stood up respectfully and sang the national anthem. They held up banners bearing messages such as "The country will have no peace as long as dictatorship lives," "Corruption is the cause of turmoil," and "The people cannot provide for parasites."

The striking students were regularly supplied with drinking water, soda, sugar, and medicine. By 10 P.M. more than a dozen of them had fainted or suffered stomach cramps and were rushed to first-aid centers in ambulances provided by the Beijing Government.

Throughout the day students and teachers streamed into the Square to show support. The first group of petitioners, from Shanghai universities, arrived at 8 A.M. Next were students from Peking University, Beijing Normal University,

[38] About resisting Japan in China's northeast in the 1930s.
[39] "Xueran fengcai," a song about China's border war with Vietnam in 1979, was sung not only at Tiananmen in spring 1989 but in the years following the June Fourth killings to commemorate its victims.

Qinghua University, and the Chinese Youth College of Political Science. In the afternoon, teachers from People's University and the Chinese University of Political Science and Law, along with doctoral students from Beijing Engineering University, arrived with banners and pennants. They were joined by more than seven hundred members of the Peace and Democracy Petition Group from Tianjin University and Nankai University. Each new support group circled the Square upon its arrival, attracting thousands of students and citizens in its wake.

A writer named Lu Yuan from the Lu Xun Institute of Literature read a "May 16 Statement" signed by several writers and scholars and said that a nationwide drive had already secured the signatures of several hundred famous writers. He also said that a march of five thousand intellectuals would begin at 1:30 P.M. the next day to support the patriotic student movement.

A teacher from Peking University then read an open letter to Party Central, the NPC, and the State Council signed by three hundred of his colleagues. The letter demanded, among other things, that the top leadership in the Party and government immediately engage in a meaningful dialogue with student representatives.

In the afternoon news of student delegates' dialogue with Comrades Li Tieying, Yan Mingfu, and others reached the Square, where it sparked considerable discussion among the protesters. Some claimed the meeting as a victory for the hunger strike, but quite a few felt it was too low-level and demanded that Zhao Ziyang and Li Peng appear personally. At midnight, more than three thousand students remained in the Square.

Li Tieying and Yan Mingfu hold dialogue with students

In view of the students' determination to continue the hunger strike, leaders involved with the issue—including Zhao Ziyang, Yang Shangkun, and Li Peng—decided to send Li Tieying, Yan Mingfu, and Wei Jianxing to speak with student representatives. The presence of Wei, who was minister of supervision, was supposed to show the students that the leadership was serious about combating corruption. The leaders also gave orders that the Beijing Municipal Government should use the Red Cross, ambulances, and hospitals to do everything possible to guard the students' health and should make sure no one died in the hunger strike.

On the morning of the fourteenth Yan met with some of the student leaders to tell them about

---

[40]There is a wall poster account of this meeting in Han, *Cries for Democracy*, 204–206.

that afternoon's planned dialogue session.[40] Although he said the dialogue could not be broadcast live, he promised that a tape of the meeting would be broadcast that evening on national television. He asked whether the student leaders had enough control over the hunger strikers to end the strike if they decided to do so. The student leaders seemed unsure of this themselves.

The session lasted from 4 P.M. to after 7 P.M., and the two sides remained far apart. Li and Yan said that the government intended to open diverse and regular dialogue channels with various groups in society, not to negotiate policy decisions but to exchange views and information. The students pressed for reversal of the April 26 editorial's characterization of their movement. Li Tieying responded that things were not necessarily developing in the way one might wish, and time would tell how the movement should be evaluated. The leaders again refused a request for simultaneous broadcast of the dialogue. The dialogue broke up with a plan to continue the next morning.

The intellectuals appeal

Dai Qing and eleven other prominent intellectuals tried to intercede with the students on May 14.

> Combined account from Letters and Visits Bureau of Party Central and the State Council, "Excerpts from twelve scholars' and writers' discussion meeting with student representatives," in "Important reception intelligence" (*Jiedai yaoqing*), May 15; United Front Work Department, "Twelve intellectuals submit an 'urgent appeal,'" in "Situation report" (*Qingkuang tongbao*), evening, May 14; State Security Ministry, "Trends in Tiananmen Square on the fifteenth," fax to Party Central and State Council duty office, May 15

After the breakdown of dialogue between the students and Li Tieying, Yan Mingfu, and others, twelve writers and intellectuals met at the offices of *Guangming Daily* at the urging of Dai Qing and eventually decided to go talk with the students. About 5 P.M. Dai Qing telephoned the United Front Work Department to express the intellectuals' willingness to urge the students to end their hunger strike and asked that the intellectuals be permitted to meet with student representatives in the Great Hall of the People. Yan Mingfu welcomed their attempt to do thought work on the students but suggested the meeting be held not in the Great Hall but in the reception room of the Letters and Visits Bureau of Party

Central and the State Council. Yan also spoke by telephone with Yan Jiaqi, who represented the scholars in the group, and expressed the hope that they would work hard to do a good job in persuading the students to end the strike.

Around 6 P.M. the twelve intellectuals—including Dai Qing, Yu Haocheng, Li Honglin, Wen Yuankai, Li Zehou, Li Tuo, Yan Jiaqi, Liu Zaifu, Bao Zunxin, and Su Xiaokang [and Su Wei and Mai Tianshu]—met with two dozen student representatives at the Letters and Visits Bureau. During the meeting Dai Qing and others drafted and made copies of "Our Urgent Appeal Regarding the Current Situation." The meeting had been going on for less than forty minutes when some of the student representatives expressed their strong wish that the scholars express their views directly to the students in the Square. At this, the scholars and writers left the meeting place and went to the United Front Work Department, arriving there about 7 P.M. Dai Qing shouted an appeal to the students: "If we're going to break this stalemate, both government and students will need to make concessions. The government should make concessions first, and the students next. As for conditions, if the students are willing to trust us, we are ready to press the government." Dai then presented the freshly drafted "Our Urgent Appeal to the United Front Work Department on behalf of the twelve intellectuals and met with Comrade Yan Mingfu.

Comrade Yan Mingfu said, "At the very least, the students should agree to evacuate the Square temporarily. What are their conditions?"

Dai Qing replied, "We've reached an agreement with the student representatives to withdraw on three conditions: Central leaders must announce in person that the student movement is patriotic and democratic, that the autonomous student organizations are legal, and that they will not settle accounts[41] later."

Yan Mingfu: "That's absolutely unworkable."

Dai Qing: "It could help to break the impasse if Zhao Ziyang and Li Peng were to meet with students in the Square."

Yan Mingfu: "The students are getting greedier, their demands are getting stiffer, and they're getting less and less unified among themselves. If they agree to stop adding conditions and to stop bargaining, I think Comrades Ziyang and Li Peng might consider meeting with them."

Dai Qing agreed to relay this message to the students and then said, "We're ready to go do thought work on the students in the Square; we're ready to try."

---

[41] *Qiuhou suanzhang,* literally "settle accounts when autumn has passed," is a phrase that the students on the Square often used to express their fear that the government might mete out heavy punishments once the movement was over.

Meanwhile, out in the United Front Work Department courtyard, some student representatives were describing the lack of unity in the student movement to scientist Wen Yuankai, philosopher Li Zehou, and Li Honglin, a former chief, now disgraced, of the Theory Bureau of the Party Propaganda Department. One student complained loudly, "We here are the official members of the Dialogue Delegation, but we don't seem to represent anybody any more. As soon we make the least bit of headway, they overrule us and nothing we said before counts."

"Who are 'they'?" asked one of the scholars.

"The hunger strikers."

About 8 P.M. Dai Qing and the other intellectuals arrived at Tiananmen Square and took seats at a "broadcasting stand" that the hunger strikers had set up. Dai Qing read "Our Urgent Appeal" aloud:

In view of the current situation at Tiananmen Square, we twelve scholars and writers make the following urgent appeal from a sense of conscience and responsibility:

1. We ask that Central leaders announce openly that this is a patriotic and democratic movement and that they will not settle accounts with participating students at any time in the future.

2. We maintain that the government should recognize as legal all student organizations that were formed through democratic processes.

3. We oppose any form of violence under any pretext against the students who are sitting in or hunger striking in the Square. History will condemn anyone who uses violence.

Dear students, we are extremely saddened and concerned by last night's news that you have begun a protest hunger strike. From mid-April on, in order to promote democracy and reform in China, you have repeatedly gone into the streets hoping to usher in a new epoch of Chinese history with your admirable, enviable, fearless, and selfless spirit. The people will long remember your historic achievements of 1989. But democracy takes time to evolve; it cannot be achieved overnight. We should be quite clear that there are people who are stirring up trouble, intensifying conflict, and worsening the situation in order to sabotage reform and the democratization process. In order to serve the long-term interests of China's reforms, in order to avoid incidents that will only hurt yourselves and comfort your enemies, and so that the Sino-Soviet summit will proceed smoothly, we entreat you to honor the highest ideals of your movement by making a temporary withdrawal from the Square.

We believe that you will choose wisely. We solemnly reaffirm that if the government does not meet the three demands we have listed, we will stand resolutely on your side to continue the fight to see them met.

After reading the appeal, Dai Qing announced to the students the conditions on which the intellectuals were recommending that the students withdraw: "If Zhao Ziyang and Li Peng come to visit you, you should then evacuate the Square, even if it's just a temporary move to Zhongshan Park,[42] in order to make room for tomorrow's state visit."

This statement provoked a tide of opposing voices from the hunger striking students:

"What good will it do just to be visited? They have to give a clear answer to our demands."

"We're not asking for alms."

"Why can't they admit we're patriotic?"

Wen Yuankai stepped forward to make his own statement: "This afternoon, we twelve university professors and scholars gathered spontaneously, from our sense of social responsibility, in order to discuss what is happening here. The twelve of us have already shared all our views on the student movement with the press. . . . Given the situation here tonight, we hope you can look at actual conditions in our country and realize that democratization is a lengthy process. No single movement can solve all the problems. You should watch for chances to make differences gradually over an extended period of time. At the same time you should be alert to the possibility that certain people might stir up trouble that will hurt democratization, not help it. That is why we are entreating you, assuming that the government meets our conditions, to withdraw from the Square and allow the Sino-Soviet summit to proceed smoothly. Remember our promise that if the government does not meet the conditions, we will stand with you."

Su Xiaokang spoke next: "Students, you have already earned a great victory. For the first time, you have shown China—and you are still showing China, both its people and its government—how to carry out a modern and democratic political movement. You're much smarter than the government, smarter than the officials, smarter than the cultural elite. The most impressive thing about your movement, ever since April 15, has been its spirit of rationality. The government and the ruling Party so far have shown themselves to be extremely inept at democratic politics, and I want to tell you that this is exactly why you must be rational: You must teach them. Do we still possess that rationality? ("Yes!" the students

---

[42]Just to the northwest of Tiananmen Square, immediately adjacent to the Gate of Heavenly Peace, the gate after which Tiananmen Square is named.

chorused.) Good! So if the government makes concessions, we can answer them with our rationality."

Then Dai Qing spoke: "We absolutely must not allow all that you have achieved to go for naught because of a tactical slipup. Were it not for you, the whole country would never know that Chinese people can be so mature or so devoted to democracy. This is your first achievement. Were it not for you, journalists would not be demanding freedom of the press, and many newspapers would not be publishing their own stories instead of simply reprinting what the Xinhua News Agency supplies. For this, too, we are in your debt. Were it not for you, the leaders would shun dialogue and never consider coming to see you. This is also your victory. . . . Students, let me repeat the two points I made a moment ago.[43] If you agree, I'll go back and talk with them. . . . State and government leaders like Zhao Ziyang and Li Peng will come to talk with you, but you mustn't make more demands on them. You should consider their positions and not demand that they make speeches or answer all kinds of questions."

Students whispered comments as Wen Yuankai, Su Xiaokang, and Dai Qing were speaking. The following were overheard and reported:

"Behold the government's lobbyists; let's not fall for their tricks!"

"We do the grunt work; now they come pick the fruit!"

"Don't believe a thing they say or do!"

"Who'd have thought they could be so spineless!"

"We don't need lobbyists!"

"They think we know nothing; all they can do is preach!"

A bespectacled student pushed his way through the crowd and shouted, "Fellow students! Fellow students! Who wants to join me in reading the hunger strike declaration three times?"

About 11:30 P.M. the scholars admitted failure in their attempt to influence the students. They left the Square and returned to the United Front Work Department, where Comrade Yan Mingfu and Comrade Li Tieying thanked them for their efforts and ordered cars to send them home.

---

[43]That Zhao and Li should come speak to the students, although the students should not expect them to answer all kinds of questions, and that the students should withdraw, even if only temporarily, to Zhongshan Park, to make room for the Gorbachev welcoming ceremony.—Comp.

May 13–14

Reports from two border regions

On May 13 and 14 thirty-two reports on student movements and related events came in from the provinces. Two of particular interest came from the Autonomous Regions of Inner Mongolia and Xinjiang.

In Huhehot, capital of the Inner Mongolia Autonomous Region, some three thousand students demonstrated continuously over the course of four days from May 11 through May 14, constituting the largest student demonstration in that city since the founding of the People's Republic of China. The slogans, banners, and speeches focused on corruption, inflation, and the inadequate funding of education. One student speaker asked people to come forward if they had information about corruption in the family of the region's most senior Party figure, Ulanfu. For the most part students kept order themselves, and onlookers appeared sympathetic.

In Xinjiang about 130 former uranium mine workers came into the capital, Urumchi, and conducted a sit-in, partly to support the students in Beijing but mainly to demand action on their own long-ignored problems of radiation sickness. They were granted a dialogue with the provincial Party and government authorities and an official of the Xinjiang Production and Construction Corps, their employer. These officials promised that the former miners' needs would be met in accordance with relevant state regulations. But they also pointed out that the method of seeking redress through a sit-in was inappropriate. The demonstrators were fairly satisfied with the answers they received. They called home to prevent additional demonstrators from coming into the capital and agreed to return to their work units.

May 15

A second dialogue with Li Tieying and Yan Mingfu

At 8:30 A.M. on May 15 Li Tieying, Yan Mingfu, and Wei Jianxing resumed their dialogue with more than fifty student representatives. Six other government officials were also present.

After three hours of effort, the meeting ended without success. The officials tried to persuade the students to end the hunger strike before more damage was done to the nation's image. They said they shared the students' sense of urgency on a host of problems, including corruption, legal construction, reform of the press system, and establishment of more democratic mechanisms for popular supervision of government. They offered to continue dialogue with the students and other sectors of society through diverse channels. But the student representatives returned again and again to the demand that the government acknowledge their movement as patriotic and constructive rather than as turmoil. Without this, the hunger strikers would not be willing to desist. But since the decision to label the student movement "turmoil" had come from Deng Xiaoping, the officials could only say that time would deliver a fair judgment.

At noon Soviet Party secretary Gorbachev arrived at the Beijing airport, and an apologetic Yang Shangkun conducted the welcoming ceremony there instead of outside the Great Hall of the People. Later, in his formal meeting with Gorbachev in the Great Hall, Yang emphasized the leadership's determination to move forward with reform. Since reform meant change, and there was no fixed blueprint, mistakes were inevitable. These words seemed to imply that Yang still sympathized with many of the students' goals and that he still hoped the crisis could be solved with moderate methods.

Beijing intellectuals demonstrate

May 15 saw an outpouring of support for the student hunger strikers from Beijing intellectuals, as reported to Zhongnanhai by the two security ministries, Beijing Municipality, and the Xinhua News Agency. The numbers of demonstrators, the units represented, the social groups involved, and the issues raised in slogans and banners increased markedly during the hunger strike's third day.

In the Square the students established a Tiananmen Square Hunger Strike Headquarters, with Chai Ling as general commander. The headquarters held a press conference for Chinese and foreign journalists at 1 P.M., during which they emphasized the students' demand that the government recognize the movement as patriotic and democratic. If the government continued to ignore them, some students would immolate themselves.

Throughout the day groups of demonstrators entered the Square to support the students. Often there were more than one hundred thousand people marching in support. They included workers waving trade union cards and ordinary citizens. There were also some staff members from government ministries and the Bank of China. The largest columns of demonstrators consisted of intellectuals from educational institutions and research institutes throughout the city. They were predominantly young, but middle-aged and older intellectuals also participated. Their slogans expressed support for the students and for democracy and criticism of the government. There were demands for freedom, attacks on corruption, protests against falling faculty salaries, and calls for an end to "old-man government."

Shortly after noon China Central Television broadcast the intellectuals' "Urgent Appeal Regarding the Current Situation." In the afternoon, some thirty thousand intellectuals from some 230 separate work units marched through the city and into the Square. There they issued a six-point "May 16 Declaration" that sharply criticized the government's handling of the crisis.[44] Four leaders of the group gave speeches urging the students to stand firm.

After two days and nights of hunger striking, nearly a hundred students had had fainting episodes, and one Beijing Normal University student was barely dissuaded from immolating himself.

Students around the country support the hunger strikers

On May 15 Zhongnanhai received reports on the student movement in fourteen provinces. They showed that the focus of the protests had shifted to expressing support for the Beijing hunger strikers.

In Taiyuan, the capital of Shanxi, more than ten thousand students from campuses throughout the province demonstrated in front of the provincial government building. Their slogans attacked corruption and the export of coal and other resources from Shanxi to other provinces. They demanded democracy and asked, "Where is China's Gorbachev?" In the afternoon the province's governor, Wang Senhao, and other officials met with thirty-three student representatives. The students criticized the facts that the new government office building had been built to an excessive standard of luxury and that members of the Provincial Party Standing Committee had been assigned above-standard housing. Governor Wang committed himself to a series of future dialogues with students and workers, and the demonstration ended that evening.

In Harbin, capital of Heilongjiang, more than nine thousand students demonstrated in front of the provincial government offices. They read a petition declaring support for the students in Beijing, and they demanded that Governor Shao Qihui come out to receive it. The governor did not appear, and toward evening the students surrounded the building but were repulsed by PAP troops. After a long standoff a vice governor came out to receive the petition. He told the students the local authorities thoroughly understood the students' wishes and would report them to the Center. He also acceded to the students' demand for a dialogue with top provincial leaders on May 20. The students, however, kept shouting for the governor to come out. Finally, about 10:30 P.M., he did, but he was unable to pacify the demonstrators. By midnight on the morning of May 16 they were still in place and the dialogue was continuing.

[44]Excerpted in Han, *Cries for Democracy*, 218–221.

Gorbachev's visit overshadowed

Twenty foreign press reports of May 15 were summarized for Zhongnanhai. Wire services noted that the journalists accompanying Gorbachev had turned much of their attention to the student movement. Kyodo News Agency noted that more than one hundred intellectuals, headed by Yan Jiaqi, had signed a petition dated May 15 calling for the release from prison of the radical dissident Wei Jingsheng and that some of the petition's signers, like Fang Lizhi, were also radical critics of the system. The French newspaper *Libération* quoted Yan Jiaqi as saying that the winds of democratization blowing from Moscow would be irresistible in China.

To much of the foreign press the events of the day spelled a major victory for the students. According to Kyodo, the government had been forced into dialogue with the hitherto illegal autonomous student organizations. But the *South China Morning Post* warned that the students would be making a big mistake if they thought they could push the government to further concessions either by making it lose face during the Gorbachev visit or by enticing Gorbachev himself to bring pressure on the Chinese authorities.

May 16

The hunger strike draws wide support

On May 16, while Deng Xiaoping met with Gorbachev inside the Great Hall of the People, thereby bringing about the long-sought normalization of Sino-Soviet relations, tens of thousands of people from all corners of society demonstrated outside in support of the students. Official reports recorded the main events.

About 1 A.M. on May 16 the offices of Party Central and the State Council broadcast a message by loudspeaker to the hunger strikers in the Square. It said that the government had already started and would continue dialogue with the students and that it was giving priority attention to the students' reasonable requests. The students, though, should consider the image and interests of the nation at the time of the summit with the Soviet leader and should also avoid damage to their health. They should end the hunger strike and return to their campuses.

Between 8:30 and 9:30 A.M. the students held their second press conference in the Square. Li Lu, a student leader from Nanjing University, joined Chai Ling, Wang Dan, and others to inform reporters that the students' determination to continue had not wavered, despite cold and hunger. Of about 3,100 hunger strikers, two hundred so far had fainted, and most of these had returned to the strike after reviving. In response to numerous questions, they emphasized that if their demands were not satisfied they would strike to the death. But the movement would remain peaceful; in fact, student monitors had already twice prevented enraged groups from trying to break into the Great Hall of the People. Although they were grateful to Yan Mingfu for saying he sympathized with their demands, they were not sure he represented the government in saying so. If he did, the government should state clearly that the student movement was patriotic and not turmoil.

Streams of self-organized supporters, from all kinds of occupations everywhere in the city, marched through the Square throughout the day. There were delegations from institutions for science, journalism, literature and art, and medicine; from government associations and ministries; from the officially recognized democratic parties; and from high schools. Over the course of the day the numbers reached an estimated three hundred thousand. They carried banners, shouted slogans in support of the students, and asked how long the government would let them fast. Citizens sent drinks and medicines and donated money.

It was learned that the AFS, who had planned the hunger strike, had originally expected the government to give in after two days. But now the AFS was making plans for a longer strike, organizing trucks to bring water, umbrellas, and hats into the Square, and directing traffic so that the trucks could get in. The Emergency Center estimated that the students could hold out for another three to four days, but after that there was a risk that some would die. By 10 P.M. the number of strikers who had fainted had grown to six hundred. The AFS reached an agreement with the Beijing Municipal Red Cross that the latter would take over care for the hunger strikers' health starting at 1 A.M. on the morning of May 17.

University presidents and professors step forward

As the strike entered its fourth day, on May 16, various groups of intellectuals stepped forth to appeal for a resolution. For example, ten senior Peking University professors issued an urgent appeal asking the government to accede to the students' demands and the students to end their strike. Ten university presidents issued an open letter urging the students to avoid further polarization, which might lead to an outcome that nobody wanted; the presidents also asked the government to open direct, face-to-face dialogue with the students as soon as possible. Eight presidents of technical schools in the capital issued an open letter in support of the ten university presidents' letter and offered to serve as intermediaries between the students and the government. And the presidents of four medical schools urged the students to eat, to take water, and to look out for their health, while also urging the government to open direct dialogue with the students. These four appeals informed the discussions at that night's emergency meeting of the Politburo Standing Committee and had an important influence on the next steps decided by the Politburo and the Elders, although not in the way the petitioners hoped.

CHAPTER FIVE

May 16–19

The Fall of Zhao Ziyang

EDITORS' NOTE: Following the diplomatic humiliation of Gorbachev's visit, fissures in the Politburo Standing Committee widened. Zhao's appeal to the students' patriotism had been ineffective, but at a Standing Committee meeting on May 16 he continued to argue that the way to end the hunger strike was to accept the students' demand to change the verdict of the April 26 editorial. Li Peng rebutted him on the grounds that Deng Xiaoping's words could not be changed.

The Standing Committee brought its disagreements to Deng's home on May 17. After hearing arguments on both sides and the views of two of his fellow Elders, Deng decided against Zhao and proposed the drastic measure of martial law. The Standing Committee then formally reconvened to adopt Deng's proposal. Zhao dissented but was outvoted. Against a background of swelling demonstrations nationwide and snowballing support for the students among intellectuals, Zhao tried to offer his resignation via Yang Shangkun but was rebuffed. He nonetheless withdrew from further decisionmaking and awaited his fate.

Taking charge, all eight Elders met on the morning of May 18 with the Standing Committee (minus Zhao) and the leaders of the Central Military Commission to solidify the consensus for martial law. The Elders felt that any further concessions to the students would spell the end of Party rule and the onset of anarchy. The remaining Standing Committee dissenter, Hu Qili, bowed to the Elders' decision, and fence-sitter Qiao Shi agreed to the deployment but expressed the hope that the troops would not have to use force.

The public in Beijing now seemed nearly unanimous in support of the students, as workers, farmers, and even military officers and police cadets marched in support. Word began to spread, however, that martial law was imminent. In some panic, student leaders advocated ending the hunger strike and called for a change in student demands, to ask for the retention in power of Zhao Ziyang and a meeting of the National People's Congress to take power out of the hands of the Elders and hard-liners.

May 16

Yan Mingfu speaks at the Square

On the morning of May 16 Yan Mingfu reported to Zhao Ziyang that the students in the Square were agitated and disunited. The situation was volatile. Their teachers and some other intellectuals had tried to persuade them to withdraw, but to no avail. The fact that the students were under the spotlight only made it harder for them to leave. Yan suggested that Zhao and Li Peng meet with some of the students to try to calm things down. Zhao replied that he realized the time for decisive action had come and promised the matter would be discussed at a meeting of the Standing Committee of the Politburo that evening.

At 5:40 that afternoon Yan Mingfu went in person to the Square to try to persuade the students to end their fast. He stressed that the future was theirs and that they were crucial to the success of China's reforms, so they should take care of their health first and foremost. They had moved the entire nation with their spirit and their resolve, he said, but now they should take care of themselves and await the day when a just assessment of their protests could come forth. If they now returned to their campuses, and those ill from fasting went to hospitals, they would not be punished, Yan said. To dramatize his sincerity, he offered himself as a hostage to accompany them during their withdrawal.

Yan's speech moved many of the students, but the situation had already gone beyond the point where benevolent advice could turn it around. The speech did have a concrete consequence for Yan himself, however: It became a major count against him when he was later dismissed from office.

Zhao Ziyang meets with Gorbachev

The Soviet leader met with Zhao Ziyang on the evening of May 16 at the same time that Yan Mingfu was speaking to the students in the Square. Zhao called on Gorbachev at the elegant state guest house called Diaoyutai.[1] Zhao remarked that Gorbachev's meeting with Deng Xiaoping had marked the restoration of normal relations between their two Communist parties. He observed that some young people now had doubts about the superiority of socialism, that these doubts

---

[1] A state guest house where high-level foreign visitors are housed. There is an account of the meeting in Michel Oksenberg, Lawrence R. Sullivan, and Marc Lambert, eds., *Beijing Spring, 1989, Confrontation and Conflict: The Basic Documents* (Armonk, New York: M. E. Sharpe, 1990), 260–264.

arose from genuine problems with Party leadership and certain entrenched habits, and that the only way out for socialism was continued vigorous pursuit of reform. It was here, too, that Zhao made his fateful comment to Gorbachev that even though Deng Xiaoping had retired from his Party posts in 1987, the Party had recognized that his wisdom and experience were essential and that for the most important questions he would still be at the helm.

Zhao's meeting with Gorbachev was reported that evening on national television and radio.

The Politburo Standing Committee holds an emergency meeting

On the evening of May 16 Zhao Ziyang, Li Peng, Qiao Shi, Hu Qili, and Yao Yilin held an emergency meeting of the Politburo Standing Committee. Party Elders Yang Shangkun and Bo Yibo also attended. The focus was on the student demonstrations. The hunger strike had evoked a strong, broad response in society, and the leaders were under pressure to find a solution.

> Excerpts from Party Central Office Secretariat, "Minutes of the May 16 Politburo Standing Committee meeting"

Zhao Ziyang: "The students' hunger strike in the Square has gone on for four days now. It's been extremely costly to their health, and in some cases has even threatened their lives. We've already done everything we can possibly do to see that they get medical attention and protection for their lives. We've had dialogues with their representatives and have promised we'll take them seriously and keep listening to their comments, asking only that they stop their fast, but it hasn't worked. The Square is so crowded—all kinds of excited people milling about with their slogans and banners—that the student representatives themselves say they have no real control of things."

Bo Yibo: "What is happening is that a minority is using the hunger strikers as hostages to force the Party and government into accepting the group's political demands. There's not an ounce of human decency in it!"

Zhao Ziyang: "If we don't get a handle on this thing quickly, if we just let it keep going, we could see a real nightmare."

Li Peng: "It's more and more clear that a tiny minority is trying to use the turmoil to reach its political goal, which is repudiation of Communist Party leadership and the socialist system. These people have already flaunted slogans about reversing the campaign against bourgeois liberalism and are on their way toward brazen opposition to the Four Basic Principles. They've spread many rumors attacking and slandering Party and state leaders, especially our comrade Deng Xiaoping, who has made such tremendous contributions to reform and opening. Their goals are to topple the Chinese Communist Party, to overthrow the People's Government that was legally elected by the National People's Congress, and to completely repudiate the people's democratic dictatorship.[2] They're lighting fires and fanning flames on all sides, secretly joining together, setting up all sorts of illegal organizations, and trying force the Party and government to recognize them so that they can establish an opposition group and lay the foundation for opposition to the Party."

Yang Shangkun: "These last few days Beijing's been in something like anarchy. Students are striking at all the schools, workers from some offices are out on the streets, transportation and lots of other things are out of whack—it's what you could call anarchy. We are having a historic Sino-Soviet summit and should have had a welcoming ceremony in Tiananmen Square, but instead we had to make do at the airport. We're supposed to have had two sessions of summit talks today in the Great Hall of the People, but we had to meet at Diaoyutai instead. That's the kind of anarchy we're in. Originally we were supposed to present wreaths at the Monument to the People's Heroes, but we couldn't. This has had a bad influence on our foreign relations. Pretty soon we won't be able to call this capital of ours a capital any more! This really is extremely serious."

Bo Yibo: "This student movement has had a bigger and broader impact, has lasted longer, and has done more harm than any past student movement. Just imagine students trying to crash through Xinhua Gate! Repeatedly invading Tiananmen Square! These things didn't even happen during the ten years of internal turmoil.[3] Up to a thousand students fasting in the Square! This never happened before in the history of our People's Republic! When the students chose Gorbachev's visit as the time for their hunger strike, they seriously disrupted the conduct of foreign affairs and sullied our national image. The spectacle these days of hundreds of thousands of people demonstrating in support of a hunger strike is something we didn't even see during the big Red Guard demonstrations in the Cultural Revolution! These people are reverting to anarchy, flouting the nation's laws, and churning up furious social tumult. This movement has

---

[2]Mao Zedong had argued that the Chinese Communist regime was a "people's democratic dictatorship" because it treated the people democratically while exercising dictatorship over the enemies of the people.

[3]A reference to the Cultural Revolution and its aftermath, 1966–1976.

already seriously damaged normal work routines, production, and daily life in the capital."

Hu Qili: "We've tried to cool this movement down and haven't gotten anywhere. Quite the contrary: With some of the students getting too emotional and with a tiny minority continually fanning the flames, the movement has veered in more complicated directions. Yesterday the demonstrations swelled to two or three hundred thousand people, and they weren't just students: They included workers, officials, members of the democratic parties, some officials and police from the justice system, grade school teachers, and high school students. People have come from the provinces expressly to support the hunger strike. When this happens, it actually pressures the students to continue striking. And when demonstrations get as large and as long-lived as this one, the tiny minority only gets more brazen and revives all its worst political slogans attacking the Communist Party and the socialist government. They focus their attacks on Comrade Xiaoping—things like 'Deng Xiaoping step down,' 'We demand that Deng Xiaoping resign from the Party,' and 'We don't need a prince-regent with Chinese characteristics.'[4] There are banners that say, 'Deng Xiaoping is ruthless; Zhao Ziyang is slick,' and 'Li Peng, step down to make amends to the people.' There's even one that says, 'Where are you, China's Walesa?' This shows that the situation is no longer an ordinary student movement but turmoil created by those who hope to gain from it."

Qiao Shi: "Things in Beijing are still unfolding, but they've already had an influence in many other cities. In quite a few places the demonstrations are getting bigger and bigger, and in some places there have even been attacks on Party and government offices. In Wuhan several thousand students are cutting off transport by sitting in on the Yangtze River bridge. It's pretty obvious that if we can't turn things around and get some stability, then everything—reform and opening, modernization—will be very much at peril. As I see it, the students have had lots of chances during this movement to compromise, but they never do. Our side can't give any more ground now, but we also haven't found any good way out of the mess. We still should do what we can to avoid confrontation, of course."

Zhao Ziyang: "The April 26 *People's Daily* editorial exposed the fact that a tiny minority is behind the turmoil. In my view the vast majority of student demonstrators are patriotic and sincerely concerned for our country. We may not approve of all of their methods, but their demands to promote democracy, to deepen the reforms, and to root out corruption are quite reasonable, and I even

---

[4]A play on Deng's own words about pursuing "socialism with Chinese characteristics."

think it's understandable when they sometimes go a bit overboard in their words and actions.

"When I got back from North Korea I learned that the April 26 editorial had elicited a strong reaction in many parts of society and had become a major issue for the students. I began to think about whether there wasn't some way to bridge the rift and get the students to settle down. I thought it might be best simply to skirt the most sensitive issue of whether the student movement is turmoil, hoping it would fade away while we gradually turn things around using the methods of democracy and law. But then on May 13 a few hundred students began a hunger strike, and one of their main demands was to reverse the official view of the April 26 editorial. So now there's no way to avoid the problem. We have to revise the April 26 editorial, find ways to dispel the sense of confrontation between us and the students, and get things settled down as soon as possible."

Li Peng: "It's just not true, Comrade Ziyang, that the official view in the April 26 editorial was aimed at the vast majority of students. It was aimed at the tiny minority who were using the student movement to exploit the young students' emotions and to exploit some of our mistakes and problems in order to begin a political struggle against the Communist Party and the socialist system and to expand this struggle from Beijing to the whole country and create national turmoil. These are indisputable facts. Even if a lot of the student demonstrators misunderstood the April 26 editorial, still it served an important purpose in exposing these truths."

Zhao Ziyang: "As I see it, the reason why so many more students have joined the demonstrations is that they couldn't accept the editorial's label for the movement. The students kept insisting that the Party and government express a different attitude and come up with a better way of characterizing the movement. I think we have to address this problem very seriously because there's no way around it. I am partly responsible for the April 26 editorial. When I was in Pyongyang, the Central Committee sent me Comrade Xiaoping's remarks and the Standing Committee's decision and asked my opinion on the draft of the April 26 editorial. I agreed with it and I said so. So I'm not saying the editorial was the Standing Committee's fault. I am willing to take upon myself full, public responsibility for the editorial."

Yao Yilin: "You can't take that responsibility, Comrade Ziyang, and the official view in the April 26 editorial cannot be changed. We're facing a serious national crisis, and we have to take a firm line. I think the Central Committee should issue these orders:

- "All levels of the Party must unite with the broad masses and do deep and detailed political work and thought work in order to build a bulwark of unified thought within a stable situation.
- "All Party members must strictly uphold Party discipline and play a vanguard role in uniting with the masses and stopping turmoil.
- "All levels of government must solemnly tighten political and legal discipline and intensify their leadership and management of all regions and units under their control.
- "Government workers across the country must stay at their jobs, fulfill their duties, and not march in the streets.
- "All industrial and commercial units must maintain labor discipline and keep production firmly on track.
- "All schools must maintain normal class schedules, and those who are boycotting classes must cease unconditionally."

Li Peng: "Comrade Ziyang, the key phrases of the April 26 editorial were drawn from Comrade Xiaoping's remarks on the twenty-fifth: 'This is a well-planned plot,' it is 'turmoil,' its 'real aim is to reject the Chinese Communist Party and the socialist system,' 'the whole Party and nation . . . are facing a most serious political struggle,' and so on are all Comrade Xiaoping's original words. They cannot be changed."

Zhao Ziyang: "We have to explain the true nature of this student movement to Comrade Xiaoping, and we need to change the official view of the movement."

The meeting decided: (1) Since the situation is extremely urgent, we need to make a complete report to Comrade Xiaoping tomorrow and solicit his views and those of the other Party Elders. (2) Right after the meeting Comrade Zhao Ziyang, speaking for the Standing Committee of the Politburo, will present a written speech to the students who are fasting in the Square.

> "Zhao Ziyang publishes a written speech representing the Politburo Standing Committee [consisting of himself and Li Peng, Qiao Shi, Hu Qili, and Yao Yilin]," *People's Daily*, May 17, p. 1[5]

Students, I would like to say a few words on behalf of myself and Comrades Li Peng, Qiao Shi, Hu Qili, and Yao Yilin of the Standing Committee of the Politburo.

[5]Early in the morning, before its publication in the morning newspaper, Zhao's speech was broadcast over loudspeakers to the students in the Square.—Comp.

Your patriotic calls for democracy and the rule of law, for action against corruption, and for further reform are extremely valuable, and Party Central and the State Council affirm them. At the same time, we hope you can remain calm, rational, self-restrained, and orderly, keeping the broader situation in mind and preserving stability and unity.

Please rest assured the Party and government absolutely will not take retribution on you after peace is restored.[6]

I would also like to tell you that the Center takes your reasonable opinions and demands very seriously. We will make further study of the opinions and demands that come from students and other parts of society and will propose and carry out concrete measures for establishing democracy and the rule of law, for moving against corruption and promoting clean government, and for increasing transparency in government.

Students, the burdens of building the Four Modernizations and rejuvenating China eventually will fall upon your shoulders. You still have a long time during which to make contributions to our nation and people. The Center hopes you will take care of your physical health, stop your hunger strike, and restore your health as soon as possible. If you do, the Center, as well as your parents, your teachers, and the broad masses, will all feel relieved. After you go back, Party Central and the State Council will continue to pay attention to your opinions and will continue and intensify multilevel, multichannel dialogue with you.

Again, I appeal to you to stop your hunger strike and hope you will restore your health as soon as possible.

Students in Shanghai and Wuhan

On May 16 students across China demonstrated in support of the Beijing hunger strike. Zhongnanhai received twenty-three reports on these activities. Among them were two State Security Ministry reports on events in Shanghai and Wuhan.

In Shanghai, around noon on May 16, more than four thousand students from twelve campuses braved a rainstorm to march on the municipal government offices, where they began a sit-in. Their slogans and banners called for the people to unite, for Jiang Zemin to step down, for support of the hunger strike, and against corruption and official profiteering. Some read "Workers, arise!" "Farmers, arise!" and "Long live the people." The students issued a list of demands call-

---

[6] *Qiuhou suanzhang*, literally "settle accounts when autumn has passed."

ing on the Municipal Government (1) to recognize the student demonstrations as just and patri-otic; (2) to forswear any reprisals against demonstrators; (3) to restore the *World Economic Her-ald,* bring back Qin Benli, and have Jiang Zemin apologize for closing the paper down; and (4) to have open dialogue on an equal footing with student representatives. They said that if the city did not agree to these demands by midnight, larger demonstrations would follow. At 10 P.M. the Shanghai Municipal Party Committee and the Municipal Government leadership agreed to meet with student representatives the next day and to listen carefully to their demands. They counseled them to take care of their health by getting out of the cold rain.

On the morning of the seventeenth, two hundred students were still sitting in and forty had signed up for a hunger strike. Later that day, more than two hundred faculty members at Fudan University signed and delivered to the city government an urgent appeal endorsing the students' demands.

In Wuhan six hundred students began a sit-in at Hubei's provincial government offices at 1:30 A.M. May 16. By evening their numbers had grown to ten thousand. They called for support of the hunger strike in Beijing and for dialogue with government officials. At 2:30 A.M., after getting no response at the government offices, about one thousand students went marching in search of the home of provincial Party secretary Guan Guangfu. After two hours of fruitless search, they returned to the government offices. Around 11 A.M. the Provincial Party Committee invited student representatives inside to "talk about the dialogue question." The students sent in five representa-tives with three demands: (1) that the student activities be recognized as upright, (2) that Guan Guangfu himself join the dialogue, and (3) that the police officers who used tear gas and night-sticks against the students on April 19 be severely punished.

By 4 P.M. there were more than six thousand participants and about four thousand onlookers. Since the provincial government had not satisfied the students' demands—which now also included publication in the local media of photos and press accounts of the student demonstra-tions—the student representatives proposed a sit-in on the Yangtze River bridge. At midnight nearly two thousand students remained on the bridge, refusing to move until the provincial gov-ernment agreed to begin dialogue.

May 17

Foreign opinion

On May 17 thirty-eight reports on foreign news coverage of the student movement and the Sino-Soviet summit arrived at Zhongnanhai. Particularly notable was an interview with the student leader Wuerkaixi in the French newspaper *Le Figaro,* which ran under the headline "We Are Ready to Lay Down Our Lives." Wuerkaixi was quoted as saying that the fasting students had no intention of blocking Gorbachev's visit to the Square, but they would not evacuate the Square, either. Asked what he imagined the Chinese government's view of this might be, he said "The government is a bunch of corrupt rotten eggs; they can think what they want." He also said, "The government and the Party are the same thing; if you oppose one you oppose the other." The recent dialogue between government officials and student representatives had been useless, he said, because the government people just kept insisting they had golden intentions but could do nothing. He said the hunger strike would continue until there was a satisfactory response; some students were prepared to fast until death, and others were prepared to die fighting if the police should crack down. On the brighter side, he said that "anything is possible," including that "Deng and Li Peng might accept our demands," although he went on to say that the student demands were by no means limited to the three or four that had been announced so far. There were others, including the important one regarding human rights.

The Standing Committee meets at Deng Xiaoping's home

On the morning of May 17 the Standing Committee of the Politburo met at Deng Xiaoping's home. Besides Zhao Ziyang, Li Peng, Qiao Shi, Hu Qili, and Yao Yilin, Elders Yang Shangkun and Bo Yibo also attended.

> Excerpts from Party Central Office Secretariat, "Minutes of the May 17 Politburo Standing Committee meeting," document supplied to Party Central Office Secretariat for its records by the Office of Deng Xiaoping

Zhao Ziyang: "The fasting students feel themselves under a spotlight that makes it hard for them to make concessions. This leaves us with a prickly situation. The most important thing right now is to get the students to delink their fasting from their demands and then to get them out of the Square and back to their campuses. Otherwise, anything could happen, and in the blink of an eye. Things are tense."

Yang Shangkun: "This student movement has gone on for more than a month now. Has that month seen turmoil in our capital? Yes. It's reached the point where we can't conduct national affairs. Things like Gorbachev's welcoming ceremony can't proceed as normal. When things get so bad that it's hard even to walk down the street or go to work, how can we talk about public order in the capital? Can we still say there's been no harm to the national interest or society's interest? This isn't turmoil? If anybody here takes the position that this isn't turmoil, I don't see any way to move ahead with reform and opening or to pursue socialist construction! But we still have to keep two groups clearly separate in our minds: the tiny minority that stirs up and manufactures turmoil and the well-intentioned students and other good people."

Li Peng: "I think Comrade Ziyang must bear the main responsibility for the escalation of the student movement, as well as for the fact that the situation has gotten so hard to control. When he was in North Korea and the Politburo asked Comrade Ziyang's opinion, he sent back a telegram clearly stating that he was 'in complete agreement with Comrade Xiaoping's plan for dealing with the unrest.' After he came back on April 30 he again said at a Politburo meeting that he endorsed Comrade Xiaoping's remarks as well as the word 'turmoil' that appeared in the April 26 editorial. But then, just a few days later, on the afternoon of May 4 at the Asian Development Bank meetings—and without consulting anybody else on the Standing Committee—he gave a speech that flew in the face of the Standing Committee's decisions, Comrade Xiaoping's statement, and the spirit of the April 26 editorial.

"First, in the midst of obvious turmoil, he felt able to say 'China will be spared any major turmoil.'

"Second, in the presence of a mountain of evidence that the aim of the turmoil was to end Communist Party rule and bring down the socialist system, he continued to insist the protesters 'do not oppose our underlying system but demand that we eliminate the flaws in our work.'

"Third, even after many facts had clearly established that a tiny minority was exploiting the student movement to cause turmoil, he said only that there are 'always going to be . . . people ready to exploit' the situation. This explicitly contradicts Party Central's correct judgment that a tiny minority was already manufacturing turmoil.

"Bao Tong drafted Comrade Ziyang's remarks, and it was also Bao Tong who asked CCTV and Central Radio to broadcast them immediately. The speech then got blown way out of proportion in *People's Daily* and other newspapers, where it caused serious confusion in the thinking of officials and the masses everywhere. The organizers and plotters of the turmoil loved all this: It stiffened their spines, added to their bile, and puffed them up. Comrades Li Ximing and Chen Xitong reported that Comrade Ziyang's speech put Beijing under great pressure. People were complaining, 'There are two different voices coming from the Center; which is right and which is wrong?'; others asked, 'You want us to maintain unanimity with the Center, but with which Center?' Comrades who were doing thought work in the universities felt betrayed and were so hurt they shed tears. Political thought work on the campuses was almost completely paralyzed, and this made the overall situation even more grave."

Yao Yilin: "Comrade Ziyang's speech to the directors of the ADB had nothing to do with financial questions. He talked only about the student movement, and if it weren't for the talk's title you'd never guess he was addressing foreigners. I think Comrade Ziyang's purposes in these remarks are clear. There's nothing wrong with his saying the student movement is patriotic, but then he went all the way over to the students' side: He said we really do have a lot of corruption and need to solve our problems through democracy and law. He completely skirted the question of whether the April 26 editorial was correct or not.

"This was an important speech. It let all the students and those people with ulterior motives get an inside look at Comrade Xiaoping's views and the opposing opinions within the Standing Committee. This only fed the flames of the student movement, until it almost got out of control. Another thing I don't understand is why Comrade Ziyang mentioned Comrade Xiaoping in his talk with Gorbachev yesterday. Given the way things are right now, this can only have been intended as a way to saddle Comrade Xiaoping with all the responsibility and to get the students to target Comrade Xiaoping for attack. This made the whole mess a lot worse."

Zhao Ziyang: "Could I have a chance to explain these two things? The basic purposes of my remarks at the annual meeting of the directors of the ADB were to pacify the student movement and to strengthen foreign investors' confidence in China's stability. The first reactions I heard to my speech were all positive, and I wasn't aware of any problems at the time. Comrades Shangkun, Qiao Shi, and Qili all thought the reaction to the speech was good; Comrade Li Peng said it was a good job and that he would echo it when he met with the ADB representatives. The tone of the speech was mild, but to judge from evidence available at the time, it had a pretty good effect. Comrade Li Peng is correct to say that my remarks were not cleared in advance with the Standing Committee. But it's always been our practice that when leading comrades talk to foreign guests they don't have to clear their remarks with the Standing Committee, except in the cases of formal talks. Usually we just prepare our own talks based on the Center's policies.

"Now, about my comments to Gorbachev yesterday: Ever since the Thirteenth Party Congress, whenever I meet with Communist Party leaders from other countries I make it clear that the First Plenum of our Thirteenth Central Committee decided that Comrade Xiaoping's role as our Party's primary decision-maker would not change. I do this in order to make sure the world has a clearer understanding that Comrade Xiaoping's continuing power within our Party is legal in spite of his retirement. I told this to Chairman Kim Il Sung on my recent trip to North Korea. So telling Gorbachev really was nothing more than following the pattern. What was different is that it got reported publicly. And why did I choose yesterday as the time to tell Gorbachev? I did it because when I got back from North Korea, I heard that Comrade Xiaoping's April 25 remarks about the student movement had stirred up some resentment in society. People said the Standing Committee had no need to 'report' to Comrade Xiaoping. And some things a lot worse than that were said. I felt I had to correct the record.

"This same question came up two days before Gorbachev got here in a meeting I was having with some workers and their union leaders. I told them about the decision at the First Plenum of the Thirteenth Central Committee, and it made things a lot better. They said they didn't know about that decision, but now that they do, fine. Some time before that Comrade Chen Xitong was in a meeting with authorities from the college campuses and was trying to refute the rumors about rule by manipulation from behind a curtain; he explained the First Plenum's decision and again the response was good. Comrade Chen Xitong told us so at the April 28 meeting of the Standing Committee. So I felt that to let this go public, to let the masses know about it, could help in cutting down on all the controversy. What I told Gorbachev was that the First Plenum of the Thirteenth Central Committee formally decided that on all matters of first importance, we will continue to make reports to Comrade Xiaoping and seek his advice. I deliberately did not mention that he has the right to call meetings and to make final decisions.

"Comrade Deng Xiaoping in fact has always supported our work, including all our collective decisions, in every way. So there's really no reason why this remark of mine should give anyone the impression that everything is decided by Deng Xiaoping. I really had no thought of doing anything to harm Comrade Xiaoping, and if I did I want to take full responsibility for it."

Deng Xiaoping: "Comrade Ziyang, that talk of yours on May 4 to the ADB was a turning point. Since then the student movement has gotten steadily worse.... Of course we want to build socialist democracy, but we can't possibly do it in a hurry, and still less do we want that Western-style stuff. If our one billion people jumped into multiparty elections, we'd get chaos like the 'all-out civil war' we saw during the Cultural Revolution. You don't have to have guns and cannon to have a civil war; fists and clubs will do just fine. Democracy is our goal, but we'll never get there without national stability. This whole incident pushes in the wrong direction: That was clear from the start. But still some comrades don't grasp the nature of the problem; they still think this is about how to handle students. Our adversaries are not in fact those students but people with ulterior motives. Their two basic slogans are 'Down with the Communist Party' and 'Overthrow the socialist system,' and their goal is to set up a bourgeois republic on the Western model. Not to understand this basic question is to mistake the nature of the movement.

"I know there are some disputes among you, but the question before us isn't how to settle all our different views; it's whether we now should back off or not."

Bo Yibo: "This movement, analyzed at its most fundamental level, is a consequence of the long-term spread of bourgeois liberalism in China. It aims at the West's so-called democracy, freedom, and human rights. We have no room for any retreat. If we go one step back, they'll come one step forward; if we go back two, they'll come forward two. We're at a point of no retreat. To retreat further would be to hand China over to them. We still, of course, must distinguish clearly between the two kinds of conflicts."

Qiao Shi: "The political schemes of people with ulterior motives are becoming more and more obvious. They use the student movement to manufacture premeditated turmoil. They have already seriously disturbed work, production, education, research, and normal life in Beijing and all across the country. Their goals are quite clear: to overthrow the leadership of the Communist Party and change the socialist order. So I think we can't yield any more, but also that we haven't yet found a good way to wrap things up. I think that we should protect the patriotism and enthusiasm of the students and the broad masses and need not hold them responsible for their sometimes excessive rhetoric. But we must expose the tiny minority who agitated and created turmoil, and we should do what we can to soften confrontations."

Yang Shangkun: "Our backs are to the wall. If we retreat any further we're done for. This student movement has not only harmed the political, economic, and social order of the capital, but it has harmed the political situation—the stability and unity—of the whole country. The crisis we face is extremely serious: This movement could lead to turmoil in the whole country and unleash forces that can't be controlled. It could turn a very hopeful China into an impossibly chaotic and hopeless China. This is a critical juncture, and we have to take steps that are careful and yet at the same time decisive to put the movement down as soon as possible. Meanwhile, we have to fix the problem of corruption if we're going to win the people's trust."

Hu Qili: "It's true that what we see before us is no ordinary student movement but a case of political turmoil that repudiates Communist Party rule and the socialist system, has clear political goals, has turned its back on democracy and the rule of law, and uses despicable political tactics to agitate among large numbers of students who do not understand what's really going on. So our first order of business should be to rescue the fasting students from the Square. It's true we can retreat no further."

Deng Xiaoping: "We've all seen how the situation in Beijing and across the country has become most grave. Especially in Beijing, the anarchy gets worse every day. Discipline and rule of law have been harmed, many universities are paralyzed, public transportation is clogged, Party and government offices are under attack, crime is on the rise, and more and more demonstrators come out every day. All this has seriously disturbed or even destroyed the normal order of production, work, study, and daily living. If we don't turn things around, if we let them go on like this, all our gains will evaporate, and China will take a historic step backward. To back down would be to give in to their values; not backing down means we stick steadfastly to the April 26 editorial. The Elder comrades— Chen Yun, Xiannian, Peng Zhen, and of course me, too—are all burning with anxiety at what we see in Beijing these days. Beijing can't keep going like this. We first have to settle the instability in Beijing, because if we don't we'll never be able to settle it in the other provinces, regions, and cities. Lying down on railroad tracks; beating, smashing, and robbing; if these aren't turmoil then what are they? If things continue like this, we could even end up under house arrest.

"After thinking long and hard about this, I've concluded that we should bring in the People's Liberation Army and declare martial law in Beijing—more precisely, in Beijing's urban districts.[7] The aim of martial law will be to suppress the turmoil once and for all and to return things quickly to normal. This is the unshirkable duty of the Party and the government. I am solemnly proposing this today to the Standing Committee of the Politburo and hope that you will consider it."

Zhao Ziyang: "It's always better to have a decision than not to have one. But Comrade Xiaoping, it will be hard for me to carry out this plan. I have difficulties with it."

---

[7]Beijing has five urban and five rural districts *(qu).*

Deng Xiaoping: "The minority yields to the majority!"[8]

Zhao Ziyang: "I will submit to Party discipline; the minority does yield to the majority."

The decisions of the meeting were: (1) the Standing Committee of the Politburo of the Central Committee of the Chinese Communist Party will resume its meeting later that evening to decide concretely how to implement martial law; (2) on the morning of the eighteenth the Standing Committee will visit fasting students in the hospital; (3) Li Peng will carry out dialogue with student representatives on the eighteenth and will ask the fasting students to leave the Square; (4) on the morning of the eighteenth the Standing Committee will report to Deng Xiaoping and other Party Elders on deployments for martial law.

After the meeting Deng Xiaoping telephoned Chen Yun, Li Xiannian, and Peng Zhen and had his secretary reach Deng Yingchao; Wang Zhen; Hong Xuezhi, deputy secretary of the CMC; Liu Huaqing, deputy secretary general of the CMC; and Qin Jiwei, minister of national defense, notifying these people of the Politburo's decision and inviting them to attend the next day's meeting.

Li Peng mobilizes his associates

That afternoon Li Peng invited Li Tieying, Li Ximing, Yan Mingfu, Chen Xitong, Luo Gan, Yuan Mu, and He Dongchang to a meeting to let them know, in advance of the formal announcement, that Beijing was headed for martial law. Quoting key phrases that Deng Xiaoping had used during the morning meeting, Li Peng said that the Party Elders were deeply concerned about the situation and felt things in the capital had to be settled before problems in other cities and provinces could be addressed. He said there would have to be new prohibitions against students from elsewhere coming into Beijing. He asked Li Tieying to scout out hospitals where it would be appropriate for Standing Committee members to visit fasting students the next morning, and asked Li Tieying, Li Ximing, Yan Mingfu, and Chen Xitong to be ready to join him in the dialogue scheduled for later the next day with student representatives. Dialogue should be with students who actually controlled things in the Square, not with officers of the AFS. The sole topic of discussion, Li said, would be how to persuade the fasting students to leave the Square. Yan Mingfu would be responsible for contacting the students.

Luo Gan then instructed the General Office of the State Council to draw up prohibitions against student travel to the capital, and these were telegraphed across the country. He Dongchang sent

---

[8]A principle of CCP "democratic centralism," according to which opinions at lower levels are concentrated at successively higher levels until a Party-wide distillate forms at the top.

out a similar notice in the name of the State Education Commission. Li Tieying set out at 10 P.M. to check on hospitals.

Meanwhile, also on May 17 but on the other side of the world, Wan Li, the chair of China's National People's Congress, was saying some very different things. While traveling in Canada, he remarked in public that the Chinese Communist Party was hard at work trying to solve some of the problems that student protesters had identified. The Party's goals, Wan said, were socialist democracy and socialist rule of law, including the sharply increased press freedom that Chinese journalists had recently been demanding. He noted that the past ten years of reform had led to spectacular economic gains but that progress in democratic reform had been slow. He said the NPC, both in recent meetings and in meetings soon to be held, was busy addressing the issues of political reform that were on the minds of students, intellectuals, and workers. The government was continuing to show restraint toward the student movement, he said; its aims were stability combined with accelerated reform.

Zhao Ziyang, Hu Qili, and Rui Xingwen welcomed Wan Li's remarks. Rui published them in the next day's *People's Daily* under the headline "Students Who Call for Democracy and Oppose Corruption Are Patriotic." Wan's remarks drew a broad and favorable popular response.

The Standing Committee resumes its meeting

At 8 P.M. the meeting of the Politburo Standing Committee resumed at Zhongnanhai. Committee members Zhao Ziyang, Li Peng, Qiao Shi, Hu Qili, and Yao Yilin attended. Yang Shangkun and Bo Yibo participated in their role as Party Elders.

> Excerpts from Party Central Office Secretariat, "Minutes of the May 17 Politburo Standing Committee meeting"

Zhao Ziyang: "The question for this evening's meeting is martial law. First we need to consider whether the situation has reached a point where martial law is our only option. Will martial law help solve the problem or only enlarge it? Is it in fact necessary to impose martial law? I hope we can discuss these questions calmly."

Li Peng: "The decision on martial law, Comrade Ziyang, was made by Comrade Xiaoping at this morning's meeting. I support Comrade Xiaoping's views on martial law. I believe that the topic for the present meeting is not whether martial law should or should not be imposed but, rather, what steps to use in carrying it out."

Yao Yilin: "I strongly support Comrade Xiaoping's proposal to impose martial law in Beijing's urban districts. Taking this powerful measure will help restore the city to normalcy, end the state of anarchy, and quickly and effectively stop the turmoil."

Zhao Ziyang: "I'm against imposing martial law in Beijing. My reason is that, given the extreme feelings of the students at this juncture, to impose martial law will not help calm things down or solve problems. It will only make things more complicated and more sharply confrontational. And after all, things are still under our control. Even among the demonstrators the vast majority are patriotic and support the Communist Party. Martial law could give us total control of the situation, yes; but think of the terror it will strike in the minds of Beijing's citizens and students. Where will that lead? . . . In the forty years of the People's Republic, our Party has learned many lessons from its political and economic mistakes. Given the crisis we now face at home and abroad, I think that one more big political mistake might well cost us all our remaining legitimacy. So I see martial law as extremely dangerous. The Chinese people cannot take any more huge policy blunders."

Hu Qili: "After much careful thought, I too have decided that I am against martial law in Beijing. In the complicated political situation we now face, we have to be wary of high-pressure tactics that could aggravate the confrontation. To be quite frank, I worry that martial law could lead to an even more serious social crisis: It could ignite new mass resistance, and it could make even more people join this student movement that should have been brought to an end long ago. It could leave us with a situation even harder to handle, and it could lead to extremes. In short, I don't see how martial law is going to help us toward a peaceful resolution of the situation."

Qiao Shi: "I've wanted to express my view all along. We can't afford any more concessions to the student movement, but on the other hand we still haven't found a suitable means for resolving the situation. So on the question of martial law, I find it hard to express either support or opposition."

Bo Yibo: "This is a Standing Committee meeting in which Comrade Shangkun and I are only observers. We don't have voting rights, but we both support Comrade Xiaoping's proposal to impose martial law. Just now everyone on the committee had a chance to express his opinion. I think we should make the opinions even clearer by taking a vote, by saying 'yes,' 'no,' or 'abstain.' This has been our Party tradition when we face important questions of principle."

Following Bo Yibo's suggestion, the five members of the Standing Committee took a formal vote. Li Peng and Yao Yilin voted for martial law; Zhao Ziyang and Hu Qili voted against it; Qiao Shi abstained.

Yang Shangkun: "The Party permits differing opinions. We can refer this evening's vote to Comrade Xiaoping and the other Party Elders and get a resolution as soon as possible."

Zhao Ziyang: "My duties must end here today; I cannot continue to serve. My view of the nature of the student movement differs from those of Comrade Xiaoping and from those of most of you here. With my different thinking, how can I carry on as general secretary? And if I can't carry on, it will make things difficult for the rest of you on the Standing Committee. So I'm asking to resign."

Bo Yibo: "Don't bring up this question, Comrade Ziyang. Didn't you agree at the morning meeting with Comrade Xiaoping that the minority should yield to the majority? Didn't you also say that it's always better to have a decision than not to have one? You mustn't drop the ball now."

Yang Shangkun: "Your attitude is incorrect, Comrade Ziyang. How can you bail out right now, when we most need unity? Whatever you do, you mustn't make things hard for the Party right at this moment."

Zhao Ziyang: "My health hasn't been good. I've had dizziness constantly for the last few days. I have low blood pressure."

Bo Yibo: "Since the Standing Committee can't reach consensus, we'll have to bring the question back to Comrade Xiaoping for a solution in any case."

At the end of the meeting it was decided that members of the Standing Committee would visit fasting students early the next morning in the Xiehe and Tongren Hospitals. On martial law, since the intractable disagreements on the Standing Committee had led to an impasse, it was decided that committee members would return to Deng Xiaoping's home the next morning to refer the question back to Deng, the Elders, and the responsible people on the Military Affairs Commission. The Elders would have the final say. This decision effectively ended the functioning of the Politburo Standing Committee of the Thirteenth Central Committee.

A million-person demonstration in Beijing

According to a May 17 report from the State Security Ministry, on the night of May 15 the number of fasting students continued to increase despite further appeals to desist, and on the night of the sixteenth city residents were kept awake all night by the sirens of ambulances taking away students who had collapsed. Zhao Ziyang's attempt at dialogue with the students on the seventeenth brought no real change, and support for the hunger-striking students continued to grow. A wide variety of the city's people took to the streets and joined the calls for leaders to resign. The ministry estimated the total number of demonstrators that day to have been 1.2 million.

According to a State Security Ministry report, demonstrators came not only from schools, even grade schools, but also from a wide range of factories, Party offices, government ministries, broadcast and print media, museums, intellectual salons,[9] hotels, food markets, department stores, and other places. Some marchers paraded with banners bearing messages that reflected their own work. Staff members from the *People's Daily,* for example, carried a banner saying "We did not write the April 26 editorial!" and people from the Beijing College of Fashion carried a banner suggesting that officials wear bikinis in order to increase the transparency of government. Other slogans or banners included "Resign already! What are you waiting for?" "When a person turns eighty he turns stupid"; "You're old, Xiaoping"; "Old-man government is due for retirement"; "Oppose the cult of personality"; "The people support the state but can also overturn it"; "Don't sell government bonds; sell the government Benzes!"[10] "Your consciences have been devoured by dogs"; "Corruption = AIDS"; and "When students fast, the hearts of their teachers ache."

The report said that with the collapse of one student after another, ordinary Beijing people worried about only one thing: getting the students to start eating again. It was widely believed that the only way to achieve this would be for Central leaders to go among the students and urge them to end the strike. If any fasting student were to die, the people would be outraged, and the situation would become harder to handle, the report warned.

The Square seethes with excitement

According to State Security Ministry reports, more than ten thousand students remained in the Square through the early hours after midnight, and they were fairly orderly. Around 6:20 A.M. students from Qinghua University launched an effort to recruit thirty students to serve as reporters on activities in the Square for audiences across the country. At 6:30 the student-run public-address system, Voice of the Movement, rebroadcast an official news report on Zhao Ziyang's recent talk with Gorbachev. As the students listened, they clearly approved when they heard Zhao acknowledging there had been errors in socialist construction, and they listened carefully to Zhao's appeal that they leave the Square. But Zhao's plea that students halt their fast drew jeers.

Around 7:15 A.M. the student public-address system called for more dialogue between students and the government and broadcast a demand that the Standing Committee of the Politburo

[9]Unofficial discussion groups for intellectuals.
[10]The Mercedes-Benz sedan had become a popular symbol of corruption by this time.

formally remove the label "turmoil" from the student movement. The broadcast also reminded demonstrators that maintaining rational behavior and public order was crucial to gaining the sympathy of observers around the country. In this regard, the broadcast continued, some improvements were in order: The students needed to stay well organized, should not show themselves pursuing amusements like playing cards, and should sleep in the Square as neatly as if sleeping in their dormitories. They needed to keep order with their own task forces on monitoring, information, and logistics. Their aim, the broadcast said, was to get the label "turmoil" removed through the power of the people, which would be a first in the history of the People's Republic of China and would of course makes some people in the Party extremely nervous.

Around dawn the number of students in the Square began to increase. At the Beijing Normal University fasting station, agents of the State Security Ministry spoke with a student "commander in chief" who was just then receiving a report from a subordinate that a total of sixty-seven fasting students had fainted. When the May 17 issue of *People's Daily* arrived, this commander in chief skimmed through it and then dismissed Zhao Ziyang's appeal because it did not satisfy the two conditions the students had put for ending their fast: (1) that their movement be declared "patriotic" and (2) that Party leaders meet with students for substantive dialogue to be broadcast live. The student leader felt that growing public support for the students would eventually force the government to accept these conditions.

Toward noon the scene became even more crowded and confused as a crowd of students who wanted to form a second group of hunger strikers pressed toward the center of the Square, disregarding appeals to retreat because of the overcrowding. Medical personnel from Xiehe Hospital, Beijing Hospital, and elsewhere circulated among the fasting students giving them infusions of glucose and telling them to drink water and to be careful of sunstroke. From time to time a student would collapse and be taken away by ambulance. Doctors commented that with so many people with weakened immune systems crowded into one place, infectious diseases could break out at any time.

The "May 17 proclamation"

The "May 17 Proclamation,"[11] drafted by Yan Jiaqi and Bao Zunxin, was broadcast in the Square on the morning of May 17 over the student public-address system. Students later collected signatures to the document from other intellectuals and presented it to Zhongnanhai at 12:10 P.M. The

[11]Text in Suzanne Ogden, Kathleen Hartford, Lawrence Sullivan, and David Zweig, eds., *China's Search for Democracy: The Student and the Mass Movement of 1989* (Armonk, New York: M. E. Sharpe, 1992), 225; and Han Minzhu, ed., *Cries for Democracy: Writings and Speeches from the 1989 Chinese Democracy Movement* (Princeton: Princeton University Press, 1990), 221–222.

statement said the collapse of seven hundred students in the hunger strike was an unprecedented tragedy in Chinese history. It blamed the government for not agreeing to the students' demands and said the government's autocratic and irresponsible behavior had led to international embarrassment. The Qing dynasty had ended seventy-six years earlier,[12] the statement went on, yet China was still ruled by an uncrowned emperor, a rotten tyrant grown muddled with age, who made all the important decisions for the nation. It declared that the fasting students had already won a great victory: They had clearly shown that the student movement was not turmoil but a heroic, patriotic democracy movement aimed at burying autocracy and dictatorship. The proclamation ended with a list of slogans, the last of which were "Long live the students!" "Long live the people!" "Long live democracy!" and "Long live freedom!"

The wall poster entitled "Rise up, Party members; resist dictatorship" was the work of four Party members in the Chinese Department at Peking University. It was posted in the Triangle at Peking University during the morning and taken to Zhongnanhai in the afternoon. Addressing Party Central and the Party as a whole, the authors said both their "Party character"[13] and their intuitive moral sense required them, at this crucial juncture, to say that Deng Xiaoping's assessment of the student movement was completely wrong and had harmed the Party; Deng should do a self-criticism and admit his mistake. The true reason there was a power struggle within the Party and the specter of turmoil in the streets, the poster stated, had nothing to do with the students. Rather, the true reason was that autocratic authority at the top had usurped proper procedure and democratic discussion. People should not recognize Deng's personal decrees, the poster said, and it called upon Party-spirited members of the Party everywhere to stand up and resist dictatorship.

Another poster, "Their Voices Are Trembling," was signed by "some students of economics at Qinghua University." It attacked "a certain doddering old man" as exercising extraconstitutional power in a way that was reminiscent of the supposedly bygone Mao era.

Other appeals and open letters that Zhongnanhai received that day came from leaders of the democratic parties and from the government-controlled Communist Youth League, All-China Youth Federation, and All-China Students' Federation, all asking for concessions to the students.

Events outside Beijing

Twenty-seven provinces reported large-scale demonstrations on May 17, sixteen of them numbering ten thousand people or more.

Harbin reported the third consecutive day of student marches. More than 25,000 students took

---

[12]There was an error in the statement here; it should have said seventy-eight years earlier.
[13]*Dangxing*, a technical term borrowed from the Soviet Union, connotes strict Party loyalty and discipline.

part–about half of the 51,700 college students in the city. The report said the protests were likely to gain strength for the foreseeable future unless something was done. The marchers were increasingly well organized: They now lined up by department and school, and monitoring teams kept order. Students had formed an autonomous organization. Slogans were getting more extreme, and participation had expanded from students and young faculty to include older faculty, officials, and reporters. Participants no longer conceived of the movement as temporary. A hunger strike was planned, and students were vowing not to yield until the situation in Beijing changed for the better. In closing, the Provincial Party Committee requested that Party Central take measures to resolve the confrontational situation in Beijing as soon as possible.

There was a fourth day of demonstrations in Shenyang. More than twenty thousand students marched, and people from research institutions and news organizations joined them. Spectators expressed open support for the students, cheering them from rooftops and sidewalks. More than ten thousand onlookers crowded Zhongshan Square, declaring, "The students are saying what is on our minds," "When students in Beijing are fainting and the top leaders still won't come out to see them, doesn't that show they value their own face more than our country?" and "If Party Central continues to refuse dialogue, we workers will rise up!" By nightfall more than one hundred thousand onlookers had gathered at the city's government building, deploring the "inhumanity" and "cowardice" of Party leaders who refused to meet with students. One factory worker said it seemed that workers would have to join the students in the streets in order to get the situation resolved. He warned that the longer the impasse lasted, the more prestige the Party would lose. The Provincial Party Committee urged Party leaders in Beijing to begin dialogue with the students as soon as possible, observing that things would get much worse if workers joined the protests.

In Guangzhou more than five hundred students appeared outside the provincial government offices beginning at 1 A.M., and by afternoon the number exceeded fifteen thousand, making this the largest demonstration in Guangzhou to date. Students carried banners bearing the names of their schools and departments; faculty and staff also turned out. Slogans included the following: "Seven hundred patriots have fallen in Beijing; what are we going to do about it?" "We can stand hunger, but not dictatorship," "If corruption does not end, our movement will not bend," "Dare to resist!" and "No more old-man government!" Students read a letter of support from local writers and university staff and a letter from a group of "ordinary women." At 9 P.M. they called on Ye Xuanping, the governor of Guangdong, to engage them in dialogue. They also presented a list of requests from their autonomous student association addressed to Party Central. The requests included recognizing autonomous student organizations as legal, granting dialogue between students and officials at the highest levels, and lifting controls on the press. At noon six young engineers posted angry slogans outside the government offices and then announced a twenty-four-hour fast and sit-in. They said the government was not responding to student demands in a clear and timely fashion and that they could not face the fasting students in Beijing if they did not themselves join them in fast.

At nearby Shenzhen University students boycotted classes, and three thousand students and faculty marched to in support of the students in Beijing.

In Chengdu about thirty thousand students, faculty, and clerical workers from many institutions gathered in the city square on Renmin South Road. The demonstration was nominally in support of students in Beijing, but just as important, it was a protest of police tactics in Chengdu. At 6 A.M. on May 16 more than a thousand police had suddenly and without warning driven away three hundred students who had been sitting in on Renmin South Road. Students lost watches and had their eyeglasses broken; some lost their footing and fell down a flight of stairs; others reported that the police had humiliated or abused female students. As a result, the demonstration of May 17 was especially acrimonious; faculty and parents called upon the provincial government to investigate the incident and punish those responsible. Workers, citizens, farmers, and even officials made contributions to the students' cause. Around 10 P.M. several hundred students announced to the crowd that they were beginning a hunger strike. Elsewhere in Sichuan more than ten thousand students demonstrated in Chongqing.

In Guiyang students began to gather in front of the railway station to support the Beijing hunger strikers, and by 1 A.M. on the eighteenth their number exceeded three thousand. They marched to the provincial government building and at dawn marched through the city streets, chanting slogans against inflation and in favor of popular unity and dialogue with leaders. One of the crowd's biggest complaints was that the provincial government had failed to lead Guizhou to economic prosperity. At 11:40 A.M. more than two thousand students returned to the provincial government offices and attempted to force their way in, but they were blocked by about a hundred PAP troops. The crowd of students then returned to the streets and continued its march. Other students joined in, including some as young as eleven years old. At 2:30 P.M. the crowd, now between four thousand and five thousand strong, came to a halt in front of the Posts and Telecommunications Building. More participants—students, ordinary citizens, reporters—continued to arrive. Around 4:20 P.M. more than three thousand students gathered outside the Provincial Party Committee building and demanded that the news media be free to cover the student protests objectively, that transportation be provided for students who wished to join the protests in Beijing, and that Party Central immediately begin dialogue with Beijing students and recognize their movement as patriotic. Provincial leaders, seeing no way to respond to these demands, ordered three thousand box dinners and prepared to let the students just sit there if they could not be persuaded to move. At 11 P.M. more than two thousand students were still in place. Police reports counted a total of more than one hundred thousand participants and onlookers in the day's demonstrations.

In Hefei more than ten thousand students, teachers, writers, editors, and others took to the streets, chanting slogans like "We don't want old-man government" and "Enough behind-the-scenes government!" Two thousand protesters from the Chinese University of Science and Technology (CUST), which had been under special pressure not to demonstrate because the campus had been the cradle of the large student demonstrations of 1986, chanted "CUST is breaking its silence!"

Foci of foreign concern

Zhongnanhai received forty-six foreign press summaries, which were organized in four categories: reports of calls for Deng Xiaoping's resignation, Zhao Ziyang's new importance as the last hope among Party leaders, increased worker participation in the demonstrations, and the issue of whether the government would crack down or engage in dialogue.

Xinhua News Agency reported from London said that experts at the Sixteenth Annual International Conference of Political Risk Services agreed that dialogue between the students and the government would help stabilize foreign investment in China; repressive measures, on the other hand, would affect China's relationship with the West and discourage foreign investment. The worst scenario was repression, according to American China specialist Larry Niksch, who was attending the conference, because it would lead to international sanctions against China and threaten Hong Kong's prosperity. The conference put China in the "moderate" category of investor risk but warned that it might be headed toward the high-risk category.

May 18

An unsent letter of resignation

At 5 A.M. on May 18 Zhao Ziyang, Li Peng, Qiao Shi, Hu Qili, Rui Xingwen, Luo Gan, and others went to the Xiehe and Tongren Hospitals in Beijing to visit fasting students. Zhao and the others repeatedly referred to the students' patriotism and spirit of self-sacrifice. At Xiehe Hospital Zhao said, "Your enthusiasm for democracy and the rule of law, for the struggle against corruption, and for furthering reform is extremely valuable. The Center takes your reasonable opinions and demands very seriously and will study them immediately and carefully. We want to improve all areas of Party and government work, and we hope all of you get your health back quickly." Zhao was even more forthright at Tongren Hospital: "The aims of the Party and government are the same as your aims; there is no basic conflict between us. You and we can stay in touch in many different ways and can solve problems together. So please don't continue fasting. You're young, and you've got a long time ahead of you for making contributions to the nation and the people, so you should take care of your health first."

> Account drawn from Central Military Commission Office, "Yang Shangkun's talk to a small-group meeting at the Enlarged Meeting of the Central Military Commission," May 23; and from *Materials for the Fourth Plenum of the Thirteenth Central Committee*, "Remarks of Comrade Yang Shangkun," Secretariat of the Fourth Plenum of the CCP Thirteenth Central Committee, June 23–24, 1989

After he visited the students Zhao went straight to his office and drafted a letter of resignation.

To the Standing Committee of the Politburo and to Comrade Xiaoping:

After much thought I have concluded that, given my current level of awareness and my state of mind, I simply cannot carry out the decision on implementing martial law in Beijing that you have decided on. I still maintain my original opinion. Accordingly, I request to resign as general secretary of the Communist Party of China and as first vice chair of the Military Affairs Commission.

ZHAO ZIYANG

May 18

After finishing the letter Zhao first sent it to Yang Shangkun, marked "extra urgent." He wanted Yang to see it before he sent it to the others because Yang was his closest confidant among the Party Elders and could help him check the letter for political soundness.

Yang telephoned Zhao as soon as he had read the letter.

Yang Shangkun: "You can't do this, Ziyang. Why send a letter like this? Can you imagine the consequences?"

Zhao Ziyang: "I can't work with them[14] any more."

Yang Shangkun: "But whatever you do, you can't do something that puts the Party in the lurch. If you resign you'll have a polarizing effect on society. And anyway, you can still get along with the others on the Standing Committee. . . . Have you thought about how you're going to explain this to the nation? To the Party? To the Politburo and the Standing Committee? And most important, to Comrade

---

[14]Meaning Li Peng and Yao Yilin.—Comp.

Xiaoping? Aren't you always saying how important it is that we guard Comrade Xiaoping's prestige? On this one, Comrade Xiaoping spoke out—and you said you agreed. So what are you, anyway—for him or against him?"

After listening to Yang's advice and getting control of his agitation, Zhao said:

"I'll think it all over once more, Comrade Shangkun. But right now my chest feels stuffy and my head a bit dizzy. I won't be going to the meeting this morning. Please tell the others I'm ill."

Shortly afterward he sent Yang Shangkun another letter:

Comrade Shangkun:
Thank you for your criticism.
In respect for your opinion I will not send my letter. But I still maintain my views, and hence my work will be very difficult. I cannot carry out this policy.

ZHAO ZIYANG
May 18

But Zhao's decision to skip the meeting that was to make arrangements for martial law hardly reduced the intensity of his worry. That afternoon he wrote again to Deng Xiaoping, urging Deng to reconsider his views, to change the official judgment of the student movement as presented in the April 26 *People's Daily* editorial, and to come out against martial law in Beijing. As a precaution, he again telephoned Yang Shangkun:

Zhao Ziyang: "Comrade Shangkun, I just wrote another letter to Comrade Xiaoping asking him to change the official view of the student movement from what's in the April 26 editorial. No matter what, I believe I have the right to express my disagreements inside the Party. I hope you can explain my views to Comrade Xiaoping one more time, and I hope he'll change his judgment on the student movement."

Yang Shangkun: "I cannot say that to him. That question is huge, you know. Changing the judgment would be a slap in the face to all the university presidents, faculty, and student activists.[15] It would leave them no leg to stand on, and we'd all come crashing down. Trust me, you're better off not sending that letter."

[15]Here "activists" refers to pro-government activism.

Li Peng's dialogue
with student representatives

At 11 A.M. on May 18, Li Peng, Li Tieying, Li Ximing, Yan Mingfu, Chen Xitong, and others met in the Great Hall of the People with Wang Dan, Wuerkaixi, and other student leaders.[16]

Li Peng opened by saying that the Party and government were concerned for the health of the fasting students and that the purpose of the present meeting was limited to the search for a way to end the fast.

Wuerkaixi responded that the students had invited Li Peng to come talk, not the other way around, so they would be the ones to set the agenda.

Wang Dan said the only way to get the students out of the Square was to accede to their two conditions for doing so: reclassify the student movement as patriotic and put the student-leader dialogue on live television. If these conditions were met, the student leaders at the meeting would work to persuade all students to leave the Square.

Wuerkaixi noted that the situation in the Square was not always "majority rule": If even one fasting student refused to leave, the others would feel duty-bound to remain. Hence the most extreme 0.1 percent could govern the behavior of the other 99.9 percent. Zhao Ziyang or Li Peng should go personally to the Square to engage students in dialogue, and the *People's Daily* should publish an editorial renouncing its April 26 statement, acknowledging the heroism of the student movement, and apologizing to the nation for its mistake.

Xiong Yan, a student at Peking University, said that history would recognize the patriotism of the student movement, so the real purpose in asking the government to change its stance was to give the government the chance to redeem itself. The people would have no trouble supporting the government provided it would admit its mistakes.

Wang Xuezhen, secretary of the Party Committee at Peking University, said he believed the students to be patriotic and committed to reform. He said the leaders should remind students that no one had called the movement as a whole turmoil. Several other students also spoke. Wang Dan then invited the officials to respond.

Li Peng began by saying he hoped no one would interrupt while the leaders were speaking. There would be plenty of time to raise questions afterward, he said.

At that point Shao Jiang, a Peking University student, interrupted to ask what the officials intended to do now that the movement was beginning to include people from the wider society.

"Are you people finished yet?" asked Li Peng. "Comrade Tieying, please say something."

Li Tieying said the leaders were worried to see the student movement develop as it had; it now affected the nation as a whole. He reminded the students that in two previous dialogues he had

[16]Transcript in Oksenberg et al., *Beijing Spring*, 269–282; excerpt in Han, *Cries for Democracy*, 242–246.

already acknowledged that most students were motivated by patriotism. But, he said, subjective desires and good intentions were not the whole story; one must also look at actual effects. He expressed concern that an increasing number of students in the Square were from outside Beijing.

Yan Mingfu said that his main concern was for the health of the hunger strikers and that ultimate solutions must be separated from the question of the hunger strike. He expressed frustration over his efforts to stay in touch with students and wondered how well student organizations were controlling the Square. Under the circumstances, he said, it might be difficult to arrange for top leaders to visit the Square. He promised that Party Central and the State Council were sincere in their commitment to solving the problems students had pointed out.

Chen Xitong said that everyone—workers, farmers, intellectuals, officials—hoped the issues could be resolved in accordance with democracy and law. Beijing had almost come to a halt and production had been adversely affected; although it was true that some workers supported the students, he added, most people in the city did not want things to continue this way. Doctors and Red Cross personnel were worried about the health of the fasting students. Students' health should not be a pawn in a political struggle or a token to be exchanged for something else.

Li Peng proposed that the Chinese Red Cross bring the fasting students immediately to hospitals and hoped that students in the Square would assist in this effort. He then said that no one had ever claimed the majority of students had been engaged in turmoil. He said the students had actually performed a service by raising the issues in a pointed manner: The government had been given additional impetus to overcome obstacles posed by forces opposed to reform.

Li asked the students to try to imagine for themselves what the outcome of the present events might be. China had seen plenty of turmoil, he said, and too often people with no intention of causing turmoil had in fact brought it about. As premier and as a member of the Communist Party, he had the responsibility to make his views known, and he did not agree with some of the demonstrators' tactics. He promised to discuss the two "issues" (his euphemism for "conditions") that the student leaders had raised, but the current moment was not appropriate. These two issues should not get tangled up with the matter of ending the hunger strike.

Wuerkaixi interjected that the best way to avoid a further tangle was for the government to offer a quick response to the two conditions for ending the fast. Wang Dan added that if any turmoil were to come about, he could confidently speak for the great majority of students in saying that responsibility would rest entirely with the government.

Xiong Yan, addressing Li Peng as "dear Comrade Li," picked out Li's reference to "signs of turmoil" in society and offered his view on the connections between the student movement and social turmoil: "None."

The Elders decide on martial law

At 8:30 that morning the eight Elders–Deng Xiaoping, Chen Yun, Li Xiannian, Peng Zhen, Deng Yingchao, Yang Shangkun, Bo Yibo, and Wang Zhen–met with Politburo Standing Committee members Li Peng, Qiao Shi, Hu Qili, and Yao Yilin and with Military Affairs Commission members Hong Xuezhi, Liu Huaqing, and Qin Jiwei and formally agreed to declare martial law in Beijing.[17]

Li Peng opened by describing the split that had emerged within the Standing Committee on the evening of the seventeenth over the question of martial law. Bo Yibo provided additional detail. Then the Elders began explaining why martial law was necessary.

> Excerpts from Party Central Office Secretariat, "Minutes of an important meeting on May 18," document supplied to Party Central Office Secretariat for its records by the Office of Deng Xiaoping

Deng Xiaoping: "We old comrades are meeting with you today because we feel we have no choice. The Standing Committee should have come up with a plan long ago, but things kept dragging on, and even today there's no decision. Beijing has been chaotic for more than a month now, and we've been extremely restrained through the whole thing, and extremely tolerant. What other country in the world would watch more than a month of marches and demonstrations in its capital and do nothing about it? Comrades Chen Yun and Xiannian came rushing back to the capital because of this, and all of us have been worried sick. I've discussed it with comrades Chen Yun, Xiannian, Peng Zhen, and others, and we all feel Beijing just can't go on like this; we have to have martial law. What's tricky is that we've never faced this kind of thing before: a small handful infiltrating into such a huge number of students and masses. It's hard to draw the lines between the camps, which has made it hard to do what we should have done long ago. Some comrades in the Party think this is a simple question of handling students and masses. But in fact our opponents are exploiting this very perception in order to drag things out and try to wear us down. At bottom they want to overthrow our state and overthrow our Party—that's what's really going on here. If you don't see this point, you can't be clear about what's going on. If you do see it, then you'll know why we need martial law in Beijing."

Li Xiannian: "I feel like the rest of you, and I think it's too bad that an accurate

---

[17]The source does not say where the meeting was held, but since the minutes were compiled by the Deng Office, it was probably at his home.

assessment of what's going on here has to depend on us old comrades. We have no choice but to show concern when things get as chaotic as they are now. General Secretary Zhao Ziyang has an undeniable responsibility here. What's the difference between what we're seeing all across the country and the Cultural Revolution? It's not just Beijing; all the cities are in chaos. Even in the Cultural Revolution nobody dared to charge Xinhua Gate; but they do now, and they beat, smash, and rob, and they lie down on railroad tracks—and this isn't turmoil? So when Comrade Xiaoping told me about the possibility of martial law in Beijing, I jumped at the chance to agree. How did we get to where we are today? I think the problem lies inside the Party: The Party has two different command centers. If there'd been no split in the Party, if the Standing Committee had been united, this chaos would never have come about. Comrades Li Peng and Yilin have told me—and so have many others—that Zhao Ziyang disagrees on this question: He's always been against the official judgment in the April 26 editorial, and he's never thought that this is turmoil. That's how a second command center emerged. If we don't put Beijing under martial law, we'll all end up under house arrest."

Deng Xiaoping: "The April 26 editorial defined the nature of the problem as turmoil. Some people object to the word, but it hits the nail on the head. The evidence shows that the judgment is correct."

Li Peng: "I resolutely support the wise plan for the implementation of martial law in the Municipality of Beijing proposed by Comrade Xiaoping and other Elders. I also want to say something about Comrade Zhao Ziyang.[18] The reason Comrade Zhao Ziyang has not come today is that he opposes martial law. He encouraged the students right from the beginning. When he got back from North Korea, he came out with his May Fourth speech at the Asian Development Bank without clearing it with anyone else on the Standing Committee. The speech was drafted by Bao Tong, and its tone was completely different from the April 26 editorial's, but it got wide distribution and had a big propaganda impact. From then on we felt it was obvious that Comrade Zhao Ziyang's opinions were different from Comrade Xiaoping's and those of the majority of comrades on the Standing Committee. Anyone with political experience could see this, and certainly the ones causing the turmoil could also see it. Comrade Zhao Ziyang did show us in advance his remarks at the meeting on the seventieth anniversary of May Fourth, but he ignored the suggestion a few of us made that he must add 'oppose bour-

[18]The switch to "Comrade Zhao Ziyang" from the more casual and habitual "Comrade Ziyang" indicates greater distance and hostility.

geois liberalization' to that speech. The student movement escalated after his Asian Development Bank speech, and now we have a million people in the streets every day, and more coming in from outside Beijing. Chen Xitong has told me that the Beijing police force is nowhere near adequate. Police have been on duty continuously for more than a month and are exhausted. So we completely support the implementation of martial law in Beijing."

Yao Yilin: "I resolutely support the implementation of martial law in Beijing Municipality. The plan was proposed by Comrade Xiaoping, and without Comrades Xiaoping, Xiannian, Chen Yun, and other Elders, it would have been hard to come to this decision. The reasons why the student movement has become so hard to deal with have directly to do with Comrade Zhao Ziyang. Since Comrade Zhao Ziyang took over responsibility for work at the Center, he effectively set the Four Basic Principles aside; worked against the policy of opposing bourgeois liberalization; seriously overlooked Party building, promotion of spiritual civilization, and political thought work; and ushered in a worsening of the atmosphere in the Party and in society, an obvious decline in the reputation of the Party among the masses, and a huge falling off of the Party's power to fight. Comrade Zhao Ziyang seldom mentioned the Four Basic Principles, let alone how to make them take hold. I remember a time, soon after he became general secretary, when he said at a Politburo meeting that the most important of the principles was Party leadership; the others could be mentioned infrequently or not at all. Comrade Li Peng objected that another of the principles, sticking with socialism, is still quite necessary, and Zhao Ziyang said nobody can say exactly what 'the socialist road' is these days. What kind of general secretary is it that does not lead the people down the socialist road, does not carry out people's democratic dictatorship, and does not make Marxism the guide?"

Yang Shangkun: "Comrade Zhao Ziyang asked me to request that his absence be excused today; he is suffering dizzy spells and has an irregular heartbeat and has gone to see a doctor. I have exchanged opinions with Comrade Zhao Ziyang many times. He has never been able to agree with the judgments of Comrade Xiaoping and members of the Standing Committee on the nature of the student movement and has wanted several times to change the judgment of the April 26 editorial. I have tried to advise him differently and have also criticized him. I have said that this is a huge problem and that to change the judgment would bring us all crashing down. The problem we now face is that the two different voices within the Party have been completely exposed; the students feel that someone at the Center supports them, so they've gotten more and more extreme. Their goals are to get the April 26 editorial repudiated and get official recognition for their autonomous federations. The situation in Beijing and the rest of the country keeps getting grimmer. So we have to guarantee the stability of the whole country, and that means starting with Beijing. I resolutely support declaration of martial law in Beijing and resolutely support its implementation."

Chen Yun: "We don't want any splits in the Party; we really need unity and unanimity. As I said in a phone conversation with Comrade Xiaoping, and again with Comrade Xiannian, the essential question we're facing here is this: Do we retreat or not? All three of us thought that to retreat would be to recognize the students' so-called democratically elected illegal organizations; it would mean we allow bourgeois liberalization and peaceful evolution. Not retreating means we stand resolutely by the policy of the April 26 editorial. So we have to stick with our principles no matter what; we have to stay the course with no change. It seems to me that if we can't even hold to these principles, then what we're doing is destroying our People's Republic—which we won from decades of battle, with the blood of thousands of revolutionary martyrs—all in a single day. And that's the same as repudiating the Chinese Communist Party. Our opponents' aims get clearer by the day: They're using turmoil to attain their political goals. They're setting up illegal organizations that they want to force the Party and government to recognize so they can lay the foundations for an anti-Party opposition group inside China. If they get what they want, China will be headed for a historic step backward, and the people will be thrown back into a morass of turmoil and disaster."

Deng Yingchao: "It's true that we have no room for retreat. Retreat means that we fall, that the People's Republic falls, that a capitalist restoration wins; it'll be what that American, Dulles,[19] hoped for: that our socialism would turn into capitalism after a few generations. The main point in implementing martial law is to get Beijing back to normal as soon as possible and to rescue the children from Tiananmen Square; to see them fasting breaks my heart."

Peng Zhen: "The situation has been getting more and more out of the students' control, and now it's moving increasingly in the opposite direction from what they expected. The people's thinking in Beijing is pretty chaotic these days—all kinds of slogans, all kinds of opinions, advocacies, all kinds of programs and whatnot—and the jumble has dragged on for days with no solution. We can't let this descend into rampant lawlessness like the Cultural Revolution. Didn't we get enough of that the first time around? Do we really want it to hap-

[19]John Foster Dulles, U.S. secretary of state from 1953 to 1959, is known in China for a policy of pushing "peaceful evolution" in socialist countries.

pen again? Without martial law, we can't restore order; without martial law, we're saying we accept indefinite anarchy. Some of the intellectuals out there marching in the streets keep mouthing the phrase 'rule of law'; but in fact, they themselves trample the Constitution and the laws, and they incite others to violate the Constitution and the laws with them. Quite a few of the students got stirred up by exactly these people. The million-person demonstrations in Beijing in the last few days are even bigger than the huge Red Guard rallies during the Cultural Revolution. Anarchy is raging again, laws and regulations aren't worth the paper they're written on, and violent tremors jolt through society. Martial law is the only cure for this kind of antidemocratic, anti–'rule of law' turmoil. How can we blindly go along with it and yield to it? Our backs are against a wall; we've got no choice."

Li Peng: "All kinds of people are strutting around on stage these days. There were posters in the crowd yesterday attacking Comrade Xiaoping, and somebody fed a lot of slander and rumors to the foreign media. Yan Jiaqi, Bao Zunxin, and others from the Chinese Academy of Social Sciences launched a so-called intellectuals' 'May 17 Proclamation' that publicly aimed its spear at Comrade Xiaoping with the most poisonous kind of slander and vilification. It called Comrade Xiaoping an 'emperor without a crown' and a 'dictator.' The relevant units are already closely monitoring the movements of these people, have secured evidence of their manipulation and exploitation of the student movement, and will expose them at the appropriate time."

Wang Zhen: "These people are really asking for it! They should be nabbed as soon as they pop out again. Give 'em no mercy! The students are nuts if they think this handful of people can overthrow our Party and our government! These kids don't know how good they've got it! When we were their age we lived in a forest of rifles and a rain of bullets; we didn't know what a peaceful day was! So aren't they dandy, now? Give them peace and they don't want it; they want to go starve themselves instead. No appreciation! What do the Party and the government owe them? Our Party is the people's Party; our government is the people's government. Out of responsibility to our sacred motherland, and out of responsibility to the whole people, I resolutely support Comrade Xiaoping's wise decision on martial law. If the students don't leave Tiananmen on their own, the PLA should go in and carry them out. This is ridiculous!"

Bo Yibo: "The whole imperialist Western world wants to make socialist countries leave the socialist road and become satellites in the system of international monopoly capitalism. The people with ulterior motives who are behind this student movement have support from the United States and Europe and from the

Kuomintang (KMT) reactionaries in Taiwan. There is a lot of evidence that the U.S. Congress and other Western parliaments have been saying all kinds of things about this student movement and have even held hearings. The Central Standing Committee of the KMT on Taiwan has passed a 'resolution' saying nonsense like 'The recent student movement on the mainland demanding freedom and democracy has already kindled the long-accumulated dissatisfaction our compatriots feel toward the violent government of the CCP. Our government and people should be more active and take more initiative in finding ways to help them, so that the mainland can reach democracy and freedom more quickly.' Members of the overseas Chinese Alliance for Democracy, which we have declared to be an illegal and reactionary organization, not only voice support for the student movement but openly admit that they advise the students and even plan how to reenter China and meddle directly. Advocates of peaceful evolution have sent back a so-called 'Proclamation to Encourage Democratic Government in Mainland China,' spouting that 'China is the China of all the people, not just a China of one Party or one faction; now is the time for the people to come forward with their political demands,' and hooting that 'the basic problem is that the people must have the power to choose which party will rule.' So you see, it was no accident that the student movement turned into turmoil. We mustn't underestimate the peril in this situation. The longer we delay, the worse it will get, and the harder it will be to extricate ourselves. The decisive measure of martial law will help to calm things down."

Li Xiannian: "Another point I'd like to make here is that the reason this thing got so big has a lot to do with our news and propaganda. The newspapers, television, and radio during these days not only haven't guided the people correctly; they've gotten in there and made it worse, encouraging the students and making it seem as though everyone in the streets is patriotic and anyone who's not demonstrating isn't. And let me say, too, that it's unthinkable that a speech by Zhao Ziyang could have better results or get a better reaction than the April 26 editorial!"

Hu Qili: "There are some things I need to think through here, and I want to consider carefully. But I'll follow Party discipline."

Qiao Shi: "For a long time now we haven't done a good job of implementing Comrade Xiaoping's Four Basic Principles and opposition to bourgeois liberalization, and the result has been a certain amount of ideological confusion. In recent weeks a tiny minority has taken advantage of ideological confusion, of the good intentions of many young students, of some mistakes of the Party and government, and of some corruption in our ranks to start plotting behind the scenes, creating turmoil, and scheming to use turmoil to reach its goal of denying Party leadership and the socialist system. I believe the time is now right for Party Central to declare martial law in some districts of Beijing. Once martial law is declared, the important thing is the threat that the army will represent. To take advantage of this threat, we must find the right moment to get the schools' Party and administrative leaders and faculty and some parents to remove the students from the Square. If we can do it this way, this would be the best way to solve the problem. We want to resolve the problem, not shed blood."

Liu Huaqing: "The scene in Beijing is like waves in the ocean that are gradually building strength, and now the waves have spread to nearly every major city in the country. Transportation is basically paralyzed in many parts of Beijing. Some workers have taken to the streets. The price of groceries has increased, periodicals and mail are not delivered on time, and garbage has begun to pile up. As I see it, Beijing is already in severe anarchy; there's no order to speak of. We have to restore order in Beijing, and let Beijing then be a model for the whole country. That's the only way the rest of the country is going to calm down. I resolutely support Comrade Xiaoping's decision to put a portion of the districts of Beijing under martial law. The thinking of the troops at present is unified and their organizational discipline is tight. The soldiers and officers will certainly be able resolutely to carry out any order from Party Central and the Military Affairs Commission."

Hong Xuezhi: "For a soldier, duty is paramount. I will resolutely carry out the order to put Beijing under martial law."

Qin Jiwei: "Obvious anarchy has already appeared in Beijing. It seems like no one needs any restraint or discipline anymore. If you want to blow off steam you just go out on the streets and demonstrate—as if demonstrating could solve any problems. Everybody demonstrating, nobody producing—that is scary! The reasons for martial law are to restore order, to clean up the confusion, and to avoid major turmoil. I resolutely support and will resolutely carry out the orders of Party Central and the Military Affairs Commission for martial law in Beijing."

The decisions of the meeting were: (1) at midnight on May 21 a portion of the districts in Beijing will be placed under martial law; (2) on the evening of May 19 there will be a large meeting of Central and Beijing Party, government, and military officials; (3) Comrade Yang Shangkun will be responsible for the action plan for the immediate deployment of troops in urban districts of the municipality and will set up the martial law troops' headquarters; (4) reports on the current situation in Beijing will go to the two senior marshals Xu Xiangqian and Nie Rongzhen, and the Party Central Committee and the Military Affairs Commission will be notified of the decision to declare martial law in Beijing; (5) because of the tense situation in Beijing and across the country, all provincial-level governments will be notified that following the large meeting of Party, government, and military officials in Beijing, their Party standing committees should report to the Center on their attitudes toward martial law.

That evening, May 18, Zhao Ziyang attended what was to be his final meeting of the Politburo Standing Committee. He was no longer a major player.

Deployment of the martial law troops

Following Deng Xiaoping's instructions, Yang Shangkun chaired a meeting of the CMC on the deployment of troops in Beijing under martial law. The meeting was attended by Yang Shangkun; Hong Xuezhi; Liu Huaqing; Qin Jiwei; Yang Baibing, chairman of the General Political Department of the PLA; Chi Haotian, PLA chief of staff; and Zhao Nanqi, director of the PLA General Logistics Department. Deng Xiaoping and Zhao Ziyang were the only CMC members who did not attend. Yang Shangkun, Liu Huaqing, and Chi Haotian reported to Deng Xiaoping immediately after the meeting.

> Excerpt from Central Military Commission Office, "Yang Shangkun's talk to a small-group meeting at the Enlarged Meeting of the Central Military Commission," May 18, as excerpted in Central Party Office Secretariat, "Daily report" (*Meiri yibao*), May 19

Yang Shangkun: "I've just finished chairing the meeting that you requested, Comrade Xiaoping. Comrades Xuezhi, Huaqing, Minister Qin, Haotian, Baibing, and Nanqi were all there. We agreed to support martial law resolutely and to carry it out to the letter. We discussed responsibilities and decided that the Beijing, Shenyang, and Jinan Military Districts should bear the main load, with other districts supporting. A martial law command center will be headed by Huaqing, Haotian, and Zhou Yibing.[20] They will report to the CMC, which will be ultimately responsible for troop deployment."

[20]Commander of the Beijing Military District.—Comp.

Deng Xiaoping: "How many PLA troops will be in Beijing?"

Yang: "Counting the armed police, 180,000."

Yang handed Deng a CMC report on Beijing troop deployment. The eventual order that was issued in Deng's name read:

> Excerpt from Central Military Commission Office, "Minutes of Central Military Commission meeting," May 18, as excerpted in Central Party Office Secretariat, "Daily report" (*Meiri yibao*), May 19

In accordance with Article 89, Item 16, of the Constitution of the People's Republic of China, the State Council has decided to implement martial law in parts of Beijing beginning May 21, 1989.[21] The following units are ordered to deploy in designated areas of Beijing on May 19 and 20: the Twenty-Fourth, Twenty-Seventh, Twenty-Eighth, Thirty-Eighth, Sixty-Third, and Sixty-Fifth Armies of the Beijing Garrison Command under the Beijing Military District; the Thirty-Ninth and Fortieth Armies of the Shenyang Military District; and the Fifty-Fourth and Sixty-Seventh Armies of the Jinan Military District.

After Deng signed the order, Yang Shangkun instructed Chi Haotian as chief of staff to meet with the commanding officers of the Beijing, Shenyang, and Jinan Military Districts to "finalize the name lists of every group army division scheduled to advance into Beijing and their exact times of departure and arrival, as well as details regarding primary duties." In the meantime, Yang Baibing was instructed to issue a political mobilization decree in the name of the PLA General Political Department to all major military districts, ordering that "all districts enforce strict discipline at this critical moment for the Party and the state; be prepared at all times and act in unison to follow the instructions of Party Central and the CMC." Zhao Nanqi was ordered to "prepare all strategic materials and provisions for combat readiness and to consult with the Beijing Municipal Committee and Government to resolve the issues of food, lodging, and supplies for the troops."

One incident stunned Yang Shangkun and the other CMC members on the evening the deployment order was issued. Zhou Yibing reported urgently to Yang Shangkun.

> Excerpt from Central Military Commission Office, "Yang Shangkun's talk to a small-group meeting at the Enlarged

---

[21]The beginning of Chapter 6 carries the information that the date was moved to May 20 after word began to leak.

Meeting of the Central Military Commission, May 23; and
from Yang Shangkun's remarks at the Enlarged Meeting of the
Politburo Standing Committee, June 20

Zhou Yibing: "Chairman Yang, we've just received a report from the Thirty-Eighth Army. The commander, Xu Qinxian, cannot carry out the order to enter Beijing to carry out martial law."

Yang Shangkun: "This is no time for jokes! This is a military order! Disobeying a military order gets you court-martialed! What do the other people in the Thirty-Eighth Army have to say?"

Zhou Yibing: "Most are ready to carry out the order resolutely."

Yang Shangkun: "This is no good. It's too important. You go talk to Xu Qinxian right away. Work on him. Tell him that whether or not he can see the logic of an order has nothing to do with whether he has to carry it out."

That night Zhou Yibing and others drove to Baoding, where the Thirty-Eighth Army was stationed.

The mood at Tiananmen

The hunger strike entered its fifth day on May 18 and agencies reported a further upsurge in citizen support. Despite a rainstorm, more than a million people came to support the students. Besides the educators, researchers, and state employees who had been seen before, today the crowd included workers from many sectors of Beijing industry and commerce. They entered the Square by car, bus, or truck, causing an enormous traffic jam that taxed the energies of the student monitors who were trying to keep a path open for emergency vehicles. The workers came in groups, organized by unit.[22] They brought food and blankets, and some contributed generous sums of money to the hunger strike. Quanjude—a famous Beijing duck restaurant—dispatched a van with "Delivering duck soup" written on the side. Even the association for the handicapped, which was headed by Deng Xiaoping's son Deng Pufang, sent one hundred thousand yuan. The slogans the workers shouted carried a sharp edge against the leadership, the Party "princes," and even the supreme leader. A slogan said, "If one man will resign, a whole nation will wish him well."

Some military personnel joined the demonstrators. They wore plainclothes and came as individuals but carried banners that identified them with the military. Police academy cadets arrived

---

[22]Implying that the Party leadership in these units had tilted to the side of the students.

in formation and in uniform. Farmers from nearby villages and faculty members of the Central Party School came as well. The themes for everyone were that the students were patriotic and that the people supported them.

The Beijing Railway Bureau reported that on May 17 more than twenty thousand students had entered the city by train from Tianjin, Hebei, Shanxi, and elsewhere. The next day another ten thousand or so came from more-distant provinces. The Beijing station master reported that if the press of students continued, the station would have trouble handling priority freight such as grain, coal, and gasoline.

In the Square emotions ran high. Early in the morning there was a rumor that the Central leaders were finally coming for a dialogue, followed by a letdown when no one came. The student public-address system broadcast open letters to the government from a group of military officers,[23] from staff of the Party Propaganda Department's Information Division, and from Beijing journalists.[24] All demanded that the government drop its objections and send people to the Square to engage in dialogue with the students. Groups of students from universities in the provinces marched in formation, some taking over the work of the exhausted Beijing student monitors. One banner read, "No food, no water, no retreat, no way."[25]

Some workers came to the Square to complain that the demonstrations had grown so large they were interfering with people trying to get to their jobs and with the delivery of food to the markets. Some blamed the leaders, who could have resolved the situation simply by coming to the Square as the students demanded.

As some hunger strikers refused to take shelter from the afternoon rains, the poet Ye Wenfu read a long poem over the loudspeaker and then announced his resignation from the Party. Parents, elderly retired officials, and middle-aged medical personnel broke down in tears at the sight of the young people's suffering. The common refrain was, "Why are the leaders so uncaring? Why have they still not come to speak with the students?" One elderly retired official remarked, "All of a sudden the people's smoldering resentment of the government has found an opportunity to flare up."

Student protests in twenty-eight provinces

In reports received May 18 twenty-one provinces reported that large-scale protests had occurred over the course of the preceding few days. In seventeen provincial capitals crowds of ten thousand or more had gathered.

---

[23]Summary of text in Oksenberg et al., *Beijing Spring*, 282–283.
[24]Summary of text in Oksenberg et al., *Beijing Spring*, 283–284.
[25]The slogan plays on the fact that *"jue"* means both "to cut off," as in cutting off food and water in order to fast, and "determined."

In Shanghai on May 17 a crowd of student demonstrators in front of the municipal government offices grew to 23,000. One hundred of them started a hunger strike, and another fifty were given a big send-off at the railway station as they headed for Beijing to join the Tiananmen strikers. A group of workers showed up in support, declaring that the official labor union no longer represented them. Deputy Party secretary Wu Bangguo and other officials conducted a dialogue with students in the afternoon. Some of the participants withdrew in protest because the student representatives had been chosen by the official rather than the autonomous student organization and because Party secretary Jiang Zemin did not take part. The remaining students pressed the leaders on their handling of the *World Economic Herald* incident, claiming it violated the Constitution. Wu Bangguo replied that the Municipal Party Committee had handled the incident in a makeshift way with the best interests of the paper in mind so the paper could continue to publish and support the reforms. Only history could determine whether the Party Committee had done the right thing. The students demanded dialogue with Jiang and demanded that the full tape of the current session be broadcast on TV. In the evening journalists from the city's official newspapers marched in support of the students.

On the following day more than one hundred thousand citizens marched in support of the students. Famous writers marched wearing headbands giving their names. Others in the crowd included professors, scientists, and some workers. The march was even joined by some representatives from municipal Party organs, the Commerce and Industry Association, and some of the minority democratic parties. High school teachers and students also marched.[26] Slogans were pointedly personal: "Missing: Deng Xiaoping, Zhao Ziyang, Li Peng," and "Xiaoping, you are wrong."

On May 17 in Shijiazhuang, the capital of Hebei, some ten thousand students and faculty and two hundred journalists and social scientists demonstrated in support of the Beijing students, shouting for democracy, dialogue, and freedom of the press. About five thousand of them broke into the provincial government complex and tried to hand over a petition demanding that the local authorities send word of the local students' support for the strikers to the authorities in Beijing. Then more than three hundred students left by train for Beijing. On May 18 the demonstrators were joined by government employees, researchers, high school students, and medical personnel, among others. The crowd of marchers and onlookers numbered around 150,000. Besides the usual slogans for democracy and against corruption, the crowd shouted that Zhao Ziyang and Li Peng should engage in dialogue and that Deng Xiaoping should resign. Some employees of the provincial People's Consultative Conference disclosed an urgent telegram they had sent to Beijing demanding that the April 26 editorial be withdrawn, that the leaders in Beijing conduct dialogue, and that the Party convene a special meeting of the Central Committee to make decisions on the major issues students had raised. The Railway Ministry reported that the number of Hebei stu-

---

[26]The security authorities would have noted this because high school students had been the shock troops of violence during the first phase of the Cultural Revolution.

dents taking trains to Beijing during the period May 16–18 had reached five thousand. Large-scale demonstrations also occurred in the Hebei cities of Baoding, Tangshan, and Handan.

In Taiyuan, in Shanxi, some 230 demonstrators started hunger striking on May 16, and the number of demonstrators in the streets reached thirty thousand. Provincial leaders went to factories and schools to try to calm emotions, generally with little success. On the morning of May 18 some violent elements attacked the provincial government building, throwing bricks and shards of glass, causing severe injury to eight people and light injury to eighty-seven police and PAP troops. About sixty demonstrators were arrested. As morning broke, an estimated 130,000 demonstrators from colleges and high schools, news organizations, the democratic parties, and some production units started to fill the streets. Slogans called for Deng Xiaoping and Yang Shangkun to resign. Early in the afternoon Governor Wang Senhao came out to comfort hunger strikers, who had been soaked by a rain- and hailstorm. Wang quickly agreed to two demands: that the province officially convey to Beijing the Shanxi students' wish that Zhao Ziyang and Li Peng hold dialogue with the students in Tiananmen Square and that the Party and government leaders in the province hold dialogue with the students on an equal footing. Sizable demonstrations were also reported in four other cities in the province.

Similar events were reported from Lanzhou, capital of Gansu; Jinan, capital of Shandong; Nanjing, capital of Jiangsu; Wuhan, capital of Hubei; Hangzhou, capital of Zhejiang; and Fuzhou, capital of Fujian. With some local variation, the pattern was the same: Students went on hunger strike in front of government offices, demanding dialogue locally and in Beijing; larger and larger groups of citizens from all stations of society—especially journalists, officials, and workers—came out in support of the students; banners and slogans named Central leaders and demanded Deng's resignation and the end of old-man government; provincial Party and government leaders conducted dialogues without finding a way to satisfy the demonstrators; students boarded trains for Beijing; and demonstrations also took place in other towns outside the provincial capital.

"The government will have to act"

The main theme of the twenty-three foreign reports passed along to Zhongnanhai on May 18 was the growing likelihood of repression. L'Agence France-Presse and the Jiji News Agency predicted Li Peng's hard line in his meeting with the students might presage a crackdown. *Le Figaro* suggested that the risk of anarchy had brought the government to a position where it would have to act and that if milder methods did not work, it would probably use repression. The Yugoslav news agency Tanjug said it was hard to imagine how the government could use force to suppress two million citizens in the capital, let alone a movement that had already spread nationwide. But the French paper *Libération* said that if the Party did not use force, it would have to find a way to restore its authority on the basis of a new kind of open politics that it might not be able to manage.

May 19

Zhao Ziyang's sorrowful speech

At 4 A.M. on May 19, following the close of the Politburo Standing Committee meeting, Zhao Ziyang and Li Peng visited the Square, accompanied respectively by Wen Jiabao and Luo Gan.[27] Knowing his political career was near an end, Zhao made remarks that brought tears to the eyes of those who heard him. "We have come too late," he said, and he begged the students to protect their health, to end the hunger strike, and to leave the Square before it was too late. The demands they had raised would be dealt with, he was sure—including the issue of whether the incident was turmoil or a patriotic movement and the larger issues of corruption and reform—but that would take time. Meanwhile, they were endangering their health and disrupting life in the capital. "We demonstrated and lay across railroad tracks when we were young, too, and took no thought for the future," he told the students. "But I have to ask you to think carefully about the future. Many issues will be resolved eventually. I beg you to end the hunger strike." He was mobbed with autograph seekers.

Zhao was exhausted, and his doctor urged him to rest. On the morning of May 19 he requested three days' sick leave.

Deng Xiaoping's sense of injury

That morning Deng Xiaoping called Yang Shangkun and asked him to come to his residence. Deng was angry.

Excerpt from memoranda of conversations supplied by a friend of Yang Shangkun who cannot be further identified

---

Deng Xiaoping: "Did you see that Zhao went to Tiananmen and spoke? Did you hear what he said? Tears were streaming down his face, and he really tried to look mistreated. He's flouted Party principles here—very undisciplined."

Yang Shangkun: "Something seemed very wrong about the tone he assumed—as if he wanted to stop working or something. He said he was 'old, and didn't matter any more.' Doesn't this amount to dragging Party differences out into the open? He just got through asking for three days' leave from the Politburo Standing Committee, claiming to be ill, but I'm afraid he's getting more stubborn about

---

[27]Report on the visit in Oksenberg et al., *Beijing Spring*, 288–290, 290–291.

his opinions."

Deng Xiaoping: "You know that I've taken a lot of heat inside the Party since this whole thing broke out. After Zhao's speech to the ADB, Xiannian told me this was the voice of a second headquarters inside the Party, and he wanted me to say something about it. Later Chen Yun, Xiannian, and others telephoned me with their views time and again. In their view, the students went to Tiananmen because the Center let it happen, and we should do something about it. But he [Zhao] was completely uncooperative—he didn't even show a sign of wanting to cooperate. I had to do what I did. He really was wandering farther and farther off."

Yang Shangkun: "I still think I should try to get him to come to the big meeting tonight. We shouldn't let things get set in stone."

Deng Xiaoping: "It's up to him. Our economy has improved a lot in recent years. The people have food to eat, and clothes to wear—as anybody can see. The economy is still the base; if we didn't have that economic base, the farmers would have risen in rebellion after only ten days of student protests—never mind a whole month. But as it is, the villages are stable all over the country, and the workers are basically stable too. This is the fruit of reform and opening. When economic reform reaches a certain point, you have to have political reform to accompany it. You know, I've never opposed political reform. But you have to consider the realities, you have to think about how many of the old comrades in the Party can accept it right now. You can't eat yourself fat in a day. It's not that easy. I'm old, and if somebody wants to say I'm senile, fine, confused, fine—but for somebody my age inside the Party, I don't think I'm conservative. Am I hanging on to power?"

Yang Shangkun: "If that were true, you could have become Party chairman when Hua Guofeng lost power. You didn't have to name Hu Yaobang for the post."

Deng Xiaoping: "These last few days I've been thinking. I've never been formally number 1 in the Party, but everybody keeps hanging around me, showing me deference. I have to give the nod on every important decision. I carry too much weight, and that's not good for the Party or the state. I should think about retiring. But how can I, right now? With all this lying before us, how could I retire? Would Xiannian, Wang Zhen, and the others agree? Stepping down is not all that easy, but our Party does need new faces and new blood."

Yang Shangkun: "The people will remember your achievements, Comrade Xiaoping. I also think they will understand and accept your decision on martial law."

Deng Xiaoping: "How is the security guard work going?"[28]

[28]Deng's change of subject here has to do with another of the several roles that Yang played for Deng. In addition to serving as president of the People's Republic, Yang was in charge of the CCP

Yang Shangkun: "We've already strengthened the guard around the Central state organs and the homes of the Central leading comrades. Some of the troops will enter Beijing this evening. Don't you think, for security, that you should move into Zhongnanhai for a while?"

Deng Xiaoping: "I've never thought of going back ever since I moved out. I'm not going anywhere. It's fine here."

Yang Shangkun: "General Xu Haidong has a son named Xu Qinxian who is chief of the Thirty-Eighth Army. Yesterday, after he got orders from the Central Military Commission, he said he wouldn't be able to carry them out. But Zhou Yibing and others from the Beijing Military District have just set this right."

Deng Xiaoping: "No military man can disobey orders, and Xu Haidong's son is no exception. You can take care of the military questions; just be sure discipline is strict and thinking is unified."

Following up on a suggestion from Li Peng's wife Zhu Lin, in the afternoon Luo Gan personally inspected and arranged for the refurbishment of the "swimming pool" quarters where Mao Zedong had lived in Zhongnanhai and suggested to Li Peng and Yang Shangkun that they stay there. Yang at first insisted on staying in Liuyin Street and not moving. Li Peng said, "Chairman Yang, this is entirely so that we can do martial law work, and it's only temporary. After martial law we can go home." That evening Li Peng and Zhu Lin, their children, and their children's families moved into the building (where they stayed until 1991). Only the next day did Yang, twenty years Li Peng's senior, accede to Li's persistent urging and move. The swimming pool, which had been open daily to staff of the Central Office and State Council Office, was closed.

At 4 P.M. that day Li Peng received Richard Woolcott, special envoy of the Australian prime minister, and David Sadlier, the Australian ambassador, in the Ziguang Pavilion. Li opened the conversation by asking, "Mr. Ambassador, did you come to Zhongnanhai today along the normal route?" Sadlier said no, "We came through the alleyways because we couldn't get through the main thoroughfares." Li Peng said, "This shows that our capital has already fallen into disorder. The disorder has already spread in differing degrees to other cities. The Chinese government will adopt a responsible attitude in taking measures to put a stop to this disorder, to restore normal social order, and to guarantee the smooth advance of our policies of reform and opening." In what seemed a hint that China might carry out martial law, Li added that "this is entirely a matter of China's internal affairs. We will resolve it appropriately. I have full confidence in this."

Central Guards Bureau (*Zhongyang jingweiju*), whose director Yang Dezhong was an old subordinate of Yang Shangkun's.—Comp.

Urgent notice from the PLA General Political Department

On the morning of May 19 the PLA General Political Department issued an urgent notice to military regions around the country, to the military service arms,[29] and to the main military organs in the capital. The notice reported that martial law would be declared in Beijing and gave instructions on how to deal with four kinds of wrong thinking that had gained some influence in the military: Some officers or troops did not take seriously the student movement's threat to stability; some thought the movement might do some good in combating corruption; some were afraid that if the troops got too actively involved in resolving civil disorders, they might be drawn into factional disputes among the masses, as had happened during the Cultural Revolution; and some felt that stemming social disorder was the job of civilian leaders, not the military.

The notice said that to deal with these attitudes, political officers should undertake three kinds of political thought work: First, they should lead the troops to a correct understanding of how important stability is for the country and to the realization that what people really want is stability, continuation of reform, and Party leadership. Second, they should help the troops and officers analyze which of the students' slogans were reasonable, which were excessive, which were just emotional, and which were truly counterrevolutionary, so the troops could dispel their doubts about the appropriateness of martial law. Third, they should help the commanding officers think through the necessity of maintaining strict attitudes of political correctness, so they could lead others in the task of ending the turmoil. The leading officers should pay close attention to social trends in the regions where they were garrisoned, be sure the troops under them were completely united, and be sure their own offices were absolutely clean so that issues about corruption did not become a problem among their own troops.

Six-point urgent declaration on the situation

The State Security Ministry reported on May 19 that Gao Shan, an official with the Office for Research on Reform of the Political System, had that morning come to the Institute for Economic Reform in China (IERC), where its director, Chen Yizi, was meeting with some twenty people. Gao told the group about events at Party Central since early May and about Zhao Ziyang's sick leave. Chen immediately declared that the group should issue a declaration and then organize staff from twenty of the ministries and commissions of the State Council to sit in at Tiananmen Square in

---

[29] The People's Liberation Army encompasses such "arms of the service" *(bingzhong)* as the ground forces, the navy, the air force, the marines, and so on.

protest. Chen led the group in drafting a "Six-Point Emergency Statement on the Current Situation," which was issued in the name of IER, the Development Research Institute of the Agricultural Research Center of the State Council, the International Affairs Research Institute of the China International Trust and Investment Corporation (CITIC), and the Beijing Association of Young Economists.[30] The main leaders of these four organizations—in particular Chen himself, Bao Tong, Du Runsheng of the Agricultural Research Center, and Li Xianglu of CITIC—were associated with Zhao Ziyang in one way or another.

The declaration opposed the impending martial law without explicitly mentioning it. It praised the students, blamed the government for the situation's deterioration, and called for an emergency meeting of the National People's Congress and for a special Party Congress, which should make decisions on behalf of the whole people to resolve the split in the leadership. The declaration was widely distributed and posted around town.[31]

Peaceful day, night of terror

According to the State Security Ministry's report on developments in the Square on May 19, the number of demonstrators marching in support of the students had diminished by as much as half. Most groups of marchers passing through the Square numbered in the tens or hundreds rather than the thousands, and the number of political slogans had also decreased. On the other hand, many students had come from universities outside Beijing to camp in the Square.

At 9:30 A.M. a handbill circulated from a group calling itself the Planning Committee for a Beijing Municipal Autonomous Workers' Federation. It called for a twenty-four-hour general strike in the city if the government did not accede to the students' demands by the next day. The student leadership was severely split, displaying coordination difficulties among four separate organizations (the AFS, the Hunger Strike Command, the Dialogue Delegation, and the newly established Association of Students from Outside Beijing). The leaders debated all day about what to do, and order in the Square deteriorated. As students from the provinces flowed in, the shortage of food, water, and facilities became more pressing. Wuerkaixi remarked that the situation was worrisome and that all the original AFS leaders except he had resigned and been replaced several times.

At 2 P.M. Voice of the Movement loudspeakers read out the six-point declaration of the four pro-

---

[30]These four organizations, the "three institutes and one association," were the major workplaces for young social scientists supporting reform and conducting policy research for Zhao. The text of the declaration is in Han, *Cries for Democracy*, 250–251.

[31]After the crackdown Chen Yizi was placed on the wanted list, but he later escaped and now lives in New York City. At the Fourth Plenum of the Thirteenth Central Committee in June, Li Peng labeled this declaration "a masterful plot by Zhao's brain trusts to put the Politburo and State Council on trial."

reform research units. Some of the parents and fellow students of the hunger strikers came to the Square to try to persuade them to end their strike. An official of the All-China Women's Federation came to the AFS headquarters and demanded that the student leaders end the hunger strike, given all the effort the strikers' fathers and mothers, as well as the state, had invested in them. A professor from Beijing Union University said society's support for the student strikers might reverse if students started to die of hunger.

Around 5 P.M. a rumor spread in hunger strike headquarters that martial law would be declared. The atmosphere in the Square became anxious. Later a large number of handbills were distributed at the Square and the railway station suggesting that the hunger strike be converted into a peaceful sit-in and that the demands be shifted to retaining Zhao Ziyang, calling a special Communist Party Congress, and calling an emergency meeting of the NPC. Around 8 P.M. some people who said they were from IER came and announced by bullhorn that Zhao had been fired, Li Peng was in charge, and force was about to be used. These speakers called for a nonviolent, nationwide general strike and for emergency Party Congress and NPC meetings. Later the Voice of the Movement broadcast an AFS decision to end the hunger strike and convert it to a sit-in.

In the early hours of May 20 the heads of student organizations in the Square announced this decision in a press conference and urged an emergency meeting of the NPC. They called for high school and grade school students to refrain from demonstrating, students from outside Beijing to refrain from coming to Beijing, and workers to refrain from striking.

On the campuses in Beijing, autonomous student federations broadcast announcements that Zhao was out, Li was in charge, and the troops were coming. The broadcasts also urged students to rush to the Square and to block intersections against the troop vehicles.

How many students from outside Beijing entered the city?

On the eve of martial law, the Railway Ministry reported to Zhongnanhai that a total of 56,888 students had entered the city on 165 trains between 6 P.M. on May 16 and 8 A.M. on May 19. The flood of students had stressed the already overstretched system. Most of the students had demanded to ride without tickets,[32] took over the trains' public-address systems, asked passengers for contributions, hung posters in and on the cars, and even demanded free food. Their rushing and overcrowding caused some of the trains to run behind schedule. There had been two cases in which students blocked the tracks—in Wuhan and in Fuzhou—which also made trains late. The ministry urged the Center to bring an end to the student movement as soon as possible and expressed the hope that local officials would try to stop the tide of students to Beijing.

[32]During the Cultural Revolution the Railway Ministry was ordered to give students free rides. Presumably, in the current atmosphere conductors were afraid to deny students the same privilege.

CHAPTER SIX

May 19–22

Martial Law

EDITORS' NOTE: The declaration of martial law in the five urban districts of Beijing elicited fierce opposition in the capital, nationwide, and internationally. Troops from twenty-two divisions moved toward the city, but many were stopped in the suburbs or blocked in city streets and failed to reach their destinations. In the first of what would be many similar instructions, on May 20 Yang Shangkun ordered that the soldiers should never turn their weapons on innocent civilians, even if provoked.

Provincial authorities voiced the requisite support for Beijing while taking actions locally to try to assure that nothing spectacular happened in their own bailiwicks. On May 21 student leaders in the Square voted to declare victory and withdraw but reversed their decision under pressure of widespread sentiment among new recruits in the Square to continue the strike.

The same day Deng Xiaoping convened the Party Elders to take charge, since the younger generation of leaders seemed unable to manage. They agreed that Zhao Ziyang, along with his Standing Committee ally Hu Qili, had to be replaced. They passed over Li Peng as a successor, vetted the names of several candidates, and began to form a consensus for Shanghai Party secretary Jiang Zemin.

The Elders also decided to summon NPC Standing Committee chair Wan Li home from a state visit abroad. Wan's conciliatory comments overseas and the notion that he might return and mobilize the NPC Standing Committee to cancel martial law appeared to be new factors prolonging the strike.

On May 22 the three remaining Politburo Standing Committee members, Li Peng, Qiao Shi, and Yao Yilin, briefed high-level officials on policy toward the movement and the decision to remove Zhao. The students in the Square seemed unable to decide whether to withdraw. Some important intellectuals were urging them to persist. In the provinces there were signs that students would try to involve factory workers in the movement.

May 19

A big meeting of the Party, government, and military in Beijing

At 10 P.M. on May 19 Party Central and the State Council convened a meeting of Party, government, and military officials, mostly holding the rank of deputy minister or higher,[1] in an auditorium at National Defense University in the western suburbs of Beijing. The purpose was to announce martial law, which, because of news leaks, now was to begin at 10 A.M. on May 20, fourteen hours earlier than originally planned. Zhao did not attend the meeting despite efforts by Li Peng's and Yang Shangkun's staffs to remind him.

> Excerpts from Party Central Office Secretariat, "Materials from the big meeting of Central and Beijing Municipal Party, government, and military officials," May 19

Li Peng spoke for the Politburo Standing Committee.[2]

Li Peng: "Based on a decision of the Standing Committee of the Politburo, today Party Central and the State Council are convening this meeting of Party, government, and military officials from Party Central and Beijing Municipality. We call urgently upon everyone to mobilize and to take decisive and effective measures to stop the turmoil, to restore normal social order, and to safeguard peace and unity in order to ensure the smooth progress of reform and opening and socialist modernization. . . .

"The current situation in the capital is grave. Anarchy is growing. Discipline and the rule of law have been broken. After great effort we managed to get things calmed down as of late April, but in May the turbulence came back. More and

---

[1]Officials throughout the Chinese system—in the government, the Party, the military, educational and cultural institutions, mass organizations, and so on, including those in retirement—hold personal ranks that are described in terms of the equivalent level in the state bureaucracy. This rank determines housing, transportation, and other privileges, the levels of personnel transfer across systems, and, especially, access to information.

[2]Text of Li Ximing's speech at this meeting in Michel Oksenberg, Lawrence R. Sullivan, and Marc Lambert, eds., *Beijing Spring, 1989, Confrontation and Conflict: The Basic Documents* (Armonk, New York: M. E. Sharpe, 1990), 298–308; text of Li Peng's speech in ibid., 309–315; and excerpts in Han Minzhu, ed., *Cries for Democracy: Writings and Speeches from the 1989 Chinese Democracy Movement* (Princeton: Princeton University Press, 1990), 255–258.

more students and others got caught up in the demonstrations; universities were paralyzed; public transportation was blocked; Party and government agencies were stormed; lawlessness increased. All this led to severe disruption of normal work, normal study, and daily life for all the people in the city. The official schedule for the Sino-Soviet summit meeting, which drew worldwide attention, also had to be altered in ways that greatly damaged the image and prestige of our country in front of the international community. . . . If we don't put a stop to this quickly, if we just let it go its own way, it will be hard to assure that it will not end in a way nobody wants. . . . We're headed for nationwide turmoil if we don't put a stop to this soon. Our country's reform and opening and our building of the Four Modernizations are already seriously threatened. . . .

"It has now become increasingly clear that a tiny, tiny minority of individuals are trying to use the turmoil to reach their political goals. They want to deny the leadership of the Chinese Communist Party and the socialist system. They openly proclaim slogans that challenge our opposition to bourgeois liberalization, and they do this in order to grant themselves an absolute freedom to oppose the Four Basic Principles without constraint. They spread numerous rumors attacking, insulting, and smearing Party and government leaders. Now they have directed their spear at Comrade Deng Xiaoping, who has made tremendous contributions to our reform and opening. Their goal is to subvert the leadership of the Chinese Communist Party, to overthrow the People's Government that was legally elected by the National People's Congress,[3] and thoroughly to repudiate the people's democratic dictatorship. They have been everywhere—instigating, networking, encouraging the establishment of all kinds of illegal organizations, and trying to force the Party and government to recognize them. They are trying to pave the way for setting up opposition groups and parties in China. If they get their way, then reform and opening, democracy and rule of law, and the building of socialist modernization will all evaporate into thin air and China will be thrown backward. A China with great hope and a great future will turn into a China with neither hope nor future. . . .

"In order to stop the turmoil resolutely and to restore order promptly, I stand before you representing Party Central and the State Council to issue these emergency calls: (1) To the students who remain in the Tiananmen Square, we hope you will immediately end your hunger strike and leave the Square to seek medical treatment in order to recover your health as soon as possible. (2) To the

---

[3]The National People's Congress nominally elects the premier and ministers of the State Council.

majority of students and to people in all parts of society, we hope you will cease all demonstrations immediately and, for humanitarian reasons, stop offering so-called support to the students on hunger strike. Whatever your motivations may be, your continued support of their fast amounts to pushing them down a road toward death. . . .

"We must take resolute and decisive measures to end the turmoil quickly and to safeguard Party leadership and the socialist system. We have faith that our action will win support from all Party members, Youth League members, work-ers, farmers, intellectuals, democratic parties, people from all occupations, and the broad masses. We will also have support from our People's Liberation Army, to which our Constitution assigns the glorious task of defending the motherland and the people's right to work in peace. At the same time, we hope that the people will give their full support to the PLA and the PAP in their endeavor to restore normal order to the capital."

Originally Zhao Ziyang was to have spoken. With Zhao absent, Yang Shangkun filled in with improvised comments.[4]

"Recently Beijing has been, in fact, in anarchy. . . . When we came here for this meeting tonight, we did it without our normal freedom of car movement. We had to take a lot of detours and had to set out an hour or more in advance in order to get here on time. If this keeps up we won't be able to call our capital a capital any more. The Beijing Municipal Government won't be able to do its job, and neither will the State Council. This is serious! In order to restore normal order, to pre-serve security, and to stabilize the situation, the PLA has had to move into certain areas near Beijing. You must have seen on your way here those military vehicles lining the streets. They belong to the PLA troops who have just arrived. We had no choice but to call them in, because the Beijing police force could no longer maintain order. Officers of the PAP and Public Security had been working almost around the clock for the past month, and many comrades, going without sleep for two or three days, were exhausted and ill. That's why we thought we needed the PLA to restore order.

"The troops that have moved to the outskirts of Beijing are in no way directed at the students; they're not here to go after the students. Their purpose is to restore normal order in the life and work of Beijing, as well as to safeguard cer-

---

[4]Excerpt in Han, *Cries for Democracy,* 258.

tain key departments and agencies, not to go after the students. This will become clear to all of you in the next few days as you watch their behavior. The PLA had to come in to restore normal order and security in Beijing and to assure that key agencies are not disturbed or attacked. This is the point I want to explain to you clearly, that the army is not here to go after the students. I hope that everyone, from every station in society, and in all the democratic parties, will support the PLA in its effort to preserve order in the capital. This is the point I want to make to you comrades."

That night Deng Xiaoping and Yang Shangkun received the following report from the headquarters of the martial law troops.

> Excerpt from Martial Law Troop Command, "Martial law situation report" *(Jieyan qingkuang baogao)*, no. 3, May 19

The Beijing Military Region, Shenyang Military Region, and Jinan Military Region have received their orders to enforce martial law and have swiftly pulled their armies together to begin ideological groundwork. The armies used circuitous and deceptive maneuvers en route to Beijing, moving quickly and in disguise, in separate groups and by diverse routes. By 10 P.M. vanguard units of the Twenty-Seventh, Thirty-Eighth, Thirty-Ninth, and Sixty-Third Group Armies had arrived inside Beijing on time and in accordance with the orders of the Central Military Commission. Most troops have by now reached their destinations and are ready to enforce martial law. A portion of the troops were blocked and surrounded on the streets and in the suburbs by students and citizens who do not correctly understand the situation. Headquarters will follow CMC orders and will gradually move troops closer to the city and to one another, maneuvering the blocked troops into their proper positions.[5]

Student protests in 116 cities

Forty-six reports to Zhongnanhai on May 19 said that major student protests had occurred that day in 116 cities. Demonstrators numbered more than ten thousand in Shanghai, Tianjin, Harbin,

---

[5]The opening section of Chapter 10 describes the troops' furtive movement into the city and citizens' reactions on June 2–3.

Changchun, Shenyang, Xi'an, Nanjing, Hangzhou, Nanchang, Wuhan, Changsha, Shijiazhuang, Zhengzhou, Lanzhou, Chengdu, Chongqing, Guiyang, Fuzhou, and Hohhot.

> Excerpt from Xinhua News Agency, "The situation in the urban areas of Shanghai on the nineteenth," report to Party Central and the State Council, May 19

More than seventy thousand people continued to demonstrate today. Some new trends were these:

1. The intensity of the protests grew as slogans directly attacked Central leaders, including some personal assaults by name: "We don't want an idiot for premier," "How long do we put up with rule from behind a curtain?" "Zhao Ziyang and Li Peng step down!" "Deng Xiaoping and Yang Shangkun retire!" "We don't want an old man's Party of Elders." Vehicles mounted with loudspeakers moved through the crowds blaring things like "Arise, workers and citizens!" All kinds of flyers and slogans were pasted onto electric poles and tree trunks.

2. Rumors arose that two or three hunger striking students in Beijing had died. Some students said they first heard this report on Voice of America. Demonstrators marched with wreaths and wore white ribbons, black armbands, or yellow flowers to show their mourning. A rumor spread that one of the dead students was named Huang Huijuan. Students gathered in front of government offices on the Bund and played funeral music, set up a twelve-foot-high statue of liberty, and hoisted a banner that read, "Huang Huijuan, the Patriotic Goddess." Students from the East China Institute of Chemical Technology worked late into the night making wreaths for major demonstrations the next day.

3. The composition of the demonstrators shifted. Until now most were from cultural and intellectual circles and from government offices, but now there are more and more grade school and high school students. Students and teachers from twenty or more high schools, normal schools, and grade schools joined the demonstrations. They held up banners reading, "Older brothers and sisters, we have arrived late!" Some grade school students went to comfort hunger striking students and to perform for them. Some junior high students actually joined the hunger strike.

By 10 P.M. a total of 203 students who had been on hunger strike at the government offices had gone to hospitals, where eighty-eight were admitted. The Shanghai Red Cross set up six examination and treatment posts in the hunger strike area and provided sixty medical workers, eleven ambulances, and one epidemic prevention vehicle.

Excerpts from Hunan Provincial Party Committee and Hunan Provincial Government, "Latest trends in our province," fax to Party Central and the State Council, May 19

Students from Changsha University continued to demonstrate, but the momentum of the protests was declining. Among the twenty thousand to thirty thousand demonstrators who remained, the number of college and high school students increased. Some workers also took to the streets in motley fashion. Banners and slogans attacking Central leaders including Zhao Ziyang and Li Peng appeared.

Among the nearly three hundred students on hunger strike at the provincial government building, twenty-six had fainted. At 3:30 P.M. a student attempted suicide by banging his head against a wall, but other students forcibly restrained him. The student said he might try the same thing again any time after tomorrow noon if provincial leaders did not come out to meet with students. Students from Hunan University distributed a "Manifesto" supporting the Beijing students and demanding investigation of Central leaders who had been responsible for major mistakes during the reforms. . . .

In the city of Shaoyang demonstrators and onlookers gathered at People's Square and by 1:20 P.M. numbered more than ten thousand. When a Volga[6] belonging to the People's Political Consultative Conference of Suining County passed by, a mob of criminals made trouble and set fire to the car. Later, another imported car and a motorcycle belonging to the Shengzi Company of Hengnan County were burned. Ruffians took the opportunity to storm the municipal Party offices, destroying the front gate and the doors and windows of the office building. By 11 P.M. seven cars had been overturned, and three cars and a motorcycle had been burned. Municipal Public Security arrested forty-five people on the scene and charged them with beating, smashing, robbing, and burning. Fourteen people, whose offenses were minor, were released after education. The remaining thirty-one were detained by law for further investigation. None of the detained was a college student.

Excerpts from Xinhua News Agency, "The situation in Fuzhou on the nineteenth," report to Party Central and the State Council, May 19

[6] A Soviet-made automobile.

Today the People's Government of Fujian Province canceled its dialogue with student delegates from Fuzhou universities, and in response nearly all the students from more than thirty universities in the area took to the streets. Many teachers joined them, as did some workers and more than three hundred professional writers and local and provincial journalists. Students and teachers from areas such as Nanping and Sanming also joined. People of all kinds, numbering in the hundreds of thousands, lined the streets to cheer the demonstrators.

Students from Fujian Normal University proposed blocking traffic intersections and railway lines as a way to express strong protest of the provincial government's cancellation of agreed dialogues. . . .

At 11:40 A.M. more than three thousand students, most of them from Fuzhou University, excitedly stormed the Fuzhou Railway Station; more than three hundred sat on the railroad tracks and disrupted use of the station for six hours. Eight passenger trains—including numbers 378, 383, 384, 478, 377, 571 and 61—and four freight trains were prevented from departing. A student representative said, "Chen Mingyi[7] has swindled us. He refuses to recognize our elected representatives and has reneged on his promise to hold dialogue with them. He even said, 'I have nothing to say to you.' This made us students very angry; it's what made us storm the railway station."

> Excerpt from Xinhua News Agency, "The situation in Chongqing on the nineteenth," report to Party Central and the State Council, May 19

As fatigue affected the students, who had been demonstrating continuously for days, they began, instead of marching, to flag down any vehicle they could to ask for rides to government offices or back to campus. This caused serious traffic tie-ups. Grain and coal reserves in Chongqing are running low, and salt is also in short supply. A cutoff of rail supplies to the city would result in great hardship. In the current chaos people have to walk to work and have trouble shopping. City residents, fearful of another Cultural Revolution, are beginning to change their attitudes toward the demonstrations from sympathy and support to resentment. They say things like, "These students didn't experience the hardships of the Cultural Revolution. What do you gain by paralyzing a country?"

[7]Vice governor of Fujian.

Excerpt from Xinhua News Agency, "The situation in Guangzhou on the nineteenth," report to Party Central and the State
Council, May 19

Students in the tens of thousands, from more than thirty universities, continued to demonstrate in the streets and to sit in at the provincial government buildings. Hundreds of editors, journalists, and research scientists from various work
units supported them. Traffic in main parts of the city was jammed several times.
The demonstrations peaked around 5 P.M., at which time more than a hundred
thousand people flanked the avenue in front of the government buildings. At 10
P.M. more than twenty thousand students were still there. For seventy-six of them
it was the third day of a hunger strike; five had already fainted and been sent to
hospitals.

Some of the demonstrations on May 19 were spontaneous, and some had been
organized by the AFS or the University Students' Association. Many teachers participated as well. The streets where the demonstrations took place were filled with
flags and banners. New slogans included "Wake up, government!" "Heaven has
eyes, but the government does not"; "The government, the government, it looks
but it doesn't see; the premier, the premier, who cares as little as he?" "Save the
CCP, save China!" "Where has our humanity gone?" "Oppose rule from behind a
curtain"; "Down with old-man government!" and "Xiaoping is too old." There
were cartoons as well. One showed a headless man in a blue Mao suit with one
hand holding a cigarette, the other stuck in his pocket. It was meant to illustrate
the government's "brainless" approach. The demonstrators had many other
activities: Students from a dance school put on performances for the hunger
strikers; sociology students took on-the-spot opinion polls to gauge reactions to
the demonstrations; others collected donations on the street. Student organizers
said their movement in Guangzhou will not end until the problems of the Beijing
students are resolved.

Excerpt from Xinhua News Agency, "The situation in Taiyuan
on the nineteenth," report to Party Central and the State
Council, May 19

Incidents of beating, smashing, and robbing have been continual since the
night of May 18. About 10:10 P.M. on May 18 a group of criminals interspersed
among the crowds under darkness of night at the intersection of Jiefang Road and

Fudong Street smashed sixty-six glass windows at the Oriental Shopping Mall. They knocked over some mannequins and then pulled out the safety dividers along a more than four-hundred-meter stretch of Jiefang Road and left the dividers lying helter-skelter in the middle of the street. When police arrived to stop them at 10:40 P.M., protesters threw bricks and bottles at them. By 5:40 A.M. on May 19 these criminals had destroyed twenty-two cars and robbed a farmer of his vegetables and milk. At 3:45 P.M. on May 19 a policeman on motorcycle duty was surrounded by a mob who first pushed and cursed him and then took off his pants, draped them over a traffic light, and shouted, "Police are sons-of-bitches!" Shanxi Province Public Security reports show that thirty-five cars were destroyed or overturned on Jiefang Road and the west end of Fudong Street during the two days of May 18 and 19. On these two days people yelled, "Down with official prof-iteering" at every passing car, and many drivers were so frightened they dared not use their cars. By 9 P.M. on May 19 Taiyuan Public Security had arrested sixty-seven vandals. None of them was a college student.

First reports on martial law in the foreign press

On May 19 the Associated Press (AP) reported that disorderly but courageous crowds blocked the way of military caravans moving toward Beijing under orders of martial law. About 10 P.M., as several thousand soldiers of the Twenty-Seventh Army were moving in military vehicles from the northern suburbs into Beijing, tens of thousands of people flocked onto the streets, shouting slogans, erecting roadblocks, and forming human walls. Reuters reported similar confrontations in the western suburbs and said the students in the Square were preparing to end their seven-day-old hunger strike. L'Agence France-Presse (AFP) reported that student leaders were reacting strongly against the specter of a crackdown, had threatened that a hunger strike of two hundred thousand people could result, and had held a news conference announcing a new decision to continue and expand the hunger strike in protest of the government's apparent decision to use force against the demonstrators.

May 20

Opposition to martial law in Beijing

In the wee hours of May 20 Li Peng signed the martial law order.

> Excerpt from "Order of the State Council of the People's
> Republic of China on the implementation of martial law in
> parts of Beijing," *People's Daily,* May 20, p. 1[8]

An outbreak of grave turmoil in Beijing has disrupted social stability, normal life, and public order. In accordance with Article 89, Item 16, of the Constitution of the People's Republic of China, the State Council has decided to implement martial law in parts of Beijing beginning at 10 A.M. on May 20, 1989, in order to curb the turmoil with a firm hand, maintain public order in Beijing, protect the lives and property of citizens, defend public property, and safeguard the normal functions of Central state organs and the Beijing Municipal Government. The Beijing Municipal People's Government will enforce the implementation of martial law and take concrete steps according to actual needs.

Mayor Chen Xitong then signed three implementing orders for Beijing.

> Excerpt from "Order of the Beijing Municipal People's Gov-
> ernment: Number 1," May 20

1. Beginning at 10 A.M. on May 20, 1989, the following districts will be under martial law: East City, West City, Chongwen, Xuanwu, Shijingshan, Haidian, Fengtai, and Chaoyang.
2. Under martial law, demonstrations, student strikes, work stoppages, and all other activities that impede public order are banned.
3. People are forbidden from fabricating or spreading rumors, networking, making public speeches, distributing leaflets, or inciting social turmoil.
4. Assault on leadership organs of the Party, government, or army, on radio or television stations, or on communications units and sabotage of key public facilities is expressly forbidden. No beating, smashing, robbing, burning, or other forms of destruction will be tolerated.

[8]Text in Oksenberg et al., *Beijing Spring,* 315–316.

5. Harassing foreign embassies or agencies of the United Nations is prohibited.

6. Under martial law, security officers, PAP, and PLA soldiers are authorized to use all necessary means, including force, to deal with prohibited activities.

> Excerpt from "Order of the Beijing Municipal People's Government: Number 3," May 20

Foreigners are forbidden from involvement in any Chinese citizens' activities that are in violation of martial law.

The martial law announcement came as a shock in Beijing and was condemned by most teachers, students, government officials, and ordinary citizens. On the first day of martial law, Zhongnanhai received more than two hundred reports on citizens' reactions to the order. Surveys found at least doubts about martial law and often frank opposition in more than 80 percent of the offices polled. Only Party organizations gave their full, but formulaic, support. A report from the Beijing Education Department noted that the order had had a counterproductive effect on some students, who had been resisting peer pressure to boycott classes but now joined the boycott.

In the early morning of May 20 copies of a handbill were distributed in the Square and the busy areas of Beijing.

> Excerpts from State Security Ministry, "The Institute for Economic Reform in China and 'Second announcement on the current situation,'" in "Important intelligence" *(Yaoqing)*, May 20

Because a small number of high-ranking leaders insist on and expand policies that have been proven wrong and are seeking to suppress this great patriotic and democratic movement, China really does face the danger of major social turmoil and national division and stands at a critical historical juncture. . . . Li Peng's speech on the evening of May 19 recklessly distorted the truth, inverted right and wrong, stirred up disturbance, intensified conflicts, ignored the appeals of all kinds of people, rejected the spirit of a series of correct speeches by General Secretary Zhao Ziyang beginning May 4, seriously worsened the situation, and brought society to the brink of turmoil. . . . Standing at this crucial moment, we once again appeal to the NPC and the CCP to call an emergency meeting and to intervene using the powers vested in them by Party regulations and the national Constitution.

That afternoon Chen Yizi, Gao Shan, and others held a meeting with members of the "three institutes and one association,"[9] which were informally known as components of Zhao Ziyang's think tank.

Chen Yizi: "Bao Tong has told me that we must protect both the Commission and the Institute for Economic Reform in China[10] because they are the backbones of the reforms. I think everyone should stop using the institute's name to stir up trouble; we really don't need any more declarations made in the name of the four units.[11] It does no one any good. And from now on, don't rely on the higher authorities for your information. We'll have to get our information through our own channels."

Someone at this meeting said that Li Peng and the Beijing Municipal Party Committee may have tricked Deng Xiaoping into approving the martial law order and suggested that someone go directly to Deng to give him a way to back out. The meeting also considered methods for blocking military vehicles. The final decisions of the meeting were (1) to compile a collection called "The Man Li Peng" in order to expose his wicked scheme to use suppression of the student movement as a stepping stone to try to become general secretary of the Party; (2) to work on senior military leaders through the children of high-ranking officials in an effort to get martial law lifted.

Luo Gan, secretary general of the State Council, obtained the minutes of this meeting and immediately forwarded them to Li Peng.

On the afternoon of May 20 several hundred editors and reporters took to the streets under a *People's Daily* banner, distributing copies of an "extra" edition of the paper as they went. This extra, which was printed in the same format and size as the regular *People's Daily,* included speeches that had been given the night before in the Square by people who claimed to be from the State Commission for the Restructure of the Economic System. Calls for "nationwide strikes by workers, students, teachers, and shopkeepers" had been omitted, however. A note at the bottom of the extra said, "Reprinted from a Peking University handbill." Students and ordinary citizens copied the issue in large numbers and spread them widely.

Qian Liren, director of the *People's Daily,* promptly announced that the newspaper had not issued an extra edition—in fact had not done so for at least ten years—and that someone must have used the paper's name without authorization. Qian forwarded a formal statement to this effect to

[9]See footnote 30 in Chapter 5.
[10]The State Commission for the Restructure of the Economic System was a ministry-level commission formally headed in 1989 by Li Peng. The Institute for Economic Reform in China, created by Zhao Ziyang and headed by Chen Yizi, was formally under the State Commission but had considerable autonomy from it.
[11]That is, the three institutes and one association.

the Xinhua News Agency for national distribution; he also launched an internal investigation of the incident and sent a report on it to Hu Qili.[12]

A handbill submitted to Zhongnanhai by the State Security Ministry indicated that workers and students were cooperating.

> Excerpt from Hunger Strike Headquarters, Autonomous Federation of Students in Beijing, and Planning Committee for the Autonomous Federation of Workers in Beijing, "Joint statement of all workers and students in the capital," handbill; forwarded by the State Security Ministry to Party Central and the State Council, May 20

In view of the perverse intransigence of Li Peng, Yang Shangkun, and other state leaders, the time has come to unite with the nation's people and use the law to relieve these tyrants of their posts. . . . In order to suppress and punish these tyrants, we ask the following:

1. That the NPC convene an ad hoc meeting to recall the premier of the State Council, Li Peng, and president of the PRC, Yang Shangkun, and investigate the legal status of all current officials who are enemies of the people. In the meantime, the NPC should set up a special court to try these tyrants publicly.

2. That citizens of Beijing oppose military control and resist the advance of troops. If troops enter the city, Beijing workers and citizens should go to the Square to protect the thousands of students who have been on a hunger strike there for eight days. Meanwhile, we urge the students to bring an end to their strike. Why should they make unnecessary sacrifices for these tyrants? We members of the working class thank these students and think the Chinese nation should be proud of them. History will remember them. Tiananmen Square will be our battlefield. We will use our bodies to protect the students, hunger strikers and sit-in protesters. We will build another Wall of the Communards[13] with our life's blood.

3. That officers and soldiers in the PLA oppose the dictators who are hoodwinking them and turn their weapons around to point at the tyrants. Our prin-

---

[12]Chapter 10 reveals that this investigation found that the extra was indeed the work of *People's Daily* staff members. But different documents describe the incident differently, sometimes contradictorily. We do not know which version, if any, is true.

[13]Karl Marx's essay "The Civil War in France" was well known to ideologically educated Chinese because it was a classic source for a concept much discussed by Mao, the dictatorship of the proletariat. In the essay Marx describes the Paris Commune of 1871 and the doomed final defense by the Communards against government guns at a wall that has come to be known by this name.

ciple is that the people's troops are our brothers, and our brothers of course protect the people.

4. That everyone disavow the martial law order that the premier of the State Council has issued. Article 89, Item 16, of the Constitution of the PRC does not empower the State Council to authorize the Beijing Municipal Government to stop citizens from exercising their rights to speak, to march, or to demonstrate, all of which are activities protected by the Constitution. Accordingly, we ask that the NPC rescind the martial law order.

5. That students and teachers boycott classes until we gain final victory.

6. That Beijing workers use all peaceful and effective means, including work stoppages, to achieve our goals.

Reports reached Li Peng and other top leaders that the Beijing AFW had organized hundreds of motorcyclists into a Flying Tiger Group to provide students and citizens in the Square and around the city with news about martial law and related topics. In forwarding these reports to Li Ximing and Chen Xitong, Li Peng commented that "this so-called Flying Tiger Group has been formed by lawless people in society; we must use resolute measures to disband it or the consequences could be catastrophic."

Thickening battle clouds

Hundreds of thousands of Beijing students and citizens set up roadblocks and checkpoints around the city in an effort to prevent troops from moving in. Many university faculty and even some Party and government officials expressed doubts about martial law. The Party Committee of the Central Academy of Fine Arts sent a telegram to the Municipal Party Committee calling for an immediate withdrawal of troops from Beijing. An English teacher at Peking University posted an announcement of resignation from the Chinese Communist Party.[14] Tens of thousands continued to demonstrate in the streets, demanding that Li Peng step down and calling on the people to resist. People began to stockpile supplies.

At 9:40 A.M. the government broadcast the martial law order over loudspeakers in Tiananmen Square. Student leaders immediately dispatched teams to intercept approaching military vehicles, prepared for crowd control and defense against tear gas, and led the students in the Square in an oath to resist. There was considerable sentiment in favor of ending the hunger strike, some students arguing that it was a futile measure against a government willing to move tanks. Around 10

[14]Text in Han, *Cries for Democracy,* 287–288.

A.M. five military helicopters circled above the Square for ten minutes, and the students shouted at them through battery-powered bullhorns, "Why have you come?" Around 5 P.M. one helicopter scattered copies of the martial law order on the Square.

The Voice of the Movement loudspeaker system broadcast a statement by Bao Zunxin, Yan Jiaqi, and other intellectuals who vowed not to yield to pressure from the government. One teacher swore he would take his own life in protest.

Yang Shangkun's order
to the martial law troops

Reports coming up the military hierarchy described slogans and posters that said, "Oppose martial law," "Oppose military control,"[15] and "Withdraw the troops and lift martial law." But more strikingly, in Beijing and major cities throughout the country the focus of popular resentment was specifically on Li Peng, Yang Shangkun, and Deng Xiaoping. There were also calls to "Give back our Ziyang."

> Examples taken from Central Military Commission, "Report on domestic situation" *(Neibu qingkuang tongbao)*, May 20; PLA Headquarters of the General Staff, "Military affairs reference" *(Junqing cankao)*, May 20; Central Military Commission Office, "Daily trends" *(Meiri dongtai)*, May 21; Central Military Commission Office, "Information extracts" *(Xinxi zhaibao)*, May 22; Beijing Military District, "Information express" *(Xinxi kuaibao)*, May 20

Slogans aimed at Li Peng included "Down with the puppet Li Peng," "Li Peng rapes the popular will," "Down, down, down with dictatorship," "Where has our conscience gone? Condemn the traitor!" "There can never be peace with Li Peng in place," "Get rid of Li Peng for the sake of the people," "Down with corrupt government," "When Li Peng is out on his ear, the people are all going to cheer!" and "As long as Li Peng stays, we'll be here for days and days." Students in Shanghai even paraded carrying Li Peng's portrait framed in black.

Slogans aimed at Deng Xiaoping included "Down with Deng Xiaoping,"

---

[15]In their slogans and handbills the demonstrators sometimes referred to martial law, properly *"jieyan,"* by the term *"junguan,"* which means "military control"; the full term is *"junshi guanzhi,"* which implies military administration.

"Down with dictatorship," "We want democracy, not famocracy,"[16] "Deng Xiao-ping step down," "A gloomy black curtain shrouds the sky, and the empress dowa-ger makes a hundred-year comeback,"[17] and "Deng Xiaoping is like the moon: He changes every fourteen days."[18]

On May 20 martial law troops from twenty-two divisions of thirteen PLA armies arrived in the Beijing area. The armies (with the number of divisions from each shown in parentheses) were the Fifteenth (2), the Twentieth (2), the Twenty-Fourth (2), the Twenty-Sixth (1), the Twenty-Seventh (3), the Twenty-Eighth (2), the Thirty-Eighth (3, plus an artillery brigade), the Thirty-Ninth (2), the Fortieth (2), the Fifty-Fourth (1), the Sixty-Third (1), the Sixty-Fifth (1), and the Sixty-Seventh (1).[19] Many were stopped in the suburbs or on city streets and were unable to proceed to their assigned locations.

The Elders became anxious when they learned that the martial law order could not be imple-mented as planned. But to Yang Shangkun, who was responsible for the practical details of imple-mentation, the situation did not seem not so bleak. Yang felt that the presence of the martial law troops had already created a strong intimidating effect, and since such an effect was one of the original objectives of martial law, he was satisfied.

On the afternoon of May 20 Yang chaired an enlarged meeting of the CMC. Hong Xuezhi, Liu Huaqing, Qin Jiwei, Yang Baibing, Chi Haotian, Zhao Nanqi, and personnel from martial law head-quarters attended.

> Excerpt from Central Military Commission Office, "Minutes of the [May] 20 Enlarged Meeting of the Central Military Commission"

Zhou Yibing: "After Thirty-Eighth Army commander Xu Qinxian disobeyed an order to carry out his martial law assignment, we obeyed Chairman Yang's order to strip Xu of his command and send him to a hospital to recover his health.

[16]"Famocracy" is invented here to mean "rule by the famous" and to translate a play on words in the Chinese original, which is *yao minzhu buyao mingzhu*.

[17]Referring to the Empress Dowager Cixi, who ruled China for many years in the late nineteenth century.

[18]The second line of the rhythmical popular saying, "Chairman Mao is like the sun, the earth is bright where it shines its rays; Deng Xiaoping is like the moon, it changes every fourteen days." The first line, which is taken directly from the Cultural Revolution paean "The East Is Red," was used in the late 1980s with a certain irony.

[19]Details on where each division was stationed and from which locations each departed en route to Beijing are listed in the Chinese manuscript. In some cases only certain regiments of a divi-sion, not the whole division, were involved. The size of a full division varied but in the infantry usually was about twelve thousand to fifteen thousand soldiers.

All members of the Thirty-Eighth Army Party Committee were firm in their determination to carry out the orders of Party Central and the CMC and in their support of decisions regarding Xu Qinxian. The Party Committee suggested that all Party committees at the army, division, and brigade levels redouble their efforts in ideological purification, sum up Xu Qinxian's mistakes as an object lesson, and take firm control of political thought."

Liu Huaqing: "How did things go with the advance of the Thirty-Eighth Army?"

Zhou Yibing: "Last night the army's command post, its 112th Division, its artillery brigade, its antiaircraft artillery regiment, and its communications regiment—nearly seven thousand men in all—moved into place in the area between Fuxing Road and Gongzhufen. The 113th Division and the Sixth Armored Division will reach the area bordered by Baojiaocun, Jiaodaokou, and Liuliqiao this afternoon. Like other units, they've been blocked and surrounded by members of the masses who do not correctly understand the situation, but they have been able to carry out their orders."

Yang Shangkun: "We must learn from the Xu Qinxian incident and be sure nothing like that happens again. A soldier follows orders. Disobedience is not tolerated."

Chi Haotian delivered an update on the number of troops that had been prevented from entering the capital or had been surrounded on the city streets or in the suburbs.

Yang Shangkun: "The first stage of our mission is complete. The troops have found ways to overcome many difficulties and have managed to carry out their orders to enter Beijing to enforce martial law in a timely manner. Beginning May 21 they should settle in for a period of rest and regrouping. The troops surrounded on the streets or in the suburbs must revise their strategies in accordance with the principles of moving from far to near, from outside to inside, and from dispersion to concentration. As they rest and regroup, troops should take particular care to strengthen political thought work and to conduct active training on command methods and on flexible response.[20] They must attend to the needs of this struggle and take up the weapons of political propaganda in concert with military maneuvers. As they rest and regroup they must broadly unfold the campaign to 'love the capital, love the people of the capital, and love the young students.'

---

[20]Presumably, on how to respond appropriately to various situations that might be encountered in Beijing.

They should send out propaganda teams to every street and alley spreading the Party's word and winning over the masses. At the same time, the troops should be mobilized to do good deeds for the masses, so all Beijing residents understand that our army is truly the people's army, a civilized army, and a mighty army."

Yang listened to reports from the officers present and then issued instructions.

Yang Shangkun: "1. Strengthen the political faith of the troops to ensure they carry out the orders of Party Central and the CMC. The situation in Beijing is highly complex, and we must remove all sources of disturbance and be sure that our actions resolutely accord with the deployment and the instructions of Party Central and the CMC. Toward those comrades who regard the turmoil with goodwill and have misgivings about martial law, we must use the spirit of Party Central and the orders of the CMC to unify army thinking. As for troops that are surrounded or blocked in the suburbs, leaders at all levels should go personally to their locations to transmit and explain the spirit of Party Central and CMC orders. This will help the troops understand the intensity and complexity of this struggle and will clarify for them the necessity and legality of martial law. Rumors are rampant in Beijing, and we must convince the people that they must neither believe nor spread rumors. Leaders at all levels should openly refute rumors about the troops. We are the people's army, and the people's army has not entered Beijing to set itself in opposition to its citizens. We are honest and upright. Under current circumstances, with so many Beijing residents ignorant of the truth, we must carry out the 'Three Opens': open unit identification, open license plates, and open display of rank. In the face of complex political storms, we must deal with turmoil with a clear head, treat chaos with toughness, and stay as united and unanimous as a slab of iron.

"2. Maintain absolute control over weapons and use them with great restraint. In line with the principle of accomplishing our mission but protecting the masses, we must be firm but flexible in following orders. This use of troops to carry out martial law involves a grave political struggle. Our Party and socialist motherland have reached a critical juncture. The troops must not hesitate or waver; they must be resolute in their actions as they shoulder this historic mission. But bad people are using the masses, who in turn are hiding the bad people. With the good and the bad mixed together in such a way, the real and the false are hard to distinguish. From a strategic point of view, we must carry out our mission of enforcing martial law while protecting the people and strive for the perfect balance between the requirements of mission and of policy. Therefore, even if troops should be beaten, burned, or killed by the unenlightened masses, or if they should be attacked by lawless elements with clubs, bricks, or Molotov cocktails, they must maintain control and defend themselves with nonlethal methods. Clubs should be their major weapons of self-defense, and they are not to open fire on the masses. Violators will be punished. Commanders at the level of regiment or above should consider organizing antiviolence teams equipped with clubs and batons.

"3. Emphasize the superior tradition and style of the PLA to instill a fearless revolutionary spirit in the officers and soldiers. The troops will encounter unexpected difficulties in carrying out their duties; some troops are surrounded as we speak. Leaders at all levels should go to the front lines to explain and publicize the superior tradition and style of the PLA to all officers and soldiers regardless of whether they are sitting in troop transports, surrounded on the streets, or sleeping in tents. Sing 'The National Anthem' and the 'Army Anthem' with them to instill in them the PLA's revolutionary heroism and spirit of collectivism, which have evolved over a long period of struggle. Once they have that spirit, they will face danger unafraid, will stand fast in the face of difficulties, will not know frustration in defeat, and will not let down even when tired."

International public opinion was surprised that the Chinese government allowed citizens to continue blocking and surrounding troops. Some attributed the phenomenon to "people power" and some, to a divided military leadership. These speculations were valid to a point, but the real reasons ran deeper.

> Account drawn from Central Military Commission Office, "Yang Shangkun's talk to a small-group meeting at the Enlarged Meeting of the Central Military Commission," May 23

That night, after Yang Shangkun had reported by telephone to Deng Xiaoping, Deng responded with the following instructions.

Deng Xiaoping: "Everyone is anxious over the current situation, so I'm calling a meeting for tomorrow to discuss the situation with Chen Yun, Xiannian, Peng Zhen, Sister Deng, Yibo, Bearded Wang,[21] and you. The two old marshals[22] are in

---

[21] *Wang Huzi*, that is, Wang Zhen. Wang got this nickname from Mao when he wore a beard in the 1930s and 1940s.
[22] Nie Rongzhen and Xu Xiangqian.

poor health, so we won't bother them. Comrade Chen Yun has suggested that you, Yibo, Li Peng, Yao Yilin, and Qiao Shi summon leaders from the province level to Beijing in order to unify their understanding. You should also convene an enlarged meeting of the CMC to ask commanders and political commissars of the major military districts to report on their situations and to clarify current conditions in order to maintain national stability."

The provinces weigh in

Zhongnanhai received 110 reports on the day's demonstrations in 132 cities across the country. The main theme of the demonstrations was opposition to Li Peng's announcement of martial law. There were slogans like "Down with Li Peng" and "Li Peng's illegitimate regime must end!" Rumors about Zhao Ziyang's fall from power circulated in many cities. Seventeen of China's thirty province-level governments expressed prompt support for Party Central, but a close look at these expressions reveals subtle gradations among them: Some provinces were closer than others in their adherence to the Center. In many cases the response was pro forma and the specific policies proposed amounted to little more than business as usual.

SHANGHAI

Shanghai was first to express support for the Center.

> Excerpt from Shanghai Party Committee, "Firmly support Party Central's important decision, firmly maintain Shanghai's normal social, production, and work order," report to Party Central in an uncoded telegram, May 20

All comrades on the Standing Committee of the Shanghai Party Committee watched with great excitement the live coverage of the great meeting of Party, government, and military officials that Party Central convened in Beijing. . . . All comrades on the Standing Committee unanimously support the report and the views that Comrade Li Peng presented on behalf of the Politburo Standing Committee. . . . Jiang Zemin, Zhu Rongji, and other Party and government leaders . . . went to the site of the student hunger strike in an effort to persuade strikers to quit and to accept medical treatment.

In the afternoon, at an enlarged meeting of the Standing Committee, Jiang Zemin expressed resolute support for Li Peng's important speech. Jiang proposed to step up propaganda in favor of stability, to enhance police vigilance, and to do a good job of "handling complicated issues under complicated circumstances."

In the evening of May 20 and on the morning of May 21 Jiang Zemin attended two briefing meetings to hear reports on how Shanghai people felt about Party Central's decision on martial law. The meetings reported that the masses had three basic worries. One was that Party Central might not be able to contain the situation even with martial law. If "the final trump card fails," chaos might spread through the whole country, and the government could fall. The second worry was that signals from the top about the student movement had been confusing—from "containment" to "tolerance" to "support" and then to "martial law"; such flip-flops made thought work hard to do. The third was that martial law, although justifiable, might cut off dialogue, and this would be unfortunate. The problems would not be resolved, on this view, until the leadership took some popular steps to eliminate corruption, stop official profiteering, and deepen the reforms. Jiang Zemin responded by saying that everyone must trust Party Central and veteran revolutionary statesmen such as Deng Xiaoping in their determination and ability to end the turmoil in Beijing.

TIANJIN

Li Ruihuan chaired a meeting of the Standing Committee of the Municipal Party Committee on the morning of May 20. He said that Li Peng's speech had great significance for stabilization of the overall situation and that Party members in Tianjin should now work to build consensus based on the speech.

This meeting also accepted the resignation, tendered earlier that morning, of Zhang Wei, Party secretary of the Tianjin Foreign Economic and Trade Commission. Zhang, age thirty-four, had studied economics at Peking University, where he had been a leader in government-sponsored student organizations and had had a reputation as a "moderate reformer." He had engaged in heated debates about democracy with the more radical student leaders Hu Ping and Wang Juntao. In 1982 he was assigned to work in Tianjin, where he served as secretary of the Communist Youth League and director of the Tianjin Economic and Technological Development Zone. In explaining his decision to resign, Zhang said:

> Excerpt from Tianjin Party Committee, "Firmly support the Center's decision, guarantee Tianjin's stability," report to Party Central, May 20

Zhang Wei: "The way things have gone breaks my heart. Why did Party Central refuse dialogue with the people on April 22? The student democracy movement would not have grown to its current size if there had been dialogue then.

... The only way to pacify the situation is through dialogue, using democratic methods. Nowadays even international affairs are conducted through dialogue, not confrontation, and yet we still choose confrontation in dealing with students. Confrontation will not end the turmoil.

"I want stability for our country, but it must be a stability based on popular consent and satisfaction, not a stability based on white terror as in the Gang of Four[23] era. I protest the use of the army against unarmed demonstrators and disagree with the decision to call the student movement turmoil. I am highly disappointed with Party Central's behavior, and this is the main reason for my resignation.... As a citizen and a member of the Communist Party, I cannot act against the people's will. When government policies that depart from the people's will interfere with the execution of my duties, I have no choice but to resign."

JILIN

An emergency meeting of the Standing Committee of the Provincial Party Committee on the morning of May 20 strongly supported Li Peng's speech and settled on the following six measures to end the turmoil in Jilin decisively.

> Excerpt from Jilin Party Committee, "Firmly support Comrade Li Peng's speech, firmly maintain unity with Party Central," report to Party Central, May 20

1. We must remain on the side of the Party Central. All our speech and behavior must be in line with Li Peng's speech of May 19. We will immediately mobilize all government offices and all enterprises, whether for-profit or nonprofit, to study and comprehend the spirit of the speech.

2. We will strengthen discipline in accordance with Li Peng's speech. Beginning today, marches, hunger strikes, and demonstrations will be illegal. All officials will stay at their workplaces today to study and discuss Li Peng's speech. Anyone who goes out on the streets to demonstrate will be subject to Party and state penalties.

3. All universities must resume classes unconditionally. Party members, school officials, and faculty members must be the first to turn themselves around. No

---

[23]The Gang of Four—Zhang Chunqiao, Wang Hongwen, Yao Wenyuan, and Mao Zedong's wife Jiang Qing—were prominent leaders during the last years of Mao Zedong's rule. They were arrested in October 1976, shortly after Mao's death; blamed for the excesses of the Cultural Revolution; and sent to Qincheng Prison, a facility for prominent political prisoners.

one may participate in or support student demonstrations, and everyone must work at convincing students to resume classes unconditionally. Party members, Youth League members, and officials who disobey will be subject to Party and state discipline.

4. We must be well prepared both mentally and organizationally to prevent further turmoil. We will also make necessary arrangements with police forces to tighten security at key institutions.

5. If violence occurs, we will end it immediately and without mercy so as to minimize damage.

6. News media must increase positive reporting and must no longer draw public attention to street demonstrations by students and the masses.

HEBEI

After a meeting of Party, state, military, and Chinese People's Political Consultative Conference (CPPCC)[24] leaders at the province level, Hebei Party secretary Xing Chongzhi filed a report.

> Excerpt from fax, Hebei Party secretary Xing Chongzhi to Zhongnanhai, afternoon, May 20

Participants at the meeting expressed unanimous support for the important speeches of Li Peng and Yang Shangkun and for all the decisions and measures Party Central and the State Council have taken or are in the process of taking in order to end the turmoil in Beijing promptly.

In the afternoon the Hebei Party Committee summoned to a meeting the leaders of the democratic parties and mass organizations, as well as some prominent nonpartisan people. Xing Chongzhi explained that there were three outlooks that needed to be revised. The first was false security: the notion that because the new China had been in place for nearly forty years, turmoil could no longer happen. Now, he said, it was possible to see that this was naive. In fact, many people both at home and abroad would like to overthrow the socialist system, as the current turmoil proved. The second problem was muddled thinking. Many people, even some officials, had not stood firm during this turmoil. They listened to rumors and made a stormy sea stormier. The third problem was complacency. Some people were so laid back they thought it was time for a good sleep. They paid no attention to the turmoil before them, and this was dangerous.

[24]The CPPCC is an assembly of distinguished persons, mostly nonmembers of the CCP, which meets to express support and make suggestions for Party and government policies, usually in conjunction with the meeting schedule of the National People's Congress.

Speaking for the Party Committee, Xing Chongzhi presented the others on the committee with three demands: 1. They should be well organized in studying the speeches by Li Peng and Yang Shangkun and make everyone align with the spirit of Party Central. 2. They should expedite every call of Party Central in order to stop the turmoil once and for all. 3. They should brace up and do a good job in every area of both reform and rectification.

Shaanxi

The Standing Committee of the Provincial Party Committee convened an enlarged emergency meeting at which it was agreed that Li Peng's speech marked a fundamental turn. Now that principles, policies, and tactics had been clarified, participants felt that the main national crisis was over but that the situation remained grim as aftershocks of the turmoil continued. The struggle had been so intense, they continued, that sudden measures, even powerful ones, might not be able to turn it around immediately. The meeting anticipated that the struggle would remain extremely acute in the next few days.

Party secretary Zhang Boxing announced eight measures on behalf of the Provincial Party Committee. These included unifying thinking, restoring normal production work and classes, forbidding Party members to take part in demonstrations, doing thought work and conducting multilevel, multichannel dialogue among students, strengthening security work, speeding up investigations of people who had attacked Party Central, avoiding intensification of conflicts, and making propaganda adhere strictly to the spirit of Party Central.

Fujian

An enlarged meeting of the Standing Committee of the Provincial Party Committee was held in the morning and all participants strongly supported Li Peng's speech. They also discussed particular measures to be taken in Fujian to safeguard peace and unity and to end the turmoil.

> Excerpt from Fujian Party Committee, "Use the Center's spirit to unify thinking, clearly and decisively oppose turmoil," report to Party Central, May 20

Chen Guangyi:[25] "What we see on the surface is a student movement, but in reality this is turmoil deliberately created by a tiny minority behind the scenes. The goal is to negate socialism and the leadership of the Chinese Communist Party. We must note especially that hostile forces abroad have never stopped their subversive activities against the Communist Party. The reactionary organization

[25]Provincial Party secretary.—Comp.

Chinese Alliance for Democracy is swollen with aggressive arrogance. The KMT authorities in Taiwan have never stopped sending spies to engage in subversive activities. We must not relax our vigilance toward any of these forces."

Chen Guangyi proposed four measures: unifying thought, curbing turmoil while ensuring normal production order, doing a good job with political thought work, and promoting both social stability and industrial and agricultural production.

GUANGDONG

An emergency meeting of the Standing Committee of the Provincial Party Committee in the morning was followed by an afternoon meeting of provincial officials at the bureau chief level and higher.

> Excerpt from Guangdong Party Committee, "Firmly support the decision of Party Central, further guarantee Guangdong's stability," report to Party Central, May 20

Lin Ruo:[26] "We stand at a crucial moment. Officials at all levels should provide bold leadership, work meticulously, face problems squarely, and perform responsibly. Guangdong is next door to Hong Kong. It has great impact on the outside world. It is therefore crucial both domestically and internationally that we stabilize Guangdong and safeguard the fruits of its reform."

Ye Xuanping, governor of Guangdong, then listed four requisites for the stabilization of the province: 1. Party members, officials, and the people in all work units would be organized to study Li Peng's speech seriously and carefully. Current affairs would be analyzed soberly to try to solve problems rationally. Nothing harmful to overall stability would be said or done. 2. Party officials would review the historical experience of Guangdong so that everyone would realize that China and Guangdong could afford no more chaos. Chaos offered no benefits and no hope and did nothing to advance reform or the cause of democracy. 3. Under present circumstances leaders at all levels, especially Party and state leaders, must use essential Party discipline in facing the complicated situation. They must lead the masses, must not join or support demonstrations or networking, and must try to guide events step by step toward a resolution. 4. All departments and work units should do their utmost to continue normal and efficient work. They must not panic or descend into confusion. Their work in Guangdong was proceeding briskly in all areas, but much

---

[26]Provincial Party secretary.—Comp.

remained to be done, and they must try their best to minimize work losses. Especially, the normal operation of certain key institutions must be ensured. Public security must be tightened to guard against criminal elements taking advantage of the situation to commit crime.

Hunan

The Party Standing Committee met at dawn on May 20 to study Li Peng's speech.

> Excerpt from Hunan Party Committee, "Do the work well, stabilize the situation, firmly maintain unity with Party Central," report to Party Central, May 20

Mao Zhiyong:[27] "Li Peng's speech and the measures of Party Central are very timely, very important. They are powerful weapons in the struggle against the current turmoil. Party committees, government offices, the military, and the civilian population at all levels throughout the province must thoroughly implement these measures in every detail. In the past few days, large demonstrations in Changsha and elsewhere in our province have caused many difficulties and problems in economic work and public safety and have led to great confusion in the people's thinking. The Standing Committee members agree unanimously that we cannot allow such turmoil to run its course and absolutely must not allow such grave conditions to continue."

Four measures were advanced to stabilize Hunan: Leaders must stabilize their units, a second group of leaders in each unit should pursue economic production, urban services departments should maintain normal service, and normal transportation services and public safety should be maintained.

Qinghai

An enlarged meeting of the Party Standing Committee on the morning of May 20 discussed Li Peng's speech and decided on measures and responses to fit the circumstances of Qinghai.

> Excerpt from Qinghai Party Committee, "Firmly support Party Central's important policy, guarantee Qinghai's stability," report to Party Central, May 20

---

[27]Hunan Party secretary.—Comp.

Yin Kesheng:[28] "The students are patriotic to oppose official profiteering, and their advocacy of democracy and rule of law is something we should affirm. But there are indeed people who are exploiting the situation to create turmoil. All provincial officials holding Party membership must study Li Peng's speech carefully to enhance their understanding and raise their morale. Everyone must remain on duty, perform work well, and try to focus the attention of people throughout the province on building the Four Modernizations."

Song Ruixiang:[29] "Qinghai is calm on the surface so far, but complicated ideological problems remain. We must conduct thoroughgoing and meticulous thought work. Right now our work should focus on schools; when thought work among students has been well done, work in factories and offices will then be easier."

Liu Feng:[30] "I support Li Peng's speech. We cannot blame the people for turmoil when so many are involved. Apart from instigation by the small minority, the cause of these events was our failure to resolve the problems of official profiteering and corruption. We should solve these problems at their roots. That is the only route to lasting peace and stability."

Dorpa:[31] "Quite a few people have been caught up in this movement, and many excessively provocative things have been said. We need rigorous policies to distinguish between provocative speech and actual wrong deeds. We must not show bad people mercy but must not be too hot-headed, either."

NINGXIA

On May 20, at a morning meeting of the Standing Committee of the Party Committee for the Autonomous Region, Party secretary Shen Daren asked leaders of the region's five leadership teams to "take a firm and overt stand in line with Party Central in ideology, action, and organization during this antiturmoil struggle that affects the future and destiny of the Party and state." Shen went on to stress how difficult the struggle would be. It might not be very difficult to put down the current turbulence, he said, but it would be much harder to resolve the underlying ideological problem and to get people to shift their outlooks. The current problem did not rest just with students or teachers but extended into culture, the news media, science and technology, and even into Party and government offices. He said that there had been a lot of confusion recently from

---

[28]Provincial Party secretary.—Comp.
[29]Governor.—Comp.
[30]Standing Committee member of the provincial Party Committee and chair of the provincial CPPCC.—Comp.
[31]Secretary of the provincial Party Discipline Inspection Commission.—Comp. Dorpa (*duoba* in romanized Chinese) is a Tibetan name. We do not know the full name.—Eds.

top levels on down and that leaders would have to get to the bottom of it. They must be ready for protracted struggle, must help people reach correct understanding issue by issue, and must be especially assiduous in doing a good job at certain key schools and workplaces to organize study sessions. Students on strike at Ningxia University, Ningxia College of Education, and the Television University were to return to classes unconditionally. The original plan to hold talks with the students would remain in force. Party and government leaders would do their best to solve the real problems the students had mentioned in their dialogues in an effort to improve the work of the Party and government noticeably and thus to help calm the students. Following the Standing Committee meeting, the Party Committee immediately issued an "Emergency Notice" mandating the study at all localities of Li Peng's and Yang Shangkun's speeches.

Guizhou

The Party Standing Committee studied Li Peng's speech on May 20 at dawn. Later in the morning members of the province's five leadership teams joined them to study the speech. The Standing Committee issued an emergency notice in the name of the Provincial Party Committee asking all government departments, districts, counties, and municipalities to organize local residents to listen to, watch broadcasts of, and then to study the speeches of the Central leaders. Provincial Party secretary Liu Zhengwei vowed to "resolutely support Party Central in its attempt to end the turmoil, to restore normal order in education, and to safeguard peace and unity."

> Excerpt from Guizhou Party Committee, "Firmly support Party Central's decision to stop the turmoil, uphold the social order of peace and unity in Guizhou," report to Party Central, May 20

Liu Zhengwei: "I support the measures of Party Central to curb the turmoil. They will be helpful in restoring normal order for production and daily life, in stabilizing the overall situation, and in assuring public safety. For some time now we have been shipping grain to disaster areas in our province. If we fail to take decisive action now, and if transportation should be disrupted, we will have real trouble when we can no longer reach those famine areas. This does not mean we do not want democracy. Any problems we have can be resolved within the Party through democracy and rule of law."

Protests by Chinese students abroad

Reports wired to Beijing from the Chinese embassies in the United States, Canada, and Sweden on May 20 showed that Chinese students and scholars abroad responded to the declaration of martial law in Beijing with angry protests.

In the United States five thousand Chinese citizens rallied in Washington, D.C., on the morning of May 20 and issued an open letter to the people of China, supporting the student movement and denouncing martial law. The letter condemned Li Peng's speech as an affront to the popular will and demanded Li's resignation and the restoration of Zhao Ziyang. It further demanded immediate dialogue between the government and the students and called upon the PLA to protect the people instead of suppressing them. The protesters marched to the Chinese embassy to deliver a copy of the open letter to officials there. Similar demonstrations took place at the Chinese consulates in New York, San Francisco, Los Angeles, and Houston.

In Canada more than two hundred Chinese students gathered at the provincial government building in Toronto on May 19 to demand a meeting with Wan Li, who had not yet returned to China. Two officials from Wan's entourage met with the students and received a petition asking Wan to cut short his visit to Canada and return home immediately. On May 20 about five hundred Chinese students protested the announcement of martial law in front of the Chinese embassy in Ottawa. This was the biggest such demonstration since the crisis in China had started, and it drew significant local media attention. Student leaders delivered an open letter to the Chinese government and the National People's Congress and then proceeded with another demonstration in front of Canada's Parliament. At the University of Victoria, Chinese students issued a statement supporting the student movement and opposing martial law.

A "cautious assessment"

Forty-five reports on the foreign media reached Zhongnanhai on May 20. In the view of many foreign media, the martial law order was a desperate move that might only make things worse. Li Peng seemed to be winning his power struggle with Zhao Ziyang. Also important was the information that the U.S. government was taking a cautious approach. Secretary of State James Baker had said it was not in the U.S. interest to see major instability in either China or the Soviet Union. When asked why the U.S. government did not support the Chinese students, Baker replied that the United States supports democracy and the freedoms of speech and assembly but that it was also very important, in the present situation, that the United States not be seen as in any way inciting political unrest.

May 21

Rumors fly

The military siege struck terror into the hearts of people in Beijing. A May 21 report from the State Security Ministry described students and citizens surrounding troops as they moved into the city and pleading desperately with them not to use force against the people. Many officers and soldiers said they had come to maintain order and pledged never to open fire on the local people. On the whole, the students and citizens seemed to be getting along fairly well with the soldiers and officers.

The report said that college students began to erect roadblocks and establish checkpoints near their campuses to prevent troops from moving in. Campus public-address systems reported news of martial law events around the clock, sometimes rebroadcasting programs from the Voice of America and spreading rumors. Some broadcasts claimed that top civilian and military leaders, such as Wan Li, Deng Yingchao, Xu Xiangqian, and Nie Rongzhen, supported the students and were opposed to any military action against them. Another said that ten provinces plus the city of Shanghai had declared independence from the Central government. A third said that 220,000 workers from Capital Iron and Steel had issued an ultimatum to Party Central threatening a strike if the government did not accede to the two student demands within twenty-four hours.

On Chang'an Boulevard, Beijing's main thoroughfare, the ministry said roadblocks appeared at virtually every intersection, while demonstrations, public speeches, and distribution of handouts continued. About one hundred thousand people gathered in Tiananmen Square during the day, and three hundred thousand were there by evening. The student public-address system at the Square urged people to exercise maximum restraint and remain nonviolent. Handbills reported clashes between civilians and military personnel at some locations and friendly interaction at others. A speaker in the streets reported[32] the death of two student hunger strikers and warned of army personnel in plainclothes who were hidden in the crowds at Tiananmen and around Beijing.

That afternoon, again according to the State Security Ministry , the AFS had convened a meeting of the leaders of all the independent student associations to discuss what to do next. Heated debate ensued over the question of whether to withdraw from Tiananmen Square. A final vote showed thirty-two in favor of withdrawal and fourteen opposed, with two abstentions. On the principle of majority rule, the student leaders agreed to withdraw and then turned their attention to composing the slogan—"Support Party reformers; down with Party conservatives"—that would

---

[32]Falsely, as far as we know.

be used during the withdrawal. They would describe the withdrawal as "demonstration, spread of information, and continuation of the student strike."

That evening, however, the number of people gathered in the Square grew rapidly. AFS leaders held another emergency meeting on the north side of the Monument to the People's Heroes. At that session, which Wang Dan chaired, the decision to withdraw was reversed. Some sources reported that Beijing intellectuals had held a meeting that morning and had "resolved unanimously to support the students in the Square and to fight the illegitimate Li Peng regime to the end." The AFS hastily arranged a news conference, and the Square's student-run public-address system, Voice of the Movement, carried a speech by Wang Dan in which he said "the students will never retreat; each school should prepare its ranks."

A report on "black hands behind the scenes"

While students and ordinary citizens continued to block martial law troops on the streets and in the suburbs, the headquarters of the martial law troops, under the direction of Yang Shangkun and Liu Huaqing, issued a "Letter to Beijing Citizens."

> Excerpt from Martial Law Command, "Letter to Beijing Citizens," May 21; published in May 22 editions of *People's Daily*, *Liberation Army Daily (Jiefangjun bao)*, and *Beijing Daily (Beijing ribao)*

1. The People's Liberation Army is a people's army under the leadership of the Chinese Communist Party.... The troops are carrying out their martial law mission in order to ensure security and to restore order in the capital. They are not in any way opposed to patriotic students.

2. The martial law troops have met with some resistance in the process of carrying out their mission. They have exercised maximum self-control out of concern for the overall situation. The broad masses have also cooperated in many different ways. The capital is currently in a state of chaos. Communications have been cut off, and certain commodities are in short supply. Security in the capital may further deteriorate, and the people are deeply worried. The martial law troops must resolutely enforce the laws and regulations of the government. It is our duty to take all effective measures to turn the current situation around. We will base ourselves on law and follow the wishes of the people in the capital,

including the wishes of patriotic students, and take resolute measures to stop the tiny minority of criminal elements who beat, smash, rob, and burn. We hope the masses of patriotic students and ordinary citizens will understand and will offer their strong support and cooperation.

3. The People's Liberation Army extends resolute support to the broad masses who demand that we punish official profiteering, oppose corruption, and promote the construction of socialist democracy and rule of law. . . . We have faith that the Party and government will take strong measures on behalf of the popular will in solving all the existing problems through democracy and rule of law.

4. The armies enforcing martial law will exercise strict discipline and will pursue education among the troops to love the capital, love the people in the capital, and love the young students. They will carry forward our army's glorious traditions of diligence and loving the people, will oppose any speech or behavior that could harm the friendly feelings between the army and the people, and will take concrete action to protect the fundamental interests of the country and people.

The tone of this letter stood in sharp contrast to what students and citizens had been expecting from martial law, and they generally reacted to it favorably. Moreover, some students and citizens were initiating face-to-face contacts with soldiers and were beginning to see them as approachable young men and fellow citizens. The sense of intense confrontation receded somewhat. Many citizens and students came to believe that "there's nothing wrong with the PLA; the problem is with the government that sent the order."

At 10 P.M. the State Security Ministry delivered to Zhongnanhai a report that caught the eye of Li Peng.

> State Security Ministry, "Activities of Chen Ziming and Wang
> Juntao with leaders of the AFS," in "Important intelligence"
> (*Yaoqing*), May 21

According to reliable sources, Director Chen Ziming of the Beijing Social and Economic Sciences Research Institute, Deputy Director Wang Juntao, and others held a secret meeting at Beijing Normal University with personnel from six sub-commands.[33] Participants included people from the Institute for Economic Reform in China, the Academy of Social Sciences, a research institute of CITIC, and members of autonomous student associations at Peking University and Beijing Normal University.

[33]The report does not explain this reference.

The group decided that the headquarters of this so-called spontaneous and loosely affiliated organization would change locations every day in order to prevent detection—and would, if possible, harbor inside the residences of high military officials.[34] For security reasons, some of the leaders will avoid appearing in public. They also decided to communicate by secret code. They will organize a special group to work on public opinion, will compile materials on "The Man Li Peng," and will set up an independent newspaper. An informed source revealed that Chen Ziming, Wang Juntao, and others have been plotting behind the scenes ever since late April. They have had many contacts with student leaders like Wang Dan. The founding of the Autonomous Student Association at Peking University and the Autonomous Federation of Beijing College Students and the student staging of a hunger strike at Tiananmen Square when Gorbachev visited all had something to do with the backstage plotting of Chen, Wang, and others. Wang Juntao, taking advantage of his status as a Peking University graduate, was able to gain trust from some members of the Autonomous Student Association at Peking University. There is information that Wang's institute not only has funded some of the student organizations in the Square but also regularly convenes radical intellectuals for all kinds of meetings. The concerned departments will watch their activities closely.

After reading this Li Peng issued an order to Luo Gan, his deputy for liaison with the Public Security, State Security, and Justice Ministries: "Comrade Luo Gan, please instruct the concerned departments to pay close attention to the moves of this organization. But keep the surveillance secret; don't tip them off." In the aftermath of June Fourth, Chen Ziming and Wang Juntao would be labeled the "black hands behind the scenes" of Tiananmen.

Meeting of the eight Elders

On May 21 a meeting was held at Deng Xiaoping's house. The participants, in addition to Deng, were Chen Yun, Li Xiannian, Peng Zhen, Deng Yingchao, Yang Shangkun, Bo Yibo, and Wang Zhen. Security had been increased for Zhongnanhai and the residences of the Central leaders since May 19. Both for Zhongnanhai itself and for the residences of those Elders who lived outside it, police strength was doubled. In Zhongnanhai light machine guns were set up, and steel plates were installed bearing spikes that would puncture the tires of unauthorized vehicles. Troops were

---

[34]Wang Juntao's father was a high-ranking military officer. Others in the group may also have had relatives who were officers.

deployed according to standard procedures for such occasions, inside the Xinhua Gate, along Nanhai Lake and on Yingtai,[35] "to guard against unpredictable accidents."

It was a comfort to Deng Xiaoping and the other Elders that it was they, not Zhao Ziyang, who controlled the military. Zhao himself lived in Zhongnanhai, where his every move could be watched, so he presented no conceivable threat. There was no basis for the popular rumor that Party leaders were moving around the city or had fled out of town or to the Western Hills. They felt perfectly secure as they gathered at Deng's residence.

> Excerpt from Party Central Office Secretariat, "Minutes of important meeting, May 21, 1989," document supplied to Party Central Office Secretariat for its records by the Office of Deng Xiaoping

Deng Xiaoping: "We can all see what's happened. Martial law hasn't restored order. This isn't because we can't do it; it's because problems inside the Party drag on and keep us from solving things that should've been solved long ago. So the trouble just gets bigger and bigger, and now it's out of hand. Other than those of us here tonight, nobody seems even able to describe the problem correctly. We need to think hard about how this whole thing broke out, and then maybe a bad thing can lead to a good thing. The people who promote turmoil have been completely exposed. They've colluded with foreign forces; even the KMT in Taiwan has tried to meddle! Their goals are to overthrow our Party and our state, to deny socialism, and to destroy the healthy situation that our policies of reform have managed to achieve after all these years of striving. Lots of people are confused in their thinking these days, but let's be clear: Our Party and state face a life-and-death crisis. Zhao Ziyang's intransigence has been obvious, and he bears undeniable responsibility. He wouldn't even attend the Party-government-army meeting that the Standing Committee of the Politburo convened. When others saw that the Party general secretary didn't show up, they all knew something was wrong. He exposed the differences within the Standing Committee for all to see. He wanted to draw a strict line between himself and us in order to make his stand clear. So we've got to talk about the Zhao Ziyang problem."

Li Xiannian: "I've said all along that the problem's inside the Party. The Party now has two headquarters. Zhao Ziyang's got his own separate headquarters. We have to get to the bottom of this, have to dig out the roots. Otherwise there can

[35]A small island near the northern side of Nanhai Lake, linked to land by a bridge, often erroneously shown on maps as a tiny peninsula.—Comp.

never again be unity of thought inside the Party. Right from the time of the April 26 editorial Zhao Ziyang wouldn't accept the 'turmoil' label. He's gone step-by-step down his own path. I knew something was wrong as soon as I heard his ADB speech, and that's why I rushed back to town. Then he stabbed Xiaoping in the back when he talked to Gorbachev. Are we to believe he didn't mean to do this? Why did he have to make the point right at that moment—no sooner, no later? He wanted the students and common people to turn their spears toward Xiaoping. Did he sound like a general secretary when he spoke to the students at Tiananmen? What did he mean by 'I'm old—so it doesn't matter any more'? And that meeting about martial law in Beijing was so important. Sure, he's allowed to take sick leave as general secretary, but he wasn't so sick that he couldn't get out of bed. He was trying to split the Party on purpose. When he opposed martial law he had his own political agenda, which was to force us senior people to hand over power and step down, so that he could go ahead with his program of bourgeois liberalization. With us senior people in the way, his hands were tied and he was stuck. Zhao Ziyang is no longer fit to be general secretary."

Wang Zhen: "Zhao Ziyang's never paid a whit of attention to people like us. Comrade Xiaoping supports him and cultivates him, and all he does is rebel. That TV film *River Elegy* that was so popular last year was aimed at glorifying him.[36] Comrade Xiaoping never appeared in it—only Zhao Ziyang. I was against it from the start. What's this "blue" civilization, this "sea" civilization, that they praise? It's bandit civilization—bandit logic—that's what! When a TV show like this gets shown—even shown twice!—what do you think it's all about if not building a Zhao Ziyang cult? This student turmoil we're seeing should've been stopped long ago. Would students have dared do this when Chairman Mao was around? When I reported to Comrade Xiaoping that I thought we should be more decisive, he said let's just watch a bit longer. But what are we watching? Aren't we just watching Zhao sit there? Quite a picture! The big number 1 boss, and doing nothing about it! On the contrary, he opposes us, opposes martial law. What he really wants is to drive us old people from power. We didn't mistreat him; he's the one who's picked the fight. When he falls it'll be his own fault. Who made him go for

---

[36] *River Elegy* was a six-part video production broadcast on Chinese national television in summer 1988. It addressed such issues as Chinese xenophobia and national pride, isolationism and wall building, authoritarian rule, and the contrast between a backward hinterland (a "yellow civilization") and a thriving, outward-looking coastal economy (a "blue civilization"). Authors Su Xiaokang and Wang Luxiang criticized "feudal" traditions of the past in order to convey criticisms of the contemporary political system that would be taboo if stated more directly. For an English translation of the text, see Richard Bodman and Pin Pin Wan, *Deathsong of a River* (Ithaca, N.Y.: Cornell University Press, 1991).

bourgeois liberalization? Then there's Hu Qili. He let the whole news scene fly out of control, and he's also against martial law. He should get the sack, too!"

Deng Yingchao: "Comrade Zhao Ziyang wavered during this movement. When he didn't carry out the resolution of the Standing Committee of the Politburo, he committed the mistake of violating Party discipline. The public admires him as a leading reformer these days, and he takes too much credit. In fact, the reform programs were the crystallization of the Party's collective wisdom and should not be credited to him. A lot of the reform programs were designed by some of you—Comrades Xiaoping, Chen Yun, and Xiannian. He only carried them out. Li Peng told me that when he wrote his Government Work Report this year, he wanted to mention mistakes the government had made in the past. But these references couldn't make it past Comrade Zhao Ziyang's desk, so the report made it seem that all the mistakes happened during the last year, when Li Peng was in charge."

Deng Xiaoping: "The trouble did not begin just last year. Three years ago it was already obvious, and it was five years ago that it first started. If there's blame, Zhao's got to share it."

Deng Yingchao: "The general secretary of the Party should be magnanimous enough to take any responsibility. This incident shows that Comrade Zhao Ziyang is not fit to be general secretary."

Peng Zhen: "I agree with all this. It's time to reconsider who should be general secretary."

Yang Shangkun: "There's no question that Zhao Ziyang has committed a serious violation of Party discipline in this matter, and no question that Hu Qili's thinking is inconsistent with Party Central's. But in my personal opinion, we should look at the big picture and make solidarity our top priority. This isn't the right moment for replacing a general secretary. Instead we could ask Zhao Ziyang for a self-criticism and avoid making big changes on the Politburo Standing Committee. Foreigners always talk about how we're split into this faction and that faction. They love it when we squabble. They've already begun to make a lot of noise along these lines."

Deng Xiaoping: "What? And what does 'independence' mean to us? Checking the look on a foreigner's face before we decide what to do? Forget about international opinion and its rumormongering, its stirring up of trouble, or whatever. The last two general secretaries didn't hold up, but that wasn't because they weren't qualified when we chose them. There was nothing wrong with them at the start. Later they both stumbled over the fundamental issue of sticking to the Four Basic Principles. The keys to the Four Principles are Party leadership and socialism. The opposite of the Four Principles is bourgeois liberalization. Each of us here has spent a lot of time in recent years talking about the need to insist on the Four Principles and to oppose bourgeois liberalization. But our general secretaries just didn't do a good job at implementation.

"In the recent turmoil Zhao Ziyang has exposed his position completely. He obviously stands on the side of the turmoil, and in practical terms he has been fomenting division, splitting the Party, and defending turmoil. It's lucky we're still here to keep a lid on things. Zhao Ziyang stimulated turmoil, and there's no reason to keep him. Hu Qili is no longer fit for the Standing Committee, either. How could we explain it to the whole Party if we kept them? They can't become models for the Party. I don't think it's a big deal to make changes in the leadership so long as we don't change the political line, the guiding principles and policies we've held since the Third Plenum of the Eleventh Central Committee, and stick with our 'one center and two basic points' policy.[37] The Standing Committee first and foremost must be a unified group. Its members must have high political consciousness, an ability to work hard and to think clearly, and skill in unifying people. A Standing Committee that is unified and hardworking can be a model for the whole Party. What do you think about all this, Comrade Chen Yun?"

Chen Yun: "I've heard what everyone's said about Comrade Zhao Ziyang, and I agree with Comrade Xiaoping. Zhao Ziyang and Hu Qili are no longer fit for the Standing Committee. The new general secretary and new Standing Committee must first of all assume a bold political profile and a tough attitude and must rigorously observe Party discipline. They must be able to listen to all kinds of opinions, not be impulsive or self-centered, and have good ability to cooperate. They have to know Marxism-Leninism, understand theory, have broad knowledge, and show good job performance. They must have a good image, be acceptable to all sorts of people, be able to draw popular support, and be stable and reliable. Comrade Xiannian has pointed out to me that Comrade Jiang Zemin from Shanghai is a suitable candidate. Every time I've gone down to Shanghai he always sees me, and he strikes me as a modest person with strong Party discipline and broad knowledge. He gets along well in Shanghai, too."

Li Xiannian: "I haven't had much contact with Comrade Jiang Zemin, but I

[37]"The guiding principles and policies we've held since the Third Plenum of the Eleventh Central Committee" refers to Deng Xiaoping's program of reform and opening. It was at this plenum, in November-December 1978, that Deng took power. "One center and two basic points" refers to centering policy on economic construction while paying attention to (1) reform and opening and (2) the Four Basic Principles. This formula was introduced by Zhao Ziyang at the Thirteenth Party Congress in October 1987.

have a pretty good impression of him, too. Back in the [1986–]1987 student movement, I remember, Shanghai handled things best. Jiang Zemin went out to the universities in person and debated with the students. He knew his facts and argued well. He took the initiative, even ahead of Party Central. He's got brains. I noticed, after the April 26 editorial, that again it was Shanghai that took the lead in pushing the spirit of Party Central. Jiang Zemin called a meeting of more than ten thousand officials the very next day, and he yanked the *World Economic Herald* into shape. That was something! That move—given what was going on—put him under tremendous public pressure, but he stood firm, didn't budge, and stuck to principle. Then, when the Party, government, and army at the Center declared martial law, again it was Shanghai that took the lead in action. This kind of firm attitude's hard to come by. In political action and Party loyalty, Jiang Zemin has been a constant. And of course, he's got a good knack for economic work. Shanghai's built a good economic foundation these last few years. I've heard Jiang talk about Shanghai programs quite a few times. He's always got it down, he's got a knack for it. And he's got a good public image—in the prime of life, full of energy. I like the idea of him as general secretary."

Wang Zhen: "Comrade Jiang Zemin has no experience at the Center. The general secretary should be chosen from the Standing Committee. Comrade Li Peng could serve as general secretary! We all saw how well he did in opposing this recent turmoil."

Peng Zhen: "Comrade Wan Li has rich work experience. He's worked at both local and central levels, knows conditions all across the country, and is in charge of building the legal system. He's got good prestige among officials and the masses everywhere. He's up to the task."

Chen Yun: "But Comrade Wan Li's a bit old. The reason we assigned him to the People's Congress was to let him gradually retreat to the second line.[38] On the Standing Committee question, I wonder if we should consider Song Ping. He's done a good job with personnel policies since going over to the Organization Department. But here I would defer to Mr. Bo."[39]

Bo Yibo: "Comrade Song Ping comes out of the planning system. He's conscientious and meticulous. He's been thorough in evaluating, training, and appointing provincial-level officials. Comrades in the organizational[40] system hold him in high regard. He holds himself to high standards and has strong organizational

[38]Chinese Communist jargon for a lighter workload, derived from military language.
[39]Bo managed top-level personnel matters for the Elders through the 1980s and best knew the qualifications of the top officials.—Comp. Chen Yun here refers to Bo Yibo as *Bo lao,* "respected elder Bo," a usage that implies not only respect but familiarity and affection as well.—Eds.
[40]That is, personnel.

discipline. He's taken an unambiguous stand on the turmoil. I agree with Comrade Chen Yun's suggestion."

Yang Shangkun: "We should find a general secretary within the current Standing Committee. Right now a lot of spears are pointed at Comrade Li Peng. The Party would get big pressure if we nominated Comrade Li Peng as general secretary. Comrade Qiao Shi is in his prime and vigorous. On the current Standing Committee he's the one with the most experience; he's been director of the Central Liaison Department, the Organization Department, and the General Office of the Central Committee; he's been president of the Party School, secretary of the Politics and Law Committee, and secretary of the CDIC. He's also served a while as vice premier and worked for a long time in the Secretariat. He's honest and able and has good prestige at the Center. I would nominate him to be general secretary."

Deng Xiaoping: "A general secretary must dare to take responsibility and show clearly just where he stands. Li Ruihuan from Tianjin is energetic, effective, and thoughtful. He's good at shaping mass opinion and at mending all sorts of conflicts—just what you need for propaganda and mobilization work. I've talked with him a few times. Don't be fooled by his carpenter background and all those model-worker hats on his head; this guy has a brain. He knows philosophy and knows how to use it in daily life. He knows how to stick to principle, and he's done a first-rate job with the economy, too. The construction and waterworks in Tianjin have popped eyes around the country in the last few years. Li Ruihuan is a doer; everybody in Tianjin praises him, and his local prestige is outstanding. We need people like him on the Standing Committee so the masses can see Party Central is sticking with reform and opening and still wants to build the economy. This could spare us some big confusion among the masses. Li would be a good choice for the Standing Committee."

Deng Yingchao: "I have a good impression of this man Li Ruihuan, too. Communist Party leaders should be populists, should keep the common people constantly in mind. We must never forget the principle of serving the people and must maintain the broadest possible view."

Li Xiannian: "I think we should let these questions of the general secretary and the Standing Committee percolate for a while. The more circumspect and careful we are, the better it will be for the Party's work and the country's future."

Deng Xiaoping: "I agree with Comrade Xiannian. Let's all think it over a few days, looking at all the comparisons every which way. Once we've thought it through, we can go to the Politburo with our proposal and suggest they call a Central Committee meeting."

Chen Yun: "I agree."

Peng Zhen: "A lot of people in society are calling for Wan Li to come home. Some of them hope he'll come back and solve this protest problem. I don't think it's a good idea for him to continue his visit to the United States: It puts pressure on the Party and on Wan Li personally, too. But it wouldn't be too smart to bring him straight back, either."[41]

Bo Yibo: "He could come back to China without coming straight to Beijing. He could go to Shanghai first."

Li Xiannian: "Good idea. And we've got to be sure he gets the true story about what's going on. Jiang Zemin could orient him."

Chen Yun: "What do you think, Comrade Xiaoping?"

Deng assented by nodding.[42]

Deng Yingchao: "In the last few days I've gotten all kinds of letters and telegrams telling me what's going on in Beijing and around the country and urging me to come forward and say something. I'm retired, but I'd still like to do what I can to support the Party. I've heard a lot of rumors flying around about martial law, saying Party Central is splitting into two factions, one supporting martial law and the other dead set against it. These rumors really upset me, and I'm thinking of writing a letter to the students and citizens of Beijing telling them I hope they'll trust the Party and government and cherish the People's Liberation Army. I hope all of us will do whatever we can to pacify the current situation as soon as possible."

Deng Xiaoping: "You are wise, Sister Deng. We should all follow your example. There's a real need in the next few days for all of us to use appropriate channels to express our views clearly and publicly on support for the PLA and martial law. I'm glad we older ones can still be useful to the Party and the country. If the rest of you agree, we can handle the questions of Zhao Ziyang, Hu Qili, and the other two members of the Secretariat[43] by temporarily relieving them of their duties until the Party Central Committee makes specific decisions. I think the Standing Committee of the Politburo should call a briefing meeting with Party, government, and military leaders right away in order to reassure people and get them thinking alike."

[41]That is, since he might side with Zhao.
[42]In the records this is denoted by *"Xiaoping tongzhi diantou."*
[43]Yan Mingfu and Rui Xingwen.

Chen Yun: "I agree completely. For now we should keep news of this meeting away from the non-Party vice chairs."[44]

This first meeting of the eight Elders set the course for replacing General Secretary Zhao Ziyang and Standing Committee member Hu Qili. They were relieved of their duties effective May 22, and the Fourth Plenum of the Thirteenth Central Committee in June 1989 made the decisions official. After the meeting the tentative list of the candidates for new general secretary and Standing Committee membership was circulated among the Elders, and the important decision to recall Wan Li—but not directly to Beijing—was announced.

In the past the pattern for appointing general secretaries had been to follow seniority within the Standing Committee. When Hu Yaobang stepped down, Zhao Ziyang, then premier, succeeded him. So when Zhao was removed, Li Peng was clearly next in line. It was therefore significant that Deng Xiaoping did not even mention Li Peng's name and that conservatives Chen Yun and Li Xiannian also passed him over. Only Wang Zhen mentioned him. Deng Yingchao, who had lobbied hard to get her foster son Li Peng appointed as premier, also said nothing for him this time around. In the past Li's two major qualifications had been that he was a "descendent of the revolution"[45] and that he "adores the old comrades";[46] why had these qualifications now lost their power? Why couldn't Li Peng get the Elders' support, even though he was the most active person on the Standing Committee in fighting for the Elders, and the one most devoted to carrying out martial law? Part of the reason must have had to do with the Elders' disappointment in Li Peng's abilities. But part, no doubt, was because of what Yang Shangkun had pointed out: Li Peng had generated great popular indignation and would not enjoy popular support as General Secretary.

The views of two marshals and eight generals

On May 21 eleven students from the Chinese University of Science and Technology went to Nie Rongzhen's residence to request a meeting with him.[47] They delivered a letter charging that Li Peng intended to clear the Square by force and imprison the students. The letter implored Mar-

[44]Meaning the vice chairs of the Standing Committee of the National People's Congress and the vice chairs of the Chinese People's Political Consultative Conference who were not CCP members.
[45]Meaning that his parents were "revolutionary martyrs." They were killed by the Kuomintang early in the history of the CCP.
[46]Meaning that he was more obsequious toward the Elders than were the other leaders.
[47]Marshals Xu Xiangqian and Nie Rongzhen were the two highest-ranking retired officers of the Chinese military. Both had opted entirely out of political affairs, and neither participated in the meetings of the Elders. In Marshal Xu's case this was related to his disapproval of the way Deng Xiaoping had climbed back to power in 1977 by promising loyalty to Mao's chosen successor, Hua Guofeng, and had then gradually engineered Hua's removal from power. Xu and Hua both

shal Nie to visit Tiananmen to show his opposition to violence against the students. After having his secretary check the accuracy of the students' allegations, Nie sent word through his secretary that troops had come to Beijing to maintain social order and that the students should withdraw from the Square and return to classes.

After this visit to Nie Rongzhen's residence, seven students went to Marshal Xu Xiangqian's home. They reported the same news they had written to Nie Rongzhen and similarly requested a reply. Xu did not meet them in person but asked his staff to reply on his behalf. The staff told the students that the troops had come only to maintain order and would avoid bloodshed. They advised the students to cooperate with the government and return to classes. The next day *People's Daily* carried a front-page report of the students' encounters with the two marshals.[48]

Xu Xiangqian and Nie Rongzhen had been among the few military leaders whom Party Central had consulted prior to deciding on martial law. Other generals, including some who felt varying degrees of sympathy for the students, were not consulted. To them the announcement of martial law on the afternoon of May 19 came as an unpleasant surprise. They felt the measure might be too drastic, and besides their views had not been solicited. On May 20 eight of them—Wang Ping, Ye Fei, Zhang Aiping, Xiao Ke, Yang Dezhi, Chen Zaidao, Song Shilun, and Li Jukui—signed a one-sentence letter addressed to Deng Xiaoping and the Central Military Commission: "We request that troops not enter the city and that martial law not be carried out in Beijing."[49] When Deng Xiaoping received this letter, he and Yang Shangkun immediately dispatched two top military leaders to pay personal visits to the generals, one by one, to explain the situation to them. Yang also personally telephoned Xiao Ke and Yang Dezhi, and eventually the minirevolt was pacified.

Chinese students overseas protest

On May 21 Zhongnanhai received thirteen reports detailing unprecedented levels of protest among Chinese students overseas. In the United States the Association of Chinese Students and

---

came from the province of Shanxi, and Xu had been Hua's strongest and most respected supporter among the senior Party elite. Xu concluded that "Deng Xiaoping is manipulative; you can't work with him." As for Nie Rongzhen, he was Hu Yaobang's mentor and friend and had not agreed with the decision to force Hu to resign.

Only ten officers in the history of the PLA had ever risen to the rank of marshal. As the sole survivors of this group, Xu and Nie had considerable influence among the military and the general public. Both believed in a soft approach toward the student movement. When they were briefed about the martial law decision, Xu Xiangqian at first said nothing but later issued a statement: "Let us hope it is never directed at the students." Nie Rongzhen's response was, "Under no circumstances should there be shedding of blood."—Comp.

[48]An account of these two visits is in Oksenberg et al., *Beijing Spring*, 316–317.

[49]A similar letter, but signed by seven generals, containing more than one sentence, and dated May 23, appears in Suzanne Ogden, Kathleen Hartford, Lawrence Sullivan, and David Zweig, eds., *China's Search for Democracy: The Student and the Mass Movement of 1989* (Armonk, New York: M. E. Sharpe, 1992), 292.

Scholars went to the Chinese consulate in New York to deliver an open letter to Wan Li, who was in Canada and about to arrive in the United States. The letter praised Wan for his popularity among the Chinese people and urged him to return to China to block the impending military crackdown on the student movement.

On the same day more than 4,500 Chinese students demonstrated in Tokyo to support their fellow students in China and to protest martial law. The students addressed an open letter to Party Central and the State Council opposing the use of force and calling for rationality and respect for the popular will. There were also demonstrations at the Chinese consulate in Osaka.

More than three thousand Chinese students rallied against martial law in Paris. In London three thousand students from mainland China, Hong Kong, and Taiwan demonstrated in support of the student movement, shouting antigovernment slogans and delivering a protest letter to the Chinese embassy, in front of which one Chinese student began a hunger strike. More than one thousand Chinese students in West Germany traveled to Bonn to sit in at the Chinese embassy, where they drew considerable media attention. Chinese students in Geneva submitted a petition to the UN secretary general and the UN Human Rights Commission, requesting intervention to abolish martial law and prevent bloodshed. Smaller demonstrations took place in the Soviet Union, Sweden, and Australia.

Cries from Hong Kong

In Hong Kong the protests against martial law in Beijing that took place on the afternoon of May 21 were the biggest demonstrations the city had seen in twenty years. Six hundred thousand people—students, teachers, social workers, laborers, women, children, old people, and members of various religious groups—participated. There were even some employees of the Xinhua News Agency, Beijing's unofficial headquarters in Hong Kong. Protesters demanded the dismissal of Li Peng, the abolition of martial law, and the withdrawal of troops from Beijing. They also called upon Wan Li to return to China to convene an emergency meeting of the NPC to review government policies.

News first of Zhao Ziyang's resignation and then of martial law caused the Hong Kong stock market to fall on May 19 by 132 points, the biggest one-day drop since October 1987. The tourist industry in Hong Kong also suffered, as the number of travelers headed for China declined rapidly during May. Business travelers were also canceling their flights to Beijing, and business shows scheduled for Hong Kong were being postponed or canceled. Foreign nationals working in China were leaving in large numbers, causing a huge demand for airline tickets from Beijing to Hong Kong. Many in financial and business circles saw martial law as a big mistake that might scare away foreign investors, cause Western nations to impose sanctions against China, and isolate the Chinese government in the international community.

May 21–22

Crosscurrents

On May 21 the General Office of the Central Committee, at the direction of Zhao Ziyang (who was still on sick leave), sent a telegram to Wan Li in Canada asking that Wan "end the visit and return home as soon as possible." When Deng Xiaoping learned of Zhao's telegram, he followed it the next day with his own, also asking Wan to cut short his state visit but only after he had had his meetings with the U.S. president, vice president, and secretary of state. Deng also specified that Wan should arrive in Shanghai first and proceed to Beijing after a few days. Deng did not mention in his telegram his plan that Jiang Zemin would brief Wan Li in Shanghai.

On the evening of May 21 Wan Li addressed more than five hundred Canadian citizens of Chinese descent at a banquet held in his honor in Toronto. He praised the students for their patriotism and their efforts to promote democracy and to root out corruption. He also called for social stability and order and the resolution of conflict through democracy and rule of law. Wan's speech bore a strong resemblance to the positions of Zhao Ziyang.

The Beijing Government and the Martial Law Headquarters issued a joint announcement on May 22 describing chaotic conditions in Beijing and making five requests of the public: 1. People should dismiss the rumors that the tiny minority of people with ulterior motives were manufacturing. Their goal was only to sow chaos. 2. People from outside Beijing should go home as soon as possible. 3. Workers of every kind were to remain on duty and concentrate on their work. 4. All martial law troops should serve their mission and people should cooperate with them. 5. Traffic police were to stay on duty, and no one else was allowed to establish checkpoints, guide traffic, or set up roadblocks.

By afternoon one-third of the public transportation in the city had been restored. Military headquarters issued a letter to all officers and soldiers, extending regards and seeking to boost their morale.

May 22 was also the day Zhao Ziyang, who still did not know the Party Elders had decided to dismiss him, returned to his office after his three-day leave; he found no documents to read and no work to do. He had already been cut off from all news of the student movement, martial law, and everything else. At the same time the Standing Committee of the Politburo had sent out telegrams summoning important provincial leaders to Beijing to hear about Zhao's dismissal.

Also that day, Deng Yingchao wrote an open letter to the students and citizens of Beijing, which *People's Daily* published the next day at Li Peng's instruction, with a photocopy of her signature to demonstrate its authenticity. The letter asked people not to believe rumors; to trust the Party, government, and army; and to cooperate with the PLA, who had entered the city only to maintain order.

The purge of Zhao Ziyang

Partly because the martial law troops were having trouble getting to their destinations and partly because rumors about Zhao Ziyang were rampant, Deng Xiaoping, Chen Yun, and Li Xiannian ordered Yang Shangkun and the three remaining Politburo Standing Committee members— Li Peng, Qiao Shi, and Yao Yilin—to convene a high-level meeting to hear analyses of the current situation from the leading Party members' groups within the NPC Standing Committee and the CPPCC and to begin the purge of Zhao Ziyang. The meeting took place on the evening of May 22. It was attended by members of the Politburo, secretaries from the Central Committee Secretariat, vice chairmen of the NPC Standing Committee with Party membership, vice premiers and members of the State Council, vice chairmen of the CPPCC holding Party membership, and members of the Central Military Commission. Even the three Politburo members holding posts away from Beijing—Jiang Zemin, Li Ruihuan, and Yang Rudai—attended the meeting. Yang Shangkun, Li Peng, Qiao Shi, and Yao Yilin all made speeches. All except Qiao Shi criticized Zhao Ziyang.

Excerpts from Party Central Secretariat, "Li Peng, Shangkun, Qiao Shi, and Yilin make a report,"[50] evening, May 22

Li Peng:[51] "Party Central has not called a Politburo meeting for some time, but the Standing Committee has been meeting and following events closely, and nearly all the Elder comrades have been involved. The general view is that the April 26 editorial was correct. What's happening now is turmoil—well-organized, planned, and premeditated turmoil whose goal is to negate the socialist system and Communist Party leadership. This has become ever more obvious. Accordingly, a number of our respected Elder comrades—Comrades Xiaoping, Chen Yun, Yang Shangkun, and Wang Zhen—and a majority of the Standing Committee all believe that we must never retreat from the position of the April 26 editorial. Of course the editorial could have been better written; it could have made a clearer distinction between the two different kinds of contradictions. But the editorial itself is not wrong. To negate it would be to pull our whole spiritual support from beneath us. . . .

"We hope the Party will not split. We want above all to stay unified. On routine matters, we might have different opinions and settle them through discussion. But this matter is different. When Comrade Ziyang came back from North Korea he made a speech to the ADB Conference on May 4. No other member of

[50] *Tongbao*, an oral report to subordinates.
[51] Text of Li Peng's speech in Oksenberg et al., *Beijing Spring*, 317–320.

the Standing Committee saw this speech in advance. He drafted it himself and sounded an entirely different tune from the April 26 editorial. The speech got wide circulation and had a big impact. From then on it was clear to everybody that there are two different views within the Party. Anyone with the slightest political experience could see it, so the ones causing the turmoil of course could see it, too. Comrade Ziyang did give the rest of us an advance look at his May 3 speech to the meeting on the seventieth anniversary of the May Fourth Movement. A number of us told him he had to add something about opposing bourgeois liberalization. But he didn't. The student movement raced ahead following that May 4 speech, and soon there were a million people demonstrating in the streets, many of them from outside Beijing. Finally Party Central had to move to impose martial law. . . .

"Another question deserves our attention: Ultimately, who is the core of our Party leadership? Who represents reform and opening up, Comrade Ziyang or Comrade Xiaoping? Everyone should keep quite clear on this point. The main principles and policies of the past ten years of reform were all put forth by Comrade Xiaoping. He is the chief architect of the policies of reform and opening. He symbolizes China's reform and opening to the rest of the world. Comrade Ziyang has also done a lot of work, but that work has been to carry out the guiding principles of Comrade Xiaoping. Comrade Ziyang has also made many mistakes in his work. When he met Gorbachev, the first thing he said was that Comrade Xiaoping is the top policymaker of our Party. He said the First Plenum of the Thirteenth Central Committee decided that all major issues had to go through Deng. What was he doing here? He was exposing Comrade Xiaoping to attack. And sure enough, the next day's slogans included 'Down with Deng Xiaoping.' If we're going to uphold Party unity and the unity of the Party core, then I say we must clearly and openly uphold Comrade Xiaoping. . . .

"I think you should know that Party Central gave its advance approval to the speech I delivered on May 19 at the meeting of Party Central and other officials in Beijing. The Standing Committee called that meeting, and it was also the Standing Committee that made the decision to impose martial law. If Comrade Ziyang cared about Party unity he should have attended that meeting. But he took sick leave. If his health was poor, couldn't he at least, as general secretary, have presided over the meeting, without giving a speech? But he wouldn't do that, either. He didn't even have to preside—others could have done that for him—but at least he could have shown up. Yet even that he would not do. Who has breached Party unity? Who has violated our Party principle of democratic centralism? The speech he gave to the students at Tiananmen in the early morning of May 19 was also nothing more than an exposure of intra-Party cleavages before the entire nation....

"This struggle is indeed complicated, and the problem got started inside the Party. Otherwise it would not have gone this far. The causes of the events run deep. We have to solve the problem at its roots inside the Party."

Yang Shangkun, in his turn to speak, began by outlining the differences between Zhao Ziyang and Deng Xiaoping on how to handle the student movement, and he then drew attention to the problem of the three institutes and one association.

Yang Shangkun: "Recently four units—the Institute for Economic Reform in China, the Development Research Institute of the State Council's Agricultural Research Center, the International Affairs Research Institute of CITIC, and the Beijing Association of Young Economists—counterfeited the masthead of *People's Daily* and distributed 'extra' editions that leaked the essence of what Comrade Ziyang has been saying. They also carried a lot of rumors—things like the 'five points' of Comrade Ziyang 'all getting vetoed'—which simply isn't the case. One of his five points was that we solve things through democracy and rule of law, and everybody supported that. Another was that we clean up corruption in business, and we supported that, too....

"Comrade Xiannian told us we've got two Party headquarters now. Which one's in charge? We've got to get to the bottom of this, and fast. Everybody sees Comrade Ziyang as a reformer, but most of his reforms came straight out of Comrade Xiaoping's work. And the disturbances have grown out of Ziyang's years as premier. Comrade Xiaoping has already told us 'the trouble didn't start just last year; it started five years ago.'"

Yao Yilin: "When Comrade Li Peng gave the government work report [in 1989], Comrade Ziyang wouldn't approve that part.[52] He made it seem all the errors belonged to Comrade Li Peng."

Li Peng: "He wouldn't admit the problems had been building up for several years; he admitted only that there'd been errors this past year."

Yang Shangkun: "All right, I'll stop here."

Qiao Shi: "This student movement started more than a month ago after Comrade Hu Yaobang's death, and it has grown steadily ever since. So far we've main-

---

[52]That is, the part about mistakes made in government work when he himself was premier.

tained a patient and restrained stance toward it. We've done our best, consistent with our principles, to meet the demands of the student leaders, and we have managed to get by for more than a month without any arrests or bloodshed. On April 18 the students presented a petition at the Great Hall of the People, and Beijing authorities sent three NPC representatives to receive the petition. The students felt they had won and said they would leave but then went and laid siege to the Xinhua Gate for two days. Some of them even pushed through the gate, shouting reactionary slogans. In short, they had plenty of chances to back off gracefully but they didn't: They just kept going. I've felt for some time now that we can't make any more concessions, but I don't know how to end this thing. If there's a concession we could have made to get it all over with, we'd have made it long ago. But there isn't. We just can't concede any more. Now we've got martial law, and although we don't want confrontation or bloodshed, it's going to be impossible to keep the soldiers entirely outside the city. In fact, a few are already inside now. Troops are in the city to maintain order and to protect key offices, the most critical offices. Nobody ever said they're here to suppress the people. Of course we have our regular police forces, but they're wearing thin and haven't had a good rest for more than a month. If this goes on much longer, those forces are going to start to think we're at our wits' end. Our best option now is to use the army as a general deterrent while watching for a chance to clear the Square—by using some police but also by mobilizing the Party and officials at the campuses and looking for help from parents. It would be great if we could solve the problem in this way. We keep putting things off because we want to avoid force or bloodshed. But dragging things out too long is a mistake. We have to go all-out to settle the matter but still avoid bloodshed. For the time being, there's no big problem just letting the army sit there on the roads, but that can't go on forever. The soldiers have to go back to their barracks someday. And if we withdraw them, the protesters are going to think they've won. I wish the NPC and the People's Congress and the CPPCC could help out."

Yao Yilin: "Comrade Zhao Ziyang opposed the majority view of the Standing Committee right from the beginning in this matter. He wouldn't carry out Comrade Xiaoping's instructions, and he exposed the internal conflicts of the Party, made the Party speak in two voices, and turned a grim social situation into something even more complicated and confusing. The reason why he publicized intra-Party differences and pinned responsibility on Comrade Xiaoping during Gorbachev's visit is obvious: He wanted to point the spear toward Comrade Xiaoping and to undo the Standing Committee's decisions. Most leading comrades resisted his efforts to split the Party and support turmoil. He couldn't change the judgment of the Standing Committee and Comrade Xiaoping on the nature of this incident, so he felt desperate and risked everything on one throw of the dice. Comrade Ziyang bears unshirkable responsibility for the situation we're in now. Comrades Xiaoping, Xiannian, and Chen Yun have all indicated that Comrade Ziyang has split the Party and supported turmoil. They are exactly right. If it weren't for him, this thing could've been stopped long ago.

"Now things are grim in many cities. Tens of thousands of workers in Beijing can't go to work, factory production is falling off, and ordinary lives are seriously disrupted. The troubles in Beijing keep getting bigger despite martial law. A tiny minority who plots and stirs up trouble has succeeded in blocking intersections in the city and bringing the entire public transport system to a standstill. They're trying to throw the city into major chaos. If we're not firm about exposing and smashing this conspiracy, the peace and security of the capital will be destroyed, life will grow hard, and even basic needs like food, clothing, and shelter will be in peril. The normal patterns of work and social life will collapse. So we must be unshakable in our resolve to restore order and restore production. We can't afford to encourage the rebels by tolerating them at all; we must show no mercy."

The students debate whether to withdraw

Of some fifty thousand students in the Square on May 22, most were from outside Beijing, and many of the Beijing students had returned to their campuses or gone home. Official records showed that at least 319 different schools were represented in the Square.

The night before, tension started to build among the total of perhaps three hundred thousand students, support demonstrators, and onlookers, as rumors spread that the PLA would storm the Square early the next morning. Around 3 A.M. on the twenty-second a self-identified AFS representative broadcast an order over the loudspeakers for the students to prepare to withdraw. The order was soon countermanded by announcements that the first speaker did not represent AFS headquarters and that the heads of various school delegations should gather at the broadcasting stand to discuss what to do. About 4 A.M. there was an announcement that the troops had agreed not to enter the Square so long as the students maintained order. Toward 5 A.M. the loudspeakers broadcast that the Beijing AFS had completed its historic mission and was going to dissolve itself, to be replaced by a new organization that would campaign for democracy and seek the support of workers and farmers. Toward dawn tension relaxed as people realized the army had not showed up.

During the day a handbill was distributed in the name of "All Beijing college students and all students from throughout the country who have participated in this democratic, patriotic movement." It announced that the students had "already achieved a preliminary victory" and that they would conduct a "large-scale, orderly, rapid withdrawal from the Square" starting at 10 A.M. After the withdrawal the struggle for democracy would continue. The handbill asked the Supreme People's Court to conduct an investigation and hold Li Peng responsible for all damage to the hunger strikers' health and all damage to the economy consequent upon the recent events. At the same time another handbill, which circulated in the name of the "AFS of university students in the capital," claimed that "what we need to do is persist; persistence is victory." This second handbill warned that if the students pulled out of the Square, the troops would be free to attack, blood would flow, the nation would fall under the terror of military rule, and reform would come to an end.

Around 3 P.M. helicopters dropped flyers that most students either crumpled up or burned. At this time there were all kinds of groups marching through the Square, carrying banners identifying the marchers' school or profession. Banners opposed corruption and martial law and called for the resignation of Li Peng and the convening of the NPC.

Around 9 P.M. Bao Zunxin, Chen Ziming, and Wang Juntao arrived and announced the formation of a newspaper to be called *News Express*.[53] Bao shouted, "Persistence is victory!" At some point during the day the establishment of a Tiananmen Square Provisional Headquarters was announced.

Around the city students set up traffic checkpoints, gave lectures, and collected contributions. They solicited contributions even on Fuyou Street, the street that runs north-south along the west wall of Zhongnanhai. School authorities reported the campuses were alive with rumors about workers either going on strike or being mobilized to welcome the troops into the city, about agents provocateurs creating incidents to justify a military attack, and about military officers issuing a declaration against Deng Xiaoping and Li Peng.

Around 10 P.M. a clash broke out between troops and civilians in Fengtai District in which sixty-three soldiers, eleven students, and twelve other civilians were injured. Ten persons were arrested.

Students get broader support

Three State Security Ministry reports on May 22 described actions by groups of intellectuals to support the students. One told of a meeting that Yan Jiaqi had chaired at the Chinese Academy of Social Sciences at which a hundred or so participants discussed what to do to oppose martial law. A second reported a meeting chaired by Wan Runnan at which he gave student leaders sugges-

---

[53]*Xinwen kuaixun*. Announcement in Ogden et al., *China's Search*, 289.

tions on how to undermine martial law. Wan was also said to have donated large sums of money to students in the Square. The third report concerned an open letter that appeared on the streets of Beijing condemning the Li Peng government.

On May 21 and 22 Zhongnanhai received seventy-eight reports describing protest demonstrations in 131 cities across China. A central theme was the involvement of intellectuals, Party members, workers, and even some soldiers.

In Shanghai rain inhibited demonstrations, but twenty thousand or more students were on the streets shouting antigovernment slogans and protesting martial law. Factory workers, professionals, and some well-known intellectuals came out to support them. In Guangzhou, 120,000 students, professionals, and local residents joined street demonstrations on May 21. The next day students demonstrating in front of the provincial government building all day long were joined by factory workers. One hundred thirty Party officials, teachers, and well-known scholars from Zhongshan University signed an open letter to Party Central asking the government not to use force against the students. In the afternoon, more than thirty thousand people rallied at the Grand Theater in nearby Shenzhen.

In Changchun more than ten thousand students and teachers, supported by other professionals, took part in street demonstrations on May 20, 21, and 22. Students built bonfires on several campuses and shouted protests as CCTV showed Li Peng delivering his speech. Students began to work in small teams, distributing and posting flyers and giving speeches at rallies. On May 21 several thousand students went to an automobile factory to seek support from workers.

In Taiyuan college students began on May 20 to shift their attention away from protests at government offices and toward the formation of propaganda teams to work among workers and soldiers. On May 22 more than one thousand students went to the Taiyuan Steel Company to distribute handouts and give speeches. Others went to military headquarters and army barracks to seek support from the troops. More than ten thousand rallied in the city's main square "to mourn the hunger-striking martyrs."[54]

In Xi'an students and teachers demonstrated in the rain on May 21 to protest the speeches of Li Peng and Yang Shangkun and the government's use of the military to suppress the students. When a rumor spread that twenty-one students from Xi'an had died in Beijing, several thousand teachers and students marched through the streets holding a coffin aloft, shouting slogans, and calling for a general strike. On May 22 more than twenty thousand students, workers, and local residents continued to demonstrate, causing a serious traffic jam in the downtown area. In front of the Municipal Trade Union building workers sat in and called for a general strike. In the afternoon a vehicle mounted with a loudspeaker drove through the streets broadcasting Voice of America and BBC radio programs. About ten thousand students went to factories and mines to

---

[54]The students in Taiyuan had heard that some of the Beijing hunger strikers had died. In fact, none had.—Comp.

instigate strikes. Yet most workers, although supportive of the students, did not want to see further unrest in the country and hoped for a gradual resolution of the issues.

In Nanjing, numerous flyers and statements were posted in the downtown area. On May 21 about ten thousand students took to the streets. The AFS set up a public-address system in the central square and broadcast an open letter from local writers to Wan Li asking that Wan convene a meeting of the NPC Standing Committee to dismiss Li Peng. Workers from the Nanjing Rubber Plant announced a strike. On May 22 a large number of journalists and writers joined the students and teachers in street demonstrations. Some journalists marched with their mouths sealed over with tape.

Pessimism abroad

On May 22 seventeen reports to Zhongnanhai showed a sharp public response in Hong Kong to the announcement of martial law in Beijing. Thirty-five Hong Kong delegates to China's NPC and to the CPPCC expressed their opposition. So did the Executive Committee of the Basic Law Consultative Committee. Two members of the committee resigned in protest. Other organizations issued statements calling on the Beijing government to avoid use of force, to abolish martial law, and to restore and protect the people's rights.

In the United States, according to reports reaching Zhongnanhai from the Ministry of Foreign Affairs and the Xinhua News Agency, President Bush called on both sides to exercise restraint and to seek a peaceful solution, but he avoided taking a clear stand on either side of the conflict. The chair of the U.S. House Committee on Foreign Affairs, Representative Stephen Solarz, warned that a military crackdown would bring sanctions against China. He agreed that a stable China was in American interests but urged the Chinese government to achieve stability through dialogue rather than force.

Winston Lord, recently relieved as U.S. ambassador to China, criticized the Chinese leaders for overreacting to the student demonstrations. He said that the students had made reasonable demands and that because their popular support was so strong, their movement would eventually survive government repression even if it came. Former secretary of state Henry Kissinger and former assistant secretary of state Gaston Sigur, however, sided with President Bush's position of not wanting to appear to be inciting student riots.

On May 21 and 22 Zhongnanhai received thirty-four foreign news reports and analyses of the situation in China. Top leaders found them "superficial" and "extreme." For example, the *Washington Post* suggested that since the workers were now getting involved, the government would find it harder than ever to satisfy the demands of the demonstrators and that China might fall into a period of political disorder similar to the warlordism that had followed the May Fourth Movement in 1919. Reuters advanced the view that martial law appeared to have failed miserably and that the only way out of the current crisis was to dismiss Li Peng, reduce the power of Yang Shang-kun, and have Deng Xiaoping retire. A French newspaper commented that disorder in China had become a threat to China's trading partners in Asia and around the world and predicted that polit-ical instability would scare away foreign investments and bank loans. But a commentary in the *Christian Science Monitor* quoted a Russian official as saying China's economic reforms could con-tinue just as well under military rule.

In general, Soviet media covered martial law only briefly and in a subdued manner. But a Hun-garian newspaper quoted Gorbachev as saying that a central theme of his visit to Beijing had been to explain to Chinese leaders that real economic reform would be impossible without political reform.

CHAPTER SEVEN

May 23–25

The Conflict Intensifies

EDITORS' NOTE: Once Zhao Ziyang was removed from office, the hard-line faction in the Party leadership began to demonize the fallen reformers. They summoned senior pro-reform leader Wan Li home to prevent him from expressing opposition to their decision. Yang Shangkun set aside his own moderation and his sympathy for Zhao to close ranks with his mentor, Deng Xiaoping.

Opposition to the Party intensified among the students and citizens in Beijing and throughout the country. Prestigious liberal intellectuals split with the Party to support the students and even appeared to be giving them tactical advice. These activities would later earn some of them long prison sentences as the alleged black hands behind the movement. The Party's opponents spoke of a Manichaean battle between light and darkness. Some students in the Square swore an oath to die rather than retreat. In fact, retreat was becoming impossible, since the stakes had become so high that the losers were inevitably going to suffer severe consequences.

May 23

Jiang Zemin is assigned to brief Wan Li

Starting on May 23 Party Central brought each provincial Party secretary and some of the provincial governors, as well as the heads of the Xinhua News Agency offices in Hong Kong and Macao, to Beijing. There they met, separately or together, with four top leaders—Yang Shangkun, Li Peng, Qiao Shi, and Yao Yilin—and received briefings on the May 22 decision to cashier Zhao Ziyang and his followers. The provincial leaders were also expected to report on what had happened in their own areas and what they had done about it and to express their support for the decisions of Party Central.

Following Jiang Zemin's May 23 briefing session with the four leaders, Yang Shangkun spoke with him alone and charged him with receiving Wan Li upon his return from the United States and conveying to him the Center's decision.

> Excerpt from memoranda of conversations supplied by a friend of Yang Shangkun who cannot be further identified

---

Yang Shangkun: "Comrade Xiaoping asked me to talk to you. Party Central has decided that Comrade Wan Li should cut short his visit to the United States and return home. The current situation in Beijing is very complicated. Certain people want to make use of Comrade Wan Li's status as chair of the Standing Committee of the NPC to stir things up again and increase their influence. So Comrades Xiaoping, Chen Yun, Xiannian, and Peng Zhen all felt it best that Comrade Wan Li return first to Shanghai, where you can represent Party Central and give him a briefing on what's happened while he was away."

Jiang Zemin: "Does Comrade Wan Li know about this plan, Chairman Yang?"

Yang Shangkun: "We've already telegraphed Party Central's decision to him. When you see him, please emphasize the following points to him:

"1. Comrade Ziyang has been relieved of his duties for openly violating the decisions of Comrade Xiaoping and the Standing Committee of the Politburo. The major mistakes of Zhao Ziyang were these:

- opposing the April 26 editorial,
- opposing martial law in Beijing, and
- mentioning Comrade Xiaoping to Gorbachev.

"Comrade Xiaoping has said these are not ordinary matters of differing opinions but matters of fundamental principle that bear on the destiny of the Party and the state. On this issue we must unambiguously uphold Comrade Xiaoping, uphold the collective decisions of the core leadership of Party Central, and uphold the unity of the Party.

"2. The entire Standing Committee of the Politburo, not just one individual, made the decision to declare martial law within the city limits of Beijing. Beijing at the time was already out of control. The students and citizens had been stirred up by people with ulterior motives and were in an excitable mood. Some people were getting fanatical and extremist. Persons with ulterior motives were set to exploit this mood to cause even bigger turmoil and to negate the Communist Party, socialism, and the Four Basic Principles. Without martial law violent instances of beating, smashing, and robbing could have broken out at any time and led to even greater turmoil. We could all have been put under house arrest. The decision on martial law was made under these grim circumstances. It was a correct decision made under compelling pressure. You must emphasize to Comrade Wan Li that martial law was not aimed at the students, let alone the citizens. It was declared in order to safeguard vital state offices and to stabilize the capital. There is no possibility whatever of a 'crackdown' as rumored in the foreign media. It's out of the question.

"3. There have been a lot of calls from the general public for an emergency meeting of the NPC, and certain members of the NPC are currently circulating a petition to do this. Believe it or not, they are doing this as we speak. The NPC Standing Committee has already passed a message through organizational channels to all NPC members asking them not to participate in things like signing petitions for emergency sessions. The breadth of the current movement and the enthusiasm of its participants are both unprecedented. But many people do not realize that its nature has changed. It's no longer an ordinary mass movement but a grave life-or-death political struggle that will determine the future of the Party and the state and the success or failure of the reform and opening. The speeches and decisions of senior comrades such as Xiaoping and members of the Standing Committee not only show the iron determination and resolute measures that Party Central will employ to stop this turmoil; they also demonstrate that it is indeed well-organized, well-planned, and premeditated political turmoil. A huge choice between right and wrong lies before us, and we absolutely must stand firm. Party Central hopes that while Comrade Wan Li is resting in Shanghai he will make an unambiguous statement."

Jiang Zemin: "Is the Party Central sending anyone to meet him in Shanghai?"

Yang Shangkun: "You're a member of the Politburo. You'll be the representative, especially since you've been handpicked by Comrade Xiaoping."

Jiang Zemin returned to Shanghai that evening.

Beijing-bound students
disrupt the railway system

That morning Li Peng issued a directive on how to stop students from around the country from flooding into Beijing. Li wrote to the minister of railways, Li Senmao, that "we must take resolute measures to prevent non-Beijing students from forcing their way onto trains bound for Beijing.

You may even stop trains if necessary." On May 23 the General Office of the State Council had already sent a report to Li Peng summarizing reports on this problem from several areas.

Excerpts from State Council General Office, "Telephone call abstracts" *(Dianhua zhaibao)*, to Premier Li Peng, May 23

Report from Anhui: Around 5 P.M. on May 22 about three hundred students entered the Hefei Train Station and boarded train number 128 (scheduled to depart at 7:30 P.M.) without tickets. After ticket checks by railway personnel, these students all got off the train but did not leave the station. After 6 P.M., another group of thirty or more students pushed into the station, demanding to board the train. A few students walked along the tracks into the railcar maintenance shed. They opened the doors of two railcars, and more than three hundred students climbed on. By 7 P.M. or so, more than seven hundred students had gathered on the station platform. They were from twelve universities, including the Chinese University of Science and Technology, Anhui University, and Hefei Polytechnic University. Provincial and municipal leaders came to the scene to try to dissuade the students, but they failed. After seeking and obtaining the permission of the Railway Ministry, we suspended the departure of train number 128; it eventually departed at 7:30 P.M. on May 23, exactly twenty-four hours late, carrying three hundred students but leaving another two hundred behind on the platform. In Wuhu City trains number 328 and number 524 were suspended because of similar problems with ticketless students.

Report from Shandong: Between 6 P.M. on May 22 and 4 A.M. on May 23, about three hundred students from Qingdao who wanted to go to Beijing to express their support for the student movement but who could not get rail tickets lay down on the railroad tracks in protest. Under Order Number 630 of the Railway Ministry, one round-trip of train number 240 to Beijing was canceled. Six trains into or out of Qingdao were delayed by five to twelve hours.

Report from Hubei: On the night of May 23 more than two thousand students from universities in Wuhan boarded train number 38, scheduled to depart Wuchang for Beijing. The students completely filled the nine hard-seat[1] railcars, and the train was severely overloaded. Wuhan's city leaders went to the scene to try to dissuade the students, but to no avail. With permission from the Railway Ministry, the trip was canceled.

Report from Jilin: On the night of May 23 more than six hundred students

---

[1]"Hard-seat" means "nonsleeper, nonupholstered," the cheapest class of accommodation on China's trains.

from universities in Changchun forced their way onto train number 60 from Changchun to Beijing. The trip was canceled with permission of the Railway Ministry. Provincial and city leaders went to the scene to try to dissuade the students; they also engaged in dialogue with student leaders, but in the end more than four hundred students conducted a sit-in on the train.

Report from Inner Mongolia: Passenger transit from Hohhot and Baotou to Beijing was cut off at 5 P.M. on May 22. Twenty-four hours later more than four hundred student protesters who had been trying to get to Beijing remained at the Hohhot train station alongside five stopped trains. This situation was the result of measures taken under Order Number 607 of the Railway Ministry to prevent students from going to Beijing. Leaders from the autonomous region government and the various universities are currently attempting to persuade students on the trains to return to their campuses.

Report from Ningxia: In the early morning of May 23 more than four hundred students boarded train number 170 bound from Yinchuan to Beijing. The trip was canceled in accordance with orders of the Railway Ministry. At 10 P.M. students still remained on board.

Report from Shaanxi: On the morning of May 23 about four thousand students entered the train station in Xi'an, demanding passage to Beijing. Under orders of the Railway Ministry, all trains from Xi'an to Beijing were suspended. At 10 P.M. there were still more than one thousand students sitting in at the train station, waiting to go to Beijing.

State Security Ministry Report from Henan: At 1 P.M. on May 23 more than two thousand students from a group called the Block-the-Army, Dare-to-Die Brigade, which had been organized under the name of the Autonomous Federation of Zhengzhou College Students, gathered at the North Zhengzhou Station, the Haitangsi Station, and other railway stations in the Zhengzhou area. They vowed "to spare no effort in blocking army troops from going to Beijing." One student, who carried a banner reading "Zhengzhou Autonomous Federation Special Monitor" said, "We organized after we got reliable information that military trains would be leaving for Beijing this afternoon." Around 5 P.M., as some of the students began heading back toward their campuses, some railway workers and people of unknown identity encouraged them to hold out to the end, even suggesting that they block the railway bridge over the Yellow River. The leader of the student federation opposed this idea. "Human bodies on that bridge would never be able to stop a train," he said. "And if we actually do block the bridge, then we really are guilty of turmoil, right? The Beijing–Guangzhou rail line is a major artery in the nation's transportation network; it affects the whole national economy. We can't mess around here." At one point a bread truck crossed the railroad tracks, and some onlookers tried to provoke the students into blocking it: "That bread's going to the army!" they shouted. On the advice of leaders of the AFS, some of the students and masses dispersed. But at 7:40 P.M. about five hundred students, after rejecting all persuasion, boarded train number 252 to Beijing.

The Beijing Garrison deploys its troops

Seeking to counter strong popular resentment of martial law within the Beijing populace, a spokesman for the headquarters of the martial law troops used a press conference with Xinhua News Agency correspondents to defend martial law. The spokesman said, "The whole purpose of declaring martial law is to protect the interests of the people and to restore order in production, work, life, and education in the capital. When people say 'Martial law is repression of the masses,' this is entirely wrong. Recently some people were spreading the rumor that the army was going to 'crack down on the students in Tiananmen Square.' By now it's quite clear that this was just rumormongering."

Asked about the legality of using troops, the spokesman said that according to China's Constitution, "It is entirely legal for the PLA to carry out its martial law duties, which are also very much needed in the current situation. Martial law troops are presently being trained to love the capital, to love the people of the capital, to love the young students, and to master policy and discipline. Filled with emotion and yet strictly disciplined, their relationship with Beijing citizens and the young students is harmonious. . . . We believe that those citizens and young students who presently do not understand or do not know the true story will, through practice, gradually shed their misunderstanding and misgivings and will work with the officers and soldiers of the martial law troops to expose the rumormongering and sabotage of the tiny minority of people with ulterior motives."

The same night Martial Law Headquarters reported to Yang Shangkun and other Central Military Commission leaders and to Li Peng and other Politburo Standing Committee members that "thanks to deep and meticulous ideological work, and with the efficient cooperation of Beijing authorities, the various troops are almost all in place. The Beijing Garrison in particular has already settled into its assigned posts."

> Excerpt from the report of Martial Law Headquarters to the Central Military Commission and the Politburo Standing Committee, May 23

As of the night of May 23 more than 2,500 officers and soldiers had assumed their positions guarding "ten designated key locations," including the Capital Airport, the Beijing Railway Station, the Telegraph Building, and others. The principles of the Beijing Garrison have been these:

1. To assure that the thinking of the troops is aligned with the spirit of Party Central. All units have organized their troops to study repeatedly and to absorb fully the important speeches of Comrades Li Peng and Yang Shangkun, the martial law order of the State Council, the order of the Beijing People's Government, and related directives from the Beijing Military Region. This study has enhanced the troops' sense of duty that they must complete their mission of enforcing martial law. For example, when troop movements were blocked, officers and soldiers took the initiative in solving difficulties by changing from uniforms to plainclothes in order to reach their assigned posts as scheduled; some traveled by foot, others by train, bus, or refrigerated truck,[2] and others by bicycle.

2. To take the initiative in doing thought work among the people in the work units where troops are stationed. Because some of the masses do not understand the presence of the troops or even harbor resentment toward them, troops have carried out propaganda among the masses, making clear that the whole purpose of enforcing martial law is to maintain security in the capital and to restore normal order and that martial law absolutely is not targeted at patriotic students, and still less at the masses, and is not intended to establish military control. Troops have made special efforts to use their own exemplary behavior and crisp military bearing to influence the masses around them. The Third Division tank regiment that has served at the Beijing Railway Station made a resounding pledge to be "a just army, a proper army, and a civilized army." Troops that moved into the offices of the *People's Daily* and the Central People's Broadcasting Station assigned soldiers to working in the kitchen, cleaning toilets, and removing garbage. Nearly a hundred troops that moved into the CCTV station had to be crowded into a corridor at the studio, but they kept it tidy and in perfect order. They maintained neat military bearing, brimmed with high spirits, and won praise from both officials and masses.

3. To take the initiative in maintaining contact with leaders of the units where we are stationed and the PAP there.[3] Leaders of the Beijing Garrison have been personally involved in assisting their troops in the work of taking up their sta-

---

[2] Since these trucks are closed, they can transport troops without their being seen.
[3] The kinds of key points and Party and government offices that the garrison troops were occupying were normally guarded by units of the People's Armed Police.

tions. They have dispatched liaison groups to help establish contacts and facilitate communications. Most army contingents have joined with leaders of the stationed units and their PAP contingents to form coordinating command groups, and these have helped considerably in solving practical problems. The Central People's Broadcasting Station provided the stationing troops with one hundred quilts, two color television sets, a daily newspaper for each squad, and a towel for every soldier. The *People's Daily* installed a special telephone for the troops, lent them a color television, gave every soldier a daily newspaper, and provided medical care to officers and soldiers. Most units helped the troops arrange for food and lodging.

On May 24 Li Peng passed this report to Luo Gan, secretary general of the State Council, and requested that Luo represent him in visiting and boosting the morale of the officers and soldiers of the Beijing Garrison who were enforcing martial law. He also instructed Yuan Mu, spokesman for the State Council, to draft a letter expressing the State Council's appreciation to all the officers and soldiers of martial law troops.

The situation in Tiananmen Square

The State Security Ministry reported on the situation in the Square on May 23. Only about ten thousand students were still sitting in, a majority of them from schools outside Beijing. Martial law troops had not entered the city, and the mood among the students and onlookers was calm. The students danced, sang, slept in their tents, or chatted in groups. The AFS, students from outside Beijing, and the Beijing Workers' Monitor Corps formed a joint coordinating organization, which announced by loudspeaker that it would keep the struggle going, maintain hygiene in the Square, and send groups around the city to explain the students' opposition to martial law. The group announced struggle slogans for the next two days, including opposition to martial law and a demand for emergency meetings of the NPC Standing Committee and the Party Central Committee to remove Li Peng from office.

At 2 P.M. four individuals threw ink-filled eggs at the official portrait of Mao Zedong on the Gate of Heavenly Peace. Students and onlookers seized the perpetrators and handed them over to Public Security. They also grabbed a foreign reporter's camera to prevent him from taking a picture, telling him that it wouldn't be in the interests of the student movement to have it taken.

During the day the Chinese Red Cross issued an urgent appeal. It asked health units to continue to station themselves in the Square to serve the demonstrators and asked that garbage be cleared away to reduce the risk of epidemic disease. To alleviate crowding, it suggested, the students should withdraw, and the government should facilitate this, should keep open the channels of dialogue, and should carry out no future retribution.

Coordinated by the Stone Company, a group of students issued a "Proposal" that called for the cancellation of martial law, removal of the troops, and convening the NPC Standing Committee and the Party Congress. In return, the students should withdraw from the Square, restoring normal order. "This withdrawal would not be a retreat but would advance the democracy movement to a new stage." The proposal drew support from sixty Peking University professors.

When Yuan Mu received the report of the Red Cross's appeal and the students' "Proposal," he felt it painted the students in too favorable a light. He also asked, "What business does the Red Cross have doing the government's job?" And "What is Wan Runnan really up to?" He passed on his concerns to Li Peng.

Demonstration in the rain against martial law

The demonstration that took place on May 23 was the largest since the declaration of martial law. It was reported to Zhongnanhai by the State Security Ministry. Bus and subway lines had been partly restored to operation, and things were calming down in the city. Around 1 P.M., about three hundred thousand people marched through parts of Beijing. The marchers were students from outside Beijing and people from the worlds of culture, finance, science and technology, industry, journalism, and government. The main slogans called for Li Peng's resignation and the cancellation of martial law. Around 4 P.M. there was a violent rainstorm that broke up some of the columns of marchers but not others.

There was wide distribution of a handbill entitled "Letter to Compatriots Throughout the Country from Intellectuals in the Capital." The letter attacked "Li Peng and his small handful of reactionaries" and demanded an emergency meeting of the NPC Standing Committee, Li's removal, an end to martial law, freedom of the press, and continuation of the democracy movement to the end.

Beijing Railway Station reported that about ten thousand students entered the city on May 23 from the provinces, the largest group coming from Henan. Some of the students said they were now staying in Beijing in two-day shifts, the better to preserve their health and spread the word of Beijing events back to the provinces.

Beijing intellectuals' declarations

At 10 P.M. on May 23 the State Security Ministry reported that some thirty intellectuals, at a meeting at the Political Science Institute of the Chinese Academy of Social Sciences, had established an Association of Beijing Intellectuals headed by Bao Zunxin. The group issued a declaration attacking "Li Peng and his small handful" for trying to use military force to suppress differing opinions within the Party and government. According to the declaration, the hard-liners had forced a decisive battle for the future of China, and the intellectuals could no longer stand silent. They demanded an emergency meeting of the NPC Standing Committee, an end to martial law, the firing of Li Peng, and respect for constitutional rights. The State Security Ministry pointedly noted that the full text of the declaration was published in the same day's issue of the *United Daily News* in Taiwan.

Another State Security Ministry report described a meeting of about sixty intellectuals and AFS leaders convened by Wang Juntao and Wang Dan to discuss coordination between the students' "Tiananmen Square Headquarters" and the Federation of All Social Sectors in the Capital (FASSC). Bao Zunxin read a statement on "the final battle between light and darkness,"[4] hailing the student movement as unprecedented in Chinese history, as spelling the end of the old China, and as opening a new era of harmony and democracy. The movement would have to press ahead until Li Peng was removed from power.

When Luo Gan received these two reports, he had them sent over immediately to Li Peng's residence. Li later said the reports were among the firmest proofs of the fact that the student movement was manipulated from behind the scenes by a small handful of people intent on opposing the Party, opposing socialism, establishing illegal organizations however possible, and deepening the crisis.

The State Education Commission issues an appeal, but demonstrations spread

On May 23 the State Education Commission issued an urgent appeal through the Xinhua News Agency, asking students to go back to classes and urging educators, journalists, and parents to persuade the students to do so. If the boycott of classes lasted any longer, it would become impossible to graduate the seniors and assign them jobs, and there would be no space in the fall for new incoming students.

---

[4] Excerpts in Suzanne Ogden, Kathleen Hartford, Lawrence Sullivan, and David Zweig, eds., *China's Search for Democracy: The Student and the Mass Movement of 1989* (Armonk, New York: M. E. Sharpe, 1992), 293–294.

Despite this appeal, reports from around the country described sit-ins and demonstrations in eighty-seven cities on May 23. The appeals heard on all sides were for the NPC Standing Committee to meet, for Li Peng to step down, and for an end to martial law in Beijing. Fifty thousand to sixty thousand marched in Shanghai under the direction of the AFS. Cultural Revolution–like phenomena appeared: wall posters, some nonstudents going onto campuses to lecture, and some students going to factories to network, or "link up." In Harbin ten thousand students demonstrated and sent petitions to the NPC and Party Central. In Changchun demonstrators numbered twenty thousand; in Shenyang, eight thousand, and students lectured at the gates of some major factories and offices.

In Jinan not only students but also, for the first time in this provincial capital, a thousand workers demonstrated. Demonstrations of more than one thousand persons were reported from six other cities in the province. Workers also demonstrated in Hangzhou, where about three hundred students announced their resignations from the Communist Youth League, some burning their membership cards. In Guangzhou a huge crowd of about four hundred thousand marched through rainstorms; the marchers included not only college and high school students but officials, citizens, workers, and journalists, as well as about six hundred supporters from Hong Kong and Macao.

May 24

Enlarged meeting of the Central Military Commission

On the morning of May 24 the Central Military Commission held an enlarged meeting, attended by the commission members and by the military commanders, political commissars, and other high officials from the three headquarters departments (the General Staff Department, the General Political Department, and the General Logistics Department), the service arms, the military regions, and the National Defense University. The meeting was held at Deng Xiaoping's behest to make sure that the top officers were unified in their thinking in support of the Center on the Zhao Ziyang matter. The centerpiece of the meeting was a long speech by Yang Shangkun explaining in detail Deng Xiaoping's views throughout the crisis.[5]

[5]Text in Michel Oksenberg, Lawrence R. Sullivan, and Marc Lambert, eds., *Beijing Spring, 1989, Confrontation and Conflict: The Basic Documents* (Armonk, New York: M. E. Sharpe, 1990), 320–327; excerpts in Han Minzhu, ed., *Cries for Democracy: Writings and Speeches from the 1989 Chinese Democracy Movement* (Princeton: Princeton University Press, 1990), 303–308.

The demands of the student movement, Yang noted, had grown increasingly radical over time, and each time the Center tried to bring it to an end through moderate means, the trouble grew worse. The root of the problem was division in the Party leadership. Although Zhao had originally assented to the April 26 editorial, after his return from North Korea he wanted its judgment to be revised. He praised the students in several speeches, most notably in the one to the Asian Development Bank, and this stimulated the growth of the movement. It was appropriate to tell Gorbachev about Deng's leading role, but by going into such detail Zhao was clearly trying to dissociate himself from Deng's policy. Zhao tried to resign and gave further encouragement to the students through his tearful appearance at Tiananmen Square on May 19. He also refused to make his scheduled appearance at the declaration of martial law. Looking back, the flaws in Zhao's work all along as Party leader were clear. Like Hu Yaobang, he had failed to carry out the struggles against bourgeois liberalization and spiritual pollution.

Under the circumstances, Yang said, the Party Elders had had no choice but to get involved. They had a clear consensus that retreat would spell the collapse of the Party and the state, which was just what the capitalists abroad wanted to see. The Party leader had to be changed, and martial law had to be declared. Contrary to rumor, Yang stressed, these decisions were carried out by proper procedure. The Politburo Standing Committee voted to fire Zhao, and the Central Military Commission members were all consulted by Deng Xiaoping in his capacity as CMC chair before he issued the orders to move troops.

Yang ordered the senior military leaders to return to their units and unify the thinking of their Party committees and subordinates. Special attention should be given to educating the troops and to gaining the support of retired comrades. The troops should do propaganda among the people to explain the army's intentions. No one, he emphasized, in the military could be allowed to disobey orders.

Students hold an oath ceremony in Tiananmen Square

The State Security Ministry reported on May 24 that public transportation in the city continued to improve. In the Square a newly formed General Headquarters for the Protection of Tiananmen Square held a ceremony in which General Commander Chai Ling administered an oath to about a hundred thousand students. The oath went as follows:

"To promote the motherland's democratization, to protect the dignity of the Constitution, to protect the great motherland from the machinations of a small handful of conspirators, to prevent 1.1 billion countrymen from being sacrificed in blood under the terror of military rule, to save the Chinese people from falling under fascist dictatorial rule, to assure that millions and millions of children will enjoy an atmosphere of freedom and democracy, I swear to devote my life and my loyalty to protect to the death Tiananmen Square, the capital Beijing, and the republic. Struggle to the end against all difficulties!"

At the meeting Wang Dan read a version of the FASSC's declaration about the decisive battle between light and darkness. Wang stressed that the students now had no choice but to continue the battle to the end, because if they retreated from the Square as losers, they would become targets of a new ideological rectification campaign.

Medical personnel continued to minister to the hunger strikers and other demonstrators to prevent deaths and the spread of diseases. In response to a rumor, the Emergency Center reported over the loudspeaker that no hunger striker had died, even though the strike had been going on for eleven days and hospitals throughout the city had treated hunger strikers 9,158 times. There were currently sixty-six hunger strikers being cared for in hospitals. Students who had given up the hunger strike in favor of a petitioning sit-in were receiving care against colds, fevers, and diarrhea.

The Public Security Ministry's regular crime bulletin reported that crime, fires, and traffic accidents throughout the city over the period May 1–21 occurred at a rate 33 percent lower than the same period the year before.

Near-term goals of the Association of Beijing Intellectuals

The May 23 meeting of Beijing intellectuals was resumed on the afternoon of May 24 at the Political Science Institute of the Chinese Academy of Social Sciences, as detailed in reports to Zhongnanhai from Beijing Municipality and the State Security Ministry. More than one hundred social scientists and journalists attended. Bao Zunxin chaired.

Bao told the group that informal preparations for the association had been underway since mid-May. Even though a final decision to organize had not been made, the fact of its existence had become public now that the group had participated in the May 23 demonstration under two large banners and now that this fact had been reported in the Hong Kong and Taiwan press. Yuan Zhiming added that the best protection for the people involved was to publish their names abroad.

Bao suggested three near-term goals for the group: the cancellation of martial law, the resignation of Li Peng, and the implementation of concrete steps toward democratization. Although Yan Jiaqi was not at the meeting, he and Bao were elected co–general convenors of the association, and the group decided to work in the Square under the leadership of the FASSC and the General Headquarters for the Protection of Tiananmen Square. At 9:30 that night two spokesmen for the group announced the association's formation in a press conference in the Square and announced plans for a demonstration the next afternoon to welcome Wan Li back to Beijing.

Anti–Li Peng handbills distributed
in Beijing

On May 24 the State Security Ministry passed along reports on anti–Li Peng, anti–martial law handbills that were widely distributed that day in the Square, on the campuses, and in some of the busier parts of town.[6]

One handbill, the "Solemn Declaration of the Autonomous Federation of Students," accused Li Peng of using martial law to mount a coup d'état. The student movement, it proclaimed, had not caused turmoil. Traffic was normal, and rates of crime, accident, and fire in the city had all declined. It was martial law that created turmoil by interfering with traffic and the movement of supplies for the city, spreading false news through the military-controlled press, setting the people against the people by organizing so-called monitoring teams to surveil the workers and the masses, and damaging the army's and the government's relationship with the people. All this was part of Li Peng's plot to seize Party and state power illegally. The NPC and Party Congress should hold emergency meetings to remove Li Peng from office and expel him from the Party, martial law should be ended, and the troops should be withdrawn. If these demands were not heeded, the handbill promised, then at an appropriate time the AFS would call for an even larger-scale hunger strike nationwide.

A group called Consultative Association of Social Sectors in the Capital issued two handbills, an "Open Letter to Beijing Citizens" and an "Open Letter to the People's Liberation Army." The first blamed the recent disturbance of life in Beijing on officials of the Municipal Government. It was they who stopped the buses and subway cars, shut down the gas stations, pulled the traffic police off the streets, and created shortages of grain, oil, and vegetables, while still demanding that people show up for work. It was they who sent plainclothes agents to incite incidents, who ordered police to beat students and citizens, and who stopped street cleaning. They then declared a state of anarchy and tried to blame it all on the students. The second open letter expressed respect and support for the troops parked outside the city but warned them there was no turmoil in Beijing. It added that they should not allow themselves to be fooled by a small handful of conspirators like Li Peng, Chen Xitong, and Li Ximing, who were trying to lead them into conflicts with the citizens that they would later regret.

The security agencies started intensive investigations into such handbills, which they viewed as key evidence of anti-Party, antisocialist activities.

---

[6]There is a series of such handbills dated May 24 in Ogden et al., *China's Search*, 303–313.

Student movement grows in the provinces

In Wuhan, large demonstrations that had been conducted daily since May 21 were having a serious impact on the life of the city. All thirty-five institutions of higher education were on strike. Students went to major factories to urge the workers to strike. They blocked the Yangtze River bridge that links the three sections of the city (Hankou, Wuchang, and Hanyang). Railway and ferry transport for both passengers and freight was affected. Traffic accidents were increasing, and social order was deteriorating.

In Chongqing many more workers than before joined the demonstrations. Students tried to force their way onto Beijing-bound trains; one was canceled, and a second was being held in the station at the time of report. In Shijiazhuang students presented a petition to the Provincial People's Congress demanding that the NPC meet to dismiss Li Peng. The Railway Ministry estimated that there were now more than ten thousand Shijiazhuang students in Beijing. Recently many of them had gotten off at the outer Beijing station of Fengtai, where they could interfere with the movement of military trains and vehicles from the southeast into the city center.

In Changsha demonstrators numbered more than ten thousand. They demanded that the NPC meet to fire Li Peng. Those sitting in at the provincial government offices and at the railway station carried out voluntary cleanup activities. Traffic conditions in the city showed some improvement. In Xi'an demonstrators were well behaved, and traffic there was near normal. Students from a school outside Guiyang forced drivers to give them rides into the city center, where they joined demonstrators demanding a nationwide plebiscite and opposition to dictatorship. Students wrote slogans on walls in oil paint so they would be hard to wash off. In Lanzhou more than ten thousand students demonstrated for the removal of Li Peng. Overall, there were demonstrations or sit-ins in sixty-eight cities, and students in thirteen cities boarded trains for Beijing.

May 25

Wan Li returns to Shanghai; Li Peng is active in Beijing

At 3 A.M. on May 25 Wan Li arrived by special plane at Shanghai's Hongqiao Airport, where he was met by Jiang Zemin, Mayor Zhu Rongji, and Ye Gongqi, chairman of the Standing Committee of the Municipal People's Congress. They escorted him to the Xijiao Guest House. Jiang personally handed over the documents the Center had prepared for Wan Li and gave him a short briefing on the situation in Beijing. Wan rested on the twenty-fifth to get over jet lag and study the documents. On May 26 Jiang gave him a full briefing.

Meanwhile, in Beijing on May 25 Li Peng signed a letter of support for the martial law troops. He expressed sympathy for the hardships they were undergoing and thanks for their discipline and self-restraint in the face of provocations from a tiny minority of provocateurs. He praised them for their initiatives in doing propaganda work among the masses and for their success in cultivating excellent relations between the army and the people. Li also signed an "Urgent Notice of the State Council on Strictly Preventing Students in the Localities from Breaking into Railway Stations and Boarding Beijing-Bound Trains by Force."

That afternoon Li met with the new ambassadors from Nigeria, Mexico, and Burma. He assured them that the government was stable and had the ability to bring an end to the situation. Martial law, he emphasized, was not the same as military control, which would occur when a government lost control and had to hand over some or all of its responsibilities to the armed forces. Li explained that martial law troops were still outside the city on the sixth day of martial law[7] not because they could not enter but because the People's Government wanted to avoid a clash between the army and the people. It would take more time to gain the full understanding and support of the people for the fact that stability and order were in their own best interests.

Hinting at the fall of Zhao Ziyang, Li assured the ambassadors that China's reform and opening did not depend on any leader other than Deng Xiaoping and that it would continue as before. He added that the current situation was entirely a domestic affair. No country should interfere, and foreign friends should wait until they understood the situation better before making judgments.

Cao Siyuan collects signatures from members of the NPC Standing Committee

On May 25 the State Security Ministry reported an effort to collect signatures from members of the NPC Standing Committee to call for an emergency meeting to remove Li Peng from office.[8] The effort was reported in that day's Hong Kong *Wenhui Daily,* and the ministry was able to fill in the background from its sources close to the organizer, Cao Siyuan.

Cao was director of the Stone Company's Social Development Research Institute and a proponent of constitutional reform and parliamentary democracy.[9] According to the ministry report, since late April he had been in frequent touch with the leaders of the AFS. After martial law was

[7]Since May 20 was the first day of martial law, May 25 was the sixth day.
[8]Under the Chinese Constitution, the National People's Congress has the power to elect and remove the premier, and the Standing Committee exercises the functions of the NPC between plenary meetings. In reality, the Party leadership decides whom to appoint to the premiership and the NPC ratifies the decision.
[9]For excerpts in English from Cao's memoirs, see Cao Siyuan, "The Storm over Bankruptcy," parts 1 and 2, ed. Catherine H. Keyser, *Chinese Law and Government* 31, no. 1 (January-February 1998): 12–93; no. 2 (March-April 1998): 11–104.

declared, with the approval of his superior Wan Runnan, Cao drafted a proposal requesting an emergency meeting of the NPC.[10] Cao took the proposal to NPC Standing Committee member Hu Jiwei, former publisher and editor-in-chief of the *People's Daily,* who not only signed it but added a line: "If the Standing Committee isn't able to meet, I recommend we hold an informal emergency meeting of the members in Beijing." Hu authorized Cao to use his name in rounding up other signatures. By May 24 Cao had collected forty-six names. (Two similar proposals gathered twenty-four and eighteen signatures respectively; taking duplicate signatures into account, fifty-seven people signed one or more of the proposals.) On May 24 Cao delivered his proposal to the NPC Standing Committee with a personal cover letter from Hu Jiwei. He also gave it to the Hong Kong *Wenhui Daily* correspondent in Beijing.

When Li Peng saw the report he ordered the NPC Standing Committee Party fraction[11] to conduct an investigation. Six members whose names were on the proposal subsequently denied they had signed it.

Citywide demonstration welcomes Wan Li back to Beijing

On May 25 Beijing Municipality and the two security ministries reported on the activities of the demonstrators. The AFS sent five propaganda teams to various places around the country to network; the first, headed by Wuerkaixi, had already left by train for Tianjin and planned to go south from there. The students sent vehicles equipped with loudspeakers around the city calling people to join a demonstration that afternoon to welcome Wan Li and to ask that Li Peng be cashiered.

From 2 P.M. on, some hundred thousand students and citizens, including workers and a variety of government employees, demonstrated for an emergency NPC meeting, the firing of Li Peng, and the return of Wan Li. A student from the command post of the large contingent of non-Beijing students said that 216 institutions of higher education were represented from twenty-seven provinces.[12] The demonstrators were more loosely organized than they had been in the past.

One of the AFS organizers revealed privately that the students were divided over whether to

---

[10]It was actually the Standing Committee that Cao wanted to convene. Procedurally speaking, a meeting of the Standing Committee would be necessary to call an unscheduled meeting of the NPC.

[11]The Party members in every governmental and nongovernmental office, enterprise, and organization belong to Party branches and cells, all of which are overseen by the Party fraction *(dangzu)* in the organization. Although the National People's Congress is the supreme organ of state power, the Party members within it (comprising a majority of both the Standing Committee and the plenary body) are subject to Party discipline.

[12]The student apparently used "province" here to mean "province, autonomous region, or directly administered city," of which there are a total of thirty.

withdraw from the Square. They had almost decided to do so but postponed the proposal after Chai Ling opposed it because, as she put it, "The intellectuals are trying to take control of the student movement in the Square."

Activities of the FASSC

A May 25 report of the State Security Ministry detailed recent activities of the FASSC. This illegal organization was formed by Chen Ziming and Wang Juntao, who headed the nongovernmental Beijing Social and Economic Sciences Research Institute.[13] These two had emerged as "the main plotters behind the scenes of the student movement," the State Security Ministry reported. Of the two of them, it was Wang who had the most contact with the heads of the AFS.

The FASSC distributed two documents in the streets of Beijing that day. "Introduction to the FASSC" laid out the organization's purposes and structure. It described itself as a mass organization formed on the basis of the patriotic democracy movement. Its purpose was to form a united front of all social groups, strengthen the forces for democracy, and support the student movement in order to push China forward on the road to freedom, democracy, rule of law, and civilization. It planned to publish a newspaper, organize monitoring teams of citizens and workers, and mobilize people to resist to the end the military control imposed by a small handful of dictators. It promised to obey the Constitution and never to dissolve no matter who opposed it, until the people themselves deemed its existence no longer necessary.

The second document, "The Present Situation and Our Policies," described the patriotic democracy movement as an epochal and decisive struggle between reform and conservatism, democracy and dictatorship, advance and retrogression, light and darkness. The FASSC called on the forty million CCP members, the members of the minority democratic parties, the retired generation of old revolutionaries, and the military to stand on the side of the movement. Emergency meetings of the NPC and of the CCP National Congress should meet to punish Li Peng and his followers and to elect a new Party Central Committee that would lead the country forward in reform. The people of Beijing should organize themselves to manage the city well, showing that there was no turmoil and no need for military rule. The FASSC called on people in the provinces—students, workers, farmers, and people in all occupations—to support the movement locally and send material support to Beijing.

---

[13]On these two activists and their institute, see George Black and Robin Munro, *Black Hands of Beijing: Lives of Defiance in China's Democracy Movement* (New York: John Wiley and Sons, 1993). After June 4 both were arrested and sentenced to thirteen-year terms for their activities as the black hands behind the Beijing events. In 1994 both were released on medical grounds. Wang went to the United States. Chen was rearrested in 1995 and released to house arrest in 1996.

Echoes from the provinces

Forty-one reports on May 25 described demonstrations and sit-ins occurring in fifty-eight cities. In Shanghai twenty thousand students demonstrated with the support of forty thousand onlookers, petitioning Wan Li, who they knew was in Shanghai, to summon a special meeting of the NPC to dismiss Li Peng. In Tianjin famous writers and other intellectuals participated in the largest demonstration to date, applauded by some fifty thousand citizens along the route. In Jinan ten thousand workers, citizens, and students marched for a second day, and students again tried to force their way onto trains. The provincial government established a special office at the train station composed of police as well as education and railway personnel to try to deal with these student assaults.

Steel workers marched in Taiyuan, marking the first entry of workers into the crisis in that city. To the applause of onlookers, they demanded Li Peng's removal and threatened to go on strike. In Hefei train number 128 for Beijing had to be canceled on both May 24 and May 25 because of student attempts to board it. Other trains were also affected. In Chengdu about forty thousand people demonstrated including workers and students from other towns outside the provincial capital. They had broad support from the populace, including a group of elderly women who, under the banner of the Grandmas' Support Brigade, haltingly delivered cup after cup of water to the marchers.

Students from the Nationalities College outside the city of Guiyang came into town to network with students at other campuses. Many of their handbills dealt with sensitive local issues: They demanded, for example, a public accounting of how the government had handled scandals relating to tax evasion by producers of cigarettes and alcohol, and they connected the province's poverty to the corruption of its leaders.

Taiwan's role

On May 25 the State Security Ministry sent Zhongnanhai two reports written by organizations in Taiwan that seemed to show Taiwan was planning to take advantage of the student movement.

One of the reports claimed that Taiwan's intelligence organs had been able to acquire timely, accurate intelligence on the student movement and on Chinese military dispositions, thanks in part to good intelligence exchange relationships between Taiwan and other countries. The report claimed that Taiwan authorities knew before Zhao Ziyang's resignation became public that the student movement had caused a split in the Chinese leadership. Taiwan had good information on the deployment of PRC troops for martial law. This information would be useful in assessing relations between the PRC's local military forces and the Communist Center and thus help to estimate the likelihood of the mainland's splitting up.

The other report, titled "Alliance Establishes a Bank Account to Assist the Mainland Democracy Movement" stated that Ma Shuli, head of the Three People's Principles[14] Alliance for the Unification of China, had opened an account at the Bank of Taiwan for citizens and groups who wanted to contribute money to support the student movement. Implying a long-term intent to promote subversion of the Communist regime, the document pledged that contributions would build a fund that could be used to support the mainland democracy activists of the future.

[14]The Three People's Principles—nationalism, democracy, and public welfare—were formulated by Sun Yat-sen as guiding principles for Republican China (1912–1949); they have continued to be honored in Taiwan since 1949.

CHAPTER EIGHT

May 26–28

The Elders Choose Jiang Zemin

EDITORS' NOTE: The leaders worked to consolidate elite support for the declaration of martial law and the removal of Zhao Ziyang, hoping to create a united front among political and military figures that would impress public opinion and eventually sway the students. For the most part, however, the obligatory expressions of loyalty to the Party line were hedged with cautions against the use of force. Wan Li's long-awaited statement from Shanghai supported martial law but also called for the government to deal with the legitimate issues the students had raised.

The Party apparatus mobilized its organizational machinery to guarantee that government, Party, and military officials and staff and their families refrained from supporting the demonstrators. The demonstrations, however, continued, although it was hard to tell whether they were expending their last burst of energy or gaining new support.

In the midst of this ambiguous atmosphere the eight Elders met at Deng Xiaoping's residence on the evening of May 27 to replace the fallen Party general secretary. The minutes of that meeting show how concerned Deng was that the switch of Party leaders and the impending suppression of the student movement not interfere with economic reform and the opening to the West. And they show the Elders' concern for finding successors who could win public support. For both these reasons, Li Peng was not a contender. Deng deferentially led the group to a consensus in favor of Shanghai Party secretary Jiang Zemin, evidently having discussed this choice in advance with his two most senior colleagues, Chen Yun and Li Xiannian.

May 26

The Party tries to build support

On May 26 Chen Yun chaired a meeting of the Central Advisory Commission Standing Committee, attended by twenty-two of its twenty-seven members.[1] Among the absentees, Zhang Aiping and Huang Hua, former foreign minister, were believed to have stayed away because of their disagreement with martial law and the treatment of Zhao Ziyang.

Chen opened with a speech urging everyone to support the Party's decisions to suppress the student movement and to punish Zhao Ziyang.[2] His remarks received unambiguous support from some members of the group. But others mixed support with reservations, saying that the students had patriotic motives, that many military officers did not like the idea of sending troops into Beijing, that they hoped the situation could be resolved peacefully, or that corruption and inflation were the ultimate causes of antigovernment sentiment. When members had spoken, the committee voted by a show of hands to support Party Central's decisions. The official media reported the next day that the committee had given martial law its "unanimous support."

That afternoon Peng Zhen held a meeting with seven leading non-Party members of the National People's Congress Standing Committee, which he had formerly chaired. Peng expressed respect for the student demonstrators' motives but said it was the Party's duty to help them avoid manipulation by a tiny minority of conspirators. He reassured everyone that the army would not use force against the students and concluded with a lengthy argument condemning bourgeois liberalization, defending the declaration of martial law, and arguing that it was all legal and constitutional. Since the present declaration of martial law did not violate the Constitution or the law, he concluded, it would be impossible for the NPC Standing Committee to reverse it.

After Peng's speech, several vice chairs of the Standing Committee expressed their views, on the one hand expressing their understanding for the declaration of martial law but on the other urging the government to accept the reasonable demands of the students.

Expressions of support for Qiao Shi

As it became apparent that Zhao Ziyang and Hu Qili were losing their seats on the Politburo

---

[1] The Central Advisory Commission is a prestigious but powerless Party body composed of retired high-ranking Party officials, both civilian and military. It was chaired by Chen Yun, the oldest of the Elders. Because of his age, it was unusual for him to appear at any meeting.

[2] Report of Chen's speech in Michel Oksenberg, Lawrence R. Sullivan, and Marc Lambert, eds., *Beijing Spring, 1989, Confrontation and Conflict: The Basic Documents* (Armonk, New York: M. E. Sharpe, 1990), 331–333.

Standing Committee, it was widely anticipated that the next general secretary would be chosen from within the current Standing Committee. This led to some subtle lobbying against Li Peng's being selected. Qiao Shi was a prominent alternative, and offices that worked under Qiao Shi did what they could to build momentum for him. For example, on May 26 the Central Discipline Inspection Commission (CDIC), an organization that Qiao Shi headed, submitted a report that seemed to be an attempt to curry favor for Qiao by toeing Party Central's line.

In addition, each of the five major units within the law enforcement system that Qiao Shi headed—the Supreme People's Court, the Supreme People's Procuratorate, the Public Security Ministry, the State Security Ministry, and the Justice Ministry—took the opportunity to express firm loyalty to Party Central.

> Excerpt from Supreme People's Court, "Conscientiously study the important speeches of Comrades Li Peng and Yang Shangkun, firmly and thoroughly implement Party Central's decisions," report to Party Central, May 26

The leaders of the Supreme People's Court and all its department heads have studied the important speeches by Li Peng and Yang Shangkun. We have also notified the various people's higher courts to study carefully and to understand these speeches in order to form uniform views and take uniform action. They were asked to stay on the side of Party Central and to implement Party decisions resolutely.

> Excerpt from Supreme People's Procuratorate, "Thoroughly implement the decisions of Party Central and the State Council without wavering, firmly strike blows against various kinds of illegal criminal activity," report to Party Central, May 26

The Supreme People's Procuratorate has notified all procuratorates at lower levels across the country to firmly implement the directives of Party Central and the State Council. They must take immediate action to cooperate closely with Public Security and other agencies to end the turmoil. They must use legal weapons to strengthen social order and must resolutely prosecute every kind of criminal activity.

> Excerpt from Public Security Ministry, "Firmly support the important speeches of Comrades Li Peng and Yang Shang-

kun, take a clear-cut stand in putting a stop to turmoil," report
to Party Central and the State Council, May 26

The Public Security Ministry has requested that police forces across the country support the speeches of Li Peng and Yang Shangkun, stay at their posts, enforce martial law as ordered by the State Council, openly oppose the turmoil, and maintain public order and traffic order in the capital city.

Excerpt from State Security Ministry, "Conscientiously study the important speeches of Comrades Li Peng and Yang Shangkun, make new contributions to guard state security, and protect stability and unity," report to Party Central and the State Council, May 26

The State Security Ministry promises to remain loyally on duty and to make new contributions in maintaining peace and unity during a struggle that could affect the fate of the Party, the future of the country, and the interests of the people.

Excerpt from Justice Ministry, "Study the important speeches of Comrades Li Peng and Yang Shangkun, firmly and thoroughly implement Party Central's decisions," report to Party Central and the State Council, May 26

The Justice Ministry vows to follow firmly the directives of Party Central and the State Council. We will study the important speeches of Comrades Li Peng and Yang Shangkun and mobilize immediately. We will stay on duty, unified, and on the side of Party Central to guarantee the smooth progress of reform and economic construction in our country.

The Party's top leadership set in motion a massive effort to carry out its recent decisions, including those on Zhao Ziyang's disgrace. The Work Committee of the Departments under the Central Committee of the CCP and the Work Committee of Central Government Departments issued a joint emergency notice demanding resolute implementation of the directives of Party Central and the State Council to end the turmoil promptly. The notices carried the following five points.

Excerpt from Work Committee of the Departments under the Central Committee of the CCP and Work Committee of [Party Committees within] Central Government Departments,[3] "Urgent notice on further organizing the broad masses of Party members and officials to study the important May 19 speeches of Comrades Li Peng and Yang Shangkun, in order to maintain firm unity with Party Central in ideology and action," May 26

1. Continue to organize Party members and officials to study the important speeches by Li Peng and Yang Shangkun on May 19. All must realize the gravity of the current situation. It is of great importance to stop the turmoil promptly, to reverse and stabilize the situation, and to uphold Party leadership and the socialist system. All must resolutely support the important decisions of Party Central and stand in line with Party Central both ideologically and in actions.

2. All Party members must strictly follow Party discipline. No one is allowed to participate in any activity that is harmful to peace and unity. All must play active roles in mobilizing the masses to oppose the turmoil.

3. All Party members must stay on duty and do a good job at work. They must submit to martial law as declared by the State Council and must take the lead in complying with the Beijing People's Government's ban on demonstrations, petitions, and student or worker strikes during martial law. They must end all demonstrating immediately and must stop going to the streets to watch or support demonstrators. All Party members must not only behave themselves but also must assist administrative leaders in uniting with the majority of the officials and masses. They must also educate their own relatives not to go to the streets and not to participate in or show support for demonstrations in Tiananmen Square.

4. All levels of the Party organization must actively assist administrative leaders in doing political and ideological work, in uniting with the majority of officials and the masses, and in playing leadership roles in stabilizing the situation.

5. All levels of the Party organization must promptly notify all Party members of the above-mentioned requirements and make sure they are obeyed.

[3]Every Party and government office is guided in its work by a Party committee made up of its leading members, and each such committee is guided by a Party committee at a higher level. In the citation, the first work committee is in charge of Party committees in central Party agencies like the Propaganda Department. The second work committee is in charge of Party committees within State Council–level offices in the government apparatus, such as ministries and commissions.—Comp.

Also on May 26 the Beijing Party Committee and the Beijing People's Government sent a letter extending regards to all officers and soldiers in the martial law troops, including units of the PLA, the PAP, and Public Security. Li Ximing, Chen Xitong, and others went to visit the troops in the evening. Li Ximing told them, "You came to the capital to enforce martial law. You have contributed greatly to security and order in the capital and to stabilization of the entire country. You are undertaking a sacred mission, and history will record your achievements." Chen Xitong said, "We are working on people's thinking at the city, district, and county levels to assure support for the army. We are trying to educate the masses to love the people's army so that you will have the best possible conditions for carrying out your martial law mission." Li and Chen assured the troops that the "broad masses" would surely support them; even people who were temporarily confused about the matter would eventually recognize their debt of gratitude.

Responses from the troops

According to reports coming in to the Central Military Commission and the Politburo, officers and troops gave unreserved support to the decisions of the Central leaders as they had been explained by Yang Shangkun.

The Beijing Military Region expressed strong support for Party Central's decisions to end the turmoil and to restore order. After studying Li Peng's and Yang Shangkun's speeches, everyone agreed the turmoil was manufactured by a tiny minority who were taking advantage of the idealism of young students to challenge the Party and the government. Their goal was to overthrow Party leadership and reject the socialist system, and this violated the Constitution and the fundamental interests of the people. In addition, Zhao Ziyang was responsible for splitting the Party, ignoring the Four Basic Principles, and encouraging turmoil; Party Elders headed by Deng Xiaoping had saved the nation in a time of crisis; and martial law was necessary, constitutional, and in keeping with the popular will. All soldiers showed strong loyalty to Party Central and expressed deep appreciation for the trust the Party and government had placed in them in this time of crisis.

The Chengdu Military Region also reported strong and unanimous support for Party Central's decisions and for the speeches by Li Peng and Yang Shangkun. Its people felt respect and admiration for Deng Xiaoping and the Party Elders for their courage in meeting the challenge, and they condemned the turmoil as an organized attempt to subvert Party leadership and the socialist system. They blamed Zhao Ziyang for violating Party principles by showing sympathy and support for the turmoil. Everyone agreed there could be no turning back in the fight against the turmoil and offered absolute submission to the command of the CMC chaired by Deng Xiaoping and Yang Shangkun. The region's Party Standing Committee resolved on May 25 to have more study sessions with officers at the regiment level and above in order to ensure ideological loyalty to Party

Central, to tighten control over the troops, and to stand alert against any hostile forces along the Yunnan and Tibetan borders.

The Party Committee of the air force also offered its resolute support for the decisions of Party Central and for the speeches by Li Peng and Yang Shangkun at the Enlarged Meeting of the CMC. The air force agreed with the April 26 editorial in the *People's Daily*. It traced the root of the problem to the split in views within the Party and urged Party Central to resolve that split as soon as possible. It supported martial law as representing the fundamental interests of the Party, the army, and the entire nation and expressed total loyalty and submission to the authority of the CMC under the leadership of Deng Xiaoping and Yang Shangkun.

The democracy movement continues

Reports from the State Security Ministry described Beijing as quiet on May 26. There were no demonstrations on the streets. Most Beijing students had left Tiananmen Square. Those remaining were largely from outside Beijing, but many of these had also gone back home. Some martial law troops in the suburbs were holding parties with the local residents, who had become more and more receptive to them. On the Square and on various school campuses posters announced a new resolution from the Autonomous Federation of Beijing Students about a Great Global Chinese Protest Day to be held on May 28.

At Peking University a wall poster signed by Wang Dan proposed a prolonged battle to promote democracy in China. Wang called for the formation of four groups of two hundred students; the groups would take turns demonstrating on the Square. The student-controlled public-address system proposed a strategy of opposing Li Peng and martial law without attacking Deng Xiaoping. Later it unveiled a plan to reorganize and militarize the autonomous student organizations and called for another round of hunger strikes on Tiananmen Square to press for the withdrawal of the martial law troops; for official recognition of the patriotic democracy movement; for the resignation of Deng Xiaoping, Li Peng, and Yang Shangkun; and for restoring Zhao Ziyang to power.

On the same day Wang Juntao, Bao Zunxin, Wang Dan, and others held a meeting at which they called for the dismissal of Li Peng, the withdrawal of the army, the mobilization of workers to strike, and the continuation of the protests on the Square until the NPC Standing Committee meeting on June 20.

On May 26 Yan Jiaqi and Bao Zunxin published an indictment of Premier Li Peng in the Hong Kong newspaper *Ming bao*.[4] The authors held martial law to be both unnecessary and unconstitutional and proposed an emergency meeting of the NPC Standing Committee to consider abol-

---

[4]Text in Oksenberg et al., *Beijing Spring*, 328–331.

ishing martial law immediately and convening the full NPC in the near future. The article accused Li Peng of two major crimes: ignoring the demands of three thousand hunger striking students and inflicting martial law upon a peaceful populace. It warned Li Peng against the further, even more serious crime of using deadly force against the people. The Chinese government immediately condemned the article as a "vicious counterrevolutionary political program."

Continuing demonstrations outside Beijing

On May 26 Zhongnanhai received thirty-one reports showing that demonstrations continued, though they were tapering off, in twenty-one provinces. In Shanghai the number of demonstrators on the streets had dwindled, but campus activity had increased. Teachers and students were making speeches calling for the student movement to expand, especially by forming alliances with workers and farmers. In Harbin some students had resumed their studies even though classes had not resumed and demonstrations continued. Many students showed concern for their academic careers, but student leaders continued to be successful in agitating for student strikes.

In Shijiazhuang the size of student protests increased for the third consecutive day, but in Taiyuan teachers said that the majority of students were losing interest and that the number of demonstrators had declined visibly. Hohhot had seen no demonstrations for three days, but fewer than a third of students remained on campus. In Xi'an more than ten thousand students and teachers held a public rally at which speakers called for continued struggle for freedom and democracy and announced the formation of a provincial autonomous student federation. In Xining fifteen students who had just returned from Beijing began a hunger strike in front of the provincial government building. In Nanjing a day of peace was followed by a day on which more than five thousand students took to the streets. In Hangzhou five thousand students gathered in Wulin Square and vowed to carry their student strike to the end. In Kunming more than a thousand students continued a sit-in, and in Guiyang 80 percent of students remained on strike.

Overseas reaction

A few of the seventeen reports on foreign comment that arrived at Zhongnanhai on May 26 drew special notice from the top Party leadership. One was an ABC-TV interview with Henry Kissinger, who characterized the "fierce dispute" in China's leadership by saying that whereas Deng Xiaoping wanted both economic reform and strong central power, Zhao Ziyang believed that economic reform had to be matched by a measure of political pluralism. Kissinger said the dispute was "tragic" because the two leaders actually shared the same goals of reform. When asked if reform in China was dead, Kissinger predicted that the economic reform would continue and even accelerate. He also believed that the Chinese authorities would take some actions against official corruption, but he did not know whether they would do it the traditional authoritarian way or by establishing some means of popular participation. Kissinger praised President Bush for his personal knowledge of China and his handling of events and noted that the Chinese government appreciated U.S. support.

The *Washington Post* commented that the ongoing political and social unrest was greatly diminishing China's influence in international affairs. It noted that many Western diplomats in Beijing had warned that if bloodshed were used to resolve the crisis, it would become impossible for their governments to maintain friendly relations with China's government. In addition 160 UN employees from seventy-four countries had written to the UN secretary general expressing their deep concern about the possibility of bloodshed and urging utmost restraint upon the Chinese government. By contrast the U.S. embassy had expressed concerns only about martial law, and Chinese officials had sent out signals indicating their special regard for the U.S. government reaction.

May 27

Wan Li's "written chat"

Wan Li's speeches during his official visit to the United States showed he understood the need for democracy and hinted at his hope he might be able to help resolve the crisis through the NPC. But he was under virtual house arrest in Shanghai, and through Jiang Zemin he had received Deng Xiaoping's demand that he express his support for the decisions of the Elders and the Politburo Standing Committee. Torn between his loyalty to the Elders and his sympathies for the people, Wan opted to abandon his political ally Zhao Ziyang and hew to the line of the Elders.

In a "written chat"[5] sent to Party Central on May 27 and published the next day by Xinhua News Agency, Wan explained that he had cut short his overseas trip for health reasons and that he was currently receiving medical treatment in Shanghai. He expressed his appreciation of the sincerity of the majority of the demonstrating students, who, in his view, only wished to promote democracy and to curtail corruption. Then he acknowledged that there was indeed a tiny minority of people who were taking advantage of the students' patriotism and conspiring to overthrow the government. He called for exposing these people while protecting the majority of the students and people.

---

[5]A statement written in an informal style.

Wan stated his support for the decisions of the Standing Committee of the Politburo and for the May 19 speeches in which Li Peng and Yang Shangkun announced martial law. He held that martial law was constitutional and was necessary to end the turmoil and restore order. He said the Standing Committee of the NPC would meet June 20 to consider all the issues the students had raised, and he hoped all patriotic citizens in China would unite under the leadership of the Party and the government.

Li Xiannian convenes a meeting of the CPPCC Presidium

On the afternoon of May 27 Li Xiannian convened the eighteenth meeting of the Presidium of the Seventh Chinese People's Political Consultative Conference.[6] Wang Renzhong, the meeting chairman, asked that all members express support for the decisions of Party Central and the State Council. Ma Wenrui, a vice chair of the CPPCC Standing Committee, "resolutely supported" the Party and government decisions against the turmoil. While conceding that some of the student demands were justified, Ma criticized their "extremism" and called for strong measures to restore order. Sun Xiaocun, the leader of the China Democratic Construction Association, supported the Center's decisions but pleaded that the students not be prosecuted. Yan Mingfu, who had negotiated extensively with the students, praised their patriotism but criticized their emotional radicalism. He urged the Party to heed the students' complaints about social injustice and official corruption, but he ended by expressing support for Party Central. Qian Xuesen[7] argued that China should focus on economic development, contending that the pursuit of superficial democracy would result in neither real democracy nor economic development.

Li Xiannian delivered the concluding speech. He reported receiving letters from members of the CPPCC and expressed appreciation for their concern and their constructive suggestions. He conceded that the students meant well, that corruption was a problem, and that democracy and law were needed. Yet he called the demonstrations counterproductive and said they sprang from a counterrevolutionary conspiracy that had been able to gain a foothold because of Zhao Ziyang's negligence. He called on the CPPCC to unite around Party Central, to support martial law, and to help the government end the turmoil.

[6]The Presidium of the Chinese People's Political Consultative Conference consists of its chair and vice chairs.

[7]Qian earned a Ph.D. in aviation and mathematics from the California Institute of Technology in 1939 and then taught at CalTech and at the Massachusetts Institute of Technology before returning to China in 1955. He joined the Communist Party in 1958 and later became the key figure in designing the delivery systems of China's nuclear weapons.

Who ordered the arrest of Bao Tong?

Bao Tong, Zhao Ziyang's secretary and closest confidant, was arrested even before the crackdown on the student movement was ordered. The reasons for the arrest were kept secret, and Bao himself was never told what they were. The handful of top leaders who were privy to the background rallied around the formal charge that Bao had "leaked state secrets." The story began on May 27 with a fax, whose full text follows, from the State Security Ministry to Li Peng.

> Coded telegram from State Security Ministry to Premier Li Peng, May 27
>
> ---
>
> After extensive investigation, it has been proven that on the night of May 17 Bao Tong called a meeting of some members of the Office for Research on Reform of the Political System. Bao revealed at the meeting that "Party Central has decided to enforce martial law in Beijing, and although Zhao Ziyang is opposed, the decision has been made and will be difficult to reverse. I hope we are all prepared for the grave situation we face; Ziyang may not last long." In his "parting words" at the meeting Bao enjoined the others "not to sell out their consciences" and not to become a "traitor" or "Judas." Hence it is clear that the secrets about martial law and the fall of Zhao Ziyang were leaked through Bao Tong.

> On the morning of May 19 Bao Tong sent Gao Shan to the IER to meet with Chen Yizi and others. Gao briefed the group on the internal workings of Party Central since early May, and the discussion led to the "Six-Point Emergency Statement on the Current Situation," issued in the name of the "three institutes and one association,"[8] which stirred up a big reaction in society. In an effort to avoid further exposure, Bao Tong instructed Gao Shan, Chen Yizi, and others to "protect the reform forces and never to make the IER, or its superior commission,[9] look bad." On May 20 Gao Shan, Chen Yizi, and others called an emergency meeting of persons concerned to pass along what Bao Tong had said.

> In addition, Bao Tong has worked closely with Yan Jiaqi, who has been highly active during the student movement, who has claimed many times to be part of "Zhao Ziyang's think tank," and who has openly proclaimed the phrase "Down with Deng and up with Zhao."

After reading the telegram, Li Peng penned the following message on it.

---

[8] See footnote 30 in Chapter 5.
[9] Apparently referring to the State Commission for the Restructure of the Economic System.

Li Peng's handwriting in large, clear characters[10] at the top of the document

Please send to comrades Xiaoping, Xiannian, and Chen Yun. The document shows that Bao Tong leaked top-level state secrets about martial law in order to confuse people's minds. I suggest he immediately be punished according to law.

The Party Elders approved Li Peng's suggestion at their meeting that night, and with their approval in hand, Li Peng issued an order to arrest Bao Tong. On the morning of May 28, while on his way to a meeting of the Standing Committee of the Politburo, Bao Tong was arrested. He was sent directly to join the Gang of Four and others at Qincheng Prison. Zhao Ziyang was put under house arrest the same day, and his staff met a variety of related fates.[11]

The Elders appoint Jiang Zemin

On the night of May 27 Deng Xiaoping, Chen Yun, Li Xiannian, Peng Zhen, Deng Yingchao, Yang Shangkun, Wang Zhen, and Bo Yibo met for about five hours at Deng Xiaoping's residence to determine a successor to Zhao Ziyang as CCP general secretary.

[10]Probably so that the Elders could read his inscription more easily. The telegram was marked "only one copy" (*zhi yifen*).—Comp.

[11]Zhao had five secretaries during his tenure as premier of the State Council and general secretary of the Party.

Bao Tong, the leader in the area of political reform, was the best known. At the time of his arrest Bao was a member of the Thirteenth Central Committee, director of the Office for Research on Reform of the Political System, and secretary of the Standing Committee of the Politburo. The Beijing Intermediate People's Court sentenced Bao to seven years' imprisonment (plus an additional two years' deprivation of political rights) for the crime of revealing state secrets.

Bai Meiqing was Zhao's secretary most familiar with economics. He served as first deputy general secretary and deputy Party secretary of the General Office of the State Council, where he was known as a meticulous analyst and skillful administrator. After Zhao's fall from power, Li Peng moved Bai Meiqing out of the State Council into a post as vice minister of commerce.

Zhang Yueqi in 1989 was deputy director of the General Office of the CCP Central Committee but lost this post after Zhao Ziyang fell. He remained unemployed until late 1990, when he was sent to Jilin to serve as deputy secretary of the Provincial Party Committee. He later became a vice chair of the provincial CPPCC.

Li Shuqiao, who had edited the Party theoretical journal *Red Flag* before coming to work for Zhao, also became unemployed after Zhao's fall until Liu Suinian, the minister of goods and materials, gave him a nonpolitical job as deputy general manager of the China Container Company in late 1990.

Li Yong was a grandson of the senior Party leaders, now deceased, Li Fuchun and Cai Chang. An unconfirmed rumor among the top leaders alleged that Li was responsible for passing news of the impending martial law to students in Tiananmen Square. Li lost his job with the fall of Zhao but soon left Beijing to be deputy general manager of the Tianjin Economic and Technological Development Zone.—Comp.

Excerpts from Party Central Office Secretariat, "Minutes of important meeting, May 27, 1989," document supplied to Party Central Office Secretariat for its records by the Office of Deng Xiaoping

Deng Xiaoping: "Let's begin by discussing a new leadership team for the Center. Let me give you my view and see if you think it's correct: New leaders for the Politburo, the Party Secretariat, and especially the Standing Committee should be chosen for their commitment to reform and opening. The new leaders should do some things to show we will persist with reform and opening so that the people can feel reassured that the new team is sincere about carrying out the policies of the Third Plenum of the Eleventh Central Committee. We must consider public perceptions when we choose the new leaders, must not let emotion sway us, and must set aside all personal grudges, even to the extent of choosing people who have once opposed us. We must take the high road of the statesman and choose people who are seen as committed to reform and opening and who have made achievements in their careers. We should be bold about putting these people into new leadership positions so that the people will see we really mean it when we talk about reform and opening."

Chen Yun: "I agree with Xiaoping's view and will add just one point. The new leaders do need to win the trust of the people and show records of real achievement. But one essential criterion is that they must dare to oppose bourgeois liberalization and uphold the Four Basic Principles. On this point we cannot compromise. Can China do without the Four Basic Principles? Can we do without the people's democratic dictatorship? Are we going to stick with these things—the people's democratic dictatorship, Marxism, socialism, and Communist Party rule—or not? These are the fundamental questions."

Li Xiannian: "We're all waiting to hear your views, Comrade Xiaoping, on the selection of the next general secretary."

Deng Xiaoping: "After long and careful comparison, the Shanghai Party secretary, Comrade Jiang Zemin, does indeed seem a proper choice. I think he's up to the task. Comrades Chen Yun, Xiannian, and I all lean toward Comrade Jiang Zemin for general secretary. What do the rest of you think?"

Wang Zhen: "If that's what the three of you think, then that's it. I don't know Jiang Zemin very well, but I trust Comrade Xiaoping to get it right. So let's have Jiang Zemin be general secretary."

Deng Yingchao: "I haven't had much contact with Jiang Zemin, but from what the rest of you say about him, he seems fine. I agree that he be general secretary."

Li Xiannian: "It's true that Jiang Zemin lacks experience at the Center. But this man has a political mind, is in the prime of life, and can be trusted."

Yang Shangkun: "It's hard to overstate how important it is that the new leadership team maintain the image of reform and opening and win the trust of the people. The country is watching us closely on this. We can't close our doors just because we're switching general secretaries. China must never again seal itself off, never go back to the closed and locked door. To do that would be frightening: The economy would not grow, people's lives would not improve, and the overall strength of the country would suffer. I agree to have Jiang Zemin as the next general secretary and also agree with Comrade Xiaoping's suggestion that Li Ruihuan from Tianjin join the Standing Committee of the Politburo. Li Ruihuan is strongly associated with reform and opening, and he really does get things done for the people."

Bo Yibo: "No one is perfect, and we're not going to find flawless people. We have to face the fact that the new leadership team will have weaknesses in its experience with politics and struggle. But the new team must be able to win confidence both within the Party and among the people. This doesn't mean we have to be happy with every member of the team—only that we should be happy with the team as a whole. Jiang Zemin and Li Ruihuan are good choices. They're both eager to go, and as long as we stay out of the way and let them go, I think they'll do well."

Chen Yun: "I think Comrade Song Ping is a good choice for the Standing Committee. He has rich political experience, knows both the Center and the localities, acts strictly on principle, is strong in Party loyalty, has high standards, and has influence. The new team should include one or two somewhat older comrades with more experience."

Li Xiannian: "I think Jiang Zemin, Song Ping, and Li Ruihuan all are appropriate selections for the Standing Committee. We shouldn't draw all the leaders from the provinces; we need some from the Center, too. Comrade Yibo is right that Jiang Zemin and Li Ruihuan both lack experience at the Center. But they are highly motivated and are ready for our support. Comrade Song Ping's rich experience should make him easily capable of meeting the challenge of membership on the Standing Committee."

Peng Zhen: "I hope the new team can be relatively stable, and that means it should have at least some continuity with the old team. We can't keep replacing people as if we're running a merry-go-round, or the new team will never be able to establish its authority or win the people's confidence, and that would hurt the

Party. We must do our best to establish the authority of the leadership core. We must let them take responsibility and delegate power as necessary. Establishing a leadership core is no easy task."

Deng Xiaoping: "I agree with Comrade Peng Zhen. Our Party didn't have a stable and mature leadership collective until the Mao, Liu, Zhou, Zhu[12] days. Before that, the leadership was always unstable and immature. Starting from Chen Duxiu and going all the way up to the Zunyi Conference,[13] none of the leaderships were really mature. During one stretch it was said that we should emphasize the leadership of the working class, so we bent over backward to find workers to be leaders. Our really mature leadership began only with Mao, Liu, Zhou, and Zhu, and the early period of that group's leadership was fine. In the later period, with the Cultural Revolution, it was a disaster. Hua Guofeng didn't get much going— only his 'two whatevers.'[14] So the actual second generation of leadership is ours, and the people have been basically happy with us primarily because we've pursued reform and opening and aimed at the Four Modernizations, and because we've made real achievements. Now we're moving to the third leadership generation, and if we want this new leadership generation to really get started and win the people's confidence, the only way is to stick with reform and opening."

Yang Shangkun: "If our new leadership team is stodgy, rigid, or mediocre, one the people won't trust and Party members won't respect, we're only asking for more disturbances—constant disturbances—down the road, and we can forget about economic growth. The students haven't gone back to classes yet; the whole thing is continuing, and if we don't pick a leadership team the people like, I see us headed for more trouble. That's why the leadership team and the reform and opening policies are so crucially connected. Comrade Xiaoping has pointed out that almost every conceivable slogan has appeared during this protest, but nobody protests reform. That's why it's crucial to stick to reform. If we don't, there's no way the country is going to live in peace."

Deng Yingchao: "Sticking with reform is our Party's guiding principle and primary focus; of course we can't give that up. But I'd like to make another point. The new Standing Committee team has to be firm against corruption. We can't

[12]Mao Zedong, Liu Shaoqi, Zhou Enlai, and Zhu De; a stock phrase of four last names that are commonly run together.
[13]Chen Duxiu was one of the founders of the CCP in 1921. At a January 1935 conference in Zunyi, in Guizhou Province, the CCP for the first time put Mao Zedong clearly in charge of the Red Army, which before then had suffered severe losses under KMT military attacks.
[14]The "two whatevers" were "We must resolutely uphold whatever policies Chairman Mao adopted, and we must steadfastly abide by whatever instructions he gave." The slogan first appeared in a *People's Daily* editorial of February 7, 1977.

face the people if we don't go after corruption, bribery, and embezzlement. We really have to get serious about this, or there's no way on earth we can explain our-selves to the people. A team that won't fight corruption doesn't measure up."

Deng Xiaoping: "I've checked with Comrades Chen Yun and Xiannian, and they completely agree with my view that the new leadership team must continue to carry out the political line, principles, and policies of the Third Plenum of the Eleventh Central Committee. Even the language should stay the same. The polit-ical report of the Thirteenth Party Congress was approved by all representatives at the time. Not a single word of it can be changed. The policies of reform and opening must not change, not for several decades; we've got to press them through to the end. This should be what we expect and require from the new gen-eration of Central leadership. Unless someone objects, I move that the new Standing Committee of the Politburo be made up of the following six comrades: Jiang Zemin, Li Peng, Qiao Shi, Yao Yilin, Song Ping, and Li Ruihuan, with Com-rade Jiang Zemin as general secretary."

At this point the Elders apparently voted.

Deng Xiaoping: "The new Standing Committee team is now determined, but we don't need to announce it right away. Let's wait until the Fourth Plenum of the Thirteenth Central Committee to publicize it officially, together with the cases of Zhao Ziyang and others."

Chen Yun: "I think we should do two things before then. The first would be to have Comrade Jiang Zemin come up to Beijing to get familiar with things here. The other would be that Comrade Xiaoping may want to notify certain members of the current Standing Committee about our decision."

Yang Shangkun: "Today in Shanghai Wan Li came out in favor of the Politburo decisions. I wonder if we should consider having Wan Li come to Beijing together with Jiang Zemin."

Peng Zhen: "Wan Li has been in Shanghai for medical treatment. There's no need to hurry him back to Beijing. If we did there'd only be more rumors about him."

Deng Xiaoping: "Let's have Jiang Zemin come first; he needs to get familiar with things. And I accept Comrade Chen Yun's suggestion that I should represent all of us to have a chat with the continuing Standing Committee members. The main purpose will be to unify thinking so the new team can get started with a clear focus and really get down to work on a few practical things that will please the people. I need to tell everybody something else, too. Li Peng has sent me materials showing that Bao Tong was the one who leaked the secret about martial law in Beijing. I'm not familiar with this man Bao Tong, but he won't get away with it—leaking Party and state secrets. Comrade Li Peng is requesting immediate prosecution by law."

Li Xiannian: "I know the man. He's over fifty but follows fashions like a youngster. He wears gaudy jackets and blue jeans inside Zhongnanhai—what kind of Party official is that? His head is full of bourgeois liberalization. Some time ago he pulled together a group of young people and called them a 'Zhao Ziyang think tank.' Our Communist Party doesn't have think tanks—never has. This is pure bourgeois stuff. A few days ago I learned from Li Peng and Yao Yilin that Bao Tong was the one responsible for that statement by the three institutes and one association. Now the truth has come out. Bao Tong has broken the law by leaking the martial law secret and should be arrested. When we arrest Bao Tong, his think tank will leak dry, and that will help end the turmoil."

Wang Zhen: "I agree with Comrade Xiannian. This guy should be arrested—arrested immediately! This is a matter of principle and we can't mess around! It's irrelevant whether he's a Central Committee member or not, secretary of the Standing Committee or not, known to us or not. What's the big deal about arresting a guy like this? We arrested Jiang Qing and the Gang of Four, we arrested the diehard followers of Lin Biao,[15] and we can't arrest him? The question isn't even worth discussing. The facts speak for themselves. Just tell Li Peng to arrest him tomorrow and put him in Qincheng."[16]

Bo Yibo: "The situation in Beijing and around the country has been improving in the last few days, but we can't rule out the possibility of backsliding. Many comrades feel it's a problem that we have martial law troops poised outside the city but allow the students to stay put in Tiananmen Square. Now that we've got the problem inside the Party solved, we should turn to ending the turmoil. We should take action, I think, but it's not easy to say just what we should do."

Deng Yingchao: "Let's take a moderate approach. We can persuade the students to go back to their campuses, use the PLA in the city to maintain order, and

---

[15]Lin Biao was deputy chairman of the CCP and Mao Zedong's "closest comrade in arms" and designated successor during the Cultural Revolution in the late 1960s. He died in an airplane crash in 1971 while apparently fleeing China after what is officially described as a coup attempt against Mao. The persons referred to as his diehard followers were Chen Boda, Huang Yongsheng, Wu Faxian, Li Zuopeng, Qiu Huizuo, and Jiang Tengjiao. They were tried and sentenced along with the Gang of Four in 1980–1981 for crimes of counterrevolution.
[16]That is, Qincheng Prison; see footnote 23 in Chapter 6.

show the common people and the majority of the young students that the Party and government are determined to address their concerns and are confident of success. This will make us popular. I hope we can restore order quickly."

Yang Shangkun: "We've always said that the PLA's move into the city will not be aimed at Beijing residents or at the masses of students. At first people didn't believe us, but now they do. We must be equally firm about stopping the turmoil and about avoiding bloodshed in doing so. These two things aren't contradictory. We do, of course, need a timetable. We can't let things drag on forever."

Chen Yun: "Yes, we must do our best both to end the turmoil quickly and to avoid bloodshed. It would be great if we could do it by the end of the month. Stability and unity of thought are the most important things."

Deng Xiaoping: "I suggest that the Standing Committee of the Politburo quickly make a decision to restore normal order in Beijing and to set a date for the Fourth Plenum of the Thirteenth Central Committee. We can't delay any longer."

The motion to appoint Jiang as general secretary and to add Li and Song to the Standing Committee had been approved by the Elders by a show of hands. But this violated the Chinese Communist Party Constitution, which stipulates that the Politburo Standing Committee should make such decisions.

Support and opposition

On May 27 and 28, Zhongnanhai received reports from the Military Regions of Jinan and Guangzhou and from the provincial Party committees of Tianjin, Zhejiang, Fujian, Jiangxi, and Inner Mongolia. All expressed support for the Center's decisions on ending the turmoil.

Meanwhile, in the Square, May 27 reports from the State Security Ministry, the Public Security Ministry, and the Beijing Municipal Government described continuing demonstrations. The student public-address system focused on Li Peng, accusing him of trying to stage a coup and refusing to recognize him as a representative of the government. Although many student demonstrators from outside Beijing had been persuaded to go home, others continued to pour in by train. One student leader forecast that calls from Chinese in the United States for a Great Global Chinese Protest Day the next day would stimulate demonstrations in Beijing of as many as three hundred thousand people. In the evening the student leaders issued a call for one more demonstration, on May 30, after which they said they would withdraw. But there were other, conflicting news releases that suggested student leaders disagreed about whether to withdraw or not.

The most notable event on May 27 was the appearance of a "Ten-Point Statement on the Current Situation"[17] from a new joint organization of protest groups called the United Conference of Patriotic Beijing Organizations in Support of the Constitution. It criticized Li Peng and his allies and praised Zhao Ziyang, but it also stated that the democracy movement was not just a reflection of intra-Party struggle, so any attempt to stop the movement by resolving the intra-Party struggle would prove futile, and anyone who stood in opposition to the movement would lose legitimacy and eventually power. It said the demonstrations would last at least until the NPC meeting scheduled for June 20.

The State Security Ministry said that Bao Zunxin had drafted this statement and that the United Conference of Patriotic Beijing Organizations in Support of the Constitution, with Wang Juntao presiding, had approved it by a show of hands. Wang had been in regular contact with student leaders, the report said, and was involved in many covert activities to organize and manipulate the student movement. This report later became the basis for the arrest of Wang Juntao, Bao Zunxin, and others as black hands, or manipulators of the student movement, behind the scenes.

May 28

Demonstrations in and outside of Beijing

Despite Great Global Chinese Protest Day activities overseas, reports from the State Security Ministry and the Public Security Ministry on student activities in Beijing May 28 said that day's demonstration was less impressive than others recently: Only about fifty thousand students participated at peak times. But Beijing residents cheered as the students continued to protest martial law and official corruption and to call for freedom of speech, for Zhao Ziyang's restoration to power, and for the dismissal of Li Peng. Demands for Deng Xiaoping's resignation seemed to have disappeared.

Most of the students on the Square, especially those who had just arrived from outside Beijing, were opposed to the idea of withdrawing by May 30. Handouts calling for another hunger strike were distributed, although it was not clear how much support such an action would have. Leaders of the AFS held a meeting and decided that despite the sharply declining numbers of demonstrators, they would remain in the Square until the opening of the NPC meeting on June 20. Bao Zunxin and Wang Juntao met secretly with student leaders at Peking University and decided to shift the focus of the movement toward mobilization of workers, farmers, soldiers, and others.

---

[17]Excerpted in Suzanne Ogden, Kathleen Hartford, Lawrence Sullivan, and David Zweig, eds., *China's Search for Democracy: The Student and the Mass Movement of 1989* (Armonk, New York: M. E. Sharpe, 1992), 329–331.

On May 28 thirty-three reports to Zhongnanhai described demonstrations in thirty-six cities. In Shanghai more than ten thousand people joined the Great Global Chinese Protest Day. In Nanjing, where more than thirty thousand people turned out, Deng Xiaoping and Li Peng were the main targets. In Hangzhou there were demonstrations on both May 27 and May 28. In Harbin about three thousand individual entrepreneurs and retired workers joined students in a demonstration in front of the provincial government building.

In Shenyang more than three thousand students took to the streets, and in Shijiazhuang students delivered a petition to the provincial government opposing martial law and demanding dialogue with provincial leaders. In Xi'an students withdrew from the city square but continued to boycott classes. In Changsha students demanding an emergency meeting of the NPC demonstrated in the rain; they called for workers to join them but got little response. In Hefei four hundred or so workers and demobilized soldiers joined more than three thousand students in a Great Global Chinese Protest Day demonstration. There were tens of thousands of onlookers.

Reactions overseas

On May 27 and 28 fifteen reports on overseas Chinese demonstrations reached Zhongnanhai. In the United States five hundred students and scholars demonstrated in front of the Chinese embassy demanding abolition of martial law and calling for an NPC meeting to resolve the crisis through democracy and law. Professor Wu Jingsheng of the University of Maryland said the Chinese associations he represented would stop cooperating with the Chinese government because of its ill-advised treatment of the demonstrators. Another report said that more than five hundred Chinese scholars and professors in the United States had signed an open letter in support of the student movement and that the letter would be published in the *New York Times* on May 30.

Hong Kong newspapers continued to cover the student activities in Tiananmen Square. On May 26 two hundred thousand young people joined a rally at Victoria Park. The next day a twelve-hour marathon concert to show support for the student movement in Beijing was held in Hong Kong.

In Taiwan the *United Daily News* conducted a public opinion poll that showed increasing popular demand for the government to issue a statement against suppression of the democracy movement on the mainland. At a seminar held by the ruling party's Research Institute on Revolutionary Practice, four panelists from Taiwan and the United States agreed that the Taiwan government's open-door policy toward mainland China had contributed to the rise of the democracy movement there.

Among twenty-four foreign media reports received on May 27 and 28, one from Britain's *Sunday Telegraph* reported on Li Xiaoqing, a granddaughter of Mao Zedong who was now living in

Australia. It said Li, once a fanatic Red Guard and now twenty-nine years old, had abandoned Communist asceticism in favor of a free and extravagant lifestyle. She studied English, was dating a wealthy and handsome Australian man, and frequented fancy restaurants and social clubs in downtown Sydney. She agreed with the Beijing protesters in condemning official corruption and calling for democratization in China.

CHAPTER NINE

May 29–June 3

Preparing to Clear the Square

EDITORS' NOTE: In the last days of May the student demonstrations wound down throughout the country, and students from the provinces began to leave Beijing. Some campuses, however, generated calls for a nationwide movement of peaceful resistance, and a hard core of students newly arrived in Tiananmen from the provinces insisted that the sit-in there should continue until the NPC meeting scheduled for June 20.

Meanwhile, the Party prepared for a possible crackdown. The troops made physical and ideological preparations to confront the students. The State Security Ministry and the Beijing municipal authorities informed the Politburo that the student demonstrations were manipulated by domestic and foreign enemies as part of a plot to overthrow the regime. This position would later form the basis of the Party's official line on Tiananmen and of its criminal indictments of the movement's leaders.

Looking past the restoration of order, Deng Xiaoping continued to focus on the fate of his economic reforms. Deng ordered the two most conservative members of the Politburo Standing Committee to give full support to Jiang Zemin and to promote even bolder reform than in the past; this, he said, was the only way to restore the Party's popularity.

The Elders met in fateful conclave with the three remaining members of the Politburo Standing Committee on June 2 to consolidate their decision to clear the Square by force. In reviewing the reasons for this action, they focused first on the use of the demonstrations by actors hostile to the regime, and second on the fact that continuing instability would damage economic reform. After the meeting Yang Shangkun issued orders for troops to begin to move toward the city center.

May 29–30

Mixed signals from the student movement

On May 29 and 30–the tenth and eleventh days of martial law–the Center received reports from the State Education Commission and the State Security and Public Security Ministries on the situation in Beijing. Life among the citizens was calm, and there were no demonstrations. Cleanup crews had been able to remove posters and handbills from some of the streets, although new posters and handbills were appearing. The State Education Commission had mobilized colleges under its control in Beijing and the provinces to work with Party members and supporters to separate the students from the hard-core organizers and get them back to classes. At Peking University students shut off the loudspeaker at the campus's west gate at the request of neighboring residents.

Students started to return to classes on some campuses in Beijing but not on those at the center of the movement: Peking University, Qinghua University, People's University, Beijing Normal University, and the Chinese University of Political Science and Law. On the Peking University campus one wall poster, signed by eight faculty members, urged students to end their boycott, since they had now made their point. But another urged continuing the struggle, and the campus loudspeaker network broadcast a call for an empty-campus movement, under which the students would go home to "agitate for revolution." The AFS at Qinghua urged students to promote widespread "nonviolent noncooperation," including strikes, demonstrations, work slowdowns, refusal to buy government bonds, and mass withdrawals of savings deposits from government banks. Beijing Municipality estimated that by May 30 about one-third of the students had left major Beijing campuses to pursue such activities.

On the evening of May 30 Wang Dan broadcast a call for society to organize itself in intellectuals' associations, trade unions, and farmers' associations, and he called for the emergence of a Walesa-like personality to lead civil society. When word arrived that the police had arrested autonomous labor organizer Shen Yinhan, some three hundred students headed off into the night to demonstrate for his release.

The Railway Ministry reported a sharp reversal in the tide of students from the provinces. Since the beginning of martial law, student trips into and out of Beijing had totaled about four hundred thousand, but the number departing was now much greater than the number entering. On May 29 alone thirty thousand students left Beijing by rail while only 180 entered. The ministry added trains and reserved 70 percent of the tickets for students. Some of the students buying tickets out of the city said that they didn't like the atmosphere in Tiananmen Square, that they were exhausted and tired of relying on the kindness of Beijing citizens for their daily needs, and that they hoped the June 20 meeting of the NPC would resolve the problems they had come to Beijing to raise.

The Goddess of Democracy

According to the State Security Ministry, student protesters in the Square on May 29 appeared lonely and listless in spite of new tents sent in from Hong Kong and the sea of banners around them. At night, however, the Square came to life with a party atmosphere. About 10:30 P.M. students from the Central Academy of Fine Arts wheeled in their Goddess of Democracy, a huge plaster statue of a female figure with flowing hair, holding up a torch, that was deliberately modeled on the American Statue of Liberty. Thousands of people watched as it went up. At midnight about three hundred students gathered to determine their next move. Chai Ling gave a speech pointing out some of the difficulties they faced, among them lack of consensus (especially disunity between Beijing and non-Beijing students) and inadequate funding. She offered to resign and proposed a democratic election to select a new leader. The students then decided to form an All-China AFS that combined the autonomous student associations from around the country. They also decided to remain in the Square until the NPC met on June 20 and in the interim to establish a unified decisionmaking body, to strengthen propaganda work, to mobilize the masses, and to raise more money.

Early on the morning of May 30 news arrived that police had arrested some of the leaders of the Autonomous Federation of Workers and the head of the Flying Tiger Group, the motorcycle brigade that worked with the students. At 9 A.M. more than four hundred students and workers staged a sit-in at the Beijing Public Security Bureau to demand the release of the arrested workers. About 10 A.M. the headquarters of the student movement held a news conference at the Square to announce that Chai Ling and Wang Dan were to be replaced by Feng Congde and Li Lu as student leaders. Li Lu set four preconditions for the resumption of dialogue with the government: (1) abolish martial law, (2) guarantee the safety of participants in the movement, (3) withdraw the troops, and (4) allow freedom of the press.

At noon the Goddess of Democracy was formally unveiled in a ceremony that included stage performances, revolutionary songs, and the reading of a manifesto. Meanwhile, the Beijing Municipal Government issued an official statement opposing the erection of the statue as a violation of its regulations.

Provincial governments and the military
continue to support the Center

On May 29 and 30 the high command of the navy and the provincial governments of Heilongjiang, Liaoning, Shanxi, Henan, Jiangsu, and Guangdong submitted reports to the Center in support of its positions on the student movement and the case of Zhao Ziyang.

The report from the navy made four main points: (1) In spite of some initial sympathy with the students, the consensus in the officer corps was that the student movement had been aiming its spear at the Party and government. The movement was premeditated turmoil, violated the Constitution, and must be stopped immediately. (2) The root of the turmoil could be traced to Zhao Ziyang, whose approach to the student movement diverged from Party Central's. Zhao was responsible for ideological confusion because he did not oppose bourgeois liberalization and did not uphold the Four Basic Principles. (3) Party Central overcame Zhao's mistakes when it published the April 26 editorial and declared martial law. These measures clarified the ideological confusion, cracked down on the tiny minority with ulterior motives, and saved the situation. (4) The crucial role that the revolutionary Elders played in this difficult crisis deserved deep appreciation.

But the navy report also revealed that some officers had doubts. Some had trouble condemning Zhao Ziyang, and some worried about instability in the Party's top leadership, which had undergone two major changes in just a few years' time.[1] Others could not understand how "a tiny minority" could have enjoyed such great popular support. Many wished that Party Central would heed the lessons of this turmoil and correct its mistakes by opposing bourgeois liberalization, eliminating corruption, and resolving the problems of income disparity and deterioration in public security.

The six provincial reports echoed one another. Each one described systematic meetings held at various levels to unify thinking behind Party Central, primarily through collective study of authoritative statements from the Center such as the April 26 *People's Daily* editorial and Li Peng's May 19 speech on martial law. The results, according to the reports, were strong support for a firm stand against the turmoil, the enforcement of martial law, prevention of further student demonstrations and resumption of classes, a ban on participation in the movement by officials or Party members, immediate clearing of Tiananmen Square, arrest of the antigovernment leaders, investigation and appropriate punishment of Zhao Ziyang, restoration of security at key institutions, upholding the Four Basic Principles, opposing bourgeois liberalization, building Party spirit, and doing political thought work among the masses.

Despite the authoritarian tone of the reports, they also reflected some genuinely popular concerns, such as continued economic growth and opposition to corruption. But items that fell out-

[1] The first major change was Hu Yaobang's dismissal as general secretary in January 1987.

side Party ideological guidelines—such as curbing inflation, banning the children of high officials from doing business privately, or avoiding bloodshed in Beijing—appeared only briefly.

Back to class but still protesting

On May 29 and 30 fifty-four official updates on student activity around the country reached Zhongnanhai. Some described university students as calming down and beginning to return to class. In Jilin Province, 81 percent of universities reportedly were back to normal. In Liaoning about 92 percent of university students had gone back to class. Xi'an was relatively quiet; most students had returned to their campuses but classes had not yet resumed. In Chongqing students were continuing to make public speeches but had stopped their demonstrations and sit-ins. In Lanzhou more than a hundred students were still encamped in the city's main square, but they "appeared exhausted" and seemed to be losing popular support.

On the other hand, in Taiyuan more than six hundred teachers and students joined a demonstration to commemorate the May Thirtieth Movement,[2] to protest against the arrest of some workers, and to show the student movement was not yet over. In Hohhot more than four thousand student demonstrators demanded that Li Peng resign. In Henan, although most students had returned to class, the number of wall posters, cartoons, and handouts on the campuses had increased, and students were continuing to give antigovernment speeches in the city square. Student boycotts in Guiyang were continuing and were set to go citywide on May 31. In Nanjing more than two hundred students, hoping to push the student movement to new heights, were planning to set out for Beijing on foot.

The report from Hefei listed various reasons why about two-thirds of the students were still boycotting class: They wanted to express solidarity with the students in Beijing remaining in Tiananmen Square; they were afraid that a return to class without any government concessions would appear to be a defeat for the student movement; they were waiting for the government to give them a face-saving exit option; and some felt that since government retaliation was inevitable in any case, they might as well protest to the hilt.

---

[2]On May 30, 1925, police under British administration in Shanghai killed thirteen "anti-imperialist" demonstrators and sparked a nationwide series of protests that became known as the May Thirtieth Movement. Observance of the anniversary in Taiyuan may have sprung in part from an interest in workers' rights, which were at stake in both 1925 and 1989, but it apparently was also used as a politically acceptable pretext for continuing the current demonstrations.

Foreign news coverage

On May 29 and 30 the Chinese leadership received twenty-seven reports on Western media coverage of China.

With martial law troops stalled in the Beijing suburbs, Western reporters had a rare chance to view PLA equipment and to see how outdated it was. The *Washington Post* reported that military trucks had to be started with a crank, that tanks broke down because of mechanical problems, and that certain Soviet-style armored vehicles were thirty years old.

The Hong Kong *Standard* published a commentary on the economic problems the turmoil might cause for the Chinese leadership. The piece said the Chinese leadership might try to counter Western sanctions, if any, by expanding economic cooperation with the Soviet Union. But, it continued, that strategy might not work because the Soviets were in the midst of major political reforms and were themselves trying to improve ties with the West. If the Chinese economy deteriorated, the government would find popular support harder to come by.

The *China Times,* a Taiwan newspaper, reported that political unrest had frightened many Taiwan investors away from the mainland. The Taiwan government expressed concern that mainland economic policies might change and advised Taiwan businesses to be careful about investing in or trading with mainland China.

May 30–31

Two briefings

On the morning of May 30 Jiang Zemin was presiding over a meeting of the Shanghai Party Committee to discuss the guidelines set out by Party Central and the State Council on safeguarding social stability against the turmoil. Suddenly he received an emergency call from the General Office of the Central Committee summoning him to Beijing. With little idea of what was happening, he boarded a special jet and arrived in Beijing that afternoon.

Wen Jiabao, head of Party Central's General Office, acting on instructions from Yang Shangkun, had arranged for Jiang to have audiences with Chen Yun and Li Xiannian that evening and with Deng Xiaoping the next morning. There is no written record of the guidance Chen, Li, and Deng gave to Jiang, but the fact that he was received individually by the three most powerful Elders—the so-called super-Elders[3]—was a sign that he was about to be appointed as the new gen-

---

[3] *Chaoji yuanlao.*

eral secretary of the CCP. It was the first procedure he went through in being inducted into the highest circle of Party power.

On May 31, after Deng had his morning talk with Jiang, he delivered an afternoon talk to Li Peng and Yao Yilin. Li and Yao may have felt their own political stars should be rising. They had championed the views of the eight Elders and had advocated the recently victorious policy of cracking down on the turmoil. Li in particular may have felt slighted that he was not chosen as the new general secretary. The transcript of Deng's remarks makes clear that his aim in addressing these two relatively conservative leaders was to warn them not to band together against the new General Secretary Jiang Zemin and not to block the policies of reform and opening.

Elaborating on some of his remarks at the Elders' meeting of May 27 (see Chapter 8), Deng emphasized the need to persist in reform and opening in order to win the hearts of the people and the need to preserve unity among the third generation of Party leaders. Deng told Li and Yao the Party must satisfy the demands of the students and citizens with concrete deeds; it could not restore its authority by an ideological counterattack on the views of the people. He urged them to set aside any preconceptions and political grudges and to manage affairs with the kind of broad vision suited to those in positions of highest power. And he closed the meeting by revealing that the Elders (whom he referred to as "Party Central") had chosen Jiang Zemin as the new Party general secretary.

Deng later transmitted the content of his talk to the full Politburo (and still later to all leaders at the province level) in order to ensure that his warnings against a conservative undermining of Jiang and possible rollback of reform be known to a wider audience.

> Excerpts from Party Central Office Secretariat, "Comrade Xiaoping's talk with Comrades Li Peng and Yilin, May 31, 1989," document supplied to Party Central Office Secretariat for its records by the Office of Deng Xiaoping[4]

"The policies of reform and opening remain unchanged and must not change for several decades. We must carry through to the end. This is the question that most concerns people both inside China and abroad. We must stick with the line, the principles, the policies, and even the language of the Third Plenum of the Eleventh Central Committee. The political report of the Thirteenth Party Congress[5] was passed by that Congress, and not a single word of it can be changed.

---

[4]Translated in Michel Oksenberg, Lawrence R. Sullivan, and Marc Lambert, eds., *Beijing Spring, 1989, Confrontation and Conflict: The Basic Documents* (Armonk, New York: M. E. Sharpe, 1990), 333–338. An edited version is contained in *Deng Xiaoping wenxuan* (Selected works of Deng Xiaoping), vol. 3 (Beijing: Renmin chubanshe, 1993), 296–301.

[5]In 1987. Its political report called for deepening the reform and even for some modest reforms in the political system.

I've consulted with Comrades Li Xiannian and Chen Yun on this, and they both concur.

"Once the turmoil passes, we will owe the people some explanations, especially on two big questions. One is our leadership changes. The new Central leadership structure should present a brand-new look and should project an image of hope and of commitment to reform. This is of utmost importance. The image is crucial! The people want actual results. If we come out with a lineup that appears rigid, conservative, or mediocre, that promises no future for China, then we'll see a lot more disturbances in coming years and may not see a moment's peace. The current trouble is continuing—the students haven't gone back to class, and even if they had, they'd still be in the streets at other times. One thing is for sure: Workers, farmers, intellectuals, and students all want reform. We've heard all kinds of slogans recently, but nobody shouts 'Down with reform!'

"Some people, of course, understand 'reform' to mean movement toward liberalism or capitalism. Capitalism is the heart of reform for them, but not for us. What *we* mean by reform is different and still under debate. But in any case, to present a fresh, reform-oriented face is of paramount importance when we select members of our new leadership team. This isn't 99 percent important; it's 100 percent important. We have to see the big picture.

"The second explanation we need to make is about corruption. We have to do some practical, on-the-ground things that show we really are serious about this problem, not just making a show of it. We've always been against corruption; I find it irritating myself! You've heard me rail against corruption for years! I've also frequently checked my own family for any evidence of violation of law or discipline. It's easy to find major cases of corruption; they're sitting there just about anywhere you look. Our problem is a reluctance to crack down. And this costs us credibility because it makes us look like we're sheltering corruption. We have to meet this challenge and make good on our promises. We've got to handle cases just as the facts dictate; a spade's a spade and that's it! We've got to win back the people's trust. We should take a couple dozen cases of corruption, embezzlement, or bribe taking—some at the province level and some national—and pursue them vigorously and swiftly. We should make everything public, decide the cases strictly as the law prescribes, and enforce the appropriate punishments, no matter who may be involved.

"A good leadership team, committed to reform and opening, should do some obvious things to really open things up. It should never pass up an opportunity, it should persist, it should get going, it should realize reform and opening, large-scale opening. I once said we should try to create a few more Hong Kongs, and what I meant by that was that we should still insist on opening, we just can't close up again. We should open up even more than before. We can't develop if we don't open. We don't have much capital, but if we open up we can increase employment and tax revenue and get some money by leasing land. Then we can benefit from growing all kinds of industries and getting more revenue. Look at Hong Kong; look at the benefits we get from it. Without Hong Kong we'd have no good information, and that's just for starters. In short, we have to be bolder about reform and opening.

"Our comrades in the Secretariat and on the Politburo, especially its Standing Committee, are in charge of important things. In considering any issue, they should always take the long, broad view. Smaller issues often have to be subordinated to the large, long-term issues. This is a crucial point. Everyone has shortcomings. All of us here have shortcomings, and so do people elsewhere. And each person has shortcomings and weak points in his own individual way. Of course a person can have bigger or smaller shortcomings, or more or fewer of them, but nobody is free of them. There can be no doubt that in terms of its political experience and fighting experience, our current leadership team has shortcomings. This is a fact.

"The CCP did not really form a stable and mature leadership collective until Mao, Liu, Zhou, Zhu.[6] The earlier leadership was unstable and immature. Beginning with Chen Duxiu and extending to the Zunyi Conference, there was no truly mature leadership. There was a period back then during which the leadership of the working class was emphasized and the Party bent over backward to find workers to be leaders. Really mature leadership did not come until the generation of Mao, Liu, Zhou, Zhu. This group did well in its early years, but it later fell into the Cultural Revolution, which turned out to be a disaster. Hua Guofeng was only a transition that can't count as a generation. He had nothing of his own, only the 'two whatevers.' So the second generation was us, and now we're in transition to a third generation. We really need to come up with a new generation of leaders.

"This leadership will have to get the trust of people; it's got to earn trust both inside and outside the Party. This doesn't mean we have to be pleased with every member of the new team, but we have to be satisfied with the collective. Every

---

[6]Deng made a similar remark in his meeting with the Elders on May 27 (Chapter 8). But he was too modest to say in front of them what he proceeds to say in the next paragraph of this briefing: that among the second generation of leaders, he is considered the chief (*lingbanren*, literally, "foreman").—Comp.

member of the group will be subject to this or that kind of complaint from some quarter, and that's fine so long as there's general satisfaction with the group as a whole. In our second generation I am viewed as the chief, but we were always a kind of collective. The people were by and large satisfied with this collective of ours because we launched reform and opening, pushed the Four Modernizations, and produced tangible results. The third generation of leadership will also need to win people's trust and achieve tangible results. Don't try to close the door! China can't possibly fit back into its former isolation. That isolation also caused disasters like the Cultural Revolution. Under conditions like that there was no way the economy could develop, no way living standards could rise, and no way the country could grow stronger. The world is galloping forward these days, a mile a minute, especially in science and technology. We can hardly keep up.

"The third generation of leaders will have to win the trust of the people, get them to trust the new leadership group, and get them to unify around a Party Central they believe in. When we assemble the new group, we'll need to look for unusually broad vision and broad-mindedness. This is the most basic requirement for our third-generation leaders. The first generation, in its early period, did have this kind of broad mind and broad vision. The second generation basically had it, too. The same standard must be set for the third and later generations. New members of the Politburo, the Secretariat, and especially the Politburo Standing Committee should be selected with reform and opening in mind. The new leading body should do some obvious things to show it is sticking with reform and opening. The people won't rest easy until they see you are at the very least committed to reform and opening and are really going to carry through with those policies as set forth at the Third Plenum of the Eleventh Central Committee.

"When we look for new leaders, we should set aside all preconceptions and look for people who will be viewed as committed to reform. We also have to set aside grudges when we pick leaders and be ready to pick even those who may have opposed us in the past. Chairman Mao, over many years, dared to work with people who had opposed him. We also need to deepen our perspective in choosing leaders. This is one kind of reform: a reform of our thinking, a liberation of our thinking. I sincerely hope we will pay attention to public opinion when we choose leaders. We can't be petty-minded or emotional; we've got to handle questions with the poise of a statesman.

"One thing we should do is rely on well-recognized reformers, and another is to have the new leadership group make a few eye-catching moves in the direction of reform and opening. A new image can be created within three or six months.

The student demonstrators have been asking nothing more than that the reforms go further, and we can show them that, all right, we're doing it! This will bring us into harmony with them, and the gap between us will disappear naturally. That gap can't be closed by writing articles or holding debates. One of the causes of the current mess is that the growth of corruption has caused some people to lose faith in the Party and government. So first of all we need to clean our own house, and we need to be somewhat tolerant when the masses sometimes go a little too far. We have to handle things with a sense of proportion and not overreact.

"Everyone who enters the top levels at the Center has to stop being what he was before. He can't just stay at the same level because the responsibilities are different. He has to change himself, including his personal style, and he has to change consciously. It's not easy to lead a country like this! The responsibilities at the top are different. Breadth of vision is the most important thing: You have to keep the big picture in mind, look out into the world, and look into the future but at the same time keep your eyes on what's under your feet. You have to look at everything!

"There is another issue. Under no circumstances should we form any factions or cliques within the Party. This Party of ours has never formed factions in the strict sense of the word. When we were in Jiangxi in the 1930s, everyone spoke of me as part of the Mao faction. But that was never the case; there never was any Mao faction. It's crucial to be able to tolerate and unite with people on all sides of issues. My view of myself is that I'm far from perfect; I've made a lot of mistakes in my time and am hardly without faults. But one reason I have a clear conscience is that I've never gone in for cliques. In the past, whenever I got transferred from one job to another, I always went alone. I didn't even bring personal staff with me. Cliques kill you! They generate a lot of blunders and breed a lot of mistakes. You two are going to be out there on the firing line, working under pressure. That's why I'm telling you all this.

"As soon as the new leadership group can establish its authority, I'm going to retire. I'm set on it. I'm going to stay out of your business. Party Central has decided that Comrade Jiang Zemin will serve as the general secretary of the CCP Central Committee. I hope everyone will respect one another, tolerate one another, and not carp at one another. I hope everyone will be able to unite around Comrade Jiang Zemin as the core. As long as the leadership collective remains united and committed to reform and opening, even just a steady, gradual change will bring great changes to China within a few decades. The key is the leadership core. I hope you'll pass my words on to all the comrades who will be going to work in the new leadership structure. I view this as passing my political legacy to you."

May 31

Mixed developments at the end of May

Party Central had asked Wan Li, despite his prestige as chair of the Standing Committee of the National People's Congress, to remain in Shanghai until he had expressed support for its recent decisions on the turmoil. Wan made such a declaration on May 27 and returned to Beijing on May 31. Privately, however, he was reported to have expressed surprise that Jiang Zemin would be the new general secretary of the Party.

Meanwhile, students in Beijing continued to protest and to shout antigovernment slogans outside Zhongnanhai. Government officials who tried to dissuade them got nowhere. In an effort to counter the effects of the student protests, the Beijing Party Committee staged "rallies against the turmoil" among farmers on the outskirts of the city. These events, and the fact that they received extensive media coverage, seemed to signal that military action was impending. Indeed, top PLA leaders, including Chi Haotian, Yang Baibing, and Zhao Nanqi were busy visiting the martial law troops in an effort to boost their morale and to inspire them to consummate their "duty to guard the motherland."

In the provinces students were headed back to class in spite of some continuing small-scale demonstrations. On May 31 the Center received reports from twenty-three provinces. The report from Heilongjiang portrayed one of the calmest situations in the country. In the provincial capital of Harbin the student movement was fading away. Students were beginning to worry about their academic careers, according to the report. Some were depressed that the government's intransigence and intimidation tactics were working. Some were ready to go back to their studies so long as they were not regarded as traitors. On May 30 the authorities at Heilongjiang University had conducted a dialogue with the AFS on that campus. The officials were candid and reasonable and did not lecture the students, and as a result the student response was good. The two sides reached a compromise by which the authorities would allow the AFS to continue in operation until normalcy returned to campus, and the AFS agreed to disband after that. The student leaders also agreed to make a good-faith effort to recall the Harbin students who had gone to join the movement in Beijing. The next day many, though not all, of the boycotting students returned to class.

June 1

An emergency report
of the Beijing Party Committee

On June 1 every member of the Politburo received a copy of a report entitled "On the True Nature of the Turmoil." Ordered by Li Peng, the report had been drafted by Li Ximing and Chen Xitong in the name of the Beijing Party Committee and People's Government. Its aims were to establish the legality and necessity of clearing Tiananmen Square. It portrayed the unarmed students and the crowds of citizens who supported them as terrorists who were preparing an armed seizure of power. It also contained the first use of the phrase "counterrevolutionary riot."[7]

> Excerpts from Beijing Municipal Party Committee and Beijing People's Government, "On the true nature of the turmoil," report to the Politburo, June 1

Long-Term Occupation of the Square is a Primary Tactic of Those Who Have Organized and Plotted the Turmoil

Tiananmen Square is the symbol of the new China, the window through which China showcases itself to the world. Over the past month and a half, and especially since the declaration of martial law, a tiny minority has organized and plotted the turmoil and has made continuous occupation of the Square an important political tactic. These people's purposes are plain.

First, they want to use the Square as a command center for their final showdown with the Party and government. On May 25 a wall poster called "A Few Points on the Current Situation" and signed "With the soldiers" appeared at Beijing Normal University. It stated that "the Square has become like a great banner for democratic patriotism, the epicenter and heart of the national movement for democracy." It argued that "the student ranks must not withdraw. To do so would be to surrender and to dissipate the prestige and appeal the movement has thus far won. It would also remove the most clear focal point for the great outpouring of support that people from all corners of society have offered to the students, and it would be a major setback for the spread of this democratic and patriotic

---

[7]The government began official public use of this term when it actually used force starting June 3 (see Chapter 10).

movement to the rest of the country." Two days later another wall poster at Beijing Normal University said, "We should streamline the student ranks in Tiananmen Square and tighten up their organization to make their command structure more efficient and their actions more deft. In this way, the group can better maintain its roles as a key front and a communications center."

From this it is clear that a tiny minority intends to turn the Square into a center of the student movement and eventually of the entire nation. If the government takes action, this minority is prepared to "take strong responses" and to use the Square "to form an antigovernment united front." Events such as the following confirm this pattern: sending a Block-the-Army, Dare-to-Die Brigade to block the martial law troops, organizing riffraff to storm Public Security and media organizations, holding news conferences, and using the Flying Tiger motorcyclists to send messages. All these activities were plotted and commanded by the tiny minority in the Square.

Second, they continue to use the Square as a center for counterrevolutionary propaganda and the manufacture of rumor. Loudspeakers that the tiny minority has installed illegally blare around the clock, attacking Party and state leaders, putting out counterrevolutionary propaganda, and urging the overthrow of the current government. They repeatedly broadcast anticommunist, anti-China propaganda in distorted reports from the Voice of America and certain newspapers and radio stations in Hong Kong and Taiwan. Certain famous bourgeois liberals, backstage plotters, and hostile elements have used these facilities to blow the horns of illegal organizations like the AFS. From time to time inflammatory rumors emerge from the Square, things like "Some elder comrades oppose martial law" or "have asked to quit the Party," "Severe divisions and antagonisms over martial law have split the army," or "Wan Li was put under house arrest when he came back from China." All these rumors issue from the Square and then permeate Beijing and even spread across the country, hoodwinking the masses and students who do not know the true story.

Third, they use the Square as their base for provoking conflicts, exacerbating tensions, and trying to cause bloodshed in order to make a national and even international impact. They believe that "if we refuse to withdraw, the government will crack down" and that "fresh blood will wake up the people and lead to a split and collapse of the government." They use money from foreign and domestic reactionary forces to improve their equipment continuously, installing new communications devices and illegally procuring weapons. One moment they set up a so-called freedom camp on the Square, and the next they put up some kind of goddess statue in front of the Monument to the People's Heroes, as if they're trying to make American freedom and democracy their spiritual support.

Students from the Central Academy of Fine Arts made this goddess statue at the request of the AFS. They first called it the Goddess of Liberty, but later they felt this was too blatant and switched to Goddess of Democracy. At first they said it would stay in the Square only a day or two, but their "Manifesto on the Goddess of Democracy,"[8] which they read at the inauguration ceremony, contained not one word about removal. On the contrary, they clamored that it was "sacred, inviolable, and the people will never tolerate any destructive behavior toward it."

The purpose of the tiny minority that orchestrated the occupation of the Square was to make it the front-line command headquarters for the turmoil, the center for counterrevolutionary propaganda, the congregating site for various hostile forces, and the base for renewed assaults on the Party and government.

The Organizers and Plotters of the Turmoil Have Continued After Martial Law to Organize Illegal Activities

After martial law was declared the organizers and plotters of the turmoil pushed a new program that consisted mainly of two items: (1) abolish martial law and (2) dismiss Li Peng and make Yang Shangkun and Deng Xiaoping retire. They have pointed their spear directly at the Central People's Government, which was formed by the legitimate authority of the National People's Congress and which represents the interests of the people of the whole country. Their criminal intent to overthrow the government has been laid bare. In pursuit of their goal they continue to organize all manner of illegal activity, exploiting the self-restraint of the government and army since martial law. The AFS has called upon students in Beijing and around the country to carry out "a complete strike, empty the campuses, and deliver the message to all the people." Some students, under AFS instigation and using AFS funds, have carried posters and leaflets into factories, farms, and high schools in Beijing, agitating for strikes and campaigning noisily to "oppose martial law" and "overthrow Li Peng." Quite a few have also gone to network outside Beijing.

Some of the behind-the-scenes plotters and organizers got so excited they couldn't resist showing themselves in public. They began openly to organize or

---

[8]Probably the same document translated in part in Suzanne Ogden, Kathleen Hartford, Lawrence Sullivan, and David Zweig, eds., *China's Search for Democracy: The Student and the Mass Movement of 1989* (Armonk, New York: M. E. Sharpe, 1992), 342–343.

support illegal organizations: the AFS, the AFW, the Hunger Strike Command, the Tiananmen Square Headquarters, and the Association of Beijing Intellectuals. They also set up new illegal organizations such as the United Conference of Patriotic Beijing Organizations in Support of the Constitution and the Autonomous Association of Beijing Residents. Under the names of legal organizations such as the Institute for Economic Reform in China, the Development Research Institute of the State Council's Agricultural Research Center, and the Association of Young Economists, they blatantly sent telegrams to army units seeking to foment dissension in the ranks. They formed special teams on public opinion, prepared for the publication of underground newspapers, and engaged in underground activities aimed at overthrowing the government. They formed die-hard bands and took group oaths in secret, pledging "never to sell out conscience, never to yield to tyranny, and never to recognize the Chinese emperor of the 1980s." At a meeting with AFS leaders at the International Hotel, the general manager of the Stone Company[9] raised six conditions for withdrawal from Tiananmen Square: "(1) Pull back the army, (2) abolish martial law, (3) dismiss Li Peng, (4) retire Deng Xiaoping, (5) retire Yang Shangkun, and (6) restore Zhao Ziyang." They also planned a so-called grand triumphal march at midnight.

Marches and demonstrations of various sizes—all organized and plotted by the tiny minority—have continued without pause in Beijing since the declaration of martial law on May 20. Records show that until May 31 at least the following numbers of work units took part in marches and demonstrations: sixty-one schools of higher education, sixty-two news or publishing units, 112 units of central Party and government organizations, four democratic parties, and students from 332 universities outside Beijing. Among the more influential of the marches were those that combined the so-called Beijing worlds of learning, education, literature, and news on May 22 and 23, the so-called great march of all citizens in the city on May 25, and the so-called Great Global Chinese Protest Day on May 28. The number of participants in these marches grew successively smaller, however, as students increasingly grew tired and bowed out. Even as AFS broadcasts were continuing all-out efforts to spur students on, student demonstrators on the streets appeared sluggish and unorganized.

As the students and masses lost enthusiasm, and especially after Comrade Zhao Ziyang took sick leave from his post of general secretary, the organizers and plotters of the turmoil turned their hopes toward an emergency meeting of the

---

[9]Wan Runnan.

Standing Committee of the National People's Congress. Yan Jiaqi and Bao Zunxin launched an offensive and gained a response from Hu Jiwei, a member of the NPC Standing Committee. At Hu's suggestion the Social Development Research Institute of the Stone Company sent out letters soliciting opinions on a "Proposal Immediately to Convene an Emergency Meeting of the NPC Standing Committee." They used a variety of reprehensible means—such as collecting signatures that were intended for different purposes and signed on different dates, misleading signatories about what they were signing, or simply counterfeiting names—in order to gain momentum and to force the NPC Standing Committee to adopt their "suggestion." Yan Jiaqi and Bao Zunxin also published an "Indictment of Li Peng" in the Hong Kong *Mingbao* newspaper, calling on "all members of the NPC to cast a sacred vote to abolish martial law and to dismiss Li Peng as premier." Then a chorus of slogans rang out, rising and falling under the baton of the tiny minority: "Hold an emergency meeting of the NPC!" "Cancel the martial law order!" "Dismiss Li Peng!" "Down with Yang Shangkun and Deng Xiaoping!" For a time the bluster was so overwhelming that it seemed it might crush the whole city.

Foreign and Domestic Hostile Forces, Organizations, and Individuals Have Offered Great Spiritual and Material Support to the Turmoil

One important factor in this turmoil has been the large amount of spiritual support and material aid that various hostile forces, organizations, and individuals at home and abroad have directly or indirectly provided to the organizers and plotters. The Voice of America has played an extremely inglorious role, only adding fuel to the flames. Every day it airs three programs, totaling ten hours or more, manufacturing rumors and inciting turmoil. Newspapers in the United States, Hong Kong, and Taiwan pile up report after report filled with distortions. They provide a forum for the tiny minority of the so-called democratic elite to publish their speeches and articles calling for the overthrow of Communist leadership and the socialist People's Republic. People from the United States, the United Kingdom, and Hong Kong have donated more than a million U.S. dollars and tens of millions of Hong Kong dollars. Some of the funds have been used to purchase tents, food, computers, high-speed printers, and advanced communications equipment.

Reports indicate that expenditure in the Square reaches one hundred thousand yuan every day. Some of this money has been used to sabotage martial law;

a person who works to set up roadblocks to block military vehicles is paid 30 yuan per day, for example. A high military official in Taiwan launched a movement to "send love to Tiananmen" by contributing one hundred thousand Taiwan dollars.[10] A member of the KMT Central Committee has set up a so-called Foundation to Support the Mainland Democracy Movement and plans to raise 100 million Taiwan dollars. So far the AFS has received more than 10 million yuan in overseas donations. Certain work units in China, like the Stone Company, have provided material aid worth several tens of thousands of yuan. Chen Yizi, director of the Institute for Economic Reform in China, which is known as Comrade Zhao Ziyang's think tank, has also secretly passed money to the AFS after the declaration of martial law. These activities warrant deep reflection.

It is precisely this spiritual support and material assistance from hostile forces, organizations, and individuals both at home and abroad that has emboldened the AFS and other organizers and plotters of the turmoil to continue to occupy Tiananmen Square and to plot even more serious acts of provocation.

The Party and Government Have Done Much to End the Abnormal Situation in the Square, But to No Avail

Following the declaration of martial law in certain areas of Beijing, and thanks to the concerted efforts of martial law troops, the PAP, the public security police, and the broad population of workers, citizens, and government officials, traffic, communications, production, and order of life in the capital have gradually taken a turn for the better. Public sentiment has also subsided considerably. However, the activities of the tiny minority to generate turmoil have not paused for a single day. Their objective of overthrowing the leadership of the Communist Party has remained unchanged, and the situation is moving day by day in the direction of counterrevolutionary riot.

Between May 22 and May 24 the Beijing Red Cross sent three different groups of people to meet with students who were sitting in at the Square to try to persuade them to see the big picture and withdraw voluntarily.

Between May 23 and May 27 Party Central, the State Council, and the Beijing Party Committee and government sent several groups of officials to contact representatives of the students who were sitting-in, trying to persuade them to withdraw from the Square. These officials said that many of the students remaining in

---

[10]About U.S.$3,900.

the Square were willing to withdraw and that after some work on their thinking, withdrawal could have been a real possibility were it not for an isolated few who shouted things like "Anybody who signs an agreement with the government will be done in!" So these efforts failed.

Party officials, administrators, and teachers at the universities made trip after trip to the Square to do persuasion work. Many students took their advice and returned to their campuses, but some, once back on campus, returned again to Tiananmen Square to sit in. Many provinces and municipalities also sent officials to Beijing on special trips to urge non-Beijing students to return home.

Officers and soldiers of the martial law troops also held many discussions with the students to exchange views about the situation and to admonish them to take the big picture and the national interest into account and to withdraw from the Square as soon as possible.

All of this work yielded little, however. Incitement by the tiny minority and support from hostile forces at home and abroad kept many students lingering in the Square. The facts show that, contrary to what kindhearted people might imagine, this turmoil cannot be ended simply by a few government concessions or just by announcing martial law. The turmoil was planned, organized, and premeditated by a tiny minority of people who are allied with hostile forces at home and abroad. This group is determined to push for a final showdown with the Party and government. Kindhearted or wishful thinking will only invite further assaults on the Party and government. The longer this drags on, the more it will cost us.

The Organizers and Plotters of the Turmoil Are Doing Their Utmost to Launch Violent Revolution

Initially, the tiny minority of organizers and plotters of the turmoil refrained from alliances with riffraff and did not engage in beating, smashing, and robbing. But as the situation evolved, they became more and more aware of the utility of these dregs of society and decided to join forces with them. They mustered local hooligans, ruffians, runaway criminals, unreformed ex-prisoners, and any others who harbored deep-seated hatred of the Communist Party and the socialist system. They pulled together terrorist groups like the Flying Tiger Group, the Block-the-Army, Dare-to-Die Brigade, and the Army of Volunteers. They boasted of plans to kidnap or detain Party and state leaders and to seize power as if they were storming the Bastille.

On May 30 the *Beijing Daily* published a news report on "The Short-Lived Flying Tiger Group" that exposed how the tiny minority manipulated this group as its communications and propaganda machine and how it was to serve as a special detachment to storm the Capital Iron and Steel Corporation and the Public Security Bureau and Traffic Brigade in Daxing County. The Tigers' activities also disturbed local residents at night. After eleven of their leaders were legally detained by Public Security authorities for investigation, some students went that same afternoon to sit in and protest at the entrance to the Municipal Public Security Bureau. The number of protesters grew to one thousand. Before long three leaders of the AFW were arrested, and at 11 that evening two hundred to three hundred students marched out of the Peking University campus holding up banners that read "Protest government kidnapping of workers" and "When lips perish, teeth get cold"[11] and chanting "On to Public Security to demand immediate release!" On May 31 illegal organizations like the AFS and the AFW continued a siege of the Public Security Bureau. This makes it quite clear that the tiny minority has joined forces with the riffraff of society.

The tiny minority also has actively instigated armed counterrevolutionary riots. On May 25 the AFS held a battlefront meeting at Tiananmen Square and decided to intensify its radical action. On May 26 it put forth a proposal to militarize itself and to dispatch five groups to mobilize the masses across the country. On May 30 a wall poster at the Beijing Institute of Aeronautics bore the title "If . . . a Single Spark Can Start a Prairie Fire:[12] An Analysis of the Prospects for Chinese Political Development Today." The poster said,

> If the top leaders of the Communist government are going to throw the wheels of history into reverse, they might force the people beyond the limits of endurance and to a point where the people rise up without the slightest fear and risk their heads and their blood to organize with open pride an armed force that could be called a "people's army" to contend with and struggle against the corrupt forces of the Communist Party. This armed force would consist of students, intellectuals, workers, farmers, and other patriotic forces from all sectors of society. It is also possible, in the event that the entire Chinese populace utterly loses faith in the Communist Party, that this army could unite with all patriotic forces with whom unity is possible, including the KMT in Taiwan, to carry out its struggle.

[11] Meaning the loss of one's close partner endangers oneself.
[12] Title of a famous letter written by Mao Zedong referring to the origins of popular revolt. See *Selected Works of Mao Tse-tung*, vol. 1 (Peking: Foreign Languages Press, 1965), 117–128.

The tiny minority clamors that it will "settle accounts when autumn has passed,"[13] and "settle them without fail." They want to get the Party, and they want to get the government. They have prepared a list of officials marked for execution. This plainly shows that the tiny minority is resolved to fight to the death against the Party and government. They will not give up until they get what they want.

Accordingly we propose that Party Central, the State Council, and the Central Military Commission take swift and decisive measures immediately to suppress the counterrevolutionary turmoil in Beijing.

Western infiltration, intervention, and subversion

On June 1 the State Security Ministry submitted a report to Party Central on ideological and political infiltration from the West. It had been prepared on instructions from Li Peng, and like the "Emergency Report" of the Beijing Party Committee, it was sent to every member of the Politburo. It was viewed as providing one of the best justifications for the military action that was about to occur.

> Excerpts from State Security Ministry, "On ideological and political infiltration into our country from the United States and other international political forces," report to Party Central, June 1

The big socialist country of China has always been a major target for the peaceful evolution methods of the Western capitalist countries headed by the United States. Since the founding of the People's Republic of China and after the failure of U.S. armed intervention, each American administration has pursued the same goal of peaceful evolution and has done a great deal of mischief aimed at overthrowing the Communist Party and sabotaging the socialist system. Carter preached "peace diplomacy," Reagan promoted "democratic movements," and Bush emphasizes "human rights diplomacy." The phraseology may vary, but the essence remains the same: to cultivate so-called democratic forces within socialist countries and to stimulate and organize political opposition using catchwords like "democracy," "liberty," or "human rights." These people also try to win over or

---

[13]See footnote 41 in Chapter 4 on the phrase "settle accounts when autumn has passed." Here the government's "Emergency Report" inverts the usage, claiming it is the students who are likely to seek revenge on the government.

split off wavering elements within the Party in hopes of fomenting peaceful evolution inside the Party, thereby causing or forcing changes in the nature of political power in our socialist state. They have done several things in pursuit of this counterrevolutionary strategy:

1. *Ideological and cultural infiltration.* No American administration, including the Bush administration, has ever relaxed the policy of pursuing ideological and cultural infiltration of socialist countries. An American diplomat has intimated privately that the U.S. government now recognizes that its earlier policies of military encirclement and economic blockade of China have all failed. From now on, its only option is to avail itself of China's reform and opening to carry out spiritual infiltration of China through economic and cultural exchange. They want to use American civilization to pull China toward liberalization.

American methods of ideological and cultural infiltration vary widely. The Fulbright program is one example. After China and the United States established diplomatic relations the United States dispatched 162 professors to twenty-four major universities across China through this program. The United States Information Agency also sends about twenty visiting scholars to China every year to give lectures at universities and research institutes in various parts of the country. Although many of these people are friendly toward our state, still, as a policy of the United States, the purpose of the program is clear. On May 6, 1989, an American government agency wired the following rather self-congratulatory statement to the U.S. embassy in Beijing:

> Given what we now see in China, it seems the professors we have sent to China have played a crucial role in transmitting American civilization, introducing American culture, and promoting democracy in China.

In recent years the United States has also sent missionaries to China to do secret evangelical work. They have come in the guise of teachers, businessmen, doctors, and technicians. One American organization, called Practical Education, has promoted American popular psychology and a number of religious theories under the cover of training teachers for China's benefit. A member of this group working at the Beijing Foreign Languages Institute boasted that "we are going to change China within three years." Their goal is to turn Chinese students into "new modern people with a different belief system."

Another example of programmatic infiltration is the Voice of America (VOA). VOA is the U.S. government's only international radio station with global reach. It is a major channel for political and ideological infiltration into socialist countries. Right from the founding of our People's Republic, VOA's

Chinese-language service has been an instrument of the U.S. government's psychological warfare against our country. In the 1950s VOA earned a notorious reputation for blatant anticommunist propaganda. It was perceived by fair-minded people the world over "as the American government's tool for overthrowing Communist parties and as the headquarters of rebellion." In the late 1970s VOA sought to reshape its image and therefore began to change its strategy. It adopted a new method of propaganda, adding more so-called news value and fact base to its coverage. After normalization of diplomatic relations between China and the United States VOA began to offer music, English lessons, and feature programs that introduced American life. The aims were to please listeners and to attract an audience. But this programming change signaled no change whatever in the goal of bewitching the Chinese audience, or "getting the audience to accept our viewpoint."

2. *The determination to cultivate pro-American forces.* The U.S. government believes that most of China's current leaders were educated in the Soviet Union and that none was educated in the United States. It wants to recruit and train a Chinese group of "U.S. experts" who can understand American policies and will be pro-American. To achieve this objective the United States has promoted "American studies institutes" at several Chinese universities. It supplies large quantities of books and materials and each year invites more than one hundred visitors to the United States through an "International Visitors' Program." Most participants are from economic, cultural, educational, and propaganda agencies of our Party and government and are either influential or potentially influential in policymaking. The program specially targets young people who are in power or who are soon likely to move into power, inviting them to travel and study in the United States. The hope is that "some day high-ranking officials will emerge from the ranks of these people." A former U.S. ambassador to China said, "We can't just look at the present, but must take the long view in evaluating the effectiveness of inviting Chinese to visit the United States."

The cultivation of a pro-America group among Chinese students studying abroad is a long-term U.S. strategy. Former American president Reagan once said at a confidential meeting that "we should view the Chinese students as a strategic investment." In 1982, after learning that there were 6,500 Chinese visiting scholars and students in the United States, Reagan said, "It would be better to have 65,000; this is a long-term investment." The United States puts high priority on winning over our students. First, the Americans focus on our best students and on the children of high-ranking officials; they try to build personal ties to them and hope they will assume important posts after returning to China. Second, they use various means to exert ideological influence on our students, helping them learn more about American democracy, liberty, and material civilization. "When they gradually become the pillars in Chinese society, their style of thinking will hasten China's evolution to capitalism." Third, they conduct counterespionage among our students. The FBI's Committee for the Management of Foreign Students handles this.[14] Even the former Japanese prime minister Nakasone was envious of American success. In a classified speech in 1985 he said the Americans had started early and made great progress in working on Chinese students; Japan had fallen behind and should work hard to catch up, to upgrade its "human investment" in China.

3. *The effort to extend feelers to the top Chinese leadership by every possible means.* Some people in the United States have homed in on leaders of certain Chinese institutions as special targets for cultivation and persuasion. These Chinese institutions include the Institute for Economic Reform in China, which is under the State Commission for the Restructure of the Economic System, the Development Research Institute of the State Council's Agricultural Research Center, CITIC's International Affairs Research Institute, the Stone Company's Social Development Research Institute, the Beijing Association of Young Economists, and others. The U.S. embassy has frequent contacts with more than twenty people from these institutions.

From 1981 to 1988 one CIA agent from the U.S. embassy in China had, by himself alone, nearly fifty contacts with fifteen people associated with the Economic Restructuring Commission, and through these contacts he gathered information on their interests. The United States believes that the education, experience, and ways of thinking of these people will come to have a subtle but strong influence on the highest Chinese leadership and decisionmaking bodies. The United States often invites people associated with the Restructuring Commission to visit the United States as "international visiting scholars." In 1988 twelve people associated with that commission received invitations to the United States, and eleven made the trip. In recommending Lou Jiwei, formerly from the Research and Investigations Department of the General Office of the State Council,[15] the same CIA agent from the U.S. embassy wrote that inviting Lou to visit

[14]In response to an inquiry from Perry Link as to whether such a committee exists, the FBI, on January 8, 2000, replied, "We do not have materials that address your topics of interest."
[15]At the time of his 1987 trip to the United States, Lou Jiwei was a deputy section chief in the Investigations and Research Department of the Office of the State Council. In 1988 he was transferred out of Zhongnanhai and before long was appointed to serve as deputy head of the System Reform Office in the Shanghai Municipal People's Government. In 1991 he returned to Zhongnanhai, and at the time of writing he serves as the vice minister in charge of day-to-day business in the Ministry of Finance.—Comp.

the United States "will help us to open the mysterious door—which so far has been tightly closed—of China's State Council."

In early 1986 George Soros, founder of the American-based Foundation for Chinese Reform and Opening, indicated that he was willing, as he had earlier been for Hungary, to fund research for China's reform and opening at a rate of no less than one million U.S. dollars per year. In June of that year Soros exchanged views on this topic with Chen Yizi, who was visiting Budapest as part of a delegation that Soros was funding. When Chen returned to China, he reported his conversation with Soros to Bao Tong. Then, in October, Chen met again with Soros, this time in Beijing, and signed an agreement with him. Li Xianglu of the Association of Young Economists was assigned to establish a temporary Beijing office for the foundation. According to Chen Yizi, Bao Tong notified Comrade Zhao Ziyang during this setup phase, and Zhao approved. Soon thereafter George Soros sent a message that he was interested in establishing personal relations with our leaders to exchange views on problems of economic reform in China.

By May 1989 Soros had wired a total of U.S.$2.5 million to China. The funds were used mainly in four areas: (1) travel expenses for people from the Institute for Economic Reform in China and its subsidiaries to visit the United States; (2) the purchase of U.S.$500,000 worth of Western books on the social sciences; (3) a U.S.$250,000 fund for the establishment of a political salon–type of social club; (4) certain cultural enterprises. Our investigations revealed that Liang Heng,[16] the personal representative of the foundation chairman George Soros, was a suspected U.S. spy. Moreover, four American members of the foundation's advisory committee had CIA connections.

In August 1988, when Liang Heng came to Beijing, the Central Committee was meeting at Beidaihe, and Bao Tong and Chen Yizi were both there. When Liang arrived in Beijing, he asked to go to Beidaihe and was turned down. Three days later Liang claimed he had talked to Chen Yizi by telephone and had learned something about the Beidaihe meeting—that there were disputes within Party Central, that things in China were worse this year than last, that complaints were everywhere, that the intellectuals were unhappy with the general state of things, and so on. Liang was scheduled to stay in Beijing for two weeks, but after only one he announced his business was finished and returned to the United States ahead of schedule. When Soros learned that conditions in China had changed, that the people he needed to be in touch with had lost their leadership positions, and that

---

[16]A Chinese living in the United States, coauthor with Judith Shapiro of *Son of the Revolution* (New York: Knopf, 1983).

his objectives in China were no longer attainable, he wrote a letter on May 23, 1989, to the Chinese chairman of the foundation,[17] proposing that the agreement end and the foundation close. George Soros had finally shown his true colors.

4. *The targeting of "future leaders."* Americans have established training and exchange centers in China to try to "cultivate" China's "future leaders." In the past few years they have set up, one after another, various "training and exchange centers" in Dalian, Nanjing, Beijing, and Guangzhou. Such training has advantages for us, but the Americans have an agenda of their own. The U.S. embassy in China is very serious about the Training Center for Industrial and Technological Management in Dalian, which it considers an outpost for monitoring China's internal affairs as well as "a window on the whole American political system" for China's future leaders. An American who works at that center has admitted that "this might be the most subversive thing we have ever done in the Communist world."

5. *Using economic and technological aid to make China dependent on the United States.* The U.S. State Department believes the United States has benefited from aspects of the Sino-Soviet confrontation over the past twenty-odd years. Now, with China's reform and opening, it believes the United States should adjust its China policy and work hard to build economic and technological cooperation between the two countries in order to use America's economic and technological power to influence the Chinese government and people. The aim is to make China dependent on the United States economically and, eventually, politically as well.

.   .   .

It is worth noting that ideological and political infiltration by U.S.-led international forces has become especially visible and blatant during this turmoil. It has taken the form of direct intervention and open support for the turmoil. During the disturbances Western political forces injected themselves in many ways—doing everything short of sending troops—all hoping to overthrow the socialist system in our country. The main signs of this were:

1. *Aggressively collecting information on internal politics and the turmoil in our country.* As soon as the turmoil in Beijing began, President Bush personally ordered the U.S. consulate general in Hong Kong to monitor events in China closely. He also dispatched to Hong Kong a small group charged with gathering information on China's internal affairs. Meanwhile, personnel at the U.S. em-

---

[17]Yu Rongguang, who was secretly a deputy minister of state security.—Comp.

bassy in Beijing constantly came out to watch the situation on the streets, and the consulate general in Shenyang recruited two or three foreign teachers at each of the large and medium-sized cities in northeast China to help in collecting information.

2. *Using all propaganda methods to help the students spread information and extend their power, and constantly intensifying the conflict by giving them pointers on policy and creating rumors.* As soon as Comrade Hu Yaobang died, foreign journalists appeared at Tiananmen Square. When university students arrived at the Monument to the People's Heroes to present wreaths on the afternoon of April 17, foreign journalists were right there to take photos, make video- and audiotapes, and do interviews with students. After the students set up their illegal student associations, foreign journalists vied with each other to report all the "declarations," "appeals," "plans," and whatnot. They also attended their news conferences and rallies and volunteered to transmit their messages all across China and to the whole world. When Peking University, Qinghua University, and three other universities called their "indefinite student boycott," the foreign press announced these plans in advance. They did the same for the demonstrations of April 27 and May 4. At every student event, foreign journalists were there ahead of time. During this period VOA spread many rumors; for example, that the workers at Capital Iron and Steel were going on strike, that the Party and government were compiling a blacklist, and so on.

At a number of crucial points they used various propaganda facilities to mislead the public egregiously. On the morning of April 20, for example, some people stormed the Xinhua Gate. All of a sudden, rumors of an "April 20 bloodbath" were spreading everywhere. Beginning April 27, as the government and students were planning a dialogue, the *World Journal*[18] in New York, in its May 1 edition, quoted a U.S. government official as saying, "The U.S. government believes that this is a cunning trick of the Communist authorities and that it might lead to splits in the student leadership and help the Communists to divide and manipulate the students." This was a flagrant attempt to poison the atmosphere of the dialogue and the relationship between our government and the students. When news of the students' hunger strike broke on the Square, the Western public-opinion machines worked overtime to depict the "solemn and tragic" atmosphere and the "widespread support" of the masses, adding fuel to the flames and encouraging the students to fast to death.

---

[18] *Shijie ribao*, a Chinese-language daily newspaper.

3. *Direct instigation by American organizations and personnel in China.* Every night for four weeks, a ranking official of the U.S. embassy in China, who said, "The American government is extremely concerned about this significant movement," met with participants in the student movement. The director of the Beijing office of the U.S.-based Committee on Scholarly Communication with the PRC[19] invited students from Peking University, People's University, and the Beijing Foreign Languages Institute to his residence many times for discussions, thereby exerting influence on them.

American students studying at Peking University, People's University, Beijing Language Institute, and nine other universities went everywhere fanning the flames. American journalists in Beijing maintained close contact with the leaders of the AFS. Journalists from the Associated Press and *Newsweek* told Wuerkaixi and others that the United States would, if necessary, provide asylum for them or help them go to the United States to study. And not only all this—they also tried to build counterrevolutionary armed forces in China. The China Study Group of the U.S. State Department submitted a report in May claiming the democracy movement in China was part of the world democracy movement. It said that China faces many problems, that racial conflicts could grow stronger, and that fifty million of China's rural dwellers have become migrant workers, constituting an antisocialist force. The report suggests that the United States look for an appropriate opportunity to provide the floating population with weapons so that it can form an armed force against the government.

4. *Exploiting Chinese students in the United States for collaboration.* After the turmoil in Beijing began, an International Scholarly Center in Newton, Massachusetts, opened four international telephone lines that Chinese students in the Boston area could use free of charge. Since May 18 Chinese students from universities such as MIT and Harvard have been in continuous contact with students in Beijing, Western Europe, and Japan. Some Chinese students from schools such as the University of California and Stanford University specialize in collecting rumors about personnel changes in the Chinese Party and government leadership; then they use the fax machine of a Chinese-language newspaper in San Francisco to send messages to universities in more than twenty big cities, such as Beijing, Shanghai, and Nanjing, misleading and agitating the public.

5. *Inciting reactionary organizations like the Chinese Alliance for Democracy to meddle in the turmoil.* The Chinese Alliance for Democracy (CAD) is a counter-

[19]Perry Link.

revolutionary organization that the scum of our nation has drummed up under the care of the U.S. government.[20] As soon as the student movement started, the CAD responded by issuing an "Open Letter to the University Students of China" signed by people such as Chen Jun, Liu Xiaobo, and CAD chairman Hu Ping.[21] The letter urged the Chinese students to "solidify the connections you have made during the student movement into a more permanent structure." The Democratic Party of China, which was founded by 108 members of the CAD, also sent a "Letter to All Chinese Compatriots" openly demanding that the Four Basic Principles be abolished. The CAD also allied with the pro-Taiwan Chinese Benevolent Association to set up a Committee to Support the Chinese Democracy Movement. They stayed in close touch with such leaders of the AFS as Wuerkaixi and Wang Dan, providing them with advice, economic aid, and propaganda equipment.

.   .   .

Reactionary forces in Taiwan and Hong Kong have run wild during this turmoil. The KMT Mainland Work Committee and intelligence agencies like the Military Intelligence Agency in the Ministry of Defense have dispatched several dozen special agents to China. In addition to collecting information, they have carried out psychological warfare, and some have even tried to contact KMT elements who have been dormant since 1949. They tried every way they could think of to infiltrate the student movement. Their main activities have been the following:

1. *Setting up special groups to direct and organize subversive operations on the mainland.* Soon after the start of the student movement, Taiwan spy organizations and hostile foreign organizations distributed propaganda materials through various means, sowing discord between the Party and the intellectuals and attacking the struggle against bourgeois liberalization. The Taiwan intelligence agents put out ten of what they called "letters of support to mainland intellectuals who dare to struggle for freedom and democracy." The letters praised Fang Lizhi, Liu Binyan, and Wang Ruowang as "pioneers of a new system and the advance guard of anticommunist national salvation." They spurred the student movement by calling it a dynasty-changing movement against "autocracy." Some

---

[20]See footnote 6 in Chapter 4.
[21]Pro-democracy activists then in the United States. Liu returned to China in late May and played a role described later in this chapter.

of their handouts and reactionary publications say, "Give up the Four Basic Principles, drive out Marxism-Leninism, annihilate the Communist Party, welcome the Three People's Principles, and expel the Dengist Gang." They attacked the Party, calling it a "dictatorial, autocratic, savage, and fascist party."

They have attacked our country as having "rule of a minority over the majority" and have urged the students to "form propaganda teams, emerge from the campuses and ally with the workers' movement, and pursue demonstrations, marches, public speeches and student strikes." The Taiwan agents and hostile foreign organizations have rushed to send people into China to network. They have come in as tourists, businessmen, visitors of relatives, and other guises. Their mission has been "to get in touch with the student movement," to incite "student leaders" to revolt, to link up with all illegal organizations, and to turn the "student movement" into a so-called all-out movement against tyranny.

2. Providing funds and supplies for the turmoil. The Taiwan regime has organized all parts of society in active support of the turmoil. The general secretary of Taiwan's National Security Council, Jiang Weiguo, launched a project to "send love to Tiananmen" by donating one hundred thousand Taiwan dollars. The Chinese Refugees Relief Association in Taiwan then contributed two hundred thousand Taiwan dollars, and Li Changyi, a KMT Central Committee member, initiated a campaign to raise 100 million Taiwan dollars for a "foundation to support the democracy movement on the mainland." Certain people in Hong Kong raised 21 million Hong Kong dollars to support the student hunger strike. Later they claimed to have raised 30 million Hong Kong dollars and planned to bring all of it into China in separate installments. They have already sent a support group to Beijing carrying one million Hong Kong dollars. And they have provided not only large sums of cash but various kinds of modern equipment such as high-power binoculars, walkie-talkies, and tents—all for the purpose of preparing the protesters sitting in on the Square for "protracted warfare."

3. Manufacturing and spreading numerous rumors. As early as the afternoon of April 17, when the students had just arrived at Tiananmen Square to offer wreaths, more than ten Hong Kong journalists from the *South China Morning Post* and elsewhere began to interview them. On April 22, soon after the illegal student organization was set up, the *Hong Kong Standard* published an editorial saying, "The student organization established two days ago is the first unofficial student organization since the founding of the PRC forty years ago; the student movement in this country has entered a new era."

When some students and masses stormed the Xinhua Gate early in the early morning on April 20, the Hong Kong press went out of its way to publicize the event. A press photographer from the Hong Kong *Express News*,[22] after taking photos in spite of orders not to, was stopped and taken away from the site. Later he filed a report saying he had been knocked to the ground and beaten by more than twenty Public Security agents in uniform. On April 20 the *Express News* published a solemn protest. Shortly thereafter, the Hong Kong *Economic Daily*[23] also claimed that their reporters had been beaten and detained. This led the Hong Kong Journalists' Association to send a letter to Xu Jiatun "demanding that Beijing explain" and further fanning the flames of public sentiment in both Hong Kong and China. The Hong Kong and Taiwan media issued many distorted and inflammatory reports about all the major events, including the demonstrations of April 27 and May 4, the student hunger strike, and the declaration of martial law.

4. *Sending special agents to meddle directly in the turmoil.* When the student movement began, KMT intelligence agencies on Taiwan escalated the delivery of inflammatory and reactionary propaganda to the mainland. At the same time they directed their underground agents on mainland to meddle directly in the turmoil in an attempt to expand the so-called democracy movement into an all-out "movement against communism and tyranny." They ordered the underground agents to watch the turmoil closely and collect information on it to send back to headquarters in Taiwan. Gradually our security agencies detected many of these counterrevolutionary activities of the underground KMT agents, and some of the agents who meddled in the turmoil were forced to surrender. On May 19 and May 27 the State Security Bureau in Beijing legally detained Taiwan KMT agents Wang Changhong, Qian Rongmian, and Liang Qiang. Other provinces and municipalities also cracked many KMT spy cases. All of the arrested confessed their crimes of meddling in the turmoil.

Many facts demonstrate that the international monopoly capitalists and hostile, reactionary foreign forces have not abandoned for a moment their intent to destroy us. It is now clear that murderous intent has always lurked behind their protestations of peace and friendship. When the opportunity arises they will remove the facade and reveal their true colors. They have only one goal: to annihilate socialism.

---

[22] *Kuaibao*, a Chinese-language daily newspaper.
[23] *Jingji ribao*, a Chinese-language newspaper.

Martial law troops await orders

On June 1 headquarters of the martial law troops sent a report to the Politburo and the Central Military Commission stating that "the officers and soldiers of the martial law troops are ready both spiritually and physically and wait only for orders from the Central Military Commission" before moving to clear Tiananmen Square. The report told the top decisionmakers that the choice was now theirs.

> Excerpts from Martial Law Headquarters, "Resolutely obey orders from Party Central, use concrete actions to stop the turmoil," report to Politburo and Central Military Commission, June 1

Despite obvious distractions during recent days, all of the officers and soldiers of the martial law troops have kept their fighting spirit strong and their morale high. Because of their high level of political consciousness and their solid political foundation—which are the results both of their regular education and of the timely and effective thought work that was done in preparation for their martial law assignment—they are absolutely obedient to the command and direction of Party Central and the CMC.

In the beginning some officers and soldiers viewed the turmoil with kind-hearted wishes and had some doubts about martial law. But headquarters has insisted on unifying the minds of the officers and soldiers of the martial law troops in the spirit of Party Central and under the command of the CMC. Our education campaign centered tightly on one theme: This is turmoil; martial law is necessary. All officers and soldiers were organized to study conscientiously the April 26 *People's Daily* editorial "The Necessity for a Clear Stand Against Turmoil." They also studied the speeches that Chairman Yang Shangkun and Premier Li Peng made at the meeting of Party, state, and military officials in Beijing. The messages from the expanded emergency meeting of the Politburo and the expanded emergency meeting of the CMC were also transmitted immediately to officers at the army, division, brigade, and regiment levels. When the troops were blocked on the streets and in the suburbs, officers at the various levels took the risk of going to the scenes in person. They boarded vehicles to transmit and propagate the principles in the Party documents. They helped the soldiers gain a deep understanding of the severity and complexity of the struggle and clarified the necessity and the legality of martial law. Party committees at army, division, brigade, and regiment levels unanimously expressed their determination to ignore all distractions, to support all CMC martial law decisions unconditionally, and to prove through concrete actions that they are firmly in line with Party Central and are absolutely reliable. Thanks to our strong emphasis on political and ideological education, the entire officer corps and all rank-and-file soldiers are able to stand firm in the midst of turmoil, fight the turmoil without mercy, and maintain iron unity in face of extremely complicated political storms. We have created the conditions necessary for a swift and thorough pacification of the turmoil in the capital. They are these:

1. *A sense of political responsibility to carry out martial law that has resulted from targeted political and ideological education.* In response to shifting situations and duties, headquarters asked each unit to undertake extensive and meticulous surveys on the thinking of all officers and soldiers. Based on the results we then produced outlines of targeted political and ideological education and instructed leaders and officers at the army, division, brigade, and regiment levels to go down into each unit and educate the troops in political doctrine, the current situation, their mission, and our glorious tradition. This work strengthened the officers' and soldiers' sense of political responsibility and guarantees a high level of unity and stability in the martial law troops. It also has inspired in all the officers and soldiers an enthusiasm to carry out martial law and to fulfill their mission with selfless dedication.

2. *Insistence on the standard of 100 percent effectiveness and zealous pursuit of crucial security targets.* The crucial security targets are the very ones that the hostile forces themselves regard as crucial in their troublemaking and sabotage. It is therefore a most difficult duty to safeguard these targets. To ensure absolute security, we first mobilized army, division, brigade, and regiment leaders to examine carefully headquarters' directives on security work. Then we examined carefully all possible eventualities, including illegal assemblies, sieges by mobs, rifle fire, bombings, arson, poisoning, and natural calamities, in each case working out well-conceived security plans and making sure all officers and soldiers are clear about security assignments, courses of action, the chain of command, guidelines for dealing with emergency situations, and the relevant rules and discipline.

We also have worked hard on security training aimed at enhancing response capability in times of emergency. Each level—army, division, brigade, and regiment—has concentrated strongly on the special nature of its assignments and has studied the possible means through which the hostile elements might generate turmoil. Each has gone through strict training in various tactics, techniques, and coordination for security and defense, has organized thirty-two large-scale exercises, and has worked out twelve contingency plans for accidental emergencies. These measures have raised the defense capability of all officers and soldiers. Finally, we have organized inspections to ensure the consolidation of our security work. After the martial law troops had received their assignments, we focused on inspecting their understanding of them. We examined their alertness level on holidays and the readiness of their weapons, equipment, and materials on sensitive days. All of this was to ensure that all troops are well supplied, are in good communication with each other, and are ready to move under any circumstances. Our quick response capabilities have been enhanced.

3. *Strict controls to guarantee stability and security within the martial law troops themselves.* The troops carrying out martial law come mostly from rural or mountainous areas and are entering an urban center. They have moved from a familiar to an unfamiliar environment, and this has given rise to the "five difficulties and one peculiarity." The five difficulties are

- resisting the strong negative influences in the bustling city,
- handling personal problems while staying on duty for such a protracted time,
- keeping things at a high standard while serving in such a dispersed pattern for such a long time,
- safeguarding weaponry when guns are allocated to the company level, when bombs are readied for use, and when troop movements are frequent, and
- controlling vehicles inside a bustling city when movements are frequent and there are no parking lots.

The peculiarity is the special status of the troops because of the political nature of this assignment.

The five difficulties and one peculiarity make management of the martial law troops more difficult and present new challenges. To assure the quality of management under such special circumstances, headquarters has done investigations and studies, has proactively explored new ideas and summarized past experiences, and has formulated "Administrative Rules for the Martial Law Troops" that establish airtight control "at all times, of all personnel, in all directions." In order to ensure the stability and safety of the martial law troops, three control standards have been set up to provide orderly management of personnel, guns, and vehicles:

A. Control of personnel. First, all officers and soldiers were organized to do careful study of the General Political Department's document called "Regulations on Private Correspondence of Army Personnel with People in Foreign Countries and Hong Kong, Macao, or Taiwan." They also studied the department's Ten Prohibitions and their regulations on secrecy. This study instilled in the minds of all officers and soldiers the concepts of preventing corrosion, infiltration, and subversion by the enemy. Extensive discussions were held on the revolutionary outlook in life, on how to distinguish glory from shame and beauty from ugliness, and on how to deal correctly with the connections between gain and loss and between pain and pleasure. At the same time the troops gained a stronger sense for law and discipline and achieved better self-control. "Every person is subject to control, every activity has organization, and every action fits the rules and regulations" became the norm. For the few problematic individuals, "three-in-one" squads of officials, company commanders, and ideological activists, by teaching in small groups, seized the initiative in turning their thought around, solved problems while they were still nascent, and thoroughly eliminated all unsafe elements.

B. Control of guns. A system of checking on and responsibility for all guns at all levels relies on leaders at every level to seize and solve the slightest sign of a problem before it can become an actual problem. Leaders must raise this issue at every meeting, and officers must check on weapons and ammunition control every time they come down to the companies. At the company level a system of daily checking—using written records and reports—has been established. So far the martial law troops have moved a company 110 times and have done 176 fully armed maneuvers, and not a single gun or single bullet is missing, nor has any incident of gun theft emerged.

C. Control of vehicles. In order to prevent vehicle accidents, education and rectification procedures have been undertaken in the ranks of drivers in all troops. Drivers have been made to study the relevant regulations of headquarters and the traffic rules of the capital city. Drivers accordingly have upgraded their sense of discipline and have achieved a good driving style. Systems have been established to plan all vehicle usage at the levels of army, division, brigade, and regiment through approval by commanders. All motorcades are led by officers, all vehicles are checked on fixed schedules, reports are required upon the completion of all trips, and all repairs and maintenance are kept up to date.

4. *Using mass work to carry forward actively our exemplary tradition and work style in civilian-military cooperation.* All officers and soldiers clearly recognize the great importance of mass work in the fulfillment of their special mission in such an unusual situation in the capital. They realize that stability in the capital will depend crucially upon close civilian-military relations and upon public under-

standing of Party Central's decision on martial law. This is the foundation and guarantee of the success of the security mission of the martial law troops. Accordingly, the martial law troops have launched extensive mass work following the guidelines of "proactivity, tolerance, and strict discipline." They are flexibly applying past experience in civil-military cooperation and have been able to enhance rapport among Party, government, and people in the capital. They have created the image of a powerful and civilized army, increased their political influence, and contributed to order and stability in the capital.

Student activities in Beijing and the provinces

According to reports from the Xinhua News Agency and the Public Security and State Security Ministries, the students on the Square appeared on June 1 to be exhausted, disorganized, and unlikely to take any more large-scale actions. Their demands had dwindled to avoidance of retaliation and, at most, legal status for their autonomous organizations. Student leaders were seeking to continue the struggle, perhaps scaling it down to some kind of "nonviolent noncooperation" movement, but were also preparing to withdraw from the Square. There were signs of internal strife within the student leadership: Some students had apparently tried to kidnap Chai Ling and Feng Congde, two of the student leaders.

On June 1 the *People's Daily* carried a letter signed by eight Peking University professors who called upon the students to return to their studies.[24] The same day, one former student demonstrator published an article in the *Beijing Daily* entitled "Tiananmen, I Cry for You" in which he described messy, chaotic conditions on the Square, expressed his disillusionment with the whole movement, and called upon the remaining protesters to withdraw. These two articles triggered a wave of protests from students in the Square and on the campuses. Some demanded the eight professors be fired, and one wall poster suggested the *Beijing Daily* be burned down. That evening Liu Xiaobo, a lecturer at Beijing Normal University, and Hou Dejian, a popular singer from Taiwan, said they would begin a hunger strike the next day.

The Jiangsu Provincial Party Committee filed an emergency report on June 1 stating that five hundred to nine hundred students from universities in the Nanjing area had set off by foot on a Long March for Democracy to Beijing to petition the government for democracy. They demanded, among other things, that the government recognize the student movement as patriotic and democratic, that Li Peng resign, that martial law in Beijing be rescinded, that the press be free, and that

[24]This was the text of the poster signed by eight professors that appeared on the Peking University campus on May 29.—Comp.

the government enter dialogue with the students. Upon receiving the emergency report, Premier Li Peng called the Jiangsu Party Committee to ask local officials to take all necessary means to stop the march. The committee immediately dispatched high-ranking officials and police to the scene and notified the authorities in locales along the route of the march that the marchers were to be stopped and were to be denied accommodations. Nine students were persuaded that day to return to their campuses. The rest forged on despite the impediments.

A June 1 report from the State Security Ministry said that work units in Henan Province were investigating workers who had joined antigovernment demonstrations. Authorities required these workers to produce self-criticisms before they could receive their monthly bonuses, and any who refused were threatened with loss of their jobs. When workers expressed resentment of these strong-arm tactics, leaders of the official trade union advised local officials to back off from confrontation.

Public Security reports from the provinces of Sichuan and Anhui on June 1 both told of accidents in which university students lost their lives. In the Sichuan incident demonstrators from the Sichuan Institute of Industry outside Chengdu were trying to flag down trucks for rides into the city. One truck failed to stop in time, killing one student and seriously injuring five. Following the incident more than a thousand students protested by setting up roadblocks and cutting off traffic for more than ten hours. In Anhui about fifteen hundred students demonstrated in support of students in Shanghai. Later a second demonstration of about three hundred paid homage to a student who was killed after falling beneath a train on his way home from Beijing, where he had gone to support the students at Tiananmen.

Other reports on June 1 told of continuing protest activities in fifty-seven cities across the country. The recurring theme was to continue class boycotts and create empty campuses. Wall posters in Tianjin and Taiyuan promoted the nonviolent noncooperation movement, and many students took this phrase as their watchword as they marched out of their schools. Students from Shanxi University caused local authorities to worry when they proposed another "long march" to Beijing. One Tianjin wall poster called on people to boycott government treasury bonds and to withdraw their savings from banks. In Changsha more than three hundred students began a hunger strike in front of the provincial government building.

June 2

The CCP Elders decide to clear the Square

On the morning of June 2 Party Elders Deng Xiaoping, Li Xiannian, Peng Zhen, Yang Shangkun, Bo Yibo, and Wang Zhen met with the Standing Committee of the Politburo, which at that juncture consisted only of Li Peng, Qiao Shi, and Yao Yilin. The topic was how to "put a quick end to the tur-moil and restore order in the capital," and the result was a decision to clear Tiananmen Square.

Li Peng opened the meeting with a report on developments, during which he quoted and par-aphrased from the Beijing Party Committee and State Security Ministry reports excerpted above. After Li's report the Elders voiced their anger at the foreign and domestic enemies who were manipulating the students, and their conviction that there was no choice left but to clear the Square by force. Nonetheless, most of the Elders hoped the job could be done without casualties, and Deng Xiaoping repeated his insistence that nothing should stop the momentum of reform and opening. After the Elders had spoken, the Politburo Standing Committee members acted: Li Peng formally moved the clearing of the Square, and Qiao Shi and Yao Yilin cast their votes in favor. Deng closed the meeting by ordering Yang Shangkun to pass the decision along to the Central Mil-itary Commission for execution.

> Excerpts from Party Central Office Secretariat, "Minutes of important meeting, June 2, 1989," document supplied to Party Central Office Secretariat for its records by the Office of Deng Xiaoping

Li Peng: "Yesterday the Beijing Party Committee and the State Security Min-istry both submitted reports to the Politburo. These two reports give ample evi-dence that following the declaration of martial law a major scheme of the organizers and plotters of the turmoil has been to occupy Tiananmen Square to serve as a command center for a final showdown with the Party and government. The Square has become 'a center of the student movement and eventually the entire nation.' Whatever decisions the government makes, strong reactions will emerge from the Square. It has been determined that, following the declaration of martial law, events such as putting together a dare-to-die corps to block the martial law troops, gathering thugs to storm the Beijing Public Security Bureau, holding press conferences, and recruiting the Flying Tiger Group to pass mes-sages around were all plotted in and commanded from the Square. The reac-tionary elements have also continued to use the Square as a center for hatching counterrevolutionary opinion and manufacturing rumor. Illegal organizations such as the AFS and AFW have installed loudspeakers on the Square and broad-cast almost around the clock, attacking Party and state leaders, inciting overthrow of the government, and repeating over and over distorted reports from VOA and the Hong Kong and Taiwan press.

"The reactionary elements believe the government will eventually crack down if they refuse to withdraw from the Square. Their plot is to provoke conflict and create bloodshed incidents, clamoring that 'blood will awaken the people and cause the government to split and collapse.' A few days ago these reactionary elements openly erected a so-called goddess statue in front of the Monument to the People's Heroes. Today they are planning to launch another hunger strike in the Square. In any case, the sacred and solemn Tiananmen Square has been reduced to a frontline command center for the turmoil, the center for nationwide transmission of counterrevolutionary opinion, the gathering place for hostile forces foreign and domestic, and a counterrevolutionary base from which to launch furious attacks on the Party and government.

"A number of illegal organizations have now exposed themselves publicly: the Autonomous Federation of Students, the Autonomous Federation of Workers, the Hunger Strike Headquarters, the Tiananmen Square Headquarters, and the Association of Beijing Intellectuals, the United Conference of Patriotic Beijing Organizations in Support of the Constitution, the Autonomous Association of Beijing Residents, and so on. They have formed special teams on public opinion, prepared for the publication of underground newspapers, and engaged in underground activities to overthrow the government. 'They formed die-hard bands and took group oaths in secret,' and they tried to instigate mutiny among martial law officers and soldiers. They are swollen with arrogance.

"Many materials show that hostile forces, organizations, and individuals both at home and abroad have directly or indirectly intervened by providing a large amount of spiritual support and material aid to the organizers and plotters. VOA every day airs three programs that total ten hours or more and that manufacture rumors and incite turmoil. Newspapers in the United States, Hong Kong, and Taiwan pile up report after report filled with distortions. When the turmoil began employees of the U.S. embassy started to collect intelligence aggressively. Some of them are CIA agents. Almost every day, and especially at night, they would go and loiter at Tiananmen or at schools such as Peking University and Beijing Normal. They have frequent contact with leaders of the AFS and give them advice. The Chinese Alliance for Democracy, which has directly meddled in this turmoil, is a tool the United States uses against China. This scum of our nation, based in New York, has collaborated with the pro-KMT Chinese Benevolent Association to set up a so-called Committee to Support the Chinese Democracy Movement. They also gave money to leaders of the AFS.

"As soon as the turmoil started, KMT intelligence agencies in Taiwan and other hostile forces outside China rushed to send in agents disguised as visitors, tourists, businessmen, and so on. They have tried to intervene directly to expand

the so-called democracy movement into an all-out 'movement against communism and tyranny.' They have also instructed underground agents to keep close
track of things and to collect all kinds of information. There is evidence that KMT
agents from Taiwan have participated in the turmoil in Beijing, Shanghai, Fujian,
and elsewhere. We have cracked some of these cases and are currently pursuing
others. The KMT from Taiwan have provided all kinds of funds and have established a Foundation to Support the Mainland Democracy Movement. Hong
Kong has also raised about thirty million Hong Kong dollars, and there are reports
that these funds have begun to be funneled into China. Reactionary organizations
have provided not only large sums of cash but various kinds of modern equipment such as high-power binoculars, walkie-talkies, and tents that have been used
during the turmoil. It is becoming increasingly clear that the turmoil has been
generated by a coalition of foreign and domestic reactionary forces and that their
goals are to overthrow the Communist Party and to subvert the socialist system."

Wang Zhen: "Those goddamn bastards! Who do they think they are, tram-
pling on sacred ground like Tiananmen so long?! They're really asking for it! We
should send the troops right now to grab those counterrevolutionaries, Comrade
Xiaoping! What's the People's Liberation Army for, anyway? What are martial law
troops for? They're not supposed to just sit around and eat! They're supposed to
grab counterrevolutionaries! We've got to do it or we'll never forgive ourselves!
We've got to do it or the common people will rebel! Anybody who tries to overthrow the Communist Party deserves death and no burial!"

Li Xiannian: "The account that Comrade Li Peng just gave us shows quite
clearly that Western capitalism really does want to see turmoil in China. And not
only that; they'd also like to see turmoil in the Soviet Union and all the socialist
countries of Eastern Europe. The United States, England, France, Japan, and
some other Western countries are leaving no stone unturned in pushing peaceful
evolution in the socialist countries. They've got a new saying about 'fighting a
smokeless world war.' We better watch out. Capitalism still wants to beat socialism in the end. None of their plots—using weapons, atomic bombs, and hydro-
gen bombs—ever succeeded in the past. Now they're trying the Dulles thing.[25] We
can't do anything about other countries, but we have to control things in China.
China can't do without socialism. Without socialism, could the Chinese people
speak with dignity? Without the Communist Party, without socialism, without
reform and opening, would we have today's China? Our People's Republic was

---

[25]That is, "peaceful evolution." See footnote 19 in Chapter 5.

built with the blood of more than twenty million revolutionary martyrs. The achievements of socialist construction came after decades of hard struggle, especially during the last ten years of reform and opening. We can't allow turmoil to destroy all this overnight. The people will never allow it. China will lose all hope if we let turmoil have its way or open the door to capitalism. The nature of this turmoil is extremely clear: Its bottom line is death to our Party and state."

Deng Xiaoping: "Comrade Xiannian is correct. The causes of this incident have to do with the global context. The Western world, especially the United States, has thrown its entire propaganda machine into agitation work and has given a lot of encouragement and assistance to the so-called democrats or opposition in China—people who in fact are the scum of the Chinese nation. This is the root of the chaotic situation we face today. When the West stirs up turmoil in other countries, in fact it is playing power politics—hegemonism—and is only trying to control those other countries, to pull into its power sphere countries that were previously beyond its control. Once we're clear on this point, it's easier to see the essential nature of this issue and to sum up certain lessons. This turmoil has taught us a lesson the hard way, but at least we now understand better than before that the sovereignty and security of the state must always be the top priority. Some Western countries use things like 'human rights,' or like saying the socialist system is irrational or illegal, to criticize us, but what they're really after is our sovereignty. Those Western countries that play power politics have no right at all to talk about human rights! Look how many people around the world they've robbed of human rights! And look how many Chinese people they've hurt the human rights of since they invaded China during the Opium War!"

Bo Yibo: "Western capitalism has decided on peaceful evolution as its long-term strategy against socialist countries. They're not the United Nations, but they want to do things that not even the United Nations can do: interfere in the internal affairs of other countries! One way or another they're always imposing sanctions or launching armed invasions. They think they've got supreme power, think they're actually the world's police. What right do they have to meddle in China's internal affairs? Who bestowed that right on them? We'll never accept any actions that violate international principles! And we never bow to pressure—not past, not present, not future. Never."

Peng Zhen: "This month or more of turmoil lets us see how important stability is. Stability is the crucial issue if China's going to shake off poverty and get to the Four Modernizations. Comrades Xiaoping, Xiannian, and Chen Yun have said it many times, and long before this incident occurred: China can't achieve anything without a stable environment. We had no real choice about martial law; we had to do it. Comrades Xiaoping, Xiannian, Chen Yun, and I all believe that from now on, whenever necessary, we must annihilate every sign of turmoil immediately and decisively as soon as it emerges. We must nip all problems in the bud, before outsiders can interfere, if we are going to guarantee state sovereignty."

Deng Xiaoping: "Two conditions are indispensable for our developmental goals: a stable environment at home and a peaceful environment abroad. We don't care what others say about us. The only thing we really care about is a good environment for developing ourselves. So long as history eventually proves the superiority of the Chinese socialist system, that's enough. We can't bother about the social systems of other countries. Imagine for a moment what could happen if China falls into turmoil. If it happens now, it'd be far worse than the Cultural Revolution. Back then the prestige of the old generation of leaders like Chairman Mao and Premier Zhou still loomed. We talked about 'full-scale civil war,' but actually no large-scale fighting took place, no true civil war ever happened. Now it's different, though. If the turmoil keeps going, it could continue until Party and state authority are worn away. Then there would be civil war, one faction controlling parts of the army and another faction controlling others. If the so-called democracy fighters were in power, they'd fight among themselves. Once civil war got started, blood would flow like a river, and where would human rights be then? In a civil war, each power would dominate a locality, production would fall, communications would be cut off, and refugees would flow out of China not in millions or tens of millions but in hundreds of millions. First hit by this flood of refugees would be Pacific Asia, which is currently the most promising region of the world. This would be disaster on a global scale. So China mustn't make a mess of itself. And this is not just to be responsible to ourselves, but to consider the whole world and all of humanity as well.

"On the topic of mistakes, we indeed have made them. I said two years ago that our biggest mistake was in education. We haven't educated our kids and students enough. A lot of thought work has been neglected, and a lot of things have not been made clear. Some people, like Zhao Ziyang, have even joined the side of the turmoil, which makes it even more our own fault that people misunderstand. We must cast a sober and critical eye upon ourselves, review the past while looking to the future, and try to learn from experience as we examine current problems. If we do this, it's possible a bad thing could turn into a good one. We could benefit from this incident. A majority of the people will sober up, and the students' thinking will sober up, too. After we put down the turmoil, we'll have to work hard to make up all those missed lessons in education, and this won't be easy. It'll take years, not months, for the people who demonstrated and petitioned to change their minds. We can't blame the people who joined the hunger strike, demonstrated, or petitioned. We should target only those who had bad intentions or who took the lead in breaking the law. Education should be our main approach to the students, including the students who joined the hunger strike. This principle must not change. We should set the majority of the students free from worry. We should be forgiving toward all the students who joined marches, demonstrations, or petitions and not hold them responsible. We will mete out precise and necessary punishments only to the minority of adventurers who attempted to subvert the People's Republic of China. We cannot tolerate turmoil. We will impose martial law again if turmoil appears again. Our purpose is to maintain stability so that we can work on construction, and our logic is simple: With so many people and so few resources, China can accomplish nothing without peace and unity in politics and a stable social order. Stability must take precedence over everything."

Li Xiannian: "We've had martial law for half a month now. The people have seen the forbearance of Party Central and the State Council. The majority of the Beijing citizens have begun to understand the martial law troops. In some other cities around the country students have begun to lose interest in demonstrations and marches. The initial thrill is over. But we're like a person with an illness: He may look okay, but the root of the disease is still inside him and could make him sick again. Tiananmen Square is now that root of our turmoil-disease. Just look at that thing—like neither human nor demon—that they've erected there in our beautiful Square! Are the people going to accept that? Absolutely not! We're never going to get a voluntary withdrawal from the Square. Tiananmen has been polluted for more than a month now, ravaged into a shadow of itself! We can't breathe free until the Square is returned to the hands of the people. We have to pull up the root of the disease immediately. I say we start tonight."

Yang Shangkun: "What's happened in the past month or so shows that the sit-in protesters and hunger strikers are not going to withdraw voluntarily. We've reached a point where we really do have to take action. We should keep a clear view of the situation, though: Whatever else we say, a majority of the workers, farmers, intellectuals, and students all favor and support reform. The fact that we're going to clear the Square, restore order, and stop the turmoil in no way means that we're giving up on reform or closing our country off from the world."

Deng Xiaoping: "No one can keep China's reform and opening from going forward. Why is that? It's simple: Without reform and opening our development stops and our economy slides downhill. Living standards decline if we turn back. The momentum of reform cannot be stopped. We must insist on this point at all times.

"Some people say we allow only economic reform and not political reform, but that's not true. We do allow political reform, but on one condition: that the Four Basic Principles are upheld. We can't handle chaos while we're busy with construction. If today we have a big demonstration and tomorrow a great airing of views and a bunch of wall posters,[26] we won't have any energy left to get anything done. That's why we have to insist on clearing the Square."

Yang Shangkun: "Troops have moved into the Great Hall of the People, Zhongshan Park, the Working People's Cultural Palace, and the Public Security Ministry compound. The thinking of all officers and soldiers has been thoroughly prepared for a clearing of Tiananmen Square. After nearly half a month of political thought work, all officers and soldiers have deepened their understanding of the severity and complexity of this struggle and have comprehended the necessity and the legality of martial law. All troop units entrusted with the martial law mission have expressed their resolution to overcome distractions and unconditionally to obey and carry out the orders of Party Central and the Central Military Commission. They are ready to prove with concrete action that the martial law troops stand in solidarity with Party Central. By now all the troop units have worked out security plans to ensure that orders are executed quickly no matter what the circumstances may be. Since arriving in Beijing all troops have implemented airtight control 'at all times, of all personnel, in all directions.' All the personnel, guns, and vehicles are under tight control, ensuring the solidarity and security of the troops themselves. Moreover, all troops have initiated civilian-military cooperation work, and this has improved their rapport with the masses from all stations in society and has given them a good social image. For these reasons I am fully confident that we can clear the Square in a peaceful way."

Wang Zhen: "We should announce in advance to those people occupying the Square that we're coming in. They can listen or not listen as they choose, but then we move in. If it causes deaths, that's their own fault. We can't be soft or merciful toward anti-Party, antisocialist elements. Military orders have to be inviolable, otherwise we have no way to enforce discipline."

Peng Zhen: "I agree that the clearing should be done as soon as possible. It's good for Beijing, good for the whole country, and good for overall stability. I

[26]Deng here uses *"daming, dafang, dazibao,"* a phrase that he used in the late 1970s to describe—and from then on to prohibit—Cultural Revolution–style "chaos."

think the students will withdraw once we've given them a clear explanation. And that's because the clearing isn't aimed at any individual student; it's only to restore the Square to its original condition and to restore normal social life and order in Beijing."

Li Peng: "I strongly urge that we move immediately to clear Tiananmen Square and that we resolutely put an end to the turmoil and the ever expanding trouble."

Qiao Shi: "The facts show that we can't expect the students on the Square to withdraw voluntarily. Clearing the Square is our only option, and it's quite necessary. I hope our announcement about clearing will meet with approval and support from the majority of citizens and students. Clearing the Square is the beginning of a restoration of normal order in the capital."

Yao Yilin: "I agree with Comrade Xiannian that the clearing should happen as soon as possible."

Deng Xiaoping: "I agree with all of you and suggest the martial law troops begin tonight to carry out the clearing plan and finish it within two days. As we proceed with the clearing, we must explain it clearly to all the citizens and students, asking them to leave and doing our very best to persuade them. But if they refuse to leave, they will be responsible for the consequences. Comrade Shangkun, I suggest you call for a meeting of the comrades in the Central Military Commission to transmit the decision of the Politburo Standing Committee and the suggestions everyone here has made. I also suggest Comrade Li Peng give a briefing on this meeting to Comrade Chen Yun and others."

That afternoon Yang Shangkun called the meeting that Deng Xiaoping had requested, after which an order went out at midnight June 2 for some of the martial law troops that were still in the outskirts of Beijing to move into the city and to advance toward designated security targets.

Unrest continues

According to State Security reports of June 2, the day began in Beijing with more than a thousand students cruising the streets on bicycles to protest the *Beijing Daily* article "Tiananmen, I Cry for You."

In the afternoon singer Hou Dejian and three intellectuals—Liu Xiaobo, Zhou Duo, and Gao Xin—formally announced that they were beginning their hunger strike. Their written declaration[27]

---

[27]Excerpted in Han Minzhu, ed., *Cries for Democracy: Writings and Speeches from the 1989 Chinese Democracy Movement* (Princeton: Princeton University Press, 1990), 349–354.

called upon the Chinese people to observe their duty as responsible citizens by supporting a peaceful democratization process. They called for an independent civil society that could check and balance the government and a government that used democratic procedures rather than arbitrary authority. "We would rather have ten devils checking on one another," their declaration read, "than one angel holding absolute power." Their statement criticized the government for suppressing a popular movement, but it also criticized the students for neglecting democratic procedures in spite of their democratic ideals. This announcement ceremony drew the attention of high-ranking people in the Party and figured in their final decision on the afternoon of June 3 (see Chapter 10) to clear the Square by force.

Reports from the localities on June 2 said that most students in medium-sized cities were returning to class but that in the big cities student resistance remained strong.

On the first night of their Long March for Democracy students from Nanjing had covered forty kilometers in spite of university officials who tagged along trying to dissuade them and police who tried to block their way. On the morning of June 2 they seemed exhausted. One hundred eighty decided to give up, but the others wanted to continue. In an attempt to boost their morale, the Nanjing branch of the AFS on June 3 held a news conference to report on the march, announced a citywide empty-campus campaign, and dispatched another hundred students as reinforcements.

June 2 reports on the foreign press included an interview the dissident astrophysicist Fang Lizhi had given to a Japanese newspaper.[28] Fang compared the student movement to its predecessor by seventy years, the famous May Fourth Movement, and praised its calls for freedom of speech, press, and assembly. He also called on elderly Party leaders to retire and commented that the government's handling of the protests may have had more to do with the power struggle inside the Party than with students on the streets. This interview may have sealed Fang's fate as a target for arrest in the wake of the military crackdown.

Meanwhile, the government was making an effort to turn popular sentiment in an anti-American direction. In government-organized rallies Uncle Sam appeared as the behind-the-scenes manipulator of Chinese dissidents.

---

[28]An interview given by Fang to a Taiwan newspaper on June 2 is in Ogden et al., *China's Search,* 353–356.

June 3

"Student weaknesses exposed by their movement"

On June 3 a report in the Hong Kong newspaper *Mingbao* attracted the attention of China's leaders. It was based on an interview with two student activists in the Square. They said that they favored withdrawing but that less-sophisticated students from the provinces, who now formed a majority of those sitting in, were against it. These students were unwilling to return home without winning the struggle against the government. The two activists complained that although the student movement was supposed to be for democracy and freedom, the students often behaved undemocratically, seizing vehicles or demanding the right to ride for free, and the student leaders took power without election and got involved in the power struggle between Zhao Ziyang and Li Peng, which should have been none of the student movement's business. One of the students, Cheng Zhen, expressed her worry that there were now all kinds of people in the Square. The situation, she said, was complex, and she hoped the student movement would not splinter and as a result provoke an actual turmoil.

CHAPTER TEN

June Fourth

EDITORS' NOTE: As soldiers entered the city in plainclothes and in uniform, instead of meeting with popular understanding they encountered anger and some violence. The leaders' hopes of avoiding bloodshed foundered on this resistance and the troops' emotional reaction to it.

After initial clashes between citizens and troops, on the afternoon of June 3 the leaders decided they now confronted a "counterrevolutionary riot" that would have to be put down by force. Yang Shangkun relayed Deng Xiaoping's instruction that in Tiananmen Square itself there must be no bloodshed. The government's internal reports claimed that this goal was achieved. Most of the deaths occurred as troops moved in from the western suburbs toward Tiananmen along Fuxingmenwai Boulevard at a location called Muxidi, where anxious soldiers reacted violently to popular anger. Troops moving on the Square negotiated a peaceful withdrawal of the people remaining there as dawn broke on June 4, but some killing of both citizens and soldiers continued during the morning hours. The populace was outraged, and rumors spread of casualties in the thousands.

In the following days the government confronted international and domestic reactions so vociferous that they threatened to fulfill Deng Xiaoping's worst fear: that a bloody denouement would make it impossible to continue reform at home and the open-door policy abroad.

June 3

The gathering storm

Reports on June 3 from the State Security and Public Security Ministries described a violent reaction by the citizens against what seemed to be efforts by martial law troops to sneak into the city in plainclothes.[1]

The reaction was triggered by an accident that began around 11 P.M. on the night of June 2. A Mitsubishi jeep belonging to the People's Armed Police ran onto a sidewalk at Muxidi, killing three pedestrians and seriously injuring one. Despite the late hour, five hundred or six hundred people quickly gathered. Police cordoned off the area and sent the dead and injured to a nearby hospital. The crowd's suspicions were aroused because the police took the perpetrators away without conducting an investigation and because the jeep had no license plates. People started to say the martial law troops were infiltrating the city in plainclothes. Some in the crowd forced their way past the police to search the jeep. They emerged with military uniforms, maps, and mobile telephones, which confirmed their suspicions.

Word spread quickly. Between midnight and 1 A.M. on June 3 the AFS, the AFW, and students groups at Peking University, People's University, and Beijing Normal University issued emergency broadcasts over the loudspeaker systems. They said large contingents of armed troops were entering the city and pressing toward the Square. They said that the troops were traveling in military and civilian vehicles and on foot—some in uniform and armed with rifles, others in plainclothes and carrying knives, metal clubs, and shovels[2]—and that students, teachers, and citizens should mobilize to set up roadblocks.

Groups of students and citizens quickly converged on dozens of major intersections. In the hours around dawn, throughout Beijing, army vehicles were blocked or overturned, tires were punctured, and approximately five hundred soldiers were surrounded in pockets. Thousands of college students rode their bicycles in a protest on Chang'an Boulevard. At approximately 5 A.M. the Voice of the Movement public-address system in the Square announced, "We have won! Look, the students and the local citizens are united!" At 6:15 A.M. sixty college students showed off helmets and boots they had confiscated from troops.

Later in the morning an electric bus lodged sideways across a road at Xinjiekou blocked a southbound bus filled with dozens of soldiers who were out of uniform. In the face of the angry crowd, they did not dare get off the bus.

[1]In the first section of Chapter 6, martial law headquarters informs Deng Xiaoping and Yang Shangkun that when the time comes their strategy will be to infiltrate the city inconspicuously. The strategy is also discussed in other sections of Chapter 6.
[2]Presumably to clean up the mess in the city.

All along the route from Jianguomen to Dongdan, east of Tiananmen Square, citizens and students surrounded and isolated small groups of soldiers. Some threw rocks. On the Jianguomen overpass citizens demanded to know why soldiers were opposing the people. Half a dozen soldiers were stripped of their shirts. Troops approaching Tiananmen from the south were stopped when citizens surrounded twenty-one army trucks and asked the soldiers questions about their units, their objectives, and their weapons; the soldiers did not reply. Most of the soldiers in this army had, according to reports, been separated from their units during the advance. They were beaten when they went to get their ammunition, and some of the wounded soldiers were kidnapped when they headed for the hospital. Beijing security personnel were beaten when they went to aid the soldiers. The ground along the way was littered with crushed provisions.

At the Xidan intersection just west of Tiananmen, dozens of soldiers sat behind closed windows in a bus that had been surrounded since midnight; citizens vented their anger by banging on the windows, cursing, and spitting. Near the Capital Theater three buses were surrounded, and the air was let out of their tires. Students boarded a bus that was carrying military gear and supplies, found guns, and displayed the guns on top of the bus. Just west of the Xinhua Gate of Zhongnanhai, the air was released from the tires of four buses carrying soldiers in civilian clothes.

Around 1 P.M. a bus filled with munitions was stopped at Liubukou (at the southwest corner of Zhongnanhai) and surrounded by several thousand people. Young men who looked like students climbed atop the bus, flashed the "V-for-victory" sign, and raised military helmets on the tips of bayonets to show the crowd. Armed police and public security personnel tried in vain to disperse the crowd. Down the street, at Xinhua Gate, a wall of PLA soldiers blocked students and citizens to prevent them from entering. At 2:30 P.M. several hundred armed policemen and public security personnel fired tear gas into the crowd of protesters, forcing them to scurry for cover. But the demonstrators counterattacked, and the police had to withdraw into Zhongnanhai through the West Gate, which they closed behind them. The demonstrators outside the gate threw rocks. Large crowds converged at the Great Hall of the People, at the Radio, Film, and Television Ministry, and the CCP Propaganda Department.

About 5 P.M. the Tiananmen command center of the AFW began supplying students and citizens with "self-defense weapons" including cleavers, clubs, steel chains, and sharpened bamboo poles. The AFW amassed more than a thousand people to knock down a wall at a construction site near Xidan, where they picked up bricks and steel beams for use in counterattack.

Around 5:30 P.M. three thousand martial law officers and soldiers who were awaiting orders began a retreat from the Great Hall of the People, eliciting applause from students and citizens. At 6 P.M. a crowd that gathered in Chang'an Boulevard was so thick that cyclists had to dismount. People brought their children out to witness the extraordinary event.

Throughout the day organized teams of demonstrators and scattered groups of students and citizens filled the Square and the length of Chang'an Boulevard, bringing traffic to a halt. Toward evening the atmosphere grew increasingly tense, with loudspeakers in the Square broadcasting reports of new clashes between police and citizens.

The order to clear the Square

At 4 P.M. on June 3 Yang Shangkun, Li Peng, Qiao Shi, and Yao Yilin called an emergency meeting on the deteriorating situation. Others in attendance were Qin Jiwei, Li Ximing, Hong Xuezhi, Liu Huaqing, Chen Xitong, Chi Haotian, Yang Baibing, Zhao Nanqi, Luo Gan, Zhou Yibing,[3] and Liu Zhenhua.[4]

> Excerpts from Party Central Office Secretariat, "Minutes of the Politburo Standing Committee meeting," June 3

Yang Shangkun: "I really did not want to call this meeting. The situation has become extremely volatile—beyond what anybody's goodwill can handle. We have to settle on some resolute measures for clearing the Square. Let's begin with you, Comrade Li Peng."

Li Peng: "Late last night a counterrevolutionary riot broke out in Beijing. A small handful of counterrevolutionaries began spreading rumors and openly violating martial law. They were brazen and lawless, and their behavior has aroused extreme indignation among the masses. We must resolutely adopt decisive measures to put down this counterrevolutionary riot tonight. Comrade Xitong, could you please update everyone on what's been happening since last night?"

Chen Xitong: "Comrade Li Peng has it exactly right: A counterrevolutionary riot has broken out in Beijing. At 10:55 last night there was a major accident at Muxidi involving a Mitsubishi jeep that the Fifth Squad of the Beijing People's Armed Police had lent to a CCTV photography crew working on the fortieth anniversary of the founding of the People's Republic. The jeep ran up onto a sidewalk, killing three people and injuring one. The instigators of the riot then grabbed their chance to start a rumor that martial law troops had already entered the city and that this advance vehicle had run over citizens; this rumor incited gullible students and citizens to block the PLA at intersections and to prevent them from entering town to enforce martial law. Early this morning people set up

---

[3]Commander of the Beijing Military District and deputy commander of the martial law troops.
[4]Political commissar of the Beijing Military District.

roadblocks at Jianguomen, Muxidi, Xinjiekou, Hufangqiao, Nanheyan, Xidan, and other major intersections to halt troop transports. People surrounded and beat soldiers and punctured tires on trucks. Some of the rioters even seized munitions and military provisions. Offices of the Central Government and other major organs came under siege. The lawless elements used all manner of despicable means to defame our soldiers, attack the martial law troops, and stir up trouble between the troops and the citizenry. The situation has become utterly intolerable. So we have to take resolute measures at whatever cost to put down this counterrevolutionary riot. Commander Zhou will tell you the ways in which the troops have been blocked; he knows these details much better than I."

Zhou Yibing: "Some of the martial law troops reached their assigned locations in the downtown area early this morning, but nearly all troops ran into resistance and blockades by students and citizens, some of whom spat at the soldiers and tried to wreck army trucks. Some troops who were trapped on the Jianguomen overpass were stripped of their shirts and publicly humiliated. Citizens blocked more than four hundred soldiers at Chaoyangmen and stoned them. A crowd at Hufangqiao discovered a plainclothes unit and chased its members in all directions. At this moment crowds are keeping soldiers at the west side of the Great Hall of the People from joining their units, and soldiers at Nanlishi Road have been forcibly searched. In a word, the martial law troops are swallowing their anger and fuming inside, struggling to restrain themselves. The political thought work people are working hard to try to keep things calm."

Li Peng: "OK, now everybody knows how things stand. At Liubukou, in broad daylight and right under our noses, the rioters seized armored cars and set up machine guns on top of them, just to show off. They even launched an attack on Zhongnanhai's Xinhua Gate and West Gate. The situation was so tense at Zhongnanhai that tear gas had to be used on the rioters. Can we tolerate all this? Yes, we can—and we have tolerated it. But we mustn't let these rioters get the idea they can take advantage of the government. That's why we have to be absolutely firm in putting down this counterrevolutionary riot in the capital. We must be merciless with the tiny minority of riot elements. The PLA martial law troops, the People's Armed Police, and Public Security are authorized to use any means necessary to deal with people who interfere with the mission. Whatever happens will be the responsibility of those who do not heed warnings and persist in testing the limits of the law."

Yang Shangkun: "You all get the picture now. I've also just been in touch with Comrade Xiaoping, and he has asked me to relay two points to everyone. The first is: Solve the problem before dawn tomorrow. He means our martial law troops should completely finish their task of clearing the Square before sunup. The second is: Be reasonable with the students and make sure they see the logic in what we're doing; the troops should resort to 'all means necessary' only if everything else fails. In other words, before we clear the Square, we should use TV and radio to advise students and citizens to avoid the streets at all costs, and we should ask the ones who are in the Square to leave of their own accord. In short, we've got to do an excellent job on propaganda work; it has to be clear to everyone that we stand with the people, and we must do everything we possibly can to avoid bloodshed. . . . The Martial Law Command must make it quite clear to all units that they are to open fire only as a last resort. And let me repeat: No bloodshed within Tiananmen Square—period. What if thousands of students refuse to leave? Then the troops carry away thousands of students on their backs! No one must die in the Square. This is not just my personal view; it's Comrade Xiaoping's view, too. So long as everybody agrees, then it will be unanimous."

The decisions of the meeting were

1. At 9 P.M. on June 3 PLA martial law troops and People's Armed Police, assisted by Beijing Public Security, will begin to put down the counterrevolutionary riot that has erupted in the capital.
2. Martial law troops will arrive at the Square at 1 A.M. on June 4 and clear it by 6 A.M.
3. Martial law troops must resolutely carry out their mission according to schedule; absolutely no delays will be permitted.
4. No one is permitted to block the advance of the troops. If blocking occurs, soldiers may clear it using any and all self-defensive means that may be required.
5. Central People's Broadcasting, CCTV, and especially Beijing People's Broadcasting and Television will broadcast nonstop emergency announcements from the Beijing Municipal Government and the Martial Law Command. Important announcements will also be broadcast over loudspeakers in the Square.

That night Yang Shangkun, Li Peng, Liu Huaqing, Li Ximing, Chen Xitong, Chi Haotian, Yang Baibing, Zhao Nanqi, and Luo Gan monitored the situation from Zhongnanhai.

June 3–4

Standoff in the Square

On the evening of June 3 Martial Law Command began its moves aimed at peacefully clearing the Square.

Excerpt from Martial Law Command, "Situation in Tiananmen Square and surrounding districts," in "Bulletin" *(Kuai-bao)*, June 3

At 6:30 in the evening the Beijing Municipal Government and Martial Law Command issued an emergency announcement stating, "Beginning immediately, Beijing citizens must be on high alert. Please stay off the streets and away from Tiananmen Square. All workers should remain at their posts and all citizens should stay at home to safeguard their lives."

The announcement was broadcast repeatedly for several hours on radio and television and over public-address systems. At the same time, student loudspeaker broadcasts on the campuses of Peking University, People's University, Beijing Normal University, Qinghua University, the Beijing Institute of Aeronautics, and other institutions were calling upon students and citizens to arm themselves with clubs and batons and to assemble at road intersections and at Tiananmen Square.

About 7:30 P.M. young men in white shirts and green pants emerged in twos and threes from the Qianmen subway station and mingled with the crowd. Unarmed and carrying identical knapsacks, they were soldiers sent by the Martial Law Command. They attracted little attention from the students and citizens and were not beaten, as soldiers around Hufangqiao had been earlier in the day.

About 8 P.M. bright lights lit up Chang'an Boulevard and the Square, where people were massing. The only vehicles on Chang'an Boulevard were the ones arrayed laterally across it as blockades. People continued to enter the Square on foot. Meanwhile, troops entered the Great Hall of the People from the west while students and citizens who watched shouted, "This is our victory!"

About 8:30 P.M. helicopters circled above Chang'an Boulevard (both East and West) and over Tiananmen Square to inspect conditions in final preparation for troop entry into the Square. One student ran breathlessly into the student command center in the Square to report, "The Western Garrison compound is packed with soldiers who are ready to move out." A female student who seemed to be in charge picked up a loudspeaker and asked the others to go back to their campuses to bring more people down to "defend Tiananmen Square."

About 9 P.M. citizens who had heard the televised announcement advising people to stay off the streets began to head home or toward the outskirts of the city to try to stop troops from entering. Only a thousand or so people were left on Chang'an Boulevard, and the huge road seemed strangely deserted. By then some troops were already lining the Square, and others were inside the Great Hall of the People awaiting orders. At the same time, makeshift "command centers" of the AFW, north of the Square, were distributing clubs, batons, and bamboo poles to the crowd.

At 10 P.M. Martial Law Command ordered units in the suburbs to enter the city, where they met with stiff resistance from citizens and students.

Pitched battle at Muxidi

Muxidi is an area about three miles west of Tiananmen on Fuxingmenwai Boulevard, which is the western extension of Chang'an Boulevard. It was where most of the deaths occurred. On the night of June 3 thousands of students and citizens had gathered there spontaneously after hearing about the impending approach of martial law troops from the west.

> Excerpt from Martial Law Command, "Situation in the Muxidi district," in "Bulletin" *(Kuaibao)*, June 3

Advance troops of the Thirty-Eighth Group Army, who were responsible for the western approaches, massed in the western suburbs at Wanshou Road, Fengtai, and Liangxiang. At 9:30 P.M. these troops began advancing eastward toward the Square and encountered their first obstacle at Gongzhufen, where students and citizens had set up a blockade. An antiriot squad fired tear gas canisters and rubber bullets into the crowd. At first the people retreated, but then they stopped. The antiriot squad pressed forward, firing more tear gas and more rubber bullets. Again the crowd retreated but soon stopped. The troops kept firing warning shots into the air, but the people displayed no signs of fear. The stretch from Gongzhufen to the Military Museum, Beifengwo Street, and Muxidi is less than two kilometers, but troop advance was slow because of citizens' interference. The crowd threw rocks, soda bottles, and other things, but troops maintained strict discipline and did not fire a single shot in return.

Believing the troops would not use live ammunition, the citizens grew increasingly bold. At 10:10 P.M. tens of thousands formed a human wall at Beifengwo Street to block the troops; the two sides faced each other over a distance of twenty to thirty meters. Some of the citizens continued throwing rocks and other objects. Using an electric bullhorn, the commanding officer exhorted the citizens and students to disperse and let the troops pass. When that measure failed, he decided to use force to assure his soldiers could reach their positions on time. Infantrymen led the way, firing into the air. Then the soldiers—with the first two rows in a kneeling position and those in back standing—pointed their weapons at the crowd. Approximately 10:30 P.M., under a barrage of rocks, the troops opened fire. Sparks flew from ricocheting bullets. When people in the crowd realized that live ammunition was in use, they surged in waves toward the Muxidi Bridge.[5] Their retreat was hindered by roadblocks they had set up, and for this reason some in the crowd were trampled and badly injured.

> Excerpts from State Security Ministry, "Situation at Muxidi on the evening of the third," in "Important intelligence" (*Yaoqing*), 2 A.M., June 4

Around 9 P.M., when the crowd at Muxidi heard that troops were about to enter the city, they began discussing ways to block them. Someone said, "Maybe we can't stop the troops, but the ones coming from the west will have to get across Muxidi Bridge." Another shouted, "We have to stop them, we can't let them get to Tiananmen on schedule!" Another said, "The troops are the people's troops, they'll never use real bullets on us. We have to try to stop them from taking up positions in Tiananmen Square." Someone blurted out, "Let's set up a roadblock!" People quickly pitched in to push electric buses onto the Muxidi Bridge to block the troops. They did not deflate the tires.

While this was going on, twenty-odd college students wearing red headbands arrived from Tiananmen. They knew the troops would have to pass through Muxidi, and they had come to mobilize the citizens to stop them. The crowd applauded. Someone yelled, "Let's break up some concrete!" and people scurried to the roadsides and began smashing sidewalk paving stones into projectile-sized

---

[5] At Muxidi, Fuxingmenwai Boulevard crosses a bridge over the Yongding River Canal.

chunks, of which there were soon piles on both sides of the street. Other people pedaled up with three-wheeled flatbeds already loaded with broken bricks and rocks. A pair of trucks arrived loaded with the same. All this activity had no organization and no directors.

The anticipation reached fruition as troops arrived. Tear gas canisters suddenly came flying over the electric buses that were stretched across the road and landed at the people's feet. At Muxidi Bridge the troops were stopped once again as citizens and students threw the broken bricks they had prepared in advance. A few dozen baton-wielding members of the troops' antiriot brigade stormed onto the bridge, where they were met with a barrage of broken bricks as thick as rain. The brigade was driven back. Then regular troops, row by row, came rushing onto the bridge chanting, "If no one attacks me, I attack no one; but if people attack me, I must attack them"[6] and turning their weapons on the crowd. The soldiers then alternated between shooting into the air and firing into the crowd. People began crumpling to the ground. Each time shots rang out, the citizens hunkered down; but with each lull in the fire they stood up again. Slowly driven back by the troops, they stood their ground from time to time shouting "Fascists!" "Hooligan government!" and "Murderers!"

It took the troops about ten minutes to cross the Muxidi Bridge and reach the subway station between Ministers' Buildings[7] 22 and 24. Citizens and students, who took cover between buildings and in the shrubbery that lay in the garden strip between the lanes of the road, kept up their verbal barrage of "Fascists!" "Murderers!" and "Bandits!" and continued pelting the troops with rocks. The soldiers pushed the electric buses and other roadblocks out of the way, then turned their weapons on the protesters again. Some soldiers who were hit by rocks lost their self-control and began firing wildly at anyone who shouted "Fascists!" or threw rocks or bricks. At least a hundred citizens and students fell to the ground in pools of blood; most were rushed to nearby Fuxing Hospital by other students and citizens.

The sound of helicopters overhead and gunfire in the streets brought citizens who lived on Fuxingmenwai Boulevard to their windows, where they cursed and threw objects at the soldiers, who therefore shot back. Bullets ricocheted off buildings up and down the five hundred meters between Muxidi and the headquarters of the All-China Federation of Trade Unions. That night three people in

---

[6] A quotation from Chairman Mao that was famous during the Cultural Revolution.
[7] Buildings where personnel at the vice ministerial level and above are assigned housing. These two have the street addresses of numbers 22 and 24, Fuxingmenwai Boulevard.—Comp.

Ministers' Buildings 22 and 24 were shot to death, including the son-in-law of Song Rufen, vice chairman of the Law Committee of the NPC.[8]

After infantrymen had cleared the street of roadblocks, returning fire the whole time, armored cars and army trucks drove onto the Muxidi Bridge. From then on there were no more lulls in the shooting. Soldiers on the trucks fired into the air continuously until people hurled rocks or verbal insults, and then they fired into the crowd. As the troops moved east along the sidewalk, the crowd maintained a distance of twenty to thirty meters, unwilling to back off further. Around 11 P.M. armed foot soldiers, armored cars, and army trucks headed toward Tiananmen.

After the troops had passed, citizens and students pushed electric buses back into the street, placing them across it, and set them on fire to block troops that were following. It was then roughly 11:40 P.M.

At midnight some citizens set up new roadblocks on the eastern approach to Muxidi Bridge. To the east of the bridge, near the subway station, lay twelve lumps of flesh, blood, and debris. The bodies of dead and wounded were being delivered continually to the door of Fuxing Hospital. Some arrived on three-wheeled flat-bed carts, others were carried on wooden doors, and some came in on the backs of motorcycles. One bloody corpse whose face was unrecognizably mangled was carried on a door. Virtually everyone at Fuxing Hospital was cursing "Fascists!" "Animals!" and "Bloody massacre!"

By 1:30 A.M. Fuxingmenwai Boulevard in the area of Muxidi was deserted and shrouded in deathly silence.

> Excerpt from State Security Ministry, "Situation in Beijing urban districts on the fourth," in "Important intelligence" (*Yaoqing*), June 4[9]

In the early morning of June 4 the crowd set up roadblocks at Muxidi. Two buses stretched across the road again blocked the way to the bridge. On the other side of the roadblocks a hundred or more army trucks reached all the way to the Color Television Center of CCTV. A dozen armored cars, each carrying eight or nine officers or soldiers, came first. The trucks in the rear carried thirty or forty

[8]This incident is discussed further in the Epilogue.
[9]The burning of the armored cars and army trucks on June 4 has long been controversial. Some people believe they were torched by the troops themselves; others assume that "rioters" were at fault. This document indicates that at least some of the vehicles were torched by civilians.— Comp.

soldiers each. These troops, having just moved from in from the west early that morning, were far friendlier to the people. At 7:10 A.M. a few armored cars and tanks sped over from Gongzhufen, preparing to break through the roadblocks on the Muxidi Bridge.

At 7:25 A.M. a yellowish-green smoke suddenly rose from one end of the bridge. It came from a broken-down armored car that was now set out to block the street. Two electric buses that citizens had set up as roadblocks were still in the middle of the road. The armored cars and tanks that had come to clear the road-blocks could do nothing but mass at the bridgehead. Suddenly a young man ran up, threw something into an armored car, and then scurried off. A few seconds later the same yellowish-green smoke was seen pouring from vehicles as soldiers scrambled out and squatted down in the street, grabbing their throats in agony. Someone said they had inhaled poison gas. But the enraged officers and soldiers managed to maintain their self-control. Some citizens came forward to mediate, and a potentially explosive situation was defused.

All that morning military vehicles became socked in, unable to move forward or backward. People riding by on bicycles often pointed at the soldiers and cursed, and some threw shards of brick. People who lived at Gongzhufen, Muxidi, and Beifengwo emerged from their houses to surround the trucks and to raise a protest with the soldiers, who sat impassively in their trucks.

At 10:30 A.M. some citizens demanded that the soldiers come down off their trucks. One person set some clothing on fire and threw it into a command car. Others followed suit, putting the torch to vehicles. Officers quickly ordered their men to retreat. After soldiers informed the citizens that one of the vehicles was an oil truck, soldiers and citizens together pushed it to the side of the road. By the time the troops were in retreat, flames had engulfed dozens of military vehicles.

All day long a steady stream of students and citizens entered and left Fuxing Hospital, where a huge crowd gathered to inquire anxiously about family members. Names of the dead—forty-two in all—were posted on the wall of the hospital's bicycle shed. The Railway Hospital counted twenty-three dead, and the Posts and Telecommunications Hospital listed sixteen. Based on these estimates, the number of persons killed citywide on the evening of June 3 must be about two hundred, with about two thousand wounded.

At 4 P.M. the morgue at Fuxing Hospital was opened to the public so that relatives could identify and retrieve bodies. Hundreds of people lined up. A record book was displayed showing the sex, age, and physical characteristics of the dead but listing few names. Inside the morgue there were two cement-floor rooms in which corpses were laid out on straw mats or white cloth. Nothing had been done to alter the victims' appearance at the time of death. Outside the hospital door, people burned paper spirit money for the dead.

Evacuating Tiananmen Square

Minutes after midnight on the morning of June 4, the Public Security Ministry sent a fax to Zhongnanhai describing how the situation in the Square and its environs had developed overnight. About 10:30 P.M. a large number of students and citizens had gathered in the northwestern corner of the Square in front of a tent where they said they were receiving the wounded from gunfire at Muxidi. Shouts arose whenever another wounded protester was brought in. Ambulances from the Beijing Emergency Center appeared in the Square several times, picking up the wounded and leaving from the southeast, but with their sirens silent.

Just west of the Telecommunications Building, two buses that had been turned sideways and set on fire were blocking all vehicular traffic on Chang'an West Boulevard. A military vehicle also stood in flames. A reporter from Xinhua News Agency said he had followed the troops from the west all the way from Wanshou Road, hitting the ground whenever he heard gunfire. After every burst of gunfire, some people fell wounded, he said, with the highest casualty rate occurring at Muxidi, where the advance of the troops had met its stiffest resistance. After passing Muxidi and proceeding eastward, soldiers in the vanguard antiriot squads were pelted with rocks and sustained more injuries than had the other martial law units.

About 11:30 P.M. the first armored car sped into the Square from Chang'an West Boulevard. Citizens and members of the AFW tried to stop it with a concrete traffic divider, and others threw Molotov cocktails. While the armored was car lodged against the traffic divider, its engine roaring, people took the opportunity to pelt it with more Molotov cocktails. A flaming bed comforter was thrust on top of it. Eventually the armored car mustered the power to roll over the traffic divider, turn around, and drive back westward in flames.

At the Xinhua Gate to Zhongnanhai seventy or eighty helmeted soldiers armed with metal batons formed a human wall in front of dozens of citizens who stood cursing them. Some of the citizens threw rocks, but the soldiers remained expressionless, held their batons across their chests, and did not react. A citizen said students had just brought a wounded soldier to the gate. The students and citizens wanted to take the soldier inside, but the soldiers loaded their rifles, shouted at them to halt, and drove them away.

By 1 A.M. on June 4 all martial law troops had entered the Square as scheduled. The following announcement was broadcast on loudspeakers for three hours and fourteen minutes.

Beijing Municipal Government and Martial Law Command,
"Emergency Announcement," 1:30 A.M., published in *People's
Daily* and other newspapers, June 4, p. 1

A severe counterrevolutionary riot has broken out in the capital tonight. Riot-ers have savagely attacked soldiers of the PLA, have stolen their weapons and burned their vehicles, have erected roadblocks, and have kidnapped officers and soldiers, all in an attempt to subvert the People's Republic and overthrow the socialist system. For many days the PLA has maintained the highest degree of restraint, but it is now determined to deal resolutely with the counterrevolution-ary riot. Citizens of the capital must obey all martial law regulations and cooper-ate with the PLA to protect the Constitution and to safeguard the security of our great socialist motherland and its capital. Citizens and students must evacuate the Square immediately so that martial law troops can successfully carry out their mission. We cannot guarantee the safety of violators, who will be solely responsi-ble for any consequences.

Excerpt from Martial Law Command, "Situation of clearing
the Square," in "Bulletin" *(Kuaibao),* pre-dawn, June 4

When they heard the announcement, tens of thousands of citizens and a handful of students began leaving the Square. By 2 A.M. the number remaining had dwindled from hundreds of thousands to only a few thousand.

During the broadcast of this emergency announcement, helmeted soldiers with assault rifles slung over their shoulders packed the steps of the Museum of Chinese History on the east side of the Square. Hundreds more stood outside the north gate of the museum. At the north of the Square a dozen army trucks were parked in front of the small bridges across the moat in front of the Gate of Heav-enly Peace, and the soldiers they had carried sat on the ground awaiting orders. To the south, armed soldiers appeared north of Qianmen and on the north side of the Chairman Mao Memorial Hall. On the east, soldiers stationed at the Great Hall of the People remained inside awaiting orders.

Excerpt from State Security Ministry, "Trends in Tiananmen
Square," third of six overnight faxes to Party Central and State
Council duty offices, 2:30 A.M., June 4

About 2 A.M. a dozen students and citizens carrying cans of gasoline tried to torch the army trucks parked at the north of the Square, but the soldiers took them into custody. Later a flurry of gunfire erupted east of the Square between Dongdan and Jianguomen. Students and citizens began running from the northeast corner of the Square toward the Monument to the People's Heroes at its center. The command center of the AFW in the Square's northwest corner was evacuated. Meanwhile, the soldiers stationed in front of the north gate of the Museum of Chinese History ran onto Chang'an East Boulevard wielding batons and assault rifles and sealed the avenue off.

> Excerpt from State Security Ministry, "Trends in Tiananmen Square," fourth of six overnight faxes to Party Central and State Council duty offices, 4:04 A.M., June 4

Around 3 A.M. roughly three thousand students were seated around the Monument to the People's Heroes. Hou Dejian, Liu Xiaobo, Zhou Duo, and Gao Xin, who had announced on June 2 that they were undertaking a hunger strike,[10] decided to urge the students to evacuate the Square peacefully. But Chai Ling, at the student command center, announced that "those who wish to leave may leave, and those who don't may stay." The group clustered around Hou Dejian then asked Chai Ling and other student leaders to send student delegates to join them in approaching the martial law troops to arrange a peaceful evacuation of the Square. Before the student leaders answered this invitation, the Hou Dejian group addressed all the students by loudspeaker:

> Dear students, all of Beijing has now begun to see bloodshed. There has already been more than enough of it to wake up the people. We know you're not afraid to die. Even if you now peacefully withdraw, you have already shown you're not afraid of death. We are like you; we are not afraid of death, either. So we hope everybody will leave the Square now. We must stick with our principles of nonviolence as we leave, so clubs, bottles, and anything else that might be used as a weapon all should be turned in at the monument. And be sure to turn over all captured firearms, too, so there are no accidents.

[10]Their hunger strike manifesto is in Han Minzhu, ed., *Cries for Democracy: Writings and Speeches from the 1989 Chinese Democracy Movement* (Princeton: Princeton University Press, 1990), 349–354; and in Suzanne Ogden, Kathleen Hartford, Lawrence Sullivan, and David Zweig, eds., *China's Search for Democracy: The Student and the Mass Movement of 1989* (Armonk, New York: M. E. Sharpe, 1992), 357–361.

When their broadcast was finished, Hou Dejian and Zhou Duo climbed into a minivan[11] to go meet with the martial law troops. But no students joined them. It was about 3:40 A.M.

> Excerpts from Martial Law Command, "Circumstances of the negotiation with Hou Dejian and others," in "Bulletin" *(Kuaibao),* June 4

About 3:45 A.M. an ambulance approaching from the direction of the Monument to the People's Heroes was halted at the Museum of Chinese History in the northeastern corner of the Square. Four middle-aged men stepped out with their hands raised. They shouted they were "Hou Dejian!" and said they had come to talk. A regimental political commissar came out to meet them. Hou and the others said, "We volunteer to take all the students out of the Square and ask the PLA not to open fire. Please give us enough time to organize an evacuation." The political commissar asked them to wait while he went to report to his superiors.

The commissar left just before 4 A.M.; this was the appointed time for preparing to clear the Square, so all the lights in the Square were extinguished. Hou's group, who were waiting at the roadside, panicked. "We're Hou Dejian!" they shouted. "We came to talk! . . . Don't shoot!" Within three minutes the commissar returned to say, "The command post accepts your request. Take the students out of the Square immediately, exiting to the south. You don't have much time. We won't open fire." Hou's group then hastened back to the Square.

> Excerpt from State Security Ministry, "Trends in Tiananmen Square," fifth of six overnight faxes to Party Central and State Council duty offices, 6:08 A.M., June 4

At four o'clock sharp all the lights in the Square went out, sending its occupiers into a panic. At the same time, the Martial Law Command continued to broadcast its "Notice to Clear the Square," now adding: "We will now begin clearing the Square, and we accept your appeal to evacuate."

The Beijing Government and the Martial Law Command then broadcast a "Notice Concerning the Immediate Restoration of Order in Tiananmen Square." It listed four demands:

---

[11]Referred to in the next document as an ambulance.

1. Anyone on the Square who hears this announcement must leave immediately.
2. Martial law troops will use any means necessary to deal with those who resist this order or disobey by remaining on the Square.
3. The Square will be under the strict control of martial law troops after it is cleared.
4. All patriotic citizens and students who do not want to see turmoil in the country should cooperate with the martial law troops to clear the Square.

At this point students who were gathered on the steps of the Monument to the People's Heroes used blankets, sticks, canvas, and other things to light a bonfire on the western side of the monument. Then they began singing the "Internationale."

Hou Dejian and Zhou Duo returned to the Square and announced over the student public-address system what had happened at their meeting with the martial law authorities. They called for an immediate evacuation. In the dark people were saying school buses from Peking University had come to take students back to campus, but this news caused no notable reaction from the students. The area was shrouded in darkness, except for the distant flames and street lamps on Chang'an Boulevard.

Martial law troops advanced toward the monument from north to south in two columns. Soldiers of the shock brigade first smashed two AFS loudspeakers, then advanced through the crowd on the western steps of the monument with their assault rifles pointed alternately into the air and at the students to frighten them off. About that time the students around the monument, who were under the direction of the General Headquarters for the Protection of Tiananmen Square, conducted a voice-vote in which those—including Hou Dejian's group—who shouted "Leave!" were louder than those who shouted "Stay!" The leader of the command post then told the students in the Square to "prepare to leave the Square in an orderly manner under your school banners; students, citizens, workers, and citizen monitors should evacuate toward Haidian District and move toward Zhongguancun."[12]

Around 4:30 A.M. the lights in the Square came back on. Students found themselves facing a large number of armed soldiers, who pressed the students closer and closer together. Tension gripped the protesters, especially when they saw rows of tanks and armored cars moving slowly through the Square from its north edge.

---

[12]Near Peking University, in the remote northwest part of the city.

The Goddess of Democracy, in the northern part of the Square, fell with a resounding thud. The tanks and armored cars kept advancing, knocking down and crushing student tents along the way, until they flanked the students on the east and west, as close as twenty or thirty meters away. From the northwest corner of the Square rows of soldiers wearing helmets and carrying batons kept pressing toward the students at the Square's center. Antiriot police in protective headgear mingled with them.

About 5 A.M. thousands of students, protected by the linked arms of monitors, retreated toward the southeast corner of the Square via the path between the grassy area and the monument. At first they moved slowly, but they soon began to bunch up as soldiers, some in fatigues, pressed toward them swinging batons. With their path to the monument blocked by troops and tanks, they threaded their way among tanks and armored cars toward the southern entrance at the east of the Square. They made an orderly retreat, carrying school flags and singing the "Internationale." Occasionally there were shouts of "Repressive Bloodbath!" "Down with Fascism!" "Bandits! Bandits!"—even "Fucking Animals!" and the like. Some spat on the soldiers as they passed.

Dawn broke about 5:20. The bulk of the students had left the Square, but about two hundred defiant students and citizens remained and were now completely hemmed in by tanks, which advanced on them slowly and patiently, gradually forcing them back. When this last group had finally been pushed from the Square and had rejoined its citizen supporters outside, some of its members mustered the courage to shout, "Fascists! Fascists!" and "Down with fascism!" In reply, officers and soldiers who were gathered at the Chairman Mao Memorial Hall fired their weapons into the air and shouted in unison, "If no one attacks me, I attack no one."[13] By 5:40 A.M. the Square had been cleared.

Many investigations have established that in the entire process of clearing the Square, martial law troops did not shoot a single person to death and no person was run over by a tank.

---

[13]As quoted above, the other half of this quotation from Chairman Mao was, "But if people attack me, I must attack them."

June 4

Death in the streets

Emotional opposition between citizens and students of Beijing and the martial law troops now reached its peak. Both sides lost control.

Excerpt from State Security Ministry, "Trends in Beijing urban districts on the fourth," in "Important intelligence" (*Yaoqing*), June 4

Liubukou, roughly 6 A.M.: When some students and citizens who had withdrawn from Tiananmen Square reached Liubukou, soldiers opened fire and drove tanks into their midst, killing eleven. Six of the corpses were not removed until 7 A.M.

Outside Xinhua Gate a dozen tanks were lined up at the red wall to protect Zhongnanhai. Electric buses and army trucks were burning at virtually every major intersection along Chang'an Boulevard.

At 6:30 around Nanheyan, just to the east of Tiananmen, a hundred or so citizens stood ten to twenty meters away from troops, taunting them and creating a dangerous standoff. When the soldiers sat down, so did the citizens; when the soldiers stood up, so did the citizens. This went on for about twenty minutes. Finally a colonel ordered the soldiers to aim their weapons at the citizens. Someone in the crowd shouted, "Run for it!" During the crowd's retreat, someone cursed angrily, "Fascists!" The word was still hanging in the air when a volley of bullets swept the protesters, leaving four citizens lying on the ground in pools of blood.

On Chang'an West Boulevard a crowd gathered near the Telecommunications Building; at the Liubukou intersection a tight row of tanks had Chang'an Boulevard sealed off. Soldiers with rifles and batons stood in front of the tanks. The two sides faced each other over a distance of a hundred meters or so. The protesters began throwing bricks at the soldiers, who responded with bricks and tear gas. The gas canisters looked like hand grenades but merely emitted a bit of stinging smoke. The bricks were useless because the distance separating the two sides was too great, and the gas had little effect on that windy morning on such a broad street. Three army trucks driving by turned back to fire on the crowd after someone shouted "Fascists!" Eight protesters were wounded.

On Taipingqiao Avenue[14] eight army trucks that protesters had stopped and then burned lay in ruins. A ninth truck had escaped torching only because it was parked beneath a power line tower; a cardboard sign on its hood read, "Power line overhead; do not torch this truck."

Some of the three hundred military trucks that had been blocked west of the Beijing College of Mines on the night of June 3 still had not moved.

From the Jinsong area to Chang'an East Boulevard, more than a hundred tanks, armored cars, and army trucks headed west[15] filled with soldiers. On top of each tank sat three soldiers with assault rifles, each facing a different direction. Whenever someone jeered or shouted, they opened fire. A soldier atop one of the tanks at Nanchizi shot and killed a citizen.

> Martial Law Command, "Situation of the martial law troops'
> advance and losses," in "Bulletin" *(Kuaibao)*, June 4

More than five hundred army trucks were torched at dozens of intersections, including Tiantan East Road, Tiantan North Gate, the west entrance of the Qianmen subway station, Qianmen East Boulevard, Fuyou Street, Liubukou, Xidan, Fuxingmen, Lishi South Road, Muxidi, Lianhuachi, Chegongzhuang, Donghuamen, Dongzhimen, Dabeiyao, Hujialou, Beidouge Zhuang, and Jiugong Xiang in Daxing County. At the Shuangjing intersection, protesters surrounded more than seventy armored trucks, stripping twenty-three of them of their machine guns.

On Chang'an Boulevard an army truck's engine was turned off and two hundred rioters stormed the cab and beat the driver to death.

Near the Capital Theater at Xidan, rioters beat a platoon leader to death, then hung his body from a burning bus, disemboweled him, and gouged out his eyes.

On the Chongwenmen overpass rioters flung a soldier over the side, then doused him with gasoline and set him on fire, and then suspended his body from the overpass.

At Fuchengmen the body of a murdered soldier was hung from a railing of the overpass.

At the Cuiwei intersection a truck carrying six soldiers slowed down to avoid hitting people in a crowd. A group of rioters then threw rocks, Molotov cocktails, and flaming torches at the truck, which tipped to the left when nails that the rioters had scattered punctured a tire. The rioters then flung burning objects into the truck, exploding its gas tank. All six solders burned to death.

---

[14] Runs north and south between Xidan and Fuxingmen.
[15] Northwest, actually. Jinsong is in the southeast corner of the city.

A June 4 report by the Martial Law Command estimated that about twenty officers and soldiers were killed. Based on June 4 reports from city hospitals, the Beijing Municipal Government estimated that more than two hundred citizens and students had died. Incomplete statistics showed that twenty-three college students lost their lives.[16]

On the college campuses students reacted with shock, anger, and grief on June 4. Virtually all teachers and students that Sunday morning exchanged information about what had happened the night before. Anxiety and terror produced a shroud of gloom. AFS public-address systems at Peking University, Qinghua University, People's University, Beijing Normal University, the Chinese University of Political Science and Law, the Beijing Institute of Aeronautics, and the Beijing Polytechnic University repeatedly broadcast programs with names like "Bloodbath at Tiananmen Square" and "The Truth About the Beijing Massacre." These reports said, "Blood flowed like a river on Chang'an Boulevard" and "The Beijing Red Cross estimates 2,600 dead."

Witnesses who said they had "escaped death" took turns at microphones describing the carnage they had seen. Funereal music played continuously, and wreaths and elegiac couplets mourning the victims appeared at campus gates. Flags flew at half staff at People's University, Peking University, Qinghua University, and Beijing Normal University. Black armbands were handed out, and even some elderly professors took part. Citizens poured onto campuses to join the mourning activities and to help the students protest the "barbarous deed" the government had committed. At Qinghua University, Peking University, People's University, and the Beijing Language Institute, students held the bodies of murdered students aloft and carried them around the campuses. At the Chinese University of Political Science and Law, the body of a student was placed on a table, surrounded with ice, and guarded by angry and grieving students and teachers. "The government has gone crazy," students and teachers were saying, "and is now driving us crazy, too."

Party and Youth League members at Peking University, Qinghua University, People's University, and Beijing Normal University announced their withdrawals from the Party and the League. Wall posters called for mass resignations from these groups. In academic departments at Peking University, Qinghua University, People's University, Beijing Normal University, and the University of Political Science and Law, people collected League membership cards for public burning. The AFS issued a leaflet.

> Public Security Ministry, "A counterrevolutionary pamphlet signed by AFS appears on Beijing campuses," in "Public security bulletin" *(Gongan kuaixun)*, June 4

Today a pamphlet from the AFS appeared on campuses and street corners in Beijing. It said,

---

[16]The Epilogue carries a later report with more precise statistics.

"This fascist massacre pushes the people of the entire nation beyond the outer limits of toleration. The blood will not have been shed in vain; the struggle must not end here. But, fellow students and countrymen, our position is firmly opposed to fighting violence with violence. The river of blood must not become an ocean. Our sacrifice has already been tragic enough. It is already enough to show clearly that the Li Peng government is the enemy of the people and that its days are numbered. We do not have our own army; we are defenseless in the face of modern, well-equipped troops. But nonviolent struggle is the people's right, and its power is beyond imagining. Our duty now is to expose to the world the true face of this bloody massacre. We call upon people in Beijing and the entire nation to strike work and boycott the marketplace, and we entreat the support of the international community.

"Fellow students and countrymen, from the beginning of this movement to the very end, we have led the masses using reason and wisdom. Now, at this critical juncture, our responsibility is even more momentous. The best commemoration of the victims will be not more bloodshed but the achievement of final victory. In peaceful struggle the people eventually will win. Eternal glory to the martyrs of democracy!

"Again we urge:

1. 'Three strikes' throughout Beijing: Strike work, strike classes, strike the marketplace.
2. All citizens withdraw all money from banks.
3. Use every possible means to spread the truth to the people of the nation."

An atmosphere of terror lay over Beijing all day on June 4. Army trucks lay burning at major intersections; center dividers were strewn all over the streets. Pedestrians were few. Stores and shops held irregular hours, and some did not open at all. Citizens began to hoard food and other necessities.

Sporadic gunfire erupted throughout the day. Someone in an armored car repeatedly fired a weapon into the air on the Fuxingmen overpass. At Baishiqiao someone kept pointing an armored car's machine gun in all directions as it drove around. In the evening a firefight broke out between soldiers and citizens at Shuangjing. Gunshots rang out at Sidaokou, Xiaoxitian, Hufangqiao, Jianguomenwai, Xuanwumen, and elsewhere.

A man claiming to be from the Chinese Alliance to Protect Human Rights distributed a "Letter to the People" on the streets of Beijing.

Excerpts from Chinese Alliance to Protect Human Rights, "Letter to the People,"[17] in Beijing Municipal Party Committee and Beijing Municipal Government, "Reflections on the Pacification Situation," June 4

There are traitors inside the Party. There are traitors inside the military. A counterrevolutionary military coup has erupted at the Center. The arch-criminals in this coup are Yang Shangkun and Li Peng. . . . Accordingly, the Chinese Alliance to Protect Human Rights calls upon all workers, farmers, and intellectuals in the nation and all PLA officers and soldiers to unite to crush the counterrevolutionary coup. First, we ask members of the Thirteenth Central Committee, the Seventh National People's Congress, and the Chinese People's Political Consultative Conference—whichever of them still enjoy freedom and mobility—to set up a provisional government in Guangzhou to lead the people in crushing this counterrevolutionary military coup. Second, for the good of the people and the future of our country and Party, we ask the officers and soldiers of the PLA to stand on the side of the people. We urge all military districts and armed forces to unite and to set out for Beijing to crush the coup. Third, we call for a united front among members of the CCP, members of the democratic parties, people with no party affiliation, and common people across the nation to use all forms of struggle (including strikes of work, classes, and the marketplace) to smash the schemers' plot to rule China. . .

That evening Chen Xitong broadcast a speech that was intended to calm the populace.

Excerpts from Beijing Municipal Party Committee and Beijing People's Government, "Comrade Chen Xitong's broadcast talk," June 4; published in *Beijing Daily (Beijing ribao)*, June 5, p. 1

In the early morning of June 3 a small handful of rioters stirred up a counterrevolutionary riot in Beijing, the capital of our great motherland. In order to preserve the socialist system, to protect the People's Government, and to ensure the security of our citizens' life and property, troops of the People's Liberation Army, Beijing Public Security personnel, and the People's Armed Police implemented

[17]Text in Ogden et al., *China's Search,* 388–390.

the resolute policy of Party Central, the State Council, and the Central Military Commission by smashing this counterrevolutionary riot with courage and fearlessness. This constitutes an initial victory in the struggle to quell the turmoil, maintain stability and unity, and smash the counterrevolutionary conspiracy. . . . [We should] spring into action at this critical moment and work closely with the martial law troops, the Public Security personnel, and the People's Armed Police to decisively and thoroughly crush this counterrevolutionary riot. . . .

During the course of this counterrevolutionary riot, a tiny minority of troublemakers and schemers has already completely exposed the true nature of its political slogans and organizational principles. They arrogantly shout that they "want to completely annihilate forty-seven million disciples of the Party" and to subvert the People's Government that has been elected by the National People's Congress. At this critical juncture the Party and government have been pushed beyond the limits of tolerance and have been forced to employ extraordinary measures to smash this counterrevolutionary riot. We have no choice. If certain people cling to their unrepentant stance by continuing to plot and to create turmoil, the People's Government and martial law troops will continue their crackdown and will punish the offenders without mercy.

The popular reaction to Chen's speech was negative, even among many Party members.

Protests by news media

As the "counterrevolutionary riot" was being crushed on June 3 and 4, the Chinese news media in the capital, led by *People's Daily,* CCTV, and the English-language section of China Radio International, showed remarkable courage in trying to report the news accurately.

Later, the Party Propaganda Department issued a report called "On the Behavior of the *People's Daily* in the Recent Events" in which it criticized Zhao Ziyang, Hu Qili, and Rui Xingwen for making statements it said had led to "major biases" in news reporting. The report said *People's Daily,* as the Party's mouthpiece, had erred especially egregiously. First, its leaders, who had been wrongheaded from the beginning, at the height of the conflict either checked into hospitals or tendered their resignations. Second, many of its editors and reporters had joined the demonstrations. Some, who thought the April 26 editorial had made them into scapegoats, made a point of taking to the streets to show their opposition to the editorial. Later some of them even published the "extra" edition about Li Peng's announcement of martial law, thereby giving the country a black eye at home and overseas. Third, when it reported the turmoil, *People's Daily* undermined Party

Central's messages with subtle subterfuge. It added flowery borders to some serious articles that Party Central had ordered it to publish, and for other stories it fashioned inappropriately provocative headlines. An unusually bold font was used, for example, for the headline "Students in Seoul Stage Hunger Strike to Protest Government Repression and Massacre."

Later that month *People's Daily* was restructured. Leaders of the old guard retired, and a new general manager and editor-in-chief took over. The three people responsible for the "extra" were punished.

Meanwhile, Luo Gan accused CCTV of loss of control and failure to follow orders while the counterrevolutionary riot was being crushed. Cameramen who had been ordered to record the clearing of Tiananmen Square refused to go, claiming they feared for their lives. Not until 5 A.M., when the Square had basically been cleared, did a camera team finally arrive, escorted by armed police. CCTV had failed to record the actual clearing process, Luo Gan charged, and had left this task to the martial law troops.

CCTV broadcasts during the period June 4–6 were somber. Anchors Xue Fei and Du Xian dressed in black and assumed an uncharacteristically doleful expression as they read the news of the crackdown. For this they were fired. Later a vice minister of radio, film, and television was fired for "supporting turmoil" because he had led some employees in demonstrating.

The English-language section of China Radio International was the first Chinese medium to announce the shocking news to the world. At 6:25 A.M. on June 4 its broadcast asked the world to remember the "most tragic events" of June 3, in which it said "several thousand people, mostly innocent citizens" had been killed by "heavily armed soldiers." It relayed eyewitness accounts of machine-gun killings and of armored cars running over soldiers who dared to hesitate. It urged its listeners to protest these horrible violations of human rights and violent suppression of the people. The person in charge of the English-language section was a son of Politburo member Wu Xueqian. Later the son was transferred and investigated, and all employees of the English-language section were forced to write detailed self-criticisms.

The report of the army that cleared the Square

The Thirty-Eighth Group Army of the Beijing Military District was the force primarily responsible for clearing the Square.

> Excerpts from Thirty-Eighth Group Army, "Accomplish the mission, conscientiously complete the martial law task," report to the Central Military Commission, June 8

On June 3, based on orders from the Martial Law Command, our group army, as the vanguard assigned the responsibility of clearing the Square, set out from the western suburbs of Beijing and advanced toward Tiananmen Square along Chang'an West Boulevard. Led by a reconnaissance battalion, the 112th Division first occupied a base east of the Military Museum as a covering force for the entire group army. Two regiments of the 113th Division then arrived at the base as an advance force. Four regiments from Fengtai, covered by a reconnaissance company, broke through rioters' blockades at four intersections and took up their assigned positions. Artillery troops cast aside all manner of difficulties to arrive at the base. A regiment of our engineer corps, swift as the wind, set out from its barracks at Liangxiang and covered a distance of twenty-four kilometers in only twenty-seven minutes to arrive at its assigned position ahead of schedule. A communications regiment overcame interference, protected its equipment with an all-out effort, and also arrived at its assigned position.

During the advance to the Square, bricks rained down on officers and soldiers, and obstacles littered the ground at their feet. Along the way they were attacked by rioters with clubs and steel reinforcing bars while a sea of smoke and fire rose in front of them. But our officers and soldiers, braving the constant threat of abduction, injury, and death itself, pushed aside burning cars and road dividers that lay strewn across the road and after four hours arrived at the Square on schedule.

The group army began to advance on Tiananmen Square at 9:30 P.M. Led by antiriot teams, the 112th and 113th Divisions and an artillery brigade advanced first, and the remaining units followed. Officers and soldiers were brave and fearless in the face of the rioters' beating, smashing, robbing, burning, and killing. Walking instead of riding and shielding their trucks with their bodies as they broke through twelve intersections, they cleared away seven blockades of burning cars and electric buses and overwhelmed a forest of roadblocks over a distance of seven kilometers. After four grinding hours they reached the front of Tiananmen at 1:30 A.M. on June 4; they were the first troops to enter the Square. The armored vehicles of the 112th Division, which was in charge of clearing and patrolling the Square, set out from Donggaodi at 9:55 P.M. on June 3. Three of the trucks arrived at the Square at 11:30 P.M. after an arduous advance. The blockaded units, who were under strict orders to meet up with the main body of the group army at the corner of Fuxingmen, increased their speed in order to do so.

The Sixth Armored Division, which began far away, moved quickly. The division's advance units, leading the Twenty-First Tank Regiment and the Anti-

Aircraft Artillery Regiment, reached Tiananmen Square at 1:45 A.M. on the fourth, and the army's base command and troops under its control and the Twenty-Fourth Armored Regiment arrived separately at 4:30 A.M. and 7:20 A.M. The remaining units of the division took up positions near the Military Museum. Before they cleared the Square, the various movements of the group army's 10,800 officers and soldiers and forty-five armored vehicles crushed the blazing arrogance of the riot elements, smashed their lines of defense on the west, and struck fear into the hearts of the diehards who were entrenched in the Square.

After the group army arrived at Tiananmen, the rioters at the edge of the Square began moving along Chang'an Boulevard to both the east and west, trying to regroup and mount a counterattack. In accordance with the deployment orders of Martial Law Command, the group army dispatched the 112th and 113th Divisions to block Chang'an Boulevard's east and west entrances to the Square and to set up cordons there. At the same time, two regiments of the Sixth Armored Division began to clear the area between Jinshui Bridge and Wumen and to block the watchtower gates flanking Wumen in order to prevent the rioters from entering the Square from the direction of the Palace Museum. These actions sealed off the northern end of the Square, thereby isolating the die-hard elements who remained in the Square and ensuring a smooth clearing operation.

The clearing itself began at 4:30 A.M. on June 4. Two thousand soldiers in artillery brigades and engineering regiments, plus forty-two armored vehicles of the 112th Division, in cooperation with fraternal units, cleared the Square, moving from north to south. Prior to that we captured six rioters—including Guo Haifeng, member of the Standing Committee and secretary general of the AFS—who were trying to burn down the Gate of Heavenly Peace, and we smashed the Goddess of Democracy, which was the rioters' spiritual pillar.

Then, led by foot soldiers, armored cars drove the crowd in the Square southward toward Zhengyangmen and quickly set up a cordon there, thus triumphantly completing our duty to clear the Square. In clearing the Square the officers and soldiers of our army and our fraternal armies maintained the highest degree of self-control from start to finish and did not kill a single person with rifle fire. Throughout the Square-clearing operations, which the whole world was watching, our army not only served the intimidation function that a mechanized army can achieve but also did a good job of displaying the image of a fearless people's army devoted to its duty.

Unrest engulfs the country

Forty-six reports to Zhongnanhai described demonstrations that burst out on June 4 in sixty-three cities across China.

> Excerpts from Shanghai Municipal Party Committee and Shanghai People's Government, "Firmly support the decisions taken by Party Central, the State Council, and the Central Military Commission to pacify the counterrevolutionary riot in the capital," fax to Party Central and the State Council, June 4

In the early morning, soon after news of the events had reached Shanghai, students from Fudan, Tongji, Jiaotong, and Huadong Normal Universities took to the streets to protest. They began by stopping military trucks and setting up roadblocks to interfere with traffic on dozens of major thoroughfares in the city. By 5 P.M. forty-two areas had been completely blocked. Seven bus lines were halted and sixty-three others had to be shortened or rerouted. The relevant municipal departments tried to clear the roadblocks in order to restore normal traffic flow. A government spokesman twice urged the students via television and radio to remove the roadblocks, to clear the intersections, and to return to their campuses; he also warned the tiny minority of plotters and organizers not to persist in their stubborn ways on the assumption that the government will be weak. Meanwhile, authorities removed more than ten roadblocks while some people from colleges and research institutes not only continued putting up roadblocks but went on protest marches and gave inflammatory speeches.

Early in the morning the Municipal Party Committee convened a meeting of the Party Secretariat as well as an enlarged meeting of the Standing Committee of the Party Committee, which was attended also by responsible comrades from district-level Party committees and responsible officials from the Party committees of municipality-level offices.[18] Comrade Zhu Rongji presided at both. After careful study and serious discussion, all present voiced resolute support for the decisions of Party Central, the State Council, and the CMC in putting down the counterrevolutionary riot in Beijing. The Shanghai Party Committee and the Municipal Government issued a "Letter to Communist Party Members and Citizens of Shanghai."

---

[18]The term *"weiban dangwei"* refers to Party committees in offices and commissions directly under the municipal Party committee and government.—Comp.

In Harbin news of the crackdown reached some campuses late on the night of June 3. Some students demonstrated through the night. On the morning of June 4 more than seven thousand students from nine universities marched to the provincial government building to protest the crackdown and mourn those who had died in Beijing. They shouted slogans like "Li Peng is a murderer." As they marched, students distributed leaflets entitled "Letter to the Citizens of Harbin" and "Latest News from Beijing."

In Changchun more than four thousand students marched twenty kilometers along Stalin Avenue to the railway station. With tens of thousands of citizens looking on, they shouted, "June fourth massacre, shocking and horrifying," "Repay the blood debt," "Down with repression," and "Down with violence." As they passed, they blanketed utility poles and bulletin boards with leaflets, which onlookers rushed over to read.

In Shenyang more than three thousand students marched to the city square in orderly fashion and to mournful music. They carried wreaths and banners that read, "Why don't you shoot us, too?," "Oppose suppression," "Punish the murderers," and so on. Tens of thousands of people watched.

In Taiyuan more than four thousand college students marched carrying banners that read, "The blood of the people will not be shed in vain," "Oppose armed suppression," "Give us back our fellow students; give us back our human rights," "Blood debts must be paid in blood," and others.

In Hohhot more than five thousand college students and teachers, most from Inner Mongolia University, took to the streets. They marched slowly, carried a dozen wreaths and several dozen banners, and shouted, "Avenge the students and citizens who died in Beijing today," "Blood debts must be paid in blood," "Punish the enemies of the people," and "Resolutely oppose suppression." Tens of thousands of citizens greeted them when they reached the city square.

In Lanzhou more than three thousand students and teachers began to march about 2 A.M. on June 4. "Dare-to-die" teams, consisting of nearly a thousand people in all, headed to the railway station, to rail crossings, and to the Yellow River bridge to block traffic. Many of the three hundred people who went to the railway station lay down on the tracks. As of 6:15 A.M. the rail and the highway arteries of the country's main thoroughfares in the northwest—the Lanzhou–Lianyungang line and the Lanzhou-Xinjiang line—were both blocked.

In Jinan more than four thousand college students marched with wreaths. They shouted such slogans as "Oppose suppression," "Oppose violence," "Down with authoritarian government," "Overthrow fascist rule," "Put down your butcher's knife, Li Peng," "Blood debts must be paid in blood," and "Give us back our compatriots." Slogans were also painted on buses and electric buses downtown. In Qingdao more than a thousand students marched under a flag of the Qingdao College of Oceanology. They held up hastily written placards and banners that read, "Down with Li Peng," "Give us back our comrades-in-arms," "Pay for blood with blood," and so on.

In Nanjing more than five thousand students marched in the rain. Students moved slowly through the downtown district, with those in front playing dirges on a tape recorder and carrying wreaths as well as a banner that read "Mourning the victims in Beijing." The banners of the Nanjing University students included "Blood debts must be repaid in blood," "The army proved with tanks and machine guns that they entered Beijing to repress students and the masses," and "Marshal Xu and Marshal Nie, what happened to your promises?"

> Excerpt from Jiangsu People's Government, "The Long March for Democracy Advance Team has been dispersed, all northbound students have returned to Nanjing," fax to the State Council, June 4

When news that the counterrevolutionary riot in Beijing had been put down reached the students who were on the Long March for Democracy, which now was at Sanjiexiang, thirty kilometers from Chuzhou, most of those students cut short their march to board buses that their schools had sent to bring them back to Nanjing. But about sixty or seventy students resolved to see the march through to the end. Therefore personnel from the Provincial Education Commission and Provincial Public Security, along with some school leaders, stopped these marchers. By 10:30 P.M. on June 4 all the marchers on the scene were in buses bound for Nanjing. A few who insisted on walking were also persuaded along the way to board a bus. A dozen or so members of the march's Advance Team had dispersed into the homes of local residents. But they were located and also persuaded to board buses.

In Hangzhou more than seven thousand college students took to the streets carrying banners bearing slogans such as "Defend justice," "Pay for blood with blood," "Wash off blood with blood," "Repay the blood debt," "Give us back our compatriots," "Condemn the national traitors," and "Down with Li Peng."

In Nanchang about two thousand college students marched in the rain. They were later joined by nearly a thousand students from the Jiangxi Institute of Finance and Economics who marched into the city across the August First Bridge singing the "Internationale" and shouting, "Avenge the martyrs!" Many students wore black armbands and small white flowers. They carried wreaths and passed out transcripts of the VOA broadcast about the killings in Beijing. Students from various colleges joined at People's Square, where they put up posters on the Monument to the Martyrs and played dirges.

> Excerpt from State Security Ministry, "Clash between Chengdu
> students and civilians and the People's Armed Police," fax to the
> State Council, June 4

A conflict that broke out between the People's Armed Police and students and civilians early in the morning was still raging at 4 P.M. At 7:30 A.M. the Chengdu Public Security Bureau announced that traffic into the square on People's South Road would be halted. Following this announcement and persuasion by police, more than half of the three hundred students who were sitting in the Square decided to leave. The fifty-one who remained were removed forcibly at 7:45 A.M. Around 9 A.M. more than two thousand students from Sichuan University, West China Medical University, Chengdu University of Science and Technology, and Sichuan College of Education marched under banners that read, "Blood debts must be repaid in blood," "Seven thousand Beijing students were suppressed," "Give us back our fellow students," and so on. They were stopped by a police cordon about three hundred meters from the square.

Around 10 A.M., when the students tried to break through the cordon, police set upon students and citizens using electric prods. After the police returned behind their cordon, the students and citizens regrouped and made another attempt, this time throwing bricks and rocks. The police then used tear gas and chased the students and citizens, beating them with their electric prods. There were some children and old people among those who were badly beaten. More than a hundred students were taken to the hospital with head injuries. This police action angered many of the citizens. About 3 P.M. the precinct station on People's East Road was set on fire. The station and some nearby stores and restaurants burned to the ground.

In Changsha roughly five hundred students marched down May First Avenue. When they reached the railway station, they rushed in with banners, wreaths, and placards and began shouting slogans as they stood or sat on the railway tracks. Some hung wreaths on locomotives. In the afternoon some two thousand students broke through a police cordon and entered the station to link up with the students who were already inside. They moved onto the tracks and blocked off all the rail exits. By 5 P.M. five trains had been prevented from entering the station, and three others were unable to leave. Security personnel and the stationmaster tried to stop the students from lying down on the tracks, but they were ignored. Students shouted, "If Li Peng dared to open fire on the people, why can't we lie down on the rails?"

In Wuhan more than ten thousand students from fourteen universities marched under banners that read, "Protest the military government's suppression of students," "Blood debts must be repaid in blood," "Avenge the martyrs," and so on. At noon the marchers blocked the main thoroughfares that link the cities of Wuhan, Wuchang, and Hanyang. At 2:44 P.M. roughly three hundred students rushed onto the tracks of the Beijing–Guangzhou line, where they held a memorial service. Northbound and southbound freight trains and a Guiyang–Beijing passenger train were forced to stop. After more than four hours of negotiations and clearing operations, rail traffic on the Yangtze River bridge resumed at 7:10 P.M.

In Guangzhou beginning in the early morning four or five thousand college students and workers took to the streets, made speeches, and sat in. By 6 P.M. two thousand students and citizens remained on the streets.

In Guiyang early in the morning, after the news from Beijing was broadcast, nearly a thousand students and citizens gathered at People's Square, where they made speeches and distributed leaflets to protest the "riot" on the part of the government. Students placed two wreaths and a white banner on the steps of the Square. The banner and the broad ribbons on the wreaths were blank except for red specks symbolizing blood.

Overseas Chinese protest

The Beijing killings of June 3 and 4 elicited vigorous protest from Chinese the world over. Fifteen reports on the reactions arrived at Zhongnanhai during the day on June 4. More than three thousand Chinese students and scholars, students from Taiwan and Hong Kong, and Chinese-Americans marched in Washington, D.C., and massed outside the Chinese embassy. Similar demonstrations took place in New York, Los Angeles, Houston, San Francisco, Philadelphia, and Chicago. The report from Canada said that fifteen hundred Chinese students, overseas Chinese, and Canadian citizens demonstrated outside the Chinese embassy in Ottawa. In Toronto twenty thousand to thirty thousand overseas Chinese, Chinese students, and Canadian citizens protested at the Chinese consulate. More than a thousand protested at the consulate in Vancouver, and smaller protests took place in other cities. In Mexico nineteen Chinese students sat in at the Chinese embassy for more than four hours and delivered a protest to the ambassador.

In England more than twenty-five hundred overseas Chinese and Chinese students marched on the Chinese embassy, where they met three hundred other Chinese who were already there. In Sweden more than a hundred Chinese students and a small group of Chinese Swedes marched to the Chinese embassy to protest and to mourn. In France more than six hundred Chinese students and scholars demonstrated outside the Chinese embassy, chanting slogans and asking all Western countries to cut diplomatic ties with the Chinese government. In Italy more than three thousand Chinese students and overseas Chinese sat in at the Chinese embassy. Thirty began a hunger strike. In Geneva about three hundred Chinese students marched with a petition to the secretary general of the United Nations, asking for UN intervention. In Japan more than two thousand Chinese students, scholars, and other Chinese carried banners protesting the killings.

In Hong Kong black placards and posters appeared on storefronts. Two million people wore dark clothes—or pure white, the traditional Chinese color of mourning. Protesters demanded that the Sino-British agreement for Hong Kong's return to Chinese sovereignty in 1997 be rewritten.

Condemnations from foreign governments

Zhongnanhai soon started to receive reports on protests by the governments of the United States, England, France, Germany, Italy, Sweden, Canada, and other countries.

The report on the United States said that President Bush expressed "deep regret" over the Chinese government's use of force to suppress the democracy movement. He said America had consistently urged the Chinese government to use nonviolent means. Secretary of State James Baker called the attack "most unfortunate" and said it made the American people "extremely concerned." Congress was pressing for stronger measures against China. Stephen Solarz, chair of the Asia-Pacific subcommittee of the House Committee on Foreign Relations, urged the recall of the U.S. ambassador and the cessation of military cooperation and commercial exchange. Senator Jesse Helms called for economic sanctions. Congress also began to discuss granting "sanctuary" to Chinese students currently in the United States.

In England Prime Minister Margaret Thatcher expressed shock and indignation over the indiscriminate slaughter of unarmed civilians, particularly in light of Britain's responsibilities in Hong Kong. The opposition party also condemned the killing and urged Western governments to take action. The Foreign Office advised British citizens to postpone visits to China. In France President François Mitterand issued a statement expressing shock and outrage in which he said a government that opens fire on its own young has no future. The general secretary of the French Communist Party expressed shock and outrage and pledged support for the Chinese people. In Sweden the prime minister condemned the use of force and urged dialogue; the foreign minister called the use of force a giant step backward in China's development.

In West Germany Chancellor Helmut Kohl expressed shock and outrage and extended his sympathy to the Chinese students. A high-ranking West German official added that although Germany did not wish to interfere in China's internal affairs, it was impermissible for a state to open fire on its own citizens; member states of the European Union, she said, should consult on an appropriate response. The German embassy in Beijing pledged to help German students in China reach safety. The Italian government condemned the use of force and urged the students to conduct dialogue with their government. There were also calls in Italy for economic sanctions. The general secretary of the Italian Communist Party delivered a letter to China's ambassador in which he said massacres have no place in a Communist movement.

June 5–10

Continuous nationwide protests

Between June 5 and 10 Zhongnanhai received nearly a hundred reports from the provinces on local reactions and on emergency meetings and police deployments undertaken in response. There were demonstrations in 181 cities, including all the provincial capitals, the major cities,[19] and special economic zones.[20] Many forms of protest, some of them violent, emerged. By June 8 the situation had begun to stabilize in some cities.

Excerpts from daily faxes from provincial Party committees and governments to Party Central and the State Council

June 5

SHANGHAI:

More than thirty thousand students brought downtown traffic to a standstill by using twelve hundred motorbuses and electric buses as roadblocks to block 122 intersections. In the suburbs fewer than a third of workers showed up at factories. Railroad operations were interrupted at five blocked crossings.

TIANJIN:

More than seven thousand students took to the streets. They carried wreaths, played dirges, and made speeches outside the municipal government building and at major intersections.

---

[19]*Jihua danlieshi* are major cities, such as Wuhan, that are treated as province-level units in the state economic plan.
[20]Areas, mostly along the southeastern coast of China, where regulations of the socialist planned economy were waived earlier than elsewhere in order to stimulate economic growth.

HARBIN:

Nearly twenty thousand students erected roadblocks at downtown intersections, bringing traffic to a halt. As many as two thousand workers marched with the students.

CHANGCHUN:

More than ten thousand students marched in the rain carrying wreaths. In the evening about fifty thousand residents and students marched down Liberation Boulevard.

SHENYANG:

More than seven thousand students took to the streets. Students went to factories to network. No university held classes.

DALIAN:

More than five thousand students marched and made speeches.

SHIJIAZHUANG:

More than eight thousand demonstrating students carried wreaths to the North China Martyrs' Mausoleum, to the Shijiazhuang Liberation Monument, and to the gate of the Hebei Provincial Party Committee and the headquarters of the Twenty-Seventh Army.

TAIYUAN:

More than fifty thousand students, teachers, and residents held a memorial meeting at May First Square.

HOHHOT:

More than ten thousand students and teachers marched, carried wreaths, and played dirges.

BAOTOU:

More than two thousand students marched and held a memorial meeting at May First Park.

XI'AN:

More than four thousand students took to the streets, and more than three thousand blocked entrances at factories, preventing workers from going to work. Seventy or more buses were used as roadblocks at major intersections, causing a total paralysis of traffic.

LANZHOU:

More than six thousand students marched in the streets and erected roadblocks, snarling traffic in the city. More than six hundred students lay down on railroad tracks at the Lanzhou Railway Station, interrupting rail traffic for five hours.

URUMCHI:

More than a hundred students staged a sit-in outside the district government building; protest posters appeared at every university.

CHENGDU:

Residents set fire to the fifteen-thousand-square-meter People's Shopping Mall in southwest Chengdu, burned down the Rose Empress Restaurant, and firebombed a movie theater and two precinct police stations. A wall of the municipal government building was toppled and its kitchen torched. Protesters invaded the ground floors of two of the largest hotels for foreign guests—the Minshan and the Jinjiang—and engaged in beating, smashing, and robbing. Fourteen fire trucks of the People's Armed Police and six ambulances were firebombed, and eight buses were destroyed. All the city's stores and shops were closed.

WUHAN:

About twenty thousand students marched and more than five thousand of them sat in at the entrance to the Wuchang Bridge, bringing downtown traffic to a standstill. Some three thousand students blocked the Yangtze River railway bridge for eight hours, and another four thousand massed in the square in front of the railway station. Six universities held memorial meetings, each attended by several thousand people. The Wuhan Steel Mill and Wuhan Heavy Machinery Factory reported that "delivery of urgently needed materials has been blocked, and we will be forced to shut down."

CHANGSHA:

More than twenty thousand students marched and were joined by at least a thousand residents and workers. They erected roadblocks at major intersections and stopped traffic.

ZHENGZHOU:

More than eight thousand students and workers made speeches and marched with wreaths to Lücheng Square, the February Seventh Memorial, and the railway station.

JINAN:

More than eight thousand students continued to march in protest.

QINGDAO:

More than six thousand students held a Memorial for June Fourth Victims outside municipal government offices.

HEFEI:

More than thirty thousand students and residents erected roadblocks at major intersections and brought traffic to a standstill.

NANJING:

More than seven thousand students massed and made speeches at Drum Tower Square. They also went to factories to urge workers to walk out. Traffic was interrupted.

HANGZHOU:

More than ten thousand students erected roadblocks and stopped all traffic except for food supply trucks. Students lay on railroad tracks at Nanxing Bridge Station and other places, bringing rail traffic to a standstill. Long lines began to form outside grocery stores.

NANCHANG:

More than ten thousand students took to the streets. The Nanchang Autonomous Federation of Students announced a strike.

GANZHOU:

More than two thousand students took to the streets and broke into the Ganzhou administrative offices, where they torched five cars, including a police car.

FUZHOU:

Nearly ten thousand students held a memorial meeting at May First Square, and several dozen writers participated.

GUANGZHOU:

Fifty thousand students and residents held a memorial at Haizhu Square.

SHENZHEN:

More than twenty thousand students and residents demonstrated, held meetings, and erected biers to mourn student victims in Beijing and to protest the use of force.

NANNING:

More than two thousand students marched.

GUILIN:

Nearly two thousand students marched.

HAIKOU:

More than three thousand students marched and made speeches at Haikou Park.

KUNMING:

More than six thousand students marched, staged a sit-in at East Wind Square, and held memorials.

GUIYANG:

More than six thousand students held a memorial at People's Square.

June 6

SHANGHAI:

Early in the morning the Municipal Government dispatched sixty-five hundred people to clear roadblocks at 120 sites, but later in the morning nearly ten thousand students and residents erected new roadblocks at 145 sites, blocking intersections and bringing downtown traffic to a standstill. During the day railroad crossings were blocked and cleared repeatedly. At 8:45 P.M. the number 161 train from Beijing ran over nine people who had gathered at the spectacle of a blocked locomotive. Five of them died. By 10 P.M. more than thirty thousand people had gathered at the scene, interrupting rail traffic and creating a disturbance. Protesters beat up the train engineer, set fire to railcars, and prevented fire trucks from entering the site. Eight railcars were destroyed. The Municipal Government sent seven hundred police to restore order.

TIANJIN:

Posters attacking Deng Xiaoping and Li Peng appeared on the campuses of the city's universities. More than six hundred students from Nankai University erected roadblocks on major streets and snarled downtown traffic.

HARBIN:

Roadblocks that had been cleared away early in the morning were set up again by students, this time using more than one hundred electric buses. Downtown traffic was snarled for a second day.

CHANGCHUN:

In the evening more than ten thousand workers, students, and residents marched and held meetings at Geology Palace Square on the campus of Changchun Geological Institute. People from all stations in society made speeches "protesting the massacre in Beijing." More than ten thousand workers from the Changchun First Automobile Works and five thousand workers from the Changchun Textile Mill rode bicycles or walked downtown to join the students. When the marchers massed at Xinfa Square outside the Jilin Party Committee headquarters the total number of demonstrators exceeded one hundred thousand people.

SHENYANG:

Early in the morning about seventeen thousand students took to the streets and blocked major intersections leading to the industrial district, preventing more than half of the workers from getting to work on time. In the afternoon more than thirty thousand students and residents gathered at the square outside the municipal government offices to hold a memorial meeting for "the martyrs of Beijing." More than four thousand workers from the Shenyang Aircraft Manufacturing Company and other enterprises joined the meetings and the march.

SHIJIAZHUANG:

Early in the morning more than three thousand students and residents attacked the headquarters of the Twenty-Seventh Army shouting, "Twenty-Seventh Army butchers!," "The Twenty-Seventh Army suppresses the people," "The Twenty-Seventh Army kills the elderly, students, and children." They rushed the gate of the army's headquarters shortly after midnight. Later, 250 policemen arrived and arrested twelve protesters who were sitting in. During the day, some three thousand of the city's college students left their campuses.

TAIYUAN:

More than one thousand students continued to demonstrate, while about five thousand left their campuses to go home.

HOHHOT:

More than three thousand students continued to demonstrate and were joined by about four hundred workers under the banner of the Autonomous Federation of Workers. One-third of the students at Inner Mongolia University and Inner Mongolia Normal University have left their campuses.

XI'AN:

More than three thousand students continued to march and to make speeches at Xincheng Square. At least five thousand left their campuses during the day.

LANZHOU:

More than two thousand students erected roadblocks to stop traffic at the Yellow River bridge. New roadblocks appeared at major intersections downtown, where traffic remained at a standstill. More than three hundred students interrupted rail traffic by lying on the rails at Lanzhou Railway Station.

YINCHUAN:

More than five thousand students and teachers marched, held a memorial to "mourn the martyrs of Beijing" at South Gate Square, and announced an empty-campus movement and an indefinite student boycott. More than one hundred thousand residents surrounded the demonstrators, making this the largest gathering in Yinchuan in a decade.

CHENGDU:

About five thousand students left their campuses. Two-thirds of the city's shops were closed. In the afternoon residents who set fire to the Sichuan Exhibition Hall and looted the Tiancheng Jewelry Store were stopped by some three hundred police from Public Security and the People's Armed Police.

WUHAN:

More than seven thousand students continued to demonstrate, stopping traffic in parts of the city. About one thousand staged a sit-in on the railroad tracks, halting rail traffic on the Beijing–Guangzhou and Wuhan–Dalian lines for three hours. More than a thousand students went to the Wuhan Steel Mill and other major enterprises to urge workers to strike.

JINAN:

More than ten thousand students took to the streets, and four thousand spoke publicly at forty or more street corners. Roadblocks built with electric buses and street dividers stopped traffic at major downtown intersections. Universities began to empty campus, and some three thousand students left school. Around 10 P.M. a confrontation occurred between Public Security from the Lixia District and a hundred or so residents who were setting up roadblocks. At 11 P.M. protesters stormed the Lixia precinct station, destroying the signboard and inquiry desk, breaking windows on the ground floor, and burning a Shanghai-model sedan. Of the fifty people arrested at the scene, none was a college student.

HEFEI:

More than eighteen hundred students went to the Hefei Steel Company to urge workers to strike. Students continued erecting roadblocks at major intersections, stopping traffic in parts of the city.

NANJING:

More than three thousand students erected roadblocks at major routes into the city, including the Yangtze River bridge, bringing downtown traffic to a halt. More than a thousand students continued to mass at Drum Tower Square, where they made speeches and relayed broadcasts from Voice of America.

NANCHANG:

More than two thousand students, answering the call of the empty-campus movement, left school that afternoon. Under the banner of the Nanchang Solidarity Union some one thousand workers and residents demonstrated outside the headquarters of the provincial and municipal workers' unions.[21]

FUZHOU:

More than a thousand students took to the streets, and another thousand responded to the empty-campus movement and went home.

GUANGZHOU:

During the day panicky Guangzhou residents began queuing up to buy rice, salt, sugar, eggs, and pork. In the afternoon about two hundred young workers and residents installed wreaths and made speeches in the vehicular lanes on Haizhu Bridge. In the evening more than twenty thousand residents and students again massed in Haizhu Square, bringing traffic to a halt.

SHENZHEN:

More than three thousand students massed in Shenzhen Cinema Square to protest the "June Fourth Massacre." High school students carrying wreaths then marched downtown, attracting twenty thousand onlookers.

HAIKOU:

Early in the morning more than fifteen hundred students and young teachers held a memorial meeting in Haikou Park, where they placed wreaths on the Monument to the People's Heroes Who Liberated Hainan.

KUNMING:

More than five thousand students continued to mass in East Wind Square, where they called upon workers to strike.

GUIYANG:

More than ten thousand students and residents continued to demonstrate in People's Square, bringing downtown traffic to a standstill. Posters with slogans such as "Hang Li Peng" and "Repay blood debts" were pasted on nearly all buses, and wall posters of all sizes appeared everywhere.

---

[21]That is, the unions sponsored by the Chinese government. The unofficial Nanchang Solidarity Union seems to have chosen its name with the Polish Solidarity union in mind.

June 7

SHANGHAI:

At Tongji University, East China Normal University, and Shanghai Polytechnic University, students stormed school auditoriums and classroom buildings, where they erected biers. Tens of thousands of students from the East China Institute of Chemical Technology, East China Normal University, Shanghai Jiaotong University, and the Shanghai Railway Medical College continued to erect roadblocks, bringing city traffic to a standstill. Rumors spread about possible martial law in Shanghai. About three thousand students left school.

TIANJIN:

The number of university students setting up roadblocks has fallen below 40 percent.

HARBIN:

Students erected no new roadblocks, and downtown traffic returned to normal. Approximately three thousand students stayed away from school. In the morning more than four hundred workers from the Harbin Bearings Factory took to the streets; that afternoon they were joined by more than six hundred workers from the Harbin Steam Turbine Factory and other plants. Some seven hundred or eight hundred students went into factories to urge the workers to strike and go out into the streets. More than fifty thousand workers could not get to work.

CHANGCHUN:

More than a thousand students from Jilin University and Northeast Normal University blocked traffic into the Number One Automobile Factory and urged workers to strike. At least a thousand workers were absent from work. As of June 7 only half of Changchun's college students remained on campus.

SHIJIAZHUANG:

More than three hundred students and residents gathered at the gate to the headquarters of the Twenty-Seventh Army. Seven began a sit-in. The chief of the army's Political Section wrote to the Provincial Party Committee, "We are deeply concerned about the rumors that are spreading that the Twenty-Seventh Army was the main force in suppressing the students and residents in Beijing. Family members are worried about two things: first, whether their loved ones in Beijing may be in danger and how long the martial law duties there might last; and second, whether people here at home might begin to view family members differently, perhaps even take them hostage, harm their children, or the like. We request that the local government work on the local people's thinking."

TAIYUAN:

About two-thirds of college students have gone home, but a minority continued to distribute leaflets on major downtown streets. The most eye-catching leaflet, signed by "all Taiyuan college students," read, "Military forces across the nation, mobilize and fight your way into Beijing. Destroy the Twenty-Seventh Army and hang Deng, Li, and Yang. Hurry, hurry, hurry!"

HOHHOT:

More than nine thousand students from seven universities, including Inner Mongolia University, responded to the empty-campus movement by returning home. Members of the Communist Party and Youth League in five Inner Mongolia University departments posted a notice of their collective resignation from the League.

CHENGDU:

Only a third of college students remained on campuses.

WUHAN:

At 5 A.M. more than five hundred students from the Chinese Geology University stopped nine buses at the Wuchang East Gate intersection and used them to block traffic over the Yangtze River bridge. At 10 A.M. more than five hundred students carrying wreaths held a memorial at Dadongmen, after which they erected roadblocks at nearby intersections. More than three hundred students from the Wuhan Institute of Iron and Steel Technology erected roadblocks around the Wuhan Steel Mill. On Wuchang bridge students and residents stopped freight train number 3981 on the Beijing–Guangzhou line. A small group damaged the locomotive and poured gasoline over the freight cars but were stopped in the nick of time by arriving police. At 10 P.M. more than three thousand students and teachers from Central China Normal University marched to colleges to demonstrate. Traffic came to a halt. Insecure residents throughout the city withdrew cash and began panic buying.

CHANGSHA:

More than a thousand residents and students continued to erect roadblocks at major intersections, bringing downtown traffic to a standstill. Four hours after they were cleared, railroad tracks were blocked again by more than a thousand students and residents.

JINAN:

More than a thousand workers, organized by the Jinan Workers Federation, carried wreaths in a protest march. Sporadic smashing and arson occurred; four cars were burned and three were overturned.

HEFEI:

More than five thousand students and residents continued to march. Only some of the roadblocks erected by students at major intersections had been cleared, leaving traffic still partially snarled. Students set up a Voice of the People broadcasting station in Municipal Government Square. It broadcast from dawn to dusk, including programs from VOA.

NANJING:

Traffic was relatively unimpeded, but at least a thousand students were still out on the streets. At 7 A.M. more than four hundred students from four colleges, including Hehai University, blocked the Yangtze River bridge with four buses, allowing only mail trucks and ice deliveries to pass. At 4 P.M. traffic on the bridge was still blocked. More than a thousand students from Nanjing University and other schools erected roadblocks at the Zhongyangmen Railway Bridge; not a single train could pass through from 8:40 A.M. until 4 P.M., when the students were finally persuaded to evacuate. Normal traffic resumed at 5 P.M.

HANGZHOU:

This was the third day students from Zhejiang University were lying on railroad tracks. At 7:30 P.M., after Deputy Governor Chai Songyue and others came to negotiate, the students left the Nanxing Bridge Railway Station; normal rail traffic resumed at 8:12 P.M. From 6 P.M. on June 4 until 6 P.M. on June 5 a total of sixty trains were stopped, forty-six of which were passenger trains; forty thousand passengers were stranded for two to three days. One hundred and sixty-six freight trains were kept from transporting a total of 98,250 tons of goods.

KUNMING:

More than a thousand students, carrying wreaths and wearing black armbands, continued to march to "mourn the student victims in Beijing."

June 8

SHANGHAI:

Electricity use in Shanghai declined steadily beginning June 3. On that day the city used 66.53 million kilowatt-hours, and on June 7 the figure had fallen to 60.28 million kilowatt-hours. This was caused by worker absence and lateness that reached as high as 34.38 percent in 997 enterprises, including enterprises in light industry, metallurgy, textiles, instruments and meters, shipping, aviation, and electrical equipment. Twelve factories stopped production, and twenty-three others cut back drastically. The number of ships waiting to be loaded reached sixteen. Clients in Japan and Hong Kong called to cancel orders. On the evening of June 7 Mayor Zhu Rongji gave a televised speech in which he emphasized that "Shanghai cannot afford any turmoil." He emphasized that martial law would not be declared in Shanghai. "Many comrades have asked us to call in the People's Armed Police, and some have even suggested bringing in the army. As mayor, I solemnly declare that neither the Party Committee nor the Municipal Government has considered calling in the army. We have never envisaged military control or martial law; we seek only to stabilize Shanghai, to steady the situation, to insist on production, and to ensure normal life." That evening tens of thousands of workers were sent out to clear away the roadblocks.

TIANJIN:

Situation normal. Li Ruihuan's catchword, "Tianjin cannot afford turmoil," has gained support from the citizenry. Most college students, except for those who are graduating, have left their campuses.

HARBIN:

No students erected roadblocks. More than a hundred students made speeches. Statistics show that about twenty thousand students, or about 40 percent of the total, have left their campuses. Those who remain at school continually receive letters and telegrams from their parents urging them to return home.

SHIJIAZHUANG:

Appropriate measures were taken on June 8 to deal with the passenger trains that had been stranded in Hebei since the morning of June 6: numbers 47 and 15 from Beijing to Guangzhou, number 5 from Beijing to Nanning, and number 149 from Beijing to Guiyang. In response to a request from railway officials, Zhengding Railway Station and other rail stations in Shijiazhuang began supplying passengers with food and water. According to a report from the branch office of the Shijiazhuang Railway Bureau, all passenger and freight trains under its jurisdiction have resumed normal operations except for passenger trains stranded south of the Yangtze River. The transportation of coal and other necessities from Hebei to Beijing was not interrupted.

TAIYUAN:

Universities issued a letter to parents asking that students return to school. Statistics show that fewer than a third of students remain on their campuses: Nine hundred of the six thousand students at Shanxi University have stayed behind; eight hundred of the twenty-seven hundred students at the Shanxi College of Finance and Economics remain on campus; barely two thousand of fifty-five hundred students at Taiyuan Polytechnic University remain; the best case is Shanxi Medical College, where twelve hundred of two thousand students remain.

XI'AN:

The situation has begun to improve. The Shaanxi Party Committee issued a policy statement calling for "restraint of rioters and avoidance of face-to-face confrontation or any escalation of conflict." Roadblocks were cleared and wall posters removed. Three of the nine campus broadcast stations that the AFS had seized were voluntarily handed back.

LANZHOU:

No marches, and the situation has gradually stabilized. The Gansu Provincial Party Committee announced six concrete measures: 1. Quick action will be taken to clamp down on leaders of the Citizen Support Group. 2. Student organizers of the AFS will receive educational work and be enjoined to shape up while they still can. 3. Yuan Mu's speech and other material from the Central Propaganda Department will be widely disseminated in order to blanket Lanzhou with the voice of Party Central. 4. Everything possible will be done to ensure smooth railway traffic on the Gansu–Shanghai line. 5. Enterprises will be mobilized to form factory-protection teams. 6. Party members who have deviated from the correct line during this movement will be disciplined.

CHENGDU:

The downtown area is relatively calm; traffic is back to normal.

CHONGQING:

Downtown traffic was paralyzed as more than three thousand students, mostly from Chongqing University, continued erecting roadblocks at major intersections. More than a thousand students marched and made speeches.

WUHAN:

At a meeting at Wuhan University the AFS decided to set up an underground radio station and relocate its printing facility. Early in the morning some five hundred students from Hubei University and other schools, under the banner of the Hubei Dare-to-Die Team, staged a sit-in outside the Wuchang Automobile Factory, stopping workers from going to work. More than three hundred students from the Wuhan College of Iron and Steel stopped trains at the rail crossing at Renjia Road and sat down on the tracks, blocking traffic for four hours.

CHANGSHA:

In the afternoon the AFS held a memorial meeting at the Changsha Railway Station; thirty thousand students and residents attended. Wreaths and elegiac couplets crowded both sides of the platform in the main hall where the meeting took place. It began at 3:50 P.M. with funeral music and eulogies and was followed by speeches from students, workers, teachers, and out-of-town students. After it ended at 4:50 P.M. a major march began, blocking traffic throughout the city.

QINGDAO:

More than five hundred students from the Qingdao College of Oceanography stopped cars and erected roadblocks, halting traffic in parts of the city.

HEFEI:

Five or six hundred students continued erecting roadblocks, snarling traffic in parts of the city.

NANJING:

In the morning more than a thousand students from Nanjing University and Hehai University, as well as some nonstudents, retook an overpass one kilometer from the Nanjing Railway Station, halting rail traffic. Meanwhile another five hundred students staged a sit-in at the south end of the highway section of the Nanjing Yangtze River bridge and at the Zhongyangmen section of the Beijing–Shanghai rail line. Traffic was blocked until 4 P.M. The Jiangsu Provincial Party Committee issued the following orders: 1. Make the students understand that the situation is now out of control and that riffraff is exploiting the students' passion in order to stir up trouble. 2. All public security personnel will warn potential troublemakers against any further illegal actions. 3. If there is an outbreak of turmoil, Public Security will "squeeze" this riffraff from among the students and severely punish them.

FUZHOU:

After the empty-campus movement began on June 6, fewer than a third of college students remained on campus. According to a report from the Provincial Education Commission that day, sixteen thousand of the twenty-three thousand students at Fuzhou University, Fujian Normal University, Fujian Agricultural Institute, Fujian Medical College, and four other institutions have left their campuses. Fewer than two thousand of the eight thousand students at Xiamen University remain on campus.

June 9

SHANGHAI:

Early in the morning more than one hundred thousand workers were sent in teams to clear roadblocks. Reserve teams of ten thousand to twenty thousand more were mobilized in every district to maintain order. Later in the morning more than six thousand students from fifteen universities, including Fudan University, Shanghai Jiaotong University, East China Normal University, East China Institute of Chemical Technology, and Tongji University, held a "memorial" in People's Square to "mourn the victims in Beijing." The participants wore black armbands, carried wreaths, and hoisted school flags as they entered the square in an orderly manner. A large wreath, about two meters in diameter, was placed to the north of the square, surrounded by a dozen smaller wreaths of various sizes.

Loudspeakers broadcast "The Truth of the Beijing Massacre" and "A Student Witness Account of the June Third Massacre." The Shanghai AFS read a declaration that said, "(1) Municipal Government leaders must have dialogue with the students. (2) Television stations must broadcast complete videotapes of the events in Beijing on June 3 and 4. (3) All flags in the city should be lowered to half staff in mourning." Around 2 P.M. protesters marched to municipal government offices on the Bund to deliver this declaration. Around 4 P.M. more than a thousand students staged a protest at the offices of *Liberation Daily* and burned a bundle of today's edition of the paper.

SHENYANG:

In a surprise raid, Shenyang Public Security arrested thirty-two nonstudents who had wormed their ways into student ranks and were leading the students in stopping cars. For the first time in a week the city was peaceful; there were no marchers on the street, workers were back on the job, and traffic was back to normal. In the early morning, following the surprise raid, "the Shenyang AFS called a meeting at Northeast Institute of Technology, where those attending felt rather panicky and decided college students should no longer be on the streets, let alone block traffic." After interrogation, eight of the thirty-two arrested people were detained; the remaining twenty-four received warnings and were released in the afternoon.

XI'AN:

Three public-address systems—at the Bell Tower, Xincheng Square, and the corner of Xiwu Road—continued to broadcast foreign news reports as well as letters and telegrams from Beijing. Students returning from Beijing made speeches on "the truth about June Fourth." Except for those at and around the Bell Tower, roadblocks have been cleared, traffic is nearly back to normal, and stores are open for business. The Xi'an Railway Station is orderly but much quieter than normal because passengers are far fewer.

LANZHOU:

Early in the morning Lanzhou Municipal Public Security sent out a huge patrol that arrested sixty-five people who had been stopping traffic and erecting roadblocks. Later in the morning the patrol twice stormed Central Square downtown, dispersing a few hundred people and arresting seventeen leaders of a Citizens' Support Group. The AFS broadcasting station called Voice of the Square was dismantled, and no student again made any speech in the square. The AFS at Lanzhou University abandoned its campus public-address system; it is unclear where the AFS leaders have gone. Two-thirds of the city's college students have left their campuses. All the roadblocks were cleared the same day they were erected. Traffic police went to work returning the flow of traffic to normal. Many stores reopened for business.

YINCHUAN:

More than five hundred students held a memorial meeting at South Gate Square. They broadcast news of the "June Fourth massacre" in Beijing, laid wreaths, played dirges, read eulogies, and made vows. The empty-campus movement reached a peak. The AFS organized students to appear on major downtown streets to make speeches, hand out leaflets, and put up posters. More than a thousand high school and college students departed for twenty outlying counties and cities, where they organized propaganda teams to tell students and residents "the truth about the June Fourth massacre."

WUHAN:

AFS organizations at all schools except Wuhan University have been disbanded. The situation in the city is relatively calm.

XIANGTAN:

More than three hundred students from Xiangtan University went to the Xiangtan Electrical Machinery Plant and Xiangtan Electric Cable Plant to demonstrate and to urge workers to strike.

HANGZHOU:

More than four hundred students went to the Hangzhou Steel Mill and to Yuhang, Xiaoshan, Shaoxing, and other cities to spread propaganda, to urge workers to strike, and to tell about "the bloody massacre on June Fourth."

GUANGZHOU:

Traffic order and social order returned to the city, and panic buying stopped. College students across the city responded to the empty-campus movement; fewer than a third remain at school. The Guangzhou AFS announced the empty-campus movement would continue through August 20.

GUIYANG:

Students at nine universities protested by joining the empty-campus movement. Statistics from the Provincial Education Commission show that not even 20 percent of students remain on campus, hence normal campus life is impossible. In the evening more than two thousand residents and students massed again at People's Square, where they made speeches and listened to loudspeakers blaring news from Beijing. One unidentified organizer said over the loudspeaker that at 10 A.M. on June 10 a detailed plan for a workers' strike, a merchants' strike, and roadblocks would be announced at the square.

On the afternoon of June 9 Deng Xiaoping gave a talk to high-ranking officials of the martial law troops,[22] and the State Council issued an "Announcement on Resolutely Preventing Disruption of Economic Order and Ensuring That Industrial Production Proceeds Normally." All province-level governments adopted procedures from the "Notice on Ensuring Urban Security and Stability" that the Party General Office and State Council had issued. The Public Security Ministry's "Urgent Notice Demanding Close Surveillance and Control of Turmoil Elements," led municipal public security offices to launch an all-out campaign to arrest student leaders and citizen activists. By June 10 this campaign effectively throttled protest activities everywhere, and an outward calm settled over the country.

June 5–20

Foreign sanctions

Abroad, 683 Chinese students announced their resignations from the CCP. Longtime friends of the Chinese government like Han Suyin[23] protested, and William Hinton,[24] an agricultural expert who had long lived in China, called upon the world to cease grain sales to China. At the United Nations a spokesman said the secretary general was "extremely depressed" over the events in Beijing but urged restraint, noting that the UN Charter opposes intervention in internal affairs of member states.

[22]See the Epilogue.
[23]Han Suyin [pseud.] is the author of more than a dozen books known for their generous praise of the Chinese Communist movement, including *Crippled Tree* (New York: Putnam, 1965), *China in the Year 2000* (New York: Basic Books, 1967), and *Morning Deluge: Mao Zedong and the Chinese Revolution* (Boston: Little, Brown & Co., 1972).
[24]An American who lived in rural China during the Mao years and wrote, among other books, *Fanshen: A Documentary of Revolution in a Chinese Village* (New York: Monthly Review Press, 1966).

Zhongnanhai received a stream of reports on how foreign condemnation was being buttressed by sanctions. In the United States President Bush on June 5 announced five measures: a temporary halt to weapons sales and commercial exports to China, a suspension of visits between U.S. and Chinese military leaders, a reconsideration of Chinese student requests to extend their stays in the United States, provision through the International Red Cross of humanitarian medical aid to the victims, and a review of bilateral agreements. The House of Representatives voted unanimously to support the president's decision on cessation of military cooperation with China, and the Senate voted unanimously to demand that the president take further measures. The U.S. government announced that some forty-five thousand Chinese in the United States would be allowed to stay after their visas expired. Mayor Edward I. Koch of New York discontinued his city's sister-city relationship with Beijing and called for renaming the intersection in front of the Chinese consulate general on Forty-Second Street and Twelfth Avenue "Tiananmen Square."

On June 20 the White House asked Western countries to suspend multilateral loans to China and said that the United States was asking international financial institutions to consider postponing new loans. The World Bank had already announced that it was freezing loans to China and was postponing deliberation on Beijing's request for two new loans.

The European Union and individual European countries joined in the condemnation and sanctions. The British government canceled a visit to England by China's minister of justice and a visit to China by Britain's minister of agriculture. France and West Germany also announced freezes in high-level contacts. Sanctions were announced by Belgium, Portugal, Austria, Greece, Netherlands, Denmark, Finland, Sweden, and Switzerland.

The Japanese ambassador to China delivered a stern protest over the wounding of three Japanese personnel when Chinese troops opened fire toward the diplomatic residences in Beijing. Major Japanese banks and enterprises recalled their staffs. Japanese banks announced they were freezing two loans to China, and the government halted one other large loan, effectively suspending all aid to China. The status of China's exports to Japan was changed from general to special, a move that required China to apply case-by-case in order to export to Japan.

Australia canceled a planned visit to China by its prime minister. New Zealand announced it was canceling the visit of its minister of police and urging its citizens not to visit China. The Brazilian government, which until now had observed a policy of never commenting on the internal affairs of other states, broke precedent to express its regret.

In the Communist world the Soviet Union expressed regret over the use of force and hoped the situation would quickly improve. Concern was expressed by the governments of Poland, Hungary, and Yugoslavia. The Vietnamese Foreign Ministry stated that Western reports of Hanoi's support for the Chinese government's actions were "pure fabrications."

Elsewhere in Asia, South Korea expressed grave concern and said the worsening situation in China might affect stability on the Korean peninsula. The president of the Philippines pledged to ensure the safety of Philippine citizens in China. The Thai prime minister expressed his worry that if hard-liners gained ascendancy in China, it would become more difficult to reduce tensions in Cambodia. The Malaysian prime minister said his government would not interfere in China's internal affairs, but he expressed regret over the deaths of so many people. The Indonesian government announced only that discussion on normalizing relations between China and Indonesia would continue as scheduled. The Singapore government declined to comment.

In Hong Kong people formed long lines outside branches of the Bank of China and withdrew a record five billion Hong Kong dollars on June 5. In Macao savers jostled at Bank of China branches to withdraw 330 million Hong Kong dollars.

In Taiwan President Lee Teng-hui protested the Chinese government's use of force and called on all peoples and nations who love freedom and respect human rights to denounce the PRC government. The Ministry of Defense ordered all officers and soldiers to terminate leave and return to base, and the government announced that it would provide Republic of China passports and financial aid to Chinese students and scholars abroad who wanted to give up their PRC passports.

June 1989 and After:
Renewed Struggle over China's Future

EDITORS' NOTE: While the Elders and the new central leaders congratulated themselves for the successful defense of Party power and expressed scorn for foreign criticisms and sanctions, Deng Xiaoping struggled to ensure that the tragedy did not push China off his preferred course of reform. At a June 6 meeting of the Elders with the Politburo Standing Committee and at a June 9 appearance at the headquarters of the martial law troops—his first public appearance after the crackdown—Deng said China must persist in economic reform and opening to the West. Political reform, however, was a different matter. Deng urged that new laws on assembly, association, and other rights, which had been in the works in the liberal period before the demonstrations, should be crafted carefully to avoid instability, and he suggested that China should avoid changing its political system to resemble those of the West.

He stressed the same themes at a June 16 briefing for the incoming Politburo Standing Committee and at a June 19–21 enlarged meeting of the Politburo. The Party must have a core, he argued, and he urged everyone present to unify around the newly chosen general secretary, Jiang Zemin. The experience of the past few months did not mean the ten-year-old policies of reform and opening were wrong. Economic growth and anticorruption measures would win back the hearts of the people, but the Party must resist measures that would weaken its control. These instructions echoed those Deng had given to Li Peng and Yao Yilin on May 31.

Yet the Party remained divided. Comments by some of the Party's senior members at an enlarged Politburo meeting of June 19–21 betrayed fears that Deng's economic reforms had gone too far in undermining political and ideological discipline. On the other hand, Zhao Ziyang's rebuttal of Li Peng's charges against him at the Fourth Plenum of the Thirteenth Central Committee criticized the Deng line from the other direction. Although Zhao claimed to have implemented Deng's orders loyally, he also argued the Party could not survive without bolder political reform. Zhao's views remained widely popular.

Deng's power was diluted after June Fourth. He faced a long struggle to restart his economic reforms.

June 6

The leaders take stock

Two and a half days after what was now officially called "putting down the counterrevolutionary riots," the healthier Elders (Deng Xiaoping, Li Xiannian, Peng Zhen, Yang Shangkun, Bo Yibo, and Wang Zhen) met with the currently serving members of the Politburo Standing Committee (Li Peng, Qiao Shi, and Yao Yilin), plus NPC head Wan Li and the incoming Party general secretary, Jiang Zemin. The agenda included restoring order in Beijing and across the country and arranging for the central committee's next meeting, the Fourth Plenum of the Thirteenth Central Committee.

> Excerpts from Party Central Office Secretariat, "Minutes of the CCP Central Politburo Standing Committee meeting," June 6, with a small number of supplements added from a tape recording of the meeting

Deng Xiaoping: "If we hadn't been firm with these counterrevolutionary riots—if we hadn't come down hard—who knows what might have happened? The PLA has suffered a great deal; we owe them a lot, we really do. If the plots of the people who were pushing the riots had gotten anywhere, we'd have had civil war. And if there'd been civil war—of course our side would have won, but just think of all the deaths! We had no choice but to come down hard. When they put down the riots, the soldiers did their best not to harm the people, especially the students. They followed our orders precisely; they protected the interests of the Party, the state, and the people. This was a very severe test and they passed."

Li Xiannian: "If we hadn't put down those counterrevolutionary riots, could we be talking here now? The PLA soldiers really are the brothers of the Chinese people, as well as the sturdy pillars of the Party and the state. But the work of putting down the counterrevolutionary riots has only begun; the situation in Beijing is still precarious. We still need to rely on our brothers the soldiers to restore order in Beijing."

Yang Shangkun: "We've paid a high price for putting down these counterrevolutionary riots. Restoring social order in Beijing should be our top priority now, and that means we've got a lot of political thought work to do."

Peng Zhen: "Putting down the riots and restoring social order relate to the big picture of the capital and the whole country. All kinds of rumors are running wild these days. We need to set things straight, and fast. On how many died, for example, the number has gone from thousands to tens of thousands, and people like VOA are making up new rumors every day. We need to come up with some positive things to say."

Bo Yibo: "I've got some material here—reports from all the big Western news services and TV networks about the so-called June 4 bloodbath at Tiananmen and the numbers of dead and wounded. Let me read it. Associated Press: 'At least five hundred dead.' NBC: 'Fourteen hundred dead, ten thousand wounded.' ABC: 'Two thousand dead.' American intelligence agencies: 'Three thousand dead.' BBC: 'Two thousand dead, up to ten thousand injured.' Reuters: 'More than one thousand dead.'" L'Agence France-Presse: 'At least fourteen hundred dead, ten thousand injured.'" UPI: 'More than three hundred dead.' Kyodo News Agency: 'Three thousand dead, more than two thousand injured.' Japan's *Yomiuri Shimbun:* 'Three thousand dead.' The impact is huge when numbers like these get spread all over the world! We need to counterattack against these rumors right now."

Li Peng: "Mr. Bo[1] is right. Yuan Mu is holding a press conference this afternoon at Zhongnanhai to release the true facts.[2] The General Office of the State Council reports that as of noon today the basic statistics—which have been double- and triple-checked with Martial Law Headquarters and the Chinese Red Cross— are these: Five thousand PLA soldiers and officers wounded, and more than two thousand local people (counting students, city people, and rioters together) also wounded. The figures on the dead are these: twenty-three from the martial law troops, including ten from the PLA and thirteen from the People's Armed Police. About two hundred soldiers are also missing. The dead among city people, students, and rioters number about two hundred, of whom thirty-six are university students. No one was killed within Tiananmen Square itself."

Qiao Shi: "Public Security reports that most of the killed and wounded were

[1] *Bo lao;* see footnote 39 in Chapter 6.
[2] Text of Yuan Mu's press conference is in Michel Oksenberg, Lawrence R. Sullivan, and Marc Lambert, eds., *Beijing Spring, 1989, Confrontation and Conflict: The Basic Documents* (Armonk, New York: M. E. Sharpe, 1990), 363–376.

city people and that these included not just rioters—who got what they deserved—but onlookers as well. None of the leaders of the illegal organizations like the AFS or AFW was killed, and no one's heard that any got injured, either. So it's going to take a lot of work to get order fully restored."

Li Peng: "No spouting of rumors can cover up the facts any more. Investigations have determined that on the night of June 3 all the leaders of those illegal organizations like the 'United Conference,'[3] the AFS, the AFW, and so on went into hiding. That Wang Dan, who'd been out in the Square almost every day, sneaked off, and the hoodlum Wuerkaixi suddenly turned chicken. He went to the Square a little after 8 P.M., and less than two hours later, when he heard we were going to clear the Square, he faked illness and stole away. The martial law troops didn't even kill people like that AFS activist Guo Haifeng—the one who wanted to use gasoline canisters to set fire to the wall of the Forbidden City at Tiananmen. They only arrested him. Facts like this can show how despicable and crazy those Western reports of a Tiananmen 'bloodbath' are."

Yang Shangkun: "Comrade Li Peng is right. We've all seen that videotape of the young man blocking the tank. Our tank gave way time and again, but he just stayed there, right in the way, and even crawled up onto the tank, and still the soldiers held their fire. That says it all! If our soldiers had fired, the repercussions would have been very different. Our soldiers carried out Party Central's orders with precision. It's amazing they could stay cool and patient in a spot like that!"

Yao Yilin: "This is like a battle in war. Our national economy's been devastated since this turmoil began. Economic life is chaotic, and it's hard to keep industry running normally. The big cities keep reporting emergencies, especially in the last few days. Old industrial bases like Shanghai and Liaoning are seeing losses of thirty to forty million yuan every day. And the country as a whole is not going to settle down until the capital gets back to normal."

Wang Zhen: "We're still going to have to rely on the PLA to stabilize things. We need to get the PLA, the PAP, and the regular police all out there hitting those counterrevolutionary rioters as hard as they can, arresting where necessary, killing when they need to, and being absolutely sure no rioters get away."

Deng Xiaoping: "This whole thing can teach us a big lesson, and if we learn it well, it will help, not hurt, the Four Modernizations and the work of reform and opening. For several years now some of our comrades have buried their heads in technical things and haven't looked at big political trends. They haven't taken political thought work seriously, haven't guarded closely enough against corrup-

---

[3] A reference to the United Conference of Patriotic Beijing Organizations in Support of the Constitution.

tion, and haven't put enough punch into their corrective measures. This incident has been a wake-up call for all of us. We'll never keep the lid on if we relax on the Four Basic Principles. Of all China's problems, the one that trumps everything is the need for stability. We have to jump on anything that might bring instability; we can't give ground on this point, can't bend at all. And we can't care what foreigners say. Let them say what they want! Anyway, it's always the same: always how benighted we are. They've been at it for years, berating us constantly, but what's it got them? All this boils down to one thing: China can't take chaos. We can't allow chaos, and we have to keep saying so, bluntly and openly. We'd be wrong not to."

Li Peng: "All the Western countries, with the United States in the lead, are issuing one or another kind of proclamation about applying sanctions against China and cutting China off from the world."

Deng Xiaoping: "Those countries like to come up with resolution after resolution about how to interfere in our internal affairs. But the interference is no big deal for us; we can ignore it if we like, or we can fight back. Those countries want to apply sanctions against us? All right, but first, let's ask them why this is any of their business. And second, if it is, then we can fight with sanctions, too. Our economic growth might suffer, but not all that much. We've done all right under international sanctions for most of the forty years of the People's Republic. So we don't have to worry too much; we can take it all calmly. This little tempest is not going to blow us over. We're not trying to offend anybody; we're just plugging away at our own work. Anybody who tries to interfere in our affairs or threaten us is going to come up empty.

"We Chinese have self-confidence; inferiority complexes get you nowhere. For more than a century we were forced to feel inferior, but then, under the leadership of the Communist Party, we stood up. No behemoth out there can scare us now. We fought the Japanese for eight years and fought the Americans in Korea for three. We have a tradition of winning even when we're outnumbered or under-armed. Our people are not going to cower before foreign invasions or threats, and neither will our children or grandchildren.

"This incident has taught us that the sovereignty and security of our country must come first. We see this more clearly than we did before. The Chinese people will never tolerate any behavior that violates international norms, nor will they bend under pressure. Our use of martial law to deal with the turmoil was absolutely necessary. In the future, whenever it might be necessary, we will use severe measures to stamp out the first signs of turmoil as soon as they appear. This will show that we won't put up with foreign interference and will protect our national sovereignty.

"In short, the indispensable conditions for reaching our own development goals are a stable environment domestically and a peaceful environment internationally. We don't care what others say about us; all we care about is a peaceful environment for our own development. We won't close any doors; our biggest lesson from the past has been not to isolate ourselves from the world—that only puts us out of touch and into a big sleep. If history confirms the superiority of the Chinese socialist system, that's enough for us. What happens with the social systems of other countries is none of our business."

Li Xiannian: "The key to stabilizing things right now is to be supertough in tracking down the counterrevolutionary rioters, especially the plotters who were organizing things behind the scenes. This conflict is a conflict with the enemy.[4] We've got to be clear on this point, because if we're not, it'll be hard to get our work going and all our future work will be vulnerable."

Deng Xiaoping: "We should mete out the necessary punishments, in varying degrees, to the ambitious handful who were trying to subvert the People's Republic—like Fang Lizhi. But we should be forgiving toward the student demonstrators and petition signers, whether from Beijing, from elsewhere in China, or from overseas, and we shouldn't try to track down individual responsibility among them. . . . We also need to watch our methods as we take control of the situation. We should be extra careful about laws, especially the laws and regulations on assembly, association, marches, demonstrations, journalism, and publishing.[5] Activities that break the law must be suppressed. We can't just allow people to demonstrate whenever they want to. If people demonstrate 365 days a year and don't want to do anything else, reform and opening will get nowhere. We've got to make it understood both inside and outside China that we're tightening control for the sake of stability, which means for the sake of reform and opening and modern construction."

The decisions of this meeting were these:

1. To convene an enlarged meeting of the Politburo from June 19 to 21.
2. To convene the Fourth Plenum of the Thirteenth Central Committee from June 23 to 24.
3. Party Central, the NPC, the State Council, the CPPCC, and the CMC must

---

[4]That is, not a conflict among the people; see footnote 31 in Chapter 2.
[5]These were laws yet to be adopted. Deng is suggesting that they should be drafted carefully so people cannot use them to threaten stability.

all quickly draft and distribute documents and regulations on the restoration of social and economic order.

June 9

Deng Xiaoping's first public appearance after June 4

Once order had been largely restored in Beijing, Deng Xiaoping made his first public appearance; on June 9 he hosted a reception for high-ranking officers of the martial law troops in the Huairentang hall in Zhongnanhai.[6] Several other leaders joined Deng in congratulating the troops.

Deng opened by calling for a moment of silence in honor of the "deceased martyrs" among the troops. "This storm," as he called the recent events, was bound to happen sooner or later. Without the Elders, he said, the situation could not have been saved. A few comrades perhaps did not understand the situation at first, but they eventually would and would thank the Center for its decisions. The goal of the people who fomented the turmoil was to overthrow the Party, state, and socialist system and to replace it with a pro-Western bourgeois republic. Their slogans about opposing corruption were a mere device. Deng praised the PLA for its restraint.

For the benefit of the Politburo members rather than the military officers who were present, Deng then turned to matters of current policy. Recent events, he said, did not prove the policy of reform and opening was wrong. The policy was correct; the problem was that political education work had been neglected. The Party should continue to pursue one center and two basic points—that is, a unified leadership navigating between the Four Basic Principles and the policy of reform and opening. He noted that although inflation and bad influences from the West had been problems recently, China's two-tiered economy—part planned, part market—must continue. China should not return to the closed-door policy of the past. Far from being at fault in the recent turmoil, reform and opening had not been pursued thoroughly enough.

In thinking about political reform, Deng added, China should stick with the model of a single National People's Congress and not go for American-style tripartite separation of powers. Student demonstrators in the United States have also been met by police and soldiers, Deng pointed out, but, he said, the Americans were suppressing students and citizens, whereas the Chinese government was putting down counterrevolutionary rioters.

[6]Text of Deng's speech in *Deng Xiaoping wenxuan* (Selected works of Deng Xiaoping), vol. 3 (Beijing: Renmin chubanshe, 1993), 302–308; translation in Oksenberg et al., *Beijing Spring*, 376–382.

That evening a simplified version of Deng's speech was made public. It stressed that the rest of the country should quickly follow Beijing in restoring order. To ordinary Chinese, one of its main messages was that Deng was, as ever, firmly in control.

June 16

Briefing the new team

Nearly two weeks after the repression, Deng Xiaoping met with the members of the new Politburo Standing Committee that was scheduled to be elected at the upcoming Fourth Plenum: Jiang Zemin, Li Peng, Qiao Shi, Yao Yilin, Song Ping, and Li Ruihuan. Although the three new members of the committee, Jiang, Song, and Li Ruihuan, had already been selected by the Elders, they had not participated in the decisions surrounding June Fourth and would not take up their Standing Committee seats until they had been confirmed at the Central Committee meeting. Yang Shangkun and Wan Li also attended Deng's briefing.

> Excerpts from Party Central Office Secretariat, "Minutes of the CCP Central Politburo Standing Committee meeting," June 16[7]

Deng Xiaoping: "Our Party now has to build its third generation of collective leadership. Let's look at our history. We didn't have a mature central leadership until the Zunyi Conference [in 1935]. From Chen Duxiu to Qu Qiubai, Xiang Zhongfa, and Li Lisan right up to Wang Ming there was never a strong Party Central. Our stable collective leadership, which gradually took shape after the Zunyi meeting, began with Mao, Liu, Zhou, Zhu and Comrade Ren Bishi. After Comrade Bishi died, Comrade Chen Yun joined, and then at the Eighth Party Congress [in 1956] the six-man Standing Committee of Mao, Liu, Zhou, Zhu, Chen, and Deng was formed. Later Lin Biao was added, and this leadership collective lasted until the Cultural Revolution. So for quite a long time, up until the Cultural Revolution, we stuck with a collective leadership around Comrade Mao Zedong as the core. This was our first generation of leadership.

"The Third Plenum of the Eleventh Central Committee [in 1978] set up a new

---

[7]Later, edited version of Deng's remarks in *Deng Xiaoping wenxuan*, 309–314; translation of Deng's remarks in Oksenberg et al., *Beijing Spring*, 382–388.

leadership collective that became our Party's second generation of leadership. You could say, to speak plainly, that I had a key position in this second generation. And I started working on the problem of a successor as soon as I could. It's true that the first two candidates I tried didn't work out,[8] but given their records—at the time I made the choices—of experience with struggle, work accomplishment, and level of political thinking, they were the obvious ones to go with. People do change, after all.

"Any leadership collective needs a core. A leadership that lacks a core is unreliable. Chairman Mao was the core of the first generation of collective leadership, and if he had not been in that position, the Cultural Revolution would have brought the Party down. I have served as the core of the second generation of leadership. Our having a core is the reason we've been able to go through two leadership transitions smoothly, without adverse effects on the continuity of Party rule. We need a core as we go into the third generation, and all of you comrades here today need to be constantly aware of this fact in the way you understand and handle things. The core we are all now agreeing to uphold is Comrade Jiang Zemin.

"Let's be clear from the outset: From day one the new Standing Committee must be careful to promote and support this leadership collective and its core. So long as we have a good Politburo, and especially a good Standing Committee, and so long as it is united and works hard and can serve as a model—I mean a model in the hard work of socialist construction and of fighting corruption—then we can withstand any trouble that might come along. But if Party Central itself loses its footing, then anything can happen. This is the crucial question. The fate of the nation, the Party, and the people all depend on having this kind of a leadership collective.

"In my talk with Comrades Li Peng and Yao Yilin, I said that once the new leadership is in place I'm going to bow out. I'll get out of everybody's way. This what I've said, and it's my final political handover. I won't, of course, turn you away if you come to ask me about things, but things are not going to be the same as before. I don't want the new Politburo or Standing Committee to announce that I still have some kind of 'function.'

"Why do I say this? It's not because I'm modest or anything like that. It's because I carry too much weight right now, and that's not good for the Party or the country and could some day be dangerous. A lot of countries around the

---

[8]Refers to Hu Yaobang and Zhao Ziyang.

world are basing their China policies on whether or not I'm healthy or even alive. I first noticed this problem several years ago. It's not healthy—it's dangerous—to let the fate of a nation hang on the prestige of one or two people. It may be fine as long as nothing goes wrong; but if something goes wrong it can be hard to fix. So once the new leadership is in place, everything will be up to you people: If you're right it's you, if you're wrong it's you, and what you achieve is yours. This way you can really concentrate on your work, and the new leadership will have a chance to learn on the job. Besides, the old arrangement wasn't ideal anyhow.

"I'm eighty-five, and at this age I ought to realize where I stand. The big picture is still the main thing. If a single person affects overall stability or gets in the way of healthy national development, it can get hard to solve problems. I can always help from the sidelines if needed, but I really don't want to hold any formal titles. . . .

"The recent events show how crucial it is that China stick with the socialist road and the leadership of the Party. If we don't, then all we'll ever be is somebody's satellite country, and if that happens, even modernization won't be easy. The world marketplace is already pretty competitive; it's not easy to break in. Only socialism can save China and turn it into a developed country. On this point the riots have actually taught us something: They've been a huge wake-up call. China has no future outside the socialist road.

"China is only a poor country, yet people speak of it as part of a 'big triangle' of the United States, China, and the Soviet Union. Why? It's because China is independent and self-governing. And why are we independent? Because we've stuck with our own brand of socialism. Otherwise we'd be aping the United States, the developed countries, the USSR, or who knows what country, and what kind of independence is that? Right now international opinion is raging against us, but we can take it; we won't let them get to us. The important thing is to keep doing our work well. The recent events have brought our mistakes out into the open. And yes, we have made some mistakes—some big ones, in fact!

"We mustn't wait for the riots to be completely put down. We should begin to examine exactly where our mistakes were and how we can correct them even as we proceed with the task of thoroughly suppressing the riots. We have to make judgments about which problems need our attention most urgently; we can't do everything at once. Right now we should concentrate on doing some things that will make the people feel happy and pleased, and at the same time we must pay attention to the issues that are crucial to our progress.

"The economy must keep going. We should do everything we can to spur development, although we mustn't, of course, expect growth to remain as rapid as it's been in the past. The main thing now is that our industrial base is weak because we're short on electricity and raw materials. Small enterprises have been encroaching on the primary resources of big industry, and this creates losses for the state. When we look at how to reverse the current economic downturn, we should identify which problems are most pressing and attend to them immediately. We should be bold and cut right through the tangles—no messing around. Hesitation could kill us. Anything that we're sure about, that's constructive, that will help our development—we should go right after. We should aim for a good rate of economic growth over the next eleven and a half years.[9] . . .

"Party Central and the State Council must have power and authority in these matters. You can't get these things done without an authority! I think we should set up a special group to study development strategy and make specific plans for the first half of the next century. The most important items would be plans for basic industry and a transport system. We should take strong measures to be sure our growth keeps going and gets a second wind. I've said before—about this crisis we've just been through—that if we can sum up lessons from the past and apply them to the future, our development might turn out to be not only better and more stable but faster as well. There's a real possibility that this misfortune can turn into a good thing. We've also got to look carefully at agriculture. In the end, the problems there might have to be solved by science. Science is a great thing; we should emphasize it. . . .

"When I talk about doing things to make the people feel pleased, I mean basically two things: One is to do reform and opening even more audaciously, and the other is to fight corruption. If we pursue reform and opening on the one hand and punish corruption on the other, these two things in combination will make our policies clearer and more able to win the people's favor. . . . The job of more opening belongs mostly to the State Council. It should stoke up its courage and let the banner of opening fly high. The main thing now is to allow risks and to not be afraid of losses. If something looks good for the long run, then do it! We've got to do more for reform and opening. Joint ventures with foreign capital are a go, all the development zones are a go. Attract foreign capital; foreigners profit, yes,

[9]The reference to eleven and a half years seems to be a reference to the time that remained before A.D. 2000, which was Deng's original target date for achieving a doubling of gross national product over the 1980 level. He may have made an arithmetical mistake, because he was speaking only ten and a half years shy of A.D. 2000. However, once he had spoken that way, many Chinese officials began to refer to the twentieth century as lasting until December 31, 2000, thus gaining an extra year within which to achieve Deng's ambitious target.

but in the end we profit, too. Right now the rest of the world is worried that we're closing up again. We should do some things to show there's no change in our policy of reform and opening—indeed that we're going even further with it.

"On the political side of reform, our first goal should be a stable environment. I tell the Americans that China's greatest interest is stability—anything that benefits China's stability is a good thing. I never give an inch—ever—on the Four Basic Principles. The Americans hit the ceiling and spread rumors, but who cares? Cutting the fat out of bureaucracies, strengthening rule of law—these are all reforms. . . . To deal with corruption, we should grab at least a dozen or two big cases, publicize them well, and prosecute them quickly. And we've got to get our Party in order. Our long-range plans might really fail if we don't get rid of corruption, especially at the higher levels in the Party. The new leadership should get on this problem right away. It's bringing the Party back to the way it's supposed to be, after all. One person slaving away here to get things done while another over there is raking in the graft—how can that work? I hope you'll make the corruption problem a special agenda item for discussion. . . .

"The job of putting down the riots should go all the way. It gives us an opportunity to uproot all the illegal organizations in the country, and that's a good thing! If we do it right we'll have won a big victory. We mustn't be soft on the biggest and most flagrant criminals. We should, of course, still make distinctions of degree, base ourselves on facts, and put things in terms of law. We still should use the policy of 'leniency to those who confess, severity to those who resist,'[10] and pursue our policies with a variety of methods. . . .

"The comrades on the Standing Committee should marshal all their energies toward building the Party. We've got to work on the Party—it's absolutely crucial."

In this speech Deng was not only laying out his instructions for the new leadership team but also setting some themes for the upcoming Fourth Plenum, where, in fact, his main points were all adopted.

---

[10]A set phrase for a long-standing policy in CCP police work.

June 19–21

An enlarged meeting of the Politburo

From June 19 to 21 the Politburo held an enlarged meeting to prepare for the Fourth Plenum. In addition to the regular Politburo members, participants included high-ranking Party members from the Party Central Advisory Committee, the State Council, the National People's Congress, and the Chinese People's Political Consultative Conference. Much of the meeting dealt with the mistakes of Zhao Ziyang, Hu Qili, Rui Xingwen, and Yan Mingfu during what was now called the "anti-Party, antisocialist turmoil." Among the Elders and other senior Party figures, Deng Xiaoping, Li Xiannian, Wang Zhen, Bo Yibo, and Song Renqiong attended, but Chen Yun, who was ill, did not; nor did Xu Xiangqian, Nie Rongzhen, Peng Zhen, and Deng Yingchao, who considered themselves retired.

Deng Xiaoping again spoke about his themes of maintaining unity and persisting in reform.

> Excerpts from "Comrade Deng Xiaoping's June 19 talk at the Enlarged Meeting of the Politburo," Secretariat of the Fourth Plenum of the Thirteenth CCP Central Committee, "Meeting materials," June 19

Our new Politburo has some older people as well as some younger ones. The old can lead the young, can help the young. The old have experience, and the young are full of energy. We need the old ones to make the transition—that's important. We need broad vision in selecting leaders. But in any case, it's crucial that the new leadership team project an image of reform and opening to people both inside and outside China. Younger leaders are crucial also because we need to give continuity to the Party's mission. In the future the leadership team will have to keep working on recruiting young people, young Marxists. They are out there: people we ourselves have nurtured, who are politically strong, and who are cultivated in Marxism-Leninism. After a lot of careful comparison we've chosen Comrade Jiang Zemin as general secretary of the Party. He is suitable and I hope everyone will support him. . . .

China is a big country. As long as our leadership remains strong and stable, no one can mess with us. We really do need a leadership collective that projects an image of reform and opening, as well as an image, both at home and abroad, of stability and unity. In fact, it needs to be a model of stability and unity. The challenge for this team is to become a collective leadership, a truly cooperative leadership that can think for itself. The members of the team must be tolerant toward each other, must be modest and yielding in their dealings with one another, must help and complement one another. I'm asking you comrades to pay special attention to this.

I also want to stress that we mustn't abandon reform and opening. If we stay in our old ruts, marching forward with blinders on, not doing any experiments or taking any risks, not paying a few prices for wrong starts here and there, then we'll never reach our long-term goals. We really do need more reform and opening; we won't get anywhere with the door closed. We should make a lot of adjustments in the next two to three years. . . .

Zhao Ziyang did some useful things on the economic front and in reform and opening during his stint at Party Central. But he blocked the Four Basic Principles and opposed Party policy on bourgeois liberalization. He seriously neglected the building of Party spirit and spiritual civilization.[11] He bears undeniable responsibility for the appearance and growth of the turmoil. I agree with Party Central's decision on how to deal with him. But here I need to make a special point: The last two general secretaries both stumbled on the questions of the Four Basic Principles and opposition to bourgeois liberalization. But this doesn't mean our original decisions to choose them were mistaken. In the end neither one of them made the grade, but at the time they were chosen—to judge from their experience with struggle, their work achievements, and their levels of political thought—they were the obvious choices. People do change; we all need to be clear on this point.

The people attending this meeting had been provided with advance copies of a report on Zhao Ziyang's mistakes that Li Peng would present to the upcoming Fourth Plenum, and each person was asked to express his opinions. Some of the senior Party members present took the opportunity to express a variety of dissatisfactions with Deng Xiaoping's reforms via their denunciations of Zhao. A sampling of these remarks follows.

> Excerpts from *Materials for the Fourth Plenum of the Thirteenth Central Committee*, "Remarks" of various speakers, Secretariat of the Fourth Plenum of the CCP Thirteenth Central Committee, June 23–24, 1989

---

[11]Respectively, loyalty to the Party among Party members and correct ideological and moral thinking among the populace.

Song Renqiong: "Comrade Zhao Ziyang's big mistake was that he separated reform and opening from the Four Basic Principles. Then he put the two into opposition with each other. He diverged from and then abandoned the Four Principles, but he tolerated, encouraged, and even supported bourgeois liberalization. This made it impossible for him to stick with socialism while he pursued reform and opening. For him socialism turned into something that nobody could define, and this led him to avoid mention of socialism, or to mention it only occasionally. Approaching reform and opening with this kind of thinking, it's no wonder he met disaster!"

Hu Qiaomu: "Comrade Zhao Ziyang never flatly championed privatization, but his reforms were always tilted in favor of enterprises that had low degrees of public ownership. His constant mantra that state enterprises should adopt the mechanisms of the township and village enterprises[12] was an encouragement to the advocates of privatization. It also caused some people who were not well versed in Marxism—especially young people—to lose confidence in socialist public ownership and to assume that for reform to go any further it would have to collide with our system of public ownership, dismantle it, and then lead to a new system. For a time this created a great hue and cry in favor of privatization. And it all happened because Zhao Ziyang and others in the Party winked at and supported people who were spreading bourgeois liberalization under such slogans as 'Liberate thought' and 'We do not oppose liberalization in the economic sphere.' Zhao and his people allowed this viewpoint to take over at the same time they were attacking and suppressing comrades who were insisting on a Marxist approach."

Jiang Hua:[13] "At a life-and-death turning point for the future of our Party and state, Zhao Ziyang supported turmoil, split the Party, gravely weakened our Party's political thought work, openly confronted Comrade Xiaoping, stubbornly clung to his erroneous position, and refused to admit his mistakes. I feel very strongly that we should strip him of all his leadership posts in the Party and set up a special investigation team[14] to look further into his case."

Zhang Jinfu:[15] "In the last few years, Comrade Zhao Ziyang has used the pre-

---

[12]In the rural economic reforms that Deng Xiaoping sponsored beginning in the late 1970s rural entrepreneurs were allowed to run profit-making industries that produced clothing, foodstuffs, and other commodities. These operations were called "township and village enterprises."

[13]A member of the Standing Committee of the Central Advisory Commission.

[14]The term "special investigation team" *(zhuan'an xiaozu)* has a chilling ring because it was used during the Cultural Revolution persecutions of the late 1960s.

[15]A member of the Standing Committee of the Central Advisory Commission.

text of 'reforming' our political thought work to slander and oppose our excellent tradition in that regard. He has spread many mistaken ideas. For several years now as general secretary he hasn't mentioned the great goals of communism or any of its highest ideals. He even used the pretext that we can't say exactly what socialism is any more in order to avoid saying we should stick with it. But then he goes aimlessly prattling about 'respecting people,' 'understanding people,' and 'caring for people'—gravely weakening the Party's political thought work and skewing it way over to one extreme. His mistakes are extremely serious."

Wang Renzhong: "Zhao Ziyang's failure to uphold the Four Basic Principles and his turning a blind eye toward bourgeois liberalization were by no means accidental or isolated occurrences. They were fundamental failures in his use of power and his style of reform and opening. In foreign policy he bowed to anti-communist, antisocialist forces and their peaceful evolution attacks, and at home he let the dream of a bourgeois republic created by his liberal brain trust go to his head. Our Party and people have paid a price in blood for Zhao Ziyang's serious mistakes. We must do more to expose those mistakes. We should get to the bottom of this and annihilate all of its effects."

Wang Zhen: "I can't stand the way Zhao Ziyang set up a personality cult and made a big deal of his personal authority. Okay, you're the general secretary, so be the general secretary; do what you're supposed to do. If you're told to do something, then do it; if not, then don't do it! Just look at that *River Elegy*![16] It drives me nuts—what's this junk about a 'blue civilization'? Dog farts! Just a naked attempt to push Zhao Ziyang's authority. And where was Comrade Xiaoping in all this? The worst was that close-up of Zhao Ziyang with the words 'a new era begins' emblazoned before him. It couldn't be more obvious that Zhao was aiming at bourgeois peaceful evolution. Zhao Ziyang is a perfect example of people in our Party who are utterly devoted to bourgeois liberalization."

Fang Yi:[17] "During his term as general secretary, Comrade Zhao Ziyang has been lax about educating people in political thought work. He has winked at bourgeois liberalization and has loved the ideas of his so-called brain trust. Some young people, as a result, have lost their confidence in socialism and communism; instead they pursue money above all else—material comforts and personal fame and fortune. The values of arduous struggle, selflessness, and helping people in need, which make up the exalted character of a Communist and are also

---

[16]See footnote 36 in Chapter 6. In *River Elegy* "blue civilization" symbolized open, modern, and democratic influences that arrived in China from overseas.
[17]A vice chair of the Chinese People's Political Consultative Conference.

the traditional virtues of the Chinese people, are regarded as out of date. A self-seeking, devil-take-the-hindmost mentality has caught on. In this recent turmoil many young people whom we ourselves had nurtured turned around and cursed us. This had a lot to do with Comrade Zhao Ziyang's failure to stress political thought work. It should be a profound lesson for us."

Yu Qiuli:[18] "Zhao Ziyang has lost the dignity of a general secretary of the Party. He made a fool of himself on May 19 when he went to Tiananmen Square, tears streaming down his face, and told the students, 'I'm old—I don't matter any more.' That right there should be enough to get him out of office."

Peng Chong:[19] "Comrade Zhao Ziyang's mistakes have been grave, and the lessons to be learned are profound. During his term as general secretary, he seriously weakened our Party's political thought work as well as the ranks of our political workers. The result is that our Party's political thought work is at its lowest ebb ever. There is a direct connection between the recent turmoil and Comrade Zhao Ziyang's laxity toward political thought work. So Comrade Xiaoping is right on the mark when he says 'we've got to work on the Party—it's absolutely crucial.' If our Party doesn't strengthen its political thought work, and doesn't conquer corruption once and for all, then we really do face the danger of losing both our Party and our state."

Wu Xiuquan:[20] "Comrade Zhao Ziyang is not fit to be general secretary of the Party. He has a knack for economic work, but he doesn't know what he's doing in political reform. What does he know? All his ideas in this area come from Bao Tong, his chief of staff. China has its own unique national situation and patterns of development; copying others mechanically will lead us straight to disaster. What's more, economics and politics go by different rules. Why did Zhao's shock-therapy price reforms fail last year?[21] Because they were too much; the people panicked. That's the way it is in China. There's a herd mentality. When the people get into their herd mentality, you can forget about all reform, and that's why we ended up with this turmoil mess that nobody wanted. When the turmoil began, Comrade Zhao Ziyang did not have a clear stand or firm attitude, and when it

---

[18]A member of the Standing Committee of the Central Advisory Commission.
[19]General secretary and vice chair of the Standing Committee of the National People's Congress.
[20]A member of the Standing Committee of the Central Advisory Commission.
[21]Reform of the Chinese economy in the 1980s faced the problem of how to deregulate prices for basic commodities such as grain and fuel, which had been fixed at artificially low levels since the 1950s. In 1988 Deng Xiaoping, accepting the argument that "short-term pain is better than long-term pain," decided to free up prices abruptly and get the pain over with. Hoarding and sharp inflation resulted, and here Wu Xiuquan holds Zhao Ziyang responsible for the mistake.

came time to call a halt to things, he was at a loss. That's why he bears undeniable responsibility and should be stripped of his duties."

These were the sharpest views expressed at the meeting. Others made pro forma criticisms of Zhao that were mild by the standards of intra-Party struggles, thus indicating either that they were reserving their opinions about the way the Tiananmen incident had been handled or even that some of them agreed with Zhao. For some of the hard-line senior members, including Deng, the most irritating point was that Zhao Ziyang refused to acknowledge that he had been in the wrong. A printed copy of Li Peng's report had been sent to Zhao, and he firmly rejected the accusations that he had "supported turmoil" and "split the Party."

How many dead and wounded?

This meeting also reviewed a report by Li Ximing on the crackdown in Beijing. The report contained official casualty figures for citizens, students, and martial law troops.

> Excerpts from Li Ximing, "Report on pacifying the counter-revolutionary riots in Beijing," report at the enlarged meeting of the Politburo, June 19

Beijing Municipality has checked and double-checked all the figures from the Martial Law Command, the Public Security Ministry, the Chinese Red Cross, all institutions of higher education, and all major hospitals. These show that 241 people died. They included twenty-three officers and soldiers from the martial law troops and 218 civilians. The twenty-three military deaths included ten from the PLA and thirteen from the People's Armed Police. The 218 civilians (Beijing residents, people from elsewhere, students, and rioters) included thirty-six students from Beijing universities and fifteen people from outside Beijing. . . . About seven thousand people were wounded. About five thousand were officers and soldiers from the martial law troops, of whom 136 were seriously wounded; about two thousand were Beijing residents. . . . No one was killed within the scope of Tiananmen itself. . . . The thirty-six students who died came from twenty different universities, including People's University, which had six student deaths; Qinghua University and Beijing University of Science and Engineering, three deaths each; seven other institutions of higher education, including Peking University and Beijing Normal University, two deaths each; and ten other institutions, one death each.

Li Ximing's figures need be viewed together with other reports about deaths of soldiers, citizens, and students. Materials from the Martial Law Headquarters, for example, show that no member of the troops that advanced on the city the night of June 3 was killed by city residents, and no soldier from the Thirty-Eighth Army, which was responsible for clearing the Square, died on June 3. Of the ten PLA soldiers who lost their lives and were later honored as Defenders of the Republic, six were from the Thirty-Eighth Army, but these men died when their military transport truck overturned about 2 A.M. This was well after the martial law troops had begun opening fire, killing and wounding Beijing citizens and students. Enraged crowds had tried to block the way as the truck passed through Cuiwei Road, and as the truck slowed people began to throw stones, Molotov cocktails, and torches at it. The truck's left rear tire was punctured by broad-headed nails that the crowd had placed erect on the road. The vehicle overturned as it was turning a corner to the right, the gas tank exploded, and the soldiers burned to death. The deaths of these six soldiers cannot properly be described as "murdered by rioters."

A report from the Beijing Public Security Bureau said, "Those killed included university professors, technical people, officials, workers, owners of small private businesses, retired workers, high school students, and grade school students, of whom the youngest was nine years old." To judge from this distribution of ages and occupations—from retired old ladies to a nine-year-old child—it would seem likely that the great majority of these people were innocent of any crime.

According to stories that circulated inside Zhongnanhai, even people close to the Party leadership were among the innocent victims. The chauffeur of Party Elder Bo Yibo was killed by PLA submachine-gun fire on Chang'an Boulevard at 8 P.M. on June 6 when he failed to stop his car on command, and the son-in-law of Song Rufen, vice chair of the Law Committee of the National People's Congress, was killed by gunfire from martial law troops at the Ministers' Buildings at Muxidi on the night of June 3. His fatal mistake was to have left the light on in his room while he watched from his window. The dead were viewed as rioters whether they were or not.[22]

June 23–24

The Fourth Plenum of the Thirteenth Central Committee

Held June 23–24 in Beijing, the Plenum approved the decisions made two days earlier at the enlarged meeting of the Politburo. Jiang Zemin was elected general secretary. Jiang, Song Ping,

[22]Few work units did anything to organize memorials for dead members. Not only did relatives receive no help from any level of government, but they have had to live ever since under the constant surveillance of Public Security. As time has passed, they have been turned into social outcasts.—Comp.

and Li Ruihuan were added to the Standing Committee of the Politburo. Li Ruihuan and Ding Guan'gen were appointed as secretaries to the General Secretariat. Zhao Ziyang, Hu Qili, Rui Xingwen, and Yan Mingfu were stripped of their Party posts.

The main agenda item for the plenum was to hear and review Li Peng's report on Zhao Ziyang.

> Excerpts from Li Peng, "Report on mistakes committed by Comrade Zhao Ziyang during the anti-Party and antisocialist turmoil," report to the Fourth Plenum of the Thirteenth Central Committee, June 23[23]

This Fourth Plenum of the Thirteenth Central Committee is based on decisions of an enlarged meeting of the Politburo that was held from June 19 to 21. Our main purposes are to discuss the errors committed by Comrade Zhao Ziyang during the anti-Party, antisocialist turmoil and to apply the necessary organizational measures appropriately. This is the most pressing issue we need to resolve in order to take the next step in putting down the turmoil, stabilizing the situation throughout the country, solidifying Party leadership, and preserving unity within the Party and between the Party and the people.

The report gave a detailed description of what Zhao had done between April 15, when Hu Yaobang died, and May 21, when Zhao sent a telegram to Wan Li asking him to return from the United States to China. It then continued.

We conclude that at a life-and-death turning point for the future of our Party and state, Comrade Zhao Ziyang committed the mistakes of supporting turmoil and splitting the Party. The nature of his mistakes and the consequences they brought are both extremely grave. He is no longer fit to go on with the important work that is currently his. We recommend that the Central Committee pass a resolution dismissing Comrade Zhao Ziyang from his posts as general secretary, as a member of the Politburo and its Standing Committee, and as first vice chair of the Central Military Commission. We also propose that a decision be made about his membership on the Central Committee, that there be a continuing investigation of his case, and that other necessary changes be made in the Standing Committee of the Politburo and in the membership of the Secretariat. . . .

The appearance and growth of the turmoil that led to the counterrevolutionary riots had deep social and historical roots. Just as Comrade Deng Xiaoping

---

[23]An English translation of this speech has been published in *The China Quarterly*, no. 128 (December, 1991), 888–901.

said, 'This storm was bound to come along sooner or later. The combination of the international climate and China's own climate made this inevitable. There was no way human will could have avoided it.' . . .

Ever since he took over work at Party Central, [Zhao Ziyang] in fact departed from the Four Basic Principles, abandoned opposition to bourgeois liberalization, and seriously neglected building the Party, building spiritual civilization, and political thought work. . . . Can we still call this Communist Party leadership? Do we not have to say that it has degenerated into something else? . . .

We have won a decisive victory in smashing the counterrevolutionary riots. Because these riots were bound to break out sooner or later in this land called China, it is better that they came sooner than later. We lose less with their coming now than if they had come later because the Deng Xiaoping generation of senior comrades—Chen Yun, Li Xiannian, Peng Zhen, Deng Yingchao, Xu Xiangqian, Nie Rongzhen, Bo Yibo, Wang Zhen, and others—are still alive and well. They were an enormous help at a crucial time in the decision to put down the riots. . . .

Our PLA soldiers are loyal to the Party, loyal to the people, and loyal to socialism. They passed a rigorous political test during this struggle. The facts show that they fully deserve to be known as the heroic brothers of the people, the stout pillars of the people's democratic dictatorship, and the great wall of steel that guards our socialist People's Republic. . . .

Comrade Deng Xiaoping's speech at the reception for high-ranking officers of the martial law troops in the capital is a defining statement for how we summarize the past, contemplate the future, and unify the thinking and understanding of the entire Party. We should take the spirit of this speech as our compass and systematically absorb the experience and lessons of our past work so that we can bring the work of the Party and government into closer accord with facts. We need to make a solemn resolution to overcome the tendency of the Party and government to drift far from the masses. We need to strengthen our close ties with the masses, revive the spirit of the revolution, restore our tradition of arduous struggle, and unite the people to continue moving forward. Accordingly, Party Central is preparing to carry out conscientious study and discussion to formulate appropriate measures. The following are a few of our preliminary thoughts:

Number one. The general direction, the principles, and the policies laid out at the Third Plenum of the Eleventh Central Committee were all correct. So was the basic program of one center and two basic points[24] that was charted at the Thirteenth Party Congress. The Four Basic Principles are the foundations of the state

[24]See footnote 37 in Chapter 6.

and must be absolutely upheld from beginning to end without the slightest vacillation. Reform and opening are the route to a powerful nation and must be carried out with the firmest resolution. We can never return to the closed-door policies of the past. We must act on the basis of our summarized experience to persist in the parts that are correct, modify the parts that are mistaken, and strengthen the parts that are insufficient. After rationalizing and reshaping everything, we should make our construction and our reform and opening more stable, better, and even faster than it was before.

Number two. In order to achieve thorough victory in stopping the turmoil and putting down the counterrevolutionary riots, we must pursue the work of ferreting out the counterrevolutionary elements right through to the end. We absolutely must not be soft. We must go all out to mobilize the masses, to strengthen the people's democratic dictatorship, to punish the widely detested criminal elements according to law, and to attack resolutely every kind of harmful activity by enemies inside or outside the country. We must distinguish rigorously between the two kinds of conflict[25] and unify with the broad masses in maintaining good social order.

Number three. We must derive lessons from this case of student movement, turmoil, and then riots. We must strengthen Party building, strengthen political thought work, and conscientiously open up the educational struggle of opposing bourgeois liberalization. We must, moreover, persist for a long time; we absolutely must not settle for a walk through, or quit half way, as we did with the campaigns against spiritual pollution and bourgeois liberalization.

Number four. We need to adopt firm measures against the flaws and mistakes that exist in Party and government work, and we need to assure that concrete correction takes place. In order to win the confidence of the people, Party Central and the State Council must find ways to get results within a short period of time on problems that concern the people most, such as conquering corruption, punishing "official profiteering,"[26] and cleaning up companies.

Number five. In the area of economic work, we need to continue to control the economic environment, reorganize the economic order, and deepen the economic reforms on every front. In particular, we really need to control the upward pressure on prices, to assure that agriculture has a good harvest, to continue to reduce the scope of capital construction, to control the increase in funds available for consumption, and to strengthen basic industry and infrastructure. We must work hard to keep the economy well regulated and overcome the difficulties that

---

[25]"Antagonistic" and "nonantagonistic"; see footnote 15 in Chapter 3.
[26]See footnote 28 in Chapter 1.

currently face us in order to maintain a rational rate of growth and to create a salutary cycle in the economy.

Number six. To keep pace with our economic reforms, we must accelerate the reform of our political system and strengthen the construction of democracy and rule of law. We should go further in bringing the role of people's congresses into play at every level, especially in their carrying out of supervision of the government according to law. At the same time, we also need to go further in bringing the CPPCC, all the democratic parties,[27] and all the people's organizations into play in the political life of our nation, and we need to work hard to create a stable, unified, and democratic sociopolitical environment.

Number seven. Western and overseas Chinese public opinion has wantonly fabricated and spread rumors about our putting down of the counterrevolutionary riots. The United States and Western Europe have led the way among foreign countries in whipping up an anti-China tide. We have faith that the rumors will eventually be seen through and that the light of truth will shine throughout the world. In these difficult times it is especially important that our entire Party, state, and people pull together to withstand all outside pressures. The Chinese people, who have risen to their feet, will not bend under any pressure. We will continue as ever to pursue an independent and peaceful foreign policy and to build friendly relations with all nations of the world based on the Five Principles of Peaceful Coexistence.[28] But when certain countries interfere in our internal affairs, we need to engage them in a struggle based on justice, self-interest, and strategy.

In response to Li Peng's report, Zhao Ziyang offered a self-defense.

> Excerpts from *Materials for the Fourth Plenum of the Thirteenth Central Committee*, "Remarks of Comrade Zhao Ziyang," Secretariat of the Fourth Plenum of the CCP Thirteenth Central Committee, June 23–24, 1989

I've carefully reviewed in my mind everything I did since the beginning of the student movement and the turmoil, trying to identify what I did that was correct and what I did that was either incorrect or inappropriate.

---

[27]The eight small noncommunist parties remaining in China; see footnote 29 in Chapter 4.
[28]The Five Principles of Peaceful Coexistence are mutual respect for territorial sovereignty, mutual nonaggression, mutual noninterference in internal affairs, equal benefit, and peaceful coexistence. China proposed them in 1953.

First, before the memorial service for Comrade Hu Yaobang there was no difference of opinion on the Standing Committee.

Second, after the memorial service I made three suggestions: (1) The memorial activities were over, so social life should resume its normal patterns; we should be firm in dissuading the students from further demonstrations and get them to go back to class. (2) We should adopt a policy of guidance toward the students, opening up dialogue with them at many levels and through many channels in order to exchange views and build understanding. (3) We should avoid bloodshed at all costs; instances of beating, smashing, and robbing or of arson or break-in should be dealt with according to law. Comrade Li Peng and all the other comrades on the Standing Committee agreed with these ideas.

Third, I was not in Beijing from April 24 until the morning of April 30, and I am not very clear on exactly what happened during those days.

Fourth, the May Fourth commemorative speech I gave in Beijing on May 3 had been reviewed in advance by comrades on the Politburo and in the Secretariat. Quite a few comrades offered opinions, and I made many changes in the draft based on what they said. I believe the meeting on May 3 highlighted two points. One is that we must continue to pursue economic and political reform simultaneously; we must not ignore political work. The other is that political reform must not lag behind and that socialist democracy and rule of law especially cannot lag behind. . . . In my personal view, these points represent the true long-term interests of our Party and state. For years I've been a bold activist in economic reform but cautious in the area of political reform; I used to call myself "a reformer in economics and a conservative in politics." But my thinking has changed in recent years. I now feel that political reform has to be a priority; if it is not made a priority, then not only will economic problems get harder to handle, but all kinds of social and political problems will only get worse. This new outlook of mine has shaped my views on some concrete questions, and I think I should use today's Party meeting to spell out these views for my comrades. They may well be mistaken, and I welcome your criticisms and help.

Fifth, the two purposes of my speech May 4 at the annual meeting of the directors of the Asian Development Bank were to try to settle the student movement down and to strengthen the confidence of foreign capital in China's stability. The initial responses to my speech were all positive. I wasn't aware of any problems. Comrade Li Peng told me it was a good speech and that he would echo it at his own meeting with the ADB directors. My speech set a soft tone, and to judge from all signs at the time, this tone did some good. Later some colleagues criticized me for not clearing my speech in advance with the Politburo Standing Committee. It's true I did not do this, but in the past we have never done this. Talks by Central leaders to foreign guests—unless they are formal meetings on written agreements—have never been sent to the Politburo Standing Commitee for advance review. It has been up to individual leaders to reflect the stance of Party Central.

Sixth, regarding the Standing Committee meeting on May 8 and the Politburo Meeting on May 10: The students, in their large demonstration on April 27, were insisting we change the official view of their movement as expressed in the April 26 editorial. This really put me in a tough spot. My impulse at the time was to sidestep the issue—to draw attention away from it by doing some eye-catching things to show we are serious about cleaning up government and building democracy—and then hope the problem would go away. . . . My basic thought was to make clean government the centerpiece of our whole political reform and then to tie everything else—democracy, rule of law, openness, transparency, supervision by the masses—to that centerpiece. I reported this idea of mine to Comrade Xiaoping on the afternoon of May 13 when Comrade Shangkun and I went to visit him. Comrade Xiaoping agreed with me. He said to grab the chance—let's get corruption cleaned up once and for all, and get more transparency, too!

Seventh, about my talk with Gorbachev: After the Thirteenth Party Congress I made it a habit, whenever I met with leaders of foreign Communist parties, to tell them about the decision of the First Plenum of our Party's Thirteenth Central Committee in which we said there would be no change in Comrade Xiaoping's position as the Party's chief decisionmaker. My purposes in doing so were to make it clear that Comrade Xiaoping's resignation from the Standing Committee had not changed this fact and also to let people know the arrangement was quite legal. I said the same thing to Chairman Kim Il Sung on my recent trip to North Korea. My telling it to Gorbachev was part of a normal pattern, and the problem arose only because—this time—the comment got publicized. . . . Comments like mine should not, by rights, have given anyone the impression that Deng Xiaoping decides everything. I never imagined that I might end up hurting Comrade Xiaoping, and I'm willing to take full responsibility if I did.

Eighth, about the Standing Committee meeting of May 16: When I arrived back from North Korea I heard that there had been a lot of adverse reaction to the April 26 editorial and that it had become a sore point among the students. I began to wonder if there weren't some way to heal the sore point and improve the students' mood. . . . I raised the matter—and this was the first time it had ever been formally raised—at the Standing Committee meeting on the evening of the sixteenth. Comrade Li Peng said that key phrases in the editorial—"this is a well-planned plot," it is "turmoil," its "real aim is to reject the Chinese Communist Party and the socialist system," and "the whole Party and nation . . . are facing a most serious political struggle"—were original quotes from Comrade Xiaoping and could not be changed. I said I disagreed.

Ninth, at the May 17 Standing Committee meeting at Comrade Xiaoping's residence, Comrades Li Peng and Yao Yilin criticized me by attributing the whole escalation of the student movement to my May 4 speech to the ADB delegates. The ferocity of their attack took me by surprise. The Standing Committee meeting then reaffirmed the judgment contained in the April 26 editorial and decided to dispatch troops to Beijing to impose martial law. I commented that having a policy was better than not having a policy but said I feared that this decision would have dire consequences and that I would have a hard time carrying it out. I spoke my mind frankly at that Party meeting, but after the meeting, and after much additional thought, I feared the limits of my ideological condition and of my understanding of events might affect or undermine the Standing Committee's ability firmly and thoroughly to carry out its policy. In my distraught and somewhat impulsive mood, it occurred to me that I should resign. But when I mentioned resigning to Comrade Shangkun, he immediately advised me not to. He said this would just agitate the masses, and he said I would not be a hindrance to the Standing Committee in getting its work done. The last thing I wanted to do was make things harder for the Party, so I withheld my resignation. But the way things were going worried me terribly, so on May 18 I wrote another letter to Comrade Xiaoping asking him to reconsider my views, and I also telephoned Comrade Shangkun asking him to put in a word for me with Comrade Xiaoping. As far as I know, it's always permitted to express dissenting views within the Party; indeed, it would be irresponsible of a general secretary to hold differing views and not voice them. As I see it now, and taking the whole situation into consideration, my impulse to resign was a wrong impulse. It's a good thing that I did not follow it.

Tenth, about my visit to the hunger strikers in Tiananmen Square on the early morning of May 19: I had wanted to go see those students ever since the second day of their strike. Several times I made plans to go, but things kept coming up to prevent it. May 19 was already the seventh day of the hunger strike, and there was a danger that deaths might start to occur. Things were very tense. I was not feeling well myself at the time but decided I just had to go. They had been fasting for seven days—all I could do was try to move them emotionally, try to plead with them to stop starving themselves. And their mood did soften a bit after I visited. That night at nine o'clock they called off their hunger strike. I cannot claim that my speech made the difference, but it surely didn't do any harm.

Eleventh, about my absence from the important meeting on May 19: I must make it clear that the Standing Committee had excused me for illness that day. Comrade Qiao Shi made an announcement to that effect at the meeting. I asked for and received three days' leave, and after the leave I no longer had a job. Unable to go to meetings, I was in the dark after that.

From what I have just said, it should be obvious that my general approach to handling the student movement and the turmoil was always to avoid confrontation with the students, to try to win over the majority among them, and to get the movement to settle down. I was constantly worried that if we took a hard line—or worse, called in troops—in a situation where we still did not have the majority on our side, it would be hard to avoid conflict and bloodshed. That would only exacerbate the problem, and even if we succeeded in putting the movement down, it would leave behind deep and lasting psychological damage.

Comrade Xiaoping recently made an extremely important speech, and I learned much from it. He said this whole upheaval happened for reasons that were beyond human will; it was an inevitable result of the interaction between the "big climate" in the outside world and the "small climate" in China. He also said it was better that it came sooner rather than later. To examine things from such an exalted viewpoint as this makes some of my earlier musings seem irrelevant. I did not see things with this kind of range and depth, and now I feel ready to rethink this problem in the light of Comrade Xiaoping's speech.

I have nothing to say about the proposals in Comrade Li Peng's report to strip me of my various leadership duties. But I beg to differ on the two charges that I "supported the turmoil" and "split the Party." It is quite true that within the bounds permitted by our Party Constitution, I expressed my differing views at Party meetings on how to handle the student movement and the turmoil. My ideas may or may not have been feasible or effective, but all of them were aimed at ending the turmoil. I never said anything to support the turmoil. No one who looks at the facts can say the expansion of the student movement or the turmoil are reasonably attributable to me. The student movement and the turmoil grew fastest, in fact, between April 23 and May 1, when I was out of the country.

Comrade Li Peng's report alleges that my speech at the Asian Development Bank meeting escalated the turmoil, but this criticism does not square with the facts. The day after my speech all the newspapers in the capital carried stories saying the students were trooping back to class. This shows that at a minimum my speech did not escalate the student movement. Then, after martial law on May 19, I no longer had a job, so of course I did not give any more speeches, and hence there can be still less reason to say I caused escalation of anything. It is absurd to argue that I missed a meeting on May 19, then went on sick leave, and then turned into the main causal force in the whole pattern of events.

As for the charge of splitting the Party, what exactly is behavior that splits the Party? There have been some precedents in our Party's history, and there are rules laid out in "Some Standards for Political Life within the Party." Never has our Party held that expression of divergent opinion—or merely registering some reservations—constituted "splitting the Party." The public speeches of Party leaders have always contained varying emphases that have stirred up this or that kind of speculation within the public; this can hardly be called splitting the Party. Comrade Li Peng's report faults me for not mentioning the April 26 editorial at the Asian Development Bank meeting and for commenting that "China will be spared any major turmoil" after turmoil had already broken out. Yet the very next day, when Comrade Li Peng spoke to the Asian Development Bank, he, too, did not mention the April 26 editorial, and he, too, commented that China was working hard to "avoid turmoil." In my view, when speeches given at different times and places display small terminological differences—or even if their general drifts are not exactly the same—such differences cannot be raised to the level of fundamental political error and be called "splitting the Party." It is even more far-fetched to say that missing a Party meeting on May 19 because of sick leave was "splitting the Party."

Since the Party Constitution allows Party members the right to plead their cases,[29] I am today defending myself against these two criticisms and hope you will give me your consideration.

Zhao Ziyang's self-defense stimulated a strong reaction in the Party. Some said he was "adamantly unrepentant" and "incorrigibly stubborn" or that "he never thought he did anything wrong." Of the three CCP general secretaries since the founding of the People's Republic, Zhao was the only one who confessed no mistakes to the organization.[30] But this may also have been

---

[29]Article 4 of the Chinese Communist Party Constitution enumerates Party members' rights, including, in item 7, "In case of disagreement with a Party decision or policy, to make reservations and present their views to Party organizations . . . up to and including the Central Committee. . . ."

[30]The two preceding general secretaries were Deng Xiaoping and Hu Yaobang. Deng engaged in self-criticism in letters to both Mao Zedong and Hua Guofeng. Hu apologized to Deng Xiaoping and the other Elders.

why Zhao did not lose his popularity even though he lost his position. From his native province of Henan to the provinces of Guangzhou, Sichuan, and Inner Mongolia, where he had worked, and to places where he had not, such as Zhejiang, Liaoning, and Heilongjiang, from high officials to ordinary citizens, people all across China continued to link the word "reform" with the name of Zhao Ziyang.

June 10–30

Rounding up democracy activists

The work of hunting down activists of the democracy movement in Beijing was shared by the martial law troops, the People's Armed Police, and the Municipal Public Security Bureau. Guidelines like the following help explain why most of those detained suffered physical abuse.

> Excerpt from Martial Law Headquarters, "Unify thinking, distinguish right from wrong, complete the martial law task with practical actions," June 10

In order to dissipate the anger and antagonism that martial law troops feel toward the residents of Beijing, to clarify the muddled understanding that many people have, to isolate the tiny minority of rioters from the vast majority of Beijing residents, and to establish correct attitudes toward the people, we need to ask all the officers and soldiers to concentrate their hatred on the small handful of thugs and rioters, to smash their evil nests, to punish the rioters, and to wrap up their martial law duties through concrete actions.

Issue numbers 26, 31, and 37 of the Beijing Public Security Bureau's *Public Order Situation (Zhi'an qingkuang)* show that 468 "counterrevolutionary rioters and creators of turmoil" had been arrested by June 10. On June 17 eight of these were sentenced to death for "beating, smashing, robbing, burning, and other serious criminal offenses during the counterrevolutionary riots in Beijing." By June 20 the number of "counterrevolutionary rioters" and "turmoil elements"[31] who had been arrested was 831; by June 30, it was 1,103. Most of the arrestees were held in temporary detention centers or makeshift jails.

Once the situation in Beijing was under control and province-level authorities throughout the

[31]The term *dongluan fenzi,* "turmoil element," seems to have entered official language soon after June 4.

country had expressed their support, Party Central unfolded a series of measures against activists throughout the country.

Excerpt from Public Security Ministry, "Notice on resolutely repressing counterrevolutionary rioters," June 12

1. Suppress and disband all illegal organizations that incited or created social turmoil or counterrevolutionary riots.

The Beijing Municipal Government and Martial Law Headquarters have declared in "Notice Number 10" that the Autonomous Federation of University Students in Beijing and the Autonomous Federation of Workers are illegal organizations and are ordered to disband of their own accord. Their members must immediately cease all illegal activity. Leaders of these two illegal organizations must immediately give themselves up to local offices of Public Security so as to receive lenient treatment. Those who fail to turn themselves in will be brought to justice according to law and severely punished.

In all other cities in which turmoil and disturbances took place, local Public Security organs should seek permission from the local People's Government to issue orders outlawing all illegal organizations that incited or created turmoil or disturbances and to order them immediately to disband and to cease all illegal activity. Leaders must register with Public Security within a fixed period of time. Those who fail to register and continue illegal activity will be severely punished according to the law. Ordinary members of these organizations, unless they are guilty of offenses under the criminal law, need not be investigated.

2. Local Public Security organs should investigate the criminal responsibility of people who have sheltered or hidden leaders of illegal organizations or of the rioting.

3. Public Security organs should seize all guns, bullets, and other army or police weapons that rioters picked up or looted during the counterrevolutionary riots in Beijing, as well as all propaganda material that illegal organizations used to incite people or poison their minds. All hidden objects of this nature must immediately be handed in to Public Security offices. Those who continue to hide such will be severely punished.

4. In accordance with the law, local Public Security organs should immediately arrest any members of illegal organizations who have fled to outlying areas and continue to network, to incite or create turmoil, or to pursue any other illegal activity.

5. All leaders of organized actions that attacked Party or government organs, radio or television stations, or other key sites; that blocked or disrupted transportation so that rail or highway transport was cut off; or that created urban paralysis should be arrested in accordance with the law and severely punished.

6. If any incident of collective disturbance occurs in any location, Public Security organs and the People's Armed Police must take resolute and decisive measures to disperse it by force. Public Security organs may arrest on the spot any elements who join in disturbances or who beat, smash, rob, burn, kill, or commit other criminal acts.

7. If the people's police encounter emergency situations of resistance to arrest, rioting, surprise attacks, looting of firearms, or other violence that harms social order and if orders to desist are ignored, they should employ firepower in accordance with the relevant provisions and regulations to protect themselves and to stop the criminal activity.

8. The broad masses must work actively to expose and report on counterrevolutionary rioters and criminal elements who carried out beating, smashing, robbing, burning, or killing. They must support and assist Public Security organs and the officers and men of the police and armed police in carrying out their duties according to law, and they must cooperate in protecting public order.

Also on June 12, the Public Security Ministry circulated to its province-level offices and to the security bureaus of the rail, trucking, and air transport systems a "Beijing Municipal Public Security Bureau Warrant for the Arrest of Fang Lizhi and Li Shuxian." On June 13 it did the same with a "Warrant for the Arrest of Fugitive 'AFS' Elements," which listed twenty-one names in order of importance: Wang Dan, Wuerkaixi, Liu Gang, Chai Ling, Zhou Fengsuo, Zhai Weimin, Liang Qingdun, Wang Zhengyun, Zheng Xuguang, Ma Shaofang, Yang Tao, Wang Zhixin, Feng Congde, Wang Chaohua, Wang Youcai, Zhang Zhiqing, Zhang Boli, Li Lu, Zhang Ming, Xiong Wei, and Xiong Yan. On June 14 came a "Warrant for the Arrest of Fugitive 'AFW' Elements" naming Han Dongfang, He Lili, and Liu Qiang.

Ten days later a warrant was issued for the arrests of Yan Jiaqi, Bao Zunxin, Chen Yizi, Wan Runnan, Su Xiaokang, Wang Juntao, and Chen Ziming.

> Excerpt from Public Security Ministry, "Warrant for the arrest of Yan Jiaqi and six others," June 24

These seven took part in the behind-the-scenes planning and direction of the counterrevolutionary riots in Beijing. . . . Public security organs in each province, autonomous region, and province-level municipality; public security organs in the rail, trucking, and air transport systems; and public security organs at all ports and border stations are to check the wanted lists and to guard rigorously against escape from the country. When a listed person is discovered he should be detained immediately and the matter reported to the Public Security Ministry.

On June 20 the Supreme People's Court issued a notice saying, "Courts at every level should in a timely manner and in accordance with law bring to trial the counterrevolutionary elements who carried out counterrevolutionary riots and instigated social turmoil and elements who committed serious criminal acts." Beijing courts responded by stepping up the tempo of their trials, but for the four months from June to September city jails still were filled to overflowing. The "counterrevolutionary elements" and "elements who committed serious criminal acts" whom they processed included Party members who had been arrested before June 4, such as Bao Tong, He Weiling, and Cao Siyuan, as well as democracy activists who had been picked up after June 4, including Liu Gang, Bao Zunxin, Chen Ziming, Liu Xiaobo, Wang Dan, and Wang Juntao.

Arrests at the province level kept pace with those in Beijing. Most of the "fugitives" and many of the "turmoil elements" in the following reports were ordinary criminals who had the bad luck to be apprehended when Party leaders had ordered a crackdown and who accordingly drew harsher sentences than usual.

> Extracts from reports of the Public Security Ministry and of provinces and cities, through June 30

SHANGHAI:

One hundred forty-three members of illegal organizations have come to Public Security to register or confess; 273 turmoil elements of various kinds have been arrested; three counterrevolutionary groups and two Taiwan-KMT spy rings have been cracked. Yao Yongzhan (alias Zhang Cai), a Hong Kong resident and major figure in the Shanghai branch of the AFS, was arrested at Hongqiao Airport.

HEILONGJIANG:

Twenty-one illegal organizations have been disbanded; 11 leaders of illegal organizations have come to Public Security to register or confess; 176 turmoil elements have been arrested.

Jilin:

Eighteen illegal organizations disbanded; 15 leaders of illegal organizations have come to Public Security to register or confess; 98 arrests of various turmoil elements.

Liaoning:

Thirty-four illegal organizations disbanded; 18 members of illegal organizations have come to Public Security to register or confess; 6 members of illegal organizations detained for questioning; 3 major figures of the AFS arrested; 6 members of other illegal organizations from other provinces arrested; 338 detentions of various turmoil elements, of which 12 have been arrested, 25 are slated for arrest, 103 are in reeducation through labor, and 198 are awaiting interrogation.

Shaanxi:

Twenty-six illegal organizations disbanded; 13 leaders of illegal organizations have come to Public Security to register or confess; 41 arrests of members of illegal organizations; 203 arrests of various turmoil elements; 3 breakups of counterrevolutionary groups.

Shanxi:

Nine illegal organizations disbanded; 16 members of illegal organizations have come to Public Security to register or confess; 218 arrests of various turmoil elements.

Inner Mongolia:

Ninety-eight arrests of turmoil elements and criminal elements of various kinds, of whom 26 were trying to flee the province, 16 were fugitives from justice in other provinces, and 56 were caught in the act; 5 rings for the protection of fugitives destroyed.

Sichuan:

Forty-eight illegal organizations disbanded; 56 members of illegal organizations have come to Public Security to register or confess; 781 arrests of various turmoil elements and members of illegal organizations; 16 rings for the protection of fugitives destroyed; 5 breakups of counterrevolutionary groups.

HUNAN:

Fourteen illegal organizations disbanded; 31 members of illegal organizations have come to Public Security to register or confess; 506 arrests of various turmoil elements; 1,327 additional persons guilty of minor offenses of beating, smashing, or robbing have been given administrative punishment;[32] 3 breakups of counterrevolutionary groups.

HUBEI:

Thirty-one illegal organizations disbanded; 27 members of illegal organizations have come to Public Security to register or confess; 216 arrests of various turmoil elements or members of illegal organizations; 5 rings for the protection of fugitives destroyed; 3 breakups of counterrevolutionary groups.

ANHUI:

Nine illegal organizations disbanded; 38 legal arrests and detentions for questioning of leaders of illegal organizations responsible for beating, smashing, and robbing, and of hard-core turmoil elements; banned the inflammatory illegal publication *Overpass*.

JIANGSU:

Fifteen illegal organizations disbanded; 18 members of illegal organizations have come to Public Security to register or confess; 113 arrests of various turmoil elements.

GUIZHOU:

Between May 21 and June 24, 6,035 fugitive criminal elements were arrested, 222 illegal groups were destroyed, 3,211 criminal cases were solved, and 1.69 million yuan in stolen money or money converted from stolen goods was seized.

> Excerpt from Party Group in the Public Security Ministry, "On resolutely striking against counterrevolutionary turmoil and riot elements[33] and other serious criminal elements," report to Party Central, June 30

---

[32]Administrative punishment *(zhi'an xingzheng chufa)* can refer to monetary fines levied by police or to short terms of detention.

[33]*Liangluan fenzi:* "elements" involved either in turmoil *(dongluan)* or in rioting *(baoluan)*.

Five hundred fifteen illegal organizations were disbanded; . . . 718 leaders of illegal organizations came to Public Security to register or confess; . . . 4,386 people were detained as members of illegal organizations or for beating, smashing, robbing, or burning; . . . 31 counterrevolutionary groups were broken up; . . . 8 Taiwan-KMT spy rings were cracked.

Despite police efforts, people as well known as Yan Jiaqi, Chen Yizi, Wan Runnan, Su Xiaokang, Wuerkaixi, Chai Ling, Feng Congde, and Li Lu made their way out of China without a single person involved breaching confidence and collecting the rewards that such a breach would have brought.

The mood on campus

A national survey conducted by the Xinhua News Agency at the end of June found university students everywhere in a mood of terror and resistance blanketed in silence.

> Excerpt from Xinhua News Agency, "The ideological condition of college students nationwide," "Proofs on domestic situation" *(Guonei dongtai qingyang),* June 29

Terror: A tense mood, under fear of punishment or arrest, pervades the universities. Leaders of the student movement have departed their campuses, and rumors are rampant about who is being picked up and when. The students who were most active in the movement are the most nervous. Some provinces have stipulated that even students who sat in to block traffic should be arrested, and many students have grown so insecure they cannot sleep well at night. A number of young lecturers at Wuhan University who had given speeches during the movement now are so terrified they sent their wives and children to their in-laws' homes and waited alone to be arrested at the university. It is noteworthy that even students who only marched in demonstrations and shouted some slogans are frightened as well. One university administrator said students "thought of the recent student movement as a patriotic movement; many took to the streets to protest against official profiteering and then were puzzled when the movement was labeled 'turmoil.' Now the common mood is worry; the students are all wondering, 'Am I going to get punished?'" A few nights ago about a hundred students were gathered at the gate of Heilongjiang University when a police car passed by.

Someone yelled "Police!" and they all scattered like animals scurrying for cover. Some students have been thinking in terms of the arbitrary arrests during the Anti-Rightist Campaign and the Cultural Revolution, so when the slightest sign of something pops up, it has an exaggerated effect.

Resistance: Nationwide about one in five university students remains defiant. These students scornfully resist government decrees and oppose efforts to put down the riots. Some have adopted a "four don'ts" policy toward the domestic media: don't listen, don't read, don't believe, don't ask. Some students make obscene comments while they watch television. Some write on the walls of their dormitories and classrooms things like "Shut up!" "Thunder from the silent zone!"[34] "China is dead!" "Where is justice?" "The government caused the turmoil!" "The truth will out some day!" "Yet another Tiananmen Incident!"[35] and so on. The students at many schools—especially the boys—sometimes seem crazed. When the lights go out at night they vent their rage with wild yelps and cries.

Silence: About one in three students maintains a purposeful silence. After June Fourth all the universities required students to reflect on their roles in the student movement. Many students kept going around in circles, willing to address only a limited number of concrete questions. On the matter of how to turn their own thinking around, they just kept silent. "I don't know" became the answer to every question, silence the shield against every arrow. When political study sessions were scheduled, some students just put up posters in their dorms and classrooms that read "silence is golden." The campuses had calmed down but had also turned as silent as graveyards. When the silence finally broke, students often avoided politics. They ignored the national news and turned to things like romance, mahjongg, and other amusements.

The moods listed above affect not only students but quite a few university officials and teachers as well. It is reported that some Beijing officials and teachers, although they did not take part in the turmoil and are now actively working on the political thinking of students, cannot make their peace with phrases like "Riots took place in Beijing." They just cannot put their hearts into uttering such language. Some feel that it is understandable if the government makes some mis-

[34]From a poem ("Untitled," 1934) by the famous modern Chinese writer Lu Xun, in which the line "thunder from the silent zone" suggests explosive anger within a repressed society. See Jon Kowallis, *The Lyrical Lu Xun* (Honolulu: University of Hawaii Press, 1996), 311–315.
[35]"Yet another" recalls the series of twentieth-century popular protests, beginning with the famous May Fourth incident of 1919 that took place at China's symbolic center, Tiananmen Square. Before 1989 the most recent Tiananmen incident was on April 5, 1976, when Beijing citizens flocked to Tiananmen to pay tribute to the recently deceased premier Zhou Enlai, but more pointedly also to protest against radical Maoists and their policies.

calculations and if the whole economy is not set right in a day but that embezzlement and corruption are unacceptable. To share ups and downs is fine, but for you to take the ups and leave me the downs is not.

An official from Peking University reports that things are tough for people from his university. When students check in at hotels, many get pushed out the door as soon as it is known where they are from. One Peking University student who was on business in Yanqing county actually got beaten up. The job assignments for seniors graduating in 1989 have been completed, but some employers, including the Central Party School, the Chinese Association of Handicapped People, and the Beijing Committee of the Youth League, have rejected certain students. This official is afraid that gifted students will not apply to Peking University this year, which in turn could lead to lower quality in the incoming class.

The report recommended that great care be taken in applying current policy to the students and that, at all costs, the numbers of those punished be strictly limited.

Chinese society fell into a deep anomie after June Fourth. Numbed, people everywhere turned away from politics. The intellectual class, and especially the students with their exuberant idealism, entered the 1990s with nothing like the admirable social engagement they had shown in the 1980s. The campuses were tranquil, and China seemed shrouded in a dour mist that harbored a spiritual emptiness. Money ruled everything, morals withered corruption burgeoned, and when all this became known on the campuses it turned students thoroughly off from politics. They now concentrated only on their own fates. Something had died.

Deng Xiaoping's struggle for reform

Deng Xiaoping now had less influence than when his previous designated successors, Hu Yaobang and Zhao Ziyang, were in office. Jiang Zemin had been the nominee of Chen Yun and Li Xiannian, and they came to dominate economic policy and personnel appointments. As a Party general secretary of the "new generation," the safest course for Jiang was to stay on the good side of all three senior figures rather than to get too closely identified with Deng. Deng's influence was further attenuated by his weak grasp of economics, a field in which Chen Yun's expertise was well known. Chen's disciples Yao Yilin and Song Ping, both old hands in the field of planned economies and former chairs of the State Planning Commission, now formed, together with Li Peng, half of the six-person Politburo Standing Committee. Deng retained only military power and with it the historical burden of having "commanded the repression."

Three times Deng convened the Politburo Standing Committee to expound on his political legacy. Each time he exhorted them to "persist with all the policies and the general line of the Third Plenum of the Eleventh Central Committee—not only with the present leadership group, but with the next one, too, and the next after that and always thereafter—because ten years of experience has shown that this policy direction is entirely correct. To abandon reform and opening would be to abandon our basic strategy for development."[36]

In November 1989, at the Fifth Plenum of the Thirteenth Central Committee, Deng relinquished his last post, chair of the Central Military Commission, and went into retirement. But he preserved a key channel of influence. Although Jiang Zemin would succeed him as CMC chair, his trusted friend Yang Shangkun would become the first vice chair, his favorite military officer, Admiral Liu Huaqing, who had been the CMC's deputy secretary general, would be another vice chair, and Yang Shangkun's cousin Yang Baibing would become secretary of the Central Party Secretariat as well as CMC secretary general, a post that would put him in charge of the CMC's day-to-day work. As this plan was being implemented between February and June 1990, a nationwide shuffle of military district commanders and political commissars, including both the PLA and the People's Armed Police, led to a shift in posture of the entire military.[37]

But history would not leave Deng Xiaoping alone. After he retired, socialist regimes fell in Romania, Poland, Czechoslovakia, Hungary, and Bulgaria. The Berlin Wall was torn down, bringing the end of German socialism and the reunification of Germany. On December 25, 1991, the red, white, and blue flag of Russia was raised over the Kremlin and the Union of Soviet Socialist Republics passed into history.

---

[36]See *Deng Xiaoping wenxuan*, 347.

[37]High military officials who lost their positions in the shake-up included Hong Xuezhi (deputy secretary general of the CMC), Guo Linxiang (deputy director of the General Political Department of the PLA and secretary of the Committee for Discipline Inspection of the CMC), Li Desheng (political commissar of the National Defense University), Li Yaowen (political commissar of the navy), Zhou Yibing (commander of the Beijing Military District), Xiang Shouzhi (commander of the Nanjing Military District), Wan Haifeng (political commissar of the Chengdu Military District), Li Lianxiu (commander of the People's Armed Police), and Zhang Xiufu (political commissar of the People's Armed Police). Following the shake-up, Zhou Yushu took over command of the People's Armed Police. The commanders and political commissars of the seven military regions of the PLA were as follows:

Region	Commander	Political Commissar
Beijing	Wang Chengbin	Zhang Gong
Shenyang	Liu Jingsong	Song Keda
Jinan	Zhang Wannian	Song Qingwei
Lanzhou	Fu Quanyou	Cao Yaoqi
Nanjing	Gu Hui	Shi Yuxiao
Chengdu	Zhang Taizhong	Gu Shanqing
Guangzhou	Zhu Dunfa	Zhang Zongxian

Four of these men—Zhang Gong, Gu Hui, Zhu Dunfa, and Zhou Yushu—received their promotions after distinguishing themselves in the "pacification of the riots." Zhang Gong, who had been director of the Political Department of the Beijing Military District at the time of June Fourth, was the first public spokesperson for the official view that "no one died inside the Square." The result was a reliable "imperial bodyguard" controlled by Deng from the top.—Comp.

These events further threatened Deng's cherished policies of reform and opening. Against the background of sanctions imposed on China by the U.S.-led Western countries after June Fourth, the fall of socialism in Eastern Europe and the Soviet Union stimulated a new Party emphasis on opposing peaceful evolution. This led to cessation and in some areas reversal of progress toward reform and opening. Again Deng exhorted the third generation of leaders to "watch things with a cool head, hold your positions, bide your time, and keep your powder dry. Stay steady under pressure. Don't be impatient; impatience will get you nowhere. Stay cool, cool, and cool again. Put your shoulder to the wheel and get your own work—your part of our work—done well."[38] Still, the "unchangeable" policies of reform and opening made little headway, and Deng's words no longer packed the punch in Beijing that they once had.

In 1992, at the age of eighty-eight, Deng set out on a second strenuous "southern tour,"[39] accompanied by Yang Shangkun. Traveling to Hubei, Jiangxi, Guangdong, Fujian, and Shanghai, he stressed repeatedly that "anyone who does not reform should step down." Deng's statements unleashed a new wave of economic entrepreneurship and an economic boom. It was his last political act. He died in 1997.

[38]Deng's remarks of September 4, 1989, in *Deng Xiaoping wenxuan*, 321.
[39]Deng's first southern tour was in 1979–1980, when China was opening its special economic zones on the southern coast.

Reflections
on Authentication

ORVILLE SCHELL

Western scholars, diplomats, and journalists have had a long and ambivalent relationship with secret or classified documents leaked from China. But whether during the imperial era, which ended in 1911, or the Marxist-Leninist era, which continues today, Chinese government has been distinguished by its lack of transparency. And so when documents that purportedly give a glimpse into the inner sanctums of the Chinese decisionmaking process surface, they naturally tend to catch our attention.

In the last century, troves of once secret documents have usually been released only after wars and revolutions enthrone new governments, which find it in their interest to reveal the malfeasance or crimes of their predecessors. Such was the case in Russia after the 1917 Revolution, when it behooved the new Marxist government to open up the archives of the tsars. A similar situation prevailed after the defeat of the Axis Powers in World War II, when the Allies found it advantageous to release captured Nazi and imperial Japanese archives. When the Soviet Union broke apart in 1991, the new Russian government also found it expedient to open once sacrosanct KGB archives to public view. And for several decades, the United States has witnessed the selective release of documents as investigative journalists have managed to wrest archives from once impermeable governmental bureaucracies via the Freedom of Information Act. In such cases, because the primary sources themselves have usually been made available, authentication has been a relatively easy process.

However, when collections of classified documents appear in the public domain and make sensitive revelations about sitting governments, a different imperative comes into play. For instance, because the war in Vietnam was still raging when the Pentagon Papers were published in 1971, their appearance was an embarrassment for the U.S. government. In fact, President Richard M. Nixon's attorney general, John Mitchell, filed a restraining order against the *New York Times* and the *Washington Post,* claiming that even the publication of excerpts (the papers consisted of forty-seven volumes, a seven-thousand-page archive) would cause "irreparable injury" to the country's national security. The case became one of the most celebrated in the history of First Amendment jurisprudence. As Justice William J. Brennan observed, "So far as I can determine, never before has the government sought to enjoin a newspaper from publishing information in its possession."[1]

Ultimately, of course, the Supreme Court ruled against the government. As Justice Brennan asserted, "The First Amendment stands as an absolute bar to the imposition of judicial restraints in circumstances of the kind presented by these cases."[2]

The question of leaked documents from a Marxist-Leninist government (or any authoritarian government), such as the one that continues to govern China, poses a somewhat different set of circumstances. This is especially true when, because there is no operable First Amendment and little prospect of getting such revelatory documents published at home, a disaffected Chinese whistle-blower has no alternative but to turn toward a media outlet abroad. Although the citizen of one country cannot, strictly speaking, use the First Amendment of the U.S. Constitution to challenge his own country's government, international standards enshrined in the Universal Declaration of Human Rights, to which China is a signatory, make it clear that free expression is a universal human right that transcends national boundaries.

But if the precedent and the right to publish documents that government leaders wish to keep secret from their own people is relatively unambiguous, what makes publishing a dossier of secret documents leaked from China especially complex is the challenging question of how to authenticate them. Whereas, by the time the documents from tsarist Russia, Nazi Germany, the Soviet Union, or the U.S. Department of Defense appeared in print, there was usually little doubt as to

---

[1] Neil Sheehan, Hedrick Smith, E. W. Kenworthy, and Fox Butterfield, *The Pentagon Papers: The Secret Secret History of the Vietnam War* (New York: Bantam Books, 1971), 655.
[2] Ibid.

whether they were real, it has proven much more difficult to arrive at such a conclusion in the case of documents leaked from an authoritarian state where a one-party political system controls the media. This can be especially true when the ruling government has a vested interest in impugning the veracity of the leaked documents in question. Moreover, if state archives remain closed to outside researchers, there is usually no way to check the authenticity of such materials.

In a country like the People's Republic of China, where various factions are almost invariably jockeying behind the scenes for more advantageous political position, one has to assume that the leakers of sensitive materials have a political agenda. This is, indeed, also the case for the Tiananmen papers. But the agenda of this volume's compiler and his sympathizers has from the beginning been quite up-front and clear: They hope to help rehabilitate the moderate wing of the Communist Party and to revive political reform in China.

But of course, there is always the possibility that some of the documents in a collection such as this one have been altered, or possibly even created out of whole cloth, in order to serve a certain faction or political viewpoint. It is always important to remember that Marxist-Leninist governments often brazenly manipulate facts and sometimes fabricate whole documentary records in order to create congenial, self-serving accounts of history.

So how do we know that this documentary record is credible? What was the process that those of us who worked on this volume underwent to convince ourselves that this record was authentic?

What has always made the challenge of authenticating leaked *hongtou wenjian,* or "red-hatted documents" (official Chinese documents distinguished by title characters written in crimson), difficult for outsiders is the fact that, politically speaking, China is still a closed society. Since no absolute corroboration of the Tiananmen papers could be made by checking archives or interviewing sources, those of us working on this project had to fall back on our own knowledge of what had taken place in China, our judgments about the motives and veracity of the compiler, and our ability to check as much of the information contained in the documents as possible with those sources that were already available to the outside world.

Our task was made more uncertain by the fact that in China's case there has been a long history of "secret" documents that have proved to be of dubious lineage. One can hardly appraise a leaked Chinese document without reflecting on the kind of perils raised by previous incidents. For example, nearly a century ago Sir Edmund Backhouse, an eccentric Oxford-educated orientalist, reportedly recovered a diary from the house of Jing Shan, an assistant secretary to the imperial family. Backhouse claimed that this diary provided a behind-the-scenes record of the tensions, disagreements, and discussions that had gone on within the imperial government during the Boxer Rebellion of 1900. The Jing Shan diary, along with a raft of other secret imperial documents, ultimately served as the basis for Backhouse's 1914 best-selling book, *China Under the Empress Dowager*, written with J. O. P. Bland, the Shanghai correspondent of the *Times* of London.

Sir Edmund's life story—masterfully chronicled in British historian Hugh Trevor-Roper's 1976 book *Hermit of Peking: The Hidden Life of Sir Edmund Backhouse*—is worth recounting here as a cautionary tale before we contemplate the question of authenticating any latter-day Chinese documents. As Trevor-Roper explained of the attitude of contemporary readers toward Backhouse's book, "Its virtues were obvious. It published many original Chinese state papers. . . . It showed an intimate knowledge of Chinese palace politics and personalities. . . . No other work presents so clear a picture of the decadent Manchu court . . . ."[3]

Never before had such an account of what went on within the walls of the Forbidden City been published in the West. But as time passed, doubts began to surface about its bona fides. Although Bland confidently wrote of the work, "The man is not born who could fake a document like that, and the original is open to anyone's inspection,"[4] his colleague at the *Times*, Beijing correspondent George Ernest Morrison, dismissed the Jing Shan diary as a fake right away.

Soon some China experts were asking to see the complete documentary record, which Backhouse promised but failed to provide. Year after year, he kept demurring, until in 1936 Backhouse finally begged off completely from his earlier promise, lamenting that he had been forced to sell the diary due to penury several years earlier. In view of Backhouse's inability or unwillingness to surrender the original documents, it was not surprising that the credibility of the Jing Shan diary began to erode. As more and more experts began to suspect and then attack its murky provenance, and after Trevor-Roper's book appeared exposing Backhouse as a man whose own life was largely woven out of fantasy and artifice, the Jing Shan diary came to be regarded as a masterful but brazen forgery.

It is also worth remembering that even though Trevor-Roper helped unmask Backhouse as a master of deceit, he himself was later taken in by another monumental hoax. In 1983 he was called upon to pass judgment on diaries allegedly

[3]Hugh Trevor-Roper, *Hermit of Peking: The Hidden Life of Sir Edmund Backhouse* (New York: Alfred A. Knopf, 1977), 88.
[4]Ibid., 102.

written by Adolf Hitler. Trevor-Roper, who had written *The Last Days of Hitler* based on his work with British intelligence during World War II, authenticated the diaries as genuine. "Whereas signatures, single documents, or even groups of documents can be skillfully forged, a whole coherent archive covering 35 years is far less easily manufactured," he authoritatively wrote in the *Times* of London. "The archive, in fact, is not only a collection of documents which can be individually tested: it coheres as a whole and the diaries are an integral part of it. That is the internal evidence of authenticity."[5] Alas, shortly thereafter forensic testing showed the diaries to be another masterful forgery. The hoax was a particular embarrassment for Trevor-Roper and serves as a reminder of what a parlous business the authentication of secret documents can be.

In modern times many documents touted as having been leaked from the People's Republic have been made available to scholars, journalists, and dissidents living around the world. With little corroboration, many have ended in one or another of the many Chinese-language newspapers, magazines, and journals in Hong Kong and Taiwan that specialize in publishing such politically sensitive materials. However, because of their uncertain pedigrees, most scholars have treated them warily as reliable sources.

In evaluating the uncertain origin of any leaked documents, it is always important for the historian to read them with a vigilant eye for prejudice: Whom does the document seem to celebrate? Whom does it seem to denigrate? The answer to such questions often provides valuable hints as to possible ulterior motives of those who usher them into public view. For in a closed political system like China's, leaked documents often serve to boost the position of one leader or faction in its political struggles against others.

A cautionary tale, more relevant to this volume, involves purported Chinese Communist Party documents that in 1983 served as the basis of a work published by the venerable New York publishing house Alfred A. Knopf. *The Conspiracy and Death of Lin Biao—How Mao's Chosen Successor Plotted and Failed: An Inside Account of the Most Bizarre and Mysterious Event in the History of Modern China* claimed to be the story of the September 1971 incident in which Marshal Lin Biao, Mao Zedong's longtime ally and chosen successor, was killed after having been allegedly involved in a plot to assassinate his patron.

The book was written by Yao Ming-le, a pseudonymous Chinese author who was said to be have been "a high-level cadre in the Security Bureau of the Central

[5]Available from www.syntac.net/hoax/kujau.php, cited from the *Times* of London, April [day unavailable], 1983.

Committee." The publisher explained that the author's identity had to remain secret because he "claims to draw on dozens of top-secret documents still being held under tight security in Chinese government archives."[6] By publishing the document simultaneously in several countries, Yao Ming-le seemed to hope that his "amazing" account would be accepted as credible and would serve as an antidote to the Party's official version of the Lin Biao affair.

Both the unnamed author of the prologue to *The Conspiracy and Death of Lin Biao* and the eminent China scholar Andrew Nathan (who is an editor of this volume) wrestled with the problem of establishing the credibility of the sources. The prologue describes Yao as being "among those shown the official documents concerning Lin Biao's death" before they were censored for public consumption. Yao was also allegedly shown "a set of private memoirs" that he was said to have quoted at length, "though for the sake of protecting individuals, they could not be used in toto."[7]

"Can Yao Ming-le be believed?" asks the jacket flap copy, anticipating the first question on every reader's mind.

> While it is obviously impossible to confirm in detail all that he says here, or to verify the authenticity of many of his sources, readings of the text by China specialists in several countries tend to support his credibility. His account is consistent with known facts and informed theories ... [and] is being published on the assumption that the story it tells is true.[8]

In hopes of bolstering the book's credibility, Knopf brought in the insightful and skeptical sinologist Pierre Ryckmans, who writes under the pseudonym Simon Leys. Leys, who had authored the scathingly critical but prescient *Chinese Shadows* in 1974, was asked to write an introduction. However, his draft was filled with warnings. "One of the main reasons why ... public opinion in the West swallowed so easily the preposterous tales hastily and crudely concocted by the Chinese propaganda organs," he said, "was simply that in the absence of any true information, even palpably false information will always appear as the next best thing."[9]

The problem Leys confronted was precisely the problem confronted by the

---

[6]Yao Ming-le, *The Conspiracy and Death of Lin Biao—How Mao's Chosen Successor Plotted and Failed: An Inside Account of the Most Bizarre and Mysterious Event in the History of Modern China* (New York: Alfred A. Knopf, 1983), front jacket flap copy.

[7]Ibid., 9.

[8]Ibid., front jacket flap copy.

[9]Simon Leys, *The Burning Forest: Essays on Chinese Culture and Politics* (New York: New Republic Books/Holt, Rinehart and Winston, 1983), 142.

editors of *The Tiananmen Papers* but compounded by the fact that he did not have a "compiler" or another Chinese interlocutor with whom he could directly speak in his quest for verification. "The publisher could only tell me that he [the author] is a Chinese whom they have good reason to trust," lamented Leys, who because "he had access to exclusive, secret information" needed "to retain complete anonymity."[10]

Such a situation left Leys as verifier with little solid ground beneath his feet. "Not knowing the author, and not being able to check his sources, I can, of course, draw no conclusion regarding the historical accuracy of his narrative," he candidly wrote. "Moreover, I do not know what the author's motivations are. Is he merely trying to serve the historical truth? What other interest may be furthered by this publication . . . ? Who is helping whom, and for what purpose?"[11]

Still trying to be of some service to the project at hand, the best this skeptic of skeptics could offer was this: "I must admit that, on the whole, the picture presented in Yao Ming-le's account is plausible and coherent." And he could also acknowledge that "the sociological accuracy of this narrative" is "beyond question." However, he hastened to forewarn readers that the account's implications "should be received with the greatest critical caution."[12]

By the end of his introduction he was still inescapably left to ask, "But is this account true?" Answering himself as positively as perhaps he could—but still with more than a hint of evasive reservation—he concluded, "At least it makes sense—which is more than could be said for the official version of the Lin Biao Affair."[13]

The publisher must have felt that Leys's introduction registered insufficiently high on the authentication meter, because after explaining that "Yao Ming-le's representative" had objected to its "excessively polemical character,"[14] Knopf rejected the effort, necessitating that a new candidate be brought in to try his hand. The pinch hitter was the respected writer on Asian affairs Stanley Karnow. But like Leys, Karnow could not help peppering his short and tentative introduction with qualifications, for instance, referring to "the presumably authoritative documents" cited as sources and using such ambiguous language as "if we are to believe Yao . . . ."[15]

And then finally, he, too, repeated the unavoidable, mantra-like question:

---

[10]Ibid., 149.
[11]Ibid., 149–150.
[12]Ibid., 150.
[13]Ibid., 151.
[14]Ibid., 141.
[15]Yao, *The Conspiracy and Death of Lin Biao*, ix, xiii.

"Can we believe all of what Yao Ming-le tells us here?" His answer was prudent: "It is obviously impossible to say with any certainty, except to note that his story confirms much of what has been rumored and reported about the Lin Biao affair in recent years."[16] And so Karnow ended up with even more ambiguity than the editors of this volume, whose judgments were greatly fortified by having access to the book's compiler.

So why did Yao Ming-le, whoever he was, risk telling his version of this story? "The time has come to tell the truth about this episode," explains the unattributed prologue. "One can and must undertake to restore history's original face, for history's sake, for the sake of those who unwittingly helped in distorting it and for the sake of those who wish and deserve to know what sort of masquerade they have been forced to witness."[17]

Now, the aspiration to banish deception, an attribute with which contemporary Chinese politics is sadly replete, is an admirable one. However, it is not a goal that is accomplished simply by means of lofty intentions and high-sounding rhetoric. Ultimately, there is no substitute for actual corroboration, and even today, eighteen years after the publication of Yao's account, corroborating sources within China are still not forthcoming, leaving its veracity to languish in that ambiguous netherworld where fact and fiction remain indistinguishable.

In 2000, however, the story told in *The Conspiracy and Death of Lin Biao* was challenged by Jin Qiu, the daughter of General Wu Faxian, the commander in chief of the Chinese air force during the early 1970s, in a scholarly work on the affair, *The Culture of Power: The Lin Biao Incident in the Cultural Revolution*. After interviewing many of the principals (including her father) and after a careful reading of Chinese sources, she noted that "speculation feeds on the absence of reliable information." She assessed Yao Ming-le's account this way: "Few students of the subject have taken this version seriously, chiefly because the sources to which Yao claimed to have exclusive access, were never made available to others."[18]

It would be wrong, however, to dismiss all leaked Chinese material and documents as worthless because of their often ambiguous origins. Indeed, over the years, much of what journalists and scholars have learned about China since Mao and how it functions has come from just such sources. And it must be said that a

---

[16]Ibid., xiv.
[17]Ibid., 12.
[18]Jin Qiu, *The Culture of Power: The Lin Biao Incident in the Cultural Revolution* (Stanford: Stanford University Press, 1999), 5.

good number of leaked Chinese Communist Party documents have managed to pass out of the shadow land of questionable lineage to be accepted as reliable. Because the genealogy of some of the documents involved is in certain ways similar to that of the Tiananmen papers, it is worth noting several such cases.

The Harvard scholar Stuart Schram has made something of a lifetime industry out of piecing together what he believes to be the authentic texts of Mao Zedong's speeches, statements, and directives. The sources of many of these texts were wall posters and tabloid-format Red Guard publications that were issued unofficially in China during the Cultural Revolution. Often these allegedly uncensored texts contained language that appears to have been deleted from the versions published in the official Party-sanctioned *Selected Works of Mao Zedong*. It was Schram's goal to restore these crucial texts to what he believed was their original form, but even he candidly acknowledged the problems of dealing with such sources: "It is necessary to say a word about authenticity, which is in reality a dual problem," he wrote in his introduction to *Mao Tse-tung Unrehearsed: Talks and Letters, 1956–71*, published in 1974. "Are the documents employed authentic materials disseminated in China? Even if they are, can the texts of Mao's utterances they contain be regarded as necessarily accurate?"[19]

On the first question, Schram seemed satisfied that the materials in his books were, in fact, widely circulated in China and viewed as authentic texts by those who read them. However, on the second point, namely, their veracity, he could only say, "I believe the authenticity of these materials to be adequately established." But then he added a caveat: "It should be stressed, that 'genuine' does not necessarily mean wholly accurate."[20] For in his research Schram had discovered that there were many discrepancies between different unofficial versions of the same speeches or directives.

Nonetheless, Schram accepted these documents as authentic. After all, they seemed consonant with everything he knew about the Great Helmsman and his manner of speaking. "One other argument, which will perhaps not appear altogether frivolous to the reader once he has savored some of these speeches," he wrote, is this: "In their scope, pungency, and verve, they are beyond the powers of any forger."[21]

The sentiment is a curious echo of J. O. P. Bland's statement that the Jing Shan

---

[19]Stuart Schram, *Mao Tse-tung Unrehearsed; Talks and Letters, 1956–1971* (Middlesex, UK: Penguin Books, 1974), 49.
[20]Ibid., 50.
[21]Ibid.

diary had to be authentic because "the man is not born who could fake a document like that." Indeed, such subjective judgments are finally cited by almost everyone who becomes involved with any compelling documentary find in whose authenticity they are inclined to believe. But such intuitions are not, of course, prima facie grounds for certifying authenticity. Stuart Schram's versions of Mao's utterances have nonetheless managed to enter the canon of source material considered to be reliable.

Another relevant case involved a book-length document that was handed surreptitiously to a Western diplomat (who was himself a respected China scholar) on a dark Beijing street in 1983. The manuscript was "A Critical Biography of Kang Sheng," an unflattering profile of the shadowy former secret police chief and architect of the Chinese gulag who was Mao's most trusted but Machiavellian hatchet man. The manuscript itself was authored by the pseudonymous "Zhongkan," who the diplomat surmised was probably a composite identity made up by using parts of the name of the deputy editor of the theoretical journal *Red Flag*, Ma Zhongyang, and the senior Party historian Li Kan. The manuscript bore a *neibu*, or "internal," classification, which meant that the material should officially only be given limited circulation, although such documents often end up being circulated rather widely, sometimes even being pirated by underground Chinese publishers for black-market commercial distribution.

As usual, there was no way to verify the manuscript's veracity by checking Chinese archives, querying the authors, or making inquiries with the publisher. And to make matters even more complicated, in writing his own book based on the material, the diplomat chose to use a pseudonym because he himself was engaged in politically sensitive government work for his own country. This served to put yet another barrier between the reader and the surety of identifiable sources.

However, "John Byron," as he called himself, clearly believed that the "critical biography" was authentic and accurate, and he used it as "the skeleton" of his own book, *The Claws of the Dragon: Kang Sheng, the Evil Genius Behind Mao and His Legacy of Terror in the People's Republic*, which was coauthored with the journalist Robert Pack. Although Byron quite honestly acknowledged that the original biography was replete with "many irritating omissions" and described it as being "frustrating as a portrait," he also found it "an irresistible invitation" to further plumb the depths of this fascinating but ruthless revolutionary. An unsigned bibliographic note, probably written by Byron and Pack themselves, insisted that "the integrity of 'Zhongkan' is beyond question" because "the author's ideological explanations never seem to compromise the honesty with which they relate facts" and because of the way the book "takes care to distinguish between truth and rumor."[22]

Finally, however, it was Byron's judgment as someone with long experience as a student of contemporary Chinese affairs that convinced him to accept the biography as "a unique document: the only book ever written for an internal Chinese audience of Party cadres and intellectuals that exposes the crimes of a top Communist."[23]

When *The Claws of the Dragon* was published by Simon and Schuster in 1992, reviewers generally accepted that the due diligence Byron and Pack had exercised by complementing the information in the leaked biography with new material from other sources, including newly researched U.S. government archives, had made the resulting effort not only reliable but informative.

.   .   .

There have, of course, been many other instances where "secret" Chinese documents have been leaked abroad. Some have ended up being viewed as having authority; others have been discounted as spurious. This short survey is meant to be not a comprehensive history of such instances but a hint of the wages of ambiguity that are often involved in evaluating such materials.

In terms of helping the reader evaluate the Tiananmen papers, I raise these various cases of historians, editors, journalists, and publishers wrestling with similar sets of documents simply as a reminder that the historical backdrop against which incompletely substantiated Chinese documents must now be considered is long and complicated.

As Andrew Nathan describes in the Introduction to this volume, those involved in this particular project struggled long and hard to come to some reasonable assessment about how to present this unusual collection. Above all, none of us wished to engage in any sort of excessive exuberance simply to help the book become accepted or to sell. Indeed, because it is our reputations that are on the line and because we are dealing with documents that are not only extremely sensitive but were received under ambiguous circumstances, we have tread cautiously. In fact, it took months before we all felt sufficiently comfortable to attach

[22]John Byron and Robert Pack, *The Claws of the Dragon: Kang Sheng, the Evil Genius Behind Mao and His Legacy of Terror in the People's Republic of China* (New York: Simon & Schuster, 1992), 489.
[23]Ibid.

our names to them. In the process, we were taken by the compiler on a curious odyssey. What is perhaps most interesting about this odyssey is that during its progress, more, rather than less, credibility accrued to the compiler. It was this slow process, as much as any particular moment of revelation or occasion of documentary confirmation, that allayed our initial fears that we might be being taken in by some elaborate and well-planned scheme of disinformation.

If the process began with a certain innate skepticism, it slowly generated an increasing level of trust, so that we ultimately concluded that the Tiananmen papers were largely credible. However, it must be emphasized again that we still have no basis for proclaiming their authenticity with absolute authority.

Our odyssey began when Andrew Nathan was approached by the compiler and then given the Chinese-language manuscript that he describes in the Introduction. He was impressed enough by the volume and scope of the collection (only a fraction of which is included in this book) to continue meeting with the compiler. As he observes, in words that echo both Bland and Schram, "*The Tiananmen Papers* possess an internal coherence, richness, and human believability that it would be almost impossible to fake."

Over the ensuing months we all found the compiler increasingly sympathetic and believable. But such cursory impressions alone were insufficient grounds to convince us to adopt these documents as a project under our names. After all, the manuscript we had been given to work with consisted not of original documents, or even facsimile copies, but of a printout of a computer transcription of original materials. They were the provenance of a political system dominated by a single Marxist-Leninist political party with a long tradition of manufacturing politically biased and factually distorted propaganda and then presenting it as fact and pseudohistory. Moreover, they were transmitted by someone who demanded anonymity and who was unwilling to reveal publicly the full dimensions of his political patronage. And if that were not sufficient grounds for doubt, the documents came from a country that has no tradition of a free press, much less a Freedom of Information Act that would allow us to coax government archives into divulging corroborating evidence.

For all three of us (Nathan, Perry Link, and myself), the final willingness to associate ourselves with this documentary collection grew out of several considerations. First, we depended on our own knowledge of the events of 1989. Two of us were in China that spring; we are all familiar with contemporary Chinese politics, speak Chinese, and have researched and written at some length about Chinese affairs in general and the 1989 Tiananmen Square period in particular.

Second, in reading and rereading these documents, we found few substantial points that contradicted what we already knew or could learn elsewhere. The documents did, of course, provide much new information, but this only tended to complement and augment our preexisting knowledge. Although some of what we learned was quite revelatory, nothing was dissonant in any significant way with what we already knew or with other verifiable sources. Moreover, we were able to check a number of facts that we do not think could have been reconstructed from the public record and to confirm their accuracy.

Third, as the materials were being translated, edited, and checked, we were learning more about the compiler—his motives, his background and social connections, how he obtained and protected the materials, and why he needed to remain anonymous. We also came to understand why he had decided to publish the materials in the United States, why he wanted the foreign-language edition to be published first and the Chinese-language edition second, and why he sought to implement this project with the help of Nathan in particular. As we resolved one question after another, we and the compiler began to trust one another more. We also came to accept the fact that we could not share with the reader all we had learned from him.

During this process, in which we also talked to other experts as well, we began to see that the issue of authentication applies differently to the different kinds of material that are presented in this collection. Among the varying types of material we confronted were reports sent to Beijing from various official agencies throughout the country; documents issued by various branches of the central governmental organizations; minutes of meetings of the Politburo, its Standing Committee, and the eight Elders; and reconstructions of important phone conversations between high leaders.

Of these, the minutes are perhaps most vulnerable to skepticism, since nothing quite like them has been released before. But in probing how such minutes were taken and circulated in China, we learned much about the official process. Understanding their genesis and their distribution did help allay our concerns about their lines of descent through the system to the compiler.

Each branch of the Chinese regime—Party Central, the National People's Congress, the State Council, the Chinese People's Political Consultative Conference, and the Central Military Commission—maintains its own "secretariat," or *mishuju,* and each secretariat has its own special "meetings department," or *huiyichu.* It is the responsibility of a specialized staff assigned to each of these *huiyichu* to take notes at the highest-level meetings, transcribe what is said into minutes, or, *jilu,* and then in addition to these minutes write summaries, or *jiyao,* of what was decided for the presiding chair to review before ordering circulation to the relevant leaders. High-level meetings are supposed to be taped, but at the time of the Tiananmen events not all of them were; in particular, the meetings at Deng Xiaoping's house were not.

Before a secretariat's confidential circulation department *(jiyao jiaotongju)* was authorized to distribute these minutes, each set had to be given its own number. Then each copy of the document was also given a serial number, the better to control errant distribution. Before any document was released, confidential secretaries *(jiyao mishu)* attached to each leader—or in the case of the most sensitive documents, the leaders themselves—had to sign for their copies in person and eventually return them in person to the originating secretariat and sign them back in. Finally, the returned documents were sealed in special hemp bags and sent off to one of two secure printing plants managed by the government for official shredding, pulping, and recycling.

The minutes included in this volume of the meetings of the Standing Committee and other high councils evidently had such a genesis and circulation. Although we were able to learn much about how the materials found their way into our hands, revelation of these details would compromise the safety of a number of people, so we must regretfully withhold them.

It was the compiler's fervent conviction that there was an important distinction between passing actual physical documents and merely the reformatted contents on to foreigners like us and hence to the world at large. This was a distinction and a sensitivity that was extremely important to the compiler for reasons that make sense in China but may seem somewhat illogical in the context of an open society. Nonetheless, they were the terms of this game, and we chose to respect them. After all, China has its own set of cultural and political imperatives that are not ours to judge for another who must live his own life in that system. Suffice it to say, there is a rather different notion of what it means to be "patriotic" extant in China. Whereas our own Western notions of "patriotism" can embrace the idea of a loyal opposition or a patriotic dissidence, in the Chinese worldview patriotism—or *aiguo zhuyi*, literally, "the ism of loving one's country"—is much more confining. Because both the Chinese Confucian and the Marxist-Leninist traditions stress orthodoxy and consensus that brook little dissent, actions that smack of disloyalty to one's leader and country have never acquired the moral sanction that could make dissent understandable as a patriotic impulse. In short, Chinese notions of patriotism do not readily extend approval to a citizen who seeks to remain loyal to something other than the ruler, the state, and the larger racial notion of "being Chinese." And thus even today,

Chinese intellectuals find the term "dissident" an uncomfortable, even dishonorable, appellation.

So in its definitions of patriotism China differs greatly from the West, even from Russia and Eastern Europe. Here the idea of "living in truth," as Václav Havel has put it, even if it involves revealing public documents that may seem to some to assail the nation and race, has nonetheless acquired an honorable cachet. Through working on this project with a Chinese who has strong feelings of loyalty for his country, we were reminded that when it comes to publishing classified documents and putting oneself into direct opposition to the state, China is culturally and politically still a very different place from the United States and the rest of the West. And thus finally, we must acknowledge that because of the cultural and political milieu from which they come and because the compiler still hopes to live and work someday in China, the Tiananmen papers are not completely analogous to the Pentagon Papers.

In the end, if the compiler's sensitivities complicated our work, they did not finally make us doubt his motives. He fully understood our concern with authenticity and did everything that he could to help us confirm them without violating the rigid political and cultural restraints he was laboring under himself. Forced by circumstances to operate in the very different, even contradictory worlds of Chinese Communist secrecy and Western scholarship and publishing, he sought to balance painful and sometimes impossible opposites. But by doing so with dignity, he ended up enhancing our confidence and helped us reconstruct, as much as possible, both the world from which these materials came and the journey they went on before being published here. In the process, he enabled us to feel much more comfortable about our involvement.

Finally, our confidence in the compiler was one of the most important factors leading us to believe in this material. It was reinforced by the fact that as we worked, we continued to be unable to discern any prejudicial or polemical agenda inherent in either his attitude or the texts themselves—other than his own agenda that he had quite candidly described at the outset.

In the last analysis, what we can say is this: To us the texts ring with an air of truth, and they dovetail in fact, tone, and political point of view with what we, as longtime observers of China, know about the events of 1989 and that country's leaders. But we cannot guarantee that these minutes, for instance, are as accurate as the Pentagon Papers or the transcripts of U.S. presidential conversations recorded during the Watergate era. Of course, the former were verifiable, written texts, and the latter were transcriptions from tapes recorded surreptitiously in the

White House.

In China during the period covered by the Tiananmen papers, on the other hand, notes were evidently handwritten by staff members from the relevant *huiyichu,* much as utterances of the emperors were once recorded by an attending amanuensis. If two note takers were on duty, perhaps from different offices, discrepancies of the kind that Schram encountered in anthologizing the unexpurgated speeches and directives of Mao Zedong might logically have occurred.

The barrier between us and the documents is, alas, still real. We have been working with sources that have somewhat mysteriously been transmitted by Chinese nationals who do not feel themselves at liberty to reveal everything they know and will not permit us to acknowledge everything we have learned. Inevitably, then, blank spaces must remain both in the fabric of authentication and in the corroborating narrative we are able to weave for the reader.

And so it is important to emphasize again that no one outside of China can completely vouch for the authenticity of these transcripts, any more than Simon Leys could vouch for the authenticity of the Lin Biao documents or Stuart Schram for Mao's speeches. After all, we were not there, nor were the original documents available to us.

The alternative to publication was to ignore this collection—in effect to yield to the Chinese Communist Party's protective shield of secrecy. Even though we are well aware of the perils of being deceived, the three of us working on this project nonetheless felt that helping to get these documents published was the responsible decision. The alternative was to eschew them and thereby engage in a form of passive suppression. Since our intention was to try to help set a distorted historical record straight, we decided we could not but proceed. We trust that our decision was the right one. However, we recognize that even as we seek to help set history right, it will, in fact, have to be history itself rather than we that will serve as the ultimate judge of this collection's veracity.

Abbreviations

ADB	Asian Development Bank
AFP	L'Agence France–Presse
AFS	Autonomous Federation of Students
AFW	Autonomous Federation of Workers
AP	Associated Press
CAC	Central Advisory Commission
CAD	Chinese Alliance for Democracy (U.S. group)
CCP	Chinese Communist Party
CCTV	China Central Television
CDIC	Central Discipline Inspection Commission
CIA	Central Intelligence Agency
CITIC	China International Trust and Investment Corporation
CMC	Central Military Commission
CPPCC	Chinese People's Political Consultative Conference
CUPSL	Chinese University of Political Science and Law
CUST	Chinese University of Science and Technology
FASSC	Federation of All Social Sectors in the Capital
IERC	Institute for Economic Reform in China
KMT	Kuomintang
NPC	National People's Congress
PAP	People's Armed Police
PB	Politburo
PBSC	Politburo Standing Committee
PLA	People's Liberation Army
PRC	People's Republic of China
ROC	Republic of China
SC	Standing Committee
SEC	State Education Commission
UPI	United Press International
USIA	United States Information Agency
VOA	Voice of America

Who Was Who

ONE HUNDRED BRIEF BIOGRAPHIES

EDITORS' NOTE: Undated information refers to spring 1989, when the events of this book took place. Thus, for example, the offices listed for Bao Tong are those he held in spring 1989. For the eight Elders and two marshals the age given is their age as of June 4, 1989.

BAO TONG. Zhao Ziyang's secretary, deputy director of the State Commission for the Restructure of the Economic System, member of the CCP Thirteenth Central Committee, director of the CCP Central Political System Reform Office, and secretary of the PBSC. Sentenced to seven years in prison after June Fourth and expelled from the Party, the highest-ranking Party figure to be imprisoned in connection with these events.

BAO ZUNXIN. Associate research fellow at the Chinese Academy of Social Sciences. One of the leaders of the intellectuals who gave support and advice to the students in Tiananmen Square. Arrested after June Fourth and subsequently released.

BO YIBO, 81. One of the eight Elders, deputy director of the CCP CAC in charge of the commission's daily work, enjoying the right to attend meetings of the PBSC. Former PB member and vice premier. Since 1982 had assisted Deng Xiaoping and Chen Yun in supervising the Party's organizational (that is, personnel) work. Retired fully from politics when the CAC was abolished in 1992.

BUHE. Chairman of the government of the Inner Mongolian Autonomous Region. Son of the late Ulanfu, who was the senior Mongolian member of the

CCP and was known as the King of Mongolia. In March 1993 appointed vice chair of the Standing Committee of the NPC.

CHAI LING. Graduate student at Peking University, general commander of the Tiananmen Square Command. Warrant for arrest issued after June Fourth, but escaped from the country. Became an M.A. student at Princeton University in 1990. Subsequently went into business in the Boston area.

CHEN JUN. Democracy activist who had been studying in the United States but returned to China in 1988. Expelled from China before June Fourth because of his membership in the "China Spring" pro-democracy group.

CHEN XITONG. Mayor of Beijing and member of the State Council. Promoted to Beijing Party secretary and PB member in 1992. Resigned in connection with a corruption scandal in 1996, sentenced to sixteen years in prison, and expelled from the CCP. Released early to house arrest on medical parole.

CHEN YIZI. Member of the State Commission for the Restructure of the Economic System and director of the Institute for Economic Reform in China. Leader of what were called the "three institutes and one association," think tanks associated with Zhao Ziyang. Warrant for arrest issued after June Fourth, but escaped from the country, first to France and then to the United States.

CHEN YUN, 84. One of the eight Elders, chairman of the CCP CAC. Considered one of the founders of the PRC. One of the top five leaders in the 1950s, along with Mao Zedong, Liu Shaoqi, Zhu De, and Zhou Enlai. Removed from power during the Cultural Revolution and restored in 1979, serving at different times as CCP deputy chairman, PBSC member, and first secretary of the CCP Central Discipline Inspection Commission. Long responsible for party organizational (that is, personnel) affairs and economic planning; considered a strong advocate of economic planning. Died in 1995.

CHEN ZHILI. Shanghai Party Committee Standing Committee member and chief of the Shanghai Party Committee's Propaganda Department. After June Fourth appointed deputy secretary of the Shanghai Party Committee. Elected to the CCP Central Committee at the Fifteenth Party Congress in 1997 and appointed Minister of Education in 1998.

CHEN ZIMING. Director of the Beijing Social and Economic Sciences Research Institute, charged with being one of the "black hands" behind the Tiananmen demonstrations. After June Fourth arrested and sentenced for the crimes of trying to overthrow the government and conducting counterrevolutionary propaganda and incitement.

CHI HAOTIAN. General, PLA chief of staff. In 1993 promoted to minister of defense and in 1994 became vice chairman of the CMC. In 1997 appointed to the PB. In 1998 reappointed minister of defense.

DAI QING. Reporter for the *Guangming Daily* and distinguished writer of Communist history; adopted daughter of the deceased CCP leader Ye Jianying. Tried to open a communication channel between the government and the students and was investigated for this after June Fourth.

DENG LIQUN. Member of the CAC. Former secretary in the CCP Central Secretariat and director of the Party's Propaganda Department. Considered a leftist in the spectrum of Chinese politics, in 1987 defeated for election both to the CCP Central Committee and to the Standing Committee of the CAC. Retired in 1992 when the CAC was abolished.

DENG XIAOPING, 85. Most influential Elder and CMC chairman. As he correctly described himself, "the core of the second generation of CCP leadership." Served as Party general secretary and member of the PBSC in the 1950s. Removed from power during the Cultural Revolution. Reappeared in 1974 and served as Party vice chairman, vice premier, and PLA chief of staff. Purged for a second time in early 1976 because of his alleged responsibility for Beijing demonstrations to mourn the death of Premier Zhou Enlai. Made his third return to power in 1976 after the death of Mao and the arrest of the Gang of Four. Served as PBSC member, chair of the CPPCC, deputy chair of the CMC, and vice premier. Died in 1997.

DENG YINGCHAO, 85. One of the Elders, widow of Zhou Enlai, and foster mother of Li Peng. Past PB member, chair of the All-China Women's Federation, chair of the CPPCC, and second secretary of the Central Discipline Inspection Commission. In retirement from all posts in 1989 but held the personal rank equivalent to PBSC member. Died in 1992.

Ding Guan'gen. Intimate and bridge partner of Deng Xiaoping, alternate member of the PB. Former minister of railways. After 1989 served as secretary of the Party Secretariat, PB member, and director of the Party's Propaganda Department.

Fang Lizhi. Astrophysicist who had served as vice chancellor of the Chinese University of Science and Technology. Expelled from the Party in 1987 because he supported the 1986 student demonstrations. Transferred to Beijing, where he served as a research fellow at the Beijing Observatory. Ordered arrested in June 1989 but sought refuge in the U.S. embassy. Went to the United States in 1991, where he eventually became a professor at the University of Arizona.

Feng Congde. Graduate student at Peking University, deputy commander of the Tiananmen Square Headquarters. Warrant issued for his arrest after June Fourth, but fled the country.

Han Dongfang. A worker in the Beijing Railway Bureau and head of the Beijing AFW. Later moved to Hong Kong, where he reports on workers' issues in China for Radio Free Asia.

He Dongchang. Vice minister of the State Education Commission, in charge of its daily work. Considered a hard-liner during the events of June Fourth. Retired in 1993.

Hong Xuezhi. PLA general, CMC member, and deputy secretary. Former director of the General Logistics Department. Retired in 1998.

Hu Jiwei. Member of the Standing Committee of the NPC, strong liberal voice in the Party. Former publisher and editor-in-chief of *People's Daily*. Effectively excluded from politics after June Fourth because of his actions at the time. Formally retired in 1993.

Hu Ping. Chairman of the U.S.-based Chinese Alliance for Democracy; former graduate student at Peking University.

Hu Qiaomu. Member of the Standing Committee of the CAC. Senior Party ideologist who had served as Mao Zedong's political secretary, PB member, secretary of the Central Party Secretariat, and president of the Chinese Academy of Social Sciences. Died in 1992.

Hu Qili. PBSC member and secretary of the Central Secretariat in charge of ideology and overseas propaganda. Served as first secretary of the Communist Youth League under Hu Yaobang in the 1960s and as minister of electronic industries and director of the Party Central Office. Removed from all posts after June Fourth. In 1991 appointed vice minister of machine building; in 1993, minister of electronic industries; and in 1998, deputy chairman of the CPPCC.

Hu Yaobang. His death at the age of 74 on April 15, 1989, sparked the student demonstrations. One of Deng Xiaoping's chief reform lieutenants until his dismissal from the post of Party general secretary in 1987 for failure to oppose bourgeois liberalization energetically enough. Important earlier posts included first secretary of the Communist Youth League, director of the Party Organization (that is, personnel) Department, and member of the PBSC.

Hua Guofeng. Mao Zedong's chosen successor, served as Party chairman and premier in the years after Mao's death in 1976. Allowed Deng Xiaoping's return to power and left office in 1980 although retaining Central Committee rank.

Huang Hua. Member of the Standing Committee of the CAC. Former ambassador to Ghana, Egypt, and Canada; 1971–1976, Chinese ambassador to the United Nations; 1976–1982, foreign minister; 1983–1988, vice chair of the Standing Committee of the NPC.

Huang Ju. Shanghai Municipal Party Committee deputy secretary and vice mayor. Became mayor in 1992 and Party secretary in 1994. Appointed to the PB in 1996.

Jia Qinglin. Fujian deputy Party secretary. Later rose to the posts of Fujian governor, Fujian Party secretary, Beijing mayor, and Beijing Party secretary. Elected to the PB in 1997.

Jiang Chunyun. Shandong Party secretary. Promoted during the 1990s to PB member, vice premier, and vice chair of the NPC.

Jiang Zemin. Shanghai Party secretary and PB member. Former minister of electronic industries and Shanghai mayor. After June Fourth became Party general secretary and a member of the PBSC. In 1990 became chairman of the CMC and in 1993 also made state president. Labeled by Deng Xiaoping "the core of the third generation of leadership."

LI CHANGCHUN. Governor of Liaoning. Later promoted to Henan Party secretary and Guangdong Party secretary and to membership in the PB.

LI GUIXIAN. Director of the Bank of China with cabinet rank. Former Party secretary of the Inner Mongolian Autonomous Region and Anhui Province. Retired from the bank in 1991 and in 1998 was elected a deputy chairman of the CPPCC.

LI LU. Student from Nanjing University, commander-in-chief of the non-Beijing students under the Tiananmen Square Command. Fled to the United States after June Fourth.

LI PENG. Premier and member of the PBSC. Adopted son of Zhou Enlai and Deng Yingchao. Had previously served as vice minister of water conservancy and electric power, secretary in the Central Party Secretariat, and vice premier. In 1998 became chairman of the NPC.

LI QIYAN. Deputy secretary, Beijing Municipal Party Committee. Became mayor of Beijing in 1993, but lost his job in 1996 in connection with the Chen Xitong corruption scandal. Then served as vice minister of labor. Retired in 1998.

LI RUIHUAN. PB member, mayor, and Party secretary of Tianjin. Formerly served as secretary in the Communist Youth League secretariat. Member of the PBSC and secretary in the Central Party Secretariat after June Fourth. After 1993 served as chairman of the CPPCC.

LI SHUXIAN. Wife of Fang Lizhi and associate professor of physics at Peking University. With Fang, took refuge in the U.S. embassy after June Fourth and later went to the United States.

LI TIEYING. Chairman of the cabinet-level State Education Commission and member of the PB. Son of early Party member Lie Weihan and Jin Weiying, who later became Deng Xiaoping's second wife. Studied in the Soviet Union, served as deputy secretary of the Liaoning Party Committee and minister of electronic industries. Continued as member of the PB and served as president of the Chinese Academy of Social Sciences after June Fourth.

LI TUO. Influential literary critic, working in the literary criticism section of the Chinese Writers' Association. Former editor-in-chief of *Beijing Literature*.

LI XIANNIAN, 80. One of the Elders and chairman of the CPPCC. Former state president and member of the PBSC. One of the few senior leaders not purged during the Cultural Revolution, he served then as PB member and vice premier. Died in 1992.

LI XIMING. Beijing Party secretary and PB member. In 1993 became a vice chairman of the NPC. Retired in 1998.

LI ZEHOU. Researcher in the Institute of Philosophy of the Chinese Academy of Social Sciences, regarded as one of China's leading contemporary philosophers. In 1993 came to the United States, where he has lived since.

LIU BINYAN. *People's Daily* reporter famous for his exposure of abuses of power, expelled from the party in January 1987 at the behest of Deng Xiaoping for supporting the fall 1986 student movement. Came to the United States in March 1988 and has not been back to China.

LIU HUAQING. General, deputy secretary general of the CMC. Former commander of the PLA navy. Served as deputy chair of the CMC and member of the PBSC after June Fourth. Retired in 1998.

LIU XIAOBO. A lecturer at Beijing Normal University, influential among young people for his thoroughgoing critique of traditional Chinese values. Jailed for a year and a half after June Fourth for his role at Tiananmen. Served three years under labor reeducation in 1996–1999 for advocating political reform.

LIU YANDONG. Second secretary of the Communist Youth League, chairman of the All-China Youth Federation, and member of the Standing Committee of the NPC. Later served as deputy director of the United Front Work Department.

LIU ZAIFU. Director of the Literature Research Institute of the Chinese Academy of Social Sciences and one of China's leading literary essayists and historians of literature. After the Tiananmen events, came to the United States, where he has lived since.

LIU ZHONGDE. Deputy secretary general of the State Council.

LUO GAN. Secretary general of the State Council and Li Peng's most trusted subordinate. Appointed in 1993 as a PB member and secretary of the Central Secretariat. Now in charge of state security, public security, the courts, and other "political-legal work."

Mao Zhiyong. Party secretary of Jiangxi. In 1998 appointed vice chairman of the CPPCC.

Nie Rongzhen, 90. One of two surviving members of the CCP's senior military leadership, the Ten Marshals. Had been in charge of military science and technology before retirement. Held personal rank equivalent to membership in the PBSC. Died in 1992.

Peng Chong. Vice chair of the NPC. Former Party secretary of Shanghai. Retired in 1993.

Peng Zhen, 87. One of the eight Elders. Retired Beijing mayor and chair of the Standing Committee of the NPC, enjoying personal rank equivalent to membership in the PBSC. Died in 1997.

Qiao Shi. Member of the PBSC and Party Secretariat, in charge of personnel, security, and intra-Party investigation and discipline. Had previously served in many posts, including running the Party's External Liaison and Organization Departments. In 1993 became chairman of the Standing Committee of the NPC. Retired in 1998.

Qin Jiwei. General, minister of defense, PB member, and CMC member; a favorite of Deng Xiaoping. Died in 1997.

Qin Benli. Editor-in-chief of the *World Economic Herald*. Fired from his job and subjected to intra-Party investigation after June Fourth. Died in 1991.

Rui Xingwen. Member of the Party Secretariat in charge of propaganda. Considered a liberal, had clashed with Jiang Zemin when Jiang was mayor and Rui was Party secretary in Shanghai. Removed from his post after June Fourth. Appointed deputy director of the State Planning Commission in 1991. Retired in 1993.

SONG PING. PB member and chairman of the State Planning Commission. Former Party secretary of Gansu. Advanced after June Fourth to membership in the PBSC and to directorship of the Party Organization Department. Considered a conservative and an advocate of economic planning; one of Chen Yun's two most trusted subordinates (along with Yao Yilin).

SONG RENQIONG. Vice chair of the CAC. Former PB member, related to Chen Yun through the marriage of their children.

SU XIAOKANG. Lecturer at the Beijing Broadcasting Institute. Coauthor of the influential 1988 television series *River Elegy* and of several works of politically incisive literary reportage. After the Tiananmen events, came to the United States, where he has lived since.

TIAN JIYUN. PB member and vice premier. One of Zhao Ziyang's trusted aides, considered an able economic administrator. Starting in 1993, served two terms as first vice chairman of the Standing Committee of the NPC.

WAN LI. Chairman of the Standing Committee of the NPC and member of the PB. Former minister of railways, Party secretary of Anhui, member of the Party secretariat, and vice premier. Retired in 1993.

WAN RUNNAN. General manager of the Stone group of companies. Fled after June Fourth and served as chairman of the Federation for Democracy in China.

WANG DAN. Freshman at Peking University and leader of the Autonomous Federation of Students. Arrested after June Fourth and sentenced to prison. Released in 1998 on medical parole and went to the United States.

WANG DAOHAN. A former mayor of Shanghai, deputy chairman of the Party's Shanghai Advisory Commission and honorary chairman of the board of the *World Economic Herald*. Has been called Jiang Zemin's mentor. In the 1990s served as head of the Association for Relations Across the Taiwan Strait.

WANG JUNTAO. Deputy editor of the privately run *Economics Weekly* and longtime democratic activist. Arrested after June Fourth and sentenced to thirteen years' imprisonment. In 1994 released to the United States on medical parole.

WANG RENZHI. Director of the Party Propaganda Department. Later served as vice president and head of the Organization Department of the Chinese Academy of Social Sciences.

WANG RENZHONG. First vice chair of the Chinese People's Political Consultative Conference and the most trusted subordinate of Li Xiannian. A former Party secretary of Hubei, PB member, and secretary in the party Central Secretariat. Died in 1992.

WANG RUILIN. Director of the Deng Xiaoping Office and Party Central Office deputy director. After Deng's retirement in late 1989 from the post of CMC chair, Wang continued as director of the Deng Office. At the same time he was promoted to the rank of general and appointed deputy director of the PLA General Political Department. He subsequently retired.

WANG RUOWANG. Writer and member of the Chinese Writers' Association, expelled from the Party in 1987 after Deng Xiaoping criticized him for supporting the student movement of the previous year. Jailed and then placed under investigation and house arrest after June Fourth. Later went into exile in the United States.

WANG ZHEN, 81. Vice president of the PRC and one of the eight Elders. A rough-spoken farmer-soldier; loyal to an old-fashioned idea of the Revolution yet gave advantages to his son in doing business. Died in 1993.

WEI JIANXING. Minister of supervision and former director of the Party Organization Department. In the years after June Fourth, served as head of the national trade union, Beijing Party secretary, and secretary of the Central Discipline Inspection Commission and was promoted to the PBSC.

WEI JINGSHENG. Famous dissident, author of "Democracy: The Fifth Modernization," in jail in 1989. Appeals for his release were part of the prologue to the events of that spring.

WEN JIABAO. Director of the Central Party Office. A former vice minister of geology and mining. Became a PB member, secretary of the Central Party Secretariat, and vice premier after June Fourth.

Wu Bangguo. Deputy secretary of the Shanghai Party Committee. Later served as Shanghai Party secretary, PB member, and vice premier.

Wu Disheng. Reformist mayor of Shenyang. Died in an airplane accident in 1993.

Wu Guanzheng. Governor of Jiangxi. Later served as Party secretary in Jiangxi and Shandong and was elected to the PB.

Wu Xueqian. PB and State Council member and vice premier in charge of foreign affairs. Former foreign minister.

Wuerkaixi. Freshman at Beijing Normal University and one of the leaders of the AFS. Fled after June Fourth and lives in Taiwan.

Xu Jiatun. Director of the Xinhua News Agency in Hong Kong, China's virtual consulate in the colony. Former Party secretary in Jiangsu. Defected in 1991 and went to the United States.

Xi Zhongxun. Deputy chairman of the Standing Committee of the NPC. Former member of the PB and Central Secretariat and a major aide of Hu Yaobang. Retired in 1993.

Xu Xiangqian, 87. One of two surviving members of the CCP's senior military leadership, the Ten Marshals. Held personal rank of PBSC member. Died in 1990.

Yan Jiaqi. Director of the Institute of Political Science of the Chinese Academy of Social Sciences. Coauthor of a highly regarded history of the Cultural Revolution. Fled after June Fourth and served for a time as chairman of the Federation for Democracy in China.

Yan Mingfu. Director of the Party's United Front Work Department. Dismissed from all posts after June Fourth. Became vice minister of civil affairs in 1991 and chairman of the China Philanthropic Association in 1997.

Yang Baibing. General, CMC member, chairman of the General Political Department of the PLA. Yang Shangkun's cousin. After June Fourth, promoted to CMC secretary general and member of the CCP Central Secretariat. Removed from military posts in 1992 as part of Jiang Zemin's consolidation of power over the military and although given a seat on the PB, lost all real influence. Retired in 1997.

YANG DEZHONG. Long-time director of the Central Guards Bureau. Central Committee member. Promoted to general in 1994. Retired in 1997.

YANG RUDAI. Sichuan Party secretary and member of the PB. In 1993 appointed vice chair of the CPPCC. Retired in 1998.

YANG SHANGKUN, 82. President of the PRC, with the right to attend meetings of the PBSC. Long-time director of the Party Central Office and close comrade of Deng Xiaoping. Retired in 1993, died in 1998.

YAO YILIN. PBSC member and senior-ranking vice premier. Like Song Ping, a trusted follower of Chen Yun, with expertise in economic planning and management. A conservative, and in 1989 the only Standing Committee member who did not meet with the students. Retired in 1993, died in 1994.

YE XUANPING. Governor of Guangdong. Son of deceased Party Elder Ye Jianying. In 1993 became vice chairman of the CPPCC Standing Committee.

YUAN MU. State Council spokesman, former journalist and Cultural Revolution activist. Close to Li Peng. Became director of the State Council research office after June Fourth and a Standing Committee member of the CPPCC in 1993. Retired in 1998.

ZENG JIANHUI. Deputy director of the Party Propaganda Department. Became director of the State Council News Office after June Fourth. In 1998 became chairman of the NPC Foreign Affairs Committee.

ZENG QINGHONG. Deputy secretary of the Shanghai Party Committee. Son of deceased former minister of interior Zeng Shan. Followed Jiang Zemin to Beijing after June Fourth and served in a series of key posts in Party Central.

ZHANG AIPING. General, standing member of the CAC. Former director of the Commission on Science and Technology for National Defense and minister of defense. Kept silent after June Fourth, a sign of disapproval. A key figure in 1992 in helping Jiang Zemin arrange the removal of Yang Shangkun and Yang Baibing from power. Continues to be one of Jiang Zemin's most respected senior military advisers.

ZHAO NANQI. General, director of the PLA General Logistics Department. Became director of the Chinese Academy of Military Sciences after June Fourth.

ZHAO ZIYANG. Party general secretary, having previously served as premier and as party secretary in Inner Mongolia, Guangdong, and Sichuan. Deprived of all posts and placed under de facto house arrest after June Fourth.

ZHU RONGJI. Mayor and deputy Party secretary of Shanghai. Later transferred to Beijing, where he became premier and a member of PBSC.

Index

Index

Index

Hu Qili
  April 26 editorial, 71, 73, 75, 124
  criticism of, 259–260
  dialogue
    with Beijing workers, 152
    with journalists, 149
  domestic press, statements biasing, 388
  hunger strike
    Politburo Standing Committee meeting
      regarding, 177, 179, 184, 189
    visit to hospitals, 199
  Hu Yaobang
    death and memorial service, 21–22, 49
    mourning and demonstrations, 47
  martial law
    decision to impose, 175, 204, 209
    Politburo Standing Committee meeting
      regarding, 191–193
  memory of, likely impact of book publica-
    tion, xxvii
  People's Daily, unauthorized edition of, 236
  press reform, 82–83, 122, 147
  replacement of, 223, 264, 438
  student movement
    Politburo meeting regarding, 58, 60–61,
      135, 137–138
    Politburo Standing Committee meeting
      regarding, 89–90, 102, 105, 107–108,
      128
    and the press, 52
    Wan Li, approval of remarks on, 191
Hu Yaobang
  death of, 19–24, 344
  Deng Xiaoping, relationship with, 140
  dismissal of, 14
  failures of, 288
  memorial service for, 49–51
  mourning for, xxxv, 24–36, 42–43, 47
  reform and divided Party leadership, 4–5
Hunan, 28–29, 62, 229, 249–250, 452
Hunan Normal University, 62
Hunan People's Government, 229
Hunan Provincial Party Committee, 6–8, 49,
  229, 249–250
Hunan University, 229
Hunger strike
  announcement of, 121–122
  appeals by university officials, 174
  beginnings of, 156–158
  condition of student strikers, report on,
    193–194
  Declaration of, 153–155
  dialogue on, 158–160, 164–165, 170–171
  Gorbachev visit as catalyst for, xxxvii
  intellectuals, attempted intercession of the,
    165–169
  leadership, disorganization among, 221
  Manifesto of, 155

  and martial law, 175, 222–223, 254
  May 17 Proclamation, 195–196
  Plan of, 156
  proposal for a, 144–145
  support for
    from the intellectuals, 171
    outside Beijing, 196–199, 227–231, 275
    spreading beyond students, 179, 196–198,
      213–214, 228, 230
    from students, 172, 182–183
    in Tiananmen Square, 173–174, 194–195,
      213–214
  Zhao Ziyang and, 152, 181–182
Hunger Strike Command, 333
Hunger Strike Headquarters, 236–237

Information, desire of leadership for,
  xxxiii–xxxiv
Inner Mongolia, 281, 451
Inner Mongolia, Military District of, 79
Inner Mongolia Autonomous Region, 170
Inner Mongolia Normal University, 404
Inner Mongolia University, 393, 404
Institute for Economic Reform
  Bao Tong, dissenting activities of, 307
  foreign infiltration of, 341–342
  indictment of, 333
  martial law, opposition to, 220–221, 235
  plotting behind the scenes, 255
  Zhao Ziyang, support of, 270–271
Institute of Printing, 38
Intellectuals
  faculty disaffection, report on, 13–14
  hunger strike
    efforts to end, 165–169, 174
    response to, 162–163, 171
  martial law, response to, 274–275, 286, 289
International Affairs Research Institute of the
  China International Trust and Investment Corporation, 221, 270–271, 341
International Scholarly Center, 345

Jiang Chunyun, xxiv
Jiang Hua, 433
Jiang Qing, xv, 313
Jiang Weiguo, 347
Jiang Zemin
  April 26 editorial, response to, 77
  career of, book publication likely to dam-
    age, xxii–xxiii
  Central Military Commission chairman-
    ship, xxxii
  general secretary
    appointment as, 308–312, 323–324, 328,
      431, 437
    consideration for, 223, 261, 297
  Hu Yaobang, mourning and demonstra-
    tions, 28

Index

MacFarquhar, Roderick, 120
Mai Tianshu, 166
Mao Zedong
  Cultural Revolution, speeches and conversations circulated during, xv
  leadership
    Central Military Commission chairmanship, xxxii
    maturity of, 311, 326–327, 426–427
    prestige of, 359
    tradition of supreme rulership, xxxi
  portrait of attacked, 284
Mao Zhiyong, 249
Martial law
  clearing the Square. *See* Military action to clear the Square
  decision to impose, 175, 189–190, 191–193, 204–211
  deployment of troops, 211–213, 227, 239–242, 282–284
  Elders meet to discuss, 242–243
  "Letter to Beijing Citizens," 254–255
  Li Peng, letter of support from, 292
  military attitudes, notice regarding wrong thinking, 220
  mobilization of support for, 298–301
  normal order, decision to restore, 313–314
  order for signed, 233–234
  purpose of, 278–279
  response to, 223
    in Beijing, 234–237, 234–239, 253–254, 268
    Chinese abroad, 252, 266
    foreign press, 253, 276
    in the government, 220–221, 234–235
    in Hong Kong, 267, 275–276
    intellectuals, 274–275, 286
    military leadership, 265–266, 282
    in the provinces, 243–252, 274–275, 287
    in the Soviet Union, 276
    students in Tiannanmen Square, 273–274, 284–285, 288–289
    in the U.S., 276
  weapons, orders regarding use on civilians, 223, 242
  Xinhua Gate, temporary declaration for the vicinity of, 33, 35
  Zhao Ziyang, desire to resign over decision to impose, 200–201
Martial Law Command
  counterrevolutionary riot, emergency announcement regarding, 378
  deployment of troops, report on, 227
  evacuation of the Square, broadcast of demands, 380–381
  military action to clear the Square, report on, 371–372, 378, 380
  Muxidi, report on battle at, 372–373

violence following evacuation of the Square, report on, 384–385
Martial Law Headquarters
  activists, measures taken against, 448
  conditions in Beijing, report on and public requests, 268
  deployment of troops, report on, 282–284
  hunting down activists, guidelines for, 447
  martial law troops, report on readiness to act, 349–353
Ma Shaofang, 158, 449
Ma Shuli, 296
Ma Wenrui, 306
Massachusetts Institute of Technology, 345
May 16 Declaration, 171
May Fourth Movement, 13–14, 363
May 17 Proclamation, 195–196, 208
May Thirtieth Movement, 322
Media. *See* Domestic press; Foreign press
Military, the
  April 26 editorial, response to, 77–80, 81
  clearing the Square. *See* Military action to clear the Square
  ideological conditions in, 9–10, 149, 349–350
  and martial law. *See* Martial law
  nationwide shuffle of officers, 1990, 456
  political importance of, xxxii
  support for martial law troops, 302
  thought work within, 144, 240–242, 283, 361
  See also People's Liberation Army and, Central Military Commission
Military action to clear the Square
  bloodshed in. *See* Bloodshed
  decision to order, 354–362
  evacuation of the Square, 377–382
  initial citizen reaction to, 365–369, 371–372
  justification for, report providing, 338–348
  leadership response to initial citizen reaction, 368–370
  martial law troops, report on readiness to act, 349–353
  military report on, 389–391
  Muxidi, battle at, 372–377
  response from
    Chinese overseas, 396–397, 416
    foreign governments, 397–398, 416–418
    the provinces, 392–396, 398–416
  violence following evacuation of the Square, 383–386
Military Affairs Commission, 211
Mitterand, François, 397
Mongolia, Inner. *See* Inner Mongolia
Muslims, demonstrations against *Sexual Customs*, 139, 145–146
Muxidi, 365, 372–377

503

Index

Index

PublicAffairs is a new nonfiction publishing house and a tribute to the standards, values, and flair of three persons who have served as mentors to countless reporters, writers, editors, and book people of all kinds, including me.

I.F. Stone, proprietor of *I. F. Stone's Weekly*, combined a commitment to the First Amendment with entrepreneurial zeal and reporting skill and became one of the great independent journalists in American history. At the age of eighty, Izzy published *The Trial of Socrates*, which was a national bestseller. He wrote the book after he taught himself ancient Greek.

Benjamin C. Bradlee was for nearly thirty years the charismatic editorial leader of *The Washington Post*. It was Ben who gave the *Post* the range and courage to pursue such historic issues as Watergate. He supported his reporters with a tenacity that made them fearless, and it is no accident that so many became authors of influential, best-selling books.

Robert L. Bernstein, the chief executive of Random House for more than a quarter century, guided one of the nation's premier publishing houses. Bob was personally responsible for many books of political dissent and argument that challenged tyranny around the globe. He is also the founder and was the longtime chair of Human Rights Watch, one of the most respected human rights organizations in the world.

.   .   .

For fifty years, the banner of Public Affairs Press was carried by its owner Morris B. Schnapper, who published Gandhi, Nasser, Toynbee, Truman, and about 1,500 other authors. In 1983 Schnapper was described by *The Washington Post* as "a redoubtable gadfly." His legacy will endure in the books to come.

Peter Osnos, *Publisher*

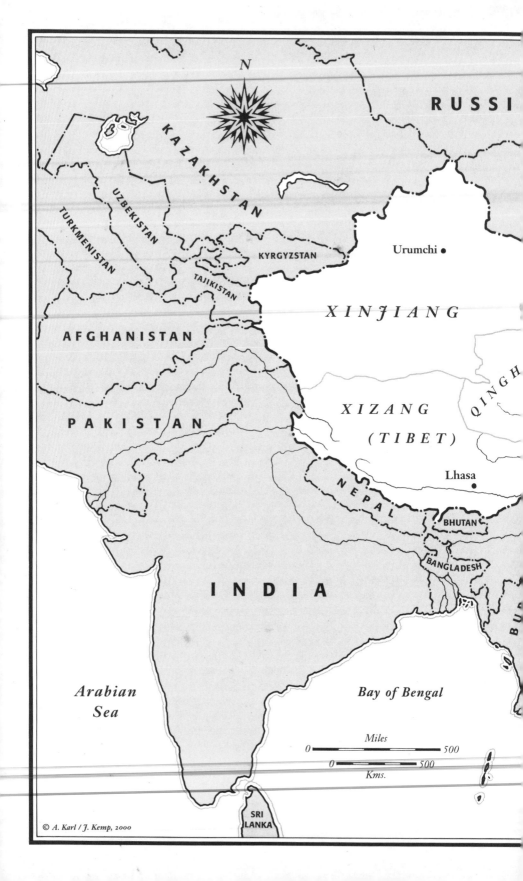

THE DEVIL'S GUIDE
TO HOLLYWOOD

THE DEVIL'S GUIDE
TO HOLLYWOOD

THE SCREENWRITER AS GOD!

JOE ESZTERHAS

ST. MARTIN'S PRESS ❦ NEW YORK

www.stmartins.com

Design by Phil Mazzone

Library of Congress Cataloging-in-Publication Data

Eszterhas, Joe.
    The devil's guide to Hollywood : the screenwriter as God! / Joe Eszterhas.—1st ed.
      p.cm.
    Includes index.
    ISBN-13: 978-0-312-35987-4
    ISBN-10: 0-312-35987-X
    1. Motion picture authorship.   2. Motion picture industry—California—Los Angeles—Anecdotes.   I. Title.

PN1996.E88 2006
808.2'3—dc22   2006043919

First Edition: September 2006

10 9 8 7 6 5 4 3 2 1

For Jenö Máté, Hungarian actor,
who played bit parts in John Wayne westerns,
and who sponsored my family's immigration
from the refugee camps of Austria to the
United States of America . . . and for Naomi, Sunlight.

"In the beginning was the Word . . ."
—John 1:1

CONTENTS

ACKNOWLEDGMENTS

For their help along the long and winding road, I thank: Guy McElwaine, Sam Fischer, Gerry and Gale Messerman, Patricia Glaser, Irwin Winkler, Norman Jewison, Craig Baumgarten, Ben Myron, Jim Morgan, Ed Victor, Alan Nierob, Richard Marquand, Paul Verhoeven, Costa-Gavras, Adrian Lyne, Alan Pakula, Steven Spielberg, Arthur Hiller, Ray Stark, Don Simpson, Jim Robinson, Dawn Steele, Arnold Rifkin, David Greenblatt, Jim Wiatt, Jeff Berg, Skip Brittenham, Bob Shapiro, Kevin Bacon, John Candy, Marsha Nasatir, Gene Corman, Patrick Palmer, Mike Medavoy, Barry Hirsch, Robert Wallerstein, Steven Bochco, Steve Roth, Richard Roth, Andrew Vajna, Mario Kassar, Lee Rich, Tony Thomopoulos, Michael Sloane, Peter Bart, Liz Smith, Army Archerd, George Christy, Michael Fleming, Lori Weintraub, Claudia Eller, Lynn Nesbit, Jerry Bruckheimer, Marty Ransohoff, Bob Bookman, Jann Wenner, Michael Viner, Alan Ladd, Jr., Frank Price, Robert Evans, Charles Evans, Sherry Lansing, Brandon Tartikoff, Jon Peters, Sylvester Stallone, Whoopi Goldberg, Debra Winger, Hunter S. Thompson, Pete Hamill, Jane Scott, Gary Kress, John Reese, Ted Princiotto, Vern Havener, Chris Matthews, Sonny Mehta, Jim Silberman, Jack Mathews, Bill Gross, Tova Leiter, Ira Levin, Tom Hedley, Scott Richardson, Gary G-Wiz, Father Bob Stec, Ron Rogers, Bob Landaw, Marshall Strome, Doug Hicks, Vernon Alden, L. J. Horton, Sue Mengers, Michael Marcus, Tom Wolfe, Philip Noyce, Karel Reisz, Bob Rafelson, Guy Ferland, Roseanne, Sam Kinison, Zelma Redding, Nelson McCormick, Paul Wilmer, Herb Caen, Bob Ranallo, Richard Rosman, Father John Mundweil, Alan Smith, Doug Buemi, Jeremy Baka, Rodman Gregg, Don Granger, Elizabeth Beier, and Matt Drudge.

Special thanks to Naomi and to my children—Joe, Nick, John Law, Luke, Steve, Suzanne Maria Eszterhas, and Suzanne Maria Perryman.

Finally, no *Devil's Guide to Hollywood* would be complete without the diabolical wit and wisdom of the players quoted in this book, some captured by me and some by others. I thank all of those people and especially the insights of my fellow Hungarian, my secret adolescent crush, *dahling*, the magnificent, the regal, Zsa Zsa Gabor.

PREFACE

They're out there by the dozens, telling you how to write screen-plays, when they don't know how to do it themselves.

Robert McKee is the most famous of them, and while it is true that he has *sold* some scripts, he has had only one feature-length film produced on cable television.

McKee's Web site points out that, at the University of Michigan, his creative writing professor was "the noted Kenneth Rowe, whose former students include Arthur Miller and Lawrence Kasdan." This is, of course, success by association, McKee elevating himself to the same creative peak where stand Miller and Kasdan by saying that he once attended the same school (which admits more than twenty thousand students each year) and had the same teacher.

McKee is a former actor who, his Web site says, "appeared on Broadway with such luminaries as Helen Hayes, Rosemary Harris, and Will Geer." He thus elevates himself to the same peak where stand those *acting* luminaries. Lo and behold, McKee miraculously turns *himself* into a *luminary*. He implies that he is as good an actor as Helen Hayes, the same way that he implied he was as *luminary* a writer as Arthur Miller.

It is a great act, brought to life by an actor who barnstorms the world doing a one-man, three-day, thirty-hour show (like Hal Holbrook doing a marathon Mark Twain): Robert McKee playing the part of successful screenwriter, the actor reciting the same lines over and over again. "It is the same fundamental lecture I have been giving for twenty years," McKee told the *Melbourne* (Australia) *Herald Sun.* "It never gets old."

Reviewing the act, *Movieline* magazine wrote, "He storms the stage like

George C. Scott in *Patton.*" *The New Yorker* wrote, "McKee, who used to be an actor, rarely speaks a sentence that does not call for a word so stressed that he bares his teeth."

McKee performs in L.A., Vegas, Miami, New York, Paris, London, and Singapore "from a script that barely changes a word from one performance to another," *The New Yorker* wrote. And McKee himself told *The New Yorker*, "I am an old actor and this is thirty hours of performance to a captive audience. It's very satisfying."

In that same interview, McKee said, "Warner Brothers said, 'Bob, we want *Jagged Edge* goes rock and roll for Cher. I wrote a thing called *Trophy,* for an embarrassing amount of money, about a rock star who murders her husband and gets away with it. They loved it. Loved it."

But alas, as much as they may have "loved it," Warner Bros. didn't make it. Nobody has made it.

I was amused to read that Warner Bros. told McKee to write "*Jagged Edge* goes rock and roll," since *I'm* the guy who wrote the original *Jagged Edge.* In other words, the great screenwriting guru, who tells the world how to write scripts, was assigned by Warner Brothers to sit down and *imitate me.* And imitate me he did: "A rock star who murders her husband and gets away with it" is how he described *Trophy.* That is a resounding echo of *Jagged Edge*'s theme of a prominent socialite who murders his wife and gets away with it.

I am led then to this conclusion: If you want to know about screenwriting, you might be better off listening to the guy who wrote the original than the guy who imitated it.

What you will read in this book is what I've learned in thirty-one years of writing screenplays.

I have written fifteen films: *F.I.S.T., Flashdance, Jagged Edge, Big Shots, Hearts of Fire, Betrayed, Music Box, Nowhere to Run, Basic Instinct, Checking Out, Sliver, Showgirls, Jade, Telling Lies in America,* and *An Alan Smithee Film: Burn Hollywood Burn.* I am now working on my sixteenth and seventeenth.

My films have grossed over $1 billion at the box office, and in 1992, *Basic Instinct* was the number-one movie of the year worldwide. I have been paid many millions of dollars for my scripts, more than any other screenwriter in Hollywood history: $4 million for a four-page outline of *One Night Stand;* $3.7 million for *Showgirls;* $3.7 million for an unproduced biography of John Gotti; $3 million for *Basic Instinct;* $2.5 million for *Jade,* and lesser seven-figure amounts for *Betrayed, Music Box, and Flashdance.*

I have been called "the rogue elephant of screenwriters" (the *Los Angeles Times*); "the Che Guevara of screenwriters (*Daily Variety*); "a living Hollywood legend" (ABC's 20/20); and "a force of nature" (*The New York Times*). My favorite quote about myself, of course, and one I use shamelessly to infuriate my critics, is a quote from *Time* magazine: "If Shakespeare were alive today, would his name be Joe Eszterhas?" (No, I will reluctantly admit that I am not Shakespeare; I am a refugee street kid from the West Side of Cleveland, in love with his wife, his children, movies, baseball, and America.)

I lived for twenty-two years in Marin County in northern California; a year in Kapalua, Maui; eight years in Malibu's Point Dume; and, for the past four years, back home in Ohio, where Naomi and I have decided to raise our four boys (so they, too, will grow up to be in love with their wives, children, baseball, and America).

But while I've lived in all these places, in my head I've lived in Hollywood all this time, beginning my days by reading *Daily Variety* and *The Hollywood Reporter*—and *then The New York Times* (starting, like George W. Bush, with the sports pages).

The lessons that I am about to pass on to you were learned in many and varied places: in so-called (and oxymoronic) studio creative meetings; on tension-laden sets; on luxurious Learjets headed for European locations; in limos moving like bulletproof armored vehicles down Sunset Boulevard in the L.A. night; on family vacations to movie-family vacation spots like the Kahala Hilton on Oahu and, later, the Four Seasons on Maui; at poker games in the Hollywood Hills and in Bel Air; at craps tables at Caesar's Palace, the Mirage, and Bellagio in Vegas; at innumerable parties in Aspen, Malibu, and the Hamptons; and at myriad power breakfasts, lunches, and dinners at Morton's, the Ivy, Elaine's, the Four Seasons Grill Room, Spago, Crustacean, Frida's, Citrus, Orsini's, the Friar's Club, the Daisy, Ma Maison, Café Rodeo, the Swiss House, Scandia, the Brown Derby, Palm, Patrick's Roadhouse, Michael's, the patio of the Bel Air Hotel, the bar at the Four Seasons Hotel and the Peninsula, the lobby bar at the Chateau Marmont, the Sky Bar, the Monkey Bar, On the Rox, La Dolce Vita, Jimmy's, La Scala on Little Santa Monica and La Scala at the beach, Nicky Blair's, Granita, Eureka, Dan Tana's, the Padrino Room at the Beverly Wilshire, the Polo Lounge at the Beverly Hills Hotel, the Grill on Dayton Way, and Nobu in L.A. and in New York.

In the world of Hollywood, the true battlefields are restaurants and bars in L.A. and New York. I have fought many battles in those places and have learned some hard-won, hilarious, and painful lessons.

I pass them on to you because my creative life has been dedicated to the belief that we screenwriters are not "schmucks with Underwoods" (as Jack Warner once called us) but that through hard work, strength of will, treachery, God's help, and big balls, we can write good scripts, protect them from being mutilated on-screen, make millions, and live lives that are self-respectful and fulfilling.

I am convinced the day will come when screenwriters will no longer be at the bottom of the Hollywood totem pole; the schmucks with laptops will be kicking ass.

Hollywood has often been a hellish place for screenwriters, but I think that with my *Devil's Guide* in hand, you'll feel less pain.

—Joe Eszterhas
Bainbridge Township, Ohio

PART ONE

PURSUING
YOUR DREAM

They Can Snort You Here!

Why do you want to be a screenwriter?

The answer I get from most young wannabe screenwriters is, "Cuz I want to be rich."

I tell them what Madonna says: "Money makes you beautiful."

And I tell them that I've made a lot of money but that I'll never be beautiful.

Why do you want to write a screenplay?

Screenwriter/novelist Raymond Chandler (*The Blue Dahlia*): "Where the money is, so will the jackals gather."

You, too, can be a star.

My biggest year was 1994. I wrote five scripts in one year. I made almost $10 million. I had houses in Tiburon and Malibu, California, and in Kapalua, Maui.

I made half a million dollars for writing a thirty-second television commercial for Chanel No. 5 perfume.

I fell in love. I got divorced. I married my second wife. Our first child was born.

I had the best tables at Spago and the Ivy and at Granita, Postrio, and Roy's. I had limos in northern California, in Malibu, and on Maui.

I ate more, I drank more, I made love more, and I spent more time in the sun than I ever had. The world was my oyster.

I became the screenwriter as star.

"Ben Hecht," his friend Budd Schulberg wrote many years ago, "seemed the personification of the writer at the top of his game, the top of his world, not gnawing at and doubting himself as great writers were said to do, but with every word and every gesture indicating the animal pleasure he took in writing well."

Robert McKee makes money, doesn't he?

When a student interrupted a McKee seminar with a question, McKee roared, "Do not interrupt me!"

A few minutes later, McKee shouted to the student, "If you think that this course is about making money, there's the door!"

I'll say this right up front: *This book is about making money.*

Money is not the best thing about screenwriting.

The best thing about screenwriting is this: I sit in a little room making things up and put my conjurings down on paper. A year and a half later, if I'm lucky, my conjurings will be playing all over the world on movie screens, giving enjoyment to hundreds of millions of people.

For two hours, the lives of hundreds of millions of people will have been made better by something that *I* conjured up in a little room out of my own heart, gut, and brain.

By then, my conjurings will have become a megacorporation employing thousands of people—from gaffers to makeup people to ticket sellers.

And it will all have begun with *me*, with *my* imagination and *my* creativity, literally communicating with the whole world.

That's the best part of screenwriting.

The money (almost) doesn't matter.

Screenwriter Jack Epps (*Top Gun, Legal Eagles*): "You do it because you love the movies. The money gets in the way. I think that if you're a good writer, the money will follow. But if you're writing for money, I don't think it's going to work. I think that very few people can make that happen." I'll say this right up front: *This book is about making money. Without losing your soul.*

Ben Hecht is no role model.

Wrote Ben: "The fact that the movie magnate is going to make an enormous pile of money out of my story and that I am therefore entitled to a creditable share of it seldom, if ever, occurs to me. I am, to the contrary, convinced that my contribution is nil. The story I will provide will be a piece of hack work, containing in it a reshuffling of familiar plot turns and characterizations."

Take it from Zsa Zsa

Actress and famed Hungarian femme fatale Zsa Zsa Gabor: "Money is like a sixth sense that makes it possible for you to fully enjoy the other five."

Getting to the Tit

An old Hollywood expression for making some big money.

If you sell a script, you'll be part of a fun and glamorous business.

When he got back to London after the *Lawrence of Arabia* shoot, screenwriter Robert Bolt told the London *Sunday Times* that the shoot had been "a continuous clash of egomaniacal monsters wasting more energy than dinosaurs and pouring rivers of money into the sand."

Dream Street

Hollywood legend: If you walk down Dream Street and somebody notices you (or buys your script), you can be a star overnight.

We have no role models.

When asked by reporters why he was a screenwriter, Ben Hecht, the most successful screenwriter in the history of Hollywood, said, "Because I was born in a toilet."

Screenwriter William Goldman (*Butch Cassidy and the Sundance Kid, All The President's Men*) described himself in the twilight of his career this way in his book *Hype and Glory*: "Couldn't walk, couldn't read, couldn't do a goddamn thing but stare the night away and block out the past."

His big brother, screenwriter James Goldman (*The Lion in Winter*), wrote this to director Joe Mankiewicz: "I need your help to write this thing. If this letter sounds prosy and dull, it's because I've been reading my script."

Screenwriter Charlie Kaufman, in *Adaptation*: "Do I have an original thought in my head? Maybe if I were happier my hair wouldn't be falling out. . . . I'm a walking cliché. Why should I be made to feel that I have to apologize for my existence?"

In the movie *Tales of Ordinary Madness*, written by Charles Bukowski about himself, a prostitute was trying to get Ben Gazzara (playing Bukowski) to stop writing and make love to her.

Watching the movie in the back of a Hollywood theater, the real Bukowski yelled, "If that were me, I would have stopped typing long ago."

Somebody in the audience told him to shut up.

"Hey," Bukowski said. "I'm the guy they made the movie about. I can say anything I want to say!"

Somebody yelled, "Oh yeah? Then shut the fuck up!"

Bukowski yelled, "Oh yeah? Fuck you!"

Cops were called. They handcuffed Charlie Bukowski and dragged him out of his own movie and locked him in jail.

You're certainly in good literary company.

William Faulkner, F. Scott Fitzgerald, Truman Capote, Alberto Moravia, Carson McCullers, John Steinbeck, John O'Hara, Dorothy Parker, Jim Harrison, Joan Didion, Ken Kesey, William Kennedy, Norman Mailer, Ayn Rand, Jay McInerney, and Hunter S. Thompson were all screenwriters at one point or another.

Faulkner even took a meeting with Sammy Glick.

After he won the Nobel Prize for Literature, William Faulkner did rewrites of these scripts: *The Left Hand of God* and *Land of the Pharaohs*. He took meetings with actress Julie Harris and producer Jerry Wald, Budd Schulberg's model for agent Sammy Glick in *What Makes Sammy Run?*

Robert McKee is an artist . . .

McKee: "People today don't respect screenwriting as an art. People didn't think this way in the 1930s, 40s, and 50s. But it takes real genius to do it beautifully."

Don't ever refer to yourself as an artist.

Novelist Sherwood Anderson said to Ben Hecht, "You let art alone . . . she's got enough guys sleeping with her."

The Revolt of the Assholes

Screenwriter John Gregory Dunne's definition of a writer's strike.

Faulkner was a mensch.

A producer, who'd begun as a press agent for studio czar Harry Cohn in the 1930s, wanted to demonstrate his knowledge of American "literatoor" for me.

"Fitzgerald?" he said. "His wife, that crazy bitch Thelma, told him he couldn't get her or any other woman off because it was too small. And that hotsy-totsy Brit gossip *kurva* he was living with out here, what was her name? Graham, that's it. *Heather Graham.* She said Fitzgerald was so ashamed of it, she never saw him with his clothes off. And then after the poor putz died, she said she'd rather make it with the size of a chimpanzee than the size of a horse. That was almost as ugly as the stuff Sally said about Burt in Playboy . . . that *fageleh* stuff that everybody talked about. Anyway. Hemingway? His bullfighting friend, that American, that gay guy, Sidney, Stanley, whatever. Stanley said Hemingway was always worried about his size. Sidney said it was the size of a thirty-thirty shell. And then there was that gay-bashing thing where Ernest sees a guy across the street who's flaming and goes across the street and beats the *fageleh* up. Faulkner? He schtupped that little secretary in town for almost twenty years. Liked her to put on little skimpy white dresses. Took her out to the beach in Santa Monica so the other guys could look through those white dresses, too. She told everybody he was a wild man—three, four times a night. Faulkner liked it here, kept coming back for the money and the pussy, just like the rest of us. Faulkner was a *mensch.*"

You don't have to be smart to be a screenwriter.

Screenwriter Sylvester Stallone was thrown out of fourteen schools in eleven years.

Be proud that Rocky is your colleague.

Sylvester Stallone even had himself photographed for a cover of *Writer's Digest*. He even sat in front of a typewriter. He even wore horn-rimmed glasses. He even said he was more a writer than an actor.

Then he stopped writing for thirty years and became an action figure and a windup toy.

But . . . at one point during those thirty years, he even smoked a pipe for a while.

He had himself photographed smoking his pipe, too, though he didn't wear his horn-rimmed glasses at the same time.

You don't want to turn into Sylvester Stallone . . . or do you?

Thirty years after Rocky, Sly and I were talking about writing.

"I used to love writing," Sly said. "I don't know what happened."

I said, "I do. You became a movie star. You've had your head in pussy all these years."

Sly said, "You're probably right."

You've got a good shot to make it.

Less brains are necessary in the motion picture business than in any other," producer Lewis J. Selznick, David's dad, told a congressional committee.

A Hollywood High:

To be overjoyed at the prospect of something great happening . . . something that will turn into shit the next day.

Maybe you might need a brainguard, too.

Producer David O. Selznick felt that a good idea was worth a million dollars, so he hired a guard to stand in front of the room where his company's scripts were kept.

He called this guard "the Brainguard."

Let's hope you get it kissed.

Legendary studio boss Harry Cohn: "I kiss the feet of talent and I kick the ass of those who don't have it."

Everybody wants to be a screenwriter.

Alice Sebold, author (*The Lovely Bones*): "We are living in the shadow of Hollywood where I teach, at UC Irvine. I was stunned at how students talked about movies when we went out to dinner, when I was expecting them to talk about novels. There is big money in Hollywood and it lures away really good minds."

David Benioff, screenwriter (*Troy*): "Thirty years ago, students probably wanted to be the next great novelist. Now many want to write the next great screenplay. Film is something young writers think about."

Jim Shepard, instructor, UC Irvine: "If you go into a classroom and ask who's read Michael Cunningham's *The Hours,* half the students will raise their hands and say they've seen the movie. All of these students are interested in writing books. But more and more are finding it hard to keep their eyes off the brass ring that film represents."

Paul Schrader, screenwriter/director (*Taxi Driver, American Gigolo*): "More literature is being written to be film-friendly. When I was a student, the writer Robert Coover said the goal should be to write a novel that cannot be adapted to film. I doubt any student aspires to that today."

Screenwriter/novelist William Goldman: "When I was a kid, novels were important, theater was important, movies were our secret pleasure. Now, movies are the center of our culture."

Screenwriter/director Nora Ephron (*When Harry Met Sally*): "Movies are the literature of this generation and all subsequent generations."

Norman Mailer: "Movies are more likely than literature to reach deep feelings in people. . . . People who can't read are quite able to reach profound reactions in the dark of a theater."

Because everybody but everybody goes to the movies.

In 1991, during the Gulf War, Iraqi airplanes dropped leaflets on our troops that said, "Your wives are back at home having sex with Bart Simpson and Burt Reynolds."

Even Richard Russo wants to be a screenwriter.

The Pulitzer Prize–winning author (*Empire Falls* and *Nobody's Fool*) has written three teleplays and an original screenplay and has also adapted Scott Phillips's novel, *The Ice Harvest,* starring Billy Bob Thornton.

Even FDR wrote a treatment.

Yes, Franklin Delano Roosevelt, as a young man, pitched a story about John Paul Jones to Jane Wells of the Paramount Famous Lasky Corporation.

Ms. Wells liked the future president's pitch and asked him to send her an outline. He sent her a twenty-nine-page treatment.

Everybody *is a writer.*

Disney Mogul Michael Eisner wrote a play called *To Metastasize a River*; famed attorney to the stars Bert Fields writes thrillers under the pseudonym D. Kincaid; ex–Beverly Hills mayor Robert Tanenbaum writes mysteries under his own name; former L.A. mayor Richard Riordan has written several unproduced screenplays; assistant U.S. attorney Dan Saunders has written a play entitled *The Death of William Shakespeare.*

Even the swamis write screenplays.

Writer Anthony Haden-Guest: "It was a crisp fall morning in 1971. Two swamis were down by the desk of the Chateau Marmont. They wore long swami hair and filthy swami robes, but the swami with blond hair was fiddling with amber worry beads in an un-guru-like fashion. 'Get this, Al,' he said apologetically. 'I can let you have a script by Thursday.'

"The other swami dropped his key on the desk with a metallic clatter. His occult pendant jangled.

" 'I don't want *a* script,' he declared coldly. 'I want *the* script.' "

Robert McKee owes his success to me and to Shane Black.

Ian Parker, writing in *The New Yorker:* "McKee became part of a great boom in screenwriting instruction which had its roots in the end of the studio system and the subsequent rise of the American auteur director: a screenwriter being one step from a director, and a director being God. The boom was further propelled by public knowledge of the multimillion-dollar fees paid to writers like Joe Eszterhas and Shane Black."

Will this be you?

Actress Hedy Lamarr discussing screenwriter Gene Markey (*Meet Me at the Fair, A Lost Lady*): "I had never been close to an American screenwriter before and I felt Gene was an individualist, one of a kind. He was bright and amusing, often brittle and superficial but at other times deep and confused. I have since learned that most screenwriters are this way. I don't know what came first, the chicken or the egg—whether they try to live up to the reputation writers have or whether their work makes them like that."

Perk of success: this is what you're working for

When my son Steve was twelve years old and the greatest Oakland Athletics fan in the world, he was desperate to meet his hero, the slugger Mark McGwire.

I called the A's publicity office, identified myself as the screenwriter of Flashdance, and the next thing I knew, Steve and I were in the A's dugout, talking to McGwire, and McGwire was telling us how much he loved Flashdance and asking me if Jenny Beals was as hot as she looked.

When my son Joe was eight years old and the greatest Cleveland Indians fan in the world, he was desperate to meet some of the players.

I read an interview in the newspaper with an Indians rookie pitcher named Roy Smith, who was quoted as saying he wanted to be a screenwriter.

I called Roy Smith and told him that if he got Joey into the Indians' dugout, I'd buy him lunch and that at that lunch he could ask me anything he wanted about screenwriting.

Roy picked out a date on which Joey could meet the Indians, but two days before the date, Roy was traded to the Oakland A's. He called me from Oakland and said Joey could meet the Indians and the A's the next time he came to Cleveland with the A's.

A week before the A's arrival in Cleveland, Roy Smith was cut by the team and sent down to the minors. I haven't heard from Roy since, but I am certain I will hear from him again if he ever gets back to the majors.

You can even turn priests on.

Through the years, a great many people have told me, like Mark McGwire, how much they loved *Flashdance*. Hundreds of women have viewed me more kindly the moment they found out I wrote (actually cowrote) the movie; some of these women even took me to bed to demonstrate to me their enthusiastic and wholehearted endorsement of the movie.

My wife Naomi's OB-GYN told me how much he loved *Flashdance* as Naomi was in her twenty-second hour of labor—sweating and nearly purple with our firstborn. He asked me, like Mark McGwire, "Is Jennifer Beals as hot as she looked?" even as Naomi groaned in pain in the background.

And my parish priest, Father Bob Stec, told me how much he had loved the movie—for other reasons, though, than McGwire and Naomi's OB-GYN. Father Bob loved the line "When you give up your dream, you die!" and said he had lived his life by that line since he'd seen the movie as a teenager.

I gave him a *Flashdance* poster and wrote that line on it and signed it.

Life-Affirming

New Age studio exec–speak for "Will it make a hundred million dollars?" It began to be used extensively after the success of *Forrest Gump*. Dreamworks chieftain Jeff Katzenberg begins each pitch meeting with a writer by saying, "Tell me how this movie you're about to pitch will be life-affirming."

What ever happened to FDR's treatment?

I t's probably still up on the shelf at Paramount.

Twelve years after he wrote that treatment, when he was president of the United States, FDR asked a lieutenant in naval intelligence to the Oval Office. The lieutenant was a former Paramount executive.

"You know why I asked you up here, don't you?" the president asked.

The lieutenant said, "Of course. It's *John Paul Jones.*"

"Whatever happened to my treatment?" the president of the United States asked.

"It's on the shelf," the lieutenant said. "Paramount hasn't rejected it, but they haven't decided anything on it yet."

Then the treatment went into storage. It now lies in a sealed locker inside a mountain in Missouri, where the studios jointly own a vast storage area of old treatments and scripts.

You, too, can be in FDR's shoes.

I certainly am.

These scripts of mine were all bought by Paramount and are still, like FDR's *John Paul Jones,* inside that mountain in Missouri: *Nark* (1981); *Dieshot* (1982); *Beat the Eagle* (1984); *Male Pattern Baldness* (1996); *Reliable Sources* (1997); *Land of the Free* (1998); *Other Men's Wives* (1999).

What are movies?

Screenwriter Dalton Trumbo: "Movies are an art that is a business and a business that is an art."

Movies are sausages.

Producer Mike Medavoy: "Getting films made is like watching sausage be produced: the finished product is great, but the process of putting it together is often messy."

Movies are selling sausages.

Director Phillip Noyce: "I realized that the Hollywood system—based as it is on the employment of branch offices all over the world promoting and selling movies—is totally dependent on a continual flow of product, and it's been set up to promote that product into the hearts and minds of people all over the world. In essence, movies represent marketing opportunities for Hollywood."

Without you, there is nothing.

I know that in theory the word is secondary in cinema," said director Orson Welles, "but the secret of my work is that everything is based on the word. I always begin with the dialogue. And I do not understand how one dares to write action before dialogue. I must begin with what the characters say. I must know what they say before seeing them do what they do."

You are more important than the director.

It all begins in the script," says director Milos Forman. "If what's happening is interesting, it doesn't matter where you shoot from, people will be interested to watch. If you write something boring, you can film from mosquitoes' underpants and it will still be boring."

Hollywood will hate you.

T he relationship between Hollywood and the writer is basically
 adversarial," says writer Jim Harrison. "The film business acts
as if it wishes it could do without writers, but it can't, and it has accepted the fact without grace."

ALL HAIL
Billy Bob Thornton!

A hard-nosed screenwriter (*Sling Blade*) who went to the wall
with several studios that wanted to change his scripts, he even
jumped atop a studio head's desk once. . . . Billy Bob is the
realization of all of our dreams: He became a movie star; he
became a rock and roll star; he married Angelina Jolie.

Tony Kushner is no role model, either.

K ushner: "I didn't write *Angels in America*. The actors wrote it,
 the directors wrote it, we all wrote it." Can you break your
Pulitzer Prize into little pieces, then, Tony, and share it with all the
others?

This is you.

S creenwriter Milo Addica (*Birth*): "The writer is the lowest man
 on the totem pole, but potentially he has the most power. He
comes up with the idea; he makes it work. You can't make a building without the blueprint; you can hire the labor and buy the material, but to make a building, you need a blueprint—which means
someone has to sit at a table, rack their brain, and figure it out.
That's what a writer does."

You ain't nothing but a **Hessian** *to them.*

J ohn Gregory Dunne: "Screenwriters are regarded in the industry as chronic malcontents, overpaid and undertalented, the Hollywood version of Hessians, measuring their worth in dollars,
since ownership of their words belongs to those who hire and fire
them."

How about sleeping with the screenwriter?

Hedy Lamarr: "The ladder of success in Hollywood is usually agent, actor, director, producer, leading man; and you are a star if you sleep with each of them in that order. Crude but true."

These are the rules of the game.

Old Hollywood adage: "In the beginning, when he is writing the script, the screenwriter has the gun. When he turns his script in, he turns the gun over to the producer. When the producer hires the director, he hands the gun over to the director. When the director turns in his final cut, he hands the gun over to the studio. The studio then takes the gun and shoots the writer, the producer, and the director. The studio then hands the gun to the stars of the movie, who are going out to publicize the film. In rare cases like *Heaven's Gate,* the studio turns the gun on itself and blows its own brains out."

The Oscar

Woody Allen: "An inanimate statue of a little bald man."

You're not in Kansas anymore, sweetie.

Mike Medavoy: "The movie business is probably the most irrational business in the world . . . it is covered by a set of rules that are absolutely irrational."

Nobody knows anything.

This is Bill Goldman's famous (and accurate) phrase, but its flip side is: *"Everybody thinks he knows everything there is to know about writing."*

Which includes the cabbie, the waitress, the director, the traffic cop, the producer, the sanitation engineer, the studio head, the massage therapist, and the star.

Scott Fitzgerald didn't know anything, either.

He did an uncredited rewrite on *Gone with the Wind.* This is what he thought of the book: "I read it—I mean really read it—it is a good novel—not very original. . . . There are no new characters, new technique, new observations—none of the elements that make literature—especially no new examination into human emotions."

He thought it was a good novel, though, right?

Poor, poor Scott Fitzgerald . . .

Can you imagine Scott Fitzgerald's pain as he rewrote Margaret Mitchell?

Fitzgerald to his editor, Maxwell Perkins: "I was absolutely forbidden to use any words except those of Margaret Mitchell, that is, when new phrases had to be invented one had to thumb through it as if it were Scripture and check out phrases of her's which would cover the situation!"

These are words Hollywood lives by.

Keep your friends close to you, but keep your enemies closer."

These words of advice were first given to me by a woman producer who still occasionally slept with her ex-husband, also a producer, even though she had remarried and was "absolutely in love" with her new husband.

Her ex-husband had beaten her, sold naked photos of her to a Web site, told the court she was a "whore and a druggie" in a custody fight, put a .45 Magnum into her mouth and pulled the trigger, and tried to blackball her in the industry.

She loathed and feared him but slept with him whenever he wanted to "keep him close" and neutralize him.

Over the years, I heard the same advice from studio head Sherry Lansing, superagent Michael Ovitz, and producer Ray Stark.

If you get reamed, take him or her out to lunch.

Mike Medavoy: "Breaking bread with them that wronged you is as common as air kissing in the movie business."

The key to winning in Hollywood is to let them think they won.

I admit there are people in Hollywood who are much better at this than I am.

Among them is director Phillip Noyce (*Sliver, The Quiet American*): "My own directorial style can be described as 'nudging'—nudging people. I don't believe much is achieved by confrontation, except resentment. I mostly get exactly what I want. But the secret of doing that in movies is to allow the other person to think what *you* want is what they really want."

Barry Diller knows what he's talking about.

The studio head and corporate mogul said, "People get corrupted. They don't lose their brains. God knows, they don't lose their talent. But part of the process of success and what it does, it corrupts in the way that it removes their objectivity, it *removes their instincts.*"

Most of what you've heard about Hollywood is true.

Screenwriter William Goldman: "Understand this: all the sleaze you've heard about Hollywood? All the illiterate scumbags who scuttle down the corridors of power? They are there, all right, and worse than you can imagine."

God bless us everyone.

Producer Robert Evans: "In this town everybody's a whore. Everybody can be bought."

You'll need to be a really good liar.

Screenwriter Dalton Trumbo: "The art of lying is the art of the practical. It ought never be indulged in for the pure pleasure of the thing, since over-usage dulls the instrument, corrodes the character, and despoils the spirit. The important thing about a lie is not that it be interesting, fanciful, graceful or even pleasant but that it be believed. Curb, therefore, your imagination. Let the lie be delivered full-face, eye to eye, and without scratching of the scalp. Let it be blunt and forthright and so simple that you can repeat it in detail and under oath ten years hence. But let it, for all of its simplicity, contain one fantastical element of creative ingenuity—one and no more—designed to capture the attention of the listener and to convince him that, since no one would dare to invent the improbability you have inserted, its mere existence places the stamp of truth upon everything you have said. If you cannot tell a believable lie, cling then to truth which is always our secret succor in times of need, and manfully accept the consequences."

It's all good news, all the time!

What absolutely no one does in Hollywood is tell you bad news. If someone doesn't like your script, they won't tell you that. You'll simply never hear from them. If somebody doesn't like your movie, they'll tell you they haven't seen it yet.

Hold out for the fifty cents.

Marilyn Monroe: "Hollywood is a place where they'll pay you a thousand dollars for a kiss and fifty cents for your soul. I know, because I turned down the first offer often enough and held out for the fifty cents."

To Do a Begelman

To commit suicide, like agent and studio head David.

Don't live in L.A.

Everyone in L.A. wants somehow to get into the movie business or has a friend or a relative who wants to get into the business. Everyone is a wannabe, already in star training.

All the wannabe screenwriters you meet will quote you classic movie lines, which you are better off not hearing and certainly not remembering.

Lines like "I will not be ignored, Dan"—written by James Dearden in *Fatal Attraction*.

And "When you give up your dream, you die"—written by Joe Eszterhas in *Flashdance*.

And "It's turkeytime, gobble gobble"—written by Martin Brest in *Gigli*.

And "How does it feel not to have anyone comin' on you anymore?"—written by Joe Eszterhas in *Showgirls*.

You don't want to live in a tabloid, do you?

Actress Jessica Alba (*Sin City*): "Literally the whole town is a tabloid. At every restaurant, every hotel, everywhere you go, people are looking at the door to see who walked in. It seems like no one is ever satisfied with their jobs or their lives, everyone is always sort of maneuvering for something else, something better."

Just another Hollywood burnout . . .

Screenwriter/novelist Jim Harrison: "I was driving on the Hollywood freeway, crossing the hill over toward Burbank, when we stopped in traffic. I looked up at the apartment buildings stacked against the wall of the canyon and on a deck a young man was standing in an open robe, whacking off and looking down at the freeway."

Forget everything you've heard about networking.

It is *not* who you know in Hollywood. If you write a good, commercial script and start sending it out—*someone* will recognize that it is good and commercial.

It is a town that runs on greed, filled with desperate people who will do anything to make money.

If they think your script will make them money, they will option or buy your script.

You can write your script anywhere. I suggest that you write it anywhere but in L.A.

You won't be able to write real people if you stay in L.A. too long.

L.A. has nothing to do with the rest of America. It is a place whose values are shaped by the movie business. It is my contention that it is not just a separate city, or even a separate state, but a separate *country* located within America.

Real Americans live in Bainbridge Township, Ohio.

If you have to go to L.A. for a meeting . . .

Do it as former Orion Pictures head Eric Pleskow advises: "Only as needed, like taking medication."

And Truman Capote gave this advice to Dominick Dunne: "Remember this—that is not where you belong, and when you get out of it what you went there to get, you have to return to your own life."

It's still bedlam.

After two weeks of writing scripts in L.A., screenwriter William Faulkner wrote home: "I have not got used to this work. But I am as well as anyone can be in this bedlam."

Don't wind up weeping into your beer.

Norman Mailer, writing to a friend in 1949: "Hollywood stinks. I'll probably stay here the rest of my life and weep into my beer about what a writer I used to be."

A *Lanzman*

A Yiddish term for a fellow Jew, it is used in Hollywood now to describe a good and loyal friend—being a *lanzman* is one rung above being a *mensch* (good people).

They can snort you there.

Producer Bert Schneider took care of an ill friend for two years. When she died, he held a party and the guests snorted her ashes up their noses.

Save the horses.

Screenwriter William Faulkner bought a horse for his daughter in Hollywood. When he realized the mare was going to foal, he drove her home to Mississippi. "I'd be damned," he said, "if I let a Faulkner mare foal in Hollywood."

This isn't the kind of place where you want to raise your kids.

I noticed our six-year-old, Joey, staring out the window of our Malibu house one sunny morning. Curious, I looked at what he was looking at.

On the patio of the house next door, a gorgeous naked young woman was with another gorgeous naked young woman.

Joey said, "What are they doing, Dada?"

I thought about it and said, "Saying hi, I guess."

Joey said, "Like doggies."

I smiled and said, "Yup."

TAKE IT FROM ZSA ZSA

Do you want neighbors like this?

Actress and Hungarian femme fatale Zsa Zsa Gabor: "Vera Krupp used to live next to me in Bel Air and they say that she got $25 million from her husband, the German armaments king, Krupp. With it, she bought the most unbelievable diamonds. Vera wasn't in the least bit overwhelmed by any of her diamonds and used to wear them while gardening or doing the dishes. But Vera lost all her money when she went to Las Vegas, fell in love with a croupier there, married him, and gave him her entire fortune. When she died, she had her four black Great Danes cremated and buried in the coffin with her."

You'll meet some mighty odd folks in L.A.

Agent Swifty Lazar: "Now, as everyone knows, I have a legendary fear of germs. The problem isn't really germs, it's the proximity of dirt that annoys me, especially someone else's dirt. Howard Hughes, on the other hand, did have a germ phobia. So that night, as I always do when leaving a public toilet, I reached for a paper towel to use on the door handle so I wouldn't have to touch it. Alas, there were none left. A few seconds later, Howard made the same discovery.

"So there we were, two germ freaks, both walking toward the door with dripping hands. I lingered, hoping to force Howard to deal with the door. But Howard saw that gambit and stepped aside, leaving me right in front of the door. Was I going to grab that germ-ridden handle? Not on your life. So we were at a standstill. Luckily, another man entered, giving us a chance to duck out before the door swung shut again."

See a proctologist often.

Playwright/screenwriter David Mamet: "Writing for Hollywood is a constant trauma."

You'll need to get yourself some Kaopectate, too.

Screenwriter William Goldman: "I bought a bottle of Kaopectate as soon as I reached the hotel. No joke. For the first several years, whenever I was in Los Angeles, I went nowhere without a bottle of Kaopectate hidden in a brown paper bag."

For almost twenty years while I was a screenwriter, I lived in Marin County in northern California and commuted to Los Angeles for meetings.

If I had a noon meeting in L.A., I'd be sitting at the bar of the terminal in San Francisco sipping two glasses of white wine at nine in the morning.

I'd have two Bloody Marys on the plane.

Upon landing, I'd go to the bar of the terminal in L.A. and drink two more glasses of white wine. Then I'd be ready for my meetings. I guess maybe Bill Goldman is smarter than I am. He limited himself to Kaopectate.

In Shallow Waters the Dragon Becomes the Joke of the Shrimp

Studio executive Dore Schary's famous line, originally applied to a down-on-his-luck David O. Selznick. Later applied to Orson Welles, producers Allan Carr, David Begelman, Dan Melnick, and directors Michael Cimino, Francis Ford Coppola, and David Lynch, among others.

If you have to be in L.A., stay at the Chateau Marmont.

Screenwriter L. M. Kit Carson: "There's several ghosts at the Chateau. The ghost would come at 3:30 in the morning. Regularly. It would wake me up and make me go to work. It was a *writing ghost.*"

If you have to rent a car in L.A.

Screenwriter and novelist Jim Harrison (*Wolf*): "Certain actors and producers are spectacularly good drivers. I'm so lousy in traffic. Having only one eye doesn't help. In fifty or so trips to L.A., I tried to drive from the airport in a rental car only once, a shattering experience. After rush hour I could drive locally, though not well, in Beverly Hills and environs, though other cars would beep at me for driving too slow. . . . A number of times I asked studios to have a five-year-old brown Taurus station wagon sent to my hotel, but they were never able to deliver."

Beware of medical help in Los Angeles.

I was hoarse. I went to see a couple of highly respected ear, nose, and throat guys in Los Angeles. They examined me and said I had a benign polyp that was wrapped around my vocal cord. They scheduled outpatient surgery at a hospital, to take place six weeks later.

My hoarseness got worse. I went to the Cleveland Clinic in Cleveland, Ohio. They told me I had throat cancer. I had surgery and lost 80 percent of my larynx.

When the head of the ENT practice read that I had throat cancer, he called my agent at William Morris, Jim Wiatt. He didn't call *me*; he called my *agent*. A doctor—calling not his patient but his patient's *agent*.

He told my agent it wasn't *his* fault. The doctor who'd first examined me was no longer with the firm, the head doctor told Jim Wiatt.

He told Jim Wiatt to wish me good luck.

Jim passed it on to me.

Beware of nurses in Los Angeles.

A young nurse who worked at a hospital in Los Angeles showed me her photo album.

It was filled with photos of delighted nurses cuddling with their famous patients. The nurses were wearing nifty little goodies from Victoria's Secret, and their patients, mostly rock stars, were niftily naked. The nurses were smiling coyly, lasciviously, joyously, teasingly, ironically, daringly, contentedly, triumphantly.

The stars in the hospital bed with them were anesthetized . . . in postsurgical comas . . . blasted out of their gourds . . . an IV sometimes still sticking in their arms.

If you're going to be in L.A. working on a script, don't take your cell phone.

The director, producer, studio execs, and any or all of their assistants, gofers, and secretaries will be bugging you all the time if you've got a cell phone.

Tell everyone that you left your cell phone home so your significant other could use it. Then tell everyone that you always shut the phone off when you're writing.

If you're Catholic, don't go to Our Lady of Malibu church.

When we lived in Point Dume, our church was Our Lady of Malibu. We'd heard of Our Lady of Lourdes and Our Lady of Guadalupe and Our Lady of Fatima . . . but we'd never heard of Our Lady of Malibu.

Lourdes and Guadalupe and Fatima were places of miracles, but we didn't know about Malibu. What had Our Lady of Malibu done? Appeared at a bonfire on the beach to tell three quaaluded surfers the secrets of the perfect and holy wave?

We went to Mass there one Sunday and I was sure the Beach Boys were making an unheralded benefit appearance, pounding out "Help Me Rhonda" to help the missions of "the Dark Continent" (as the sisters in grade school used to say).

But it wasn't the Beach Boys. It was a local Malibu group doing "Kyrie Eleison" surfer-style.

If you're staying in a hotel in Beverly Hills, don't go for a walk at night.

The cops will arrest you and take you to jail.

Nobody walks at night in Beverly Hills. Read Ray Bradbury's short story "The Pedestrian," which is about a man who goes for a walk in Los Angeles and is taken to a mental institution. Bradbury wrote the short story in *the 1950s*!

If you're writing in L.A. . . .

Drive down to the Formosa Café and get a whiff of what Hollywood used to be like. Elvis used to hang there; so did Robert Mitchum; so did Tuesday Weld. You'll run into some people if you're lucky.

The last time I was there, I ran into Sean Young, no longer a movie star but still a fine woman who likes to drink beer.

And stay away from the Rose Café. . . .

It's where all the wannabe screenwriters hang out, exchanging ideas, talking about movies, popping their pimples, sharing their dreams.

It is a stultifying, suffocating place fueled by ambition, greed, and envy.

If you share your dream with anybody here, chances are it'll be ripped off and wind up in a script that will never be sold.

TAKE IT FROM ZSA ZSA

Don't buy any parrots in L.A., either.

Actress and famed Hungarian femme fatale Zsa Zsa Gabor:
"On my way to the kitchen, I passed Caesar's cage. Our eyes met and the parrot fixed me with what, at the time, seemed to be an evil eye . . . and in the clearest voice possible pronounced the words 'Fuck you!' I fetched a piece of orange for Caesar, careful to avoid his eyes. In silence, he ate it. I breathed a sigh of relief. Prematurely. Because from that moment on, all Caesar would say to me, and to anyone who crossed the threshold of our house, was 'Fuck you!'"

Go shake Bob Walker's hand.

Drive out to Malibu and check out a little gallery in the Cross Creek Center called TOPS. It's owned and managed by Bob Walker, also known as Robert Walker, Jr., who was going to be a big movie star—until one day he just left it all behind and decided to live like a human being. If you're lucky, you'll run into him and can shake his hand.

Everything in L.A. is so inbred.

Robert Walker, Jr., is the son of the actors Robert Walker (*Strangers on a Train*) and Jennifer Jones (*Duel in the Sun*).

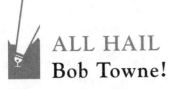

ALL HAIL
Bob Towne!

Yelling that he was being cheated by Warner Bros., screenwriter Robert Towne drove to Warner head Terry Semel's house in the mideighties and screamed obscenities outside his bedroom window.

The Auteur Theory

It will be the bane of your existence as a screenwriter and is the biggest single reason why movies are so awful today.

In France, where directors also write the scripts they direct, they are viewed as "the authors" of their films. They own the film's copyright and distributors can only release their films, not interfere with them.

American directors—who mostly don't *write* their films—began viewing themselves as "auteurs" in the seventies, looking for the same kind of critical canonization French directors were getting.

A generation of American film critics—some of them failed screenwriters like Roger Ebert and Pauline Kael and Janet Maslin—supported these American directors and extended the "author" label to them.

The auteur theory is hypocritical and corrupt—*unless the film's writer and director are the same.*

Try not to "go Hollywood."

Screenwriter William Faulkner, a good ole boy from Oxford, Mississippi, took to wearing sunglasses while he wrote his scripts in his studio office in Hollywood.

And I, the street kid from Cleveland, allowed myself to be talked into putting blond highlights in my hair—which I grew to mid-back length—while I lived in Malibu on a bluff overlooking the sea.

I shopped at the same market as Tom and Nicole for recently arrived fresh truffles and got a black Dodge Ram pickup truck the same month that Steven Spielberg and David Geffen got theirs.

I had Sunday brunch at Wolfgang Puck's Granita, listening to violinist David Wilson play his boulevardier chansons, avoiding eye contact with the likes of Gwyneth Paltrow, who kept staring at me one day.

Her stare said, There's that misogynist, sexist asshole who wrote *Showgirls* and *Basic Instinct.*

I did *not*, however, wear sunglasses while I wrote my scripts—though I did wear them everywhere else . . . even, to my first wife's great annoyance, in airports at night.

Don't piss off the most powerful man in Hollywood.

He's not a star or a studio head. He's not a director or producer. He's a lawyer. And he's over seventy years old.

His name is Bert Fields. He's the most powerful man in Hollywood because if he sends someone a letter threatening to sue, the recipient of that letter is better off simply giving Bert what he wants, instead of going to court to argue with him. He is a brilliant litigator, maybe the best in America. He's also a writer (of thrillers) and a Shakespearean scholar. (Didn't I tell you *everyone* in Hollywood, *even the most powerful man in Hollywood,* wants to be a writer?)

Patricia Glaser is the second most powerful person in Hollywood. Don't piss her off, either.

She, too, is a lawyer. She, too, is a brilliant litigator, maybe the best in America. Behind her honeyed West Virginia drawl is a stone-cold killer (whose childhood dream was to succeed Mickey Mantle in the New York Yankee outfield).

Patty Glaser doesn't fear Bert Fields; she jousts with him publicly. She told *The New York Times* that a letter from Bert Fields was "a B.F. letter." The whole town knew that "a B.F. letter" meant a "big fucking letter" and not "a Bert Fields letter."

If you get a threatening letter from Bert Fields, hire Patty Glaser immediately.

Forget Bert Fields and Patty Glaser. Don't ever—ever—piss these people off. . . . These are the most powerful people in Hollywood.

Scientologists.

Studios are terrified of them because they represent a lot of big stars.

Other people are terrified of them because they have a reputation of not tolerating anyone who, they feel, is *trying to piss them off.*

And no, I am *not* trying to piss them off!

PERK OF SUCCESS: YOU, TOO, CAN WEAR SUNGLASSES AT NIGHT

I was wearing the hottest thing in town. Spielberg had one . . . and Geffen . . . and I got mine before Jeff Katzenberg did.

They cost four hundred dollars a pair, but they were in such short supply that some people were offering a thousand dollars for them.

They were the best pair of sunglasses Chrome Hearts on Robertson had ever made—but that's not why everyone (me, too) wanted them. They wanted them because—if you rubbed the glass—ingrained in the glass very delicately, facing out, so you could see it if you really looked, were these words: Fuck you.

PERK OF FAILURE: YOU DON'T WANT TO WEAR THIS HAT

I saw two screenwriters recently at the farmer's market in L.A. wearing ball caps that said DON'T SHIT ON MY HEAD.

A Hollywood parable . . .

A Rwandan tracker who appeared in *Gorillas in the Mist* was invited to attend its New York premiere by the producers.

The tracker had never been on an airplane. He had never been in New York. He had never been in America. He had never been out of the Rwandan mountains.

But he somehow got to New York.

And there was no one at the airport waiting for him.

He *walked* from Kennedy Airport to Park Avenue, where the producer who'd invited him lived.

The doorman turned him away. The producer was out of town.

The producer got back the next day and found the tracker waiting for him—squatting beneath the emergency stairway at the back of his apartment house.

Don't contemplate your navel.

Producer Sean Daniel, after superagent Michael Ovitz left the Creative Artists Agency: "First the fall of the Soviet Union and now the fall of CAA."

If you have to live in L.A., you simply have to have a pool.

California has, like, half the swimming pools in the whole USA," said actress Drew Barrymore. "After you're successful, you can't *not* have a pool. Here, a house without a pool is like a neck with no diamond necklace."

Look out! The pool underneath you is empty.

Jim Harrison: "My friend the novelist Tom McGuane used to compare the whole Hollywood experience to being on a high board, mostly at night, and possibly the pool beneath you was empty. I habitually think of it as being stuck on a shuddering elevator, always caught between one floor or another, always in transition up or down."

You don't want to leave a suicide note like this one.

Actor George Sanders left this suicide note: "I am leaving because I am bored. I feel I have lived long enough. I am leaving you with your worries in this sweet cesspool. Good luck."

I probably shouldn't mention that he was once married to Zsa Zsa Gabor.

And I certainly shouldn't mention that after their divorce, he married one of her sisters.

The Movie God

The explanation for all the insane, inane, moronic, crazy, surreal, hilarious, tragic things that happen daily in Hollywood.

As in: "There is nothing to explain it except the movie God."

PART TWO

LEARNING THE BUSINESS

LESSON 2

Use Your F-Bombs!

Want money and fame?

Producer and studio head Mike Medavoy: "Don't *do* something to be remembered; it is the things you *do* that are remembered."

There are some good reasons to want to be famous.

Comedian Bobcat Goldthwait: "Fame is like a big eraser. It's strange, now that I'm famous, in my parents' opinion, all the shitty things—all the wreckage of my past—is erased. . . . Now it's like I was never the kid who got arrested—now I'm the wonderful son."

You will be world-famous!

William Goldman: "There hasn't been a truly famous writer since Hemingway died. At a Knicks game last year, Norman Mailer was introduced to the crowd and half a dozen people around me said, 'Who?' and one guy went so far as to ask, 'Who did he play for?'"

Bullshit, Bill. When I walk down the street people ask me for my autograph. In L.A., I can't even stand in theater lines or in restaurants without being bothered. I've done the *Today* show half a dozen times; I've done *Good Morning America* and CNN's morning show and a whole half hour of *Hardball* and Deborah Norville and Greta Van Susteren and . . . More people went to see *Showgirls* because of my name than because of anyone else associated with the movie.

And no matter what you say, Bill, you're famous, too.

Nowdays, you can be famous.

UCLA screenwriting professor Richard Walter in his novel, *Escape from Film School*: "Back in the 60s, there was not a single screenwriter—not one—I or anyone beyond the industry had ever heard of. It was not that there were no great screenwriters—quite the contrary; it was merely that none had ever been heard of. Screenwriters wrote; they were not written about."

Are you really sure you want to be famous?

One of the most famous screenwriters in the world is Laura Hart McKinny, who teaches screenwriting at North Carolina College of the Arts.

She is one of the most famous screenwriters in the world, but she has never written a screenplay that has been made into a movie.

The reason she is one of the most famous screenwriters in the world is because of her former boyfriend.

His name is Lt. Mark Fuhrman, formerly of the Los Angeles Police Department. Laura was going to collaborate with Mark on a screenplay about L.A. cops, so she made a lot of tape recordings with him about his true-life experiences. Her tapes wound up smack-dab in the middle of the O. J. Simpson murder trail.

There's a lot to be said for not being famous.

Actor Paul Newman: "I stopped signing autographs after I was asked to sign one while standing at a urinal in a restaurant. I was already quite cool about the idea after being asked for about the thousandth time, 'Can you remove your sunglasses so we can see your blue eyes?' I started saying, 'I'm so sorry, but if I take off my glasses, my pants fall down.'"

Actor Robin Williams: "The paparazzi follow me into the men's room. They say, 'Robin, can you hold it up? Could you make the puppet talk? Oh, you're having a bowel movement? Oh, great! It's *Live-Stools of the Rich and Famous!*"

You better stay forever young . . . or else!

Mike Medavoy: "This is a business that eats its elders instead of its young."

Are screenwriters the victims of ageism?

There has always been the issue of ageism directed toward screenwriters, directors, producers, and actors in Hollywood.

An agent sets up a meeting for a screenwriter with a studio executive.

The agent says, "How old are you?"

The screenwriter says, "I'm twenty-eight."

The agent says, "Let's make it twenty-three."

How do you define success?

Director Richard Quine (*Sex and the Single Girl*): "The definition of success is to be doing better than your best friend."

If you make it, you won't have any friends.

In direct proportion to how successful one is, that's how much the need is to chop him or her down," said actor/producer Michael Douglas.

Producer Bernie Brillstein: "You're no one in Hollywood unless someone wants you dead."

Marilyn Monroe: "It's funny how success makes so many people hate you. I wish it wasn't that way. It would be wonderful to enjoy success without seeing things in the eyes of those around you."

Question: What things, Marilyn?

Mike Medavoy: "Friendships are a funny thing in Hollywood. Everyone talks about what good friends they are with everyone else. In truth, most people in the entertainment industry have many acquaintances and few friends, at least in the way I define friendship. In a movie script, you can create a fifteen-year friendship in fifteen minutes. In real life it takes fifteen years."

Some canaries make it and some don't.

My fellow Hungarian, actor Tony Curtis: "The Mocambo was on Sunset Boulevard in the middle of the Strip. It had a bar, a dining room, and a dance floor with a small stage, and along one long wall were cages with yellow canaries. We'd go there on weekends for an evening on the town, and I was always intrigued how those canaries were able to survive in that smoke-filled, noisy club. One night I found out. I happened to look over when one of the canaries toppled off its perch and fell to the bottom of the cage, dead. A waiter standing nearby just whipped out a fishnet from his pocket, opened the cage, and scooped it up. Another waiter came up instantly and replaced the poor dead canary with a live one. Nobody noticed it but me. So that was the mystery of the dead yellow canary. Some make it in Hollywood, and some don't."

Audience-Attuned

If you write movies that make a hundred million dollars each, you're audience-attuned. Otherwise, you're just another dumb schmuck writer.

You, too, can enjoy their pain.

Producer Peter Guber: "As I was to learn and experience in Hollywood, it's not so much your own success that is relished, but more your friends' failures."

How to make it in Hollywood . . .

Legendary light-heavyweight champion Billy Conn: "He was a nice fellow. I hit him in the balls and knocked his ass through the ropes in the thirteenth round. You're supposed to do everything you can to win. Hit 'em on the break, backhand 'em, do all the rotten stuff to 'em. You're not an altar boy in there."

Studio head L. B. Mayer: "There's only one way to succeed in this business. Step on those guys. Gouge their eyes out. Trample on them. Kick them in the balls. You'll be a smash."

To Do an Ovitz

To commit an act of homophobia in public; like agent Michael, who, some said, committed such an act in the pages of *Vanity Fair*.

They lie, they cheat, and they steal.

Studio executives do not like to deal with honest men," said screenwriter/novelist Raymond Chandler.

Hire a good accountant.

Accountants," said screenwriter Dalton Trumbo, "are the most important people in the world."

Let your accountant be your rabbi.

My accountant said to me, "In Hollywood, you only get ripped off by your friends and the people you trust."

Invest wisely.

A well-known director in his sixties made millions of dollars and invested much of it years ago in a ranch in Wyoming. He visits his ranch three or four times a year but says he doesn't really like to go there.

"Every time I'm there," he says, "I think this is what my career amounted to—millions of dollars of horse shit."

Save your money.

Sugar Ray Robinson, boxing champ, years after his retirement: "Do I still own a flashy Cadillac? No more. The car I drive now is a little red Pinto. *But I've been there.*"

TAKE IT FROM ZSA ZSA

Tips to save money in Hollywood . . .

Actress and famed Hungarian femme fatale Zsa Zsa Gabor: "When you open a new five-pound can of Beluga caviar and you are not able to eat it all right away, put what's left over back into the refrigerator, where it will keep for five days, then you will always have nice fresh caviar handy. . . . Another hint to save you a lot is to never throw away any truffles. If, for instance, you open a can and you don't use them all in the pheasant Souvaroff or whatever you're making, don't throw them in the disposal for garbage, but freeze them and they will be as good like new later."

One good way to avoid writer's block . . .

Advice to legendary producer David O. Selznick from his father: "Spend it all. Give it away. Throw it away. But get rid of it. Live expensively. If you have confidence in yourself, live beyond your means. Then you'll have to work hard to catch up. That's the only fun there is: hard work."

The Three Cs

The "Three Cs" are what old-timers say Hollywood was once all about: "cocktails, cards, and cunt."

Schtup Music

An old producer's term for romantic music.

If you make it, you're going to need an accountant.

If you don't get one, you're going to spend all your time book-keeping and worrying about taxes—not writing.

You have to pick your accountant carefully, because some people have been robbed blind: Allen Funt, the creator of *Candid Camera*, lost everything he had to an unscrupulous accountant. Your fellow screenwriter Sylvester Stallone lost millions, too, to an accountant.

But for a set figure each month, based on what you've earned, you can get full-scale protection . . . the kind of protection where you won't even receive your own bills, since everything will go to the accountant.

Just make sure you get a weekly cash-flow report, *signed* by your accountant.

You, too, can be addled by accountants.

Jim Harrison (*Wolf, Revenge, Legends of the Fall*): "Entering a bank made me sweat, lawyers frightened me, and accountants addled me so that I couldn't write for a day or two. Despite learning how to make money I couldn't quite figure out that I had to give half to the government."

PERK OF SUCCESS: MY ACCOUNTANTS ALMOST KILLED ME.

The day after I had my first meeting with accountants, I had a full-blown anxiety attack that was initially misdiagnosed as a heart attack.

Your accountant may fire you.

This is especially true if you have gotten behind on paying your taxes. The good accountants in L.A. all have excellent relationships with the IRS.

The IRS knows that if you are being represented by an accounting firm it's done business with, the odds are very good that you won't be cheating on your taxes—which makes an audit of your returns a waste of time. So it won't audit you if you are represented by one of these firms.

But if you can't pay your taxes, your accounting firm will worry that your problems will affect its relationship with the IRS, and its other clients, so it will quickly rid itself of you.

Sometimes the accounting firms get rid of a client too quickly and regrets it. Sharon Stone's accounting firm got rid of her the year before she starred in *Basic Instinct*. They made a big, big mistake.

Congealed Snow

What screenwriter Dorothy Parker called Hollywood money.

Hire a good lawyer, too.

Peter Guber: "In business, you don't get what's fair. You get what you negotiate."

Be sure to hire a damn good lawyer.

John Gregory Dunne: "The attitude studio business affairs attorneys seem to take toward writers is that a writer's time is nowhere near so valuable as that of a director, producer, or star; that the writer always needs money; and that stalling is a tactic that will ultimately cause the writer who is a little short on the do-re-mi to cave in."

You're going to need an agent, too.

There's no heart as black as the black heart of an agent," my longtime agent, Guy McElwaine, once told me.

You need an agent right now, right this minute.

The playwright Brendan Behan sold the rights to all of his plays at the pubs where he drank—sometimes to customers, sometimes to bartenders, sometimes for as little as a couple of drinks.

It's still the same old story.

Sixty years ago, studio head Howard Hughes sent his executives a memo saying he only wanted to make movies "about fighting and fucking."

It's always been a meat market.

Marilyn Monroe: "Expensive cars used to drive up beside me when I was standing on a street corner or walking on a sidewalk and the driver would say, 'I could do something for you in pictures. How would you like to be a Goldwyn girl?' I figure those guys in those cars were trying for a pickup and I had an agent so I could say to those fellows, 'See my agent.'"

It is still the same old meat market, too.

Producer Brian Grazer and I were driving back to town after a meeting in the Valley, when Brian spotted a gorgeous young woman walking down the street.

He pulled over, got out, and said, "Hi, I'm Brian Grazer, the producer. Has anyone ever told you you should be in movies?"

She gave Brian a dazzling smile and said, "Thank you. My agent tells me that all the time. I'm represented by CAA. Here's my agent's card."

Don't be too sure.

Well, that's the last cock I have to suck," said Marilyn Monroe after she signed her first big studio contract.

You see what I mean?

I crawled the hill of broken glass and I sucked and I sucked until I sucked all the air out of my life," Sharon Stone told me after she became a big star.

It helps to be Hungarian, though.

I am Hungarian-born. I dallied with the star I created, Sharon Stone. André de Dienes was Hungarian, too. He dallied with the star he photographed, Marilyn Monroe. The famous William Morris agent Johnny Hyde was part Hungarian (Ivan Haidabura). He also dallied with the star he created, Marilyn Monroe.

But it's not enough to be Hungarian.

In the early days of the film business, there were so many Hungarian filmmakers in L.A. that there was a sign at the MGM commissary that read "IT'S NOT ENOUGH TO BE HUNGARIAN. YOU STILL HAVE TO PAY FOR THE CHICKEN SOUP."

The Panic List

Allegedly kept by the studios, it is a list of those who badly need money and will work cheap. The only time I heard direct mention of it was in a studio meeting with a Paramount executive, who suggested hiring a well-known director for one of my scripts and said, "He's on the panic list. He just bought a house on Martha's Vineyard and needs to go to work."

ALL HAIL
Hail Paul Rudnick!

He not only has put together a lengthy and successful career as a screenwriter but, as columnist Libby Gelman-Waxner in *Premier* magazine, he has also wickedly trashed most of the town's heavyweights and gotten away with it.

Don't gamble.

Gambling is part of ancient Hollywood tradition, going back to David O. Selznick losing much of what he made. David Begelman, agent/studio exec/embezzler/suicide was addicted to gambling.

I saw producer Don Simpson lose thirty thousand dollars in fifteen minutes at Caesar's Palace in Las Vegas.

If you're successful, you'll be invited to industry poker games—some are legendary. Don't do it.

I was even introduced to a little man who was the industry's bookie to the stars. He was very rich and knew the works of George Bernard Shaw inside out.

TAKE IT FROM ZSA ZSA

Don't marry a writer.

Actress and famed Hungarian femme fatale Zsa Zsa Gabor: "Even though painters and sculptors and composers and writers have a romantic reputation all over the world, in my opinion they are worthless as ex-husbands, or as husbands, or as anything else you may have in your mind to do with them, except if you want to have a beautiful nude statue made of you. Honestly, no woman, even if she is the most alluring creature that ever existed, can win out when she is competing for a man's attention with his precious muse. Artists spend all their time thinking about imaginary beauty. . . .

"Let's face it, nine times out of ten intellectual men would rather go to bed with a good book. Which just goes to show how unintelligent an intelligent person can be."

If you get married, do it in Portofino.

This, too, is an old Hollywood tradition. David O. Selznick was married there . . . and I had an agent who was married there—at the Splendido Hotel—three times to three different women.

I stayed there once, when I was already married to my first wife, Geraldine, and happened to arrive the first day that the Splendido opened for the season. In the dining room that night, Gerri and I found ourselves surrounded by German couples in their seventies and eighties.

"All Nazis," our American waiter told us. "They came here to hide after the war, and on the first day that the hotel is open each year, they flock here to celebrate surviving another year without capture."

Always let them pick up the check.

Only pick a check up if you're out with another screenwriter . . . and if you're doing better than he/she is.

Agent Swifty Lazar, describing gossip columnist Walter Winchell: "He had a great way of not reaching for a check. He'd feign a move toward it, but if someone made the slightest protest, he'd redirect his hand and pick up his water glass. In all the years I knew him, I never saw him pay for a meal."

You're dealing with horribly spoiled people.

Actress Hedy Lamarr: "If a man sends me flowers, I always look to see if a diamond bracelet is hidden among the blossoms. If there isn't one, I don't see the flowers."

I sent Sharon Stone a hundred red roses once. She sent me a card thanking me.

I sent her a gold bracelet. She called and asked me to dinner.

Everything you've ever heard about Hollywood parties is true.

Actress Hedy Lamarr: "At one magnificent party (for which I bought a gown that cost me two weeks' salary) I excused myself to fetch a scarf that was in the sleeve of my fur coat. I couldn't find a maid, so I went into the darkened master bedroom, where many furs were laid out on the bed. And when I got into the room I could see and hear that wasn't all that was laid out on the bed. A man and woman were right on top of all the furs, taking desperate advantage of the occasion. I merely said, 'Excuse me,' reached under the young girl, and pulled out my green scarf. They never stopped for one moment. Later on I saw the two of them formally dressed, sipping champagne cocktails. They knew it was me, but they didn't seem the slightest bit embarrassed. Nor was I."

Avoid Hollywood parties.

Screenwriter/novelist Charles Bukowski wrote this after getting home from a Hollywood party: "Sitting naked behind my house, 8 a.m., spreading sesame seed oil over my body, Jesus, have I come to this? I once battled in dark alleys for a laugh, now I'm not laughing."

F-bomb the world!

Tom Tapp, the editor of *VLife* magazine, published by *Daily Variety*: "Among moguls, crude language is part of routine business. In turn, the executives who work under them don't exactly censor themselves. One network honcho is so well-known for his foul mouth that it's become a calling card. Such language is not necessarily derogatory. It's a colorful patois that can often be complimentary. Everyone understands this."

Even Mel Gibson, *The Passion of the Christ* director and a devout Christian, described the man in charge of distributing the movie as "a very smart fucking guy."

Bill Clinton belongs in Hollywood.

Producer David Geffen took his boyfriend to meet Bill Clinton in the Oval Office.

Clinton said, "Is that a fuckin' reporter?"

"No, he's with me, Bill," Geffen said.

"Oh," Clinton said, "I thought he was a fuckin' reporter."

If you want to sound like a real Hollywood pro . . .

Always refer to MGM as "Metro" and Twentieth Century–Fox not as "Fox" but as "Twentieth."

Dirt Sandwich

Popularized by Sharon Stone's reference to a boyfriend as such, it's an old Hollywood term for someone who rips you off, someone who leaves a bad taste in your mouth.

Be nice to the Godfathers.

I met Sidney Korshak, mob lawyer and Hollywood Godfather, in producer Robert Evans's screening room moments after a young woman in her twenties had finished going down on him. Sidney was in his late seventies.

I'd stumbled into the screening room (literally) as the young woman was leaving and as Sidney was getting his pants up off his ankles.

I introduced myself and said it was a pleasure to meet him, and Sidney said likewise, reached out a hand, shook mine, and finished zipping himself up.

I went into the nearest bathroom and washed my hands just as the same young woman was coming out of it. A bottle of mouthwash was on the sink.

As I spent more time in Evans's house, I realized there were bottles of mouthwash everywhere.

Hey, Sidney, I liked Estes Kefauver.

Sidney Korshak once blackmailed Senator Estes Kefauver, the head of a Senate rackets committee, by showing him a photograph of a naked young woman going down on the senator in a Chicago hotel room.

TAKE IT FROM ZSA ZSA

Don't ask a Hungarian to help you.

The young Zsa Zsa Gabor went to see an old Hungarian friend, the producer Alexander Korda, when she got to Hollywood. She asked him to help her get an acting career started.

He said, "Take your clothes off."

She fled.

Remain philosophical.

An angry housekeeper who arrived and found a disastrously messy house said to the producer who owned it, "There's shit everywhere."

The producer said to her, "There's shit all over the world."

Think Yiddish, Dress British

A saying of Harry Cohn–era studio heads.

And William Morris was Jewish, wasn't he?

William Morris agent David Wirtschafter described the industry's perception of the agency this way: "In the minds of our competitors, we're still a lot of old Jews dropping dead in our offices."

But Walt Disney was a schmuck.

Everybody argues about who is entitled to call it "my film."

Screenwriters hate it when a director or producer refers to "my writer."

And during an interview with a reporter involving a financial question, Walt Disney said, "Before answering, I'd like to ask *my Jew* to come over and help me on this one."

Unelectric

Uninspired, flat, dull, benighted—the opposite of producer Peter Guber, known in the industry as "the Electric Jew."

The Blue in the Toilet Bowl

An old-time studio term for a successful WASP in Hollywood.

Never underestimate how scared everybody else in town is.

I said this on ABC's *20/20*: "People in Hollywood pee themselves the moment their feet hit the floor in the morning."

Don't count on anything.

Actress Hedy Lamarr: "That's how it always is in the entertainment industry, your feet are always treading Jell-O. From one minute to the next everything changes."

Take this to heart.

Producer Ray Stark gave me this advice: "Don't let anyone push you around, do what your heart tells you to do, and don't borrow any money."

To Cut Down on Your Cream

To stop living excessively, to save for a rainy day.

Do what Sharon does.

Sharon Stone keeps a large punching bag in her garage and pounds on it every day.

I created a monster.

Actress Sharon Stone: "I've got the biggest balls in Hollywood. It's good that they're scared of me. The longer they stay scared, the longer I keep my job."

If you don't like your own writing, do something else for a living.

William Goldman: "Since I don't much care for my writing, *Princess Bride* is the only picture of mine I can look at without embarrassment."

Why does your butt hurt after you've taken Robert McKee's course?

The New Yorker wrote: "McKee, who is sixty-two, and likes to wear dark shirts with two buttons undone at the neck, suggesting a career in extortion, lit a cigarette, then walked down the street while listening to an agitated young man say that the last time he had heard McKee speak the effect had been so overwhelming that he had fallen ill. 'All the stuff you don't want to face, which is to say emotional truth, the stuff of good story telling, it was coming out!' the young man said, very fast. 'It was coming out in such a way that it caused this pain in my back, because subconscious growth is such a painful process.'"

I shouldn't be telling you all these things.

Screenwriter Dan O'Bannon (*Alien*): "Most of what is written on how to write a screenplay is written by people who don't know how. . . . There aren't that many who do know how, and those who do know how tend not to tell. For the very obvious reason: they don't want to train their own competition. These are not un-knowns, but it's on the level of the mortuary trade—it's passed on by word of mouth."

The Screenwriter's Lament

"The fucking you get isn't worth the fucking you get."

LESSON 3

Don't Let 'Em Fart at Your Ideas!

If you're nineteen years old and writing your first script, know this: Life will get easier.

Paddy Chayefsky (*Network, The Hospital*): "Nineteen-year-old writers want more out of their writing than mere satisfaction. They want approbation, to change the world and many other things. Besides, at nineteen, he doesn't know his ass from his elbow."

Don't be a screenwriter; be a writer who just happens to write for the screen.

Don't spend all of your time in dark theaters watching movies. Live. Love. Immerse yourself in the messy entanglements of *real,* not *reel,* life.

Listen to human beings talk, not characters created by other screenwriters who spend all their time in dark movie theaters.

Use the events and the human beings of your everyday life to create a fictional world that *real* people, not *reel* people, will recognize, understand, and be moved by when they see what you have created.

You scare the living shit out of the studios.

Paddy Chayefsky: "When the studios hire a director, they can see him direct, or an actor act, or a typist type, but they can't see a writer think, and that frightens them."

Darling and Honey

These are two of Hollywood's most meaningless and overused words and greatest clichés. In the past few decades, there has been a trend away from using these words, although longtime Paramount head Sherry Lansing insisted on calling everyone "darling" and "honey," perhaps as a homage to Hollywood's Golden Age.

Robert McKee and I agree about one thing.

McKee: "Movie-making is a collaborative endeavor—requiring great skill and talent by the entire cast, crew, and creative team—but the screenwriter is the only original artist on a film. Everyone else—the actors, directors, cameramen, production designers, editors, special effects wizards, and so on—are interpretive artists, trying to bring alive the world, the events, and the characters that the screenwriter has invented and created."

You're the storyteller, not the director.

The director takes your story and characters and translates it and them to the big screen.

If anybody in your presence refers to the director as a "storyteller," deck him (or her).

In musical terms, *you* are the composer; the director conducts the orchestra.

The director is passé.

William Goldman: "There is a theory put forward by some (Gore Vidal for one) that the true influence of the director died with the coming of sound. In the silent days, Griffith could stand there and, with his actor's voice, he could talk to Lillian Gish or whomever and literally mold the performance with long, heated verbal instructions *while the camera was rolling.* Not anymore. Now the director must stand helpless alongside the crew and watch the actors work at their craft."

You are more important than the director.

Sometimes even directors admit this. Famed director Akira Kurosawa (*Rashomon*): "With a good script a good director can produce a masterpiece; with the same script a mediocre director can make a passable film. But with a bad script even a good director can't possibly make a good film. For truly cinematic expression, the camera and the microphone must be able to cross both fire and water. That is what makes a real movie. The script must be something that has the power to do this."

Aren't you worried about your next job, Bill?

Screenwriter William Goldman: "Directors—even though we all know from the media's portrayals of them that they are men and women of wisdom and artistic vision, masters of the subtle use of symbolism—are more often than not a bunch of insecure lying assholes."

You're the asshole responsible.

Screenwriter Robert Towne: "Until the screenwriter does his job, nobody else has a job. In other words, he is the asshole who keeps everyone else from going to work."

They all know you're the asshole responsible.

Actress Barbara Stanwyck: "The performer can't work miracles. What's on paper is on the screen. If it isn't there, it isn't on the screen."

Without you, nobody gets paid.

Mike Medavoy: "Writers get directors. Directors get actors. And the right combination of all three gets the money."

Don't let 'em fart at your ideas.

Producer Bert Schneider could fart whenever he wanted and farted often during story meetings with screenwriters at ideas he didn't like.

Like I said, damn it, don't let 'em fart at your ideas.

Screenwriter Robert Carson was summoned to producer David O. Selznick's house to pitch a script.

Selznick was in the bedroom, lying down, in pain from an attack of the stomach flu.

Carson said, "David, I don't think you're really in any shape to listen to a story."

Selznick said, "That's all right—go ahead."

Carson told his story.

Selznick listened in bed as he groaned, strained, and passed gas.

The next day, he informed Carson that he was passing on his project, too.

The War Zone

Beverly Hills, Bel Air, the Palisades, north to Malibu and Point Dume and Carbon Beach . . . where most of the industry's wealthiest and most powerful "player" warriors live.

Haunt streets, saloons, and whorehouses.

Ben Hecht: "I haunted streets, whorehouses, police stations, courtrooms, theater stages, jails, saloons, slums, madhouses, fires, murders, riots, banquet halls and bookshops. I ran everywhere in the city like a fly buzzing in the works of a clock, tasted more than any fit belly could hold, learned not to sleep, and buried myself in a tick-tock of whirling hours that still echo in me."

Live your life fully so you can write fully.

Screenwriter Michael Blake (*Dances with Wolves*): "Characters do come out of the thin air. I think writers acquire characters by living a life in which something is risked. It's only by being defeated, rejected, exalted, by going through all the peaks and valleys, that you can acquire anything worth writing down."

Don't see a movie; read a book.

Director Akira Kurosawa: "In order to write scripts, you must first study the great novels and dramas of the world. You must consider why they are great. Where does the emotion come from that you feel as you read them?"

See some good movies.

Screenwriter Michael Blake: "My approach to learning how to write screenplays was to watch the best movies. I tried not to watch lousy movies, because I didn't think I could learn anything from them. I didn't take any classes. I just kind of dreamed it."

Don't see too many movies.

Novelist Charles Bukowski: "People who hang around celluloid usually are."

Don't turn into a film geek.

It's okay to see movies, but it's not okay to get caught up in movie trivia if you want to write screenplays—that is, to become a film geek who can tell you the name of the DP on the movie *Two-Lane Blacktop,* directed by Monte Hellman . . . or the name of the character in Jack Nicholson's first bit part.

Knowing these things will clutter up your brain. Knowing these things won't help you become a screenwriter.

Knowing too much about movies can be hazardous to your creativity. Put that energy into learning about real life and the loves, hopes, aspirations, guilts, failures, and dreams of the human beings around you.

There's hope for you; Faulkner couldn't write screenplays, either.

Jim Harrison: "A good screenplay takes a sizable measure of talent and I hadn't yet studied the genre. Later on at Warners when I read a half dozen of William Faulkner's screenplays I was appalled and amused by how terrible they were."

To Do a Joe Eszterhas

To get out of town and live somewhere in flyover country, in some town no one has ever heard of.

Put a piece of paper up above your writing desk.

Mine says, "The first thing a writer must do is protect his own ass."

Novelist/screenwriter Jim Harrison's says, "You're just a writer."

Novelist Mickey Spillane's used to say, "Fuck 'em if they can't take a joke!" After he was born again, Mickey replaced that with "Oh Lordy! Oh Jesus!"

Repeat to yourself: "I've got nothing to lose."

That's what screenwriter Callie Khouri kept telling herself as she wrote her first screenplay. "I've got nothing to lose. I've got nothing to lose. I've got nothing to lose!" She was writing a groundbreaking and original script, which won the Academy Award for Best Screenplay: *Thelma & Louise*.

Exempt yourself from shit.

Novelist/screenwriter Harlan Ellison has a typewriter emblazoned with "I am an artist and should be exempt from shit."

ALL HAIL
Harlan Ellison!

The screenwriter/novelist did an interview with a magazine and posed for the photograph accompanying it. He was nude.

The caption read, "The writer at work; naked and unashamed."

"Fuck You" Money

You know you have "fuck you" money when you tip the bathroom attendant ten bucks for handing you a towel and then, after he looks at you quizzically, you hand him another ten and smile as you walk out the door.

Sit on your damn butt.

What's the key to being a successful screenwriter?

I say it's "*sitzfleisch*"—a German term that means the ability and the strength to sit on your ass.

According to my writer/producer friend Bill Froug, it's "the seat of the pants to the seat of the chair."

Ego is good.

Paddy Chayefsky: "The most impure motives are useful to a beginning writer. Just to get your name in the papers is not an improper motivation for a writer, when you're a kid, when you're young. The need for fame and notoriety, I think, is part of the package that brings you into show business."

When Paddy was at the height of his fame, he was the only screenwriter to get his picture—of him beating away at his typewriter—on the posters for his movies.

I tried like hell to equal that but couldn't do it. I did get the line "From Joe Eszterhas" splashed across the poster for *An Alan Smithee Film: Burn Hollywood Burn*. I also got the same words onto the T-shirts made to promote the movie, which, alas, was a critical and commercial disaster.

Hollywood is the kingdom of greed.

It doesn't matter if you are a convicted child molester; it doesn't matter if you once pissed on a studio executive's new Tibetan rug; it doesn't matter if you bitch-slapped David Geffen at the Ivy; it doesn't matter if you told the press how Sherry Lansing saved the best Paramount scripts for her husband to direct.

All that matters is that someone who reads your script believes that money can be made making it into a movie.

Be polite at all times.

My fellow Hungarian, actor Tony Curtis: "Universal sent me to Chicago on tour for a picture. I made an appearance at a theater, and while I was there I met a beautiful girl who worked in the Universal distributing office, and I asked her if she'd go out with me after I finished the tour that day. She said yes, so we had dinner, and I took her up to the hotel room. We necked on the couch and got semi-undressed, and she started to go down on me. About the fourth stroke, she stopped and looked up at me and said, 'If my mother could only see me now.' I said, 'Darling, it's not polite to talk with your mouth full.'"

When speaking to people in the industry, try to put things in Hollywood terms.

Producer Robert Evans to director Larry Kasdan: "I'd give up a blow job to direct this picture."

Practice humming.

You, too, can sound authoritative.

Producer Robert Evans says his deep baritone is a result of many years of practice.

Humming, Evans says, deepens the voice.

Evans hums all day, every day.

Never stand anyone up for a meeting.

I had a breakfast scheduled with agent John Gaines, but I got back to my hotel at five o'clock in the morning, after extensive late-night research. I knew I'd never make the breakfast. So I called to cancel. At five in the morning. To cancel an eight o'clock date.

John said, "I've never had anyone call me at five in the morning to cancel breakfast."

I said, "I didn't want to be rude and stand you up," then hung up . . . and laughed myself to sleep.

Always treat superstar actors with the proper respect.

When screenwriter/novelist Charles Bukowski met Arnold Schwarzenegger, he said, "You're a piece of shit."

You, too, can be Jack Nicholson's bodyguard.

Screenwriter/novelist Jim Harrison: "Several times when traveling with Jack Nicholson, I suppose partly because of my poor tailoring and thickish appearance, I had been mistaken for his bodyguard."

TAKE IT FROM ZSA ZSA

Don't let yourself get horsewhipped.

Zsa Zsa Gabor: "Once she arrived in America, my sister Magda also started acting, winning parts in several plays. Then she married an Irish screenwriter. Unfortunately, though, he was continually drunk. Magda complained to Father, who promptly horsewhipped the screenwriter and arranged for Magda to divorce him."

Your time is more precious than theirs.

A producer sent me a two-page outline of a story he wanted me to write. To each page was attached a thousand-dollar bill.

I read the two pages and then, just to be fair to the man, reread the two pages.

I didn't like the story and wrote him a note telling him that . . . and also thanking him for the "beer money."

You, too, can be Robert Evans's writer.

R obert Evans took two writers with him to the island of Maui, where they all stayed at the Ritz-Carlton, which overlooked the sea, and helped Bob write his autobiography.

One "writer" was sixteen, the other seventeen. They looked like corn-fed farm girls. During the day sometimes, while Evans slept, gathering his energy, they enjoyed manicures and pedicures in the hotel salon.

Evans introduced them to everyone they met as "my writers."

A Mush Pit

A place where a lot of women looking to become stars hang out to meet powerful men in the industry—to get a knee up the ladder. Producer Robert Evans's house is a well-known Hollywood mush pit.

You won't get a Land Rover, either.

O n *Lethal Weapon 3,* the studio gave the director, Dick Donner, and the star, Mel Gibson, gift Land Rovers.

Shane Black, the screenwriter who invented the entire franchise, didn't get one. He didn't even get to write the sequels.

If you make it, they'll ask you to steal from yourself.

M ike Medavoy: "The natural instinct of studio executives is to pigeonhole creative people and ask them to repeat themselves."

I got pigeonholed.

I had a meeting with Cuba Gooding, Jr., about playing soul singer Otis Redding in my script *Blaze of Glory.*

I wrote it after *Showgirls* and *Jade* and was happy that since the critics had clobbered me for excessive sexuality, there was no sex in this script.

"I want to talk to you about that," Cuba said. "You're the guy who wrote *Showgirls* and *Jade*. That's what you do—I mean, can't we put some sex in this script?"

PERK OF SUCCESS: YOU DON'T HAVE TO GET YOUR TEETH FIXED

"I could never be attracted to a man who had perfect teeth," Marilyn Monroe said. "A man with perfect teeth alienates me. I don't know what it is, but it has something to do with the kind of men I have known with perfect teeth. They weren't so perfect elsewhere."

Learn all you can about modern art.

Steven Spielberg has an extensive collection; the real reason producer David Geffen and once-superagent Michael Ovitz hate each other is because they are jealous of each other's art collections; and—get this—director Arne Glimcher (*Mambo Kings*) was an art dealer (Ovitz's) when he began directing movies.

Don't write an adaptation of The Great Gatsby.

Gatsby has been filmed four times. It has failed at the box office four times. Being assigned to adapt *Gatsby* for the screen is the filmic equivalent of what city editors on newspapers used to do to rookie reporters: assign them to interview the mother of the Unknown Soldier.

Don't let your urine rise to your head.

It's an old industry saying.

When the agent Michael Ovitz told me his foot soldiers would put me into the ground, he was letting his urine rise to his head.

When I told the director Arthur Hiller he was a "doddering old fuck," I was letting my urine rise to *my* head.

Other urine risings:

The director Paul Verhoeven saying to me, "I am the director, ja? You are the writer. You will do what I tell you to do."

And me saying to Paul: "If you use that tone of voice with me again, I'm going to come across this fucking table at you."

(Notice how artfully I used my f-bomb in that last sentence.)

Choose your projects wisely.

In the 1980s, "the Polish Prince," crooner Bobby Vinton, asked me to write the screenplay of his "true life story."

It was a tortuously tough decision . . . but I turned the Polish Prince down.

Fartland

What Hollywood executives call the Midwest, the heartland.

Mel Brooks caused the impeachment of Bill Clinton.

The former president of the United States, William Jefferson Clinton, watched *Blazing Saddles* in the White House screening room twenty-four times.

I wonder if Mel Brooks feels responsible for what happened with Monica.

Writing during a Writers Guild strike can be extremely lucrative.

The Guild strike had been going on for several weeks when the producer flew up to see me at my home in northern California.

If I rewrote the script that would soon go into production, he said, he would pay me $200,000.

He would put the money into a bank account in Dubrovnik, in what was then Yugoslavia.

No one would ever know, he said. Not the IRS and certainly not the Writers Guild, which forbids doing any writing during a strike.

Did I do it?

Ha! What are you—nuts?

If you live in L.A., don't get involved in Writers Guild politics.

Don't join any committees or go to too many meetings. The people who get involved in Writers Guild politics are people who don't, or can't, write all that much—or all that well, or all that well anymore.

They'll pay you for writing nothing.

I made a deal with ABC Films in the early eighties to write a script about the wheat harvesters who travel from state to state in the summer.

I was to be paid $350,000.

I went off to Nebraska and Iowa for two weeks to interview the harvesters.

When I got back, ABC informed me that their marketing people had concluded while I was doing research that a film about wheat harvesters wouldn't be commercially successful.

So ABC wanted me to write a film instead about Ross Perot.

My agent said not a chance—the deal we had made called for me to write a script about wheat harvesters.

ABC Films paid me the full fee—$350,000—for what amounted to two weeks' research.

Don't buy the mink coat yet.

This advice was given to me by *F.I.S.T.* producer Patrick Palmer after everyone involved loved my first-draft screenplay.

He was right. The movie went into turnaround; then forty pages had to be cut from the script; then $7 million had to be cut from the budget; then Robert De Niro wouldn't respond to the studio's offer to star in the film; then Sylvester Stallone played the lead instead of De Niro; and after all that, the movie failed both critically and commercially.

With a mentor like this, you, too, can cowrite Predator.

Robert McKee was the closest thing I've had to a mentor," said screenwriter Jim Thomas on McKee's Web site. Thomas is listed as the cowriter of *Predator, Executive Decision,* and *Mission to Mars.*

A screenwriter got JFK elected president.

The day of the West Virginia primary, which decided the Democratic nominee in the 1960 race, John Fitzgerald Kennedy was relaxed and in the best of humor.

He told reporters he'd watched a movie the night before and had gone to bed early.

He didn't tell them it was a porn movie called *Private Property.*

He didn't tell them he hadn't gone to bed alone, either.

My point is this: Someone wrote *Private Property.* Did he know that he would one day relax and perhaps inspire the future president of the United States?

TAKE IT FROM ZSA ZSA

Don't go to bed with Hungarians.

Zsa Zsa Gabor: "Tony Curtis is also Hungarian and we were cast in the same movie. We got on very well. We shot our love scene at the studio. The script called for me to be in bed with Tony and I was seminude through most of it. After one take, the director said, 'Let's do another take!'

"Whereupon Tony ruefully admitted, 'But I can't retake it. That would be impossible.'"

Don't step on any big toes accidentally.

I wrote a script about a man who kills his wife, and the film's producer told me that if I wanted to get it made at *this* studio, I'd have to change the ending: It would have to be an innocent man falsely accused of killing his wife.

"Why won't they make it the other way?" I asked.

He told me why: The studio head was a venerable and truly respected former producer, now a very wealthy man. But he hadn't always been wealthy. He'd come to Hollywood as a penniless wannabe screenwriter and met a wealthy, socially elite widow. He married her and some years later she committed suicide and he inherited all of her money.

Then he met another wealthy, socially prominent widow and married her, too. And she, too, committed suicide some years later and he inherited all of *her* money, as well.

Demand your payment on time.

Screenwriter Dalton Trumbo to producer Sam Spiegel: "Listen, I have a gun and I will shoot you if I don't get my money today."

To Spiegel

To manipulate, flatter, seduce, cajole, con, like producer Sam.

Spiegelese

A line of BS that sounds terrific and is designed to take advantage of you, it was originated by Sam Spiegel, producer, but perfected by David Begelman, who spoke perfect Spiegelese and became a top-ranked agent and then a studio head and then (flat broke) a suicide. "How *cheesy,* wags said, to commit suicide at the Century Plaza, of all places, not at the Bel Air, the Chateau Marmont, or a bungalow at the Beverly Hills Hotel."

Three's Company, but Four Is an Orgy

Old Hollywood rule, allegedly first said by Mae West, then later by Zsa Zsa Gabor.

Learn to recognize bullshit when you hear it.

A director called and told me he'd read my script and was interested in directing it. He said, "I don't want to exploit your script. I want to pay homage to it."

I hung up on him.

If you want to sell your script, be capable of anything.

Actress Sigourney Weaver was in the middle of her gynecological exam when the doctor said, "I have written a screenplay. Could you possibly read it?"

Move to the Midwest.

Discussing a script, producer Sam Spiegel said to screenwriter Harold Pinter, "They won't understand it in the Midwest."

Pinter said, "Fuck the Midwest!"

Spiegel said, "Do you want to fuck the *whole* of the Midwest?"

It's okay to live in your car.

Michael Blake did before he sold *Dances with Wolves.*

I was so poor before I sold my first script that I was working as a bartender and going through my pockets looking for forgotten change.

L.A. has lots of places where you can work all day without paying too much—the Rose Café, the Farmers Market, in the company of other screenwriters.

And many young screenwriters swear that the El Pollo Loco diet is healthy, too, besides being filling.

Forget playing video games; watch Tracy and Hepburn instead.

The old Tracy and Hepburn movies are a dialogue treat, as are the films of Preston Sturges and Woody Allen. They're fun to watch, and good dialogue exercise, too.

It's okay to have literary influences.

Screenwriter William Faulkner referred to his penis as "Mr. Bolton," a play on the name of a character from D. H. Lawrence's *Lady Chatterley's Lover.*

Don't have an affair with a script girl.

Screenwriter William Faulkner did; he had a lengthy affair with a script girl. After he died, she wrote a book about him. She wrote that for most of his life he was impotent. She even wrote that he ran the water in the bathroom so no one could hear his bodily functions and that he took a bath before they made love. He had the "prettiest little feet," she wrote, and always kept a handkerchief around in case he coughed.

Don't have an affair with an actress, either (heh-heh-heh).

Sally Field did an interview for *Playboy* magazine in which she said "there were always" men around Burt Reynolds. It came at the same time that Reynolds had lost a lot of weight, thanks to a broken jaw. The Field interview led to rampant and false rumors that Reynolds was gay and dying of AIDS.

There are many in Hollywood who think that single Sally Field interview destroyed Burt Reynolds's career.

Never lie to yourself.
Michael Moore, after his famous Bush-bashing acceptance speech for *Bowling for Columbine,* asked Academy president Frank Pierson, "Did I make an ass out of myself up there?"

To Do an Eric Red

To flip out and lose it suddenly. Red, the talented screenwriter of *The Hitcher* and other action-noir films, drove his car one day into a bar full of people in Westwood.

If you want to be a movie star, write a screenplay.
Sylvester Stallone wrote *Rocky.* Billie Bob Thornton wrote *Sling Blade.* Matt Damon and Ben Affleck wrote *Good Will Hunting.*

Then they stuck to their guns and said they wouldn't sell their scripts unless they could play the star parts.

Producers argued with them and offered them vast sums of money not to act in their films. They turned the vast sums of money down . . . and became movie stars and multimillionaires by holding firm.

Don't try to figure out the next trend before you write your script.
There was an investor who thought *Heaven's Gate* was going to be such a big hit that dozens of other Westerns would be made, so he *bought all the horses* used in *Heaven's Gate,* thinking he'd make a fortune renting movie-trained horses out to other film companies.

Well, after *Heaven's Gate* became one of the biggest disasters of all times, he was stuck with all these unemployable horses.

What did he do with them?

Well, they shoot horses, don't they?

It doesn't pay to go out to lunch with other screenwriters.
Ben Hecht: "Would that our writing had been as good as our lunches."

The Cocaine Highway

Sunset Boulevard in Los Angeles.

If you need drugs to write.

The valet parkers at a lot of "hot" Hollywood restaurants will be able to help you.

For many years, the valet-parking guys at a famous Sunset Strip restaurant had the best coke in the business, until they all got busted. Some people said the real reason people ate there was for the coke, not the food.

ALL HAIL
Peter Viertel!

The author, who wrote the screenplay of *The Sun Also Rises*, had a reputation for "looking great in bathing suits" and for coaxing "everyone" to be "naughty."

TAKE IT FROM ME: IT'S OKAY TO DEVELOP SOME SCHOLARLY INTERESTS

My lifelong scholarly interest has been Zsa Zsa Gabor.

There is a story that I just can't get out of my head about Zsa Zsa, who is a fellow Hungarian, a story that I'm fixated on. It's a true story.

Zsa Zsa and Marlon Brando are on The Tonight Show *with Johnny Carson. Zsa Zsa is saying something—they are on the air—and Marlon interrupts her rudely and says to Johnny, "I don't know why Zsa Zsa has to talk so much. With those boobs she really doesn't have to say anything! Do you want to know what I want to do with that girl, Johnny? I want to fuck her!"*

Then Marlon turns to Zsa Zsa and says, "A man can only do one thing with you, Zsa Zsa—throw you down and fuck you!"

Call yourself on the phone.

If you want people to think you're important, have yourself paged by friends at the Polo Lounge or at the pool of the Beverly Hills Hotel.

Producer Robert Evans once took a phone call from director Roman Polanski while being interviewed for ABC's *20/20*. An ABC staffer picked an extension up and found Evans speaking to dead air. Bob had faked the call from Roman.

Your script can burn.

Screenwriter/novelist Charles Bukowski: "Usually what the greatest actor of our day and his friends do after eating (if the night is cold) is to have a few drinks and watch the screenplays burn in the fireplace. Or after eating (on warm evenings) after a few drinks the screenplays are taken frozen out of cold storage. He hands some to his friends—keeps some—then together from the veranda they toss them like flying saucers far out into the spacious canyon below. Then they all go back in knowing instinctively that the screenplays were bad."

Don't work in a studio office.

Screenwriter William Faulkner: "It's like a hospital prison corridor. Those damned gray walls, those damned wide corridors, all those closed doors. And everything so damned hushed and still. I hate it."

Believe in God-incidence.

As a young journalist at the Cleveland *Plain Dealer,* I did an interview with soul singer Otis Redding after a concert at a place called Leo's Casino. Otis and I hit it off and I found him a generous and truly soulful man.

The next afternoon, he got on a little plane in Cleveland and the plane crashed at a lake in Wisconsin and Otis Redding died.

My interview with him was his last.

Nearly thirty years later, listening one afternoon to one of his songs, I thought back to that interview with Otis and I heard a voice telling me to write his story.

The next day, I sat down and called his widow in Macon, Georgia, did a month's worth of research, and started writing.

In Hollywood, sometimes even God can't help you.

Otis's widow loved the script so much that she kept it under her pillow for a month and prayed that someone would make it.

Eight years later, no one has made it.

Don't write any personal pet projects.

Look what happened to Oliver Stone: *Alexander.* Kevin Spacey: *Beyond the Sea.* Martin Scorsese: *Gangs of New York.* Bill Murray: *The Razor's Edge.* Francis Ford Coppola: *One from the Heart.* And Joe Eszterhas: *Telling Lies in America.* All personal pet projects. All box-office disasters.

Everything in moderation . . .

Novelist and screenwriter Dominick Dunne: "Drunk, I once set my room on fire in the Volney Hotel in New York, where I was living. Another time, I was in the closet with people I didn't know using Turnbull and Asser ties to find a vein to shoot cocaine. One of the strangers died. I ran. Then, when I was stoned again, a crazed psychopath beat me, tied me up, put a brown grocery bag over my face, and dropped lighted matches on the bag. I lived."

Try to write a "fuck film" like Love Story.

According to Paramount's research people, that's what *Love Story* was.

Why? A guy took his date to see *Love Story*. They held hands and cried when she died at the end. Then they went back to his place and vigorously showed their appreciation that *they* were alive.

Any publicity is good publicity.

The week after his eleven-year-old daughter, Marci, was abducted, Calvin Klein sold a record number of blue jeans: 200,000 in a single week.

Help those who have helped you.

I got more exposure from the *Today* show than any screenwriter in history thanks to a *Today* show producer who had befriended me.

When he told me that he wanted to write television sitcoms, I fixed him up with a TV agent.

You can make directors beg to work with you.

Director Phillip Noyce: "I liked the script of *Sliver* a lot. Or at least I liked the idea of jumping on the Joe Eszterhas bandwagon."

LESSON 4

Beware of the Back Pat!

You'll need to ward off evil spirits.

When he was a young director, Marty Scorsese wore a gold talisman to keep evil spirits at bay, as well as an American Indian pouch filled with holy objects.

The Jack Story

Superagent Jeff Berg told me this old Hollywood story in an effort to calm me down about what I saw as a potential problem.

Jeff said, "A guy is driving down an abandoned country road and gets a flat tire. He opens his trunk and finds he doesn't have a jack. He looks around, freaks, and says, 'Oh, God, what am I going to do now?' He doesn't see any houses anywhere. He starts walking down the road—angry, worried, fearful that he is in Deliverance country and anything can happen to him. He can wind up like poor Ned Beatty in that movie. He turns a corner and there's a big house in front of him. He walks up warily. Norman Bates can be in there. A beautiful woman opens the door. He asks the woman if she's got a jack. Of course she does. She walks back to his car with him. She helps him fix the tire. She asks if he wants a cold beer. She walks back to her house with him. They have more beers. She fucks him atop the kitchen table. They fall in love. They marry. They have blond, blue-eyed children. They live happily ever after."

The moral of the story: Don't turn every mini problem into "a jack story."

You've gotta be Sammy Glick.

Paul Schrader (*Taxi Driver, American Gigolo*): "No one succeeds in film if he's not hustling. The first thing you think of when you wake up in the morning is 'Who can I hustle?' And the last thing you think of before you go to bed is 'Who can I hustle?'"

Get arrested.

Screenwriter Stuart Beattie (*Collateral*): "My business manager once gave me this great advice. He said, 'If you are not kicking down enough doors to sell your script and knocking on enough windows to get arrested, you are not trying hard enough.'"

Beware of the back pat.

If a director or producer shakes hands with you and at the same time reaches around you and rubs your back with his left hand, run.

He's looking for the soft spot where he can best stick the knife in your back.

You, too, can give a studio head an orgasm.

Jaws producer David Brown: "The only orgasm that Lew Wasserman [the longtime Universal chieftain] ever had in his life was when he saw the opening numbers for *Jaws*."

This is what your brilliant, literary script is really about.

Producer Scott Rudin: "A movie is about two movie stars."

Avoid spending time with Sherry Lansing.

Raymond Chandler: "These Hollywood people are fantastic when you have been away for a while. In their presence any calm sensible remark sounds faked. Their conversation is a mess of shopworn superlatives interrupted by four telephone calls to the sentence. Ray Stark is a nice chap. I like him. Everybody at the brothel is nice."

They've made us settle for a Polish starlet.

Frank Pierson, screenwriter (*Dog Day Afternoon*) and Writers Guild president: "Screenwriters have accepted the idea of being third-class citizens, the industry's pain in the ass. Our position is that maybe someday we could forget the old joke about the Polish starlet. You know, she thought she could get ahead by fucking the writer."

I struck out with the Polish starlet.

I tried like hell to get Polish starlet Joanna Pacula to leave a party at Robert Evans's house with me and go back to my hotel room, but it was no-go.

These are our male role models.

Many screenwriters have bedded movie stars: Charles MacArthur teamed up with Helen Hayes, Norman Mailer with Shelley Winters, Thomas Wolfe with Jean Harlow, Paddy Chayefsky with Kim Novak, Arthur Miller with Marilyn Monroe, Pete Hamill with Shirley MacLaine, John O'Hara with Marlene Dietrich, Robert Graves with Ava Gardner, Romain Gary with Jean Seberg, Tom McGuane with Elizabeth Ashley and Margot Kidder, Tom Green with Drew Barrymore, Peter Viertel with Deborah Kerr, James Jones with Montgomery Clift, John Monk Saunders with Mary Astor.

Get in touch with your feminine side.

The only good artists are feminine," said Orson Welles. "I don't believe an artist exists whose dominant characteristic is not feminine. It's nothing to do with homosexuality, but intellectually an artist must be a man with feminine aptitudes."

Norman Mailer has a feminine side.

Said Shelley Winters of Norman: "Norman's not capable of sleeping with a starlet and using her and then just saying 'That was great, kid. Goodbye.' Unlike most men in Hollywood, he's actually a feminist. He sees women as people, not just sex objects. He reveres women. He feels there's a kind of respect they must have. He didn't treat me like a dumb starlet, he just couldn't do that. In fact, I remember times when he was in a restaurant with me and Burt Lancaster. Pretty, sexy girls would come over and sit down and be introduced to 'Norman Mailer, the writer.' And Norman would cool it. He wouldn't be rude or anything, he'd be charming and with that funny little grin of his he has, he'd flatter them and compliment them. But as far as I could see, he wouldn't make dates with them. Now maybe he tells people different, but from what I saw over the years in Hollywood, my impression—from a woman's point of view—is that he never treated a woman like a hunk of meat."

Find yourself a smart mate.

I take my wife, Naomi, into most studio meetings with me. Before he was the governor of California, Arnold Schwarzenegger relied on his wife, Maria, the same way.

Says studio head Mike Medavoy about trying to get Arnold to star in the *Sixth Day*: "Maria Shriver made notes on all the drafts of the script. She saw her role as her husband's advisor and protector. In one meeting, she was the only one who had problems with the material, so I began addressing my questions to her, as if she were the one who had to be fully sold on the material. In a way, she was. No matter how much money we paid Arnold, he wasn't going to do the movie unless both he and Maria felt comfortable with the script."

Does anyone realize that Maria Shriver is running the state of California?

We all have our own trophies.

I'm jealous that Bill Goldman has won two Oscars and I've won none.

But I bet Bill Goldman is jealous that I've bedded Sharon Stone.

Larry McMurtry says what you're doing isn't even hard work.

Screenwriter/novelist Larry McMurtry: "So much has been written about the miseries of screenwriting or, more precisely, about the miseries of the screenwriter's lot, that I, for one, am sick of reading it. I think it is time to redress the balance, to treat Hollywood fairly, and to suggest that screenwriting, far from being hard work, might actually be considered to be a form of creative play."

PERK OF SUCCESS: YOU CAN MAKE THEM BABY-SIT YOUR DOG

Screenwriter John Milius, at the height of his success, forced producers to make side deals with him. Not only did they have to sign a contract for him to write the script; they also had to baby-sit his dog on certain days so he could write that script.

ALL HAIL Harlan Ellison!

After he won a copyright court battle with Paramount over a TV show, the screenwriter/novelist bought a billboard just outside the Paramount lot.

It read WRITERS—DON'T LET THEM STEAL FROM YOU.

Unemployable

The biggest scare word in Hollywood—as in, "You'll never eat lunch in this town again." As in, "NO—MORE—MONEY!"

Your film can become a joke at the Oscars.

Discussing my film *Showgirls,* Whoopi Goldberg said at the sixty-eighth Academy Awards, "I haven't seen that many poles mistreated since World War Two."

Make 'em feel smart and you'll get your way.

I learned this trick from screenwriter Waldo Salt (*Midnight Cowboy*). He'd finish his script and then tear six or seven pages out of it and turn the script in to the studio.

The studio execs would sometimes—not always—notice that something seemed to be missing from a sequence and suggest that he fill it in with some scenes.

Seemingly acting on *their* suggestions, he would then put the pages that he had torn out *back* into the script.

The studio executives would then praise him for listening to, and acting upon, *their* suggestions.

When you're not writing, read stage plays.

Reading plays is great training for writing dialogue; think of it as doing push-ups for the ear.

Don't, however, read playwrights like Mamet or Pinter and Beckett, who are so stylized that their style can creep into your head and stylistically affect what you write.

Reading plays from the thirties and forties is ideal training because plays in those days were much more accessible than they are today.

Hollywood won't corrupt you, but your family might.

Screenwriter Dalton Trumbo: "I begin to realize why people believe the legend that Hollywood corrupts writers. But they're quite wrong. All Hollywood does is give them enough money so they can get married and have kids like normal people. But it's the getting married and having kids that really corrupts them."

Pay for your own drinks.

If a studio has flown you to L.A. for a meeting and is picking up your hotel bill, don't put any drinks you may have had in the bar on it.

A studio accountant will let the executive in charge of your project know how many drinks you had. If you had more than a few, the studio will decide that you have a drinking problem and will not hire you for the project.

And, obviously, don't charge to your hotel bill any hookers, sex toys, or jewelry bought in the store in the lobby, either.

See Thunder Road.

Hunter S. Thompson: "Between Mitchum and Burroughs and Marlon Brando and James Dean and Jack Kerouac, I got myself a serious running start before I was twenty years old, and there was no turning back. Buy the ticket, take the ride. So welcome to *Thunder Road,* Bubba. It was one of those movies that got a grip on me when I was too young to resist. It convinced me that the only way to drive was at top speed with a car full of whiskey, and I have been driving that way ever since, for good or ill."

PERK OF SUCCESS: SLEEP WITH THE STAR

Even if you're married—it's worth the memory.

Don't lose your head in the process, though. Paddy Chayefsky and Kim Novak had a brief affair. "He was awestruck, really, that someone like Kim Novak would be interested in him," said a producer. "Kim had Paddy thinking he was seven feet tall, a blond, blue-eyed WASP." Said another producer: "This was a sensational-looking woman. She had a pair of tits you would not believe, and she never wore a bra."

Paddy believed his friend Irwin Shaw's dictum that "the writer only has one obligation—to stay alive and try to please himself."

But he lost his head. He told his wife that he wanted a divorce because he was in love with Novak.

His wife, luckily, said, "Don't be ridiculous!"

A week later, Novak dumped him.

So you're a little nuts, so what.

I know it wasn't really sane to tell those Disney executives to "get your hands off my dick" in the Disney conference room . . . or to send a memo to a director that caused him to suffer a heart attack.

But all writers are a little nuts. The people who know me and love me have made peace with that.

As the writer/director Garson Kanin said of his friend Paddy Chayefsky: "I think it's fair to say—and nothing against him—Paddy was a little crazy. I don't think there is any important writer who is completely sane. If he was, he wouldn't be a writer—or a painter, or a poet, or a sculptor. I don't mean clinically insane—but his reactions aren't normal, and his perceptions certainly aren't normal. And Paddy, more than most, was a little bit cuckoo."

It is not who you know.

All it takes to become a successful screenwriter is to *sell one script*.

One person has to read your script and believe that he/she can make money off of it. *They* can't begin *making* money, of course, until they pay *you* some.

Spend your time on your butt, working on that one script instead of trying to seduce people into being your friends—so they can be there to buy your script, if and whenever you finally get around to writing it.

They'll do everything they can to stop you from being a star.

It is not in the studio's interest for a screenwriter to become a star, the way directors become stars.

If a screenwriter becomes a star, studio execs won't be able to tell him what to write.

If a screenwriter becomes a star, he'll wind up in the papers and on TV, criticizing studio heads.

Everyone knows directors are controllable and they *need* the studios to be able to work.

But those crazy asshole writers—all they *need* to go to work is a piece of paper and a pencil.

Don't break your own heart.

Shane Black was the hottest young writer in town, selling original spec scripts for lots of money. He was a savvy, well-read guy with balls.

The Long Kiss Goodnight was his pet project—a brilliant script that director Renny Harlin and his wife at the time, Geena Davis, turned into a turgid and empty film.

Shane stopped writing for a long time after that nightmarish experience and tried to make it as an actor. The reason he stopped writing was that his heart was broken, but that's only half the story.

The reason his heart was broken was that he had broken it himself. He had let Renny Harlin cajole and charm him into making fatal changes to his script, the changes that ruined his own script and doomed his own movie.

After many years, Shane came back to direct his own script—one way of making sure you don't break your own heart again . . . unless, of course, he listens too closely to his producer, Joel Silver, who is, unfortunately, a friend of his and very good at cajoling and charming.

Don't write for "blood money."

"Blood money" is when you're rewriting someone else's script, and you change anything and everything in the script—plot points, characters, and especially characters' names—not because the changes are creatively necessary but so you'll get screen credit and the money that's tied to you getting that credit.

There is a story, hopefully apocryphal, about a screenwriter assigned to adapt *The Great Gatsby*. The screenwriter changed the name "Gatsby" to "Farrell" and the title to "The Great Farrell" in an attempt to get screen credit and more money.

Sometimes the damn place just makes you cry.

Corky was a sweet little man who poured the stiffest drinks at the Hideaway Bar at the Beverly Wilshire Hotel.

Jack Lemmon and I would sip our drinks there on soggy or smoggy L.A. afternoons.

Corky had a laugh that made Jack and me laugh, and he told the dumbest jokes in Southern California.

One day, I walked in and there was a new guy behind the bar and Jack was floating his scotch high up in his eyeballs.

Jack told me that Corky had met a guy right there in the Hideaway Room who'd taken him home, then left his body in a Dumpster.

No more laughs and jokes. No more hiding in the afternoons at the Hideaway Bar. Jack and I both started to cry, realizing that sometimes there is simply no shelter from the town's degradations.

You don't want to get in a creative disagreement with a Scientologist.

While they're nice folks, scientologists don't like to be messed with.

I once threatened to take Sylvester Stallone on in a fistfight. I once threatened to break a studio executive's knees. I once told the most powerful man in Hollywood to go fuck himself and the foot soldiers he rode in on.

But under no circumstances would I get into a creative disagreement with a Scientologist.

Besides, I don't think the Dogon fighting stick or the Tibetan rock or the hunting knife I carry are any match for their E-meter.

You don't want to mess with that E-meter, either.

Scientologists have this machine called the E-meter. They will have someone read your script and E-meter it before one of their people commits to do the movie.

It's more than enough, in my experience, for a screenwriter to deal with a director, a producer, studio notes, a star's ego, et cetera.

Trust me on this: You don't need to deal with an E-meter.

Oscarosis

A disease whose main symptom is that the victim is willing to do anything—*anything*—to win an Oscar.

With actors and executives, act like you're a playwright, not a screenwriter.

Actress Jill Hennessy (*Crossing Jordan*): "When you're an actor working in the theater, you would never say anything to the writer, never alter the dialogue, never dream to ask for changes."

Good ideas can come from great gossip.

In *Sliver,* Sharon Stone spends a lot of time looking through a telescope at her New York apartment building neighbors. I got the idea from a friend of Jackie Kennedy's who told me Jackie loved to do the same thing.

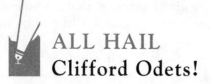

ALL HAIL
Clifford Odets!

Agent Swifty Lazar: "Clifford Odets was a wily client. One day he called me. He was so in debt, he said, that he'd sold his art collection. But he had an idea for a movie, *Page One*. I knew he was spitballing, but I took him over to see Jerry Wald and Jerry bit. Jerry sent us out to Darryl Zanuck.

"I got Odets two hundred thousand, a small fortune for a screenplay in those days. . . . A month later, Odets invited me to pick up the script. When I walked into his cottage, he was holding a six-hundred-page screenplay—a document about five times longer than a standard script.

"Odets said, 'I'll cut it if they pay me.'

"I soon realized that Odets had planned this caper. . . . I got him some additional money. Odets started cutting away. He trimmed it down to three hundred pages, and then I had to get him some additional money to cut it to two hundred. At that point, he announced he wanted to direct the movie. . . . They let him direct the picture. . . . It was a ghastly movie that died on Pico Boulevard and should never have been released."

The word Death in a title is death at the box office.

It will bum audiences out and let them know they're in for a depressing experience. I've heard at least three producers tell me this.

Each time I've said, "Have you ever heard of something called *Death of a Salesman?*"

If you sell the concept for a script, demand a hotel suite in which to write it.

Many screenwriters claim to get in touch with their muses *best* at places like the Dolder Grand in Zurich, the Dorchester in London, the Kahala on Oahu, the Ritz-Carlton on Maui, or the relatively cut-rate Beverly Hills Hotel and Chateau Marmont in L.A.

While vacationing with my family at the Kahala once, we were sitting on the beach when we saw John Gregory Dunne and Joan Didion walking along the beach, their heads down, *matching sweaters tied around their hips,* lost in *serious thought.*

A producer and his family sat near us and I asked him what Dunne and Didion were doing here.

"What do you think?" the producer said. "Can't you tell? Writing. Working."

If you make it, directors will resent the amount of money you make.

Director Phillip Noyce: "I continued to work on a script of *The Sum of All Fears.* Paul Attanasio [*Donnie Brasco* and *Quiz Show*] wrote another draft with a lot of input from myself and, particularly, my business partner Kathleen McLaughlin. He was paid more than a million dollars to rewrite the screenplay, which, due to another commitment, he ended up doing in about ten days. Nice work if you can get it!"

You didn't write Gone with the Wind.

I was at a shop in Los Angeles in the mideighties and the store owner asked me what I did for a living. I told him I wrote movies, and when he asked me which ones, I told him my last movie was *Flashdance*.

"Hey," he said, "you must have worked with my niece." He told me her name.

I'd never heard of his niece and asked what she did on the film.

He said, "She wrote it, too."

I said, "No, she didn't."

He said, "Yes, she did."

I said, "Is her name up on-screen?"

He said, "She wrote the damn movie; that's what she told me."

I discovered that his niece had been brought in to do some "polishing" on the script but didn't do enough work on it to get any credit from the Writers Guild.

It was my first introduction to a whole subgenre of screenwriters in Hollywood: those who claim to have "written" a movie but don't have any writing credit on it.

You're a writer, not a social butterfly.

I ran into him by the pool of the Four Seasons hotel in Beverly Hills. He came up and introduced himself and told me his story.

He was a successful and well-known attorney from Chicago but had always wanted to write for television, so one day he took a leave of absence and came out to L.A. He was living at the Four Seasons.

He'd given himself six months. He'd be at the Four Seasons for six months and in that time he would have as many meetings with television producers and executives and showrunners as possible. If it didn't work out in six months, he'd go back to Chicago.

I got a note from him about a year later. He was back with the law firm in Chicago. It hadn't worked out in L.A.

"But I'll always know that I tried," he wrote. "I didn't futz around. I really, really went for it."

I remembered what I had told him when we met: "Stop running around meeting people. Go back to Chicago and write something."

I hoped that's what he was doing.

You, too, can con the MPAA.

When the MPAA ratings board saw *Basic Instinct,* they gave the movie an NC-17.

As long as Sharon uncrossed her legs, the board told us, the NC-17 would stand.

I told the studio PR people to tell the MPAA that this wasn't a sex scene; this was a confrontation scene between an empowered and liberated modern woman and her male-piggy poe/leece inquisitors.

The "empowerment" argument swayed the MPAA and saved the beaver. Paul Verhoeven only had to take a few snips from the, um, *focal point* of the scene to satisfy the ratings board.

You never know how they'll film the scene that you wrote.

I wrote an extravagant dance sequence for Jennifer Beals in *Flash-dance.*

Some studio wizard suggested cutting the sequence in half and rewriting it, but I convinced them that a big dance movie had to have a lot of dance in it.

Since Jenny couldn't dance very well and certainly couldn't do a big dance sequence, the director hired a "dance double" for Jenny named Marine Jahan.

But it still wasn't enough to convince the audience that Jenny Beals could dance, because Marine Jihan couldn't do the floor spins.

So the producers brought in someone who could do the floor spins perfectly—a guy, who had to wear a wig and shave his legs . . . but who refused to shave his mustache.

If you slow the film down and look very closely, you can see Jenny Beals spinning around, wearing leotards and a mustache.

Don't die with the wrong people.

That's what happened to screenwriter/novelist F. Scott Fitzgerald, whose last girlfriend was gossip columnist Sheilah Graham.

Graham had once been previously married to a man who was twenty-five years older and arranged dates for her with wealthy men. She and her husband lived off the gifts given to her by the wealthy men she went out with.

To Do a Belushi

To OD on drugs, like actor John.

Some people do, temporarily, know some things about making hit movies.

Producer Jerry Bruckheimer, producer Brian Grazer, the late producer Don Simpson, producer/director George Lucas, and producer/director Steven Spielberg all know some things.

Producer/director Ivan Reitman *knew* some things, but he has forgotten them. So has Francis Ford Coppola.

After *Flashdance, Jagged Edge,* and *Basic Instinct,* I knew some things about making hit movies, too.

But after *Sliver, Showgirls,* and *Jade,* I, like Ivan and Francis, forgot what I knew.

PERK OF SUCCESS: YOU, TOO, CAN GET FRANKIE AVALON TO SING FOR YOU

He knew who I was, and somebody at our table, as a joke, told him that it was my wife Geraldine's birthday. So Frankie Avalon sang "Happy Birthday" for her.

It wasn't her birthday at all, but she'd loved Frankie Avalon as a teenager, and when he sang happy birthday to her, she cried. She told me after our divorce that it was one of her greatest thrills as a screenwriter's wife.

Billy Wilder was a sexist pig.

Screenwriter/director Billy Wilder had a recurring fantasy that he told friends about: He wanted to invent a mattress that would make a woman disappear after he'd made love to her.

In her place would appear three of his friends around a card table.

Wilder said that if men were forced to choose between sex with a woman and playing cards, 98 percent would choose cards. (Not me, babe.)

If they say it won't work, it probably will.

I was once told by a studio head that movies set on farms didn't sell because "dirt doesn't sell." Then the film *Witness* came out. It was set on a farm and it was a smash.

Paddy Chayefsky was told by a studio head that movies "with funeral scenes" don't sell. Then *The Godfather* came out. It had a funeral scene and it was a smash.

I was told by another studio exec that "courtroom dramas don't sell." I wrote *Jagged Edge* and it was the number-one movie in America for more than a month.

The truth is that anything that is well written, well directed, and well acted can sell.

Bull-whip every Hollywood astrologer you meet.

Author Hunter S. Thompson: "There is a ghastly political factor in doing any business with Hollywood. You can't get by without five or six personal staff people—and at least one personal astrologer. I have always hated astrologers, and I like to have sport with them. They are harmless quacks in the main, but some of them get ambitious and turn predatory, especially in Hollywood. In Venice Beach, I ran into a man who claimed to be Johnny Depp's astrologer. . . . I took his card and examined it carefully a moment, as if I couldn't quite read the small print. But I knew he was lying, so I leaned toward him and slapped him sharply in the nuts. Not hard, but very quickly, using the back of my hand and my fingers like a bull whip, yet very discreetly. He let out a hiss and went limp, unable to speak or breathe."

PERK OF SUCCESS: YOU, TOO, CAN WIN AN INDUSTRY AWARD

Screenwriter Dalton Trumbo, in a note to himself: "Develop the idea that no moderately competent hack in any field of Hollywood endeavor can spend ten years in the community without winning a wide assortment of plaques, medals, and certificates of merit."

Leave a message at 1:30 P.M., during lunch hour, on his answering machine.

Do this when you don't want to talk to that studio executive but want to make it appear that you do.

But if you get a message back on *your* answering machine during lunch hour, it might really be time to talk to him.

You're not going to be in The Dictionary of Film.

A magazine wanted to do a profile of me and assigned the job to David Thomson, the critic and author of *A Biographical Dictionary of Film,* recognized as a classic film book.

I had lunch with David Thomson, a pleasant man, at the Lark Creek Inn in Larkspur, California, and told him I wasn't going to let him do the article.

He seemed shocked. "But why not?"

I said, "Because I've read your dictionary and there are hardly any screenwriters in it; there are all kinds of actors, directors, producers, even cinematographers, but not one screenwriter."

David Thomson said, "What does that have to do with anything? Just because you're a screenwriter doesn't mean I can't write about you in a publication."

I said, "But you obviously don't believe very many screenwriters are important enough to include in *A Biographical Dictionary of Film*."

"No," he said calmly, "I don't suppose I do."

So I didn't let him do the interview—enjoying the fact that I, a lowly screenwriter, was denying him a paycheck.

Keep your name out of the trades.

Mike Medavoy: "I told my writer clients to ignore the big-splash announcements in the trades about some unknown writer getting big bucks for a script, because often these guys are never heard from again."

Don't be anybody's N word.

According to screenwriter Buck Henry, screenwriter Robert Towne became "Warren Beatty's nigger."

Don't take yourself seriously.

Producer Gerry Ayres: "Bob Towne would love to work for money on rewrites on which he got no credit, and would do it quickly. Over three weeks, he'd have a whole new script ready. But something that had his name on it would become all involved in the neurosis of completion and failure and would take forever."

Scald 'em with chicken soup.

Mike Medavoy: "I had lunch with Paddy Chayefsky. We were talking about directors for Paddy's script *Network* and Paddy asked me what I thought of Sidney Lumet.

"'Sidney Lumet to do *Network*?' I gasped. 'What was the last funny movie he made?'

"In response, Paddy turned his bowl of chicken soup over on the table.

"'You're right, Paddy,' I replied, 'he'd be great.'"

If you make it, don't brag about it.

My fellow Hungarian, actor Tony Curtis: "It was a miserable, rainy late afternoon, my chauffeur drives me down Forty-eighth Street, and who do I see out front, standing under the marquee, but Walter Matthau. He's got a long, heavy coat on and looks as grumpy as he's ever looked in his life . . . he's looking out at this cold miserable world he's got to live in. He hates it. I'm getting this reading as I'm sitting in my limo, warm and comfy, looking at this poor guy on the sidewalk staring into the gutter and saying to himself, 'What's ever going to happen for me? Nothin'.' You could see that on his face.

"So I say to the driver, 'See that guy standing under the awning? Drive up to him as slowly as possible, and when we're alongside of him, stop.' He says okay, so we drive up, and I see Walter watching this limousine come rolling up, and it stops right where he's standing. I roll the window down, I look at him, and I say, '*I fucked Yvonne DeCarlo!*'

"Then I just rolled that window back up and told the driver to get the hell out of there."

To Do a Hughie

To trip on your own dick, like actor Hugh Grant.

The definition of "creative differences" . . .

The producer had a reputation for having a nasty temper, so some people were surprised when he was named to take over the studio.

He soon developed a conflict with a lawyer in Business Affairs who kept questioning some of the personal expenses that the new studio head was writing off—expenses like an airplaneful of orchids sent to an actress girlfriend in Rio.

The studio head told the lawyer several times to back off. The lawyers' *friends* told him to back off.

Yet he kept after the studio head, questioning expenses in meetings—expenses like twenty thousand dollars for a party involving three girls who worked for a club in Vegas.

One day, at a meeting in a studio conference room full of executives, the lawyer nitpicked about some suspicious expense. The studio head punched him in the mouth, judo-chopped him in the throat, and kicked him in the head and ribs while the other studio executives sat there and did nothing.

The lawyer was taken by ambulance to a hospital. He recovered quickly. He left the studio and received a $5 million settlement.

Raymond Chandler, role model . . .

Producer Ray Stark told screenwriter/novelist Jim Harrison that as a young agent one of his jobs was to get Raymond Chandler off the floor of his apartment, where he sometimes slept fully dressed in a drying pool of his own vomit.

Never hug an actress on a soundstage.

You'll screw up her hair, costuming, and makeup. She'll hate you.

LESSON 5

Don't Let 'Em Bleed on You!

You're on your own.

After I sold *Basic Instinct* for $3 million to Carolco, Disney studio honcho Jeff Katzenberg wrote a memo lamenting the fact, and studio heads got together in meetings to discuss ways of keeping future script prices down. (*Daily Variety* reported both the memo and the studio meetings.)

The Writers Guild should have filed an antitrust action against the studios for conspiring to keep writers' prices down, but the Guild, great on matters of health plans and insurance and awful on matters of creative rights, did nothing.

The multimillion-dollar script frenzy ended within six months, making it pretty clear that the studios had successfully put the writers back in their places: the schmucks at the bottom of the totem pole.

In 2001, the Guild threatened a strike. One of its main demands was the elimination of the directors' possessory "Filmed by" credit.

When the Guild made progress on financial fronts, it simply—without even an explanatory statement—dropped its demands about the directors' possessory credit, and signed a new contract with the studios.

Be an outlaw.

John Milius (*Apocalypse Now, Dirty Harry*): "I liken myself to a successful outlaw. To be worth a shit in the world, you've got to blaze your own trail. Nothing else is any good. Whatever you're going to do you're going to do alone."

Even Mailer lost his soul.

Sandy Charlebois Thomas, Norman Mailer's secretary: "Something happened to him out in Hollywood. He's talked to me about being corrupted out there. He was young, suddenly very famous, and he was wined and dined. He discovered if he did the cutest little things, people just fell all over him."

Don't let 'em bleed on you.

Stanley Jaffe, producer and former head of Paramount, would yell at people with such force that blood would flow from his nostrils.

Don't do it.

Screenwriter/playwright David Mamet: "Working as a screenwriter, I always thought that 'Film is a collaborative business' only constituted half of the actual phrase. From a screenwriter's point of view, the correct rendering should be 'Film is a collaborative business: bend over.'"

Slug some more Kaopectate, Bill.

Screenwriter William Goldman: "It's probably not unwise to try to remember why movie people have kept the tranquilizer business booming; after a debacle, it's hard to get work; after two, it's hard to get television.

Can I have a slug of your Kaopectate, Bill?

Your last movie has bombed at the box office. Good luck. You're in a heap of *creative* trouble. Everyone in every story meeting or phone conference will now think that they know more than you do.

They may have thought that *before* your movie failed, but now that it has, *they* know that *you* know that you have to listen to their ideas.

Don't be a road map.

Screenwriter Terry George (*Hotel Rwanda*): "Film today is more and more concentrated on the amusement park element. If a writer can attach an actor or a producer who has some clout, then you can arm yourself; otherwise, a script simply becomes a road map to attract money and talent."

I've moved out of Malibu, thank you.

Screenwriter Milo Addica (*Birth*): "Most writers just want to get their movie made, and it doesn't matter how. I think I am not in that category. I like to get my movies made by the right director, so that I can have a body of work I can look back on and be proud of. Otherwise, I would not be doing anything I am doing now. I would be in Hollywood trying to make my first million and move up to Malibu."

They want to control you.

Novelist/screenwriter George Pelecanos: "When I was a kid, I used to watch *Twilight Zone,* as everybody did. The reason I watched it—although I didn't know enough intellectually then to know why I was watching it—it was written by novelists like Richard Matheson. I always wondered, Why don't they do that more? Because, damn, novelists sure could use the work; I mean, just to get that extra thirty grand or whatever the scale is for a script and a story is a huge amount of money to most novelists. I think one of the reasons they don't—actually what a producer told me one time is, 'We can't control you guys.'"

They'll spring the monster on you.

John Gregory Dunne: "A producer and writer were arguing vigorously against the changes the studio was demanding in a picture already in production. The president of the Disney division overseeing the picture suddenly demanded silence. He was, he said, forced by the writer's intransigence to 'take the monster out of its cage.'

"In the silence that ensued, the division president reached under the table, pretended to grab a small predatory animal from its lair, and then, as if clutching the creature by the neck in his fist, exhibited his empty, clawlike hand to the people around the table. He asked the screenwriter if he saw the monster. The writer, not knowing what else to do, nodded yes.

"'I'm going to put it back in its cage now,' the executive said, drawing each word out, 'and I never want you to force me to bring it out again.' Then he mimed putting the monster back into its cage under the table. When he was done, the executive asked the writer, 'Do you know what the monster is?'

"The writer shook his head.

"The executive said, 'It's our money.'"

Don't let 'em tell you what to write.

I did what they said," Marilyn Monroe said, "and all it got me was a lot of abuse. Everyone's just laughing at me. I hate it. Big breasts, big ass, big deal."

They'll even try to take your brains.

Monroe Stahr, the producer in F. Scott Fitzgerald's final novel, *The Last Tycoon*: "I never thought I had more brains than a writer has. But I always thought that his brains *belonged* to me—because I knew how to use them."

Robert McKee taught him . . .

A young screenwriter who'd attended Robert McKee's screen-writing seminar sent me a script. It was about a young screen-writer who'd attended the Robert McKee seminar, hadn't learned anything, and wound up homeless in Santa Monica.

The script was awful.

It helps to know how to fight.

Screenwriter J. P. Miller said this about Paddy Chayefsky: "Paddy was an extraordinarily good human manipulator. He knew his way around a scrap as very few writers do. Most writers, if they get into a fight or a bad situation on a movie, call their agents. But Paddy knew Hollywood and he wouldn't back down. He would go head to head with anybody—and at the same time he had this in-credible writer's sensitivity. That's a rare combination which many of us don't have. He was that rare breed of talent and fighter."

You don't ever need a job this badly.

During a script meeting, a producer suggested something that screenwriter William Goldman thought was "a moron point."

Goldman: "I wanted to scream so loud. I wanted to choke the asshole. But I was so sweet. I took notes. I grunted and nodded. I smiled when it was conceiv-ably possible."

Kick 'em in their ass!

Screenwriter/novelist Raymond Chandler: "I don't care about the money. I just like to fight. I'm a tired old man, but it takes more than a motion picture studio to push me around."

Kicking ass can do you good.

Paddy Chayefsky: "I stormed and ranted. And the more I ranted, the more the studio people respected me."

I got into so many nasty fights with studio execs over my fifteen movies that the *Los Angeles Business Weekly* quoted an anonymous screenwriter as saying this about me: "At the heart of the Eszterhas phenomenon is titillation. There is a sense of danger about him, violence. For a lot of movie executives, who have no life experience, he's exciting, exotic. They get a sense of danger by being in business with him."

Clench your fists; throw a fit.

I once told a group of Disney executives in a crowded conference room to "get your hands off my dick and tell me the truth."

Billy Bob Thornton, back in his screenwriting days, leaped atop a studio executive's desk and threatened to strangle the man for ruining his script.

"Sometimes I find myself dealing unpleasantly with people," said Paddy Chayefsky, "talking to them as if they were animals."

A producer describes Chayefsky at a meeting this way: "When he was crossed, his entire body would tighten like steel. He'd scowl, clench his fists, glare, then the verbal avalanche would begin. He could level armies with that tongue of his if he didn't explode first, because his whole body would shake in a fit of apoplexy. For the most part, he looked like a monster child having a tantrum."

Pretend you're Clint Eastwood.

After seeing *The Outlaw Josey Wales,* Warner Bros. studio executive David Geffen said to director Clint Eastwood, "I only want to suggest one thing: I think it would be better if it was twenty minutes shorter."

Clint said to David, "I'm glad you took the time to see the picture, and I appreciate your comments. But why don't you study the picture some more and see if you have any more thoughts. When you do, give me a call over at Paramount."

David said to Clint, "Why over at Paramount?"

"Because that's where I'll be making my next movie," Clint said.

David said, "The picture is perfect. I wouldn't change one frame. Thank you very much."

Clint said, "Thank *you.*"

Don't ever quit a job.

If you've been hired to work on a script and you loathe the director and the producer and you feel that what you wrote is being truncated and transmogrified into dog shit, don't quit. Keep telling them that you are "ready, willing, and able to perform"—legalese right out of the contract that you signed.

If you are pleasantly intransigent, they will fire you. That's what you want. You'll be paid in full and the trades will report that because of "creative differences," you've left the project.

He was talking about Hemingway, honest, not about me.

Screenwriter/novelist Raymond Chandler: "He never really wrote but one story. All the rest is the same thing in different pants—or without different pants. And his eternal preoccupation with what goes on between the sheets becomes rather nauseating in the end. One reaches a time of life when limericks written on the walls of comfort stations are not just obscene, they are horribly dull. This man has only one subject and he makes that ridiculous. I suppose the man's epitaph, if he had the choosing of it, would be: Here Lies a Man Who Was Bloody Good in Bed. Too Bad He's Alone Here. But the point is I begin to doubt whether he ever was. You don't have to work so hard at things you are really good at—or do you?"

Our scripts turned Garbo into a recluse.

Screenwriter/playwright Mercedes de Acosta, an intimate friend of Greta Garbo, said Garbo's reclusiveness was caused by disappointment in herself "for not fighting harder for better scripts."

In other words, bad screenplays screwed Garbo up.

If you make an ass of yourself, don't make an even bigger ass out of yourself.

Screenwriter/novelist Anne Rice looked silly when she said the biggest movie star in the world at the time, Tom Cruise, was too short to play her character Lestat in *Interview with a Vampire*.

But she looked even sillier when, after seeing the film, she took a two-page ad in *Daily Variety* saying how much she had loved Cruise . . . and the film.

ALL HAIL
Ben Hecht!

Agent Swifty Lazar: "No one was better at beating the moguls at their own game than Ben Hecht. The deal I made for him with Sam Goldwyn certainly proves that he had Sam beat.

" 'I get paid two thousand dollars per day—in cash,' Ben told me. 'I want it in hundred dollar bills on my desk, or I don't show up for work the next day. And, by the way, there's a very pretty girl who's a wonderful secretary. You've got to get her a contract while I'm still out here. She'll make a thousand a week. I know that sounds like a lot, but she's a great actress and a great typist—and I want her to have a part in the picture.'

" 'Can she really act?' I asked.

" '*She* thinks she can. *I* think she can. Nobody may agree with us, but I can tell you right now. I'll fight for her.' "

Don't join a writing committee.

The writing committee is a relatively new phenomenon, first seen when a few writers (very few) began getting more publicity on their films than the directors they were working with.

So the directors decided to bring not one writer on board a project, but *half a dozen*—on the theory that if there were half a dozen cooks in the kitchen, it would be obvious that the director was the auteur chef who told them what to do.

Don't do "quick job" rewrites.

These are rewrites done at the behest of the director or a studio days before a movie goes into production.

There is no time to write anything except what the director or studio tells you to write.

Screenwriter William Goldman has done many of them.

"I make a point of never reading anything I've written in these rewrites," he says.

Be respectful of those whose work you adapt for the screen.

I adapted Brian Moore's novel *The Doctor's Wife,* and on the front page of my script I wrote, "Screenplay by Joe Eszterhas, from the novel by Brian Moore."

The executive in charge of the project at United Artists, Marcia Nasatir, said to me, "In all my years in the business, I've never seen the screenwriter put the novelist's name on the title page of the script."

I did the same thing with Ira Levin's *Sliver.*

I did it because I knew that without their *novels,* without the story and characters *they* created, I wouldn't have this job of *translating* their work from book to screenplay.

This is what you do when you are asked to rewrite the last draft of Gone With the Wind.

Ben Hecht read the previous seven drafts, which had been done by different writers. He turned his rewrite in *three days* later. And he never read the novel.

Write original screenplays, not rewrites.

Director David Lean: "We want someone who has written original stories. We don't want a scriptwriter who has spent his time embroidering on other people's ideas."

The more writers on a movie, the worse it will be.

If a character has been rewritten by, say, six or eight or ten writers, that character will not have a distinctive and original voice; the voice will be a hodgepodge of a bunch of characters' voices, as each writer envisions the character *for himself.*

The actors aren't smart enough to realize that their lines are being homogenized, and directors feel that *their imprint* on the film will be more felt the more writers there are on it.

Even the Writers Guild is happy about all the writers employed—the wealth is spread, there are fewer unemployed writers, and they're all being paid handsome sums to fuck one another's work over.

Oh yeah? Then how come Premiere *magazine named me one of the one hundred most powerful people in Hollywood?*

Screenwriter William Goldman: "There are still a few lost souls who actually think that screenwriters have some authority. If only it were so. We have none. . . . There are lots of reasons. We're not, most of us, so terrifically talented. And we're so easy to fire—at least half of the people in positions of authority in Hollywood know the alphabet. You don't fire composers often; editors are safe, too. But it's not unusual, despite what you see on the credits, to have two or three or eight writers write on one film script. As well as being inept and disposable, we're also, truly, disliked. Why? Because you can't make a movie without us. If it's going to be a decent flick, it better have a decent screenplay; directors know this and it drives them maaaaaaad."

Don't sprinkle their piss.

If, that is to say, the studio execs agree to kill the script they are asking you to rewrite.

If you can create a whole new plot with all new characters, then it's probably worth putting your creativity to work on the rewrite.

Otherwise, you're just being asked to pour the director's or the producer's or the studio execs' piss into the stew.

They piss into the bottle, hand it to you, and let you sprinkle it into the script however you want. But it's still piss—and it's *their* piss.

The Robert Towne award goes to . . .

I may not be the slickest screenwriter in Hollywood," said William Faulkner, "but I know how to fix a screenplay."

Faulkner rewrote Hemingway.

Everybody out here rewrites everybody else," said screenwriter William Faulkner as he adapted Ernest Hemingway's *To Have and Have Not*. Ironically, adapting the Hemingway book was Faulkner's greatest success as a screenwriter.

But I didn't rewrite Gore Vidal.

Vidal did an adaptation of Lucian Truscott's novel *Dress Gray,* which Paramount wanted me to rewrite.

I tried to explain to the Paramount executives that I wasn't comfortable rewriting Gore Vidal, but they didn't understand why not.

I didn't rewrite William Goldman, either, but I should have.

Bill wrote an original script about Ross Perot that ABC Films wanted me to rewrite.

I tried to explain to the ABC executives that I didn't feel comfortable rewriting Bill Goldman, but they didn't get it.

Time to retire, Bill.

William Goldman: "No matter how much shit you may have heard or read, movies are finally only about one thing: THE NEXT JOB."

He even capitalized those three words in a book to make sure you got the point.

It's time to get off our hands and knees.

Norman Mailer, writing to a friend in 1949: "We found us a house high above Sunset Boulevard in the hills west of Hollywood, and can see half of that horrible city that lies below us . . . the writers are walking around on their hands and knees, not knowing where their next job is coming from."

Sometimes you won't get any credit for what you've written.

Director Phillip Noyce: "Steve Zaillian wrote the script of *Patriot Games* that we shot. Uncredited, because the Writers Guild decides on credits, and they usually give it to the original writer. In this case, two of them: Peter Iliff and Donald Stewart—the guy who wrote *Missing*. Their names are on the credits, but eighty percent of what was shot was written by Steve Zaillian."

Don't break Milton Berle's rule.

Uncle Miltie said, "Don't tell jokes only the band laughs at."

I wrote a whole movie filled with esoteric in-jokes about the movie industry—*An Alan Smithee Film: Burn Hollywood Burn.*

No one understood the in-jokes. And no one went to see the movie.

Write an animated film.

Screenwriter Nicholas Kazan (*Reversal of Fortune*): "*The Incredibles* was the wittiest film of the year, as witty as *Sideways* and maybe more. There was a degree of verbal and visual wit that you just don't see anymore, that we saw in the films of the 1930s, 40s, and 50s—the good ones. They had a lot of great writers then who were allowed to write, and today there are a lot of brilliant writers who are not allowed to write—no one is interested in wit, except in animation."

Bill Goldman should have been a mailman.

Goldman: "In twenty-five years of movie work, I've never been late. I do crazy things to make that happen sometimes—once I called in and said I'd be late and asked for a week's extension, got it, then went into sleepless overdrive and turned the screenplay in by the original date. The work may stink, but it arrives."

You're not doing slave labor, are you?

Screenwriter James L. White (*Ray*): "When I started working on the *Ray* script with director Taylor Hackford, our workday would start at 9:00 A.M. and sometimes go until two in the morning. I was doing that seven days a week! We would go for stretches of a month and a half or two months, and in the last days I can recall two occasions where we would actually be up straight through for twenty-four to thirty-six hours."

When all else fails, those jealous of you will say your script doesn't "play."

That's after you've sold it for a lot of money and the studio is sending it around to directors and actors.

Some midlevel studio exec you've never met—but who is pushing some other script to be made—will say "Sure, it reads like it's brilliant. It makes sense why we bought it, but my gut is that it doesn't play."

If everyone passes on your script, he will say, "See, I told you so."

If it gets made and fails, he'll say, "I kept trying to tell all of you."

A successful screenwriter's writing schedule . . .

Screenwriters John Gregory Dunne and Joan Didion liked writing at the exclusive Kahala Hilton Hotel on Oahu.

Dunne: "Our schedule did not vary: a sunrise swim, breakfast, then four hours' work in the suite; an hour for lunch, then two more hours' work in the afternoon; another swim, then three more hours' work before a late dinner. After dinner, we went over the day's pages, then printed out a schedule of scenes for the next day."

The way to celebrate an option . . .

Screenwriter/novelist James Brown: "When an independent producer in New York options my third novel, I am excited but cautious. . . . I run out and buy an eight-ball of methamphetamine because it is cheaper and stronger than coke, a few cases of Budweiser, a half gallon of Smirnoff, Dewar's scotch, and Seagram's 7 and invite my friends over for a party. But most of them are busy for some reason and what few do show end up leaving early when I make an ass of myself."

If you make enough money to buy two houses, at least don't build your own road to reach them.

Screenwriter Albert Maltz on his friend and fellow screenwriter Dalton Trumbo: "There is no question that Trumbo had talent for much greater literary work than the film work that he produced. The reason he never did what he could have done was this obsession of his with making money and living in a grand manner. I never knew what made it necessary for him to have both a house on Beverly Drive and a ranch that he had to build a road to get to. It kept him writing, and writing, and writing, though. Why *do* writers write, after all?"

The deal every screenwriter should aspire to . . .

Yes, I did sell a four-page outline for $4 million, but . . .
Paddy Chayefsky made a deal with a studio, which paid him $1 million for the script. They had a year to make the movie.

If production didn't start within the year, Paddy could sell his script elsewhere . . . and keep the million dollars.

Don't think twice, it's all right.

Screenwriter William Faulkner, writing from Los Angeles to his New York agent: "Things are going pretty well. My father died last month, and what with getting his affairs straightened out and getting Hollywood out of my system by means of a judicious course of alcohol in mild though sufficient quantities before and after eating and lying down and getting up, I am not working now."

Maybe it's not all right.

At a script meeting with director Howard Hawks, screenwriter William Faulkner, who had been seen sipping earlier on a silver flask, said, "This is what I think, Howard."

He smiled, raised his hand to make a point, fell on his face, and passed out.

Bob Towne is a big William Faulkner fan.

While waiting for executives Barry Diller and Michael Eisner to decide whether they would release his movie *Personal Best,* Bob Towne kept pouring scotch for himself from Diller's bar. He passed out on the couch before they came back into the room.

PERK OF SUCCESS: A NEW PURDY SHOTGUN

Screenwriter/director John Milius always demanded a brand-new Purdy shotgun as part of his screenwriting deals.

He told friends he needed the guns so he could arm a battalion in case it was necessary to overcome the government. Every studio making a deal with him complied. His friends say Milius could now arm a small army.

Words to live by . . .

Paddy Chayefsky's last words: "I tried. I really tried."

Don't buy a Hungarian dog.

Robert Towne did—a rare komondor, so big that it wouldn't fit into the back of his car. So Towne let the dog ride next to him in the front seat and put his wife in the back. Then he and his wife got divorced.

LESSON 6

Don't Take Your Clothes Off!

If you really want to learn about the industry . . .

Hide in a bathroom stall in the men's room of The Grille in Beverly Hills any weekday lunch hour, overhearing conversations. At the end of that time, you will have learned everything you need to know about Hollywood.

Don't obsess about getting rich.

Paddy Chayefsky: "You make a lot of money and you never get rich."

Research all celebrity auctions you may be involved in.

A man paid thousands of dollars at a celebrity auction to have lunch with me. He wanted to be a screenwriter and used the lunch to get screenwriting tips.

His name was Jerry George. He was an editor of the *National Enquirer.* I used the lunch to get celebrity tips. I asked him more questions than he asked me.

It's possible I learned more from Jerry George in that lunch than he learned from me. And it didn't cost me anything

Don't ever write a script for a movie-star couple who are allegedly in love.

It will fail.

Consider: *Shanghai Surprise* with Sean Penn and Madonna; *The Getaway* with Alec Baldwin and Kim Basinger; *Husbands and Wives* with Woody Allen and Mia Farrow; *Mortal Thoughts* with Bruce Willis and Demi Moore; *Proof of*

100

Life with Russell Crowe and Meg Ryan; *Made in America* with Whoopi Goldberg and Ted Danson; *Eyes Wide Shut* and *Far and Away* with Tom Cruise and Nicole Kidman; *Bounce* with Ben Affleck and Gwyneth Paltrow; *Gigli* with Ben Affleck and Jennifer Lopez.

You, too, can live the screenwriter's life.
Hunter S. Thompson described his "workdays" in Hollywood as "Violence, joy, and constant Mexican music."

PERK OF SUCCESS: YOU, TOO, CAN GET MAXFIELD'S ON MELROSE TO SEND YOU A $150,000 SELECTION OF GOLD AND DIAMOND CROSSES

If, that is, they know you've sold a lot of scripts for a lot of money. Then they'll send you their selection of crosses—wherever you are in the world—by FedEx by ten o'clock the next morning, and trust you to send the unbought crosses back to them.

Help those who've helped you.
Marcia Nasatir was a studio executive at United Artists when she discovered me, in 1974. She had read a book that I had written, which had been nominated for the National Book Award.

As the years went by, my career as a screenwriter prospered, while Marcia had turned to the shaky world of independent production.

In 1991, after I wrote *Basic Instinct,* I was the hottest screenwriter in Hollywood and Marcia was in New York, a producer trying to find hot scripts and put films together.

I asked if she wanted to produce my latest script with Irwin Winkler, one of the town's hottest producers. She was happy and grateful, but, unfortunately, we never got the movie I had written made.

My agent at the time said, "If you really want to say thank you to her for the help she was to you and pay her back, maybe next time you should give her a script that's not about the president of the United States having sex with a cow."

This industry is much more inbred than the music business.

Producer Don Simpson died of a heart attack while straining on the toilet. He was reading a book about Oliver Stone. (Elvis also died of a heart attack while straining on the toilet. He was reading a book about Jesus Christ.)

If you write a hit movie, don't write the sequel.

Your vision didn't include a sequel: your vision was for one story, which they are now asking you to stretch to two.

Remember that piece of rope can only stretch so far without snapping.

When MGM asked me to write the sequel to *Basic Instinct,* it was easy for me to pass: I'd get millions from a sequel whether I wrote it or not, according to my contract for *Basic Instinct.*

I had other incentives to pass, too. The studio executive in charge of the project, Lindsay Doran, told me she thought the original was "sexist" and "misogynistic" and said, "We have to figure out a way not to make the sequel like that."

I didn't remind her that the original had made nearly $500 million worldwide at the box office.

I didn't tell her that a French newsmagazine picked the release of *Basic* as *the* worldwide event of 1992—not in entertainment, but in world news.

I didn't tell her that, thanks to her attitude, I thought my characters Nick Curran and Catherine Tramell were in the hands of a *politically correct ideologue.* But I knew that any sequel they might make would be a disaster.

I'm glad I didn't write the sequel to Basic Instinct.

Written by Henry Bean and Leora Barish, it turned out to be the disaster of the year, getting reviews that made my reviews for *Showgirls* look terrific in comparison.

Typical was David Thomson's review in *The Independent on Sunday* (London): "Everyone now marks Sharon Stone down as the chump who enabled them to do the remake . . . And Sharon Stone, for the first time in her life, has been publicly disgraced. Now it is hard to see where she can go—except to the kind of roles Joan Collins played when television had soap operas."

Its opening weekend box office was $2 million—unfathomably abysmal—the numbers were similar all around the world.

Thanks to Henry Bean and Leora Barish, I finally got some damn good reviews for the original.

The trades wrote: "Part of this disaster is the fault of the abysmal script (I can't believe I'm saying this, but: Joe Eszterhas, we need you!).

The Toronto Star: "Missing in action in the sequel are Michael Douglas, director Paul Verhoeven, and writer Joe Eszterhas, who are sorely missed, as is any semblance of a coherent plot."

The Guardian (London): "The original *Basic Instinct* had style, of a barking mad sort; Eszterhas's screenplay had its own beady-eyed narrative drive."

The Denver Post: "With *Basic Instinct,* Eszterhas, the one-time writer for *Rolling Stone,* became screenwriter as rock star."

The New York *Daily News*: "Written as a fever dream by Hollywood bad boy Joe Eszterhas, the original introduced into the pantheon of femme fatales a wealthy thirty-year-old widow with degrees in literature and psychology."

The Independent (London): "Mounted on the different testosterone drives of Joe Eszterhas, Paul Verhoeven, and Michael Douglas (major league hard-ons)— *Basic Instinct* was a trash masterpiece, deliriously inventive, hatefully incorrect, and exhiliratingly sure of its bad taste."

The Weekly Standard: "Only once, really, did a genuinely filthy mainstream Hollywood picture strike it big, and that was the original *Basic Instinct*—a brilliantly made thriller in which a bisexual woman goes around San Francisco killing men with an ice pick. At one moment, *Basic Instinct* is the ultimate male fantasy about a completely uninhibited woman, while at the next it's the ultimate male nightmare about a woman so cold she would kill you as soon as look at you. It's lascivious and puritanical in equal measure, a movie that says sex will probably kill you and, what's more, you'll deserve it. But man, what a way to go. *Basic Instinct* became a sensation because it rides its mixed messages all the way to a daringly unrealized conclusion that leaves us in perpetual doubt as to who the real killer is. That playful trickery is entirely absent from the endless and lethargic sequel."

The Village Voice: "The original *Basic Instinct* was both a manifestation and a critique of sex panic, an effortless distillation of a late '80s/early '90s zeitgeist: the end of second-wave feminism, the peaking of AIDS anxieties, the dawn of the Clinton years. Stale and corny, *Basic Instinct 2* isn't even accidentally relevant."

On the other hand, some critics still want me dead.

Even though I had nothing to do with the sequel, the *Arkansas Times* wrote in its review of *Basic 2:* "It's the kind of movie that makes me wish Joe Eszterhas's mother had left a few more dry cleaning bags around when he was a kid."

Thanks to the sequel, I'm a director.

The Sunday Independent of Johannesburg, South Africa: "We all remember that famous scene—the flash—with Sharon Stone in *Basic Instinct*. It was trashy film, but Joe Eszterhas directed it with the flair born of knowing delight in trashiness."

If it's a bad movie and it fails—well, what the hell—blame it on George W. Bush.

Paul Verhoeven, who turned down a lot of money to direct *Basic*'s sequel, said this about the sequel's failure: "Anything that is erotic has been banned in the United States."

Did you know they paid me homage in Basic Instinct 2?

That's what a critic said, discussing a scene in the film where someone is reading a Hungarian-language primer.

I don't think that the critic knew that one of the movie's producers was Hungarian, as was the cinematographer. And the producer's girlfriend had a small part.

So the Hungarian homage may have been addressed to *all* the Hungarians making the film, an homage made by Hungarians to Hungarians, dancing merrily off the sinking ship.

I did not pleasure myself . . . , I swear I didn't. . . .

Reviewing *Basic Instinct 2* in *The Weekly Standard,* John Podhoretz wrote: "The only person who'll enjoy this travesty is the exiled Eszterhas, who'll no doubt be pleasuring himself as his pagan goddess thuds to earth."

Yeah, okay, but she's still got chutzpah.

After the failure of the sequel, Sharon Stone announced that she would direct either another sequel or a *Basic Instinct* television series.

A producer friend told me, "What happened to the sequel says nobody even wants to see her pussy anymore, let alone her movies."

Beware of quisling screenwriters.

Notice how often critics and film journalists write that such and such a screenwriter worked on a film, doing an uncredited polish or rewrite.

The critics and journalists are leaked this information by the director or the studio. The screenwriters they plug are either the director's friends or the studio's lackeys.

The reason the names of these screenwriters are leaked to the press is to take credit *away* from those writers who *really wrote* the script and who may have gotten into defiant creative disagreements with the director or the studio.

Don't take a screenwriting course in Cleveland, Ohio, either.

Bob Noll teaches screenwriting at both John Carroll University and the Cleveland Play House. His credits? Producer and co-director of the local weekly children's show *Hickory Hideout* on Cleveland's Channel 3.

He was also a child actor and worked in local theater.

His advice about how to write a good script?

"Step one: Put a character in a tree. Step two: Shake the tree and let loose ravenous animals to prowl beneath it. Step three: Get the character out of the tree—survival optional."

Sometimes everything goes wrong on your movie.

Director Phillip Noyce, on *Sliver*: "On *Sliver* I just became so tired I couldn't get off the floor. I had to have doctors constantly injecting me with vitamins. I was trying to give up smoking at the time and I don't think I was all that stable myself, as I had been inhaling up to six packs a day previously. . . . I was terribly addicted and had decided to give up before *Sliver*. This probably wasn't a good idea for my equilibrium. But every day of pressure on the *Sliver* set caused bad nicotine-induced panic attacks, so the chaos of the whole thing was not something I could blame on others. The film had become a Hollywood nightmare—with a producer [Robert Evans] who, from the beginning, had dreamt of his movie being directed by someone else, a writer [Joe Eszterhas] who had abandoned a best-selling novel to pen his own version of the story, an actress [Sharon Stone] who I couldn't communicate with and who loathed her co-star and producer, and a cinematographer [Vilmos Zsigmond] who was creating beautiful images at a snail's pace, on a set that made more noise than the actors when they spoke their lines. At night I dreamt of turning up at a schoolboy rugby match and then running onto the field only to discover I'd left my football boots at home. I'd wake with a deep sense of dread. Facing another day at the factory that filmmaking had become."

Never mind all that, the real reason Sliver *failed.*

Two of the key elements (screenwriter and cinematographer) were Hungarian.

Time is your best ally.

When *Betrayed* was released in 1988, the critics said it was "an unrealistic apocalyptic vision."

Just a few years later, neo-Nazi Timothy McVeigh, the spittin' image of the Tom Berenger character in *Betrayed,* blew up the federal courthouse in Oklahoma City.

When *Showgirls* was released in 1995, critics said it "maligned and libeled" Las Vegas, "a place of family values."

Just a few years later, Vegas casinos were playing topless stage shows and casino buses were taking tourists to lap-dance bars.

If you get lucky, you'll find partners.

I hooked up with three directors twice: with Richard Marquand on *Jagged Edge* and *Hearts of Fire*; with Costa-Gavras on *Betrayed* and *Music Box*; with Paul Verhoeven on *Showgirls* and *Basic Instinct*.

I hooked up with the producer Irwin Winkler (*Rocky, Raging Bull*) four times: on *Betrayed, Music Box, Basic Instinct* (he was replaced by Alan Marshall), and *Sacred Cows* (unproduced).

ALL HAIL
Harlan Ellison!

The screenwriter/author claimed that the script of *The Terminator* was a rip-off of both a novelette and a TV script that he had written. He sued and won.

After he won, he bought a full-page ad in the trades, which said, "The film acknowledges the works of Harlan Ellison."

Use Frank as your role model.

I was appearing as myself in *An Alan Smithee Film: Burn Hollywood Burn,* and Arthur Hiller, the director, did two takes and wanted to do more.

I said no, that two were enough, then got up and walked off the set.

Arthur gaped, but what could he do? I wasn't going back to do any more takes.

I learned that from Sinatra. Frank did two takes—no matter who the director was—and no more.

Can you be a person of integrity as a screenwriter?

Screenwriter/novelist Raymond Chandler: "All progress in the art of the screenplay depends on a very few people who are in a position to fight for excellence. Hollywood loves them for it and is only too anxious to reward them by making them something else than writers. Hollywood's attitude to writers is necessarily conditioned by the mass of its writers, not by the few who have what it calls integrity. It loves the word, having so little of the quality."

Keep everything close to your vest.

Producer David Merrick once got a phone call telling him his building would be blown up in two minutes. He told no one else, ran out of his office, yelled, "Take any messages!" to his assistant, then scurried to the elevator and out of the building.

Hit 'em back.

When MPAA president Jack Valenti told people that I was "desperately ill and needed immediate medical attention," I reminded people that Jack Valenti was the White House aide who briefed Lyndon Johnson in the West Wing bathroom each morning and handed him the toilet paper under the stall before he got his gig at the MPAA.

If they kick the living shit out of you, smile and say, "Is that the best you've got?"

I won the Hollywood Women's Press Association's Sour Apple Award—following in the footsteps of Norman Mailer and Howard Stern . . . for acting boorishly and believing my own publicity.

When I received the award at the Beverly Hilton Hotel, I said this:

"Mel Gibson said that if I came here to accept this award, I should wear a bulletproof vest. I've brought my wife with me instead. I pity any potential assassin who may be lurking here. Naomi keeps a riding crop next to our bed, you know.

"I know that this award is given for believing your own publicity and I thought what I'd do here today is share some of my recent publicity with you. I'm doing it, of course, so that you will have no lingering doubt in your minds that you have given this award to the right person.

"The Portland *Oregonian* said about me: 'He is an imbecilic ape of a screenwriter.'

"*Time* magazine said, 'His movie is ludicrous, he can't write.'

"*The Boston Globe* said, 'He types, he doesn't write, and if the stories about his manual typewriter are accurate, he can't type very well, either.'

"A small-town paper in Florida said, 'He is the overwriter—overweight and overpaid.'

"*The Miami Herald* said, 'It's hard to believe this is the same man who wrote *Music Box* and *Betrayed*. With age, his brains seem to have lowered gravitationally to another part of his anatomy.'

"Ladies and gentlemen, allow me to thank you. I am proud of you for giving this award to a screenwriter instead of Jim Carrey, the actor who was my main competing candidate. This is a landmark day for screenwriters! Good Lord, I have defeated the biggest movie star in the world!

"Eat your heart out, Jim. The apple is mine!"

You'll need some K-Y jelly.

Producer Robert Evans: "You've gotta scare the piss out of 'em to close a deal. You've gotta make 'em feel that if they don't do the deal, you've got somebody waiting in the wings who will. Fear is the K-Y jelly that gets the fucking done. Without that jelly, the deals don't close."

Mark Twain, Homer, and Shakespeare were in the same boat you're in.

Novelist/screenwriter Raymond Chandler: "No writer in any age ever got a blank check. He always had to accept some conditions imposed from without, respect certain taboos, try to please certain people. It might have been the church, or a rich patron, or a generally accepted standard of elegance, or the commercial wisdom of a publisher or an editor, or perhaps even a set of political theories. If he did not accept them, he revolted against them. In either case they conditioned his writing. No writer ever wrote exactly what he wanted to write, because there was never anything inside himself, anything purely individual that he did want to write. It's all reaction of one sort or another."

Thank God for television.

Mike Medavoy: "The audience certainly recognizes a second-rate product when it sees it. It ought to: it grew up watching second-rate stuff on television."

Don't become a complete cynic.

Have a touch of cynicism, but only a touch," wrote Raymond Chandler. "The complete cynic is as useless to Hollywood as he is to himself. He should be scrupulously honest about his work, but he should not expect scrupulous honesty in return. He won't get it."

Some people might begrudge you your success.

When he heard that *Time* magazine was thinking of putting producer Robert Evans on its cover, studio chief Frank Yablans said to Evans, "If you're on the cover of *Time* without me, I will make each hour of each day of each week that you're here so miserable you'll be sorry you're alive."

Help those who've helped you.

Two young guys wrote a script that was butchered by the director and the studio. The producer stuck up for the writers but couldn't protect them from the director and the studio.

The script that was butchered was called *Assassins,* starring Sylvester Stallone and Antonio Banderas. The screenwriters were Larry and Andy Wachowski. The producer was Joel Silver.

Because Joel Silver stuck up for them, Larry and Andy gave him their next script. It was called *The Matrix.*

P.S. *Assassins* was a disaster.

This can metaphorically happen to you.

At first I was shocked," Marilyn Monroe said. "I hadn't been around enough to know what was going on. He had a suit on, so I didn't think he could hurt me. When I started thinking about a new dress I wanted and couldn't afford, well . . . I was pretty drunk, too, so I said okay. I still wasn't sure what he wanted to do. He asked me to take off my clothes. I thought that was a pretty good deal for fifteen dollars."

PERK OF SUCCESS: YOU, TOO, CAN GET THE BEST TABLE AT SPAGO

I do, sometimes on only an hour's notice. And Wolfgang always comes over to my table and often he even sits down. Hallelujah!

We even had dinner together while vacationing in Hawaii. He even gave me career advice: "Don't ever turn your back on Michael Ovitz! He never forgets."

Wolfgang is a good guy. He has the same respect for screenwriters that he has for directors and movie stars—as long as they've all had some hit movies.

Leni Riefenstahl smiled in her grave.

The Writers Guild gave its Best Original Screenplay award to the liberal propagandist Michael Moore for his script of *Bowling for Columbine,* a documentary.

In other words, Moore didn't write it; he interviewed people and edited what *they* said into a political polemic.

Memo to Michael Moore.

Old Hollywood saying: "If you want to write a message, use Western Union."

Don't let anyone impugn your integrity . . . not even Farrah Fawcett.

In the book *American Rhapsody,* I wrote that Farrah Fawcett pooped on the front lawn at a party she was attending. In an interview with a New York gossip columnist, Farrah denied it. I wrote the gossip columnist a note:

"I sure don't see why she's denying it. In an interview in the September *Movieline* magazine she said, 'If I'm on location in the woods and my trailer is miles away, I will go to the bathroom in the bushes. There's no way my makeup lady would do that, for instance, but that's who I am.' Farrah clearly loves nature; she is, after all, a country girl from Texas.

"Let me say in defense of Farrah that we've all been in situations like that. It's tough when nature calls so rudely. As they say in Ohio, where I'm from, 'When you gotta go, you gotta go.' I remember nearly causing an international incident once—when I asked a limo to pull over between Tel Aviv and Jerusalem and took a hike into a field.

"Also, this party where nature called Farrah so rudely was held at the agent Arnold Rifkin's house. I was at a party on another occasion at that house and I remember my wife, who was very pregnant at the time, had to use the bathroom. But the bathroom was locked. Some sniffling people were having a lengthy Hollywood conference in there. So I certainly understand the same thing could have happened to Farrah. Some sniffling people may have been having a lengthy Hollywood conference in the bathroom and Farrah couldn't get in there and nature called."

A pratfall is better than a kiss.

If you want to write a hit movie . . .

Remember screenwriter Preston Sturges's (*The Power and the Glory, Strictly Dishonorable*) eleven rules for writing a hit movie:

1. A pretty girl is better than an ugly one.
2. A leg is better than an arm.
3. A bedroom is better than a living room.
4. An arrival is better than a departure.
5. A birth is better than a death.
6. A chase is better than a chat.

7. A dog is better than a landscape.

8. A kitten is better than a dog.

9. A baby is better than a kitten.

10. A kiss is better than a baby.

11. A pratfall is better than anything.

Don't write a script set in a jungle.

Actors will avoid your script. Actor Christopher Walken: "Just a month ago I shot in a place in Hawaii where they made *Jurassic Park*. I mean, I didn't know there was a place like that: it was so pristine. . . . But I'll tell you, I would have to really need money to do another jungle movie. I'm never going back to the jungle. It's a nightmare. Getting up at night and turning on the light in the bathroom? You see lots of, you know, scary things. I'm never going back."

They were honorable hookers.

During the blacklist, screenwriters like Dalton Trumbo sometimes wrote ten scripts a year under pseudonyms for relatively little amounts of money.

Because it was so difficult for them to get work, they did what Trumbo did. Trumbo agreed to rewrite and rewrite until the producer was "satisfied"—no matter how many drafts the producer wanted him to do and no matter *what* the producer wanted him to write.

Trumbo didn't care. He just wrote what he was told to write.

Since this became somewhat common practice during the blacklist, some producers ever since have expected "their writers" to write this way. If you're ever asked to do this, tell your producer you want to check it out with your lawyer.

You're a bust-out loser if you do this.

Dalton Trumbo: "In order to earn what I do earn I have felt compelled to make a policy of absolutely guaranteeing my work. Thus I may rewrite a script three or four times. Certainly it's not worth it for the one fee involved, but the man comes back if he gets this kind of service, and thus I am assured of a continuing income."

Those old lefty screenwriters really were hacks.

Screenwriter Dalton Trumbo: "I am obliged to warn you in advance that an original screenplay, designed for sale on the local market, involves a combination of prose and conviction and sentimentality that appalls even me, who am used to it, and would appall you even more. The only thing which makes it possible for a self-respecting writer to engage in such an enterprise is that the story is never published, and is read only by Hollywood."

Those old lefty screenwriters had some big balls, too.

Dalton Trumbo: "And so it chanced in Hollywood that each blacklisted writer, after swiftly describing that long parabola from the heart of the motion picture industry to a small house in a low-rent district, picked himself up, dusted his trousers, anointed his abrasions, looked around for a ream of clean white paper and something to deface it with, and began to write. Through secret channels, and by means so cunning that they may never be revealed, what we wrote was passed along until finally it appeared on a producer's desk, and the producer looked upon it and found it good, and moneys were paid, and the writer's children began contentedly to eat. Thus the black market."

Free at last, free at last.

Blacklisted screenwriter Dalton Trumbo, writing to a friend: "Perhaps I should not be as angry as I am against the weaklings, cravens, and liars who have succeeded in banning me from motion pictures. For I feel a sense of relief and a sense of buoyancy at no longer being an employee, at no longer being under the absolute necessity of earning, say, $75,000 a year. I'm sure I should never have had the courage—or perhaps one should say foolhardiness—to have left it voluntarily. My feeling now—as of today, that is, with the hope of succeeding elsewhere still strong in me—[is] that I shall never return to films, that if Metro asked me back tomorrow with all forgiven, I should refuse. Hunger, of course, could in time alter that decision. But for the present it stands."

There are no heroes.

Said agent Ingo Preminger: "Nobody used blacklisted writers for the sake of giving them a chance, or for being interested in justice—everybody—whether it was Kirk Douglas with *Spartacus* or my brother Otto with *Exodus*—they all did it for business reasons. These blacklisted writers were bargains. You go to a bargain sale and the blacklist was a bargain."

My friend Phillip Noyce is part of a vast Commie conspiracy.

When he read the script of his novel *Patriot Games*, author Tom Clancy faxed the producer, expressing his belief that "Hollywood was under siege from Communist infiltrators."

Said director Phillip Noyce: "As soon as Clancy read the script he sent us a massive fax accusing us of running some sort of Hollywood, left-wing, liberal fellow-traveling club."

If your film wins an Oscar, they'll probably "forget" to thank you.

On *Forrest Gump,* everyone involved with the film who went up onstage forgot to thank the man whose novel it was based on: Winston Groom.

And on *American Beauty,* the director and the star forgot to thank the man who wrote the original screenplay, Alan Ball.

An Oscar is a pain in the . . .

Steven Spielberg, his Oscar in hand: "You know what gets tired? You think it's your legs that'll get tired, but it's not. It's your arm. Your arm gets tired holding it."

Listen up, Michael Moore.

Paddy Chayefsky said this when accepting an Academy Award: "I would like to say, personal opinion, of course, that I'm sick and tired of people exploiting the Academy Awards for the propagation of their own personal propaganda. I would like to suggest to Miss Vanessa Redgrave that her winning an Academy Award is not a pivotal moment in history, does not require a proclamation, and a simple 'Thank you' would have sufficed."

If you're walking down a red carpet and the paparazzi are taking your picture.

Goldie Hawn: "Just turn your head and smile, but don't stop. Never stop."

At least your script can't get flashlighted.

Until a few years ago, at Academy screenings for best documentary, committee members voted with flashlights. If, at any given point, three-quarters of the flashlights in the room were on, the documentary was stopped and shitcanned.

Make sure you've really won the Oscar before you go up there to get it.

Will Rogers, host of the 1933 Academy Awards, announced best director by saying, "Come on up and get it, Frank!" Frank Capra got up and was on his way to the stage when he realized that the award was Frank Lloyd's.

Make 'em use their rubber bullets.

The Academy Award producers have a serious contingency plan in case someone flips out up there in front of 600 million people and won't stop talking.

They begin with blinding spotlights and end with rubber bullets—really.

His nomination got Trey Parker laid.

Screenwriter Trey Parker: "I was in a strip club in Vegas at four o'clock this morning. I was pretty fucked up, but I do remember looking at a stripper and yelling, 'Hey, you wanna go with me to the Academy Awards nominee lunch tomorrow?' And she looked down and yelled 'Sure!'"

If you desperately want an Oscar . . .

Three statuettes ripped off in the late 1990s were never recovered by police. They're out there somewhere—all you need are connections.

If you win an Oscar, display it proudly.

Screenwriter Ben Hecht used his as a doorstop in his home in Nyack, New York.

If you're not nominated for an Oscar . . .

Hungarian composer Béla Bartók said, "Competitions are for horses, not men."

I've never been nominated for an Oscar, but . . .

Jon Bon Jovi asked me to fly to Budapest, Hungary, with him and introduce the band onstage in the Hungarian language. And Sam Kinison dedicated a CD to me.

It's a bird, it's a plane, it's a screenplay!

At the sixty-sixth Academy Awards, a screenwriter hired an airplane that towed a banner behind it proclaiming WORLD'S FUNNIEST SCRIPT, along with a phone number.

It didn't do him any good. The script remains unsold.

PART THREE

GETTING READY TO WRITE THE SCRIPT

LESSON 7

Avoid the Woodpecker!

Inhale a writer you admire.

Knowing nothing about writing a play, Paddy Chayefsky taught himself playwriting by sitting down at the typewriter and copying Lillian Hellman's *The Children's Hour* word for word.

He said, "I studied every line of it and kept asking myself, Why did she write this particular line?"

WRITE WHAT YOU KNOW . . . *F.I.S.T.*

I grew up on the west side of Cleveland among working-class folks, many of whose parents were involved in the union struggles of the 1930s and 1940s.

The first script I wrote was called F.I.S.T. and was about a union's struggles in the thirties and forties.

Do your research . . .
BASIC INSTINCT

When I was a police reporter in Cleveland, I knew a cop who was also a television cameraman on his days off. He'd been involved in several police shootings. He craved action. He couldn't stand to be away from the scene, even on his days off, which is why he did the cameraman gig. He liked it too much. He got sucked too close to the flame. I remembered him twenty years later when I wrote the burned-out cop Nick Curran, who got sucked too close to the flame in Basic Instinct.

ALL HAIL
The Old Macho Bastard!

Selznick told Ernest Hemingway that, as an homage to him, he would give him fifty thousand dollars from the profits of *A Farewell to Arms,* even though that was not in the contract.

Hemingway wrote him a note back, telling him that since Selznick's forty-one-year-old wife was playing Hemingway's twenty-four-year-old Catherine Barkley, any profit on the movie was unlikely.

But if a miracle somehow occurred and the movie did go into profit, Hemingway told Selznick, he could change the fifty grand into nickels . . . and shove them up his ass . . . until they came out his ears.

High Concept

The best high-concept definition of a film I've ever heard is producer Robert Evans's description of his film *The Cotton Club*: "Gangsters, music, pussy."

Don't pitch a story; write it.

Don't sit there like Willy Loman with a roomful of imbeciles who see shoe salesmen pitching their wares all day. If you do this, you'll demean yourself and it will harm your creativity.

If you really believe in your story, believe in it enough not just to chatter about it but to sit down and *do the hard work and write it.*

It is the only honest way to sell a script. With a pitch, you're trying to convince the studio that you *will* write a good script. Instead, *just write the good script.*

If they buy it, chances are good that they will piss in it less . . . because it's all done and ready to be cast and produced.

And, too, if it's already written and ready to go, they will pay you more for it than as a "pitch"—especially if you can get other studios interested in buying it.

One of the reasons I've made so much money on my scripts through the course of my career is that most of my sales have been scripts I just sat down and wrote and then sold . . . instead of "pitching" them to the imbeciles.

Real writers sit down and write: wannabe writers sit around and talk.

In a town full of cons, writing a spec script is an act of integrity.

It's the honest way to go for both you and the studios you are trying to sell it to.

As a spec script, something that you have already written in toto for no compensation, it's right there in front of your potential buyers. You're not selling them a hustle: your promise in a pitch meeting that you'll write and your promise *how* you'll write it.

You're selling the thing itself—boom!—it's right there on the table, take it or leave it.

It's the most honest way for you to deal with *you,* too. You can sell it to a whole *bunch* of possible buyers in a script auction instead of the one or two you'd pitch it to. If you get two or more wannabe buyers bidding against each other, the sky is your limit.

I sold *Basic Instinct* for $3 million because every production entity in town except one was bidding on it.

The greatest fun in screenwriting is *not* getting paid a lot of money . . . and it's certainly no fun trying to hustle the Neanderthal who doesn't even read and barely watches movies into being impressed with your pitch; the great fun in screenwriting is writing your first draft without anyone else's ideas cluttering or polluting it. Just you and your muse and the empty page or blank screen. Creating. Playing God.

Why would you turn down being God for playing Willy Loman selling his shoes to an imbecile studio exec?

Pitching your script can hurt your writing.

Director David Lean: "These American screenwriters really frighten me. They talk so well and write so badly. I have now worked with five of them, and not one has come along with a big original idea. We *need* an original idea. Hence my fright."

There is no risk to writing a spec script.

Not selling it is not a risk.

I didn't sell several—*Magic Man, Blaze of Glory, Platinum*—but by writing each one I got better at writing scripts; I learned form and structure on each one. It was like going to school.

And even though no one bought those unsold-at auction scripts, a lot of people read them and admired them—which is how many years later I sold *Magic Man* (I retitled it *Telling Lies in America*). A producer who'd read it during the failed auction recommended it to a young director, who fell in love with it.

Ron Bass is Willy Loman.

Screenwriter Ron Bass (*Rain Man*): "I was sitting with David Madden [a studio executive] and I was pitching him. At the beginning, I used to have fifty different ideas, a carpetbag; I would go and I would pitch six or eight things at a time. I pitched him, over the course of a day, about six or seven ideas and two different main ideas. . . . I work in this very strange way where I book myself way, way, way ahead. I'm usually booked for two or three years in advance; that's the way I work. I have a lot of things going at the same time. I'm usually writing six or seven things at the same time, different drafts at different stages."

Here comes the woodpecker!

One studio exec gave writers three minutes to pitch their stories. He had an aluminum pole in his office with a woodpecker on top of it. When the writer began the pitch, the exec prodded the woodpecker and it made its way down the pole—hammering away loudly with its beak—as the writer chattered on about his idea. The woodpecker got to the bottom of the pole exactly three minutes later, when the writer had to finish his pitch.

You don't want to do your work at a urinal.

Ben Hecht walked into a restaurant rest room and found Sam Goldwyn standing at a urinal. Ben stood at the next urinal and pitched Sam a story. Goldwyn had prostate problems, so Ben had a long time to pitch. When Sam finally shook off, he told Ben he'd buy it for $125,000.

Don't become "a good meeting."

John Gregory Dunne: "Screeenwriters known in Hollywood as 'good meetings' are those with the gift of schmoozing an idea so successfully—as if getting that idea down on paper was only a matter of some incidental typing—that studio executives pressed development funds on them."

Don't listen to morons like this.

In his book *Screenwriting from the Heart: The Technique of the Character-Driven Screenplay* (the reading line of which describes it as "An Indispensable Guide to Developing Dramatic and Passionate Screenplays Based on Compelling Characters"), Professor James Ryan writes: "To begin a pitch you should first lure someone with a tease, such as 'Did you ever think what it must be like to have sex with someone in your office? It doesn't just happen in the Oval Office. Maybe your girlfriend has dumped you and you are hurt and vulnerable, or maybe you found out that your lover is two-timing you.' The pitch then continues to the story. . . . You may notice that I tied the tease to the current events of that time in the Oval Office. . . . However trite it may seem, it's good strategy. Giving a pitch . . . is about being simple and *shameless* in your effort to grab the listener's suggestion."

Always go to a pitch meeting with a witness.

Try to convince your agent or your agent's assistant to accompany you. If you can't convince them, go with a friend, whom you should call your "writing partner."

They will be less likely to rip you off if they know you had a witness in the room—and if they do rip you off, you can go to court with a chance to win.

Who is this goofball?

Professor James Ryan in *Screenwriting from the Heart*: "A producer asked me to take the concept of the film *The Man Who Came to Dinner* and change it into *The Woman Who Came to Dinner*. He had a producing deal with a well-known actress and thought this screenplay would provide an excellent vehicle for her talent. Written by the Epstein Brothers, *The Man Who Came to Dinner* was based on the Kaufman-Hart play about a pompous New York critic, Monty Wooley, who accidentally slips on ice, breaks his leg, and is forced to stay with a midwestern family during his recovery, driving them crazy with his arrogance and grandiosity. At the time we were pitching this project in Hollywood, *Jurassic Park* had just opened and everyone was taken with its blockbuster success. When we sat down to discuss the project with a studio executive, my producer introduced me in this way: 'James has a really great story to tell you. Just like *Jurassic Park,* this story is about a dinosaur that descends upon an unsuspecting midwestern town.'"

Take notes for yourself after a pitch meeting.

Describe what you pitched, what you said, and what those in the room said to you. Be very detailed about everyone who was in the room.

Then mail these notes to your lawyer, keeping, of course, a copy for yourself.

Bill Goldman and I agree on something.

William Goldman: "I have only tried one 'pitch' in my life and that was for friends, and I was so awful I quit halfway through."

Send those that you've pitched an e-mail.

The e-mail should begin by saying how much you enjoyed the meeting, and end by detailing everything that you said and that they said.

Yes, of course they will know why you sent the note, but it will make it less likely that they will steal your ideas.

Pukeheads

A studio exec's term for those screenwriters who are nervous doing a pitch.

WRITE WHAT YOU KNOW . . .
MUSIC BOX

As an immigrant kid in Cleveland, I played with kids whose fathers were raving anti-Semites and whom other Hungarians in Cleveland were calling "war criminals."

Many years later, I wrote a script called Music Box about a Hungarian-American lawyer who defends her father against criminal charges for activities back in Hungary during World War II.

DO YOUR RESEARCH . . . BASIC
INSTINCT

One night when I was a young man, I was with a girl I'd picked up at a go-go bar in Dayton, Ohio. She was one of the dancers.

We went to a hotel and, after what we'd done what we went there to do, she pulled a cute little .22-caliber revolver on me and asked if I had any real good reason why she shouldn't pull the trigger, considering the way her life was going and considering how used she felt at that moment.

She told me I wouldn't be the first guy she'd pulled the trigger on, and I believed her . . . and somehow talked her out of pulling it on me.

When I was writing Basic Instinct many years later in a little room of my house in San Rafael, California, I remembered the girl in that hotel room in Dayton, Ohio.

If you've pitched a story and they want you to give them an outline . . .

Fudge. I do this all the time. I explain in the first paragraph of the outline that it isn't an outline. It is a document containing "notes in the direction of a story."

This wording gives you a legalistic out in case your script doesn't reflect what is in the outline that isn't an outline.

Don't talk your story away.

Keep what you're writing to yourself. Don't expend the energy you'll need to write it by talking your story instead, telling friends in bars, restaurants, and beds what you're working on.

I've heard too many good stories from screenwriters who talked but never wrote them. I've come to the conclusion that your characters get angry at you if you speak about them . . . and stop you from giving birth to them on the page in revenge.

Remember: Real writers sit down and write; wannabe writers sit around and talk.

Screenwriter Robert Towne is famous in Hollywood for talking terrific scripts that never get written. Towne even had an agent once who heard so many brilliant and unwritten scripts from Towne that he started writing their plot summaries down. He proposed to Towne that they form a production company together and assign the unwritten Towne stories to other writers. Towne, horrified that his agent was taking notes about what he was telling him, fired the agent instead.

There is another reason not to tell anyone what you are writing. It isn't as likely that you'll be ripped off if you stay mum. Rip-offs are common in Hollywood; some of the town's most successful writers have plagiarized. A screenwriter won an Academy Award by ripping off a novel written by one of his college professors; the studio paid a hefty six-figure sum to settle the suit.

Write your script; don't schmooze your producer.

Producer David Geffen, discussing screenwriter Robert Towne: "Bob was a very talented writer, although an extraordinarily boring man. He always talked about himself. He used to go to Catalina to write and would describe to you in endless detail watching the cows shit."

She wouldn't have liked Bob Towne.

Hedy Lamarr: "In my experiences with writers, I found that those who talk less are more talented. I sat a whole evening with Otto Preminger and Tennessee Williams and Mr. Williams said just ten words."

It's okay to plagiarize yourself.

Ben Hecht based his 1958 film, *The Fiend Who Walked the West*, starring a young Robert Evans, on his 1947 hit film, *Kiss of Death*, starring Richard Widmark.

I based my 1983 film, *Flashdance*, on the Dutch film *Spetters*, directed by Paul Verhoeven. Then I based my 1995 film, *Showgirls*, directed by Paul Verhoeven, on *Flashdance*.

It might be fair then to say that my friend Paul Verhoeven was the creative spark behind both *Flashdance* and *Showgirls*. I'm certainly happy he didn't direct *Flashdance*, though, because he probably would have had an affair with Jennifer Beals, and Lord knows how *Flashdance* would have turned out.

You can rob yourself blind.

Raymond Chandler did it all the time, turning sketches into short stories, stories into novels, and novels into screenplays.

As he said, "I am the copyright owner. I can use my material in any way I see fit. There is no moral or ethical issue involved."

Chandler was once lambasted for plagiarizing himself—by a reader named E. Howard Hunt who, twenty years later, was one of the burglars involved in the Watergate break-in.

Hunt obviously didn't have any issues with someone stealing from *other* people.

Eugene O'Neill plagiarized Raymond Chandler . . . or did Raymond Chandler plagiarize Eugene O'Neill?

My ideas have been plagiarized," wrote Raymond Chandler. "Throughout the play *The Iceman Cometh* O'Neill uses the expression "The Big Sleep" as a synonym for death. He is apparently under the impression that this is a current underworld or half-

world usage, whereas it is a pure invention on my part. If I am remembered long enough, I shall probably be accused of stealing the
phrase from O'Neill, since he is a big shot."

I swear I wasn't influenced by reading Hungarian plays.
Orson Welles said, "Every Hungarian play is plagiarized from
another Hungarian play."

WRITE WHAT YOU KNOW . . .
TELLING LIES IN AMERICA

*I went to a Catholic high school in Cleveland, where I was the
victim of a great deal of prejudice because I was an immigrant
and because I was poor. I dreamed of overcoming all that
animosity and becoming an American writer one day.*

Thirty years later, I wrote Telling Lies in America, *the
story of a kid at a Catholic high school in Cleveland who is the
victim of a great deal of prejudice because he is an immigrant
and because he is poor. He dreams of overcoming the
marginalization and being a famous American writer
someday.*

DO YOUR RESEARCH . . .
FLASHDANCE

*I researched a script about pipeline welders for a script about
the Alaska pipeline. The script, called* Rowdy, *was never
made into a film.*

*Four years later, I used all the research I had done about
the pipeline for the young woman that I made a welder in*
Flashdance.

The most important part of what you write is what will be left out.

T he hell of good film writing," Raymond Chandler wrote, "is that the most important part is left out. It's left out because the camera and the actors can do it better and quicker, above all quicker. But it had to be there in the beginning."

WRITE WHAT YOU KNOW . . .
CHECKING OUT

In my midthirties, I suddenly began experiencing panic and anxiety attacks, during which I felt I was going to die. I wrote a script—Checking Out—about a man who begins having anxiety and panic attacks and is convinced he is going to die.

After I wrote the film, I stopped having the attacks. I had cured myself with my own writing.

When the movie failed both critically and commercially, I had a couple more attacks.

The "asshole guy" might read your script.

B y writing screenplays for Hollywood production, you are writing for studio executives who don't read anything, except maybe their readers' summaries about scripts.

Oh, they might skim through *Vanity Fair* to see the new chichi Prada and Dolce ads. But they don't read books or scripts. They are about as illiterate as most people who want to write scripts . . . as illiterate, maybe, as *you*.

Some go to the greatest lengths to avoid reading. I know a studio exec who gives the comedies his reader says he should read to his wife's gynecologist and the dramas to his own proctologist.

I know another illiterate exec who's made everyone believe that he's got dyslexia; consequently, he has his assistants tape a script (even then he will sometimes fast-forward through it).

The fact that most studio execs don't read books or even scripts isn't good news . . . if you want to write a literate and literary script that the critics would praise but no one would see.

If, however, you want to write a script of a movie that everyone would see, like *Basic Instinct* and *Jagged Edge* and *Flashdance*, then these semi-illiterate and illiterate studio execs might be your perfect first audience.

WRITE WHAT YOU FEAR . . .
BIG SHOTS

While I was having my panic attacks, I worried what would happen to my ten-year-old son, Steve, if I died. So I sat down and wrote a script called Big Shots, *which is about a ten-year-old boy who loves his father very much and whose father dies.*

When they were about to film the script, the producer met my son Steve and wanted to cast him in the film as the kid whose father dies. I stopped it because I was afraid that if Steve played the kid whose father died, then I might die.

When Steve graduated from high school, I gave him the Rolex Submariner that I always wore, and which was featured in the movie. It was the watch that the fictional kid always wanted and which he got after his father died.

I felt odd giving Steve the watch . . . since I was very much alive.

You'll probably be rewritten.

In some ways, this has always been the case in Hollywood. Witness what F. Scott Fitzgerald said during his Hollywood years: "If one writer on a picture is good, ten are ten times better."

I was very fortunate in this regard: Of my fifteen films, I had sole credit on nine.

Francis Ford Coppola caused the carpet bombing of Cambodia.

The night before American fighters carpet-bombed Cambodia, Richard Nixon watched *Patton* in the White House over and over again.

Paddy Chayefsky got Arnold elected.

Thanks to his line—"I'm mad as hell, and I'm not going to take this anymore!"—Arnold Schwarzenegger was elected governor of California.

James Cameron has blood on his hands, too.

Hasta la vista, baby!" Cameron wrote in *The Terminator*. It, too, became a slogan of Arnold's gubernatorial campaign.

WRITE WHAT YOU KNOW . . .
BETRAYED

I attended every one of my son Steve's Little League games and found racist and anti-Semitic epithets carved into some of the grandstands—in liberal Marin County, northern California.

I wrote a script about the rise of neo-Nazis in America, Betrayed.

It was filmed in Lethbridge, Canada, and one day during filming, missing Steve, I wandered down to a local field and watched some Little Leaguers play a game. And I noticed that the grandstand I was watching the game from had the same kind of anti-Semitic epithets on it that I had seen in Marin County.

Don't try to discover the hot new thing.

Mike Medavoy: "I'm always suspicious of the hot new thing. You can really get burned attempting to make films like the ones that worked last month or last year."

Write what your heart tells you to write.

It might lead you nowhere. I've always loved old-timey honky-tonk country music . . . Ernest Tubb and Hank and Ray Price and George Jones.

I decided one day that I was going to put my love of real country music up on the big screen. I wrote an old-timey country musical, called *The Honky-Tonk Opera,* which was more a stage musical than a movie. Once I had the script written, I didn't know what to do with it. For one thing, somebody would have to write the music—all I had were the words.

I sent the script to Tom Ross, who had been the head of CAA's music division. He loved it. He said he could envision stage versions of *Honky-Tonk* produced in places like Nashville, Vegas, and Houston after the movie's release.

Tom felt we needed "a country music partner," so we made a trip to Nashville, trying to convince country-music record executives Tony Brown, Joe Galante, and Mike Curb to come aboard as coproducers. Curb, the former lieutenant governor of California, went for it. He was a huge name in country music—among his artists at Curb Records were Tim McGraw, Faith Hill, and Jo Dee Messina.

With Ross and Curb attached to the project, my agents went out to sell the script. They got nowhere. Potential buyers didn't know what to do with it. Old-timey Hank Williams country music? Say what? A tear-jerking celebration of love and America? *Huh?* By the guy who wrote *Basic Instinct* and *Showgirls?* Oh boy. Where was the sex? (There was no sex.)

I went to David Geffen, who'd produced both films and plays, and asked him to read the script and tell me his opinion. He read it and told me that it was "unproducible."

I thanked him and put *The Honky-Tonk Opera* into a drawer. It's still there . . . where my heart had led me.

Only shitheads do shitwork.

Oscar-winning screenwriter Bill Goldman: "Screenwriting is shitwork. Brief example: *Waldo Pepper. Waldo* was basically an original screenplay of mine. I say 'basically' because the pulse of the movie came from George Hill, the director, and we worked for ten days on a story. . . . Okay, we open in New York and three daily papers are split—two terrific, one pan. In neither of the laudatory reviews was my name even mentioned. But you better believe I got top billing in the pan. I had screwed up George Hill's movie. Nothing unusual at all about that—it's SOP for the screenwriter. That is simply the way of the world. You do not, except in rare, rare exceptions, get critical recognition."

The moral of the story: Don't work with any director for ten days trying to come up with a story. Don't let the screenplay be "basically" yours. Make sure the "pulse" of the movie comes from you and not the directing.

If you do all those things, you won't be doing shitwork.

Do your research.

Ben Hecht: "The producer wanted my script to top all the other gangster pictures. So I had my secretary go out and see all the gangster pictures playing. She scouted up all the dead people in each picture. In one film nine people were bumped off, so I went to the producer and said, 'We're going to kill twenty-five people!'"

LESSON 8

Ideas Are Poison!

Go outside the box.

Screenwriter/director Jean-Luc Godard: "A film should have a beginning, a middle, and an end, but not necessarily in that order."

Violate everyone's privacy.

To write the way real people talk, *listen* to the way real people talk. Pretend you have a scanner in your head and, as people talk, imagine their words running across the screen, complete with punctuation marks, to "see" the words more clearly.

A friend of mine who is a screenwriter taped his own phone calls but felt after awhile that his conversations were becoming stilted because he knew he was taping them. So he put a tiny microphone into a flowerpot near a table at a bar and listened to the conversations at that table while he sat across the room with a tiny transmitter in his ear.

I have another friend, a phone repairman in L.A. He sits atop a telephone pole for hours every day listening to strangers' conversations. He wants to be a screenwriter.

PERK OF SUCCESS: YOU, TOO, CAN GET A FREE LEXUS

When I wrote An Alan Smithee Film: Burn Hollywood Burn, *I wrote several Toyota Land Cruisers into the script.*

I got a call from a Lexus representative, who told me that if I changed the Toyotas in the script into Lexuses, I'd get a free Lexus delivered to my house in Malibu.

In what was probably the most stupid move of my life, done for obviously perverse reasons, I turned my free Lexus down.

WRITE WHAT YOU KNOW . . . RELIABLE SOURCES

When I was a young newspaper reporter, I covered a hostage situation where a gunman was holding his ex-girlfriend hostage.

Twenty-five years later, I wrote the story as Reliable Sources *and sold the script to Paramount for $2 million.*

Don't write a Western.

The odds are overwhelming that it won't be made, and that if it is, it will fail. Almost every year or so, there is a failed attempt to do a Western—some, like Larry Kasdan's *Wyatt Earp,* have been especially good, but the public doesn't seem interested.

A producer said to me, "A Western in space, yes, a hip-hop Western, yes, but a Western with horses, absolutely not.

A Tender Love Story

That, according to director Jim Cameron, is what *The Terminator* was. Cameron used the very same words to describe *Titanic*.

"*The worst thing that could happen*" *is the worst thing you can do.*

A lot of screenwriters write scripts this way!

A man is happily married and has three beautiful children. What's the worst thing that could happen to him? His wife dies. Okay. *Now* what's the worst thing that could happen? His kids die, too. Okay. *Now* what's the worst thing that could happen? He falls in love with the wrong woman. *Now* what's the worst thing that could happen? She steals all of his money. *Now* what's the worst thing that could happen? He becomes a homeless person. *Now* what's the worst thing that could happen? He finds himself asleep at night atop his wife's grave. *Now* what? He gets pneumonia. *Now* what? He dies. *Now* what? The person who receives the kidney that he left to medical science rejects his kidney and dies, too.

And on and on and on.

Do not allow that sentence—What's the worst thing that could happen?—to enter your thoughts as you write.

No more Travis Bickle . . .

If you want to sell your script, give your main characters lots of friends, extended families to cheer him/her on.

Studios love this—studio execs feel that if an audience sees a lead character being cheered on-screen, then the audience will automatically like him.

Studio research on *Top Gun,* for example, discovered that audiences weren't cheering the movie at its end. The studio inserted a scene that had been shot earlier, which showed all the other pilots cheering on-screen at the end.

After that scene was inserted, audiences everywhere cheered the ending of the movie.

DO YOUR RESEARCH . . . AN ALAN SMITHEE FILM

A director came to have lunch with me at my home in Malibu. His name was Stuart Baird. He was formerly a film editor and he had just directed his first big action hit. He was a Brit who'd worked with Ken Russell and was dressed all in khaki. I liked him and we talked for hours.

A couple of weeks later, I sat down to write An Alan Smithee Film: Burn Hollywood Burn, *which is about a former film editor who directs his first film. My lead character, the director, Alan Smithee, is a Brit who has worked with Ken Russell and dresses in all khaki.*

When the film was released, Stuart Baird went to the producer and said, "That bloody Hungarian—he stole my whole life in one bloody lunch."

You're better off getting the rights.

My movie *F.I.S.T.* was about Jimmy Hoffa. But United Artists didn't have the rights to Hoffa's life and didn't want to pay to acquire the rights, either; so throughout the writing of the script, I had to be careful not to get too close to the details of Hoffa's life (even though I knew and the studio knew that I was writing about Hoffa).

It was a nightmare because I had to be as concerned about what the lawyers would think as what the director, producer, and studio executives would think.

Angie Dickinson inspired Basic Instinct, Sliver, Showgirls, and Jade.

I was staying overnight in a producer's guest house in Beverly Hills and dreamed all night about sex.

I don't dream often about sex, but on this night I kept having a vision of endless coupling with women whose faces I didn't recognize.

The dreams were only of the act itself—without tenderness or feeling—sporting, athletic, as though I were riding a mechanical bull.

I awoke worn-out, drenched in sweat, and with the kind of painful erection I'd had when I was thirteen years old.

The producer asked me how I'd slept, and I lied and said fine. Then he told me that his guest house had been the place where JFK trysted with Angie Dickinson when he came to town.

A couple weeks later, as I was waiting for a cab in the portico of the Beverly Wilshire Hotel, I watched as a little Mercedes convertible pulled up and a stunning older woman got out and walked toward me into the hotel.

As Angie Dickinson passed me, I couldn't help winking at her, and she gave me a knowing, dazzling smile.

Be nice to those you've wounded.

Don't try to take credit away from the first writer, who thought the basic concept up. After I rewrote *Flashdance,* there wasn't much left of Tom Hedley's original script except the title and the concept of a working-class girl wanting to be a ballet dancer.

It was enough, though.

In its arbitration, the Writers Guild ruled that the credit should be: Screenplay by Hedley and Eszterhas, story by Hedley.

While in my heart I felt that I should have had story credit along with him, I understood that without him, we would've had nothing. So, after the arbitration was announced, I called Tom Hedley and congratulated him.

ALL HAIL
Nunnally Johnson, Charles MacArthur, and Joel Sayre!

Told by Dave Chasen one night that his restaurant was about to close, the three screenwriters picked Chasen up, took him outside, came back in, and locked the door.

DO YOUR RESEARCH . . . AN
ALAN SMITHEE FILM

In my film An Alan Smithee Film: Burn Hollywood Burn, the lead character, Smithee, has two props that he carries throughout the film: his Dogon fighting stick and his Tibetan rock. They are his talismans, holy objects he carries for luck.

Stuart Baird didn't carry those things around, but I did. I keep those holy objects near me—even now, as I write this.

I made my holy objects famous! I put them up on the big screen!

You're not writing children's books.

Professor Andrew Horton, of Loyola University, in his book *Writing the Character-Centered Screenplay*: "Want to get a good feel for writing screenplays? . . . Check out an armful of children's books from the library. I'm serious. Comic books do much the same thing—after all, they're written in 'frames' with speech bubbles. But children's books have become incredibly inventive and VISUALLY IMAGINATIVE JOURNEYS for kids."

Avoid writing about living people.

In my Otis Redding script, *Blaze of Glory,* I wrote about Zelma, his wife, and his friend and manager, Phil Walden.

Zelma loved the script and her depiction and had no problems. Initially, neither did Phil Walden, who publicly said he loved the script.

But after a couple of weeks, he changed his mind. While both Phil and one of his brothers had managed Otis, in my script, for reasons of dramatic tension, I showed only Phil (no brother) representing Otis.

Understandably, Phil's brother didn't like being left out of the script, and Phil, no doubt not wanting to make his brother unhappy, turned against the script—one reason it hasn't been made in all these years.

Write what you know . . .
FLASHDANCE

When I was nineteen years old, I dated a twenty-four-year-old woman from the West Side of Cleveland who worked for Republic Steel as a welder. She'd once dreamed of being a ballet dancer and went to every ballet performance in the city.

Twenty years later, I wrote the story of the young woman who wants to be a ballet dancer and works as a welder—Alex, in Flashdance.

Expose all your family secrets.

You know all the family secrets—how Uncle John used to dress up as a woman on weekends and how one of his kids spotted him getting out of a car downtown; how Aunt Emily disappeared at the wedding reception for forty minutes with the best man.

Change all the names, of course, and if you sell your script and Uncle John sees himself on-screen, pretend that it has nothing at all to do with him. Chances are he won't confront you because *he won't want* the comparison to be made by anybody.

If someone in the family asks you how you came up with that particular story, just smile and say that your writing has nothing to do with you, that there's a twisted little person inside you who makes all this stuff up.

Your toys can inspire you.

An African Dogon hatchet that I bought at an antique fair became the murder weapon in *Jade.*

My favorite antique manual typewriter became the McGuffin in *Jagged Edge*—the clue that gives Jeff Bridges away as the murderer.

Compounded irony: I actually wrote the script of *Jagged Edge* on the very antique manual typewriter that was the McGuffin in the script.

If you're good in the sack, you can make 'em laugh.

Comedian Jay Leno: "No one thinks they're a bad lay. Everyone figures 'I may be fat and acne-riddled or stupid, but I know, in the sack, I'm the greatest thing in the world' . . . and it's the same thing with comedy. Telling someone they have no sense of humor is like telling someone they're bad at sex."

If you want to win an Oscar . . .

Paddy Chayefsky gave this advice to Gore Vidal: "If you want all the prizes, you gotta write shrill."

"He had a point," said Vidal.

Winner's Walk

The passageway at the Academy Awards between the stage and the press room—the route taken by all Oscar winners.

If you want to win an Oscar, fight the good fight.

A Holocaust-related film was, for many years, a good bet to be nominated for an Oscar; in later years, it was a film about civil rights and black empowerment.

Today's hot Oscar subjects are gay rights and gay empowerment.

An Oscar-winning producer said to me, "The Holocaust battle has been won. We're winning on women's empowerment, too. The best indication of that is the record number of copies sold of Hillary's book. The real door-to-door political street fighting is about gay rights and gay marriage now. Those are the movies the Academy wants to reward, and there are a lot of shrewd people in this town who always figure out what the Academy wants to reward, before they sit down and go to work."

POWs

Past Oscar winners.

If you write this script, you're probably a sure bet for an Oscar.

The script is about a saintly black man with a newly discovered mental illness who was abused by white foster parents as a child, and who has surgery now to become the woman he's always wanted to be, so she can help other black children abused by white foster parents.

In the first half of the movie, he's played by Denzel Washington. In the second half, the starring role is played by Halle Berry.

They both win Oscars—for Best Actor and Best Actress, respectively—as does Michael Moore for Best Director.

Trophy Girls

Bimbos who carry the statues at awards shows.

Or, if you want to win an Oscar, try writing about . . .

A saintly heroic woman, a saintly heroic gay man or woman, a saintly heroic black man or woman, a victimized woman, a gay man or woman, a black man or woman . . . *who frees him or her,* or *himself and herself* from *victimization* and *empowers* any of the above gender/color combos, as well as anyone with autism, Tourette's, or, best of all, a bizarre new neurological disorder that only Oliver Sachs knows about.

Don't write any John Wayne–type parts.

With the exception of Russell Crowe and Mel Gibson, there are few stars able to play supermacho parts today. Many of Hollywood's top male movie stars are either bisexual or gay. If they're not bisexual or gay, their feminine sides overpower their manhood. Look at how Orlando Bloom and Colin Farrell and Brad Pitt failed, respectively, in *Kingdom of Heaven, Alexander,* and *Troy.*

Are My Nipples Even?

The greatest concern of starlets who appear on awards shows.

Another surefire formula for a quick script sale . . .

Write a script about a young woman battling cancer, whose best friend is a gay man and who has an adopted black daughter and a mutant but cuddly and ugly dog.

If you want to sell your script, don't kill off your lead character.

John Wayne made over two hundred movies; he died in only eight of them, including his last one, *The Shootist.*

Sylvester Stallone had a full-scale hissy fit when my script of *F.I.S.T.* called for him to die. Studio lawyers had to force him to die.

If you write a real man's man . . .

Do to him what Jim Brooks did to the Jack Nicholson character in *As Good As It Gets.*

Turn him inside out. Show him to be the asshole that he is and, at the end, show him reborn as a touchy-feely man who has great disdain for the way he used to be—cure him of his psychic, spiritual cancer and show how happy he is to be healthily reborn.

Or do to him what Marty Brest did to the Ben Affleck character in *Gigli*: "It's turkeytime," and he gobble-gobbles and maybe he'll even stop calling that poor kid "a fucking retard," as he's done through the whole movie.

To simplify this: If you have an old-style man's man in the beginning of the movie, castrate him gradually in the second and third acts—and at the end, show how happy he is about his gelding.

Write strong and independent female characters.

Your women have to be smart, tough, streetwise, courageous, heroic, and good. They have to be smarter than their male costars and they have to have women friends they bond with. It helps if they have gay friends—male or female—and it's not even harmful to have *them* be subtly bisexual.

While they may kiss men on-screen and condescend to them and patronize them and make love to them (in darkly shot scenes), there should be something in their persona that says, *All men are assholes.*

If you're male and trying to write a female character . . .

Screenwriter/director Ron Shelton (*Bull Durham*): "Write a woman's character as a man, then change any specifics, and you'll find there're very few things you have to change."

Write a buddy movie about two women.

You'll sell the script, though the movie might fail.

Director/screenwriter Anthony Minghella, discussing *Cold Mountain*: "I wanted to make a movie about . . . the joy that occurs when men are away and women find each other and help each other. The relationship between Ruby and Ada, the wit of it, and the idea that there could be this exchange of gifts between people, that you could help somebody else and they could help you and you would grow with them and laugh at them and laugh with them. Such a relief not to have made a movie in which the two women are fighting over the same guy."

You can get away with trashing straight white males.

There is no male counterpart for the National Organization for Women (thankfully). There are no male lobbying or pressure groups. And, as a group, straight white males have been so beaten down by their wives and girlfriends (and by media coverage, especially TV ads) that many believe they really *are* and *have historically been* villains and/or assholes.

Redeeming Social Values

The values (liberal, progressive, or elitist—that's your choice) shared by most Hollywood studio heads, producers, directors, stars, screenwriters, and all those others who want to work in this town again.

Too Ethnic

A story that is too Jewish or too black.

I don't shoot my villains.

Screenwriter Herman Mankiewicz (*Citizen Kane*): "In a novel a hero can lay the girls and marry a virgin for a finish. In a movie this is not allowed. The hero, as well as the heroine, has to be a virgin. The villain can lay anybody he wants, have as much fun as he wants cheating and stealing, getting rich and whipping the servants. But you have to shoot him in the end."

Orson Welles agrees with me: He said, "Most heavies should be played for sympathy."

No Denzel in bed with Gwyneth . . .

After *Monster's Ball,* it's possible to get a movie made that includes torrid sex between a white man and a black woman—but the reverse won't fly.

Denzel Washington or Jamie Foxx in bed with Gwyneth Paltrow or Charlize Theron (or even the dark-hued Angelina Jolie)? Forget it.

Hollywood executives are secretly still afraid there would be riots, lynchings, and God knows what else in the streets.

Richard Pryor and Margot Kidder got it on in a movie called *Some Kind of Hero* many years ago; the footage was so hot that it can still be seen at certain producers' parties, along with Mickey Rourke and Carrie Otis in *Wild Orchid* and, for comic relief, Sharon Stone and Billy Baldwin in *Sliver.*

Don't be afraid to write sex scenes.

Nothing risqué, nothing gained," said Jayne Mansfield, sexy actress.

Showing a little flesh won't hurt your movie.

Actor James Coburn: "A little titty never hurt anyone."

Swimming pool scenes are fine.

Louis B. Mayer: "You'd be surprised how tits figure in a hit movie."

But write genteel sex scenes.

Consider Louis B. Mayer *leching* with Hedy Lamarr: "If you like to make love—fornicate—screw your leading man in the dressing room, that's your business. But in front of the camera, gentility. You hear? Gentility!"

"Side-Al" Nudity

The kind of nudity on-screen that is usually rated R but tries very, very hard to get a PG-13.

DO YOUR RESEARCH . . . JADE, BASIC INSTINCT, AN ALAN SMITHEE FILM

We had both come and we were smoking our obligatory cigarettes in a motel overlooking Venice Beach. A four-story mural of Morrison as the Lizard King was outside our window. Some guy down on the beach was playing his bongo drums.

I was with a producer's wife who had once wanted to be an actress. She had picked me out at a dinner party, asked for my phone number, called me, set up the date, and made the reservation at the motel under a false name.

I asked her why she was crying.

Because she came here often, she said, with guys like me.

Sometimes, she said, she cruised Pico or Ocean in her black Porsche and picked guys up, usually Latinos, right off the street and brought them here for the afternoon.

I laughed and told her not to worry about it. Vivien Leigh, I told her, used to drive to bars in Compton and pick guys up and do them in her Bentley. Clara Bow used to pick guys off the street in a red convertible roadster. Jean Harlow did cabdrivers while wearing a black wig.

"Guys cruise the streets all the time," I said to her. "What's the big deal? Women in Hollywood have always been more empowered than in other places."

> *She stopped crying and smiled at me. "You're really very sweet, aren't you?" she said, and we went back to doing what we'd been doing before.*
>
> *The guy on the beach was still bambing away at his bongos.*

They'll confuse you with Larry Flynt.

Director Milos Forman: "When the Nazis and Communists first came to Czechoslovakia, they declared war on pornographers and perverts. Everyone applauded: who wants perverts running through the streets? But then, suddenly, Jesus Christ was a pervert, Shakespeare was a pervert, Hemingway was a pervert. It always starts with pornographers to open the door a little, but then the door is opened wide for all kinds of persecution."

Cover your own ass.

Cover yourself. Before each sex scene write, "It is dark; you can't see clearly"—just in case the director wants to shoot your script as an NC-17 or "a deep R" . . . and blames you for pornography if the movie fails.

You're asking for trouble if you write a scene with male frontal nudity.

Director Jean-Jacques Annaud: "The penis is a terrible, terrible actor. It is an actor who overacts."

And stay away from that backdoor hanky-panky.

Louis B. Mayer: "A woman's ass is for her husband, not theater-goers."

You can be your own test market.

If you're writing a script with a sexual content and find yourself getting a hard-on or a wet-on, it's okay. If you're getting turned on, it's not unreasonable to suppose that the viewer of the film might be turned on, too.

If, however, this happens to you while you're writing something without *any* sexual contact, seek company . . . or the company of a shrink.

Don't write a script with a lot of sex.

You won't get it made. They don't make movies like *Midnight Cowboy* and *Clockwork Orange* anymore. *Eyes Wide Shut* and

Crash and *Henry and June* and *Tie Me Up! Tie Me Down!* and *Showgirls* all failed at the box office.

Showgirls (my film) was the greatest commercial and cinematic disaster since *Heaven's Gate* and *Ishtar*. It failed because of liberal political correctness and conservative fundamentalism and because it was a bad movie.

I deserve the credit for it: I almost single-handedly killed off the sexual-content movie in America.

Violence is still fine, though—the bloodier and the more sexless (witness Tarantino) the better.

But you can go absolutely apeshit on the violence.

Director Phillip Noyce, discussing *Sliver*: "The MPAA have a phobia about seeing people joined together in lovemaking. So they wanted us to cut down on the amount of material where Sharon and Billy seemed to be truly coupling. I would cut it and they would say, 'No, no, no still too much.' I would try cutting it again. 'No, no, no still too much'—and this went on endlessly. Yet in any film that I have made in the U.S., there has never been any discussion with censors about violence."

Try to write a French movie.

Ron Shelton: "The French can make comedies about someone sleeping with their cousin. If that happens in an American movie, somebody gets their heads blown off."

If you write a violent movie . . .

You'll need some very good reviews to give it some respectability. That way, audiences can feel they're buying a ticket not because they want to see bloody, gruesome violence but because they want to see artistic accomplishment.

This doesn't mean that even without good reviews your violent movie won't be a hit—witness *Jagged Edge* and *Basic Instinct*.

Don't write another Dirty Harry.

Novelist/screenwriter George Pelecanos (*King Suckerman, A Firing Offense*): "You could never make a picture like *Dirty Harry* today because it's about a cop who, you know, shoots unarmed people and steps on 'em when they're wounded and beats 'em up and so on. And on the page [the studio executives' notes] say: *'Well, I don't really like this guy'*—like everybody has to like the protagonist of these movies. I don't understand that. Is that person interesting or not? That's what matters."

Crash-and-Bash Pictures

You know what they are. Please don't write them. Please don't want to write them. Everybody is writing them. Be the exception.

Whiz-Bang

As in, "We need a little bit more whiz-bang in the opening sequence," meaning action, visual pyrotechnics, more smoke and wacko camera angles.

The Whammo Chart, aka the Eleven-Minute Commandment

A formula invented by producer Larry Gordon for action films. The chart calls for an action sequence every eleven minutes. Time Joel Silver films like *Die Hard, Lethal Weapon,* and *Predator* and you'll see how religiously Joel believes in Larry Gordon's eleven-minute commandment.

If you're bored with your mate, do lots of research.

Studio executives are suckers for authenticity. Interviewing people, they can understand; creative genius, they can't.

In the course of my unhappy first marriage, I did studio-expensed research in the following locations: the south of France, Israel, Zurich, London (four times), Paris (three times), Hawaii (five times), and Los Vegas, of course (which I researched *in depth* innumerable times, and ways, for *Showgirls*).

About sitting down and writing—it's okay to be scared.

Screenwriter and director Billy Wilder: "I was only nervous when confronted with an empty page. One with nothing on it."

Don't do an outline for yourself.

It will lock the characters in step too much and not give them enough room to plot the course of their own actions in the script.

Give them the freedom to tell you what it is they want to do or say.

Do a character sketch for yourself instead.

Spend a page on each character. His/her back story, background, physical descriptions, interests, relationships, dreams, failings.

Do it for all the major characters.

Study it for a week, reread it and think about it as much as you can, and revise it as the week goes along.

At the end of the week, do a final version of it, and start writing your script.

Keep your character sketches handy and reread them as you continue to write your script.

Before you write anything, think about designing a jacket for your script.

Lloyd Levin, who worked for studio head Larry Gordon at Fox, took him a novel called *Nothing Lasts Forever,* by Roderick Thorp.

Gordon took one look at the book's jacket and said to Levin, "I don't need to read it. Buy it."

Old Hungarian saying . . .

The moment you begin writing is the moment "the monkey jumps into the water."

Go jump already!

Don't play it safe.

Screenwriter Larry Gelbart (*Tootsie*): "In half a century, we've gone from *Citizen Kane* to candy cane. That's what comes from playing it safe."

Shut up, don't worry so damn much about it, sit down, and write.

Raymond Chandler: "Ideas are poison. The more you reason, the less you create."

This is the most fun you're going to have.

Ron Shelton: "The best part of screenwriting—you do it alone. The stuff that scares most people is why I love it: the blank page, and you're alone. There's no committee, there's no bureaucracy, you're the boss, you're the czar, you're *"everything."*

Go for it—get some boos.

Bob Dylan said, "If you haven't done anything, you've never been booed."

This is what you should do.

Screenwriter Dan Harris (*Imaginary Heroes*): "My script is my head vomited up on paper."

PART FOUR

WRITING THE SCRIPT

LESSON 9

Slit a Vein and Drip It on the Page!

Follow your bliss . . . or your body part.

I know it sounds like the worst New Age line you've ever heard (Joseph Campbell), but it's true. Write the story that's in your heart and gut and whatever other body parts you write from.

I've always been accused of writing from—Oh well, never mind. My wife, who loves me, says I'm a kinder and gentler Joe these days. *Ha!*

Buy yourself a good chair.

You can get them for sixty or seventy dollars at places like Office-Max. The less discomfort you have while you're writing, the more you can concentrate, and thus the better your script will be.

Don't sit there for hours.

Get up every hour or so and walk around for five or ten minutes. Otherwise, you'll ruin your back, your prostate, and possibly your relationship with your wife and kids. Say hi to them, give them a hug, drink some water, and go back to work.

You've got to forget about the money.

Writer/producer William Froug: "If you think about how much you can sell it for while you're writing it, you're lost."

Try to have fun writing your script.

Albert Einstein: "The highest level of creativity unfolds through play."

Keep some holy object near you as you write.

It has to have some relationship to what you're writing about: For my Otis Redding script, *Blaze of Glory,* it was a boyhood photo of Otis that his widow, Zelma, gave me; for *Basic Instinct,* it was a gleaming silver ice pick that I had found at a flea market; for *Music Box,* it was a photo of a group of Hungarian Jewish women being led by Hungarian gendarmes to a train.

Sometimes some unholy object will do, too.

For *Showgirls,* it was a pair of my wife's black lace panties.

Screenplays are a bitch to write.

One man wrote *War and Peace.* Thirty-five screenwriters wrote *The Flintstones.*

You don't have to love writing a script.

Screenwriter William Faulkner: "If I never do another one until I'm old and bent and grey, it will be too soon."

All you have to do is slit a vein and let it drip on the page.

Ron Shelton: "The hard part is getting from thinking about the script to the first page of writing. I might think about it for years. By the time I write page one, I like to have so much of it inside me it practically explodes onto the page."

Just write your first sentence.

Writing the first sentence," my writer friend Will Froug said, "is the toughest part of writing a script."

Don't be afraid to ask God to help you.

Ron Shelton: "For the first thirty-five years of your life you run from the Church, and somewhere in your thirties and forties you make peace with it and embrace it as a part of who you are, and thereby liberate yourself from it. I realized I could take from it those elements that comforted me and helped me to cope, and discard the rest."

Robert McKee says you have to defeat your fear.

McKee: "You have to think like an artist. If you know you're in over your head, and that doesn't intimidate you, you might just make it. The hard part is getting in the chair and writing. It takes tremendous willpower and discipline and the only way to defeat the fear is to gain the self-confidence that comes from knowing you've mastered the art form."

To Robert McKee: It's okay, Bob, I get scared, too.

Ian Parker in *The New Yorker:* "McKee motivates writers for a living, but he has not been able to get this book done. When I asked him why, he said, 'It's a good question. Why haven't I? Fear is part of it.'"

If you've written the first page, the rest is easy.

Now you know you can do it, because you've already done it once. All you have to do is do it about 110 more times. *But you've done it.* So what's the big deal?

Don't keep messing with the first scene.

Screenwriter Anna Hamilton Phelan (*Gorillas in the Mist*): "Don't go back and fix that first scene. Don't go back and fix that dialogue. Write yourself a little note saying 'Put in first scene such and such,' if you happen to think of something, then get a little stickum and stick that somewhere on the wall. But don't go back, because going back is a trap. It keeps you from going forward. It keeps you from going ahead. Your first enemy, of course, is yourself. Yourself is also that little critic that sits on your shoulder and says, *"This is terrible."*

Don't rush to finish your script.

Ben Hecht wrote *The Unholy Garden* in two days, dictating it to two secretaries. Sam Goldwyn congratulated Ben on his brilliant work. The script was shot without a word changed.

"It was one of the worst flops ever turned out by a studio," Ben said later.

Take your time writing your script.

I wrote *Basic Instinct* in a blind frenzy while listening almost nonstop to the Rolling Stones.

I didn't outline the script and I didn't know my ending until I was almost two-thirds finished.

It exploded out of my head—I kept hearing lines of dialogue and had to hurry to keep up with the voices I was hearing. I woke up at four in the morning and wrote lines of dialogue down.

I wrote it in two shifts each day—from nine in the morning till one in the afternoon and from three in the afternoon to eight o'clock at night.

From the time I began writing till the day my agent sold it at auction: thirteen days.

No Attachment to Outcome

This is *Gorillas in the Mist* screenwriter Anna Hamilton Phelan's phrase: "When I get bogged down I say 'No attachment to outcome.' Don't worry about what's going to happen to this. Just write the next word."

Shut the world down.

I have found that for me, the best time to write is from seven in the morning till one o'clock in the afternoon. I get up at six, shower, drink some carrot juice and tea, and am at my writing desk by seven. I don't take calls when I'm writing; my wife disturbs me only for emergencies.

I quit writing at one and have lunch with my wife. Sometimes I take a nap after lunch, but I'm back at my desk at three. Then I edit what I've written, sometimes rewrite it extensively, and make a note about scenes I'm going to write the next day.

I'm usually finished with that by five o'clock. I walk five miles then and spend the rest of the night with my family.

Put your laptop away.

I write my first drafts longhand. That's right—*longhand*, with a *pencil*. I feel it puts me more in touch with my characters.

I go to my laptop on my subsequent drafts.

That's a lie. I don't know how to *use* a laptop—I go to my manual Olivetti Lettera typewriter—but you can use *your* laptop while sipping a double latte at Starbucks. In my drinking days, *I* used to suck on a bottle of Jack Daniel's as I wrote—the only danger was that I sometimes couldn't read my own handwriting the next day.

Go sit in the tub.

Screenwriter Dalton Trumbo, revered as one of the legendary screenwriters of Old Hollywood, wrote most of his screenplays in the bathtub.

I've written a lot of scripts in the tub, too, but I'm Hungarian-born, and Hungary (a landlocked country) has more public baths than any other country in the world.

It also has the highest suicide rate in the world. That means that if your script is not going well, you can just slide down in the tub and . . .

If you're masturbating and writing a script, stop masturbating (but keep writing).

Screenwriter Dalton Trumbo: "It is then, while panic tightens my sagging throat, that I whisper to myself: It's true, after all. It *does* make you crazy. It *does* cause the brain to soften. Why, oh why did I like it so much? Why didn't I stop while I was still ahead of the game? Was it only one time too many that caused this rush of premature senility? Or a dozen times? Or a thousand? Ah, well—little good to know it now: the harm's done, the jig's up, you're thoroughly addled, better you'd been born with handless stumps."

Write six pages of script a day.

Stick to this schedule no matter what. You'll have a finished first draft in roughly twenty days.

Then go back and edit what you've written. Spend no more than five days on this edit.

Then rewrite your script from page one—with your edits. Spend no more than one week on this rewrite—that means twenty pages a day.

Put the script away for a week; don't even look at it.

Then edit it once again. Spend no more than four days on the edit this time.

Then rewrite it again from scratch with your edits—taking another week. This will be *your third draft.*

Now begin the process of trying to sell it—this, your official *first draft.*

At least write something every day.

John Lennon once said, "I haven't picked up a guitar in six years. I forget how heavy they are."

If you don't feel like writing today . . .

Comedian Rita Rudner: "People don't want to get up and drive a truck every day either, but they do—that's their job and this is my job."

Don't watch TV if you're writing.

Hunter S. Thompson: "No music and bad TV equals bad mood and no pages."

Don't watch any movies while you're writing.

You don't want to wind up "borrowing" from or paying "homage" to whatever it is you're seeing. There is a tendency while you're writing your script to feel lost and desperate, as in, Oh, Jesus God, I know this isn't "working." All you need is to watch some stupid movie that will give you a bad idea.

Keep your brain as inviolate and isolated as possible from *everything* while you're writing.

Music can help you.

As I said, when I wrote *Basic Instinct*, I played the Stones all the time, especially "Sympathy for the Devil," over and over again.

All the music in the film was supposed to be Stones music and "Sympathy for the Devil" was to play over the final credits.

The studio even bought the rights to "Sympathy" from the Stones for $750,000, but the director, Paul Verhoeven, changed his mind about using the song in the film, and the Stones were $750,000 richer.

Don't smoke while you write; if you smoke, stop!

Screenwriter Albert Maltz about his friend, screenwriter Dalton Trumbo: "He's a very feisty man, you know, a regular fighting cock. It's that damned cigarette smoking of his that put him in the shape he's in today. He just couldn't stop. He used to smoke the things one after another."

So did I. I smoked four packs a day and *always* chain-smoked when I was writing. I started smoking when I was twelve years old.

In 2001, when I was fifty-seven, I was diagnosed with cancer of the throat and 80 percent of my larynx was surgically removed.

I had a trache tube for months afterward and had difficulty breathing and swallowing.

I finally stopped smoking and have been smoke-free now for five years.

After I stopped smoking, I couldn't write for a year and a half. I can write now, finally, without missing the cigarettes.

Don't do what Dalton Trumbo and I did to ourselves; stop before it's too late.

Pay attention to every word.

Comedian Joe Bolster: "The difference between a laugh and no laugh is often a single syllable. You remember the 'Where's the beef' campaign? Initially, it was 'Where's *all* the beef?' But the director took out 'all' and without [him doing] that, it probably wouldn't have been as effective."

Keep a night-light, pen, and paper on your nightstand.

You never know when you'll wake up with a script thought in your head. That's how I came up with the ending of *Basic Instinct*.

I literally dreamed the final scene, with the ice pick under the bed. I woke up and jotted it down and used it when I wrote the ending.

Treat yourself well after a good day.

The novelist H. G. Wells told interviewers that after a good day's writing, he always celebrated by having sex.

Don't think you're better than your audience.

Ben Hecht did: "But among all my fantasies is none of writing and directing a movie that becomes the most famous movie of the week or even the month. I know why I don't have this fantasy. It is because my mind balks at the partner in this daydream—the audience. I have never fancied the pleasures that come from its applause and approval."

Write cinematically.

Raymond Chandler said to a friend, "I suppose you know the famous story of the writer who racked his brains [about] how to show, very shortly, that a middle-aged man and his wife were no longer in love with each other. Finally he licked it. The man and his wife got into an elevator and he kept his hat on. At the next stop a lady got into the elevator and he immediately removed his hat. That is proper film writing. Me, I'd have done a four-page scene about it."

Don't Mist the Orchids

Don't lay on the sentimentality too thickly.

"What's wrong with sentimentality?" a reporter once asked William Faulkner.

"People are afraid of it," he said.

Don't use voice-over unless you absolutely have to.

Most studio executives and directors view a voice-over as the kiss of death, to be used only if a movie's structure doesn't hang together.

If you hear a voice-over in a movie, it's a possible sign that the movie was, and/or still is, in great creative trouble.

HOW TO DEAL WITH WRITER'S BLOCK . . . THE HOTEL ROOM SOLUTION.

Screenwriter Jordan Roberts (Around the Bend): "I can only write in hotel surroundings. I like isolation, I like loneliness, and there's nothing lonelier than a hotel. When I'm lonely, I write more intimately. I need to be away from everything, including family and friends, so that I'm so desperate I will actually bother to write."

Each morning, reread what you wrote the day before.

Do this first thing in the morning, before you start writing for the day. Don't edit any of what you wrote the day before; just read it a couple of times to put yourself back into it.

As you approach the ending, reread the entire script each morning before you start writing. I find that doing this inevitably leads me to my ending.

Don't worry about writing too much in one day.

Ben Hecht sometimes wrote entire scripts in three or four days. I am not advocating that, but I have found that on occasion I've had banner writing days, where I've written twenty to thirty pages in a single day, barely able to keep up with my characters' voices.

Just go with it, keep going, and when you are finished—*only then*—see how much of it works.

But, whatever you do, keep to your minimum—*six pages every day.*

If you feel you're roaring along . . .

Don't take the weekends off. Just keep writing. Try to explain to your loved ones what is going on. But even if they don't understand—even if they're pissed off at you, ignore them: Keep writing.

If, on the other hand, you don't feel like you're roaring along, take the weekends off, spend time with your loved ones, and air your mind.

Don't write on speed or cocaine.

It will affect the rhythm of your scenes. You're too wired or too zippy on either drug to get your rhythms right. I know; I've been there.

Don't write on booze and cigarettes, either. I've been there, too. I used to love writing on black coffee, cognac, and endless cigarettes.

Since I like writing and always wrote a lot, I smoked lots and lots of cigarettes and drank lot and lots of cognac.

That's one big reason 80 percent of my larynx is gone and I hack for an hour each morning until I get the phlegm off of what's left of my throat.

Don't think about the budget.

In my experience, if you write something really good, they will somehow come up with the money to film it.

In other words, the budget shouldn't shape your script; your script should shape the budget.

Let only your imagination limit you.

Don't worry about how they will actually film something. With technical advances and computerization, *anything* can be filmed.

Don't write camera angles into your script.

And don't mention POV (point of view), either. Don't do *all* of the director's work for him. Let him earn his wage by doing *something*.

You don't have to be rooting for anyone in your script.

As much as some studio executives feel that it is, a script is not a football, baseball, or basketball game.

If the story is fascinating enough, if the world it depicts is seductive enough, if your characters are interesting and complex enough, you don't need someone to wave the pom-poms every time he or she speaks.

I point to *Basic Instinct* as my best example. Its two central characters were both flawed and gray. The movie was the number-one movie of its year and made nearly half a billion dollars.

If you tell me that the reason it made so much money was because of that split-second beaver, I will tell you that even Sharon, who puts a very high price indeed on her beaver, would argue with you.

Structure your individual scenes the way you structure your script.

A scene should have a beginning, a middle, and an end. The end of the scene should have the same kind of impact that the end of the script must have. So build your *scenes* to a climax.

How to deal with writer's block . . . the robert towne solution

If you can't write it, and if nothing works, do what Robert Towne does. He goes out to lunch with agents and producers and tells them the details of the story that he is blocked on. They beg him to write the story instead of telling it, and Bob goes home and doesn't write it; he abandons it. But at least he's impressed agents and producers, sellers and buyers, about how creative he is.

Each page of your script is a minute on screen.

But don't worry about this in your first draft. My first draft of *F.I.S.T.* was almost three hundred pages and I had a monologue that went on for seven pages—seven minutes.

Old rule: If it's there, you can always trim it. But if it's not there, you're in trouble.

Don't show the script to anyone as you write it.

Don't even tell anyone what you write each day. It is between you and your muse. Don't confuse your muse with anyone else at this point—your director, producer, agent, or significant other.

Only when you are finished with your script should you show it to anyone.

The easier your script reads, the better.

Most studio executives I've met think that if it takes them longer than forty-five minutes to read a script, then that script isn't very good.

Considering that most studio executives I've met are, charitably, slow readers—they don't *all* necessarily move their lips when they read—keep it simple, stupid . . . and readable.

A Good Set of Bones

A well-structured script with a strong "spine."

Don't lock yourself into your ending.

As you write, your ending will gradually become apparent to you . . . almost as though it were a ship coming out of the fog.

Keep it in mind, but don't let it block you from considering other endings—the ship coming out of the fog may be the wrong ship.

William Wyler agrees with me.

The director said, "A lot of people come to me with great openings. I don't want a great opening. I want a great ending, because with most stories you can't find a good ending."

Take George Foreman's literary advice.

The former heavyweight champ said, "So many people, especially young people, think that everything now is about digital and television, but nothing will ever surpass the written word. Character has to be written about. Writers used to give us character but now too many writers have abandoned character."

Take Mike Tyson's literary advice, too.

The people want to be lied to on a grand scale," said former heavyweight champ Tyson. "They want heroic characters. The people don't want to believe their idol is a freak; that he likes to get fellatio. They don't want to believe that he might want somebody to stick their finger up his butt."

Begin with your characters, not the plot.

Novelist Flannery O'Connor: "In most good stories, it is the character's personality that creates the action of the story. If you start with a real personality, a real character, then something is bound to happen."

The Core of the Character

What is it that makes your character tick?

You can't, of course, put it that simply when you are asked this question—What is the core of the character—by the producer, director, studio execs, and actors.

Be prepared to make up a whole bunch of fancy-sounding Freudian, Jungian, Shakespearean, Homeric *bullshit* about what makes your character tick.

If you have problems with your plot, you're not alone.

Oscar winner Alvin Sargent (*The Way We Were*): "When I die, I'm going to have written on my tombstone, 'Finally, a plot.'"

HOW TO DEAL WITH WRITER'S BLOCK . . . THE PAIN IN THE ASS SOLUTION.

This has always worked for me: Let's say I'm on page fifty-seven when I'm blocked. I go back to page one and retype the whole thing.

Through the process of retyping all the scenes, I have always found where I went wrong—and why, feeling that I went wrong, I shut down.

I have found that actual scene or sequence and, by rewriting it as I retype it, I have unblocked myself.

I know it's a terrific pain in the ass to go back to page one and retype the whole damn thing, but it's always worth it.

Character is everything.

Novelist/screenwriter Larry McMurtry: "Movies have largely lost interest in character. It is not without significance that two of the most publicized characters in the cinema have been a shark and a mechanical ape."

Listen to the voices of your characters.

Screenwriter William Faulkner: "I listen to the voices, and when I put down what the voices say, it's right. Sometimes I don't like what they say, but I don't change it."

Let your characters live.

Have a rough idea of where you're going with your story but not too clear an idea. Let your characters talk to you and determine their own way—within boundaries that are not clearly marked.

You'll know you're doing well when your characters start taking over and are nearly giving you dictation, which sometimes comes so quickly that it's tough to keep up with; when your characters are literally talking to you; when words and images are coursing through your brain (without drugs) at a meth-fueled pace.

Deliver the Moment

Realize your story; empower your characters to live up there on-screen.

Write human beings, not scenes.

Novelist Eudora Welty: "The frame through which I viewed the world changed, too, with time. Greater than scene, I came to see, is situation. Greater than situation is implication. Greater than all of these is a single, entire human being, who will never be confined in any frame."

Don't "nice" your script up.

Don't purposely set out to make your characters more likable and sympathetic so your box office will be bigger. Audiences aren't stupid and will smell the bullshit as it's being heaped on them from the screen.

Let your characters be themselves; don't make them share your opinions and convictions.

Screenwriter William Faulkner kept using the phrase "A character of mine once said" throughout his life.

Don't burden your lead character with too much back story.

The only time you need any back story at all is if the back story is relevant to the plot. This usually happens only in a thriller.

Otherwise, the personae of your lead actors is, in a sense, all the back story you'll need. It is part of what actors are paid for: They superimpose the public's perception of their personalities onto that of your characters.

The word *perception* is key here. For example, it doesn't matter if your male romantic lead is gay in real life and favors rough sex . . . as long as the public perception of him is that of a nice-guy heterosexual Romeo. It is also true that in Hollywood some of the gay romantic leading men who like rough sex are married and have kids (to make sure that the public perception of their images is a positive one).

Take your time revealing your main character.

Mystery goes a long way—don't tell me everything I need to know about him/her in the first ten minutes unless you're writing some real simpleminded television script.

Keep surprising me with little character twists all the way to the third act; unless you're going for a great big cathartic twist at the end of the movie, your main character should be completely defined by the beginning of the third act.

A Built-in Sphincter

A character who brings comic relief to a drama. My character Sam Ransom (Robert Loggia) in *Jagged Edge* was a built-in sphincter; he played it well.

A Black Shirt

A major character that you know will die.

Don't write a "leggy" script.

Even though character-driven scenes will be the first ones to be edited for time and budget reasons, these are the scenes that will give depth to your script. Give it some heart; otherwise, as they say, your script will be "all legs"—all plot, racing from one point to another.

The Meat of the Thing

The climactic moments that lead up to the moment of catharsis.

Don't show your characters smoking in your script.

For many years, because I smoked four packs of cigarettes a day, because I thought smoking was cool, and because I resented what I deemed to be politically correct assaults on my smoking, I showed my characters smoking in my scripts.

I didn't care if I was glamorizing smoking or causing young people to start smoking.

Then I got throat cancer. I consider my cancer my personal punishment for glamorizing smoking on-screen.

Don't bring the same karma upon yourself that I brought upon myself.

Let's repeat that.

Kirk Douglas: "Hollywood started me smoking, literally putting a cigarette in my hand. Who knows how many moviegoers have started smoking because of what they have seen on the screen? Too many movies glorify young people smoking. It doesn't have to be this way."

Conflict means spinal fusion.

The most important component of the spine of your script is conflict, and the dramatic tension that flows from it.

Without the introduction of conflict, you can't hold your audience; they'll get restless and leave what you've put your heart and soul into, going for the urinal or the candy counter instead.

Conflict doesn't have to be physical, of course; it can be cerebral, understated, and subtle. But it has to be there.

You can combine conflict with attraction and create a spicy and often sexy stew that will both hold and amuse your audience. I did that in *Betrayed, Jagged Edge,* and *Basic Instinct.* There was conflict between Tom Berenger and Debra Winger, between Jeff Bridges and Glenn Close and between Michael Douglas and Sharon Stone. But, as in real life, the conflict led to attraction, or attraction was part of the conflict.

The most hard-hitting of all conflicts is when the heart is in conflict with itself, when the heart is torn. In *Betrayed,* Debra falls in love with Tom even as she knows that he is a neo-Nazi murderer. When she kills him, she blasts away a part of her own heart. In *Jagged Edge,* Glenn falls in love with Jeff, saves him through her own skills and strength gained in prison, and then discovers that he is a murderer and that he's been using her all along. And in *Music Box,* we see the deadliest conflict of the heart: A woman who adores her immigrant father winds up protecting her son from being poisoned by her father's cruelty and racism.

When my friend Richard Marquand was shooting *Hearts of Fire,* he called me from the set one day to tell me that Bob Dylan and Rupert Everett, who played rockers vying for the same young woman, were getting along so well as actors that it was impossible to bring out the underlying conflict their characters were supposed to have between them on-screen.

Richard said, "I've decided just to let their characters be friends."

I said, "You can't do that. If there's no conflict between them, there's no triangle. If there's no triangle, the movie isn't about anything."

"I'm not disagreeing with you," Richard said. "But there's nothing I can do about it. Bob and Rupert like hanging out, and every time Rupert looks at Bob, Rupert says, Bob makes him laugh. And neither of them really want Fiona. Rupert, as you know, is gay, and Bob says he doesn't want to kiss Fiona."

I said, "He won't kiss Fiona? Why the hell not?" I'd had a long afternoon in New York getting to know Fiona—we'd begun with two bottles of Cristal at Tavern on the Green—and I thought her eminently kissable.

"I'm not certain," Richard said. "I think it has something to do with his newfound Christianity. He says he doesn't want to be seen kissing anyone on the big screen."

I realized we had a love triangle where the two guys didn't want the girl for different reasons and liked each other more than they liked the girl.

I feared the movie was dead. And it was. When it was released after Richard's death, there was no underlying tension to it, no conflict—just an actor and two tired rockers making tired, friendly, "Have a nice day" faces at everybody.

Categorical Imperative

The underlying thrust of your script—the motivation that gives it
power, that makes your hero go the extra mile to achieve what he wants.

Tone is everything.

The tone of your script is even more important than the structure of it. It is the key to your script's success. If your tone is
off, the movie will not work.

No matter how good the structure is and no matter how sharp the dialogue,
your script is hostage to its tone.

In my experience, hitting exactly the right tone comes with rewriting and
polishing. It is like selecting the right volume on a stereo or like the volume of
an actor's performance: If it's even slightly off, it's all over.

A Built-in Spine

What the movie is about—the drama at its core.

Slug it out with your second act.

The second act is the most difficult to write because the first and
third acts have built-in, surefire dramatic potential.

But in the second, you have to move your story and your characters along as
speedily as possible.

The director of *Jagged Edge* (Richard Marquand) and I kept taking the film
out to preview audiences and getting dismal responses. But when we cut eight
minutes from the film's second act, audiences erupted at the end of the movie
with applause.

Adrenalizer Scene

If things are slowing down, you inject one of these into the spine of the script.

Don't worry about first- or second-act curtains.
You don't need them. Just follow a general three-act format, but you don't have to pay off each act by giving it an ending. Your need is for one ending and one ending only—at the end of the film (the end of the third act).

Does Your Story Hang?

Does your story climax? Is it well-structured?

Don't be afraid of ambiguity.
The ambiguous ending of *Bridge on the River Kwai* was thanks to producer Sam Spiegel, who believed "that the audience should make their own choice."

Producer David Selznick believed in ambiguous endings, too: "Let the audience write their own ending."

Ambiguity can make you a lot of money, too.
Surveys after the success of *Basic Instinct* showed that many people were going back to see the movie twice, or even three times, because they were involved in arguments with others about who the killer was.

I was asked over and over again about the ending of the movie by people who recognized me.

"Catherine did it, right?"

Or: "She didn't really kill anybody, did she?"

My answer to every one was this: "Go back and see the movie again. Pay close attention; there's a clue near the end that will answer everything for you. If you still don't get it, see it again."

Needless to say, I had significant "points" in the movie. And made more money every time someone bought a ticket.

But if you want to sell your script, an ambiguous ending can be risky.

Michael Douglas had a full-rupture hissy fit over the ending of *Basic Instinct*. He wanted to blow Sharon Stone away at the end. He said the film "lacked redemption" and would fail at the box office.

The studio didn't like the script's ambiguous ending, either, and the only reason it stood is because the director, Paul Verhoeven, wouldn't allow the film to be focus-grouped. The focus group would certainly have voted down the ambiguous ending.

If you're writing a mystery, let it be a mystery to you, too.

I think the true test of a successful mystery, one that will fool audiences, is to be able to switch the last scene and still have the movie make complete sense.

Take the last scene of *Basic Instinct*. It would have made sense if Nick had killed Catherine, and it would have made sense if Catherine had killed Nick. But the ambiguous ending—the ice pick under the bed—was the most surprising.

The same thing is true with *Jagged Edge*. It would have made sense if the tennis pro had been revealed as the killer at the end instead of Jeff Bridges, but it wouldn't have been as daring. Partly because Jeff Bridges was the perfect casting for a killer—until *Jagged Edge*, he had always played some variation of the homespun, down-to-earth good ole boy.

It's okay to leave audiences confused at the end of your movie if you're writing a mystery.

If they're somewhat confused, they'll talk about your movie with others—and they'll argue about what happened at the end.

In the case of *Basic Instinct*, they argued about what the ice pick under that bed meant. Did it mean that she'd kill Michael? Or did it mean that she wouldn't use that ice pick on him because she loved him.

With *Jagged Edge*, as Siskel and Ebert discovered, people weren't sure *who* that was on the floor when the mask came off. Was it the tennis pro (played by actor Marshall Colt), or was it Jeff Bridges? So a lot of people went back to see it again—and the movie made a lot of money.

If you leave them confused, though, make sure they *like* the movie. Because if they don't like it, they'll never go back to see it again and they'll trash it to their friends.

My feeling is that people like to be fooled by a mystery's ending—to be taken in some direction they never expected—but a lot of studio executives would disagree with me. Their feeling is that a movie (even a tough mystery) needs a soothing last scene, one that will make people leave the theater happy—the classic television ending.

I point to box office. *Jagged Edge* and *Basic Instinct* both had surprise endings that faked audiences out. Both were huge hits.

Spell it all out in your script.

Leave as little as possible for the director to screw up. View what you're writing not as a blueprint for a film, but as literature. Lie to yourself—tell yourself that not only may millions of people see your movie but millions may read this script that you're writing.

So it has to be . . . perfect!

You can subvert your future director with beats and adverbs.

When you write a scene, control how the scene is paced by indicating "beats"—screen moments. If you indicate in the script when a character is to deliver a line of dialogue (after two beats, say) and then the actor is exposed to your description in the script, he will be influenced by your vision (no matter what the director tells him).

And if you describe how your character is to say a line (sweetly, with an edge, with a grin, etc.) and the actor reads your description, it will affect his performance.

Through the course of fifteen films, I had only one director who caught on to my game and stripped the script of beats and adverbs before he gave it to actors: Costa-Gavras.

"Why?" Costa said. A long beat . . . and then (sweetly): "Because I am the director and not you, okay?"

Use your iron.

Screenwriter/director Paul Thomas Anderson (*Boogie Nights*): "Screenwriting is like ironing. You move forward a little bit and go back and smooth things out."

Try not to masturbate too much while you're writing your script.

In a survey done a decade ago, it was determined that writers masturbate more than people in any other profession.

If you do, you'll go blind and grow hair on your palms and . . .

You will take that creative edge that should be going into your script and put it into your hand, so to speak.

How to deal with writer's block . . . the lamborghini solution

If you live in L.A.—which I told you not to—go over to Budget in Beverly Hills and rent a Lamborghini for the weekend. Drive it out to Joshua Tree National Monument and then back. Tell yourself that if you finish your script and it's a hit movie, you'll be able to buy yourself one of these babies.

You'll finish the script (I promise).

More is more.

On the first draft of an original screenplay, don't make it too tight and lean. Don't worry if it's around 140 pages; producers and studio people have a theory that anything can be cut down. But if it comes in at around one hundred pages, many of them will ask, "Where's the beef?"

Screenwriter Michael Tolkin (*The Player*): "The director is someone who can take all the intentions and make sense of them for the reality of a production. All scripts are too long, all written scenes are too long, all dialogue is too wordy; this is the inevitable dividend of being written in a room, usually alone."

If you write a script that's too long.

Cheat on the margins. Extend and lengthen the margins on your page. Chances are good that the person timing your script (a minute a page is the rule) won't notice what you've done.

The downside is what happened to me on *Betrayed*. My script was about thirteen pages too long, but it read great. I didn't want to ruin how it read by cutting it down. So I extended the margins on both sides and at the bottom, too.

Halfway through the shoot, I got a call from the producer, Irwin Winkler, telling me that half the script had been shot and that at this rate it would be a three-hour movie.

I had to fly to the *Betrayed* set in Canada and cut my script—cut from the parts that *had not yet been shot*.

Cutting that way, I'm sure, threw the whole movie out of whack. It's not impossible that extending my margins ruined the fundamental structure of the movie.

But, as I said, the script read beautifully. It was passed around town and admired, and when the movie failed, there were those who said they're read the script and it was brilliant and that obviously Costa-Gavras, the director, had ruined it.

Tighten your script as much as you can.

Poor you. As studio head Arthur Krim said, "There's always going to be another turn of the screwdriver."

If your script reads beautifully, rewrite it.

A good script is about character and action, not language. If the language is literary and gets in the way of dialogue and action, it should be a short story or a novella, not a screenplay. In a script, the simpler the better.

It's okay to repeat yourself in a script.

An old studio rule: Never use anything once that you can use twice.

Pick your characters' names for how they sound.

For *Basic Instinct,* I named my burned-out, streetwise homicide detective Nick Curran because I thought the name made the character sound cool and tough. Catherine Tramell, I thought, sounded classy and vaguely threatening.

Sharon Shone thought I'd named her after a tramell, "a death shroud in Scottish mythology," and complimented me for my subtlety. I shouldn't have corrected her, but, being Hungarian, I couldn't help myself. She didn't believe that I'd named her after Alan Tramell of the Detroit Tigers, one of my favorite baseball players.

The truth is that I've named a lot of my characters after ballplayers; I keep the *Baseball Encyclopedia* near my desk.

I also tend to use first names that are classic and old-timey; I think there are way too many Brets and Austins and Dylans (even Jaggers) on the big screen. A Jack, I think, is ageless; a Dylan, I fear, might be out of style in a few years, replaced by an Eminem or an Usher.

Don't name your characters for personal reasons; it never works out well.

I gave a villain in *F.I.S.T.* the first and last names of an editor I had clashed with at the Cleveland *Plain Dealer* in my reporting days: Tom Vail.

I gloried in the notion that this person who had fired me from the paper would recognize himself on the big screen as a bad guy.

At the time, I didn't know that studios vet with a research firm all the names in scripts they are filming.

In this case, the firm's report came back with this notation: "Tom Vail was once Mr. Eszterhas's editor at the Cleveland *Plain Dealer* and fired him."

Don't ever name a character after the man or woman you love.

I learned the lesson painfully: Nomi Malone of *Showgirls* was named after my beloved wife's childhood nickname, Nomi—the name I called her in intimate moments.

Not anymore. Not after a stark-naked Elizabeth Berkley came up to her on the set and said, "Hi Nomi, I'm Nomi." Not after *Showgirls* turned into one of the great bombs of film history.

Some names can get you big laughs.

Every time this TV newsman introduced himself in *Jagged Edge,* we got big laughs from preview audiences. We couldn't figure it out until I changed the guy's name.

His new name was Tom—no laughs. His old name was Dick—big laughs. A producer friend told me that the name Peter on-screen always gets the same reaction.

Sometimes you can have a little fun with your names.

New York Times film critic Janet Maslin was always more than a little hard on my movies, once even calling me "the Andrew Dice Clay of screenwriters."

When I wrote *An Alan Smithee Film: Burn Hollywood Burn,* I created a fictional character named Janet Maslin, a critic and desperate wannabe screenwriter who hated the work of the fictional character Joe Eszterhas.

The studio's lawyers made me change the name of the fictional character Janet Maslin, first to Sheila Maslin and then to Sheila Kaslin.

I made sure, though, that the director, Arthur Hiller, cast an aesthetically challenged woman as the fictional Sheila Kaslin.

You can get a LITTLE cute naming your characters.

In the movie *Sliver,* one of the characters is talking on the phone to her agent. She says, "You're a sleazeball, Michael. You're a bully. You're two-faced, Michael. You're a sad excuse, Michael, for a human being."

You'll notice the constant reiteration of the name Michael.

I had very publicly fired my agent, Michael Ovitz, four years earlier.

How to deal with writer's block . . . the Viagra solution

A screenwriter I absolutely, categorically won't name told me this story. He was blocked writing a script and he took Viagra. He figured if Viagra helped one thing, it might help another. He was still blocked, though, after he took the Viagra.

But now he was blocked and had a big hard-on. He called his girlfriend and said he was on his way over to see her. They got into an argument when he got there and he stormed out and went home, where he sat down and tried to write. He was still blocked.

But now, his hard-on was making him so uncomfortable that he couldn't even sit at his desk anymore. He lay down in bed and tried to figure out how to get himself unblocked. After awhile, he found himself unblocked with one thing but not with the other.

Don't try to write classic lines of dialogue.

If you write them, you'll write them accidentally, not purposely. They'll pop out of the material.

I've written two famous, or infamous, lines through the course of fifteen scripts.

Flashdance: "When you give up your dream, you die."

Showgirls: "How does it feel not to have anyone comin' on you anymore?"

Twenty years after I wrote that line (the former, not the latter), my parish priest told me it had been the inspiration of his life.

Take it from zsa zsa

At all costs, don't write lines like this.

Actress and famed Hungarian femme fatale Zsa Zsa Gabor: "I adore George [Sanders] in that movie because he was so rude with women, saying the words of Somerset Maugham, like: 'All women are like little beasts. You have to beat them and that's when they love you.' "

No one can predict what will become a classic line of dialogue.

The studio felt strongly that the last line of *Jagged Edge* would be an oft-repeated one.

After a bloody, nerve-racking battle between a masked Jeff Bridges and Glenn Close, private eye Robert Loggia looks at Jeff's body on the floor and says, "Fuck him. He was trash."

Nobody remembered or repeated the line. Some people, focus groups showed, didn't even hear it.

A Three Beat

Three lines of dialogue—the last line (the three beat) pays the first line off.

Read your dialogue aloud to yourself.

When you think you are finished writing your script, organize a reading with your significant other and your friends. The more you *hear* the words you've written, the more you'll want to polish the words to get them just right.

Play your dialogue back to yourself on tape.

I'm convinced that the really smart wannabe screenwriters driving aimlessly around the 405 or the 10 in L.A. aren't doing it because they read *Play It As It Lays*.

They're doing it because they're listening to tapes of themselves reading their screenplays.

You're better than a tape recorder.

Paddy Chayefsky: "I'd like to find a tape recorder as clever as I am in dialogue. The whole labor of writing is to make it look like it just came off the top of your head."

If you can come up with a good title, you're halfway there.

To boffo box-office heaven, that is, although the road to a good title, even a bad title, can be a circuitous, even byzantine one. Consider the following.

While everyone involved with the production agreed that *F.I.S.T.* was a great title, it didn't matter. The movie itself didn't work and *F.I.S.T.* tanked.

Flashdance was a great title. Indeed, while most of his script was gone in my rewrite, Tom Hedley, the original screenwriter, had come up with that great title.

Jagged Edge was a great title, but it wasn't mine. My title for the movie was *Hearts of Fire*—a crazily misfired title for this tough courtroom drama. The title *Jagged Edge* was the brainchild of a studio assistant who pored through every word of my script and found the description "knife with a jagged edge" for the murder weapon.

I used *Hearts of Fire* again years later for a rock-and-roll movie with Bob Dylan and Rupert Everett. It didn't work for *that* movie, either. Nobody saw it. The movie was so bad that it literally *killed* the director, my friend Richard Marquand.

My favorite title was *Telling Lies in America*, an offbeat piece about a young Hungarian man who wants to be a writer. The original title was *Magic Man,* and I changed the title so that studio execs reading *Telling Lies in America* wouldn't know it was the same script they'd read ten years ago.

The only way to outwit their computers and avoid old readers' reports was to change the title. I was pulling a scam, and the scam gave me the best title I'd ever come up with.

What do you expect from a young man who wound up making millions for the made-up stories—the *lies*—that he told to the world?

My worst title was probably *An Alan Smithee Film: Burn Hollywood Burn.* Too clumsy, too gawky, too geeky. I like the movie (I'm one of the few), but I hate the title.

That was God speaking to me.

My script entitled *Love Hurts* was in its brown envelope and I was almost out of the house on my way to Federal Express to send it to my agent, when I suddenly thought of another title for it: *Basic Instinct.*

I ran back inside the house, unsealed the envelope, and typed up a new cover page.

Did you see Anhedonia?

Woody Allen wanted the title of *Annie Hall* to be *Anhedonia* ("the inability to feel pleasure"). His cowriter, Marshall Brickman, wanted the title to be *It Had to Be a Jew.*

Save your titles.

I wrote a script about two little boys who go off on an adventure together. I called it *Pals.* I sold the script with that title to Lorimar Pictures. The studio didn't like the title and came up with a new one: *Big Shots.*

Years later, when Richard Marquand and I were talking about making a movie about a hardhearted man and his relationship with two little kids, I called it *Pals.* The title was again changed by the studio, this time to *Nowhere to Run,* although the studio had previously called it *Lion on the Lam* (yup, you read it right).

Since all these years have passed, and since I have four little boys now, I am planning to write a new script about a hardhearted man and his relationship with four little kids and calling it *Pals* (just kidding).

You can recycle your titles.

My movie *Betrayed* was first called *Sins of the Fathers,* then *Father of Lies,* then *Heartland,* and then *Eighty-Eight.*

My movie *Music Box* was at first called *Sins of the Fathers* and then *Father of Lies.*

You can't copyright a title.

In 1927, Ben Hecht wrote an original screenplay called *American Beauty.*

In 2000, another *American Beauty* (1999) won the Academy Award for Best Picture.

They can steal your title.

The producers were working on a script with playwright Bernard Slade, who also had a play running in London that was called *Fatal Attraction.*

The producers decided not to make the script Slade was working on, then went on to work with a young writer named James Dearden on a thriller. The thriller became a hit movie.

It was called *Fatal Attraction*—nothing but a coincidence, of course, nothing at all to do with Bernard Slade's play.

HOW TO DEAL WITH WRITER'S BLOCK . . . THE BROKEN TOE SOLUTION.

My wife bought me a heavy rock at an art fair. On it were written the words Writer's Block.

I kept it on my writing desk.

One day, blocked on a script, I smashed my desk with my fist and the Writer's Block fell on my big toe.

It hurt like hell. I put ice on it, but it still hurt like hell.

I went to the doctor and he said the toe was broken. There was nothing he could do, though, except put a bandage on it and tape that toe to another one.

I hobbled back home, sat back down at my desk, and found myself, miraculously, unblocked!

I moved my Writer's Block from my writing desk to my bedroom nightstand as a possible talismanic weapon in other creative situations.

My big toe still hurts, six years later, when cold weather sets in. The doctor says I've got arthritis in it.

There are obviously pluses and minuses, ups and downs, to a Writer's Block.

You're finished writing your script—this is your greatest moment as a screenwriter.

Playwright Robert Anderson: "I feel best about a play when I finish writing it, just before I send it off to anybody. I've written it, but no one has seen it, no one can say anything about it, no one can piss in it."

Hold on to the first draft of your script as well as all notes you may have taken in longhand.

You never know. Most scripts will rot away in storage somewhere, but . . .

I still have my rough draft of *Basic Instinct,* written on my manual typewriter and entitled *Love Hurts,* with notes to myself (in the second draft) in the margins.

Last year, a French movie memorabilia freak who loved the film offered me $500,000 for it. I turned him down. I figure that by the time my grandchildren sell it, it well be worth more than the $3 million I got for writing it.

I know that sometime in the future, the director of *Basic Instinct,* Paul Verhoeven, will be able to finance a movie with what *he'll* get for my first-draft script of *Showgirls.* Not because of the value of my script, but because each scene of his script is scrawled over with his pencil drawings of the way he saw the scene on-screen. Paul's script is an erotic comic book of breasts, butts, and vaginas, accompanied by my words translated into Paul's Dutch.

I know Paul also has, but probably won't sell, the scented pair of panties Sharon took off and handed him the morning he shot the beaver in *Basic Instinct.*

Once you finish your script, you don't have much control.

Novelist/screenwriter George Pelecanos: "There are so many things that are out of your control as a screenwriter. It's not just the 'evil producers.' It's also actors, directors, editors, cinematographers, the crew—anything that gets between you and your words, from when you're sitting in your room to the time it's up on the screen."

Make lots of copies of your script.

Thinking about posterity, send your script to friends and relatives and as many libraries as will accept it.

Screenwriter/novelist Raymond Chandler: "There is no available body of screenplay literature because it belongs to the studios, not to the writers, and they won't show it."

What can you do to prevent being ripped off?

It's not easy to do anything about it. You can do a few things to protect yourself, but not many. The day that you finish an outline or a script, send it to yourself in the mail. When you receive it, make sure *not* to open it and make sure you put it away in a safe place. That way, if you're ripped off somewhere along the line, your lawyer can dramatically open the envelope in a courtroom and prove (a) that you wrote it and (b) when you wrote it.

Just as important: You can send an idea, a script, or an outline to the Writers Guild of America and register it—even if you're not yet a member of the Guild. (You can even do it on-line. It will cost you twenty dollars if you're not a member.) If you're ripped off, you can then refer to the contents and the date in court.

If you are about to have a meeting with a studio executive, a development person, a producer, a director, an assistant to any of the above, or an agent to pitch a story, as soon as you get home from the meeting, write a memo describing the details of the meeting as well as the details of the story or stories that you pitched. Same drill as before: Put the memo in an envelope, send it to yourself in the mail, and don't open it when it comes back to you.

Besides these things, there's not much you can do if you're ripped off except sue. But suing is probably worth it. There are law firms that will take your case on a contingency basis. Studios and production entities usually don't want to go to court. So the chances are better than even that you'll make some bucks with a settlement.

Don't ever tell the press what you're writing.

I was ripped off with my very first movie, *F.I.S.T.*

Shortly after stories in the trade papers reported what *F.I.S.T.* was about, an Oscar-winning screenwriter—ironically, from my hometown—made a deal with a network to do the same story on television.

Because TV movies take a much shorter time to make, his film—*Power*—came out before *F.I.S.T.* did. So when *F.I.S.T.* came out, it appeared that I'd ripped off *Power*.

I was pissed, especially because I knew that this same Academy Award–winning screenwriter had been fired from my hometown newspaper—where I, too, had worked, albeit many years later—for stealing a watch from the scene of a jewelry store robbery that he was covering.

Interestingly, I, too, was fired from that same newspaper—not for stealing a watch, but for calling my editor some bad names in an article in a national publication.

A pox on both our houses, I say: He's a thief; I'm an ingrate.

The best way to avoid being plagiarized.

Jay Leno: "You have to write faster than they can steal."

R E E L S P E A K

Parallel Creativity

The phrase that will be used by someone who has plagiarized you.

PART FIVE

SELLING THE SCRIPT

How Do You Feel About Going to Bed with an Agent?

You've written your script. You need an agent or somebody in the business to read it. What can you do?

If you've read other screenwriting books, this is where everyone fudges. "Well," they say, "it's hard"—or they tell you to look up some agents' names in *Writer's Yearly* and send your script around.

This is what you do if you are a sexy, relatively good-looking man or woman willing to do *anything* to succeed.

You buy a plane ticket to L.A. You check yourself into a cheap motel in the Valley. You rent a car. You dress yourself up *good* to show your *assets*. Then you drive down to the bar of the Four Seasons or the Peninsula or the Mondrian in Beverly Hills or Hollywood and you pick out someone who looks like an agent or a development person (not that difficult to pick out: Prada or Armani black uniform, Cristophe haircut). And then you let yourself be picked up by him or her and you go home or upstairs in the hotel and you *fuck that person's brains out.* You fuck like you've never fucked before. You fuck like it's the bang of the century in *Basic Instinct.*

And before you leave, you give the person your script.

Let's go over that again.

Did you hear me right, though? Was I actually saying . . . was I advocating *whoring* there?

No, no, no! Forget everything you've just read. That's truly diabolical advice and I'm not the devil, am I? *Am I?* I'm a former altar boy, a devout Catholic. I even carry the cross on some Sundays at the Church of the Holy Angels in Bainbridge Township, Ohio.

The kind of diabolic advice you've just read is given by the most jaded and corrupt Hollywood veterans, the kind of nontalents who tell you that it's not *what* you know but *who* you know that will make you successful.

So I was just kidding, okay? Playing a devilish joke on you. I was kidding the same way I was kidding when I told teenagers to bring their fake IDs to see *Showgirls.* I was kidding then, too, but America didn't get the joke. So I thought I'd put it into boldface type this time: **You do not—do not, do not—have to pop an agent to make it!**

What you have to do is much less demanding (both physically and morally). You have to sit in a comfortable chair and make up a story that hundreds of millions will want to see.

And while you don't have to sleep with an agent, nobody is saying your story can't include a bit of sex and violence. You can still carry the cross to the altar, even after writing *Basic Instinct* and *Showgirls.* You don't have to be cynical yourself to write about corruption and corrupt people (either in a script or in a book cynically entitled *The Devil's Guide to Hollywood*).

Don't follow Madonna's example.

She appeared in the office of Barbara Boyle, Orion's head of production.

She dropped to her knees and sexily said, "I'll do anything to get this part."

Boyle said, "I'm happily married and I'm straight."

Madonna said, "You should try everything once."

Madonna got the part in *Desperately Seeking Susan.*

Don't follow Warren's example, either.

When Warren wanted to convince studio head Jack Warner to make *Bonnie and Clyde,* he grabbed Warner by the knees, fell to the floor, and said, "I'll kiss your shoes here. I'll lick 'em."

Jack Warner was not convinced.

He said, "Yeah, yeah, get up, Warren."

If you need the home address and phone number of an agent who'd be perfect to help you, this is what you do.

Go to Variety.com and read stories about screenwriters selling scripts to the studios for big bucks. Make a list of five screenwriters.

Call the Writers Guild of America West and identify yourself as an assistant to producer Scott Rudin (or Joel Silver, Jerry Bruckheimer, or Edward

Pressman). Ask the Guild to tell you the names of the agents representing the five screenwriters you picked from the Variety.com site.

Armed with the names of the five agents, get in touch with a Los Angeles private eye and make a deal with him to get you the home addresses and phone numbers of the five agents. (There will be a fee involved here, but it will be well worth it.)

Send your script to the home addresses of the five agents and wait a week. After a week, call them at home and ask if they've read your script. If you get any kind of positive (or frightened) response, convince the agent to meet with you at his office.

If you get a rude refusal to read your script, take it in stride and keep sending your script to the agent's home once a week.

Always be very polite. Most agents are abject cowards. If you keep bugging them (nicely), sooner or later they'll read your script—or have it read by an assistant—and see you just to be rid of you.

A more traditional way to find an agent.

Screenwriter/director Ron Shelton (*Bull Durham*): "The best way to get an agent is to send the manuscript to every agent ten times. That's how I got an agent. I spent three years sending my script to everyone who would read it and knocking on doors. I sent it everywhere. Everyone in town is always looking for something they can sell. Get a list of the agencies that read unsolicited manuscripts."

Or you can do what Andrew Kevin Walker did.

He worked at Tower Records in L.A. for three years while writing the script he entitled *Seven*.

When he was finished, he called the Writers Guild with a list of writers who had written scripts about mass murderers. He asked for the names of their agents.

Then he called the agents, but, of course, he couldn't get through to them directly. However, he spoke to their assistants, who told him that they wouldn't accept unsolicited screenplays.

And then, brilliantly, he pitched his script to the assistants very simply: "It's about a serial killer who kills according to the seven deadly sins."

He went down the list, pitching to the assistants, until one of them said, "Okay, send it. I'll read it."

She did, loved it, and gave it to her boss.

Seven, a brilliantly written piece, became one of the biggest hits of 1995. And Andrew Kevin Walker quit his job at Tower Records.

Or you can join the Church of Scientology.

Many big-time Hollywood actors belong to the Church of Scientology, and you just might meet them if you join. If you meet them, you just might get a chance to slip them your script.

On the other hand, screenwriter Floyd Mutrux, a longtime member of the Church of Scientology, hasn't had very many movies made, making me think that the rumored rigorous discipline of Scientologists might not be worth the access to a star.

On the other hand, there's that machine called the E-meter that vets each screenplay its members are asked to star in.

If that's really true, though, I wonder how *Eyes Wide Shut* got past the E-meter for Tom Cruise.

If you don't want to become a Scientologist, this is what you can do to get your script read by someone important.

- You can skydive from a rented plane onto Steven Spielberg's Pacific Palisades estate and hope your daredevil exploit impresses the house manager enough so that she will give your script to Steven.

- You can streak naked through the shower room at the Riviera Country Club and hand your plastic-bagged script to Sylvester Stallone. (If he likes it, you'll probably have to share credit with him.)

- You can swim to shore off Brad Pitt's Santa Barbara estate and leave several copies of your script around the pool, then race back to the beach and swim back to your boat before security gets you.

- You can visit the Coppola Winery in the Napa Valley, shake Francis's hand, and slip him a couple of C-notes to get your script to Sofia.

- You can pretend to be an exterminator and show up at the door of David Geffen's estate in Malibu. Since Malibu always has a rat problem, chances are excellent that someone will let you in.

- You can go down to Maxfield's on Melrose or Chrome Hearts on Robertson and slip a clerk a couple of twenties for some Maxfield or Chrome Hearts boxes. You can then send the boxes (with your script inside) to the agents, producers, or directors of your choice.

  Maxfield's and Chrome Hearts boxes are almost always immediately opened by the addressees themselves, not assistants, because the addressees are afraid their assistants will steal whatever goodies are inside those boxes. Also, if the agents, producers, or directors are successful, chances are excellent that he or she shops at Maxfield's or Chrome Hearts.

- You can go down to the Coffee Bean on Sunset and slip your script to Jennifer Aniston.

    My brother-in-law, a sometimes-aspiring screenwriter, drinks double lattes there but so far has not had the cojones to slip any of the beautiful people there his masterpiece. He does, however, keep a chart on his wall of the stars he's sighted at the Bean, along with time and date of sighting and witnesses.

- You can go down to the office of Dr. Robert Koblin on Robertson or that of Dr. Edward Kantor off Wilshire Boulevard and wait around. Koblin is an internist who treats many of the most powerful people in the industry; Kantor is known as the "ENT man to the stars." These folks who walk into these offices may not exactly be happy to see you there waiting for them with your script, especially if they are in pain or stressed to the max, but you've got a living to make, don't you?

    And as my director friend Richard Marquand used to say, "Fuck 'em if they can't take a joke!"

You can follow them into the john.

Mike Medavoy: "I'll be using the men's room at the AMC Century 14 and some one will hand me a script. 'You should make this script,' the man will say; 'it's a lot better than the last film you made.' There hasn't been a woman in the men's room yet, but there will be."

A Script Stalker

A screenwriter capable of following you anywhere or doing anything to get you to read his/her script.

Even Steven Spielberg needs an agent.

Steven Spielberg hadn't had an agent in many years. He felt he didn't need one. Then he sent Tom Cruise a script he wanted Tom to do with him. More exactly, he sent Tom's agent at CAA—the Creative Artists Agency, run by Michael Ovitz—the script he wanted Cruise to do, an old F. Scott Fitzgerald short story.

Steven didn't get an answer—not a yes, nor a no—for six months.

At the end of six months, Steven Spielberg signed CAA up as his agents—so he would get an answer from Tom Cruise.

He got his answer: Tom Cruise said no. He didn't want to do that script with Steven, although he did hook up with Steven about a year later.

Steven Spielberg must have felt he needed an agent pretty badly.

It couldn't have been easy for Steven, the most powerful director in Hollywood, to sign up with CAA.

He knew that before he married Kate Capshaw, CAA head Michael Ovitz had chased her around his office.

Why Steven Spielberg has never been represented by Jeff Berg at ICM . . .

Jeff's brother, Tony, said, "A Steven Spielberg film is a classic example of a third-rate melodrama elevated way beyond its depth. I can't think of a filmmaker whose stuff I like less. His work is so manipulative."

Mike Medavoy isn't smart about everything.

When his client Steven Spielberg didn't walk out on his deal with Universal as he had recommended, agent Medavoy fired Spielberg. Medavoy: "I'm just glad that wasn't the defining point of my career."

An agent will help you to hold on to your aureole.

Writer/director Elia Kazan: "Let your agent tell the lies. Get a hireling to drop the axe so that you never fog your aureole of culture and gentility."

Your first agent won't be your last agent.

I had an agent who told me we'd spend decades together; six months later she stopped being an agent and became a very successful interior decorator in New York.

I had an agent who said, "My job isn't to give you advice. My job is to respond. When you say 'Jump,' I say 'How high?'" I fired him.

I had an agent who told me it would take him two weeks to read an original screenplay I'd written. I figured he was too busy to be my agent or that he moved his lips when he read. I fired him.

I had an agent who spoke with a thick English accent many years after she'd spent six months working in London. After awhile, the accent was driving me nuts. I fired her.

I had an agent who, in the middle of a negotiation with a studio, disappeared for ten days. Nobody knew where he was. He finally reappeared and whispered to me, man to man, that he'd gotten hold of a "big bag" of cocaine and had been in Puerto Vallarta with a well-known sexpot movie star. I fired him *after* he concluded the negotiation successfully. It's not impossible that I fired him because I was jealous.

I had an agent who was depressed and gloomy much of the time while he was representing me. A producer friend and I had a bet that one day he'd drive into the desert (he liked to go to Joshua Tree alone on weekends) and blow his brains out. But we were wrong. He went on Prozac, stopped being depressed, stopped driving out into the desert, married a beautiful, smart woman, and is now one of the most powerful men in Hollywood. I fired and rehired him *twice* in my career. I like him.

I had an agent who was one of the coldest people I've ever met and one of the smartest. We had nothing to talk to each other about besides business—our conversations usually lasted thirty seconds or less. I finally fired him because, although he was very good as an agent, I just couldn't tolerate his coldness anymore. He wrote me an affable postcard after I fired him, wishing me the best of luck. It was the warmest communication he'd ever had with me. He also said that sooner or later he knew I'd rehire him because I'd realize just how good he was as an agent. A couple years after he sent me the note, I rehired him. I was with him for a couple years, until his coldness got to me again and I fired him once more.

Don't let your agent give you creative advice.

Whatever he tells you will be stupid.

It's what George Bernard Shaw said to Sam Goldwyn: "Mr. Goldwyn, all you want to do is talk about art and all I want to do is talk about money."

I knew an agent who not only hired a reader to read all scripts for him but then hired another reader to read that reader's reports and compress them into one paragraph—or no more than thirty words.

A Rainmaker

An agent who makes a lot of money (with successful clients) for an agency.

Agents have their own agendas.

The morning that we began the *Basic Instinct* auction, I asked the head of my agency, Jeff Berg of ICM, who he thought was going to buy it and how much he thought it would sell for.

Jeff said he thought Mario Kassar at Carolco would wind up buying it for $3 million.

Jeff ran the auction himself. Everyone in town except Fox played and bid against one another. And at the end of that long day, Mario Kassar of Carolco bought it for $3 million.

How did Berg know? Was there a side deal between ICM and Carolco that I didn't know about? Was there a kickback to ICM? Not that I was ever able to uncover, but I was suspicious.

Of course it's also possible that Jeff Berg is more than just one of the smartest people in Hollywood. It's possible that Jeff is a genius and a seer.

R E E L S P E A K

The *Ubermenschen* of Hollywood

What CAA agents, led by Michael Ovitz, were known as in the 1990s.

How you can tell that your agent cares about you . . .

He calls you three times a week at least. He has nothing really to say to you, so he says, "I'm just checking in," thinking, maybe, that you've turned into a hotel.

He kisses you on both cheeks every time he sees you. He tells you he loves you every time he sees you.

How you can tell that your agent doesn't care about you . . .

He calls you three times a week at least. He has nothing to say to you, so he says "I'm just checking in," thinking, maybe, that you've turned into a hotel.

He kisses you on both cheeks every time he sees you. He tells you he loves you every time he sees you.

You're part of the ebb and flow.

There is an ebb and flow in the client business," agent Jeff Berg once told me. "You lose a client and you ask yourself, How can I get a new one?"

You don't want a sweet and adorable negotiator.

Legendary former agent Freddie Fields: "What excuse do you have, what defense against a proper negotiator, when you've been bettered? You call him a killer, a cold-blooded guy. They're all overused terms. There's no such thing as a sweet, warm, adorable good negotiator."

Try to find an agent who's seen it all.

Like my longtime agent Guy McElwaine—studio head at Warner Bros., Columbia, and Rastar; married seven or nine times; represented Frank Sinatra, Judy Garland, Peters Sellers, Yul Brynner, Burt Reynolds, Sharon Stone, Richard Pryor; married on three separate occasions to separate women at the Splendido Hotel in Portofino, Italy; once made love to Natalie Wood on top of a pool table in a bar where the jukebox was playing Sinatra; once won a white Lincoln Continental in a poker game from golfer Johnny Miller; once pulled producer David Geffen off a conference table when he was about to duke it out with Warner Bros. head Ted Ashley.

Be a pain in your agent's ass.

Screenwriter Anna Hamilton Phelan (*Gorillas in the Mist*): "My agent gave me the best advice an agent had ever given me. He said, 'I represent a lot of big people. I'm going to forget about you unless you bug me. You have to call me. You have to call me three, four times a week and you have to make me crazy. Make me hate you. If you don't, I'm going to forget about you, and this is not going to go anywhere.'"

Tumeling

Where agents want to be: at the center of the action.

If you've written a new script and want to give it to your new agent . . .

Wait until the next time he's flying to New York and give it to him the day before he leaves. He'll be captive for five hours, and that means:

1. **He'll probably be able to finish the script before he lands.**

2. **He won't stop reading it to take any phone calls.**

ALL HAIL
Irving ("Swifty") Lazar!

David O. Selznick, the most powerful producer in town at the time, said of him: "There is one man who is single-handedly ruining the motion picture industry as we know it. The ridiculous prices he demands for books and plays and writers will surely be the end of us all."

To Wirtschafter

To lose clients because of stupid things you said during an interview—like William Morris agent David Wirtschafter, who lost clients after an interview he did with *The New Yorker* magazine.

What was that about the black heart of an agent?

When agent Marty Baum retired from CMA, where he'd worked for many years, his fellow agents gave him a Cartier tank watch. He discovered that it was a Hong Kong knockoff.

I wouldn't hire this guy.

A CAA agent hustles new clients by saying, "I want to be your asshole," or "I want to be your bitch."

Try to get your agent to lie for you.

This won't be easy, because your agent will have better relationships with studio executives (whom he's known for a long time) than with you. But if you can somehow get your agent to do it, it will pay off big-time.

In 1980, I wrote a spec script called *City Hall* and sent it to my agent. He loved it and decided to auction it. He sent it out to Paramount, Universal, Warner Bros., and MGM at the same time. Within hours, Paramount, Universal, and MGM passed. Warner Bros. was thinking about it.

I asked my agent to tell Warner Bros. that one of the three who'd passed wanted to buy it. He said he couldn't lie to people he'd had a relationship with for a long time. I reminded him of my two little kids, the house we had just bought, the mortgage payments owed, the college educations I would one day have to pay for.

He interrupted me and said, "You really are a Hungarian, you know."

He called Warners and told them Paramount wanted to buy *City Hall* and he was only calling to inform them of this. Warners decided they wanted to buy it, too—but came in at a low figure. He told them Paramount was at a higher figure. Warners then came in so high that it set a new industry record for a spec script, beating the price for William Goldman's *Butch Cassidy and the Sundance Kid*.

Shortly afterward, the Warners executives who bought the script were fired. Almost twenty-five years later, *City Hall* is still up on the Warner Bros. shelf— unmade. The money they paid for it, though, has long been spent.

Don't be fooled by the paintings on the walls.

I had an agent who lived in a posh Beverly Hills house with spectacular art on the walls—sometimes.

Sometimes when I saw him, the art was there, but sometimes the walls were bare.

One of his colleagues explained it to me: The paintings were rented. Some months he was able to foot the bill and other months he wasn't.

As a matter of fact, I discovered, the house was rented, too, and both the Jaguar and the Mercedes were leased.

It's okay to be a pawn in their game.

If you write scripts that are made into movies, agencies will kiss your butt.

This isn't because they care about you—you are, after all, nothing but a schmuck writer—but because they can use you to convince superstar actors to let them represent them.

The superstar actor will think that if this agency represents him, he will get first crack at your script.

Michael Ovitz was a con artist.

When superagent Michael Ovitz graduated from Birmingham High School in Encino, California, he received an award of merit at the senior breakfast. It was for being "class con artist."

Michael Ovitz was a frat boy.

When superagent Michael Ovitz became president of his fraternity at UCLA, his fraternity brothers called him "King" Ovitz.

Michael Ovitz was a narc.

When the members of the rock band Sly and the Family Stone took a look at their new agent, Michael Ovitz, one of them yelled, "Narc!"

Michael Ovitz was a mensch.

This is how Mike Medavoy first met agent Michael Ovitz: "I'd never talked to him before, but I knew who he was and took his phone call. He said to me, 'My name is Mike Ovitz. I don't know you, but I intend to be your best friend. I want to come and see you.' I asked when. He said, 'Now.' Fifteen minutes later, he appeared at my door."

Michael Ovitz was a healer.

When superlawyer Bert Fields's wife was ill with cancer, agent Michael Ovitz arranged for the best specialists at UCLA to treat her. When screenwriter Robert Towne's Hungarian dog bit him severely, Michael Ovitz arranged for the best specialists at UCLA to treat him. When I hurt my back in Santa Fe, New Mexico, Michael Ovitz called me and offered to fly his acupuncturist to my home in Marin County.

Michael Ovitz was my fairy godmother.

The first thing Michael Ovitz asked me at our first meeting— this was about six years before he told me that his foot soldiers would put me into the ground—was this: "What's your biggest dream? I need to know so I can make it come true."

Michael Ovitz was Magic Johnson and Aristotle combined.

Superagent Michael Ovitz, explaining his success: "Read *The Art of War* and *Tao Teh Ching,* get it flavored by a little of Aristotle, and watch the Los Angeles Lakers do a fast break. It's like watching a Swiss watch work as they drive down the court, five guys; Magic Johnson would look, fake, and rarely take the shot. That was my philosophy."

Michael Ovitz used Robert Redford.

I'm not worried about the press," agent Michael Ovitz told me at a meeting in September of 1989. "All those guys want is to write screenplays for Robert Redford."

Michael Ovitz was Citizen Kane.

When he began representing Bill Carruthers, producer of game shows, Michael Ovitz asked him to give his wife, Judy, a spot as a model on the show *Give and Take*.

Michael Ovitz was a killer.

On rare occasions when he told something to his friends confidentially, Michael Ovitz said, "This is a private conversation. If you ever repeat it, I'm going to kill you."

Michael Ovitz was the Godfather.

After his first meeting with agent Michael Ovitz, comedian David Letterman told a friend, "I've been to see the Godfather! I had a meeting with the Godfather!"

Michael Ovitz was the Antichrist.

NBC president Don Ohlmeyer called superagent Michael Ovitz "The Antichrist." Producer David Geffen then commented, "Apparently Don Ohlmeyer thinks more highly of Michael Ovitz than I do."

Nobody punked Michael Ovitz!

When I read that Michael Ovitz blamed his demise on what he called "Hollywood's gay mafia," I remembered something he'd said to me in our famous meeting in 1989, during which he'd threatened to destroy my career if I left his agency.

"You think you're just going to leave this agency and I'm just going to take it?" he said. "Nobody makes a faggot out of me—nobody!"

How did Michael Ovitz get away with acting like the Antichrist?

Mike Medavoy: "Ovitz got away with it because people thought he had his hand on some kind of nuclear launch button. The moment fear of him disappeared, he became fair game for everyone who resented his methods."

I punked Michael Ovitz.

If you make me eat shit, I'm going to make you eat shit," superagent Michael Ovitz told me at a meeting in September 1989.

I even stole Michael Ovitz's best line.

Ten years after Michael Ovitz told me his foot soldiers who went up and down Wilshire Boulevard would "put me into the ground," and several years after Ovitz left CAA, his former agency asked me to appear in their annual video.

I improvised my line on the video: "My foot soldiers who go up and down Zuma Beach will put Mike Ovitz into the sand."

Michael Ovitz believed what they wrote about him.

In the 1990s, Michael Ovitz said to reporters, "I understand I am the single most powerful force in the entertainment industry." Ten years later, he was out of the business.

Now Michael Ovitz is a fucking bum.

Years before I had a public fight with him and fired him, Michael Ovitz tried to convince me to let him represent me.

I had a big meeting with him in a CAA conference room, where a bunch of other agents were present, and said no thank you to Ovitz's pitch and walked out of the room.

Ovitz called Don Simpson, the producer I was working with at the time, and said, "Who is this fucking bum to do this to me?"

Michael Ovitz had a role model.

When Tommy Dorsey wanted to leave MCA, his agent, Billy Goodhart, said this to him: "Tommy, if you continue this bullshit, making everybody miserable, you see these balls?" He bent over and grabbed his own balls. "I'm gonna cut yours off. Not only won't you be working for MCA, you won't be working for anybody else for maybe the rest of your life. You have something to say, put it in writing. Now get the fuck out of here—you irritate me."

A threesome: Michael Ovitz, Roseanne, and Zsa Zsa.

After Michael Ovitz threatened to destroy my career, Roseanne Barr, whom I'd never met, sent him a note with the words "Fuck you!" scrawled all over the page.

I was flattered . . . until I heard that after my fellow Hungarian Zsa Zsa Gabor was arrested for a scuffle with a Beverly Hills cop, Roseanne sent Zsa Zsa a note that said, "Fuck them all!"

The Writers Guild can be punked, too.

When I was in a public battle with agent Michael Ovitz—and he was denying the threats he had made to destroy my career—I asked the Writers Guild for support.

The Writers Guild issued a statement saying that "if Ovitz did the things Eszterhas alleges," he was wrong.

In other words, instead of supporting me, the Writers Guild was publicly questioning my integrity. And, of course, they launched no investigation of Ovitz or agency tactics.

The president of the Writers Guild at the time was George Kirgo, a television writer represented by the Creative Artists Agency, headed by Ovitz.

We'll Kill for You!

The sentence with which superagent Michael Ovitz concluded his pitches to prospective clients.

I tried that same phrase out on a literary agent who wanted to represent the books I wrote. "I want you," I said, "*to kill for me!*"

The agent, Ed Victor, urbane, sophisticated, and very *literary* (he lives in London) blanched, and looked like he was having cardiac arrhythmia.

This is the agent you need.

George Shapiro, a William Morris agent, had his assistant answer the phone by saying, "George Shapiro's office—kill for the love of killing."

Most agents don't read books.

When Julius Caesar Stein was running MCA, the superagency of its day, he decorated the building with antiques he bought in England.

The bookcases he bought needed books, so he bought roomfuls of leather-covered books he called "furniture books."

No one who worked at MCA ever read the leather-covered books, but Tennessee Williams, who was represented by MCA, told his friends, "If you're ever in the building, take five or six books. They'll never miss them."

Your agent can screw up.

Agent Swifty Lazar: "When I sold *Rich Man, Poor Man,* I made a great mistake—and, over time, it cost me my friendship with Irwin Shaw [the author]. The lowliest writer who sells his book to television gets, by union contract, at least a guaranteed minimum for repeat showings and spin-offs. In Irwin's contract, there was no such provision. I know what I was thinking—I'd had such a struggle selling it that I believed it would never get beyond the option stage—but I should have protected Irwin better. I had no excuse."

It's okay to fire your agent.

Sean Penn: "Changing agents is like changing lounge chairs on the deck of the *Titanic*."

If you make it big, you don't have to return your agent's call.

Sydney Pollack on not returning agent Michael Ovitz's calls: "Sometimes I didn't take his calls. And he would say, when I finally did, 'Did you get my message? You didn't return my call.' And I would tell him, 'I didn't return your call, Michael, because there's nothing to say. All you want to say to me is, 'I'm just checking in.'"

If you're angry at your agent.

Director Sam Peckinpah liked to get drunk and then hurl knives at a dartboard. He'd ask his agent over sometimes to hold the dartboard.

If you're successful enough, your agent will clean up the poo-poo.

Mae West told her agent, my fellow Hungarian Johnny Hyde, who would later make love to Marilyn Monroe, to clean up the poo-poo whenever her pet chimp had diarrhea.

I told that story to one of my agents, and she said, "That's what we do all right; we work with chimps and clean up their poo-poo."

But it might be smarter if you clean up the poo-poo.

Today's agent might be tomorrow's producer and next month's studio head.

Mike Medavoy: "In the entertainment industry, people change jobs faster than they change cars, girlfriends, clothes, sometimes even underwear."

Underwear?

If your agent dies, forget about him.

Agent mogul Julius Caesar Stein of MCA asked in his will that his clients Benny Goodman and Dinah Shore perform at his funeral.

When Stein died, both Goodman and Shore declined, citing previous commitments.

PART SIX

FILMING THE SCRIPT

LESSON 11

Steal As Much Memorabilia from the Set As You Can!

Your new agent has submitted your script to a studio. He tells you that a "studio reader" is reading it. Who is a studio reader?

The studio reader who first gets your script and either recommends it or not to the studio execs is your worst enemy.

This person is a wannabe screenwriter trying desperately to break into the business. He wants to shout out his own erudition and cinematic skills by impressing the studio execs—by deconstructing, castrating, disemboweling *your* script—and telling the execs how *he* could and would make it better.

Few readers ever *praise* a script, because they know that very few scripts ever become hit movies. They don't want to put their own pimply, pale skinnies on the line in support of a script that will probably never be made and would probably be a disaster even if it were made.

When I auctioned the script of *Basic Instinct,* a reader at Warner Bros. trashed the script and advised the studio not to bid on it. When the studio discovered a few hours later that everyone else in town was bidding on it, the Warner's executives decided to bid on it, too, although they hadn't read it and their reader had advised against it. The reason, of course, was that they figured if *everyone else* was bidding to buy it, the script *had to be good* and their loser reader/wannabe screenwriter *had to be wrong*.

The execs could have shut themselves off in their offices and read the script; it would have taken them an hour to two (even if they moved their lips while reading).

But since they all hated to read, they didn't read it; they just automatically *bid on it.* They ultimately bid $2.5 million; it sold for $3 million. And when the auction was over, they fired their reader/wannabe screenwriter for making an obviously bad call.

When *Basic Instinct* made $500 million, their woeful, misbegotten reader was captured by the studio's foot soldiers one night (at Starbucks), driven to the back lot (near the water tower) at Warner Bros., and beheaded.

Oh no, all those readers have been McKee'd.

Robert McKee's Web site bio says, "Several companies such as ABC, Disney, Miramax, PBS, Nickelodeon and Paramount regularly send their entire creative and writing staffs to his lectures."

If the first studio passes on your script . . .

Sugar Ray Robinson, former middleweight champion of the world: "You never know how tough you are till somebody knocks you down and you decide whether you wanna get yourself up or not."

A Calling-Card Script

A script that you don't sell but that studio execs read as an indication of your talent. Figure it his way: Even if you don't sell the script that you've put your heart and guts into, it still might get you a writing job—although this kind of figuring can get a bit overdrawn at times. I spoke to a wannabe screenwriter once, who said, "I haven't sold anything yet, but I've got six or seven really great calling-card scripts."

Cover the Waterfront

It once used to mean something very different, but now it means getting your script to as many potential buyers as possible if you're trying to sell it on a spec basis.

A Pussy Hair Away

According to producer Robert Evans, this is a deal that's almost but not quite done.

After several months of trying, your new agent has sold your script to a studio. They ask you how long it took you to write it. Lie.

After I had sold *Basic Instinct* for $3 million, many people asked me how long it had taken me to write it.

I had my answer down pat: "Well, I've probably been working on this script for most of my life. It's about homicidal impulse and thrill killing, and I was fascinated by those things even twenty-five years ago, when I was a journalist. I remember I interviewed a mass murderer named Edward Kemper when I was writing for *Rolling Stone* magazine, and before that, when I was a reporter in Cleveland, I interviewed two kids there who'd killed their parents, Freddie Esherick and Treva Crosthwaite. And I'd known and worked with cops from the time when I covered the police beat in Cleveland to the time I interviewed narcotics agents for *Rolling Stone*. I actually had my office in Cleveland in the basement at Central Police Station. I even covered a shooting where eight policemen were shot down in the streets a couple hundred feet in front of me. And I did a profile of a burned-out cop very much like the Nick Curran character in my script; he was involved in so many shootings, he was suspended from the force. And, from the point of view of the other central character, Catherine Tramell, well, I've already written three films where women were manipulated by men—*Betrayed, Jagged Edge,* and *Music Box*—and I wanted to write a story about a woman who is so smart and so sensual that she can manipulate even the smartest streetwise homicide cop. And, of course, I'm a writer and the central character of this piece is a writer. I wanted to get into the whole notion of becoming your characters, of getting too close to the fire and getting burned. So, as you see, this script comes from deep in my soul, and maybe the reason it was sold for so much money is because the buyers sensed the authenticity, the reality, of it."

This was all true, but it was also malarkey. Because while it was true that I had done all the things I referred to in my little speech, it had taken only thirteen days from the moment I had the idea to the moment my agents sold the finished script at auction.

Truth is, I had gotten $3 million for maybe ten days' writing.

I certainly wasn't about to tell anyone *that*.

Had I said that, many people in Hollywood would immediately have said, "Never mind that it sold for three mil, if all it took to write it was ten days, then it's a piece of shit." (Few in Hollywood knew or would have cared that it took William Faulkner *six weeks* to write *The Sound and the Fury,* one of the most complex *novels* of our time.)

Only after *Basic* was a smash did I tell the press that it had taken just thirteen days from inception to sale.

I told the truth, then, to flip a gigantic bird in the face of Hollywood.

Thirteen days and five hundred mil! I can do that and you can't!

But nowhere have I revealed my real motive for writing that script. In 1980, I had set a record for a spec script by selling *City Hall* for $500,000. I had broken my own record a couple of years later by selling *Big Shots* for $1,250,000. Then a writer named Shane Black had broken my record by selling *The Last Boy Scout* for $1,750,000.

I read about Shane's sale—and my record being broken—on the front page of the *Los Angeles Times* while I was vacationing at the Kahala Hilton in Hawaii. Shane's sale pissed me off. I wanted my record back. I wanted to see an article on the front page of the *Los Angeles Times* about me setting a *new* record.

I flew home from Hawaii and sat down immediately and started writing the most commercial script I could think of.

Twelve days later, I had my record back. I had the article on the front page of the *Los Angeles Times* about *my* new record. And I had my $3 million.

Arthur Miller lied, too.

He didn't tell anyone for many years that he wrote the first draft of *Death of a Salesman* in one day and part of a night.

Always lie about how many drafts you've done.

Tell the studio or the producer that it's your fifth or sixth draft but that it's just the first one you're turning in.

Gore Vidal tells this story: "After about three weeks, I turned in my first draft. The producer couldn't believe it, he wanted me to work forever and ever because he wanted his money's worth. I remember telling him, 'Yes, but what I do in the first draft is generally the best, and people usually end up going back to it.' He said, 'No, no, no, no, we must work harder."

ALL HAIL
William Saroyan!

Agent Swifty Lazar: "One day L. B. Mayer mentioned that he was looking for some new stories. By coincidence, Saroyan had just called me—he always rang when he was broke. I explained what Mayer was looking for and urged him to come up with something. I then told Mayer that I had a Pulitzer Prize–winning writer with a great story. A few days later, I brought Saroyan to Mayer's office. As Saroyan took him through the plot, L. B. Mayer began to tear up—he was a real crier. My heart was less moved: I knew Saroyan was making it up as he went along.

"'That's terrific,' Mayer said, when Saroyan finished weaving his tale. 'Now go wait outside and I'll talk to Irving about it.'

"Saroyan dutifully strolled out to the parking lot.

"'How much?' Mayer asked.

"'He wants one fifty,' I said.

"'He's got it.'

"I went to Business Affairs to work out the payment: fifty thousand up front, fifty thousand when he hands in half the story, then a final fifty thousand when he turns in the ending. Elated, I hurried out to the car to tell Saroyan I'd gotten him fifty grand to start.

"'What's the total?' he asked.

"'One hundred fifty.'

"'Get me the one fifty. I need all of it right now.'

"'You're crazy.'

"'Tell him I want the one fifty now or no deal.'

"I went back to Mayer's office and explained the situation—and he agreed to give Saroyan a check in full. I raced back to Saroyan and told him I'd deposit the check, take my commission, and give him the rest tomorrow.

"'No, I want the money in cash, now.'

"'You're crazy, can't you wait two days?'

"He apparently couldn't—his bookies had threatened him.

Back I went to Mayer, who called Business Affairs. And they arranged for the bank to bring the money over to the studio in hundred-dollar bills. I took the loot to the parking lot, and stood with Saroyan as we counted the money out on the hood. With every ten thousand he took, I'd take a thousand for myself, until I had my fifteen grand and he had the rest. Then he went off to pay his bookie."

Get a piece of the ice pick and white scarf sales.

My lawyer got me a healthy percentage of the merchandising from *Basic Instinct* after a long struggle with the studio's Business Affairs lawyers.

Of course, there *was* no merchandising for *Basic Instinct*.

If you sell your script, try to get a credit as executive producer, too.

There are so many producer credits these days that your agent shouldn't have much of a problem getting this in your contract.

If you get the credit, it means you'll get your name on-screen and on the poster (the "one sheet") twice—as writer and executive producer.

Seeing your name on-screen twice might help the audience think that this is *your* movie and not the director's.

What kind of power does being executive producer of your film give you?

None.

I know. I executive-produced many of my films. Anyone from the actor's manager to the producer's son to the director's mistress can get a producer credit today.

"Producer" and "executive producer" credits have become more or less meaningless except for people like Jerry Bruckheimer, Brian Grazer, or Scott Rudin, who truly are old-time Sam Spiegel–like producers.

What being the executive producer of your film might give you—if your agent insists—is your own *director's chair* with your name imprinted on it.

Naomi and I have several of these scattered around the house. Our cats love them, but because of their height, they're a potential death trap for toddlers.

So take care. If your *director's* chair breaks your child's neck, well, that would be the ultimate irony, wouldn't it?

Back-End Points

What Eddie Murphy referred to as "monkey points," a percentage of profits. They are called back-end points not just because the terms are defined in the back of a contract but because—since the points never pay off, due to the studio's accounting practices—they stick it up your back end.

ALL HAIL
Preston Sturges!

He was the first screenwriter to get a percentage of his film's profits. He sold *The Power and the Glory,* an original script, in 1930 for a small advance and big back-end points.

Now that you've sold your script, you're really in deep shit.

Mike Medavoy: "The average studio now has thirty people doing story notes, twenty people playing producer (and taking screen credit for it, too), and focus groups composed of disaffected Generation Xers causing entire films to be reedited into cookie-cutter models."

Google the studio execs you'll be meeting with.

The first time I met Brandon Tartikoff, I was armed with every detail about the life of Ryne Duren, a near-blind former New York Yankees relief pitcher who, I knew, was one of Tartikoff's heroes.

As soon as I walked in, I spotted a framed baseball card of Duren on a wall. I was off to the races, talking about Duren, telling Brandon things even *he* didn't know. The object of my meeting was to try to get Brandon to approve my friend Tom Berenger in the cast of *Sliver.* Thanks, I am convinced, to Ryne Duren, Brandon agreed to cast Tom "as a favor" to me.

Prepare for your creative meetings.

I realized a few hours before Jimi Hendrix's sister and brother-in-law were to come to my house in Malibu that I didn't have any paintings of Jimi on my walls, while I did have paintings of Dylan and the Stones on display.

I quickly called a friend who had a Ronnie Wood print of Jimi, and he took it off his wall and messengered it to my house. I put it up on my wall, replacing Dylan just as Jimi's sister and brother-in-law were pulling into my driveway.

They were impressed by the print of Jimi they saw on the wall, but ultimately they turned down my offer to do a script of Jimi's life.

If you're going to your first studio meeting and you're terrified, remembering this will terrify you.

Keep in mind what Mike Medavoy, former studio head, said about studio people: They don't change their underwear all that often.

If you have a meeting at the studio, don't park on the lot.

Screenwriter James Brown: "I meet with the producer at Warner Bros. At the main gate that afternoon is a long line of cars waiting for the guard to check them through. Ahead of me are a Mercedes, two BMWs, and a Porsche. I am driving an eleven-year old Nissan pickup with a broken muffler, and it's loud. People are staring at me and I'm suddenly self-conscious. On a whim I put it into reverse, and instead of parking on the studio lot as I was instructed to do, I leave my old truck at a meter down the street and walk back to the guard's booth."

Don't take any breakfast meetings.

Novelist/screenwriter Jay McInerney: "A breakfast meeting is the nastiest and most inelegant of Hollywood inventions."

Tell the people who want to meet with you for breakfast that you write at night and don't get to bed till five or six in the morning.

Try to avoid meetings with a whole roomful of studio executives.

John Gregory Dunne: "To attend one of those meetings is to understand the cold truth of the saying that a camel is a horse made by a committee."

Check your crotch before a meeting.

Comedian Alan King: "Never walk into a meeting with a creased crotch."

Don't wear shorts to a studio meeting.

There is a dress code you should follow—jeans, sneakers, vintage rock-and-roll T-shirt or new Tommy Bahama silk shirt (not oversized, but hanging out), and a baseball cap (not a MLB hat or a trucker's hat—they're for star actors—but the kind that sits snugly over your head and doesn't sit like a crown up there). Shades are okay, but they should be taken off as soon as you walk into the room.

If you go to a script meeting at a studio, hug everyone there.

Hugs are much better now than they were in the past," a retired agent in her seventies said to me. "People are in much better shape than they were in the old days, when a hug meant being bounced off of some fat belly."

If you're sitting in a story meeting . . .

Let them talk first, even if they want *you* to.

Dodge and say, "You know, I'm really interested in hearing your ideas. I've always been much more of a listener than a talker."

Someone in the room will invariably say, "That's why you're such a good writer."

Smile shyly then and, looking humble, say, "Thank you."

In a story meeting about a script they haven't yet bought . . .

Say as little as possible.

There are probably people in the room who will steal what you are saying and plug it into another project they are overseeing.

The surest way for a studio to get a bunch of fresh ideas on a doddering project is to do a series of meetings with auditioning screenwriters who want to be hired for the project.

Chances are good that the studio will steal your ideas and then hire a "pro" who doesn't do auditions.

The studio will then give the this so-called pro their "notes," incorporating all the ideas that the studio execs stole from all the screenwriters they auditioned.

In a story meeting after they've bought your script . . .

Understand that no matter how friendly these people are being to you, all they really want to do is to *impregnate* your script with their syphilitic story ideas.

You can do a little kissy face, and you can even do a little petting, but don't let them stick it in. Once they stick it in, they will not pull it out before the movie comes out.

When the movie comes out, it will minimally look like them and not like you.

If you let them stick it in often, the movie won't look like you at all. It will be all theirs.

Know, too, that if the movie is stillborn, the film doctors will blame *your* script for its demise. The name on the script will be yours, not that of the studio executives who stuck it into you.

Steal their cigars.

Screenwriter Calder Willingham felt producer Sam Spiegel was picking on him unfairly during their story meetings. So each time Spiegel went to the bathroom, Willingham stole one of his cigars.

Studio execs know they can't write.

That's why they need *you*.

So as you sit there in a meeting with them, don't take notes on the stupid ideas they are telling you, and don't tell them how smart they are, because underneath their BS, they know they can't write.

Don't be afraid to tell them they don't know what they're talking about; *they know they don't* and in their hearts (deep, deep in their plaqued-up hearts) they agree with you.

To put it in Hollywood terms:

They won't respect you if you swallow. So gag.

And spit it back up in their faces if you don't like the taste of it.

It's okay to throw up after a meeting.

Screenwriter/playwright Harold Pinter: "As soon as he read my script *Accident,* the producer Sam Spiegel summoned me to his office. He began his commentary by saying, 'You call this a screenplay?' He then said, 'You can't make a movie out of this. Who are these people? I don't know anything about them. I don't know anything about their background. I don't know what they're doing. I don't understand what they're up to. I don't understand one thing. I think you have to seriously rethink the whole script.'

"I said, 'No, I'm not rethinking it. That's it.' When I got out of there, I was sick on the pavement."

Your script is probably doomed.

Director Jean-Pierre Melville: "I'll tell you what makes a good film. Fifty percent is the choice of the story. Fifty percent is the screenplay. Fifty percent is the actors. Fifty percent is the director. Fifty percent is the cinematographer. Fifty percent is the editor. If any of these elements goes wrong, there goes fifty percent of your film."

If they can't find a director willing to direct your script . . .

Remember that Elia Kazan, John Ford, Howard Hawks, Nicholas Ray, Carol Reed, William Wyler, and Fred Zinnemann all passed on directing *The Bridge on the River Kwai.*

If they can't find a producer willing to produce your script . . .

Remember that producer Sam Spiegel passed on the first James Bond script, saying, "It's utter nonsense."

If they've been trying to cast your script for six months without success . . .

Remember that Albert Finney and Marlon Brando turned down playing the lead in *Lawrence of Arabia.*

If you want Spielberg to read your script and Tom Hanks to star in it . . .

Convince Lori Goddard, who highlights hair in Beverly Hills, to read it.

If she likes it, she can tell Kate Capshaw about it—Lori does Kate's highlights.

If Kate likes it, she'll tell her husband, Steven Spielberg, about it and Steven will read it.

If Steven likes it, he'll tell his friend Tom Hanks to read it, too.

Don't worry about getting a big star into your film; stars don't matter.

When we got Sylvester Stallone into *F.I.S.T.,* coming right off of *Rocky,* we were overjoyed. The movie tanked.

Jeff Bridges hadn't had a hit movie in many years when he did *Jagged Edge;* nevertheless, the movie became a hit.

Sharon Stone was perhaps the biggest star in the world when she did *Sliver,* coming right off of *Basic Instinct.* It didn't matter. The movie failed.

Nobody had ever heard of Jennifer Beals when she did *Flashdance;* despite that, the movie went on to make $500 million.

I got Sylvester Stallone, Jackie Chan, and Whoopi Goldberg into *An Alan Smithee Film: Burn Hollywood Burn;* the movie bombed.

Also think Harrison Ford in *Random Hearts,* Kevin Costner in *The Postman,* Sean Connery in *The Avengers,* John Travolta and Dustin Hoffman in *Mad City.*

How not to deal with the director of your film . . .

You don't have to bend over *this* low . . . or stick it up in the air *this* high.

Screenwriter Ron Bass (*Rain Man*): "I wasn't smart enough to get it right away, but Steven Spielberg was extremely patient with me. He talked with me until I started to realize this was not only something to get behind but was really a much better way than I'd been going. Then we started to meet with Dustin Hoffman and Tom Cruise. There were four-way meetings at Steven's house at the beach. Tom was in many of them and Dustin was in all of them. *They were cowriters.* It was just unbelievable. We invented scenes together; we invented the character together.... I can't tell you how much Dustin contributed and how much Steven contributed. Then I went away and wrote this long draft. Dustin really liked it and Tom really liked it. Steven liked it, but he felt it needed more work than the actors did. So we continued to meet and talk about what it needed. And then we reached a moment in time when Steven realized that he wasn't going to be able to do the movie . . . so [Dustin] went to Sydney Pollack, obviously one of the great directors who's ever directed.... And he's a very gracious guy.... These are like the nicest guys, these directors. They're not only great directors, they're also really great people to work with."

Don't be open to too many ideas about changing your script.

You're the writer; *they're* not. Plus this: Most of *their* ideas will be asinine. Believe me: I've heard *thirty years* of asinine ideas.

Gather around, class, here's point number one: A gaffer on the *Betrayed* set told me he had an idea about my script that he wanted to discuss with me. I grabbed him by his lapels, bounced him off the wall, and hit him in the liver with a beautiful left hook.

Point number two: I carry a hunting knife with me to studio meetings sometimes. I began one meeting by taking the knife and sticking it into the middle of a studio conference table, a stunt I had learned while I was a writer at *Rolling Stone*.

Point number three: I left a gigantic dent in a William Morris Agency's conference table by smashing it with my African Dogon walking stick.

Class dismissed, boys and girls.

If they mess with you, give them a little taste of the old ultraviolence.

Fight the morons if they want to change what you've written.

Paddy Chayefsky: "You spill your guts into the typewriter, which is why you can't stand to see what you write destroyed or degraded into a hunk of claptrap by picture butchers."

After a young director butchered one of my scripts behind my back, I sent him a twenty-page memo when I discovered what he had done. The memo questioned his brains, his lineage, and his masculinity. He had a heart attack after reading the memo and almost died. He was in his *thirties*.

Don't let 'em convince you to rewrite it.

A playwright completely rewrote his play when producers told him it was unproducible. They also told him to change the title to *Free and Clear.*

He threw his rewrite away and decided to go with his original title. Arthur Miller did very well, thank you, with *Death of a Salesman.*

ALL HAIL
Harlan Ellison!

When *Star Trek* producer Gene Roddenberry rewrote one of Ellison's scripts, the screenwriter/novelist publicly said this about him: "Gene Roddenberry has about as much writing ability as the lowest industry hack."

If your script gets butchered, Robert McKee may have done it.

McKee told a reporter in Melbourne, Australia, that he works for studios sometimes as a "story doctor."

This is a doctor whose patients (his own scripts) have all died (unproduced) except for the one patient who lived and became a television movie.

First he teaches you how to write and then he kills what you've written.

Don't worry about hurting their feelings.

I've said things like this to studio execs:

"You don't know what the fuck you're talking about."

"That's the stupidest thing I've ever heard in a meeting like this."

"I make more money than you do, so don't give me any suggestions."

One executive called me "temperamental."

Another executive said, "That's why you write so well. Because you believe in yourself so much."

Another thanked me for my "passion" and said, after I'd insulted her, "That's why you're so successful, because you're so passionate."

I grabbed her and kissed her hard, put her across her desk, knocking the silver-framed picture of her husband and kids down, and tore her black Prada. (Just kidding, and apologies to Mickey Spillane, Frank Miller, Michael Ovitz, and my friend Gloria Steinem.)

If the studio gives you script notes . . .

Tear them up.

That's what screenwriter/novelist Michael Crichton does when the studio gives him notes. When he finishes writing his first draft, he walks away and says, "Thank you very much and fuck you."

Most of the people who are writing these memos today have MBAs, don't read, are too busy writing script notes to see too many movies. Their references in the script notes are to other movies—none going back past 1985—few of which they've actually seen, and certainly none shot in black and white.

If you listen to the suggestions contained in these notes, it's possible that you'll get your script made, but it is also very possible that critics will eviscerate it (and you) and other studio execs won't hire you to do anything else or buy any of your other scripts.

Buy your own shredder and carry it with you.

Screenwriter Julian Fellowes (*Gosford Park*): "A screenplay is a collaborative business because making a movie is collaborative. You write synopsis after synopsis until you find one that's agreeable to the executives. Then you write your first draft and get sixty pages of notes from producers and 150 pages from the studio, then you write the second draft and the director comes in with 400 pages of notes, and then the star does their thing. I understand all of that, but there is a time when you get a little tired trying to accommodate a billion different interests, of the fact that your business is one of compromise where your voice is constantly being given direction."

You didn't have to do it, Ben; you elected to.

Ben Hecht wrote, "My chief memory of movieland is one of asking in the producer's office why must I change the script, eviscerate it, cripple and hamstring it? Why must I strip the hero of his few semi-intelligent remarks and why must I tack on a corny ending that makes the stomach shudder?"

The director tells you to rewrite your script in a way that you know will damage and possibly destroy it. What do you do?

William Goldman: "This is not an isolated incident. It happens to us all. And it happens a lot, usually because of star insecurity, but directors can fuck things up pretty good, too. I did what Michael Douglas wanted. The alternative, of course, was to leave the picture. Which would have been stupid, I think, because the instant I am out the door, someone else is hired to do what I wouldn't."

This is the moment when you separate the writers from the whores. I was confronted by the same dilemma—with the same star.

Michael Douglas (and the director, Paul Verhoeven) wanted me to make a bunch of changes to my first draft of *Basic Instinct*. Convinced that the changes would destroy the film, I refused.

I publicly walked off, which made me look like the greatest intransigent asshole in the world, because I had been paid $3 million for the script.

I kept arguing publicly that the script should not be changed, putting a lot of pressure on Verhoeven (and Gary Goldman, the writer he brought in to rewrite me).

And guess what happened? Because of how hard I fought, because I had publicly walked off, and because I refused to mutilate my own child, Verhoeven, after working with the new writer, changed his mind.

He went back to the first draft of my script and shot it. He fired the other writer. He made Michael Douglas accept the fact that my script could not be changed. And he publicly apologized, saying that he hadn't understood "the basement" of my script and was wrong.

I saved my script from being destroyed by my intransigence and my willingness to fight.

Our scripts are our babies; we create them. Bill Goldman mutilated his own baby and advises that you should mutilate yours—at the behest of a star or a director.

Please don't do that.

I don't know how you (and Bill Goldman) can look yourself in the mirror once you do that.

P.S. The script that I wouldn't change was the biggest hit movie of the year. The script that Bill Goldman changed was a disaster.

If you start rewriting, you can be rewriting for years.

From the time screenwriters John Gregory Dunne and Joan Didion began work on a script called *Golden Girl* until the time it was filmed as *Up Close and Personal,* they did *twenty-seven* drafts of the script over the course of *six* years.

What can they do to you if you refuse to make their changes?

Nothing.

They can fire you and bring another writer in to do their dirty work.

Chances are good that they'll even pay you fully. They can't blackball you, because the town runs on greed and tomorrow you might write something that would make some studio or producer $100 million.

Steven Bochco, probably the best writer working in television, once said, "What are they gonna do? Take me out on the back lot and shoot me? What are they gonna do? They can't take my typewriter; it's mine. They can kick me off the lot, but I'll just write another one."

The agent Michael Ovitz once wanted me to do something I didn't want to do, and I wrote him a letter that ended this way: "So do whatever you want to do, Mike, and fuck you. I have my family and I have my old manual imperfect typewriter and they have always been the things I've treasured the most."

Notice how Bochco and I love our *typewriters?*

Spell it out for 'em.

If they want you to rewrite your script in a way you disagree with, point out to them that *script* is the root of the word *scripture,* as in Holy Scripture.

They wanted Paddy to do some rewriting, too.

So don't get discouraged if you're asked to rewrite. But Chayef-sky said, "Can you believe it? These *cruds* want rewrites."

Don't explain anything to anybody.

Screenwriter Dan Pyne (*Pacific Heights*): "When you go to make the movie, you've got to be able to explain to everybody on the movie, from the director on down, what that core idea [for the script] was so that they can see where you started. You have to strip it all back away."

No, you don't. Your deal is to *write* it, not to write and *explain* it. To begin with, have no discussions with anyone on the set except the director. Explain this by saying the director is in charge of the set and you don't want to put yourself in a situation where you're undercutting the son of a bitch.

Otherwise, you'll be having creative discussions with the stars, the gaffers, and the makeup people, who stand around doing nothing and want to express how creative they all are.

Don't strip it away for them. Tell them it's complex and works on different layers, so everyone is free to interpret it according to his or her *own* layer.

Try to do what I did when anyone I met who had seen *Basic Instinct* asked me to tell them if Catherine really did it. I said, "I'm not allowed by contract to tell you that. But go see it again and look for a clue that will definitely give you the answer."

Don't ignore it, fight it.

Screenwriter Jeffrey Boam (*Indiana Jones and the Last Crusade, Lethal Weapon 2*): "I get notes on a script from the lowest-ranking junior executive's assistant reader, who suggests rewrites for dialogue. And I have to endure this. I throw the notes away. I ignore them. I just pay no attention to them at all. You shouldn't fight it. You should just ignore it."

No, Jeffrey. You *should* fight it. You should write the person who sent you the notes a memo, pointing out how stupid, insipid, and benighted his or her ideas are. You should point this out at length and in great detail. And you should send a copy to all the other executives, the producer, and the director.

Your movie has been cast and shooting has begun. They want you to go to the set. What do you do?

Hell no, don't go.

Screenwriter John Gregory Dunne: "I think the writer's presence on the set is just another element in what is often a volatile mix. Tension is the given of a movie, and it has less to do with ego than with the intensity of short-term relationships, a lifetime lived in a seventy-day shoot; if there are location romances, there are also equally irrational location hatreds. If the writer is hanging around, actors ask for a script fix, or why a speech from draft eight can not be substituted for the one in the scene just setting up. I also never speak to a star actor on a set unless spoken to first; this is the actor's office and in his office he or she sets the rules."

In my own experience, everyone will come up to you and present some dumb-ass idea to incorporate into the next scene.

If an actor is having a problem with the director, he'll try to get even with the director by sucking up to you and trying to get you to take a position against the director.

If the director is having trouble with an actor, he'll recruit you to talk the actor into doing the scene his way, not the actor's.

The actor Peter Lawford saw that Dalton Trumbo was on the set of *Exodus,* the script of which Trumbo had written. He went over to Trumbo and asked if he could discuss his character with him.

Otto Preminger, the director, saw Lawford huddled with Trumbo and yelled to Lawford, "You are not to discuss the script with Mr. Trumbo. He is here as a guest and not as a writer."

Lawford said, "Yes, Mr. Preminger," and hurried away from Trumbo.

Don't get too excited watching your film's dailies.

Sam Goldwyn said, "If everyone likes the dailies, the picture's gonna stink."

Try to get videotaped copies of the dailies of your film.

Do this for posterity, of course, and also for eBay, if times get tough in the future.

I've got all the dailies of *Sliver,* including three full tapes of Sharon and Billy "rutting," as Robert Evans, the producer, termed it.

"They're like horses at each other" was the way Evans described it.

Anybody interested?

Steal as much memorabilia from the set as you can.

Everybody does it. If you don't do it, the director will.
Dick Donner has a house in Montana furnished mostly with props and sets from his movies. I visited Steven Spielberg's house in the Palisades years ago and it was filled with what he called "toys" from his sets.

A friend of mine stole the real ice pick from *Basic Instinct* (Planet Hollywood was displaying a phony one for a while), and someone stole my old Royal typewriter—the typewriter I'd actually used to write the script and which also had a cameo in the film—from the *Jagged Edge* set.

The Theory of Creative Conflict

As defined by producer Sam Spiegel: "Films that run smoothly are colorless—only those which are produced in strife have an outstanding merit."

A Production Fuck

An affair that lasts only as long as the shoot.

You can make sure your film will be distributed.

Afraid that Disney wouldn't release *An Alan Smithee Film: Burn Hollywood Burn,* I was ready to show it myself in church halls and school cafeterias.

So I had a copy of the negative illicitly duped, and then I *stole it* (a federal offense)!

I still have it in a closet in the baby's room, hidden underneath a big box of old toys.

Sit in the back row at a studio screening of the rough cut.

John Gregory Dunne: "Don DeLine, the head of production, was sitting directly behind us, and I wished we were sitting behind him so that we could measure his reaction, see where he took notes."

If the Writers Guild arbitrates your screen credit . . .

Remember that the Writers Guild committee that will decide whether to award you screen credit (and more money) is made up of people like you—writers who want credit (and more money) on their writing projects.

The people on this committee *want* to award you the credit, so make it easy for them. Give them a lengthy, scholarly, lawyerly document pointing to all your plot, character, and name changes—and be sure to use a lot of yellow Magic Markers.

I know a screenwriter who, in an effort to get screen credit, sent the Guild committee a document that was longer than his script.

You might have to stand in line to get your screen credit.

John Gregory Dunne: "Prevailing industry wisdom is that the more writers there are on a script, the better that script will be. On our version of *A Star Is Born*, eight of the thirteen writers who actually worked on the script filed for credit.

Scratch and claw for your credit.

Screenwriter Budd Schulberg: "The billing on *On the Waterfront* soured the sweet taste of all of it for me. There was Sam Spiegel's billing twice as big as life, while the name of the writer, and in this case the originator of the project as well, is either left out entirely or reduced to almost ridiculous minuteness."

Your director will try to screw you with your screen credit.

Two easy and common ways:

1. Your name as screenwriter stays up on-screen for three seconds; the director's name stays on-screen for eight seconds.

2. Your name on-screen—in black letters—is against a black background, so the audience can hardly make it out. The director's name—also in black letters—is against a crisp white background, so it is glaringly visible.

If the movie has little to do with the script that you wrote, take your name off of it.

Unless you want to paint the scarlet letter on yourself, don't let your name be on something that isn't yours.

I realize giving up the credit may cost you money, but I argue that you will damage yourself more by feeling like a hypocrite or a hooker.

When I saw the final cut of *Nowhere to Run* (starring Jean Claude Van Damme), which was based on my script *Pals,* I didn't recognize it as mine. I told the studio I wanted my name off of it.

The studio said no. They wanted to use my name in the trailers for the movie, running the line "from the writer of *Basic Instinct,* Joe Eszterhas."

I went to the Writers Guild and demanded that my name be taken off, but the Guild said I couldn't do it—I'd been paid too much money by the studio.

So I petitioned the Guild to give credit to the two guys who'd rewritten me, as well. I was told that it was the first time in Guild history that a writer had petitioned for credit for his "competing" cowriters.

The two guys who had rewritten me got credit behind me, and that way, at least, I was able to spread the blame for the mess that was on-screen.

If they ask you how you like the movie you wrote, tell 'em the truth.

Director Joseph von Sternberg: "When he saw the movie he wrote and I directed, Ben Hecht told the press that he was about to vomit, his exact words being—'I must rush home at once, I think it's mal de mer.'"

Try to find something positive to say about your film.

Sharon Stone, after the release of *Basic Instinct*: "At least it proves I'm a natural blonde."

You might have to drink whiskey from a vase.

If you're attending the first screening of the film and you wrote the script, that is.

Tennessee Williams, attending the first screening of his film *Suddenly Last Summer,* drank whiskey from a vase and muttered, "Who wrote this shit?"

Watching your movie might hurt.

Jim Harrison: "Sitting there in the dark before the projector starts you have the distinct feeling you might be raped by an elephant or, if your imagination is running to the sea, a whale."

Don't tell your friends when or where your movie will be screened.

Actor/producer Danny DeVito: "I've heard stories where people have actually paid other people to call newspapers and say they've seen screenings of movies that were bad—just because they wanted to sabotage the movie. That happens all the time."

Do whatever you can to stop the studio from market-researching your film.

Director Phillip Noyce: "Then we did the first screening for a recruited audience on the lot at Paramount, as was customary for a Paramount film. The guys from a company called National Research Group, run by Joseph Farrell, would go out to malls and cinemas and recruit an audience for these previews. In Los Angeles people are pretty used to being invited. It's a way of getting the lowdown on films many, many months before their release, and, in a town devoted to the entertainment industry, it's also become a way for the ordinary man and woman to have their say. *They can become not just a film critic but a film executive.* The tick of their pen, the cross of their pencil, can decide the fate of the movie they're judging. The preview audience's power has been further increased since the late 1990s by advance reviews appearing on Internet sites such as 'Ain't It Cool.' "

Don't go to any focus-group screenings.

L.A. is a city full of make-believe film critics who wanna be screenwriters. They turn out en masse at focus-group research screenings.

Every twit out there thinks he's a critic, and they all think they know better than guess who?

Not the director, because the director knows things about camera angles and cameras that they don't.

Not the actors, because, well, they're handsome or beautiful or, minimally, graduate students of the Method.

Okay, all together now, they think they know better than—*ta da*—the highly paid, millionaire screenwriter!

And here are all these twits, gathered together in this room, part of a focus group, with the screenwriter usually there, and they have a chance to tell him (with studio execs listening) how it *should have been* written.

And maybe, in the process, they'll be discovered by the director or producer—it's their big chance at the brass ring, at discovery, at stardom, if they can just sound smart enough about what the screenwriter did wrong.

I saw one guy in his late thirties in three of my focus groups at research screenings—*the same guy at three of them,* at *Jagged Edge* and *Betrayed* and *Music Box*—and in all three cases, the guy lectured me about how bad my ending was.

See your films in a theater with real people.

Most people in Hollywood see movies in a screening room or on their home screens. But it's important for a writer to see how a film affects real people—especially the impact your own lines of dialogue and your story have on them.

This should be the final part of your creative experience of writing a screenplay. It begins in a little room, with you sitting there all alone, making it up, and it ends in a big room, with hundreds of people communicating to you their reactions to what you've written.

If you don't experience what you've written with an audience, then you're not bringing your communication process to a conclusion.

Avoid the industry premiere of your film.

Mike Medavoy: "Industry screenings might be the ultimate hypocrisy in a business that can be very hypocritical. The audience is usually composed mostly of the filmmaker's genuine friends, who applaud and laugh at all the right moments. They want the studio executives in the audience to hear what a great film it is so the studio will support their friend's film with marketing dollars. The studio executives tend to be a group of people who either inherited the film from a previous regime or don't want anything to do with what they think is a potential turkey, so they walk out and praise the film in Hollywood doublespeak. Typically, they can be heard telling the producer and director things like "You did it again" or "What a picture!" neither of which says what it really means. Those executives also know they might need that producer or director in the future. So in the end, everyone runs from a failure and tries to walk alongside a success."

Make sure you're part of the junket interviews.

Some directors like to exclude screenwriters from these interviews because the journalists who fly in from everywhere are bought and paid for—literally. The studio covers all their expenses. That means they're not going to write anything bad about your movie or, if you're there to be interviewed, you—not unless they want to lose their sunny weekends sitting by the pool at the Four Seasons, enjoying anything they want to order from room service.

Wash your hands of any blood.

If your script becomes a movie and on the first weekend of its release some sick freak in Omaha kills his girlfriend in the same manner in which you killed one of your characters, forget about it.

Remember that Mark Chapman had a copy of *Catcher in the Rye* in his pocket when he shot John Lennon. And keep in mind that more killers have carried the Bible in their pockets during the act of murder than any other book.

Your words can become toys and trading cards.

Traveling through Italy while *Flashdance* was being released there, I started collecting *Flashdance* trading cards. Each shot of the film I had cowritten had been turned into a trading card. I saw little Italian kids flipping the cards against the curb and trying to win them from one another.

Screenwriter Dan O'Bannon (*Alien*): "When *Alien* was made, I went into a Thrifty Drug and there was a little *Alien* doll in the toy stand. When your work begins to become somewhat influential like that, you do see pieces of yourself come floating back in the oddest places."

If your movie fails, they'll blame the marketing department.

When three straight MGM films with big budgets and big stars failed miserably—*Windtalkers, Hart's War, Rollerball*—the studio didn't fire its head of production and didn't hesitate to make new development deals with the screenwriters and directors of those three disasters. Instead, the studio got rid of two people in the marketing department.

Aw, stop whining already.

Screenwriter/director Larry Kasdan (*Body Heat*), talking about screenwriting: "The movie comes out and there's the pain that your movie never got made; there's this other movie instead. But everyone says *you* wrote it, and they blame *you* for it anyway. So you're getting it from both sides: from inside and outside."

Pissing on Your Leg

What audiences do when they don't like something they see on-screen— that, at least, is how Warren Beatty puts it.

If your movie fails, blame it on the director.

Tell everyone he trashed your script and/or let the actors improvise.

As my good friend Don Simpson used to say, "It's not how you play the game; it's how you place the blame."

Or blame it on the good old USA.

In an interview in Budapest, Hungary, director Oliver Stone blamed the failure of his film *Alexander* on American audiences. "Americans aren't interested in history," he said, "and can't concentrate enough for a three-hour film."

And talk about how huge it is in Croatia.

Oliver Stone, discussing the failure of *Alexander*: "Europe was spectacular. Not the major territories—that's in January. What's positive is that it opened in various regions very strongly— Russia, Sweden, it moved down to Croatia. And then you go down to Turkey, Taiwan, the Asian side. Then to Bangkok and the Philippines. That was very, very encouraging. I don't follow these things—I'm told it's like Number One."

Or use Shakespeare, Marlowe, and Goethe as your alibi.

Oliver Stone, discussing the failure of his film *Alexander*: "I mean—why didn't Shakespeare touch Alexander, or Marlowe or Goethe? Alexander was famous. Nobody touched him. Why? Because there's too much success. He's too much—too much for people."

In other words, while Shakespeare, Marlowe, and Goethe chickened out, at least Oliver tried!

But you won't be able to fool Robert J. Hurns of Mount Prospect, Illinois.

After reading Oliver Stone discussing the failure of *Alexander,* Mr. Hurns wrote a letter to *The New York Times* (January 2, 2005):

"The failure of his film wasn't due to a lack of interest in Alexander the Great, but rather to the unwillingness of moviegoers to invest their time and money in a product associated with Oliver the Opinionated.

"Mr. Stone states that Alexander was 'too much' for Shakespeare, Marlowe and Goethe. The true epic here is that of Mr. Stone's bloated ego."

Once you write some hit movies, you'll have much more power.

Screenwriter Jeffrey Boam (*Indiana Jones and the Last Crusade, Lethal Weapon*): "I get no more respect now than I did when I first started. Absolutely none . . . I feel that I've earned more respect than I'm getting. And that my ideas shouldn't be dismissed out of hand, which they often are. I'll throw out an idea at a meeting, and the director or producer or the studio executive will say, 'I hate it.'

They won't explain to me why; they feel like they don't have to. They're not curious to know how I would actually execute this idea. They stop me and say, 'That's terrible. We don't like it. Move on.' You know, just like I'm the errand boy."

If you let 'em treat you like an errand boy, Jeffrey, then you're an errand boy.

If somebody says "I hate it," one possible answer, with your record of hit movies, is, "Oh yeah, how many millions have your movies grossed, asshole?"

In my experience, I've found that most producers, directors, and studio execs don't know how to deal with that word—*asshole*—when it's directed at them, possibly because deep in their hearts they know that they're . . .

If your movie fails, there's a good chance that one day it will be remade. Samuel Goldwyn: "It's a mistake to remake a great picture, because you can never make it better. Better you should find a picture that was done badly and see what can be done to improve it."

PART SEVEN

WORKING WITH THE DIRECTOR

LESSON 12

He's a Passive-Aggressive Snake!

Defining the director . . .

Screenwriter William Faulkner describing his director friend Howard Hawks: "He's a cold-blooded man, but he will protect me if I write a script that will make money for him."

Another definition of the director . . .

The starlet offers the director a blow job for a bit part.
The director says, "What's in it for me?"

It's all about the next job, isn't it, Ron?

Oscar-winning screenwriter Ron Bass (*Rain Main*) on the director: "He's a *fascinating* guy. He's a *brilliant* guy. He's really a *challenging* guy. . . . Everything he wanted to do, even when I didn't see the sense of it at the time or I didn't see where he was going, it all did make sense and it was all going toward *a vision that was his vision.* . . . This was my first lesson in trying to let go of my vision of the piece and understand that there comes a point when the director's the guy who's got to make the movie, and you really have to be *servicing his vision.* . . . I see the film and I say at the end of it, 'Boy, *he's a lot smarter than I was* and smart enough to realize it.' . . . *The director is the author of the film.* . . . The farther I go in my writing career, the more I enjoy what I'm doing, *the more sympathetic and admiring I am of directors.* I think directing is the lousiest job in the world. . . . *The directors are the victims.* They are controlled by the movie. They are the victims of the flaws in my script."

Directors can plagiarize anything they want.

If *they* steal, it's called an *homage.* The director Brian De Palma has done whole film-length homages to Hitchcock—*Sisters, Blow Out, Obsession.*

Directors are petty despots.

Director Ken Russell to screenwriter Paddy Chayefsky: "What's it to you whether you like the set or not? You're only the writer! . . . Take your turkey sandwiches and your script and your Sanka and stuff it up your ass and get on the next fucking plane back to New York and let me get on with the fucking film."

Avoid auteur directors.

The director's job is to put *your* vision up on the movie screen.

If you work with an auteur director, he will steal *your* vision and change it enough so he can call it his own.

Stanley Kubrick, perhaps the best director in the world, wanted to direct Paddy Chayefsky's *Network.* Paddy wouldn't work with him and stopped the studio from hiring him. *Network* won the Oscar for Best Screenplay and was a huge worldwide hit. It remained very much "a Paddy Chayefsky film," not "a film by Stanley Kubrick."

An Ambience Chaser

A director who uses smokepots in every scene.

Don't work with any director who's just won an Oscar.

That director will be so impressed with his accomplishment that he won't work again for many years.

Robert Redford didn't work again for eight years after he won for *Ordinary People*; Warren Beatty didn't direct again for nine years after *Reds*; Milos Forman didn't direct for five years after *Amadeus.*

What these guys all did, though, for all those years they didn't direct, was *develop* properties.

They worked with screenwriters like you, trying to get a script in good-enough shape to shoot. The fact that they found no scripts in all that time good enough to shoot may have had something to do with how petrified they were to direct after winning an Oscar.

R E E L S P E A K

To Do a Cimino

To direct a film that fails so badly that it kills the studio, like Michael's *Heaven's Gate*.

ALL HAIL
Bruce Vilanch!

Never mind all the producers and directors and hosts, Bruce Vilanch, screenwriter, has been writing the Academy Awards show for fifteen years and is its true voice.

Work with a director when he is "briefly, temporarily, human."

Producer Robert Evans: "The time I want to work with a director is when he's just had a gigantic failure. Think Cimino after *Heaven's Gate*, Spielberg after *1941*, Coppola after *One from the Heart*, Verhoeven after *Showgirls*. That's the time to work with them—when, briefly, temporarily, they're human."

Try to work with directors who began as producers.

Joe Mankiewicz, Alan Pakula, and Irwin Winkler all began as successful producers and then became successful directors. Knowing so much about film, there is less chance that they view themselves as omnipotent auteurs.

If you hook up with the wrong director, it can be hazardous to your health.

Raymond Chandler: "I went to Hollywood to work with Billy Wilder on *Double Indemnity*. This was an agonizing experience and has probably shortened my life."

Directors resent the money you're paid.

Director David Lean wrote a memo to the producer about Michael Wilson, the screenwriter they'd been working with on *Lawrence of Arabia*.

Lean wrote, "He's shot his bolt as far as this script's concerned and whether he's bitter with you and me or both of us we've got to lump it. I only note him because I hope you are not proposing to give him the two and a half percent profit because, softy as I am, I would resent it very much."

Some directors will try to take your credit away from you.

Screenwriter Walon Green (*The Wild Bunch*) on director Bob Rafelson: "If he wrote ten words, he'd say he wrote the whole thing."

A Credit-Card Filmmaker

A guy who's broke and can't pay for an option on your script but wants to direct it—though he's only directed a couple of TV ads in regional markets—and wants to sit down with you first to share some ideas he has about the script.

ALL HAIL
Director Philip Noyce!

My friend Phillip refuses to take the "film by" credit on any of his films.

He explained it to me this way: "I don't deserve it any more than you deserve it or the stars deserve it or the DP deserves it or the editor deserves it or et cetera, et cetera, et cetera."

Beware of world-famous, highly publicized auteur directors.

Film editor Lou Lombardo, who worked with both men, compared Sam Peckinpah and Robert Altman this way: "Peckinpah is a prick and Altman is a cunt."

Don't work with a busy director.

Director Jon Avnet and screenwriter John Gregory Dunne were having a script discussion on the phone, when Avnet got another call and told Dunne he'd call him right back. He called him back *eleven days later,* but explained that he'd been very busy.

A director can agree to direct your script for the wrong reasons.

Director Phillip Noyce, on directing *The Saint*: "It was an opportunity at the time to create a franchise. Although in the end, what I really found attractive about it was the opportunity to choose my own location to set the story. So, it became as much about the adventure of making the film as the adventure of the story of the film. It was as much about the adventure *off the screen* as the adventure *on the screen.* I satisfied my curiosity about post-Soviet Russia during the making of that movie."

In other words, Phillip just wanted to take an extended trip to Russia.

Some directors are only as good as their wives.

Bob Rafelson's and Peter Bogdanovich's best work was behind them the day Bob divorced Toby and Peter divorced Polly Platt.

Directors are incessantly looking for their next job.

The director Adrian Lyne and I were discussing *Flashdance* many years after we'd made the movie. A young supporting actress in the film had died tragically, as had studio executive Dawn Steel and our producer, Don Simpson.

"But that's nothing compared to *Superman,*" I said. "George Reeves, the guy who played him on TV, was murdered. Look what happened to Christopher Reeve, and then there was poor Margot Kidder, found wandering around that guy's backyard out near the airport."

"Bloody hell," Adrian said. And then he added, "Do you think there's a movie there? Our sequel? *The Curse of Flashdance?*"

If you wrote and directed it, then you're an auteur.

If you're the screenwriter, you are not the author of the film; you, the director, the producer, the actors, the editor, and the cinematographer are *collaborators.*

That's why it's immoral and absurd for directors to take a credit that reads "a film by Bill Hotshot."

Newspapers and magazines, staffed by reporters and critics who'd love to make screenwriter wages, rub this in. They refer to movies as simply "by" the director.

Don't ever refer to a movie as the director's possession; that's incorrect and morally wrong.

It is not George Roy Hill's *Butch Cassidy and the Sundance Kid.* It is not Steven Spielberg's *E.T.* It is not Sidney Lumet's *Network.* It is not Sam Mendes's *American Beauty.* It is not Clint Eastwood's *Million Dollar Baby.* It is not John Avildsen's *Rocky.* It is not Ridley Scott's *Thelma & Louise.* It is not Richard Marquand's *Jagged Edge.* It is not Paul Verhoeven's *Basic Instinct.* It is not Billy Friedkin's *Jade.*

It is just as wrong to refer to a movie as the screenwriter's possession, but it's a helluva lot of fun.

It is William Goldman's *Butch Cassidy and the Sundance Kid.* It is Melissa Mathison's *E.T.* It is Paddy Chayefsky's *Network.* It is Alan Ball's *American Beauty.* It is F. X. Toole's and Paul Haggis's *Million Dollar Baby.* It is Sylvester Stallone's *Rocky.* It is Callie Khouri's *Thelma & Louise.* It is Joe Eszterhas's *Jagged Edge.* It is Joe Eszterhas's *Basic Instinct.* It is Joe Eszterhas's *Jade.*

When working with the director, always say "my movie" while talking to him.

This is, of course, your revenge for what you will see on-screen and in ads: a film *by* the director.

Just because the Writers Guild doesn't even care about this usage doesn't mean you can't get your sweet little pound (okay, ounce) of flesh.

Orson Welles told the truth.

Welles told French critic André Bazin, the father of the auteur theory, this: "Directing is an invention of people like you. It's not an art, it's at most an art for one minute per day."

Yours is a creative art; the director's is interpretive.

Screenwriter/novelist Donald Westlake: "I am not a proponent of the director's auteur theory. I think it comes out of a basic misunderstanding of the functions of the creative versus interpretive arts."

You've got the power.

A screenwriter and a director were on a trip, scouting locations. The script called for "white houses dotting the hillsides." The hills they were looking at were perfect except for the fact that blue houses were dotting the hillside, not white ones.

The director, a freak for authenticity, turned the location down because of the blue houses.

The screenwriter took the script out of the director's hands, then crossed the word *white* out and replaced it with the word *blue.*

The director approved the hillside.

The vision is yours, not the director's.

I had an agent named Rosalie Swedlin, who, after a research screening of my film *Betrayed,* turned to the director (Costa-Gavras), who was standing next to me, and congratulated him for his "vision."

I fired her the next day.

Anybody can direct.

Producer David O. Selznick: "There is no mystery to directing. I don't have time. Frankly it's easier to criticize another man's work than to direct myself. As a producer, I can maintain an editorial perspective that I wouldn't have as a director. I consider myself first a creative person, then a showman, and then a businessman."

You, too, can give your director directing lessons.

Director David Lean not only asked screenwriter Robert Bolt to read his script of *Lawrence of Arabia* but also taped Bolt reading it. When shooting began each day, Lean listened to Bolt's recording of that day's scenes before he started shooting.

Directors can't write.

Vincent Canby of *The New York Times* wrote, "Mr. Cimino has written his own screenplay whose awfulness has been considerably inflated by the director's [Mr. Cimino's] wholly unwarranted respect for it."

When will they ever learn?

Martin Brest directed the hit movie *Beverly Hills Cop,* written by Danilo Bach and Daniel Petrie, Jr. He then directed the hit movies *Midnight Run,* written by George Gallo, and *Scent of a Woman,* written by Bo Goldman.

And then he directed *Gigli,* which he also wrote. It was one of the biggest cinematic disasters in years.

Stay away from Michael Cimino.

Michael Cimino directed *The Deer Hunter* brilliantly. He didn't write it. He won the Oscar for Best Director; the movie won for Best Picture.

Then he directed *Heaven's Gate*. He wrote it. It became the greatest financial and critical disaster in film history.

Michael Cimino has directed many films since then. He has cowritten or written all of them. All of them have failed.

He is rewriting himself now. He is sometimes seen around Hollywood wearing dresses and a wig.

Renny Harlin's writing advice . . .

Harlin (*Cliffhanger, Exorcist: The Beginning*): "I don't want accidents, I want disasters. I don't want dirt, I want filth. I don't want a storm, I want a hurricane. I don't want fear, I want panic. I don't want suspense, I want terror. I don't want humor, I want hysteria."

Directors confuse psychodrama with drama.

Adrian Lyne, the director of *Flashdance,* tried to talk me into having Alex, the central character, be raped by her father at the age of eight.

Larry Peerce, the original director of *Love Story,* wanted Ryan O'Neal to be a returning Vietnam veteran suffering combat flashbacks.

No wonder he screwed up my script of Jade.

Billy Friedkin, to an interviewer in 1967: "The plotted film is on the way out and is no longer of interest to the serious director."

Your director will hate you because you can write.

On July 18, 2003, Alessandra Stanley wrote this in *The New York Times*: "Mr. Affleck and Mr. Damon, who were themselves awkward newcomers when they won an Oscar for best screenplay for their first film, *Good Will Hunting,* sponsored a competition for thousands of unknown, inexperienced writers and directors, summoning the semifinalists to the 2003 Sundance Film Festival. Erica Beeney, 28, whose screenplay about a troubled teenager in Shaker Heights won first place, was teamed with Efram Potelle and Kyle Rankin, both 30, long-time friends and directing partners. . . . The two directors' desire to exclude the reticent Ms. Beeney becomes increasingly obvious in each episode. By this Sunday, she had finally moved from wounded perplexity to sarcastic rage. 'Do phones work?' she finally barks at Mr. Potelle when she realizes that they have once again made last-minute changes behind her back. She bonds with the slick producers who report to Miramax and try to keep the directors' inexperience and egotism in check."

Writing is more difficult than directing.

Writer/director Elia Kazan: "Writing, in case you don't know it, is much harder than directing films. It may be the reason why I, perverse I, do it."

A director isn't a writer or an artist; he's a general.

Director Orson Welles: "A poet needs a pen, a painter a brush, and a director an army."

Directors are artists.

Director Herbert Brenon delayed shooting a scene while an assistant searched Hollywood for a fifty-pound note.

When the note was brought to him, Brenon sealed it in an envelope and handed the envelope to the actor, who, the script said, was carrying a brown envelope with a fifty-pound note in it.

It's the scenery that makes a great movie, not your script.

Director David Lean in a memo to his *Lawrence of Arabia* producer: "Listen to me. The thing that's going to make this a very exceptional picture in the world-beater class are the backgrounds, the camels, horses, and uniqueness of the strange atmosphere we are putting around our intimate story.... This is our great spectacle which will pull the crowd from university professor to newsboy."

What to do when a director calls you to tell you he likes your script.

When Barbet Schroeder called screenwriter/novelist Charles Bukowski to tell him he liked *Barfly*, Bukowski said, "Fuck off, you French frog!"

Directors certainly haven't changed much.

Ben Hecht, discussing a first meeting with a director in 1937: "I've never met anyone so eager to flaunt his stupidity, low-grade human values and jackass vanities in the world."

Directors hate what they do.

Director Stephen Frears (*My Beautiful Launderette*): "There's nothing more loathsome than actually making a film."

Directors use people.

They don't say, "He's perfect—we'll cast him." They say, "He's perfect—we'll use him."

Don't give any ideas away.

The director Ivan Reitman was the producer of *Big Shots,* a comic adventure about two little kids.

As Ivan and I talked for days about the script, I suggested putting adult stars Arnold Schwarzenegger and Danny DeVito into the kids' parts.

A couple of years after *Big Shots,* Ivan made a comic adventure about two adult kids. It was called *Twins* and starred Schwarzenegger and Danny DeVito.

Big Shots failed, but *Twins* was a huge hit.

Most directors are passive-aggressive snakes.

This will seriously complicate your life.

It means they won't tell you if they dislike your script or something in your script. They'll rewrite it themselves behind your back or try to get a screenwriter friend to do it. Or they'll tell you they love your script but that the studio wants another writer to come in and do some "very minor rewriting . . . nothing more than some touching up, really."

They hate confrontations and will agree with you about most things and then do exactly what they want to do when you aren't on the set. And if you see the finished film and then confront them and say, "What the fuck did you do to my script?" they'll say, "What do you mean? I didn't change a comma."

Or: "I didn't have a choice. The studio ordered me to make those changes. I didn't want to tell you because I knew how bloody upset you'd get."

Or: "I was just trying to prevent you from getting hurt."

Or: "The star just didn't want to do the scene. I tried to insist on doing it the way you wrote it, but you know how arrogant he is. Defending your script almost cost me my job."

Martin Scorsese is paranoid.

Martin Scorsese puts a mirror on top of the monitor while he's filming, so he can see who's standing behind him, watching.

When he was shooting *Gangs of New York,* producer Harvey Weinstein put a giant truck mirror on Scorsese's monitor. Written on it were these words: "Caution, objects in the mirror are larger than they appear."

In the middle of the jumbo mirror was Weinstein's huge face.

The director always thinks he is the star.

According to Hal Ashby's producing partner, Charles Mulvehill: "Hal felt the picture should be the star, not the actor. But what that meant is that the star was the director, Hal Ashby."

ALL HAIL
Barbet Schroeder!

He's a director, I know, but still . . .

Learning that the studio had just pulled the plug on his film, he bought a Black & Decker circular saw, took it into the office of the studio head, plugged it in, turned it on, and held the blade over the studio head's hand, threatening to slice his finger off.

At that moment, the studio head changed his mind and decided to make Barbet's film.

Directors have always been full of it.

Screenwriter Ben Hecht: "My movie, *Underworld*, was the first gangster film to bedazzle the movie fans; there were no lies in it—except for a half dozen sentimental touches introduced by its director, Joe von Sternberg. I still shudder remembering one of them. My head villain, after robbing a bank, emerged with a suitcase full of money and paused in the crowded street to notice a blind beggar and give him a coin—before making his getaway."

You don't want to get this close.

According to the producer Gerald Ayres, who worked with them, screenwriter Robert Towne and director/star Warren Beatty liked having sex with different women at the same time in the same room.

Hanging out with your director can be deadly.

Screenwriter/film critic James Agee went off to write at the San Ysidro Ranch, near Santa Barbara, with director John Huston. They drank and played tennis, and Agee had a heart attack and almost died.

ALL HAIL
Carole Eastman!

Screenwriter Eastman (*Five Easy Pieces*) "felt she would become polluted if she had to talk to the director," said her friend Richard Wechsler.

You don't want a director as your best friend.

When director Bob Fosse was dying, he asked his best and oldest friend, Paddy Chayefsky, to look over his will.

"Hey," Paddy said to Fosse, "why am I not in your will?"

"I'm taking care of my wife and my kids," Fosse replied.

"Fuck you, then," Paddy said. "*Live!*"

Don't be anybody's "pocket writer."

This can happen when you get to be pals with a director. In most cases, a director will be pals with you if you do exactly what he tells you to do, *if you write what he tells you to write.*

If you do that, he will then bring you into his future projects (written by others) and get you a lot of money to rewrite those scripts.

Kurt Luedtke (*Absence of Malice*) and David Rayfiel (*The Firm*) made a lot of money being director Sidney Pollack's "pocket writers." As a result, though, they were mistrusted by other directors, who feared that if they worked with them, these writers would pass their ideas on to their pal Pollack.

If you're working with a director, don't just "come up with the details."

Screenwriter José Rivera, talking about working with director Walter Salles on *The Motorcycle Diaries:* "Some of the best collaborative work I have ever done with a director was with Walter because he doesn't rewrite you. He makes very precise and interesting comments on everything you've written, and some of them yield new things . . . He would have an idea and I would come up with the details."

Directors like being deified.

Billy Friedkin about Alfred Hitchcock: "I don't give a flying fuck about him, and I'm not a worshipper of his, nor have I ever set out to emulate him. But I'm glad that people deify directors because I make more money that way."

But you don't really have to deify your director.

Screenwriter Brian Helgeland on director Dick Donner: "With his leonine head and booming voice, he seems more like a movie star than the stars he's directing. When Donner shouts action on a set, it's the voice of God coming down from on high."

Oh gag me!

Screenwriter Darryl Ponicsan on director Martha Coolidge: "She values words, but she knows the silences are worth more. A rambling rose rambling down a Texas street says more than words can convey. Come to think of it, so does this photograph of Martha."

Please pass me that barf bag.

Screenwriter Jeff Davis, asked to adapt a novel for director William Friedkin, whose wife, Sherry Lansing, headed Paramount at the time and who hadn't had a hit movie in thirty years, said, "To be writing a psychological horror film for William Friedkin, the man who set the standard in the genre by directing what is considered to be the scariest and most viscerally disturbing movie of all time, is more than a writer could hope for."

You can get up now, sweetie.

Ronald Harwood won Best Adapted Screenplay for *The Pianist* and said in his acceptance speech, "Roman Polanski [the director] deserves this."

ALL HAIL
William Goldman!

He wrote an article in *Daily Variety* saying that Martin Scorsese did not deserve to win an Oscar for *Gangs of New York*: "*Gangs of New York* is a mess."

He also wrote that he would never forgive Miramax for "hyping the Oscar to Robert Benigni, the scummiest award in the Academy's history."

Don't ever trust your director.

Jean Renoir, the king of auteur directors, said, "Is it possible to succeed without any act of betrayal?"

You can't ever overestimate a director's ego.

Billy Friedkin told screenwriter William Peter Blatty that he refused to cast Marlon Brando in *The Exorcist*. Blatty: "His reason was that if he cast Brando, it would be Brando's picture, not his."

Where do their brains go? Be prepared for the director of your film to have an affair on the set with the lead actress.

It happened to me twice—with Costa-Gavras and Debra Winger on *Betrayed* and, more famously, with Paul Verhoeven and Elizabeth Berkley on *Showgirls*.

Costa's affair didn't hurt *Betrayed,* but Paul's destroyed *Showgirls*.

After the film bombed, I said to Paul, "When a man gets a hard-on, his brains slide into his ass."

Paul laughed; he didn't argue with me.

But they can't walk the walk.

Directors know they can't write, but they try to make up for this by *talking* about writing.

They are similar to the screenwriting teachers in this regard—the teachers who can't write scripts but tell you how you should write them.

Directors will talk to you about the "through line" and "the arc," ask "Where is the redemption?" . . . and refer to "deep in the subtext" and "the door to the character's motivation."

Some directors, interestingly, have taken screenwriting courses from the likes of Robert McKee, but even those who haven't have learned how to speak this cinema-lit psychobabble.

They can't write, but while *you're* writing, they have to do *something* creative—they can't even cast or scout for locations until you're *done* writing.

So what they do to kill time while you're creating the movie is to talk to you about how to write—like the baseball-hitting coach who never got out of the minors telling major leaguers how to hit a curveball.

A good director is worth waiting for.

Costa-Gavras, the director of *Z,* called me in 1977, after he'd read my script of *F.I.S.T.* He said, in very broken English, that he loved the script but that he couldn't speak English very well.

But he was taking Berlitz courses, he said, and when his English got better, he'd call me back and maybe we could do something together.

Eight years after that first phone call, he directed my script *Betrayed.*

Don't completely dismiss your director's ideas.

Director Costa-Gavras saved me from an ending to *Music Box* that, I think, in retrospect, would have hurt the movie. I will always be grateful for the way he slugged it out with me and convinced me that my ending was wrong.

On the other hand, dismiss most of your director's ideas.

Costa-Gavras had an idea for the ending of *Betrayed* that, I was convinced, would destroy the movie.

We slugged it out for two days and, at the end of those days, he reluctantly agreed with me that he was wrong. I will always be grateful for that, too.

LESSON 13

Every Good Director Is a Sadist!

If you argue with your director, go for the jugular.

Sam Spiegel, arguing with Elia Kazan, said to him, "What the hell do you know? You only know about testifying on your friends."

On *An Alan Smithee Film: Burn Hollywood Burn*, I said to Arthur Hiller, "You don't know what the fuck you're doing, you doddering old fuck." (I apologized later.)

Are you masochistic?

Producer David Merrick: "All good directors are sadists. I won't put up with it from mediocrities, but for genius I'm willing to be a doormat."

Your disagreement with the director can get ugly.

Working on *Lawrence of Arabia*, screenwriter Carl Foreman and director David Lean got along so badly that they were even arguing about whether a character would scratch his face or not.

Foreman accused Lean of being "an art house director." "You have made only small British films," Foreman said. "You have no experience of the international market."

Lean attacked Foreman in an eight-page letter to the film's producer, which began: "This is not meant to be an attack. But when one gets into the scenes in detail, they are awfully rough and ready, and in many cases cheap and derivative."

In a creative discussion, use any lethal weapon you can.

Director Jack Garfein (*The Strange One*) had survived concentration camps, and when a screenwriter wasn't listening to him about the scene he wanted, Garfein asked, "Why are you arguing with me? Don't you know I am an Auschwitz victim?"

The way to talk to a director . . .

Producer Robert Evans: "I don't want a director to talk with me and then leave and say, 'Gee, what a nice guy.' I want him to say, 'That bastard.' 'That son of a bitch!' Because then they always come back and say, 'You were right. Let's talk.'"

To Do a Terry Malick

To acquire a towering international reputation for very little work.

Break his ribs.

When screenwriter/actor Sylvester Stallone had a creative disagreement with director Ted Kotcheff (*The Apprenticeship of Duddy Kravitz*) on the set of *First Blood,* Sly smashed a jarring left hook into Ted's rib cage, breaking three ribs.

Brass-knuckle him.

If a director insisted that Frank Sinatra do more than two takes of a scene, the director got a visit at home that night from Frank's pal Jilly Rizzo.

Jilly carried a pair of brass knuckles given to him by Frank and inscribed "To Jilly with love from Frankie." Jilly would show the director he visited these brass knuckles.

Shoot him.

Screenwriter Abraham Polonsky about director Elia Kazan: "I'll be watching, hoping somebody shoots him."

Yes, I know, I know—Abe *might* have had personal issue with him: Kazan testified in front of the House Committee on Un-American Activities; Polonsky refused to testify and therefore became a blacklisted screenwriter.

Spit in the producer's face and call him a pig.

That's what Katharine Hepburn did when she finished the last shot of *Suddenly Last Summer.*

She spit in the director Joe Mankiewicz's face and called the producer "a pig in a silk suit who sends flowers." Then she spat on the floor.

Seduce his wife.

I was introduced to Martin Scorsese a few years after I publicly fired his good friend and agent Michael Ovitz. Marty looked at me superciliously, barely taking my hand.

I knew he was the King of the Auteurs, while I was the auteur-slayer. I knew how seriously he took himself, while I prided myself on being the "rogue elephant" of screenwriters.

I knew all those things about him and I knew a whole lot more that he didn't know I knew, things I had learned from one of his wives, things she had told me after we'd made love on the kitchen floor of Marty's house while Marty was off on location, shooting, being the auteur.

Throw something in his face.

Angry at Roman Polanski, Faye Dunaway peed in a coffee cup and threw it into his face.

Did poor Francis lose his marbles?

When studio head Mike Medavoy arrived on the set of *Apocalypse Now* in the Philippines, director Coppola spoke to him mostly in the language of the natives he'd been living with.

Coppola said to Medavoy, "Maybe it should be a perpetual work in progress. I don't know if I want to finish it this year. I might want to finish it next year. Or maybe I should just start improvising and see where it goes."

Francis can teach you how to write a screenplay, though.

He can do this for you, even though he hasn't written anything in decades, even though he spends most of his time these days greeting tourists at his Napa Valley winery.

If you pay Francis $3,250 plus air fare to Belize, you can stay at his Blancaneaux Lodge, sleep in teak cabanas, drink wine shipped from Francis's vineyard, and talk about writing a script—not with Francis, no, since he'll be back home in Napa greeting tourists, but with the editors of his *Zoetrope* magazine.

Francis who?

Accepting her Oscar for Best Original Screenplay, Sofia Coppola thanked no writers for inspiring her. She did, however, thank a long list of directors.

Not among them, however, was her father, Francis Ford Coppola.

She did thank her mother "for inspiration."

No wonder Francis went bankrupt.

ABC offered Coppola $10 million for the TV rights to *Apocalypse Now*. He held out for $12 million. After the film came out and failed commercially, he sold it to ABC for $4 million.

The gods get angry sometimes.

Because he was the director, Francis Ford Coppola was able to hire his father, Carmine, to do the score for *The Godfather*.

Carmine did the score so well that he won the Oscar for Best Original Score.

But on the way back from the stage to his seat, he dropped the Oscar and it shattered.

Were they also screenwriters?

When two studio executives from Columbia Pictures showed up on the set of *The Cincinnati Kid,* director Sam Peckinpah had them stripped, hog-tied, and left in a seedy motel far away from the set.

ALL HAIL
Norman Jewison

Yes, I know he's a director, but he's a man I admire, and he's also a friend of mine.

A male star threw a punch at Norman on the set, then came back and apologized and said he was ready to go back to work.

Norman said, "After you apologize."

"I just apologized," the star said.

Norman said, "You have to apologize to everybody. The whole crew. You insulted them."

The star apologized to the whole crew.

Directors are human.

Director Victor Fleming suffered a nervous breakdown during the shooting of *Gone with the Wind*. Francis Ford Coppola had a near breakdown/heart attack during the shooting of *Apocalypse Now*.

Director Robert Harmon suffered a heart attack while reading a memo I'd sent him, questioning his ability to direct *Nowhere to Run*. Harmon recovered and went on to botch the movie, just as I knew he would.

I swear, though, that I didn't know—didn't know, did not, did not *know*—that Harmon had a preexisting heart problem when I sent him my near-lethal memo.

Directors are feminists.

Sam Peckinpah: "Women have very complicated plumbing that I'm fascinated with."

Another romantic director . . .

Director Blake Edwards said about his wife, Julie Andrews, "She has lilacs for pubic hairs."

A director is a visual artist.

More than anything, he's a painter—but he likes to think of himself as a writer.

Gus Van Sant did oil paintings before he began to direct films, and he still paints. Peter Weir says he wishes he could "cram my trailer full of Gauguins and van Goghs and all the great art in history." Paul Verhoeven is a comic book artist who actually draws images of the scenes on the pages of the screenplay. Adrian Lyne knows more about modern painters than most art critics. Howard Zieff, Jerry Schatzberg, and Stanley Kubrick all began their professional careers as photographers.

In theory, to have a man who is a visual artist direct a script written by someone who works with words sounds like the perfect combination. Except that the director always tries to tell the writer what to write, while the writer never tries to tell the director how to compose his images on the screen.

Director Michael Mann is an especially brilliant visual stylist.

Gusmano Cesaretti, a respected still photographer, has been Michael Mann's associate producer since the 1970s. After he reads the script of whatever Mann's upcoming film is, he goes out and shoots thousands of stills of images that might work in the film.

As Mann shoots the movie, he tries to fit photographer Cesaretti's images into "his" film.

Some directors love torturing the actors.

Walter Salles (*The Motorcycle Diaries*): "We asked the actors to arrive four months prior to the shoot in Buenos Aires and then we started to do a series of seminars on Latin American history; on the cinema of the 50s. We did seminars on Incan history; we studied the music of the 50s in Latin America, with the help of professors from Buenos Aires University—all this was done to create a collective starting point, where the actors and the technical crew could have a really ingrained sense of what this journey was about."

Orson Welles was a liar.

Welles said he wrote the character of Harry Lime in *The Third Man*. "I wrote everything to do with his character, I created him all around," Welles said. "It was more than just a part for me. Harry Lime is without doubt part of my creative work."

The Third Man was written by Graham Greene. Welles *played the part* of Harry Lime. He wrote no dialogue for the character.

Orson Welles was a big fat liar.

The only film I wrote from the first to the last word," Welles said, "is *Citizen Kane*."

Welles directed *Citizen Kane*, but he didn't write it. It was written by Herman J. Mankiewicz.

You'll meet all kinds.

When Joe Mankiewicz was on the set directing, he always wore white cotton gloves. He had eczema, which broke out on his hands whenever he was nervous. He was always nervous on a set.

Director Jack Clayton (*Moby Dick, The Innocents*) chain-smoked on the set, drank brandy and sodas nonstop, and wore a Bedouin knife strapped to his right leg. He once said to his producer, "Don't speak while I'm talking or I'll have you thrown off the set."

You might even run into some Hungarian hack.

Legendary director Michael Curtiz, who was Hungarian, was often used by the studios to replace other directors. He was famous for getting the script on Saturday and beginning to shoot on Monday.

Hitchcock was a great auteur.

In a letter to the head of MGM after he'd written the screenplay of *Strangers on a Train*, Raymond Chandler wrote, "Are you aware that this screenplay was written without one single consultation with Mr. Hitchcock after the writing of the screenplay began? Not even a telephone call. Not one word of criticism or appreciation. Silence. Blank silence then and since. There are always things that need to be discussed. There are always places where a writer goes wrong, not being himself a master of the camera. There are always difficult little points which require the meeting of minds, the accommodation of points of view. I had none of this. I find it rather strange. I find it rather ruthless. I find it almost incomparably rude."

To Do a Jim Cameron

To have the kind of huge success that frightens you out of doing any more films.

Robert Altman is an asshole.

That's what producer Don Simpson, a friend of mine, thought: "We made *Popeye* and we hated Altman. He was a true fraud . . . he was full of gibberish and full of himself, a pompous, pretentious asshole."

Don Simpson was right about Robert Altman.

Ring Lardner wrote *M*A*S*H* and director Altman praised his script in early interviews.

After the movie was a hit, Altman said that he had tossed out Lardner's script and written it himself.

The movie's producer, George Litto, said, "Bob was never one to acknowledge a writer's contribution. The movie was ninety percent Ring Lardner's script, but Bob started saying he improvised the movie. I said, 'Bob, Ring Lardner gave you the best opportunity you had in your whole life. Ring was blacklisted for years. What you're doing is very unfair to him and you ought to stop it.'"

Howard Hughes's masturbatory vision . . .

He took over directing *The Outlaw* from Howard Hawks. His camera angles were always in dominant positions over Jane Russell, who was nineteen years old during filming. His biographer Charles Higham wrote, "No other individual in commercial Hollywood had so completely released his sexual urges on screen."

Directors are occasionally self-aware.

A book published in Holland about director Paul Verhoeven is entitled *Verhoeven: Poet or Pervert?* Paul told me that he came up with the title.

Never mind everything else, Billy Friedkin is an honest man.

Friedkin: "The day after I won the Oscar was the only time I ever went to see a psychiatrist. I was profoundly unhappy. I told him I won an Oscar and didn't think I deserved it."

Beware of English directors.

The English were supposed to be so nice," Marilyn Monroe said. "But they treated me like a freak, a sex freak. All they wanted to know was whether I slept without any clothes on, did I wear underwear, what were my measurements. Gosh, don't they have women in England?"

It's tough for a director to share credit with Henry James.

Woody Allen had lunch with Peter Bogdanovich shortly after Bogdanovich wrapped *Daisy Miller.*

Allen: "He spent the whole meal agonizing. He didn't know what the credit should read. A Peter Bogdanovich Film of Henry James's Novella? Henry James's Novella Directed by Peter Bogdanovich? Henry James's *Daisy Miller,* a film by Peter Bogdanovich? Peter Bogdanovich's *Daisy Miller*, from Henry James's Novella?"

Directors have taste.

Costa-Gavras directed two of my scripts—*Betrayed* and *Music Box*—showing, I think, great taste in choosing them.

I don't know why he passed on directing *The Godfather.*

First-time directors are piglets.

On HBO's *Project Greenlight,* directors Kyle Rankin and Efram Potelle did the following things on-camera:

1. Tried to fire a boom-mike operator because he had "a bad attitude."

2. Wasted most of a day's shoot talking to producers as cast and crew stood around doing nothing.

3. Asked that the screenwriter and the producer communicate with them through index cards.

4. Demanded a free car when learning that the screenwriter had been provided a car to use.

After all, they were first-time directors.

Don't hold your breath.

"Eventually," wrote screenwriter/novelist Raymond Chandler in 1951, "there will be a type of director who realizes that what is said and how it is said is more important than shooting it upside down through a glass of champagne."

If you consider yourself a writer, don't direct.

Playwright Robert E. Lee: "Becoming a director diminishes the writer. He may have more control and more power, but he loses the writer's perspective, the chance of looking at something with a broad, objective eye."

"More and more writers are becoming directors," wrote Raymond Chandler in 1957. "But in essence they cease to be writers, because a writer creates his own world on his own terms, in his own way."

ALL HAIL
Anatole Litvak!

Yes, he was a director . . . but we're hailing him anyway for creating one of old Hollywood's legendary moments.

One night at Ciro's—as fancy and celebrated then as Spago is now—Anatole Litvak sank to the floor, put his head in Paulette Goddard's lap, and did naughty things there.

Don't be so sure you can direct.

After a week's production on *Personal Best,* screenwriter turned director Robert Towne was a month behind schedule.

Directors know there are screenwriters out there who hate them.

Steven Spielberg, Bob Zemeckis, and Michael Mann describe themselves as "weapons enthusiasts" and can sometimes be seen at various L.A. "shooting clubs."

All three also describe themselves as liberal Democrats who "believe in gun control."

Let's hope David Benioff doesn't hate any directors.

Screenwriter David Benioff (*Troy*) describes himself as a "weapons enthusiast," too; and according to gun club owners, he can outshoot Spielberg, Zemeckis, and Mann.

Was he a screenwriter?

Police arrested a man trying to break into Steven Spielberg's Pacific Palisades mansion. The man had a gun, a knife, rolls of duct tape, whips, a dildo, and various objects described by police as "torture instruments."

The man told police he wanted to rape Spielberg and kill him.

PART EIGHT

WORKING WITH THE PRODUCER

LESSON 14

Is His Heart Full of Shit?

Your producer can be your greatest ally.

When a woman got up at a *Betrayed* screening and started yelling about how much she disliked the movie, producer Irwin Winkler, a literate and sophisticated man, yelled this at her: "Shut up! Sit down! Throw her out! Get her the fuck outta here!"

Pray for a good producer.

I got very lucky with two of my scripts—*Betrayed* and *Music Box*. Irwin Winkler produced both of them.

I saw what made him a great producer on the *Betrayed* set. He was there from seven in the morning until seven at night every day. It was a hundred degrees outside, and under the bright lights in a suffocating barn, it was much hotter than that—but Irwin was there for every single day of the shoot.

One day he was so exhausted and dehydrated that he got dizzy and had to be driven back to his hotel. I warned him about his health, and Irwin said, "I know. But all directors are a little nuts. The best directors are more than a little nuts. I want to be there to make sure we don't experience any unexpected improvisations or unwarranted flights of frenzy."

Irwin was talking about Costa-Gavras, a man we both loved and greatly respected, but still . . . *he was a director.*

The definition of a good producer . . .

Novelist/screenwriter John Gregory Dunne: "If Don Simpson didn't like something, he hit you right between the eyes with it; he did not send eleven pages of notes to an agent, with orders not to show them to the writer, and then go pissing and moaning to the studio. Okay, he said, let's fix it, and we would sit down and do it. What the really good producers do is make you enthusiastic by the sheer force of their personalities about the most problematic ideas.

If your producer is pissing you off, remember that you've got him by the balls.

Playwright/screenwriter David Mamet: "The problem for them is, the story is the one thing that producers can't do."

The most respected producer.

Sam Spiegel is admired by today's producers as the "producer of all producers." He produced *The African Queen, The Bridge on the River Kwai,* and *Lawrence of Arabia.* He won *three* Oscars.

When he first came to America from Europe, he told his sister, "I'll either become a very rich and famous man or I'll die like a dog in the gutter."

He bounced checks constantly. He even pimped for a while. He even went to jail in San Francisco for fraud.

Sam Spiegel's résumé . . .

Before Sam Spiegel produced any movies, he had an affair with a wealthy divorcée. He stole her George Bernard Shaw first editions, he stole her car, and he stole her ex-husband's walking stick.

He was arrested in England for fraud: the nonpayment of his apartment bill. He went to Brixton Prison and was allowed one phone call.

He called a studio executive in Hollywood and tried to set up a film deal.

If your producer asks you to send him your script before you send it to the studio.

Don't do it. Your deal isn't with the producer; it's with the studio—and by contract, you have to deliver the script to the studio. What the producer is trying to do is to get a free draft of the script from you.

If you send it to him first, he will tell you how you can make it "better" before the studio sees it. Chances are, if you listen to his ideas, your script will be worse than it was before he told you his ideas.

"Tell me everything you have in mind."

This is William Goldman's spin on what to say to a producer. Take out a notebook and say this to the producer, who will have nothing to say that he would want written down . . . so your meeting won't last long.

Producers want to get paid, too.

If you're a screenwriter, you're paid when you start writing the script or when you sell it. But if you're a producer, you're paid only when the movie starts shooting.

Consequently, the producer will do everything he can to get you moving along on the script as fast as possible—so he can get paid.

You're better off ignoring his notes.

Screenwriter/novelist James Brown: "The producer is an articulate, intelligent man, and during the course of our meeting he gives me several pages of notes, all of them insightful. I want to do a good job, and once more I'm willing to mercilessly cut and chop, create new scenes and eliminate others. Inside of six months we have a strong screenplay with the original vision of my novel still intact. The producer shops it around to actors, directors, and studio executives. A year passes. No luck. The call comes from Vermont, where he is vacationing, and I can sense by the tone of his voice that he's given up. 'You wrote a good script,' he tells me, 'but they're all saying that it's too soft.'

"My phone stops ringing. My book mysteriously disappears from the bookstores. I think it's all over and then out of the blue he phones again to tell me, in short order, that I'm fired."

ALL HAIL
Gore Vidal!

Screenwriter and novelist Vidal (*Myra Breckinridge*): "I was having a meeting with a producer and I said to him, 'Look, I'm tired shitless of your complaints. You don't know what you're talking about. You know marketing, you may know how to make deals, but you don't know how to make movies, and you intrude on other people who are talented and do.' He exploded. 'How can you say that to me?' he said. He was halfway across the room. 'I will hit you!' he said. Then I started toward him and said, 'I am going to throw you out of this window.' And I came at him. We were about three feet apart and he was running toward me and he couldn't stop because of how much he weighed—he was very heavy. He veered off to the right and ran into a wall. I heard his nose crack against the wall."

A producer today isn't what a producer was yesterday.

Mike Medavoy: "Producer credits today are given out like lollipops in a pediatrician's office—to managers, wives, girlfriends, lawyers, and development executives. They are the ego badge of the business.

Schnorrer

A flimflam man who can talk you into and out of anything . . . especially your wallet. It's a term usually applied to producers.

You, too, can be a producer today.

The Assassination of Richard Nixon boasted *sixteen* producers.

That sound you just heard was Sam Spiegel and David O. Selznick rolling over—and over and over—in their graves.

Beware of producers' offices that are in fancy buildings but have no furniture.

I had a meeting once with a well-known producer in an office like this and called my agent as soon as the meeting was over to tell him that I didn't trust the fact that there was no furniture in the office.

"They just moved in," my agent said; "the furniture is on the way."

Two weeks later, the producer declared bankruptcy and closed his office.

Producers are intellectuals.

Icon producer Sam Spiegel said his two favorite things in life were "great food and very young girls."

Producers are honorable people.

Said writer/director John Huston about producer Sam Spiegel, the winner of three Oscars for best picture: "If you had committed murder, a totally unjustified act of which you were guilty as hell, Sam would be one of the two or three friends you would turn to, certain that Sam would help."

TAKE IT FROM ZSA ZSA

You don't want to seduce your producer.

Actress and Hungarian femme fatale Zsa Zsa Gabor: "Everyone thinks that the one kind of man you find most in Hollywood is the ugly, vulgar producer who smokes big fat cigars. This image is, of course, exaggerated. Some of these ugly, vulgar producers smoke little thin cigars, and nowadays some of the producers are young bearded men who smoke pot."

Producers are demanding.

Producer Charles Evans advanced me $2 million to write the script of *Showgirls*. When I was more than a month late turning it in, he threatened to sue me unless I agreed to rewrite for free a script that he owned called *Bloodlines* (after I finished writing *Showgirls*).

When I finished *Showgirls* and Carolco agreed to finance the project, Charles Evans received $3.7 million—a $1.7 million profit on his $2 million investment.

But even after he made such a whopping profit, he still insisted that I had to rewrite *Bloodlines* for free.

My lawyers told me I had no choice but to rewrite it. I did.

But my rewrite somehow wasn't very good. *Bloodlines* was never made.

No one can force you to write anything.

Alas, as hard as I worked on that free and forced *Bloodlines* rewrite—as much of my heart and soul and guts I put into it—alas, alas, alas, my rewrite was god-awful. But I completed it and Charles Evans couldn't sue me.

Joel Silver is demanding, too.

What do you want out of life?" someone asked the producer Joel Silver.

Joel said, "*Everything!*"

So was the great Selznick.

Producer David O. Selznick, looking back at his career: "I was a pig. I worked so hard and waited so long, I got piggish and wanted everything."

How to deal with a European producer . . .

Quote Paddy Chayefsky to him in your first meeting. Paddy said, "You America-haters bore me to tears. Europe was a brothel long before we came to town."

The Nipple Check

A producer's role at the casting call.

A powerful producer like my friend Robert Evans can change the course of history.

Evans told me this story: "I called Henry Kissinger and invited him to *The Godfather* premiere in 1972. I needed Henry there for the publicity. Henry said he couldn't come—something about the war and the Paris peace talks and having to fly to Moscow the next morning. I reminded Henry how often he'd stayed in my guest house. I didn't hear any more about the Paris peace talks. Henry didn't fly to Moscow the next morning. He flew to *The Godfather* premiere."

TAKE IT FROM ZSA ZSA

Actress and famed Hungarian femme fatale Zsa Zsa Gabor: "I was in Boston, touring in Blithe Spirit, and Henry Kissinger made a date with me to fly down and take me out. But on opening night, he called and canceled. A trifle piqued, I asked why. And Henry gave me the reason—a reason that even I couldn't quibble with: 'I can't fly down because we are invading Cambodia tomorrow. It is a big secret, you are the first person outside the White House who knows about it.'"

It's all about whose is bigger.

Producers have big egos.

The first time that producer Sam Spiegel met director David Lean's girlfriend, he tried to seduce her.

ALL HAIL
Irwin Shaw!

The novelist and Sam Spiegel didn't get along and Spiegel criticized Shaw's work behind his back to other Hollywood producers—thereby stopping Shaw from getting screenwriting jobs.

To get even, Shaw began having an affair with Spiegel's wife.

ALL HAIL
Irwin Shaw!

Sam Spiegel dumped the wife that Irwin Shaw had seduced and remarried.

And one day Irwin Shaw was having lunch with a mutual friend and the friend said that Sam Spiegel's new wife was supposed to be "great in the feathers."

So Irwin Shaw seduced Sam Spiegel's new wife and began an affair with her.

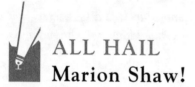

ALL HAIL
Marion Shaw!

Shaw's wife, Marion, found out about the affair and, at a dinner party, she stuck her foot out and tripped Spiegel's wife, who broke her ankle.

ALL HAIL
Omar Sharif!

Sam Spiegel discovered Omar Sharif in obscure Egyptian films. He made him an international star.

In return, Sharif seduced Sam Spiegel's wife and had an affair with her.

ALL HAIL
John Huston!

Angered that Sam Spiegel's wife was flaunting jewels while he was broke, *African Queen* director John Huston began an affair with her.

"John was very cruel to her," a friend said. "He really abused her.

Sam Spiegel's was bigger than Mike Todd's.

Sam Spiegel took his new wife to the Lido in Venice. Producer Mike Todd went over to their table.

"Hey, angel face," Todd said to Spiegel's new wife. "Do you know where you were last year on this exact same date at this exact same time?" Sam Spiegel said to his new wife, "Never mind."

But Mike Todd continued: "You were sitting right here, at this exact same table, with me, angel face."

Don Simpson admired Sam Spiegel.

Don didn't date; he fucked," said a former assistant.

Simpson said, "When you meet a lady and she says, 'Would you like to make love?' well, the first thing I like to do is fuck, not make love."

Because they're all empowered . . .

Screenwriter Nick Kazan: "Why is it that, in Hollywood, every producer, studio executive, and development person just out of college feels entitled to make suggestions on every script they receive? How can they be so confident of their opinions? Are they truly unaware of the damage they can do?"

What's it really like being a producer?

Sam Spiegel, who had escaped from Hitler's Germany, said, "It's better than being a lamp shade."

"Some producers have hearts full of shit."

Director Elia Kazan said that about Sam Spiegel.

Because we're scared to speak up . . .

Screenwriter Nick Kazan: "Why do we writers accept notes (from producers, studio executives, development people) which will destroy what we have so painstakingly created?"

Don't throw the damn thing back at 'em.

Producer William Sackheim was known for throwing across the room scripts that he didn't like.

If someone throws your script across the room, pick it up, tear off the first page, and make whoever threw it eat it.

Producers have impeccable taste (oh yeah!).

Respected Broadway producer Cheryl Crawford turned down a new play Arthur Miller offered her.

She wept bitterly at the opening night of *Death of a Salesman.*

These are the kind of people who give you notes on your script.

Jed Harris was Broadway's most famous stage director when he saw Arthur Miller's *Death of a Salesman.* Harris called it "a stupid play" and said "there is no drama in an ass like Willy Loman."

It takes one to know one.

Otto Preminger, the director, and Sam Spiegel, the producer, met in Hollywood for the first time—they had known each other previously in Europe.

Preminger said to Spiegel, "You are the greatest, most treacherous son of a bitch that every lived. . . . You end up in Mexico where you get involved in selling dope. You also get arrested on a white slavery charge. You get thrown in prison. Somehow or other you bribe yourself out of prison and you sneak illegally into the United States at Tijuana."

Spiegel looked at him sorrowfully and said, "It wasn't Tijuana."

Showman

The highest praise for a producer whose name, identified with a project, immediately gives it status: Sam Spiegel, Mike Todd, David Merrick, Irwin Winkler, Alan Carr, David O. Selznick, Jerry Bruckheimer, Joel Silver, Brian Grazer, Scott Rudin, Steven Spielberg, and Cecil B. DeMille are showmen.

Nazis yes, producers no . . .

Screenwriter/playwright/director David Mamet: "It occurred to me that there are films about good Nazis, but there are no films about good producers. Every producer in every movie is bad. Of course, that makes sense, because all of the films about bad producers are written by writers."

Don't bugger any boys in the backseat of the Porsche, either.

Producer Don Simpson, on why he was fired by Paramount as vice president of production: "They fired me for doing coke. They fired me on a fucking morals clause in the contract. They had executives buggering boys in the backseats of their Porsches and they fired me on a fucking morals charge."

Some producers really know how to hype their films.

Executive producer Robert Redford, discussing *The Motorcycle Diaries*: "There's a lot that's touching, there's a lot of humor, there's a lot of comedy, but it's real. It's honest comedy that comes out of real experiences, particularly with the young guys on what starts as an adventure. But there's also a lot of poignancy, and a lot of powerful emotional stuff in it, that's also real, and for that reason, it's all the more powerful."

Some producers really, really know how to hype their films.

Executive producer Robert Redford, discussing *The Motorcycle Diaries*: "When you see the film, you'll see that they really went through something to tell their story. Exactly what the characters actually went through. They followed the path that was absolutely authentic—the actual path they took on the motorcycle. They went to all the same places. And you see it, but more importantly you feel it. And if you feel it, then you're going to feel how Ernesto Guevara was affected by it."

Some producers really, really, really know how to hype their films.

Executive producer Robert Redford, discussing *The Motorcycle Diaries*: "This is a great story. This was not an easy film to make. They went to some really extreme locations that were next to impossible in some cases. The weather, you had the threat of violence along the way, political violence. You didn't know how things were going to go. You were going to go into some pretty hot areas. So that's all evidenced in this film."

Some producers know how to hype the directors who work for them, too.

Executive producer Robert Redford, discussing Walter Salles, the director of *The Motorcycle Diaries*: "Walter's work draws you in because, first and foremost, he is a natural storyteller. He blends, in a visually compelling manner, a specific world of characters, places and struggle that subtly reveals larger threads of shared human experience and emotion that link us all."

Robert McKee took producer Don Simpson's film course.

Producer Lynda Obst: "Don created the three-act structure that we all use, the one that Robert McKee and Syd Field [another screenwriting teacher] use and take credit for. Don made up this logarithm. There is the hot first act with an exciting incident, and the second act with the crisis and the dark bad moments in which our hero is challenged, and the third act with the triumphant moment and the redemption and the freeze-frame ending."

Some producers are true liberals.

During the South Central riots of 1992, producer Bert Schneider said, "I wish they'd come up here [to Bel Air] and burn my house down."

Some producers really respect screenwriters.

Producer Bert Schneider walked past writers' offices on the Columbia lot, banging on their doors and yelling, "Get out from under your desk, motherfucker! I know you're in there. Why don't you go write something, turn something in, you jerkoff!"

ALL HAIL
Charles MacArthur!

In the middle of a script dispute, MacArthur (*The Front Page*) knocked producer David O. Selznick over a bed.

Selznick's agent brother, Myron, jumped on MacArthur's back to try to stop him, but MacArthur hurled himself on Selznick and bit him in the leg.

"Dracula!" Myron Selznick screamed.

A Pisher

An old term used by producers for a nobody.

Many producers are happy and well adjusted.
The secret to happiness is whores," said "the producer of producers," Sam Spiegel.

If he speaks Hungarian, he's not all bad.
Sam Spiegel spoke fluent Hungarian.

Unfuckable

A producer's term for an actor or actress whom he doesn't want to cast in the movie.

Because they can't do what we do.

Screenwriter Nick Kazan: "If we refuse to make destructive changes, why are we considered 'difficult' rather than 'principled and passionate'? Why are we not considered experts, both in general and, most especially, on the distinct universe of the script which we have written?"

A powerful producer can even move the White House.

When I needed serious government help with a personal problem (a psychotic brother-in-law), I went to Robert Evans, who was walking around his house those days with a commander in chief ball cap from the Bush White House.

Evans got the government involved for me and solved my problem.

Press secretary Marlin Fitzwater had been a guest in Evans's guest house.

Bring 'em a towel from the rest room.

A producer and I met in the little bar at La Scala on Little Santa Monica. He proposed a deal and it sounded good to me. We shook hands on it.

I told my agent about the deal and the agent said, "Forget it. There's no way I'll let you make that deal."

The producer went ballistic when he heard we had no deal.

Six months later, he asked me to dinner. His wife joined us. We went back to La Scala on Little Santa Monica.

We had a couple of martinis at the bar. He said to his wife, "You see this stool I'm sitting on? He fucked me right here on this stool. Right here."

She laughed and laughed. The producer sort of smiled, but he wasn't laughing. I was laughing, but I was forcing it.

I went into the bathroom and got a paper towel. I took it out to the bar and told the producer to stand up a second. He did and I put the paper towel under him on the stool.

Now he started to laugh. He laughed and laughed, and so did his wife and I.

"You son of a bitch," the producer kept saying, sitting on the paper towel, but he was still laughing.

To Do a Burt Weisbourd

He was the hottest producer of the early eighties, the producer of
Raggedy Man and *Ghost Story*. He was working with Robert Redford
on *Red Headed Stranger* when, word is, he went up against Redford
and got into a major battle with the star. He went from being one of the
hottest producers in town to getting out of the business.

Give 'em music lessons.

Screenwriter Nick Kazan: "The next time someone reads your
script and either really hates something that you know works or
makes cavalier and foolish suggestions . . . perhaps you should ask
them: Did you ever hear a song for the first time and hate it and
then two weeks later find yourself singing it?"

Producers outbid themselves sometimes.

Producer Charles Evans bid on a house that he wanted to buy.
He forgot that he'd already made a bid; then heard about another bid, which was really *his* bid.

So he made another bid, bidding against himself, and bought the house.

Creative Parasite

A wannabe producer who pals around with you and cultivates your friendship in the hope that if you sell your script, you'll get him the job of associate or executive producer on the movie is guilty of creative parasitism.

Producer Don Simpson was the reincarnation of David O. Selznick.

Screenwriter Nunnally Johnson, who turned down working on
another project with Selznick: "Working with you consists of
three months of work and three more of recuperation."

Joel Silver stopped when he was seven.

Screenwriter Ben Hecht to producer David O. Selznick: "The trouble with you, David, is that you did all your reading before you were twelve."

This producer's a real clown.

David Nicksay was once employed as a clown by the Ringling Brothers and Barnum & Bailey Circus. He even graduated from clown school.

Producers have to start somewhere.

Irwin Winkler, the Oscar-winning producer, once worked as a "laugher" for live television.

Nobody messes with Sean Connery.

Producer Peter Guber was going to tell Sean Connery about a new ending needed for a movie.

When Connery poked his finger in Guber's chest and said, "Now what's all this shit about not shooting the ending we want?" Guber backed off and said, "No, I just came by to wish you luck."

David Geffen is tougher than Michael Ovitz.

Said Ovitz to producer Geffen: "You're so smart, so bright, so aggressive. . . . I wish to God you could take all your venom and turn it into something positive. Your whole life is so negative. It's not enough for you to win. You have to have everyone else do poorly around you. They have to do badly. I don't get that, David. If you keep saying bad things about me, I'm going to beat you up."

In the end, it's all BS.

Producer Peter Guber: "Success is more attitude than aptitude."

Some studio bosses can't read very well.

One studio head hated reading so much that he sat with an assistant for an hour a day as the assistant told him the plot summaries of the scripts the agencies had submitted.

That's the sound of one hand clapping.

Peter Guber: "The perception of power is power."

Stay away from hands-on producers.

I will not work for dominating people like Selznick or Goldwyn," said Raymond Chandler. "If you deprive me of the right to do my own kind of writing, there is almost nothing left."

The producer was a pimp.

David Merrick defined producer Robert Evans this way: "He's Paramount's vice president in charge of procurement."

Robert Evans's role model.

Joe Schenck, powerful studio head and producer, was known for discovering and "sponsoring" women in Hollywood. He prepared them for other men and even marriage to other men. He took care of them and asked for "a little consideration along the way."

One of the women Joe Schenck discovered and sponsored was Marilyn Monroe.

Don't take any meetings at a producer's house.

Marilyn Monroe: "He had me come over to his house. It was a mansion. I had never been any place like that. He had the greatest food, too. That's when I learned about Champagne. What I liked was hearing about all the stars I had seen in the movies. He knew them all. He seemed to have this thing about breasts. After dinner, he told me to take my clothes off and he would tell me Hollywood stories as he played with my breasts. What could I say? He didn't want to do much else, since he was getting old, but sometimes he asked me to kiss him—down there. It would seem like hours and nothing would happen, but I was afraid to stop. I felt like gagging, but if I did, I thought he'd get insulted. Sometimes, he'd just fall asleep. If he stayed awake, he'd pat my head, like a puppy, and thank me."

Producers can be assinine.

On my film *Jagged Edge,* producer Marty Ransohoff kept trying to get rid of Glenn Close, claiming, "Her ass is too big."

After lunch with Helen Mirren, producer Sam Spiegel said she was wrong for the part in his film. "Her ass is too big," he said.

A Truffle Nose

A nose that can find a treasure (truffles) hidden in the brush.
    A nose only a successful producer can have.
    A pig's nose, since it is pigs that discover truffles.

Powerful producers can afford to wear dirty, smelly toupees.

Producer David Merrick ordered a toupee from the man who made Fred Astaire's. But Merrick never cleaned his toupee. It smelled. He didn't even put it on carefully, letting it look like a dirty, smelly napkin atop his head. It was Merrick's way of showing contempt for the people he worked with. He had so much power, he could walk around in a dirty, smelly wig . . . and not even bother about how he looked.

And they call Thalberg a genius.

Irving Thalberg passed on a movie and said to his boss, Louise B. Mayer, "Forget it, Louis. No Civil War picture will make a nickel." He was talking about *Gone With the Wind.*

In need of producorial stimulation . . .

Screenwriter Eleanor Perry and her director husband, Frank, wrote this note to a producer: "I'm afraid that both of us seem now to require your direct stimulation before we embark or agree on truly significant changes, in short, we need you."

Don't steal the crumpled paper.

English screenwriter Ivan Moffat (*Giant, Black Sunday*) on working with an internationally acclaimed producer: "He was crablike and all-controlling. He would hold on to everything. I had idly taken a crumpled piece of paper from his desk. He said, 'What is this, Ivan? No, please.' And I had to put it back. On Saturday or Sunday, he would call up, saying, 'Ivan, where are you going? Please leave a number. We might have to work.' There was never any question of our working. I said something flippant at dinner with him once. He said, 'Ivan, hold the humor.'"

Not only can you get snorted; you can get chomped, too.

Director Robert Parrish (*Casino Royale*), speaking about a well-known producer he had worked with: "He never chomped on a cigar. It wasn't his style. He was too much of a gentleman to be caught 'chomping' anything, except maybe a script or a screenwriter."

Murder is always an option.

At 3:30 A.M., screenwriter Budd Schulberg's wife awoke, to find him not in bed.

He was in the bathroom, shaving.

She said, "Why are you shaving so early?"

He said, "Because I'm driving to New York to kill the producer."

He would've loved Heidi Fleiss.

A Fox executive welcomed producer Sam Spiegel to New York. "I proposed showing him places like the Metropolitan Museum," the executive said, "and all he wanted to go and see was Polly Adler's—the best whorehouse in town. Sam spent the whole night there. I had to buy the place out—it was over nine hundred dollars."

The best producers are the best liars.

Director Elia Kazan said producer Sam Spiegel could lie "without betraying a tremor of his facial muscles. He kept me intrigued just to see how he got away with everything."

David Geffen is refined.

When producer David Geffen went to a high-toned reception for Princess Margaret, he wore blue jeans.

He went up to her and said, "Hi ya."

I'm not going to mess with David Geffen.

Writer Tom King did—in his book, *The Operator*. Only a few years after writing the book he died at a young age—of natural causes, of course.

Did you say that to Tom King, David?

Whenever producer David Geffen gets angry at someone, he says, "I hope you die!"

You have to love David Geffen a lot.

David Geffen said this to screenwriter Robert Towne about why he wouldn't work with him again: "You just didn't love me enough, Robert."

I always liked Michael Eisner.

Michael is a liar," David Geffen said about Disney chief Michael Eisner. "And anybody who has dealt with him—genuinely dealt with him—knows he is a liar."

But what if David Geffen is lying?

I worked with Michael Eisner on *Flashdance* and enjoyed working with him. He disagreed with me sometimes, but he never lied to me—as far as I know. It is possible, therefore, that David Geffen is lying when he calls Michael Eisner a liar.

On the other hand . . .

I've dealt with David Geffen, too, and he never lied to me, either.

But he obviously wanted to fuck Tom Cruise.

After he read the script of *Risky Business,* producer David Geffen told the director, "I want you to cast someone in the role of Joel that I would want to fuck."

Who's that holding Ron Bass's Oscar?

Peter Guber produced *Rain Man* with his partner Jon Peters, even though director Barry Levinson rarely saw them on the set.

Yet Peter was photographed with "his" Oscar after the Academy Awards.

Alas, it wasn't his Oscar; it was *Rain Man* screenwriter Ron Bass's Oscar—Peter and Jon had asked Ron to "borrow it for the photographers."

Why weren't the photographers taking Ron Bass's picture with his Oscar?

Because photographers aren't interested in taking screenwriters' photographs.

They're not *all that* interested in taking producers' pictures, either, but they are more interested in producers than screenwriters.

Peter Guber doesn't exist; Peter Bart invented him.

Peter Guber produced *Flashdance,* though I never once saw him during the making of that movie. He also produced *Midnight Express,* though the director, Alan Parker, said that he rarely saw him during the making of that movie. And he produced *Rain Man,* though the director, Barry Levinson, said that he rarely saw him during the making of that movie.

Don't be a pawn in these games.

Powerful producer Irwin Winkler once asked me to write the "true story" of media baron Rupert Murdoch. I turned him down.

Powerful producer Scott Rudin once asked John Gregory Dunne and his wife, Joan Didion, to write "the true story" of entertainment mogul Barry Diller. They turned him down.

Tough-guy producers are easier to work with.

John Gregory Dunne: "In general, we prefer doing business with the bully boys than with the smoothies. The clout of the bully boys allows them to act as a buffer between you and the studio, shielding you from those mind-deadening omnibus meetings at which everyone present feels the necessity to say something; the bully boys do these meetings, and give you only the notes they think are worthwhile. If you let them know you will yell back at them when they yell at you, then they are more prone to listen—or else they fire you quickly; the smoothies just jerk your chain and smile as they measure your rib cage—for the ribs between which they will slip the stiletto."

At all cost, even if you're secretly writing a tell-all, appear loyal.

Producer Peter Guber: "In Hollywood, even the appearance of disloyalty can shoot down even the most promising future."

Avoid the producer who is a wannabe director.

Watching the filming of *Duel in the Sun*, producer David O. Selznick interrupted filming, dashed over to Gregory Peck and Jennifer Jones, and splashed more makeup blood on them.

The director, King Vidor, got up off his chair and said, "David, you can take this picture and shove it," and left the set.

Producers know how to cheer themselves up.

On days when he was depressed, producer Robert Evans said to his staff, "Go out there and find me some money!"

Producers are survivors.

Before he became my friend and, on several films, my producer partner, he had worked in a bookstore in Mill Valley, California, and owned an art theater with its own restaurant in Sonoma County. After he and I parted ways, he partnered with someone else—this time in a new Italian restaurant in Beverly Hills, where he also became the maître'd.

If a producer gets bored, he can always change his name.

My friend Howard Koch, Jr., a very successful producer and truly nice guy, decided one day that he didn't like his name anymore.

So he changed it. He became "Hawk" Koch.

He asked his friends to call him that, and he called himself that on all of his future film credits.

Everyone called him Hawk. Everyone liked Hawk better after he became Hawk.

A Velvet Octopus

A producer who wraps his arms around you with great affection and takes from you for free what you should be paid for: idea, outline, option, or script.

Don't ever let yourself be caught by a velvet octopus.

Make the producer swim for your script.

John Huston wrote the first eleven pages of his script and handed them to producer Sam Spiegel. Spiegel started reading the pages, but Huston's pet monkey grabbed the pages from him and threw them into the swimming pool. Siegel jumped into the pool and swam underwater to retrieve the pages.

Make him hire armed guards to keep you at bay.

Producer David Geffen hired armed guards to keep screenwriter Robert Towne out of those theaters in New York and L.A. that were showing Towne's *Personal Best*.

One way to get even with a producer.

Actor Timothy Bottoms disliked Dino De Laurentiis so much that he pissed on his shoes during the production of the movie.

If you're a writer, don't be a producer.

I never wanted to be a producer, but I had more movie ideas than I had the time to write them all. Plus, I was intrigued by the notion of setting up a production company that would give screenwriters more control over their scripts and more participation profit than they'd ever had before. And I had two good producer friends—I'll call them Ben and Bill—whom I enjoyed hanging out with.

So the three of us started to set up our own production company. We even had the name for it: Renegade. We had the company icon all worked out, too. Our films would begin with a steel door slamming shut and then being sprayed by bullets that spelled out R-E-N-E-G-A-D-E. We even designed and ordered three beautiful varsity jackets with the Renegade logo on the back and the names Joe, Ben and Bill scripted on the front. We also had office space picked out and—*get this*—studios ready to begin bidding against one another to make a deal with us.

And then, suddenly, in the Hungarian way, with a great big bang (not a whimper) Renegade *imploded*.

Ben and Bill, I noticed, didn't like each other and were trying to score points against each other—with me—behind each other's backs. I finally realized that it was normal behavior—because they weren't friends; they were—individually—*my* friends. I liked hanging out with Ben and with Bill—*individually*. There were serious strains in the subtext when *all three of us* were together. Each guy was jealous of the other's friendship with me.

That was one good reason to forget about Renegade.

The other was that I fell in love with Bill's wife and married her.

PART NINE

DEALING WITH THE STUDIO

LESSON 15

You're a Jackass in a Hailstorm!

Barry Diller ruined movies.

According to producer/studio boss Mike Medavoy: "Barry Diller's Paramount regime was the beginning of the movie by committee syndrome that pervades Hollywood today.

"Diller and his lieutenants began setting the agenda at the script stage. Previously, it was left up to the director and the screenwriter to work out what the movie would say and how it would be said, and then run it by the studio for input. But at Paramount, the executive would get involved with the first draft of the script, typing up voluminous notes for the filmmakers.

"Next, they would hold story meetings so the executives and filmmakers could float their ideas, many of which were undoubtedly in conflict with one another. It was then left up to the filmmakers to cut and paste it all together."

Killer Dillers

Executives hired by Barry Diller in whatever enterprise he is involved in.

Ingratiate yourself with your superiors.

In an effort to convince me to change the ending of my script, a studio head listed for me all the television series that he had written, worked on, or supervised.

I said, "I know you've done all those things. That's exactly the problem."

Insult their pampered white asses.

I am extremely allergic to big shots of all types wherever found," said screenwriter/author Raymond Chandler. "I lose no opportunity to insult them whenever I get the chance."

They begrudge you the money they have to pay you.

Playwright/screenwriter David Mamet: "In my experience, almost every financial interchange with Hollywood ends with an accusation by the corporation of theft. 'You didn't do what I wanted, you didn't work hard enough, you intended to defraud me.' These are the recurring plaints of industry. They may be translated as: You forgot to work for nothing."

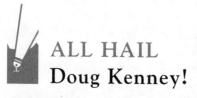

ALL HAIL
Doug Kenney!

Doug Kenney, the screenwriter of *Caddyshack*, hated the poster for the movie so much that he confronted studio head Mike Medavoy outside his office and the two wound up grappling on the ground.

The poster was changed.

R E E L S P E A K

The Green Light

The decision by a studio to film (green-light) a script.

Until recently, this was the decision of the studio head—he took the blame when the movie failed, or got the credit when it was a hit.

Today, though, many studio heads have figured out that they'll last longer in the job if they alone don't make the decision to green-light.

So, at many studios today, a committee makes the decision to green-light a script. The committee is made up of the top execs on all levels—even publicity, advertising, and marketing.

Since you can't fire the whole committee (*all* the executives) and have a studio left, *everybody* holds on to their jobs.

Thanks to The Mummy, *we got Graham Greene.*

*T*he *Quiet American* was green-lighted by Intermedia Films only when Brendan Fraser agreed to take the supporting role. Brendan had just starred in *The Mummy Returns* and the studio felt he was a big-enough star for it to be able to take a chance on Graham Greene.

Sherry Lansing speaks doublespeak.

*D*irector Phillip Noyce, discussing *The Saint*: "At the end of the first screening, Sherry Lansing, the head of the studio, was genuinely crying. She said it was a brilliant film and it was *Doctor Zhivago*-ish. . . . Later I did feel resentful that Sherry Lansing had initially been so enthusiastic about the movie, only to eventually talk me into cutting those things which had most moved her when she first saw the film."

A Bomb Thrower

A studio executive who disagrees with a reader's coverage of a script will be known as a "bomb thrower."

To Do a DeLuca

To be caught publicly in flagrante delicto—as was then New Line head Mike De Luca at a party at then agent Arnold Rifkin's house (with the sister of a William Morris agent). To trip on your own dick.

With ding-a-lings like this in charge . . .

David Picker, the former head of United Artists, MGM, and Paramount, looking back on his career: "If I would have reversed all my decisions—if I hadn't made the pictures I did and made the pictures I didn't, the results would have been exactly the same."

A studio boss is an orchid.

Studio mogul Louis B. Mayer: "You see, wherever I go there are girls who want to become actresses. I have a sixth sense for it. She would follow me into my stateroom, if I snapped my fingers, and stay all night. Just for a bit role in any picture. But I am not interested in fast affairs. I am interested in *relationships*. I am a human being. I need warmth—like an orchid."

To Sweat Dollars

To wait for the box-office results from your film's opening weekend.

It's not about money, it's about getting laid.

An agent told Hedy Lamarr this story: "Phil Kamp has had an office at a major studio for four years and he has never made a picture. He's a distant relative of the president of the studio. He just auditions girls. That's his whole life. He gets a salary but he's a producer who doesn't produce. Phil is so dedicated to his art that he occasionally goes to another city and there he tries another variation. He puts in ads for a secretary to a movie producer—if he were to advertise for an actress it would look suspicious. As a producer, girls who are really secretaries often want to be actresses. Phil does well both in and out of town."

They'll want you to write dishonest stories.

Paramount studio head B. P. Schulberg: "We can't afford to alienate our movie audience by telling them the truth about themselves."

Creative Executive

There's no such thing. It's an oxymoron, like "lady producer."

The barbarians are inside the gates.

Frank Pierson, screenwriter (*Dog Day Afternoon*) and president of the MPAA: "We had been having too much fun to notice: the barbarians were inside the gate. . . . We began to see Harvard Business School MBAs sit in on our story conferences. Lawyers multiplied."

They don't like to say no.

Columbia studio exec Peter Guber was instructed by his boss, Leo Jaffe, to tell the once-powerful Jack Warner, now an old producer, that his movie *1776* was being canceled.

Guber went to see Warner but didn't have the guts to tell him.

Leo Jaffe didn't have the guts to tell him, either.

1776 was made . . . and bombed.

Dumb Fuck Films

The late director Hal Ashby's movie company, generally thought by Hollywood cynics to be the best name of a production company ever.

Lew made a big boo-boo.

Not long before his death, former Universal tycoon Lew Wasserman said, "Sold the company to the Japanese. It wasn't the price that was wrong, but the sale itself."

What if he had hemorrhoids?

Harry Cohn, the Columbia czar, said, "If my fanny squirms while I'm watching it, the movie is bad. If my fanny doesn't squirm, it's good."

A Civilian Question

A stupid question asked at a story meeting—the kind of question asked by someone outside the industry, a "civilian," who doesn't know anything.

Those poor scared studio execs . . .

Screenwriter/novelist Raymond Chandler: "Sometimes I feel kind of sorry for the poor bastards. They are so damn scared they won't make their second or third million. In fact, they are just so damned scared, period."

We've all got a spiritual side.

The wife of a studio exec said to me, "Jack was so wound up, we really needed a relaxing evening. We went to a séance for Henry Fonda and Katharine Hepburn."

Hollywood Sperm

The children of studio executives.

Lew had a big problemo.

Lew Wasserman said, "I was unfortunate not to have a son, only a daughter."

They're all sleep-deprived.

The wife of a studio exec told me that he woke up many nights yelling things in his sleep.

Things like:

"He's going to hand *me* my head on a platter? I'm going to hand him *his* head on a platter!"

"He wants to see a professional? I'll show *him* a professional!"

"The hat has been thrown in the ring! So he better be ready!"

"If he tries to take credit for this movie, I'll fucking kill him."

Three-Piss Picture

Jack Warner felt that if he had to go to the bathroom during a screening, the movie would fail. A movie that would be a disastrous embarrassment was "a three-piss picture." Nobody could ever convince him that he had a weak bladder.

They live in the reel world.

Sony had financed the ill-fated Roland Joffe–directed *City of Joy,* set amid the dire poverty of India.

A few months later, Mark Canton, Sony's head of production, was showing me around the studio lot, which was in the midst of massive construction. Bulldozers were everywhere; much of the lot seemed to be in ruins.

"This," Mark Canton greeted me, "is our *City of Joy.*"

Dick Zanuck's dad "passed" on Marilyn.

Studio chief Darryl Zanuck refused to cast Marilyn Monroe in any "serious" roles.

Marilyn said, "I would have been happy to do anything—*you know*—to get him to let me try something different. He wasn't interested at all. Every other guy was. Why wasn't he?"

Suckfish

The junior executives who scuttle the corridors at a movie studio. Also known as "hall mice."

I hope he got Bill Goldman's next job.

James Ryan, adjunct professor of playwriting at the New School in New York City, writes in his book *Screenwriting from the Heart,* "Most executives who run Hollywood, in my experience, are incredibly bright and often very well educated."

Sorry, but this won't work.

Discussing the making of his *Blue Dahlia,* Raymond Chandler said, "I threatened to walk off the picture, not yet finished, unless they stopped the director putting in foolish dialogue out of his own head."

A Halfway Girl

A studio executive who slept her way not to the top, but to the middle.

They're all fans of Robert McKee.

Screenwriter Dan Pyne (*Pacific Heights*): "Maybe that's who's taking all these screenwriting courses—story editors or producers who want to write one. I met up with a guy yesterday, a very nice guy from Disney. He wants me to read something . . . if he writes it. For them, it's all about writing that one script and then cashing in on it. Whereas, I think, for the real writers, it's about a career."

Bob's lucky he's still alive.

In a disagreement with Universal titan Lew Wasserman, director Bob Rafelson said, "What's this fuckin' bullshit?" and swept all of Wasserman's medals and awards off his desk.

A Total Fucking Disaster

The worst kind of disaster, a movie that does such a belly slam that it clears all the water out of the pool, a movie like my *Showgirls* (before it became a cult classic).

Make 'em show you theirs first.

If you're sitting in a meeting with a young studio exec who says, "Tell me what you've done," reply this way: "You first."

Michael Eisner's is bigger than yours.

Screenwriter John Gregory Dunne ran into Disney chairman Michael Eisner at Morton's.

Dunne: "I asked him how his heart was, and Michael said it was fine. He had come through his bypass surgery in good order. 'You know,' I said, 'I had the same operation,' and without missing a beat, Eisner replied, 'Of course, mine was more serious.' I have rarely been struck dumb, but this seemed to be 'mine is bigger than yours' Hollywood-style."

Putting Your Dick on the Table

What studio bosses do when they agree to pay a big star $20 million to do a movie. They put their "dicks on the table"—ready to be chopped off if the movie fails.

Harry Cohn had big balls.

My fellow Hungarian, actor Tony Curtis: "Some people were glad the studios were disintegrating, because they hated the moguls, Harry Cohn in particular. I always liked Harry, myself. One day I got an inside look at the way he operated. He liked to see me, and I'd stop by now and then, just to talk. One day I'm in his office with a friend, just sitting there, talking, and Harry's buzzer rings. He says to the secretary, "Well, send her in." And in walks this beautiful girl, maybe twenty years old, just a magnificent young woman in a beautiful silk summer dress. . . . She takes a look around, nervously, and says, 'Harry, I have to talk to you.' He says, 'So talk.' She looks at us and says, 'Harry, I'd rather not talk in front of these gentlemen.' He says, 'Anything you've got to say, you can say in front of them.' She takes a deep breath and says, 'Harry, I can't go on this way. You promised to take care of me, put me in a movie. It's been eight months now, and it just can't keep on like this. You have to do something, or I'm going to have to call your wife.' He looked at her, picked up the telephone, dialed the number, held out the phone to her, and said, 'Tell her yourself.' . . . She just slowly walked out. After a silence my friend had the nerve to ask, 'Harry, was that really your wife?' Harry Cohn just looked him straight in the eye and said, 'You'll never know.'"

ALL HAIL
Ben Hecht!

This is the advice screenwriter Ben Hecht gave to a director who had been asked by Columbia chief Harry Cohn if he was a member of the Communist party.

"Tell him to go fuck himself," Hecht said. "It's none of his goddamn business. Ask him if he's a Jew."

Hecht didn't call Cohn by name. He called him "White Fang."

Perry King gave birth to Sylvester Stallone.

Arthur Krim, the respected octogenarian head of United Artists, signed Sylvester Stallone up for *Rocky* after he saw *The Lords of Flatbush* and was impressed by the actor he thought was Sly in that movie. It was only when *Rocky* was released that Krim realized he'd confused Sly in *Flatbush* with another actor in that film, Perry King.

Without Perry King's acting ability, the world today would be without *Rocky* and Sylvester Stallone.

Spitballing

Usually used as "just spitballing," as in "We're just spitballing here." Often used in creative meetings by studio execs who (1) are trying to write your story for you and (2) know that what they're suggesting is stupid. Therefore they cover themselves by saying, "We're just spitballing here, right?" or "This isn't a very good idea, probably but we're just spitballing here, aren't we?"

Ingratiate yourself with your superiors.

Jack Valenti, the head of the Motion Picture Academy of America, and I were on the *Today* show.

Jack was berating me (I deserved it) for telling teenagers to use their fake IDs to see *Showgirls,* an NC-17 movie.

Jack, exasperated and angry with me, said, "Oh, you're just here publicizing your movie."

And I said, "So are you, Jack."

Stereotypes

A word used by directors, producers, and especially studio executives to get you to rewrite a character. If you force them to admit that a character is acting in a realistic manner, then they tell you that while the behavior is realistic, it's also stereotypical.

The word is frequently used when discussing black or gay characters.

Jack Valenti is not an Oliver Stone fan.

Said Jack about Oliver's *JFK*: "Young German girls and boys in 1941 were mesmerized by Leni Riefenstahl's *Triumph of the Will* in which Adolf Hitler is pictured as a newborn God. Both *JFK* and *Triumph of the Will* are equally a propaganda masterpiece and equally a hoax. . . . Does any sane human being truly believe that President Johnson, the Warren Commission, the CIA, the FBI, the Secret Service, local law enforcement officers, assorted thugs, weirdos, all conspired together as plotters in Stone's wacky sightings?"

Studio execs feel no pain there.

A Warner Bros. executive who didn't think *Bonnie and Clyde* was releasable said this after a preview audience got up and cheered it at the end: "Well, I guess Warren Beatty just shoved it up our ass."

Send Me Some Pages

What producers, directors, or studio execs say when they are worried your script won't be any good. Don't ever send anyone pages from your script until you are finished with the script—then send the script in toto. Their hope is that if you send pages before you're finished, they can tell you where to take the story from there . . . or tell you to start all over again.

DBTA

Dead by the third act . . . this usually refers to the protagonist's best friend or partner, killed off by the third act . . . usually to motivate the protagonist to take revenge for his pal's death.

Studio execs have impeccable taste.

I still think *Pinocchio* is a perfect movie," said Dreamworks coboss Jeffrey Katzenberg. "Perfect story, perfect characters and stunning animation."

Off Point

A scene that doesn't work.

Lew tells me it ain't so.

When I was a young screenwriter, I ran into Universal potentate Lew Wasserman and his wife, Edie, one morning near the deli Nate and Al's on Beverly Drive. I introduced myself and said that I knew that both Lew and Edie were from Cleveland, like me.

Then I said that I had a gangster friend in Cleveland named Shondor Birns, who'd told me that Lew had worked handling the racing wire across the street from the Theatrical Grill on Short Vincent Street (before he became a mogul).

Lew Wasserman looked at me, smiled, and said, "You got some bum information. I never did that."

Then he said, "Is Shondor Birns still alive?"

I said, "No, he got blown up in a car bomb on the West Side."

Lew Wasserman smiled and said, "There you go," and walked away with Edie into Nate and Al's.

That Doesn't Work

Usually uttered by producers and studio execs, it means "I don't like it."

What does Mike Medavoy know?

Director Bob Rafelson went to studio head Mike Medavoy's office to tell him that Arnold Schwarzenegger would be perfect in *Stay Hungry.*

Medavoy said to Bob, "I've known you were crazy for years and now I'm sure of it. This guy has an Austrian accent and he doesn't look anything like a traditional movie star. Get out of my office."

Your Script Is Too Soft

By this, they mean it's too arty, too lyrical, not dramatic enough, lacking enough violence for a box-office hit.

Studio execs are very busy people, too.

Louis B. Mayer and his executives spent weeks trying to figure out how many times the MGM lion should roar on-screen at the beginning of a film. They finally settled on two loud growls followed by a yip.

Tweaking Your Script

If a director, producer, or studio exec tells you that your script is "terrific" but needs "a little tweaking" it means you are about to be paid off and another writer will soon come in and rewrite everything you've written.

In short, it means they hate your script.

You're a jackass in a hailstorm.

Jack Valenti did give screenwriters some good advice.

Jack: "I do get frustrated; in fact, I do get depressed from time to time. But I've learned something. If I just hunker down, as LBJ used to say, like a jackass in a hailstorm and wait till the storm passes, it's going to be all right. If I look down on a day or two, I know on the third day I'm gonna start rising again."

A Round Conversation

One that is going nowhere.

Give studios you've been in business with before a first chance to read a brand-new script.

Just make sure the brand-new script doesn't have too many coffee stains on it.

They have to pay you, but they don't have to thank you.

Columbia studio boss Harry Cohn: "The word gratitude is not part of the Hollywood dictionary."

ALL HAIL
Harlan Ellison

When screenwriter/novelist Ellison felt that a studio executive had lied to him, he messengered the man a dead gopher.

Bullet Points

What studio execs call their most important notes on a screenplay. Screenwriters say they're called "bullet points" because these are the points that will kill the script.

This Is the Best First Draft I've Ever Read

Producers and studio execs say this when they know that an awful lot of work will have to be done on the script and when they want to cajole you into doing more drafts than what your contract calls for.

Garbage

This is what studio executives call the dialogue of a screenplay.

Sweet Jesus . . .

Academy Awards producer and former studio chief Joe Roth had this idea to start the show the year after *The Passion of the Christ* was released: "I say, bring Billy Crystal out in a loincloth, carried on a cross through the Academy."

PART TEN

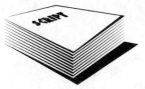

INSPIRING THE ACTORS

LESSON 16

Their Shorts Have Skid Marks, Too!

Don't star-fuck.

William Goldman, on the making of his *Marathon Man,* starring Laurence Olivier: "But that moment—when the actor of the century asked me would I mind if he switched six words around—is the most memorable incident of my movie career. Olivier. Calling me 'Bill.' Olivier. Asking *me* would I mind. That's high cotton."

Actors have a social conscience.

Shooting *Viva Villa* in Mexico, Lee Tracy took a piss off of his hotel balcony while Mexicans beneath him were marching to celebrate their national independence.

In order to avoid an international incident, Tracy had to be replaced.

Do not genuflect before stars.

William Goldman: "Stars do not—repeat—do not play heroes—stars play gods. And your job as a screenwriter is to genuflect, if you are lucky enough to have them glance in your direction. Because they may destroy your work, will destroy it more often than not—but you will have a career."

Listen to me carefully: I am my own best example. You don't have to genuflect to anyone to have a lengthy and profitable screenwriting career.

You'll pick up a lot of rug burns and need to carry mouthwash with you. (We already know that Bill used to carry bottles of Kaopectate.)

Aw, come on, their shorts get skid marks, too.

Screenwriter John Gregory Dunne: "I have a confession to make: I have a hard time calling Robert Redford 'Bob.' He is younger than I am, and yet I would let his diminutive cross my lips only if I could not get his attention by catching his eye or clearing my throat. To me, he is Robert Redford. In an era of faux egalitarian familiarity, when presidential contenders pass themselves off as Bill or Phil, 'Bob' is somehow diminishing; it would be like calling Woodrow Wilson 'Woody.'"

ALL HAIL
The Old Scum-Sucking Swine!

Hunter S. Thompson was the only writer I've ever known who could make groupies out of movie stars.

Johnny Depp slept in a little room, which was filled with brown spiders, in Hunter's basement.

Sean Penn, Jude Law, and Benicio Del Toro were all friends who tried to cheer Hunter up when he was depressed by reading to him . . . from his own writings.

I asked Hunter once how he was able to do this to actors.

"They're actors," he said, "I show 'em my guns. I let 'em play with 'em. Actors like to play with guns."

Actors ruined everything a long time ago.

Producer David O. Selznick: "I don't mind spending money, but there's no more reason to believe that Marlon Brando is a producer than Karl Malden is. We always have difficulties but actors used to accept discipline. I've called Jack Barrymore into my office for not knowing his lines; he was contrite and apologetic. I had to speak to Leslie Howard, who was embarrassing Vivien Leigh by not being prepared for a scene. But you never had to speak again. They recognized their fault and corrected it."

TAKE IT FROM ZSA ZSA

Don't marry an actor.

Actress and famed Hungarian femme fatale Zsa Zsa Gabor: "When you are married to an actor, you have the feeling you are nothing but an understudy to him. He only has eyes for himself. It is really the one situation I know of where, with just two people, you have a triangle! Both of you, madly in love with him. They probably have these big ego problems because deep inside, they are not secure, like little boys. There is a saying that an actress is something more than a woman and an actor is something less than a man."

Please, Bill, you're embarrassing me.

Screenwriter William Goldman: "I have worked with Redford. I have been in a room with Beatty. They are brilliant men, passionate about what they produce, and boy are they not dumb. Well, Michael Douglas is their equal. And Douglas did something no other actor did with me—he spent *time*. On the script. Going over it and over it. Actors just don't do that. They are simply too busy. But Douglas spent literally days locked in a room with me and with Stephen Hopkins, who did a wonderful job directing the movie."

Oh boy, Bill, I know you think it's about *the next job,* but you don't have to be this *desperate* to get one, do you? You "have been in a room with Beatty"? Hallelujah, man! They're "brilliant" and "passionate" and "wonderful"? Have you no gag reflex left?

Michael Douglas, in my experience, is not brilliant and may very well, in some cases, be dumb. This is the guy who wanted to change the ending of *Basic Instinct* because he said it wasn't "redemptive." Pressed, he said he was the star of the movie and "she one-ups me at every turn." The ending he wanted was for himself to shoot Sharon in the final scene. Even when the movie came out and was a huge hit, he kept bellyaching and asking, "Where's the redemption?"

If he's so brilliant, then why doesn't he understand that not every movie has to end (especially in film noir) with redemption? And that ambiguity is a much more interesting way to go than redemption, which is, at the same time, a disguised way of soothing a star's ego.

You don't want theater tickets, do you?

Agent Swifty Lazar: "The actor Jacob Adler induced some actress to sleep with him, only to have her hit him up for money. 'Mr. Adler,' she told him, 'I need bread!' To which he replied, 'Then fuck a baker. Fuck an actor, you get theater tickets.'"

This means Robert McKee is a great actor.

The better the actor," said screenwriter/novelist Truman Capote, "the more stupid he is."

Billy Friedkin agrees.

Friedkin: "I'd rather work with tree stumps than actors."

To get actress Angie Everhart into the right frame of mind for her character in *Jade*, Friedkin slapped her. He also slapped a bit actor, a priest, on the set of *The Exorcist*.

Mike Nichols agrees, too.

Asked how many smart actors he knew, Nichols said, "One and half—Anthony Perkins is smart, and Richard Burton is something."

Barbara Kingland, who had an affair with Richard Burton when she was thirteen, was impressed by all the wise things Burton was always saying to her—until, when she was older, she found them in *Bartlett's Familiar Quotations*.

Drew Carey studies Robert McKee.

Comedian Drew Carey has taken Robert McKee's screenwriting course twice—which means he's spent sixty hours listening to him.

John Cleese studies Robert McKee.

The comedian John Cleese has taken the Robert McKee screenwriting seminar three times. In other words, he's spent ninety hours listening to McKee.

Joan Rivers studies Robert McKee.

Comedian Joan Rivers has taken Robert McKee's screenwriting course—but only once.

Actors can be smart.

Debra Winger called me at midnight in California from the *Betrayed* set in Canada. She said she had a script idea.

I listened. Then I told her why her idea was uninspired.

She listened. Then she said, "You're right, damn you!" and hung up.

An Immersive Actor

An actor who never steps out of the part, a potential Oscar winner, a phony, a pain in the ass.

But actors aren't geniuses.

Montgomery Clift turned down the Marlon Brando role in *On the Waterfront*, the William Holden role in *Sunset Boulevard*, the Paul Newman role in *Somebody Up There Likes Me*, and the James Dean role in *East of Eden*.

Actors aren't narcissistic, either.

Jennifer Aniston: "The last thing we think about is our looks, even though people think we do, because our wardrobe and hair are so great."

Actors are human; they're insecure, too.

If an actor says, "My character wouldn't do that," it usually means the actor is afraid he can't act that scene.

Jim Carrey: "When the camera's on, I'm a desperate motherfucker."

Actors are dumb.

For many years, Robert De Niro, always brilliant on-screen, couldn't even say two words on his own. He'd sit there, not speaking, stuck inside the mannerisms of the last character he'd played on-screen—woefully, miserably, pathetically lost without the words of a script.

But actors are no dummies.

When she was in her midforties, Sharon Stone legally adopted a woman as her grandmother.

The woman was a multizillionaire wife of a New York City parking magnate.

Actors are sensitive.

Sharon Stone told the English press that she was so "traumatized" by having to do killing scenes in *Basic Instinct* that during those scenes, she asked that paramedics be near with a tank of oxygen and a mask in case she passed out.

It was a complete crock. She was as ruthlessly efficient in her killing scenes as she was in her sex scenes.

Actors are so very sensitive.

Sharon went up to the *Basic Instinct* cinematographer with a gun in hand and waved it in his face.

"If I see one ounce of cellulite on-screen," she said, "you're a dead motherfucker."

You, too, can create a monster.

Sharon Stone: "People who have seen *Basic* stand two feet away from me. They speak to me in careful tones. They don't condescend to me at all anymore."

Beware of "ach-trusses."

Sharon Stone put a clause in her *Diabolique* contract that she wouldn't do any nudity.

Here's my two bucks.

Sharon Stone to Carrie Fisher: "I've often thought that if I could get a 900 number and charge all the people who say they've had sex with me—or say they know someone who's had sex with me—two dollars a call, I'd never have to work again."

Maybe it's not such a good idea to sleep with your leading lady.

Actor James Woods to actress Sharon Stone: "Look, Sharon, maybe everyone can't wait to get in there, but once they get it in, the big problem is getting it out again."

Some actors have guts.

As feminists everywhere were trashing *Basic Instinct* after the movie's release, actress Demi Moore, who had been offered the Stone part, told the press that she was upset at herself for having turned it down.

She particularly liked the scene where Catherine Tramell is interrogated by a roomful of policemen. Demi thought it was "the best female empowerment scene in movie history."

The Suicide Years

Used in reference to actresses who are in their thirties.

Actors are nutcases.

Marlon Brando's contracts for many years specified that he could leave the set in the midafternoon to see his shrink.

Actors can't write.

Hudson Hawk, one of the great total disasters of our time, was cowritten by Bruce Willis, who also cowrote the title song, which also bombed.

Not even Warren can write.

John Gregory Dunne: "Warren Beatty does not write as much as he supervises, in the manner of an architect. *Teams of writers* in effect work under the pseudonym Warren Beatty."

Be careful making suggestions to actors.

Said George C. Scott to Paddy Chayefsky when Paddy tried to give him some acting tips: "You do your fucking writing! And I'll do the acting!"

But actors can be mellow.

George C. Scott (*Patton, The Hospital*): "I've always been mellow. I have been the most mellow son of a bitch you've ever seen."

Actors will do anything to upstage one another.

Zero Mostel always ate a big dish of black beans and onions before the premiere of a play he was appearing in. He did that so he could fart easier (and louder and smellier) to distract the other actors.

Actors can be cheap.

Two actors I've worked with—Ryan O'Neal and Maximilian Schell—*took* all the clothes that they wore in the film they had just finished shooting.

Ryan O'Neal left the set so quickly with his new Armani suit that he had to be chased across town to bring it back—Arthur Hiller, the director, wanted to do another take.

Actors can be pissy.

This is especially true on a set, where they're pumped full of diuretics like Diazide, which make them go to the bathroom three times an hour (that would make anyone irritable).

They take the pills to look lean and hollowed out for the camera. Some actors—like Jeff Bridges and Michael Douglas—put twenty pounds on between movies and have to go on a rigid crash diet before the shoot. And *then* they have to gobble their piss pills on the set.

To Do a Pee-Wee

To be caught in a dark place playing with it.

Actors are somewhat competitive.

Anna Magnani watched Marilyn Monroe accept a prize from the Italian industry and yelled this from the audience: "*Putana!*" (Whore!)

They're so worried about wrinkles.

When Marilyn Monroe died, hair designer Sydney Guilaroff, one of her best friends, said, "I'm glad she died young. She could never have stood getting a wrinkle on her face. All she had was her beauty."

HOLLYWOOD PARABLE

Dr. Haing S. Ngor worked as a gynecologist in Cambodia. When the Communists took over the government, he and his wife were taken to a prison camp as slave laborers.

He was crucified in the camps and had part of his right little finger chopped off. His wife, pregnant with his child, was beaten to death.

He escaped to a Thai refugee camp. The director Roland Joffe met him and asked him to play a lead part in his film The Killing Fields. *He agreed to do the part only because he had promised his wife that he would do his best to tell the world of the horrors that had taken place in Cambodia.*

He received a Golden Globe Award and an Academy Award for his performance, the first nonprofessional actor in nearly fifty years to win the Oscar. He played other roles in film and television but spent much of his time involved in Cambodian relief efforts.

In February 1996, he was standing in the driveway of his Los Angeles apartment when he was shot to death by three young men. They were members of the Oriental Lazy Boyz street gang and were trying to rob Dr. Ngor.

He resisted. He didn't want to give them the locket around his neck. Inside it was a photograph of his dead wife.

If an actor has good lines, you'd better believe that he improvised them. Director Richard Marquand and I loved Robert Loggia's performance in *Jagged Edge* because he was the ultimate pro. He hit all his marks, said all his lines, never asked a question about his character's motivation, and never improvised.

When the movie became a big hit, Bob Loggia told his many interviewers that he had improvised *most* of his lines.

He stopped saying it when Richard told him that if he said it one more time, "I'm going to tell the press that you're a bloody bald-faced liar."

Robert Loggia was nominated for an Academy Award for his performance in *Jagged Edge*. He thanked neither me nor Richard.

In the beginning was the word.

Actor Chris Cooper (*Adaptation*): "Last night I tried to make a little bit of a joke at the very opening of a speech. I'm a guy that always needs a script. I can't talk off the cuff and be witty."

Who do you want me to be?

Actor John C. Reilly (*Chicago, Gangs of New York*): "I don't know who I am unless you tell me who I am—or who you want me to be. I'm still figuring out who I am, you know?"

Sometimes it's up to you to convince an actor to take the part.

Director Phillip Noyce (*Sliver*) describes a meeting he and I had with Sharon Stone to convince her to take the part of Carly Norris in *Sliver*: "On that occasion, which was quite tense going in, Sharon asked Joe if he'd like a massage. . . . It's true that I stopped talking. But not because I was sexually moved by the sight of a fifty-year-old man lying on the floor moaning as Sharon Stone was massaging him while sitting astride him. I stopped talking simply because he was so grotesque in the sounds he was making that it seemed ridiculous to continue trying to convince Sharon to do the part. And so I stopped talking and let the two of them play with each other on the floor. After massaging Joe, Sharon agreed to take the part of Carly."

If you have actor friends, try to get them to do a reading of your script.

Screenwriter Nicholas Kazan: "A reading won't always validate the writer's view . . . and that's its beauty. It simply exposes the text, usually revealing problems of some sort."

You don't want Edward Norton starring in your movie.

He was so disgusted by the quality of the scripts he was getting that he took Robert McKee's course, too, and he now *rewrites all the scripts he agrees to act in.*

Since he is a star, directors and studio execs try to flatter him into starring in their film by letting him do whatever he likes to the screenplay.

Try to stop Dustin Hoffman from being cast in your film.

Dusty is a huge fan of improvising a script. He will take a scene in the script that takes a minute and use it as a basis of improvisation with the other actors. They'll improvise for a half hour and then ask the writer to rewrite it in a way that they discovered while they were improvising.

Penis Extension

A Robert Evans phrase for a male star with "eruptability and swagger."

If Warren Beatty has anything to do with your film, stop working on it.

The joke in Hollywood is that Beatty, the great auteur, can turn a "go" movie into a development deal.

He'll get involved, work with six writers, rewriting your script, then *pull out of the project.*

He wanted to play the lead in my film *Jade,* but the director knew that if Beatty got involved, he (the director) would be out of a job. So he blocked Beatty from getting involved by making sure the studio didn't make Beatty's very expensive deal. The way he made sure of that was by discussing it with his wife, who ran the studio.

The director was Billy Friedkin, his wife Sherry Lansing.

Beware the unprepared actor; he could give you the performance of a lifetime.

Marlon Brando arrived on the set of *Apocalypse Now* without having read either the script or the novel on which it was based. He was so overweight that he could be shot only from the neck up.

Oh, but to be a star.

Hedy Lamarr: "To be a star is to own the world and all the people in it. A star can have anything: if there's something she can't buy, there's always a man to give it to her. Everybody adores a star. Strangers fight just to approach her. After a taste of stardom, everything else is poverty."

If an actor is looking for you, run!

Keanu Reeves was looking for a writer on the Academy Awards show.

"You're one of the writers, right?" he said to Bruce Vilanch, holding a script.

"This is really important. In this line 'This shocking, brutal, hilarious adventure is called *Pulp Fiction*.'"

Keanu looked at Vilanch.

Vilanch said, "So?"

Keanu said, "I want to change it."

Vilanch said, "You want to change it?"

Keanu said, "Yeah."

Vilanch said, "What do you want to change it to?"

Keanu said, "Can I say 'entitled' instead of 'called'? 'Entitled *Pulp Fiction*.'"

Vilanch said, "I don't see why not."

Keanu said, "Okay, good."

Maybe you can learn to eat glass.

Agent Swifty Lazar: "One night a well-respected French writer named Joseph Kissel was a guest at the home of Lewis Milestone, a fine director who did *All Quiet on the Western Front*. Kissel, a monster of a man, had mastered the art of eating glass.

"Humphrey Bogart had never met Kissel. . . . It was early in the evening when Kissel encountered Bogart in the foyer and asked him if he could eat glass. Bogart admitted he could not.

"'I can,' the writer boasted.

"'Well, eat this,' Bogie said, pointing in the direction of an eighteenth-century mirror. And before you knew it, Bogie had smashed the mirror and handed a piece to Kissel. And Kissel immediately swallowed half the piece Bogie had given him.

"'If you can do it, I can do it,' Bogie said.

"He tried, but all he did was cut up the inside of his mouth."

Actors bring their own strengths and weaknesses to the part.

Robert Redford belches a lot, one reason he's mostly so cool and poker-faced on screen.

If Redford gets interested in your script, delete any scenes where he might be laughing.

Actors live their parts.

Hedy Lamarr: "How deeply do actresses become involved in their roles? Very deeply. I know when Ida Lupino did a string of neurotic characters, it had a definite effect on her. The doctor recommended happier pictures. The same thing happened to Bette Davis. I remember that during the making of *Samson and Delilah* my libido was definitely aroused."

Sometimes, very rarely, very very rarely, once in a blue moon, hardly ever, an actor will improvise a line better than any writer could have written it.

At the Academy Awards, after a streaker crossed the stage, actor David Niven said, "Isn't it fascinating to think that probably the only laugh that man will ever get in his life is by stripping off his clothes and showing his shortcomings?"

Actors really do respect, um, the screenwriter.

Tim Robbins: "There are the scripts you don't want to touch at all, that are so brilliant that you just have to figure a way into the character, and that's your job. There's other stuff that you have to fill out on your own and flesh out on your own. I try not to get involved with rewriting. I don't think it's necessary for an actor to do that. I think it's necessary for an actor to say, 'This doesn't really ring true. Is there something else we can do here?' But only after really trying. Sometimes actors can be wrong about their instincts and, without trying to go to a place emotionally out of some kind of reluctance, think they need a rewrite. But I trust—99 percent of the time—the writer's instinct."

I wasn't a dirty old man then, but maybe I am now.

When she was cast as the lead in my film *Jade*, Linda Fiorentino told *Daily Variety*, "It's an absolutely brilliant screenplay."

When *Jade* failed, Linda Fiorentino told reporters, "I had a lot of doubts about the script. It reads like it's written by a dirty old man."

Actors are ingrates.

I asked Paramount to cast Tom Berenger in *Sliver.* Tom and I were friends—we had met on the *Betrayed* set.

Paramount didn't want to cast him—he hadn't had any hit movies and he was drinking too much.

I finally went to Brandon Tartikoff, the head of production at the time, and asked him as a personal favor to me to cast Tom.

Brandon finally agreed—but told me I owed him a big one.

During the shoot, I discovered on the set that Tom was indeed drinking too much—he had vodka bottles in his trailer that he was sucking on, but I stood by him. The studio didn't replace him.

When the movie was released (and failed), Tom told *USA Today*, "Yeah, well, Joe can be real sleazy sometimes."

Actors have short memories.

Asked at a New York political fund-raiser what children should say no to, Arnold Schwarzenegger, whose movies have included more than five hundred shootings, maimings, or knifings, said, "How about violence? We should say no to violence."

Actors are loyal.

David Caruso, about my film *Jade*: "You'll see. *Jade* will be rediscovered by audiences in the future. In fact, I will make a prediction that this film will have a resurgence."

Gina Gershon, about my film *Showgirls*: "I'm not embarrassed saying I was in that movie. And I can't tell you how many people still come up to me and tell me how much they liked that movie. I think the *Showgirls* phenomenon has to do with the media. There were such high expectations that by the time the movie came out, it was bound to fail. And then when the critics started blasting it, people were scared to have their own opinion. I don't think it was as bad as some people said."

Shit happens to actors, too.

Hedy Lamarr: "At times, sex has been a disruptive factor in my life. The men in my life have ranged from a classic case history of impotence to a whip-brandishing sadist who enjoyed sex only after he tied my arms behind me with the sash of his robe. There was another man who took his pleasure with a girl in my own bed, while he thought I was asleep in it."

It ain't easy to be a star.

I stopped believing in Santa Claus at an early age," said Shirley Temple. "Mother took me to see him in a department store and he asked me for my autograph."

R E E L S P E A K

To Do a Garry Shandling

To sue, as Shandling did, your own agent or manager—an absolute no-no in the business. Look at what's happened to Shandling's career in the past five years: nada.

No hobbies, no kids, no nothin' . . .

Christopher Walken (*The Deer Hunter, King of New York*): "I hardly turn down anything, that's true. I don't have hobbies. I don't have kids. I really like to go to work. And when you're working, you want to stay a little bit fit and thin—so you look nice and your diet's better."

Macho Isn't Mucho

Said first by Zsa Zsa Gabor. In today's industry, macho definitely isn't mucho.

Try to avoid Method actors.

My fellow Hungarian Tony Curtis: "At the studio's urging I made a stab or two at the Method school of acting. . . . They called it sense memory. You had to recall the feeling of an icebox, or the exact sensation you had when you held a glass ball in your hand or felt the fabric of your tie. It was valid enough for some young actors, because it gave them something to do. But the truth is, acting was the only profession *people thought about a lot* and *did* very little. . . . It was a mind fuck: Go off in your head somewhere and find some other reality for what you were doing, *regardless of what the script intended*."

Poor Victor Mature . . .

Hedy Lamarr complained to director C. B. DeMille that in every scene she had with Victor Mature, her back was to the camera.

De Mille said, "Do you think there are any men in America who would rather look at Victor's face than your ass? Up to this point in your life, every man in the audience wanted to marry you. After this picture every man will want to go to bed with you. I have taken you out of the living room and brought you into the bedroom."

R E E L S P E A K

To Do a Jennifer Grey

To get the kind of plastic surgery that destroys your career.

It helps if the director is your ally and not the star's.

Director Phillip Noyce, discussing *Sliver*: "We were only a few weeks from shooting and basically Sharon was saying she wanted to start back with the script at square one. My own loyalty to Joe Eszterhas, as well as the practicality of the situation, meant that I had to say 'No, we're not gonna do that.' That was the issue— whether we were going to rewrite the script from the first page, and that was the issue on which I took a stand. I gave her the appearance of submitting, whereas in fact we did shoot Joe Eszterhas's script. But I allowed Sharon to feel she had won—that she was the most powerful person in the relationship. Joe Eszterhas has failed to understand that you can often achieve exactly what you want to by appearing to let the other person win."

The star is not your script's ally.

Producer Mace Neufeld described Harrison Ford's contribution to the script of *Patriot Games* this way: "He's always looking to eliminate false notes, writer's directions that look good on paper but just don't work."

Some screenwriters hate actors.

Author/screenwriter William Saroyan hated Marlon Brando. He had his reasons.

1. When he was a young man, Saroyan discovered that Brando had seduced his wife, Carol.

2. When he was an old man, Saroyan discovered that Brando had seduced his daughter, Lucy.

Why Marlon Brando could seduce both Mrs. and Miss Saroyan . . .

An actor friend of Robert Duvall's told him that as far as sex is concerned, "acting is the greatest leg-opener in the world."

You're lucky you're you and not Tom Cruise.

Screenwriter William Goldman: "It's shitty work. Not the money, not the power, that's all neat. But have you ever been on a movie set? Death. It's all mechanical stuff. Done in quick snippets. Sure, there's craft involved in sustaining a character over a four-month shoot—but most stars only play themselves, so even that isn't so hard. Ask anyone—movie acting is the snooze of all the world. So it's shitty and it's phony and the fame doesn't last. No wonder they're crazy. Maybe the real wonder is that they're not crazier than they are."

Actors are bullies.

Ryan O'Neal, sometime producer, played a studio executive in my film *An Alan Smithee Film: Burn Hollywood Burn.*

The script called for him to hit a *National Enquirer* reporter named Alan Smith, played by a real *National Enquirer* reporter named Alan Smith.

O'Neal, a Hollywood lothario, had reason not to like the tabloids . . . and Alan Smith, who had written about him in the past.

So when the scene was being filmed, Ryan hit the real Alan Smith so hard that he almost broke the man's jaw.

"Score one for us," Ryan O'Neal said.

If you're really pissed off at an actor, touch him or her.

What's awful about being famous and being an actress," said famous actress Winona Ryder, "is when people come up to you and touch you. That's scary, and they just seem to think it's okay to do it, like you're public property."

ALL HAIL
Mercedes de Acosta!

The screenwriter/playwright seduced both Greta Garbo and Marlene Dietrich.

A friend said she looked like "a Spanish Dracula with the body of a young boy."

She was known in society circles as "the dyke at the top of the stairs."

You're too smart to learn anything from actors.

Professor James Ryan in *Screenwriting from the Heart*: "Having worked early in my career as a professional actor in stage, film, and television, I tried an experiment. I got my writing students on their feet doing improvisations. It helped enormously even if they were lousy actors. They began to understand that good dramatic writing is acting on the page and there must be truthful moment to moment behavior for their characters. I devised 'simple-stupid' exercises to get all their 'learning' out of the way, so that they could access their deeply felt imagination and find that place in themselves that would give them a sense of prowess—a feeling of being alive and true."

H—E—L—P!

Forehead

One of Arnold Schwarzenegger's favorite words—it means a stupid person or a person who argues with Arnold. Most of the legislators in California are "foreheads."

Lame-o

Jack Nicholson's version of "forehead."

Their PR person will decide about your script.

Actress Sally Field said, "I hesitate to say that Pat Kingsley does my public relations. It's way beyond that. I send her material, the scripts I'm thinking of doing or developing. And I'm not the only one who does. Jim Brooks, Goldie Hawn—a whole bunch of people ask her about scripts, about writers."

Oh, wasn't Jim Brooks a writer once?

The screenwriter/director, according to Sally Field, sends his scripts to Pat Kingsley, PR person, for advice.

A writer who sends his script to his PR person? *For advice?*

This is the meaning of "star power."

Screenwriter/director Billy Wilder: "There was an actress named Marilyn Monroe. She was always late. She never remembered her lines. She was a pain in the ass. My Aunt Millie is a nice lady. If she were in pictures, she would always be on time. She would know her lines. She would be nice. Why does everyone in Hollywood want to work with Marilyn Monroe and no one wants to work with my Aunt Millie? Because no one will go to the movies to watch my Aunt Millie and everyone will come out to watch Marilyn Monroe."

You, too, can leave your wife.

Mike Medavoy said this to Kevin Costner after meeting him for the first time: "You know, I have this sense that I'm sitting here with someone who is going to become a great big star. You're going to want to direct your own movies, produce your own movies, and you're going to end up leaving your wife and going through the whole Hollywood movie-star cycle."

Stars are better with their mouths closed.

Screenwriter Robert Towne: "What was once said of the British aristocracy, that they did nothing and did it very well—is a definition that could be applied to movie actors. For gifted movie actors affect us most, I believe, not by talking, fighting, fucking, killing, cursing, or cross-dressing. They do it by being photographed. The point is that a fine actor onscreen conveys a staggering amount of information before he ever opens his mouth."

Work with actors who are unknown.

Producer Sam Spiegel: "When actors are still comparatively unknown, they are easygoing and amiable. When they lose their sense of proportion, they become lionized and begin to believe their own publicity."

A complete unknown can be better in a part than Robert De Niro or Gene ("the Hack") Hackman.

Director Phillip Noyce: "Between a beginner and an experienced actor there is a huge gap. And often it's better not to fill that gap, because someone with absolutely no experience, and therefore no technique, can be just as good as the most experienced actor. With experience come actorly tricks, acting techniques that can make a performance false."

If you marry an actress, don't write a script for her.

Arthur Miller wrote *The Misfits* for Marilyn Monroe. This is what she had to say: "Arthur did this to me. He could have written anything and he comes up with this. If that's what he thinks of me, well, then I'm not for him and he's not for me. Arthur said it's his movie. I don't think he even wants me in it. It's all over. We have to stay with each other because it would be bad for the film if we split up now. . . . I think Arthur secretly likes dumb blondes. Some help he is."

Find your own Marilyn Monroe and have a fling with her.

Mexican screenwriter José Bolaños found the actual Marilyn. He was one of her last lovers. This is what she said about him: "He's the greatest lover in the whole wide world. I heard he writes some of the worst movies in Mexico. Silly romances. But what do I care? Everything else he does is incredible."

ALL HAIL
Mercedes de Acosta!

Truman Capote designed a game that he called the International Daisy Chain. Its goal was to connect people through the people they had slept with.

Capote said that the best card to have in the game was screenwriter Mercedes de Acosta because she had slept with so many people, "you could get to anyone from Francis Cardinal Spellman to the Duchess of Windsor."

You, too, can marry a movie star.

Paul Bern wrote screenplays for German films directed by Ernst Lubitsch and Josef von Sternberg.

That's not what made him famous. What made him famous was marrying sex bomb Jean Harlow.

When Harlow married him, she said, "He doesn't talk fuck, fuck, fuck, fuck all the time."

He was just another impotent screenwriter.

Screenwriter Paul Bern killed himself after two months of marriage to Jean Harlow.

The studio wanted to make sure the public didn't blame Harlow in any way for her husband's suicide. They made up a story that Bern killed himself because he was suffering from "underdeveloped genitalia"—a real problem, considering he was married to the world's greatest sex bomb.

Keep your casting ideas to yourself.

Novelist Margaret Mitchell suggested that Groucho Marx be cast as Rhett Butler in the film version of her novel, *Gone With the Wind.*

Don't fly on the same plane with actors.

We were flying from Dubuque, Iowa, to Chicago in a puddle jumper after the *F.I.S.T.* premiere—Norman Jewison, the director, and I and the actors Kevin Conway and Cassie Yates.

We got caught in a thunderstorm and the little plane started to be buffeted about in the wind.

"Oh shit," Norman Jewison said to me. "If this thing crashes, I'm only going to get the second paragraph. The actors always get the lead—and you, the screenwriter, will be mentioned somewhere deep in the middle of the story."

Don't have a movie star for a friend.

Remember that the word *star* spelled backward is *rats.*

LESSON 17

Just Say the Fucking Words!

Even Bill Goldman wrote a tell-all.

Bill Goldman wrote about going bikini shopping with Elizabeth Hurley; Norman Mailer wrote about his great lust for Marilyn Monroe; Arthur Miller wrote a play about Marilyn Monroe, his wife; and then there was the screenwriter who wrote about rolling around on the floor with Sharon Stone.

Movie stars are right not to trust writers.

Warren Beatty shouldn't ever be without his watercooler.

When studio head Frank Wells denied director and star Warren Beatty's request for a watercooler in his office, Beatty took *Heaven Can Wait* away from Warner Bros. and went to Paramount.

Actors are teenagers undergoing a sexual identity crisis.

Sir Laurence Olivier: "To oneself inside, one is always sixteen with red lips."

TAKE IT FROM ZSA ZSA

Actors are like children and children are simple.

Stallone fights like a sissy and Sean Penn can't fight.

When Sylvester Stallone claimed in interviews that he had written *F.I.S.T.* (it had taken me years to research and write the script), I challenged him to a fistfight by saying I'd been in more barroom brawls and claiming that he "fought like a sissy."

My father, who loved me, said "I've seen *Rocky*. I've seen him fight. Challenge him to fight, yes, but do not under any circumstances fight him. He will beat you bloody." I took my father's advice.

At dinner one night, screenwriter/novelist Charles Bukowski told Sean Penn that his wife smelled "like she'd been sucking donkeys off all day."

Sean jumped up and challenged Bukowski to fight. Bukowski, then in his seventies, said, "Sit down, Sean, you know I can take you."

A Blood Star

An action star like Van Damme, Stallone, Seagal, or the governor of California.

Don't get caught in a cross fire between two superstars.

When Sly Stallone was directing John Travolta in *Staying Alive*, they got into a hellacious battle royal over the script.

Sly wanted me to do a rewrite incorporating both of their thoughts. I had a meeting with the two of them in Sly's trailer and saw that they were a thousand miles apart.

Sly and I had had a previous battle over *F.I.S.T.*, so I said to him now, "Sly, you fucked me with a tree trunk on *F.I.S.T.* What do you want to fuck me again for?"

Both Sly and Travolta laughed—they thought that was really funny.

I didn't do the rewrite.

You, too, can be a star maker.

Jennifer Beals, Sharon Stone, and Gina Gershon became stars playing the characters that I created.

All three of them denied it and said they became stars thanks to their own talent.

But none had any explanation for why they didn't become stars after playing other screenwriters' parts.

Actors know how to flatter you.

An actress in a Harold Pinter film said that saying Pinter's words was like "blowing air into yeast when making bread."

Liv Tyler is obsessed with me.

Liv Tyler did an interview in which she said *she* was the inspiration for *Showgirls*. She said I had become obsessed with her after seeing her play a stripper in an Aerosmith video.

She said, "Joe Eszterhas thought the video was brilliant. It gave him the idea for *Showgirls*. He tried to get me to take the lead in the movie, but I didn't want to get into that kind of thing."

It was news to me.

I'd never seen the Aerosmith video; neither had Paul Verhoeven, the director of *Showgirls*.

I'd never met or spoken with Liv; neither had Paul Verhoeven.

I didn't even know that Steven Tyler had a daughter named Liv; neither did Paul Verhoeven.

ALL HAIL
Tim Robbins!

The actor thanked novelist Dennis Lehane and screenwriter Brian Helgeland "for the writing of this amazing script" before thanking the director and producers as he accepted his Oscar for *Mystic River*.

THE HELL WITH TIM ROBBINS

In The Player, *he plays a sleazy studio executive who murders the screenwriter.*

Actors, like writers, don't like to think of themselves as liars.

Actress Melina Mercouri: "My colleague says that all actors are liars. But my colleague is an actor. So he is lying, yes? So therefore actors are not liars. Therefore he speaks the truth and therefore actors are liars, so therefore he lies and so on and so on."

You, too, can get even with an actor who treats you badly.

John Barrymore already had an opossum, a kinkajou, a mouse deer, and six dogs, which had been born during an earthquake—it was his theory that dogs born during earthquakes are more alert than others.

And then, as a gift from an English actress, John was given a monkey, which bit everyone in the house except him. The monkey would sit next to his feet for hours, gazing at him fondly. It was only after he'd been forced to give the monkey to the zoo that a vet told him the monkey had been transfixed not by his personality but by the booze he'd smelled on him. So John made weekly visits to the zoo to breathe on his monkey.

And then a screenwriter who secretly despised him gave John a vulture. Not just any vulture, but a king vulture, which became John's best friend. He named the vulture Maloney. He'd take Maloney out on the yacht, and the crew would be horrified as the big vulture sat on John's shoulders, nibbling at John's eyeball, holding his beak out for a kiss. They sailed happily up and down from Santa Monica to Santa Barbara, but one day John realized that Maloney wasn't happy. Maloney wasn't eating properly. John realized he wasn't able to feed Maloney what he required: partially but not *completely* decayed meat.

So he took Maloney ashore, kissed him farewell, and sailed away.

From then on, for the rest of his life, thanks to a diabolical screenwriter who hated him, John Barrymore did little but drink, a brokenhearted old actor pining for his vulture.

You can get even with an actress, too.

On the set of one of her earlier movies, Sharon Stone's prima donna act pissed off the crew so badly that *they pissed* into a bathtub before Sharon got into it for her scene.

What you write can destroy someone's career.

They told her she was going to be a big movie star and she almost believed it. She had done the television and the stage work, and here she was, at twenty-seven, costarring in a big movie with a big star at a cheap hotel out in the middle of nowhere, with only her pills and her little Baggies of coke to keep her company, to make her forget how much she hated the script. (They weren't such little bags, really; they were pretty big bags, a last-minute gift from her agent in L.A.)

She had a 5:00 A.M. wake-up call, and here it was, 2:00 A.M., and she couldn't get to sleep. She kept thinking about how awful this script was. She went out on her patio and practiced deep breathing for a while, noticing the balminess of this Iowa summer night, the softness of the corn-scented air.

She went downstairs, her pills and her Baggies in her purse, and got into her rent-a-car. Just a little drive around the blacktop and dirt roads was what she had in mind. But somehow she found herself flying down the interstate, popping another pill.

She lost track of much of the next couple of days. She woke up in the desert sun, out of pills, out of coke, trembling, knowing that it was over, that everything she had worked for was gone, knowing now that she would never be a star.

Beware of "serious" actors.

Laird Cregar was the best fiend you've ever seen on-screen. He was a talented actor with a weird, off-kilter face and a swollen body. Playing monsters and freaks, he'd go into makeup at the start of each film and ask them what they were going to do to his face, and they'd smile and say, "Nothing."

He read a sensitive book about an inward young guy with an inferiority complex. At his suggestion, a studio bought the book, but then the people there turned the inward young guy into a rapist and a murderer and cast Laird in the part.

When the shoot ended, Laird had plastic surgery done on his eyes, his nose, his jaw, and his ears. He wouldn't ever allow himself to be cast as a fiend again.

He was going to turn himself into a romantic lead. All he had left to do was to lose the weight.

He lost thirty pounds. Then he suffered a heart arrhythmia from the weight loss and died.

The pain, the pain . . .

Marlon Brando to Mike Medavoy: "Can you imagine going to work every day and pretending to be someone else?"

Just say the fucking words!

Faye Dunaway asked Roman Polanski about her character's motivation in *Chinatown*.

Roman said, "Say the fucking words. Your salary is your motivation."

Sharon didn't like Billy.

Sliver director Phillip Noyce: "Billy Baldwin knew that Sharon Stone hadn't wanted him in *Sliver* and their relationship was always tense. I ended up having to shoot many of their close-ups with only one of them in the room at a time, because they didn't want to look at each other."

Why didn't Sharon want Billy to costar with her?

Because she wanted Billy's older brother, Alec. Sharon said, "Alec can put me over a table anytime he wants."

What did Billy Baldwin have to say about that?

Billy called Sharon "a paean to lipstick lesbianism."

Comedians can kill you.

Producer Bernie Brillstein: "The words of comedy are death—'I killed them, I laid them in the aisle, I blew their head off, I murdered them'—it's all death—it's how far you can take a human being."

Who the hell is Hedy Lamarr?

Hedy Lamarr: "I enjoyed the location trips to desert towns in Arizona. The nights were mellow and romantic. Making love out of doors is so much more thrilling. Add a cowboy who never heard of Hedy Lamarr and the situation is ideal."

My friend Phillip Noyce fell in love with Angelina Jolie.

Director Phillip Noyce, discussing *The Bone Collector*: "In the second half of the schedule I was shooting predominantly with Angelina Jolie. Usually in the morning when I woke up, I couldn't wait to get to the set to work with her. I was impatient to continue what became a sort of love affair, being connected in this weird manner, through the lens, through the story, through the strange relationship between performer and director. I had the same connection with Nicole Kidman. I loved her, adored her; she was the angel who couldn't do a thing wrong."

The Crack of the Ass

The line at which most actresses stop when it comes to shooting nudity. There is usually a clause in their contracts that specifies that in a scene in bed, the bedsheet will be high enough so that a "crack of the ass" is visible.

My friend Phillip didn't just fall in love; he went stark raving gaga apeshit.

Some directors can fall gaga apeshit over their actors.

Phillip Noyce, discussing Angelina Jolie: "When I first met Angie I felt a sense of discovery, of being there when something wonderful is being formed. You could see tremendous talent as well as hunger, a hunger for work, good work, a love of trying things, a love of giving herself up to the character, to the lens, to the moment. . . . Porcelain isn't fine enough to describe how fragile she is. She's not burned out with the joy of performing. She's in her element because she can set parameters for a character, whereas I suspect she doesn't know her own boundaries emotionally and physically. She's very courageous as an actress. Angelina will go anywhere, or at least she'll try going anywhere that the director suggests."

Clint is Marilyn in drag.

Clint Eastwood's ex-lover said that Clint listened to hours and hours of audiotapes of Marilyn Monroe—to get his hushed voice just right.

Dustpan Hoffman, movie star . . .

As a young actor, Dustin Hoffman was known to his friends as "Dustbin" and "Dustpan." But after he was cast in *The Graduate*, all of his friends called him "Dusty."

Dennis Quaid asked God to take it all away.

Actor Dennis Quaid (*Far from Heaven*): "I wasn't really prepared for the sort of attention I got. When it started happening, it was just too much—and I was also fueling it by getting loaded a lot. There was so much coming at me at one point that I remember just asking God to take it away from me."

Tom Thumb's boots . . .

Tom Cruise didn't mind being cast with Brad Pitt in *Interview with the Vampire,* but he demanded that his costumer be allowed to make him boots that made him look taller than Pitt.

Her acting teachers killed Marilyn.

Marilyn Monroe's drama coach, Michael Chekhov, told her to spread her arms wide and stand with her legs apart so she could imagine herself becoming larger and larger.

She had to say to herself, "I am going to awaken the sleeping muscles of my body. I am going to revivify and use them."

Then she was to kneel on the floor and imagine herself getting smaller and smaller, until she became a speck on the floor.

She did these exercises every day for six hours.

Bogie was a wuss.

At a party he was attending with Lauren Bacall, his wife, Humphrey Bogart got angry when a sailor pinched Bacall's butt.

Bogie and some friends locked the sailor in the bathroom and called the Shore Patrol to come and arrest him.

Billy Wilder, who witnessed it all, said, "That was Bogie, the hero of *Casablanca.*"

Michael Douglas looks better with Botox and surgery.

Bogart once said to his cinematographer, "I like my lines and wrinkles, so don't try and light them out and make me look like a goddamn fag."

Dustpan is a hypocrite.

He starred in *Straw Dogs,* one of the bloodiest of all the films directed by Sam Peckinpah. Years later, he first turned down *Captain Hook,* the Peter Pan remake to be directed by Steven Spielberg, because, as Dusty's agent said, "The script is too violent."

Montgomery Clift in The Bridge on the River Kwai . . .

Producer Sam Spiegel was interested in casting Montgomery Clift in *The Bridge on the River Kwai.* He asked him to dinner in New York.

Clift arrived sky-high on pills. He would say things out of the blue, like "The sky is blue." He ordered a martini and then ordered two more. He ordered both steak and lamb chops—rare. He ate the steak and the chops and spit meat and blood all over the table. Then he lay down in the booth and went to sleep.

The producer changed his mind about casting him.

Only if it's a real honker . . .

While nose jobs hurt the careers of Jennifer Grey, Carol Burnett, and Roy Scheider, Peter O'Toole had such a beak of a nose that he would always have been a character actor without surgery.

Brando was stupid.

Brando not only sold off his gross points in *The Godfather* for $100,000 but then asked for $100,000 to attend the twenty-fifth-anniversary party of *The Godfather*'s release.

He didn't get it and didn't go. He would have received at least $8 million had he not sold his gross points.

Kate Nelligan was too smart.

Screenwriter/playwright Harold Pinter: "The porter called to say that a young actress named Kate Nelligan was on the way up to meet us and I can always remember Mike Nichols saying 'I feel sorry for young actresses. Can you imagine coming up to meet Sam Spiegel, Harold Pinter, and me—it must be terrifying.' And the next thing we knew, she walked into the room and took us to the cleaners. She was totally self-possessed, absolutely on top of everything, and made us feel that we didn't know what we were doing. *She didn't get the part because of that.*"

TAKE IT FROM ZSA ZSA

Zsa Zsa killed Clark Gable.

Zsa says that Clark's favorite food in the whole world was the artery-busting Hungarian favorite kolbasz, smoked and dried sausage.

She introduced Clark to it and he loved it so much that she would take a bunch of it over to his house each week—even the week that he died of a massive heart attack.

Elizabeth Taylor killed his dream.

Richard Burton, who said he was "a pockmarked boyo from Wales," didn't want to be an actor. He said he should have been a coal miner.

His dream was to own a big house filled with books and little else. He wanted to spend his life reading his books.

The Italian dwarf, movie star . . .

He is the actor whom Paramount executives referred to as "that Italian dwarf" before they cast him in *The Godfather.*

George C. Scott was George Lincoln Rockwell.

George C. Scott hated black people so much that *Islands in the Stream* had to be shot in Hawaii, on Kauai, where there were no black people—so Scott wouldn't get into trouble in the bars at night.

The few blacks necessary for scenes in the movie, set in the Caribbean, had to be flown in.

Vacuum the Dustpan.

Dusty went to story meetings for years with his own personal "dramaturge"—the playwright Murray Schisgal. Dusty wanted screenwriters he was working with to "work with Murray" as they wrote their scripts.

After they had worked with Murray and the script was finished, Dusty often brought in another personal pet writer just to rewrite his character's dialogue— that's how Malia Scotch Marmo wound up getting a shared screenplay credit on *Hook.*

The moral of the story: After Dusty and Murray and Malia are done with you, you might not recognize your own script.

Kim Novak almost killed Sammy Davis, Jr.

Columbia studio czar Harry Cohn once asked mobster Mickey Cohen to kill Sammy Davis, Jr., because Sammy was having an affair with Columbia star Kim Novak.

Cohn worried that if the affair became public, Novak's career would be finished.

Drew's father was an actor, too.

Actress Drew Barrymore: "My father said, 'Hey, Drew, you want to give me an autograph, too? How about putting it on a check?' "

David Caruso sleeps with a mirror.

My lead actor in *Jade,* David Caruso, said, "I'm nowhere near as sexy as I come off on-camera. Film just loves me."

Sandra Bernhard defines whores.

I cast her in *An Alan Smithee Film: Burn Hollywood Burn.* I think she's a brilliant actress.

She once said, "I find people in the porn world are very lively and animated. So what if they screw for a living? I like a lot of them better than the actors in Hollywood—who are the real whores, to be perfectly honest with you."

I wonder if Grace Kelly ever slept with Joe Mankiewicz.

Gary Cooper told friends that Grace Kelly liked going to bed wearing nothing but white gloves.

Coop said, "She gave the impression that she could be a cold dish until you got her in bed . . . then she could really explode."

Tim Robbins is full of . . . himself.

Actor Tim Robbins: "The best directors I've worked with would never consider themselves auteurs or experts or anything. Those experiences taught me that the open ear, the open mind, the open heart can produce such great work from the actor. If an actor comes on the set and the director is viewing themself [sic] as the person who knows everything, the person that has all the answers, then you're not going to create an organic performance. You're going to create someone's idea of a performance. And the really great directors know that and are able to inspire their actors to create by giving them a confidence in themselves and a worth in themselves. Then actors feel like they belong there. They feel like they are contributing something significant, that they aren't just saying lines, that they are bringing who they are as people to the project and are fully appreciated for that."

R E E L S P E A K

A Quality of Eruptibility

Absolutely necessary for a lead male part, making every female viewer believe that the actor playing the part would go to bed with her.

A Quality of Availability

Absolutely necessary for a lead feminine part, making every male viewer believe he could bed the starlet playing the part.

Val Kilmer is an imbecile.

Asked by the Academy to nominate the three best film moments of the century, Kilmer nominated three of his movies (one of them was *Batman Forever*). He enclosed a postcard to the Academy that said, "I can't help it, these are my three favorite movies."

The Pesci is beginning to stink.

Actor Joe Pesci, after winning Best Supporting Actor for *Good-Fellas,* went offstage and collapsed on the floor, clutching his Oscar and mumbling, "I can't believe this! I can't believe this!"

Yes, but did she clean the blood off the coat hangers?

Joan Crawford had all of her furniture and even her walls coated in plastic so she could clean them better.

Is that why he changed professions?

Harrison Ford, carpenter, was hired by John Gregory Dunne and Joan Didion to remodel their Trancas house.

Julia Roberts's virgin eyes . . .

When she moved into an apartment complex, Julia Roberts had notices sent to the other tenants, telling them they were not to speak to her or even look at her if they ran into her in the corridor.

Barbra Streisand did the same thing when she was doing a gig at a hotel in Vegas.

And Hillary Clinton did the same thing with Secret Service agents in the White House.

Is Tom Thumb the new Burt Reynolds?

Mimi Rogers, discussing soon-to-be-ex-husband Tom Cruise: "Here's the real story on why we broke up. Tom was seriously thinking of becoming a monk. At least for that period of time, it looked as though marriage wouldn't fit into his overall spiritual need. And he thought he had to be celibate to maintain the purity of his instrument. My instrument needed tuning. Therefore, it became obvious that we had to split."

James Woods's Krazy-glued penis.

When she broke up with actor James Woods, actress Sean Young put mutilated voodoo dolls on his front porch and told friends she was going to Krazy-glue his penis to his thigh.

The one-sheet tells all.

If the stars' faces aren't on it, their careers are fading. Check out Harrison Ford and Michelle Pfeiffer, missing from the *What Lies Beneath* one-sheet, and Sylvester Stallone, missing from the *Cliffhanger* poster.

He, too, was a big-mouth Hungarian.

Hungarian screenwriter Andrew Solt told his friend Zsa Zsa Gabor that Ingrid Bergman, on *Joan of Arc*, the picture he had written, slept with everyone on the set, including the electricians, and that when she was through with the electricians, she had them fired.

If Bruce Willis is a real asshole, then say he's a real asshole.

At a writer's seminar on Maui, Shane Black (*Lethal Weapon*), who was sitting next to me, said, "Okay, I'll say it, Bruce Willis is a real asshole."

Okay, maybe my physical proximity to Shane made him say it.

PART ELEVEN

SURVIVING THE CRITICS

LESSON 18

They Want to Kill You, Rape Your Wife, and Eat Your Children!

The definition of a critic . . .

Ben Hecht: "A person who smiles when he calls you a son of a bitch."

Comedian Dick Shawn: "A critic is someone who comes in after the battle is over and shoots the wounded."

Don't read your reviews.

William Faulkner never did. "Who knows the faults of my work better than I do?" he said.

His brother said, "He was simply protecting himself from hurt."

Never mind the damn critics; maybe you've just written Dr. Zhivago.

Dr. Zhivago was hammered by the critic when it was released. It is now considered perhaps the greatest movie of all time by many writers, directors . . . and critics.

The best way to deal with a bad review . . .

When critic Louis Kronenberger panned one of Ben Hecht's plays, Hecht threatened to castrate him.

Bruce Willis might be an asshole, but he's got a pretty good idea here.

Bruce Willis: "What I had hoped for her [the critic] was that she became so famous that she had to start worrying about her life, that she had to start feeling that she was threatened, and then had to sleep with a gun by her bed every night because she thought that she was so famous someone was going to do something to her or attack her. And then one night she finally realized the sick life she was living, and she just put the gun in her mouth and blew her fucking brains out."

They have a (tawdry) living to make.

Most film critics also do filmmaker interviews for the publications they work for. Their income depends on their access to stars.

So let's say Steven Spielberg has directed a new movie starring Julia Roberts and written by John Doe.

Let's say this new movie is awful. The critic for your local metropolitan paper or TV station knows he will need interviews with Spielberg and Roberts in the future. He reviews the film nevertheless and says that the movie isn't very good. He knows that if he says a bad movie is good too often, his readers will dismiss him as a street-corner hooker.

But if the movie isn't very good, then whom should he blame? Spielberg? Roberts? Or the screenwriter, John Doe, whom he will never need to interview because (A) the public could give a flying fig about who the screenwriter is, and (B) because there are almost no screenwriters who are stars (and whom he will ever need to interview).

This, more likely, will be the critic's capsule review: "Julia Roberts shows flashes of brilliance with some of her obviously improvised lines of dialogue. But Spielberg, who has given it a heroic try, is ultimately brought down by John Doe's hackneyed and cliché-ridden screenplay."

Now you're talking, Billy boy!

William Goldman: "Directors have no vision. . . . One of the reasons the media gushes about them is this—they don't know shit about the movie business. They are filling columns or minutes for circulation or ratings. And since they want to feel important, the people they interview have to be fabulously important. The *hottest* young star, the *most brilliant* director. That kind of madness."

They want to kill you, rape your wife, and eat your children.

No critic working today compares the first draft of an original screenplay with the finished movie.

Doing this would show the critic—especially in a misfired movie—who is to blame.

What if the script was brilliant and a moronic director destroyed it?

Critics claim that it would take too much time for them to read the script of a movie, but I'm convinced they don't want to know if a director has butchered a brilliant script.

Critics *purposely* blind themselves to any information that would force them to praise the writer and damn the director or the star.

This is because their bread and butter depends on access to the directors and the stars. And because they hate you—because they want to *be* you.

Aw, come on! Rape your wife and eat your children?

Yup.

Because you're a screenwriter and they're self-styled "film experts" who can't write screenplays.

Because you make big bucks and they make peanuts, even in comparison to what you make if you write *unsuccessful* movies.

And because they don't think it is fair that they know all this movie trivia and you don't, and still you're the one writing screenplays!

They want to be you!

Consequently: If you've written a good movie, don't expect them to praise you. They might not even mention you in their review, and they'll certainly heap lavish praise upon the director for "creating" a great movie.

If, however, you've written a movie that winds up being bad on-screen, they'll not only mention you; they'll blame you for *everything*—even bad acting. The actor, they'll say, just couldn't do anything with your lame lines of dialogue.

Some critics are so shamelessly biased that they'll even praise an actor's performance while bashing your script—as if the performance were created by the director's notes and not your story, character, and lines of dialogue.

Who are these miscreants?

Hollywood Reporter columnist Ray Richmond, himself a some-time film critic: "They are at once heavily ego-driven and desperately insecure. Film critics are movie geeks who write as much to impress other critics as they do to inform their audience. They're obsessed with being taken seriously, which can manifest itself either via quotes in movie ads or their anointing by the critical intelligentsia as one of their own. Yet while critics sport the iconoclast's soul, it's mitigated by an almost child-like need to be loved—not necessarily by the public but by their peers. They pine to be members of the club and at the same time somehow outside it, but not so much that they appear to be snobbish. This is why most would never be caught dead lavishing too much worship on a mainstream blockbuster . . . unless of course their contemporaries did too (such as in the case of *Spider-Man 2*). Then it would be cool."

How these miscreants see themselves.

Film critic A. O. Scott in *The New York Times*: "Criticism always contains an element of autobiography, and it is not much a leap to suggest that more than a few have seen themselves in *Sideways*. (Several have admitted as much.) This is not to suggest that white, middle-aged men with a taste for alcohol are disproportionately represented in the ranks of working movie reviewers; plausible as such a notion may be, I don't have the sociological data to support it just yet. But the self-pity and the solipsism that are Miles's less attractive (and frequently most prominent) traits represent the underside of the critical temperament; his morbid sensitivity may be an occupational hazard we all face."

Critics are hustlers who want to be screenwriters.

Consider James Agee, Peter Bogdanovich, Barbara Shulgasser, Paul Schrader, Jay Cocks, Paul Attanasio, among others—all critics who made it to be screenwriters or directors.

What better way to advertise that you know something about writing screenplays than to pick apart the screenplays of the movies you're reviewing—knowing that producers and studio execs will read your review if it's coming from a relatively prominent place.

They'll hang you by your themes.

I've always been fascinated by the notion that we don't ever know one another—that lovers and family members may not really know their mates or parents.

I played with that theme in *Betrayed, Music Box, Jagged Edge, Basic Instinct,* and *Sliver.*

According to the critics, though, screenwriters aren't allowed to have themes. However, novelists and directors are.

But the critics said there was no theme to my work. I was, they said, "plagiarizing myself."

If you write witty dialogue . . .

Be prepared for the critics to call you not a witty writer, but a wordsmith.

No matter what you do, the critics will define you.

Critics have defined me as the man who writes about sleazy sex. To reach that conclusion they have ignored most of my films: *F.I.S.T., Checking Out, Big Shots, Hearts of Fire, Betrayed, Music Box, Nowhere to Run, Telling Lies in America,* and *An Alan Smithee Film: Burn Hollywood Burn.*

You, too, can laugh all the way to the bank.

In every bad review I got for *Basic Instinct, Showgirls, Sliver,* and *Jade*, the amount of money I received for the script was always in the review—often in the first paragraph.

William Goldman, speaking about *Butch Cassidy and the Sundance Kid*: "My very late great agent, Evarts Ziegler, had secured $400,000 for the screenplay. A lot of money today. Back then, record-shattering. It made all the papers, not just *Variety*. And a lot of people wondered what the world was coming to, a western selling for that. It's my belief that the reason the reviews were so shitty is because of the money I got. A lot of people were pissed, a lot of these people were critics. For them the title of the movie really turned out to be this: *Butch Cassidy and the Sundance Kid $400,000*."

If they were pissed about Bill Goldman's $400,000, imagine how apoplectic they must have gotten when I got $2.5 million for *Jade*, $3 million for *Basic Instinct*, and $3.7 million for *Showgirls*. Or how insane they must have been when the movie they'd unanimously trashed, *Basic Instinct*, became the biggest-grossing film of the year wordwide!

In the old days, they openly took bribes.

Syndicated columnist Jimmy Fiddler revealed that he was offered $2,500 for a favorable review of Errol Flynn's *The Prisoner of Zenda* and turned the money down because the movie was so bad that he felt he couldn't take it without looking like a simpleton.

Running into Fiddler at a party later, Flynn decked him—at which point, Fiddler's wife stuck a fork in Flynn's ear.

They can be bribed? You damn betcha!

Martin Kaplan, associate dean of the USC Annenberg School for Communication and former Disney executive: "Studios know that many in the entertainment press don't have the budgets or the scruples to turn down all-expenses-paid junkets to Disney World, to New York, or the set in New Zealand. A bag of swag, or a signed photo of the reporter in a bear hug with a smiling super-star, isn't a guarantee against a critic's pan, but it can't hurt."

They're just damn whoors.

Many listen to the studio publicity people who call them and ask, "Couldn't you say this about the movie?" and then tell them what to write.

The reason many critics listen is because they like going on those press junkets, where the studio pays for everything.

They like the Christmas gifts they'll receive if the studio is pleased with the things they write during the year.

And they like to see their names in big letters in full-page ads paid for by the studio in *The New York Times* or *USA Today*.

Harlots, harlots everywhere!

Mike Medavoy: "Back in 1971 *The New Yorker*'s Pauline Kael could anoint a picture like *Last Tango in Paris* simply with a review. But by the end of the eighties, there were so many movie critics that their impact had become watered-down as their opinions piled up. Every small town has its own movie critic, and there are reviewers out there working for dubious-sounding organizations who will say something great about any piece of junk just to see their names in the ads."

Liar, liar!

A reporter named Lenny Traube, writing for the *Western Queens Gazette* in Astoria, New York, described an interview he did with me at a place called Mary McGuire's restaurant on Broadway.

He wrote: "Joe Eszterhas, the bearded millionaire screenwriter, turned up at Mary McGuire's on Broadway following a script session at the Kaufman-Astoria studios and passed on the following to his eager interviewer, yours truly."

Lenny Traube then quoted me at length about my past movies and future projects.

The only problem was that I'd never spoken to anyone named Lenny Traube or anyone else from the *Western Queens Gazette*. I had never been in Astoria, New York. I had never been at the Kaufman-Astoria studios. I had never been at Mary McGuire's restaurant.

Lenny Traube had made the whole thing up and had plagiarized other interviews I had done during the previous six months.

When I threatened to sue, the *Western Queens Gazette* apologized and admitted that Lenny Traube had made it all up. They begged me not to sue. They even offered to do a lengthy (this time real) interview with me.

I didn't do the interview.

I didn't sue, either, although I should have.

Let's make critics real people, not cinema geeks.

Here's how to clean up film criticism—how to take the corruptions out of it, how to stop the payoffs and the junket swag and strip critics of their power.

It's easy, really. In the interest of fairness, newspapers should rotate their film critics every six months. Film critics should not be people who have seen ten movies a week for years and years.

Their expertise should not be in the technique of moviemaking. They shouldn't be cinema geeks who spend most of their time in dark theaters.

They should be reporters from the newspaper's other beats—sports, news, the style sections, the obituary pages—who, for six months, get to review movies—not from a technical viewpoint, but from a human point of view—and who aren't afraid to tell us without mincing words (for fear of antagonizing studios) how they feel about the movie they've just seen.

Take their names away from 'em.

I said this to a studio executive: "If you think critics are supreme egotists who like to see their names displayed in full-page newspaper ads, why don't you leave their names out of the ads? Just go with the publication they work for. If all the studios did that, maybe critics would write less grandstanding reviews."

She said, "No, we need their names, even if nobody's ever heard of them. Because if we get thrashed by all the major media outlets, we will still have reviews from John and Jane Doe from obscure radio stations around the country, who will give us the review we need to plaster on a full page."

Be patient—once they kick the holy hell out of you, they just might praise you.

While, after its release, feminists bashed *Basic Instinct* unanimously (Tammy Bruce, the then president of the L.A. chapter of NOW, even stood in a picket line), months later feminist author Naomi Wolf wrote, "What was so cathartic about *Basic Instinct* was here was not a cartoon villainess like in *Fatal Attraction*— not a misogynist two-dimensional nightmare—but a complex, compelling Nietzschean *Uberfraulein* who owns everything about her own power. She's rich. She's not ashamed of being rich, which is transgressive in the ideology of femininity."

Yale lecturer and revisionist feminist Camille Paglia wrote, "Woman is the bitch goddess of the universe. . . . Sharon Stone's performance was one of the great performances by a woman in screen history."

When my film *Jagged Edge* was released, it was panned by the critics, dismissed in a few paragraphs by *The New York Times*. Ten years later, in an article about modern classic thrillers, the *Times* included *Jagged Edge*.

Pauline was the worst!

Canonized as "the Divine Redeemer" of film critics, Pauline Kael viewed James Toback (*Fingers*) as a creative genius.

That's all you really need to know about her.

Plus the fact that she stopped writing criticism when Warren Beatty hired her to become part of his production company. Then, when he fired her about a year later, Pauline started writing reviews once again.

A Feedable Critic

Screenwriter/director Buck Henry: "Everyone knew that Pauline Kael was feedable, that if you sat next to her, got her drunk, and fed her some lines, you could get them replayed in some other form."

Pauline liked to hang out.

To Pauline Kael, Altman was a cinematic god. She called *M*A*S*H* "the best American war comedy since sound came in."

Screenwriter Joan Tewksbury, who worked with Altman, said, "Bob could cultivate Pauline. She would come to the sets, go out to dinner with him, hang around his office."

How did Mailer know this?

He called Pauline Kael "the first frigid of the film critics."

A Paulette

Disciples of Pauline Kael.

Was he talking about Pauline or Roger Ebert?

No, Raymond Chandler was referring to Edmund Wilson, the top literary critic of his day, when he called him "a fat bore . . . who made fornication as dull as a railroad time table."

The next time you listen to Ebert . . .

Remember that he is a failed screenwriter, whose sole credit is *Beyond the Valley of the Dolls.*

Gene Shalit is a circus clown.

Paddy Chayefsky called NBC's Gene Shalit "a professional clown" and added that TV critics are "frustrated actors who try to be cute in ninety seconds."

Charles Champlin was a good friend.

When *F.I.S.T.,* my first movie, was released, Norman Jewison, the director, told me that the film critic of the *Los Angeles Times* had seen it and loved it.

"That doesn't really mean a whole helluva lot, though," Norman said.

"What do you mean?" I said. "It's the *Los Angeles Times.* Who's going to write the review it?"

"Charles Champlin," Norman said.

"He's a very respected guy," I said.

"Sure he is," Norman said. "But he's a good friend of mine. I even blurbed his last book."

"So what," I said. "He liked it."

"He certainly did," Norman said, and grinned.

"But he's a friend of yours," I said.

"He certainly is," Norman said, still grinning.

If Rex Reed gives you a bad review . . .

Ben Hecht and his writing partner, Charles MacArthur, saw a critic in a restaurant who had trashed their latest film. Hecht encouraged MacArthur to go over and punch the critic out.

MacArthur said, "It's not worth it—I'll just send him a poison choirboy."

They gave me my props.

Many critics said *Basic Instinct* was written "from the crotch . . . from his loins . . . by his penis."

Those reviews obviously impressed many women who read them and then, after reading them, sought me out.

A Popcorn Movie

They are movies like *Flashdance* and *Jagged Edge* that overcome negative critics and wind up doing huge business. In other words, they are
movies that people who've seen them tell other people about. Mike
Medavoy: "Studio owners have been known to tell production people,
'Make popcorn movies; that's what people want.'"

Maybe he thought Mike Ovitz would help him sell his script.

A reporter working for *Details* magazine asked me how I felt
about the distress I was causing Michael Ovitz "and his family" by telling the world that he had threatened to destroy my career
unless I continued to let him represent me.

From a writer's point of view, who is the best film critic working today?

From a writer's point of view, there are no good film critics
working today.

There weren't any good film critics working yesterday, either (except for
maybe Graham Greene).

And there won't be any good film critics working tomorrow, either.

From a writer's point of view, as my late director friend Richard Marquand
advocated, "All critics should be taken into the backyard, lined up alongside the
garage wall, and shot."

Forget about critics.

Marilyn Monroe said: "I don't care about the critics. I don't care
about anybody. The only people I care about are the people in
Times Square, across the street from the theatre, who can't even get
close as I come in."

They even beat up on Arthur Miller.

A 1991 *New Yorker* article referred to Arthur Miller (*Death of a
Salesman, After the Fall, The Misfits*) as "a critic's punching bag."

Leave the sons of bitches hanging.

Many film critics supplement their income by teaching film
classes at various schools around L.A. and New York. Their
salaries depend to a great extent on being able to get "stars" to do
free Q and As sessions for their classes.

If, while doing an interview with you, they ask you to make a guest appearance in their classes, always say yes. The interview with you or their review of your movie will appear long before your scheduled appearance in one of their classes.

Then, a day before your scheduled appearance, call the person and, faking a hoarse voice, tell him you've got the flu.

Since my throat cancer, I don't even have to fake my hoarse voice.

It pays to be friendly with Daily Variety.

Getting great coverage from *Daily Variety* translates into dollars and cents. If a studio knows that your profile and your relationship with *Daily Variety* can get it positive front-page coverage, that studio is more likely to make a deal with you.

You can use Variety to close your deals.

Another way to profit from a good relationship with *Daily Variety*: When a deal isn't quite done, leak the story as a fait accompli to *Daily Variety*—it will make the deal more likely to get done if everyone is already talking about it.

It worked when I leaked that Paul Verhoeven was directing *Showgirls,* before he'd actually decided to direct it. Everyone told Paul what a great idea it sounded like, and he closed his deal.

It didn't work when I leaked that Cuba Gooding, Jr., would play Otis Redding in my script *Blaze of Glory.* Cuba got pissed that *Variety* was writing about something he hadn't yet decided to do, and he immediately pulled out of the project.

I had outfoxed myself.

This *Variety* device to get deals done was something I called "the Mike Fleming Net," after the *Variety* writer who wrote all the stories about new deals.

Columnists like Cristal.

If you want her to mention you and to mention you nicely" producer Irwin Winkler said to me about entertainment columnist Marilyn Beck, "send her a bottle of great champagne each Christmas."

I did . . . and she did.

A Chatter Chippie

A Hollywood gossip columnist.

Disrupt traffic, break windows, and slit tires.

A group of Writers Guild officials sat in my dining room in Malibu, telling me how awful it was that the *Los Angeles Times* was increasingly giving the "Film by" credit or simply the "by" credit to directors.

I said, "What are you guys doing about it?"

One of the Guild people said, "We're setting a series of cocktail events up where *Los Angeles Times* and other journalists can come by and meet screenwriters once a week."

I said, "Why are you doing that?"

One of them said, "So they can get to know screenwriters, write about them, and elevate their profile."

I said, "That won't do any good. Those journalists are jealous as hell of screenwriters. Those bastards would die to make the kind of money a lot of screenwriters make."

One of them said, "Well, what would you do?"

I said, "I'd set up a picket line outside the *Los Angeles Times* building to protest the 'Film by' credit. I'd make a lot of noise, disrupt traffic, break some windows, slit some tires, and get our feelings on the front page of every newspaper in the country. SCREENWRITERS RUN AMOK—that'd be a great headline."

The Writers Guild people got out of my house very quickly.

Isn't there something wrong here?

Many newspapers are already using the "by" credit.

Here is what it looks like: *Daisy Miller* by Peter Bogdanovich; *The Color Purple* by Steven Spielberg; *Gone With the Wind* by Victor Fleming; *The Godfather* by Francis Ford Coppola; *War and Peace* by King Vidor; *Huckleberry Finn* by William Desmond Taylor; *The Ten Commandments* by Cecil B. DeMille; and *The Bible* by John Huston.

PART TWELVE

THE HAPPY ENDING

LESSON 19

Fight, Write, Throw Up, and Keep Writing!

It's okay to be jealous of other screenwriters.

Novelist and screenwriter Gore Vidal: "Every time a friend succeeds, I die a little."

Robert McKee can get jealous, too.

McKee: "Would you rather get paid $25,000 to have your story on the screen exactly as you wrote it, or get paid a million dollars by a studio and have your script butchered by development executives? Nine out of ten screenwriters want the latter. These people are not artists. They have no integrity and they get what they deserve—to have their names associated with bad films."

You don't get it, Bobby. The name of the game is to get the million bucks and *still* get it made exactly as you wrote it . . . which is exactly what I have done with many of my movies.

Your movie needs a little luck.

The advance word on *The China Syndrome* was bleak. The movie lacked any buzz; everyone expected it to bomb.

Three days before it was released, a nuclear catastrophe at Three Mile Island got the attention of the whole world. *The China Syndrome,* a movie about a nuclear catastrophe, was a smash hit.

You need a little luck, too.

A reporter for ABC television did a lengthy *20/20* piece about my screenwriting success. I had just sold several scripts for millions of dollars and I had just fallen head over heels with the love of my life. I was floating when I did the interview.

ABC's correspondent Judd Rose told me off-camera in the course of our day together that he felt like his luck in life had run out. He was a young man and he had recently been diagnosed with an inoperable brain tumor.

For luck, I gave him a beautiful antique Hawaiian walking stick, one of my most treasured objects.

But a couple of years later, Judd Rose died.

Avoid the gods of irony.

Mike Medavoy: "The gods of irony wield a lot of power in Hollywood."

Don't let it kill you.

Producer Alan Carr died as a result of the failure of his Academy Award telecast; director Richard Marquand died as a result of the failure of his film *Hearts of Fire*; Paddy Chayefsky died as a result of his directorially butchered film *Altered States*.

If you fail, don't kill yourself.

Writer and producer Dominick Dunne: "For me, the pain of failure exceeded by far the joys of success. My plight was hopeless. I almost jumped in front of a train in Santa Barbara. At the last second I let it pass me. I had a major flirtation with a kitchen knife that I took to bed with me. The love that I felt for Los Angeles turned to hate. I ran from there."

R E E L S P E A K

Creatively Reliable

A person who is so screwed up on drugs or booze that he is personally unreliable . . . but can still function as a screenwriter.

Remember that chicken shit can turn into chicken liver.

My film *Showgirls*, trashed as one of the worst movies ever made when it was released, is now a cult classic.

A sequel and a Broadway show are planned.

Remember that chicken liver can turn into chicken shit, too.

*T*itanic, the world's most successful film in history, winner of God knows how many Academy Awards, was voted one of the worst movies of all time in 2003 by the viewers of England's BBC.

You don't want to turn into Joe Gillis.

*I*n *Sunset Boulevard,* Joe Gillis, screenwriter (played by William Holden), wound up as the kept man of a broken-down movie star who hadn't made a movie in decades. She spoiled him, belittled him, and finally killed him. In the last scene of the film, we see him floating facedown in her swimming pool.

Someone asks him in the film, "Don't you sometimes hate yourself?"

Joe says, "Constantly."

This is the way Joe Gillis describes himself: "Nobody important, really. Just a movie writer with a couple of B pictures to his credit. The poor dope."

Don't let this be your self-portrait.

*W*illiam Goldman: "Everybody knows that writers are miserable—the line between novelists and alcoholics is constantly talked of. But we're weird. We're antisocial, and if you've seen us on the tube, you know that, except for Gore Vidal, we're not a whole lot of fun. You expect the unhappiness."

If you're a boozer, go clean yourself up.

I did. I was the complete functioning alcoholic. I never staggered or slurred or passed out. I rarely even had hangovers.

But I started drinking when I was fourteen, and by 2001, I was drinking a fifth of tequila, bourbon, or gin a day and two bottles of white wine or two six-packs of beer.

I developed throat cancer and had to detox before the surgery. After the surgery, to have a chance to live, I had to stop smoking and drinking.

I did. I've been sober five years. It was the most difficult thing I've ever had to do in my life, but I did it. So can you.

Remember that first and foremost you're an entertainer.

*D*irector Phillip Noyce: "I first became interested in movies as a result of my fascination with the traveling tent shows that came to my small country town when I was a child. And my fascination with the tent shows was an attraction to the ability of the performer to engage the audience. So I've always seen myself as an entertainer of the public. Nothing gives me greater pleasure than to sit in a cinema where one of my films is screening and to feel the pleasure that I'm giving to the audience. That's what makes it all worthwhile. I'd make films for nothing if they told me there was no other way of getting a film financed, just so that I could continue to feel the thrill of that contact with a satisfied public as you take them into the make-believe world that you've created for them."

Hold on to the magic.

I liked the cinema better before I began to do it," said Orson Welles. "Now I can't stop myself from hearing the clappers at the beginning of each shot; all the magic is destroyed."

You can become an echo.

If your script doesn't sell, there's still hope for the future. My script about soul singer Otis Redding, *Blaze of Glory,* wasn't made for eight years—until the Ray Charles biopic, *Ray,* became a hit movie—and then suddenly my phone didn't stop ringing. People were now showing interest in *Blaze.*

Screenwriter Larry Gross bought the rights to and adapted two Andre Dubus short stories. He couldn't sell his script for *twenty years*—until another Dubus piece, *In the Bedroom,* became a hit movie.

"My partner and I dusted off the script," says Gross, "did a couple of more changes, and all the reasons people had passed on it now were ignored because it was from the author of *In the Bedroom.*"

And you can create an echo.

When I wrote *Flashdance,* there hadn't been a hit musical in many years; after the movie's success, there was suddenly a vast variety of musicals being filmed.

Ditto with *Jagged Edge.* There hadn't been a hit courtroom mystery in a long time; after *Jagged Edge*'s success, one after another were released.

If everybody passes on your script . . .

Producer Robert Evans's favorite saying is "Aw, fuck 'em. Fuck 'em all!"

If you get discouraged . . .

Remember that while *Confederacy of Dunces* is now hailed as the funniest novel ever written and won the Pulitzer Prize, every single publisher passed when it was first sent to them.

You're in good company: Screenwriting almost killed Raymond Chandler, too.

The last picture I did at Paramount," said the novelist/screenwriter, "nearly killed me. The producer was in the doghouse—he has since left—and the director was a stale old hack who had been directing for thirty years without once achieving any real distinction. Obviously he never could. So here I am, a mere writer and a tired one at that screaming at the front office to protect the producer and actually going on the set to direct scenes—I know nothing about directing—in order that the whole project might be saved from going down the drain. Well, it was saved. As pictures go, it was pretty lively. No classic, but no dud, either."

The film Chandler was talking about was the noir classic *The Blue Dahlia*.

Don't look to Marilyn for inspiration.

John Kennedy Toole, unable to sell his novel *A Confederacy of Dunces,* drove to California and visited Marilyn Monroe's grave.

He then drove back home to Louisiana and killed himself.

Be philosophical about life.

While the PC police were organizing posses everywhere to lynch me for the sex in *Basic Instinct, Showgirls,* and *Sliver,* the president of the United States and his intern were practicing analingus in the Oval Office.

Don't get bitter.

Screenwriter and author John Fante (*Ask the Dust*) was sixty-nine years old and a resident of the Motion Picture and Television Hospital. He was blind. Both of his legs had been amputated.

He said, "The most horrible thing that happens to people is bitterness. They all get so bitter."

If you get discouraged . . .

Remember that fabled (and smart) studio head Frank Price had first crack at a Steven Spielberg project and passed. The project was *E.T.*

Come on, you've only had one cable movie made, Bobby.

Robert McKee: "What I teach is the truth; you're in over your head, this is not a hobby, this is an art form and a profession, and your chances of success are very, very slim. And if you've got only one story, get the fuck out of here. . . ."

Try not to burn out.

Screenwriter Dalton Trumbo: "For several years I have disliked motion pictures and planned tentatively to get out of them. . . . I have an overpowering desire never again to have anything to do with this depraved industry, and an equally overpowering desire to get what cash I can and blow."

R E E L S P E A K

Analysis Paralysis

The definition of Hollywood burnout. For example:

The writer who has writer's block.

The director who wants to himself rewrite the script.

The studio head who is afraid to say yes or no to a movie.

The agent who drives out to Joshua Tree in his new Porsche and sits in the car for three days drinking vodka and popping pills, watching the sunsets and sunrises.

The superstar actor who becomes a shoemaker's apprentice in Italy.

The actress who gets a nose job that ruins her career.

The producer who decides, at the age of sixty-two, that he's gay.

There are a thousand other symptoms of the same malaise.

The only cure? *Get the hell outta Dodge—now!*

If you get discouraged . . .

Remember that when a screenwriter changed the title to something else, put his own name on it, and sent it to most of the production entities in Hollywood, there were no takers.

The original title of that script was *Casablanca.*

If you can't sell your script, enter the competitions.

Some agents read the scripts of competition winners and some producers assign readers to the winners' scripts, too.

There seem to be more and more of these competitions each year, but some of the more established ones are the Nicholl Fellowships in Screenwriting, the Chesterfield Film Company's Writer's Film Project, and the Writer's Network Screenplay and Fiction Competition. Check the Internet for others.

If things go bad screenwriting, you can always try to write a novel.

There is no director, producer, star, or studio head to work with. You will get no "notes" from anyone. You will have an editor who will make "suggestions" to you. You can take those suggestions or leave them. No writer will replace you if you leave the publisher. You'll be paid whether you listen to the suggestions or not.

Sounds like bliss, right?

You can free yourself by writing a novel.

Screenwriter/director/novelist John Sayles (*Matewan*): "There's a basic structure to movies. It's rigid and reductive. In a movie, you only deal with core relationships: a protagonist, an antagonist. But in a novel you can do whatever you want. You can introduce characters that disappear for a hundred pages, you can have a dozen plot lines that interweave and overlap. In a novel, you get to be God. That doesn't happen in the movies."

Steven Bochco thinks writing a novel is fun.

Bochco (*Hill Street Blues, Death by Hollywood*): "Television and film are such streamlined story mediums. You can't really meander about, whereas a novel is an interior experience. Once you have your map, once you know your final destination, you can take all these pit stops along the way. You can take side trips and digress, riff on something and come back to the main road. It's so much fun."

If you write a novel, you gotta go platinum or else.

John Sayles: "Getting a second novel published is even harder than getting a first novel published. It's no longer enough to be a good writer; now you have to be a good writer whose first book went platinum."

It isn't bliss.

Publishing isn't what it once was. By their preorders, booksellers determine how many copies of a book a publisher will print.

In film terms, that's letting the exhibitors, the individual theater owners, determine how many prints a studio will make.

If you're already writing your novel . . .

Remember that booksellers have so much power that they can determine the jacket of your book. This is what often happens when Barnes & Noble doesn't like a cover. The publisher prints up a new one.

Another reason not to write novels . . .

One time when Irish author Carlo Gébler was doing a book reading, a group of drunken students in the audience started fighting.

"Do you want me to finish?" he asked.

"Not really," someone yelled.

Carl Hiaasen, my favorite mystery novelist, went to a book reading in Arkansas and discovered that an Arkansas Razorbacks game was taking place at the same time. He did his book reading for the few book salesmen who showed up.

Novelist William Trevor went to a reading, found no one there, and read for the cabdriver who'd brought him. He discovered after he finished reading that his cabbie had charged him for his reading time.

You might want to try gay porn.

Screenwriter/novelist Gigi Grazer (*Stepmom*, *The Starter Wife*): "Writers, or any artists, should constantly be reinventing themselves, whatever that means—plays to screenplays to novels and back again, or second wife to mistress to third wife to gay porn, whatever works. Life feeds us. If we stagnate, there is no material."

Be proud of being a screenwriter.

Don't take any shit from anyone who asks you why, if you're so unhappy being a screenwriter, you're not writing novels instead.

Paddy Chayefsky: "I consider writing novels déclassé. After all, drama has been around since the Orphic rites; the novel has been around only since Cervantes or thereabouts."

If you wind up writing television because you can't get a film job . . .

You're in good company.

David O. Selznick, the greatest creative producer in the history of Hollywood, wound up working in TV after he went broke.

If you can't write screenplays, then take over the studio.

That's what the legendary studio boss Darryl F. Zanuck did.

When he began his career, he was a screenwriter on the Warner Bros. payroll, making a hundred dollars a week.

If you can't make it as a screenwriter, there's still hope.

If you're Tom Cruise or Jack Nicholson or Barbra—one of *those* people—what are you supposed to do? Stand out there on the side of the road on the 405 or I-10 and change the tire?

Yourself? Getting your hands dirty? Dirtying your new Gucci embroidered jeans?

That's what gave my friend Hank an idea. He had been writing and trying to sell screenplays for eight years, without success. One year, he even slept in his car; his office was the Kinko's on Lincoln Avenue.

Then, one beautiful socked-in L.A. day, he was driving along the 405 in his beater and there was a brother standing on the side of the road next to a Rolls-Royce. Hank saw that it was Eddie Murphy, and that got him thinking.

Hank had a friend who had a friend who was an accountant for people like Harrison Ford and Richard Dreyfuss and a lot of other big-time directors and producers. He went to his friend, who went to *his* friend, the accountant, and got Hank an appointment with him. And the accountant *loved* Hank's idea.

The accountant gave Hank's number to all of his clients and the clients gave his number to big-shot friends of theirs, and pretty soon Hank's phone started to ring.

If they needed to take any of their cars (some had six or seven) to be serviced, Hank took it for them—drove it there, had the work done, and drove it back home for them.

If they broke down on the road, or had any other difficulty, Hank drove to the scene, fixed the car if he could, or drove it to the shop if he couldn't and then waited with them while the limo he had called for them arrived.

Hank has a staff of four now. As a sideline, he's starting his own limo company. A good-looking guy, he's even dating a couple of his clients, sometimes even showing them one of his scripts.

You don't want to die like Clifford Odets did.

The world-acclaimed playwright was employed as a segment writer for the television show *Paladin,* starring Richard Boone, when he died of cancer at age fifty-seven.

A friend said, "He was miserable out there. All of his dreams were of escaping from it, of writing plays and coming back to the theater. He never made peace with his defeat."

Go get some rhinoplasties.

Trevor Mills, a screenwriter who lives in Austin, Texas, couldn't sell a script, so he spent nine thousand dollars on a chin implant and two rhinoplasties to make himself look like Keanu Reeves.

He still couldn't sell a script after his surgeries, but he was thinking about studying acting.

Jim Harrison wants to be Jack Nicholson.

Screenwriter/novelist Jim Harrison was on a Mediterranean cruise with Jack Nicholson. Harrison said later, "It would be a tiny port and there would be all these women screaming 'Fuck me, Jack! I love you, Jack! I'm yours, Jack!' I remember thinking, What does that do to your head?"

Kevin Costner does Jim Harrison a favor.

Jim Harrison and Kevin Costner were sitting together in a bar. Jim pointed out to Kevin after their third beer that Kevin had gotten a dozen notes from ladies in the bar and that he had gotten none.

To make him feel better, Kevin offered to give Jim some of his notes.

Your teeth can be discolored and you can still score big-time.

Paddy Chayefsky, by all accounts, was a singularly unhandsome man—small, overweight, his teeth discolored, his hair balding. He usually reeked of tobacco and garlic. Yet he got the sex symbol of his age to go to bed with him.

Does anybody think that had a little to do with the quality of his writing?

I don't flatter myself, either. In the period of my life when I bedded the sex symbol of my age, I, too, was an unhandsome man—overweight, my teeth discolored, my hair down to my butt. I usually reeked of tobacco, garlic, and alcohol. And yet the sex symbol of my age slept with me, too.

If you keep writing, if you don't give up, then you, too, can follow in our footsteps.

Billy Wilder was a gigolo.

If you can't sell your script, maybe you can sell yourself.

That's what Billy Wilder did when he couldn't sell his scripts in Berlin. He became a gigolo.

If you get discouraged . . .

Paddy Chayefsky said, "In spite of everything, screenwriting is better than threading pipe."

You don't want to get old in Hollywood.

Bert Fields, one of the most powerful attorneys in Hollywood, wrote this in a short story entitled *The Heart of the Matter*: "On his sixty-fifth birthday, the actor sits alone on his terrace finishing a bottle of Cristal. The city lights stretch out before him. Millions of homes, millions of families. Husbands coming home to wives, kids, even dogs. He's got his butler . . . and sometimes his lawyer. His agent has died. It doesn't matter. No scripts come in anyway. He shakes his head, smiling sadly . . . remembering. He wonders whatever happened to his wife. He feels the need for people, noise, something. He dials his lawyer, gets an answering machine. He dials his favorite restaurant. They're fully booked. For a few minutes, he stares out at the city. Then he rises slowly from the chair, blows a kiss to the lights, and climbs the stairs to the bedroom, where the .38 special lies waiting in the drawer."

Unless you're Clint Eastwood (who's Marilyn in drag). . .
Clint: "Some people glow really early, in their twenties and thirties, then in their fifties they are not doing as much. But I feel that growing up and maturing, constantly maturing—aging is the impolite way of saying it—I like to think there is an expansion going on philosophically."

A Chocolate Life

Hollywood retirement: champagne, caviar, fresh flowers delivered every day, and all the chocolate you can eat.

No matter how old you are, you can always learn more about film.
Director Akira Kurosawa, at age eighty-two: "I'm just beginning to understand what cinema can do."

Did I tell you to get the hell out of L.A.?
Raymond Chandler: "No doubt I have learned a lot from Hollywood. Please do not think I completely despise it, because I don't . . . but the overall picture, as the boys say, is of a degraded community whose idealism even is largely fake. The pretentiousness, the bogus enthusiasm, the incessant squabbling over money, the all-pervasive agent, the strutting of the big shots (and their usually utter incompetence to achieve anything they start out to do), the

constant fear of losing all this fairy gold and being the nothing they have really never ceased to be, the snide tricks, the whole damn mess is out of this world . . . it is like one of these South American palace revolutions conducted by officers in comic opera uniforms— only when the thing is over the ragged dead men lie in rows against the wall, and you suddenly know that this is not funny, this is the Roman circus, and damn near the end of civilization.''

If you reach a certain point, quit screenwriting.

I mean it. I bartended for a while.

Screenwriter Jeffrey Boam: "I have a schedule, I have a secretary and a producing partner and a development person, and I feel like I'm no longer living the quiet, contemplative life of a writer. I'm not getting that benefit anymore, and I've gotten to the point where I'm losing my patience with directors and producers. I feel 'Why do I have to please these people? Why do I have to knock myself out to please them? Come back to them with idea after idea after idea. They're all good, but they reject them so often. I'm just sick of it.''

Time to go bartend, Jeffrey.

You can get drunk and dance in your bare feet.

Screenwriter William Faulkner: "Anybody who can sell anything to the movies for more than $50,000 has a right to get drunk and dance in his bare feet.''

Peter Bart doesn't have any balls. Or . . . Take notes for your Hollywood tell-all. Or . . . Sidney Korshak was a sleazeball.

Variety editor Peter Bart, in his book Shoot Out: "One night I wandered home, dead tired, and found myself leafing through the journal I had been keeping—notes that I would someday turn into my 'definitive' book about life at the studio. I was riveted as I relived these day-to-day experiences—encounters with Mafioso and managers, with the Roman Polanskis and the Sidney Korshaks. I'd even noted down one conversation with Korshak, the ever-somber attorney who had started out serving Al Capone and ended up mentoring stars and studio chiefs. 'Peter,' he said, 'do you know what's the best insurance policy—one that guarantees continuous breathing?' I thought this an odd question, but I asked for his answer. 'It's silence,' he intoned. He said it as though he had just imparted great wisdom, and in a sense he had. This was, after all, advice emanating from someone who was arguably the industry's most talented 'fixer.' I decided it was advice worth taking. I would stay at Paramount, but I would shred my notes.''

That's crap. Moustache Pete Omertà stuff. Write everything down and keep your notes, and if you feel like it, write the book that tells all. I've written two of those already.

If they screw you over, write about it.

It's okay to bite the hand that feeds you.

Ben Hecht, the king of all screenwriters, wrote the scripts for three films that satirized Hollywood: *Actors and Sin,* in which an old actor kills his actress daughter so she will not wind up being a nobody like him; *I Hate Actors,* in which a celebrated and successful script is written by a nine-year-old child; *The Scoundrel*, in which a producer says, "Don't use that line; it's twenty-five years old." (The line is "I love you.")

I wrote a script called *An Alan Smithee Film: Burn Hollywood Burn*, which made fun of most of the players in town. In my first draft, I used real names, not made-up ones. I will sell that draft on eBay someday.

(Just kidding, I *think*.)

You're a writer, not the owner of a writing factory.

Ben Hecht hired writers to "block out and draft" scripts, which he then revised and called his own. Ernest Tidyman (*The French Connection*) did the same thing after he won the Oscar. While Ron Bass (*Rain Main*) denies that he runs a writing factory, he does hire assistants and researchers, who accompany him to studio meetings.

The trouble with doing this, of course, is that word spreads quickly, and that studios will think twice about hiring you if they think *you're* doing what *they're* doing: grinding out sausages.

Nobody ever accused William Goldman of running a writing factory, but he does write *quickly*. When he wrote three scripts in one year and none of them was produced, word spread that he was grinding out sausages. His phone didn't ring for years.

Don't die wearing a diamond ring.

Famed producer Mike Todd's remains were stolen from a Chicago cemetery so the thieves could get the big diamond ring he was famous for wearing.

Anthony Pellicano will unearth you, too.

The infamous Hollywood private eye's first claim to fame was finding Mike Todd's remains. Alas, when the Pelican found the body, the diamond ring was gone.

If you're asked for casting advice, take great care.

My first draft of *An Alan Smithee Film: Burn Hollywood Burn* called for Anthony Pellicano to play an infamous Hollywood gumshoe named Anthony Pellicano.

I called Anthony and sent him the script and he happily agreed to play himself in the film.

When I cast Sly Stallone in the lead part, Sly had only one demand: that Anthony Pellicano not be in the film.

I don't know why he made that demand and I was smart enough not to want to know. I didn't ask him.

I called Anthony and told him I had to write him out of the film or I'd lose Sly.

Anthony called Sly a bunch of names but said he understood that Sly's presence in the film gave us our financing for it.

I changed the Anthony Pellicano character's name in the script to the fictitious Sam Rizzo.

My agent called me a couple of weeks later and said he had a friend who had read the script and was desperate to play the Sam Rizzo part. It was Harvey Weinstein, then the head of Miramax and one of the most powerful people in town.

I cast Harvey and called Anthony and told him that Harvey Weinstein would be playing the part.

Anthony said: "*Harvey Weinstein?* Harvey Weinstein is going to *play me?* He's a fuckin' wuss. He can't play *me!*"

I said, "No, he's going to play Sam Rizzo."

Anthony said, "There is no fuckin' Sam Rizzo! Sam Rizzo is *me!*"

Anthony said: "I oughta get my baseball bat and go visit the set."

But Anthony laughed. He was making a little joke.

The joke was funny, but . . .

Anthony invited himself over to my house in Malibu.

"I've got a lot of stories you'd be interested in hearing," he said.

Something told me I wasn't interested in hearing Anthony's stories.

I never invited him over to my house.

That may have been the smartest move I've ever made in Hollywood.

Raymond Chandler was just jealous of writers who made more money than he did.

After I sold a four-page outline for $4 million, I tried not to think about what Raymond Chandler had said about screenwriting in Hollywood: "The big money still goes to the wrong people."

Perk of success: olfactory pleasures

You will know the smell of freshly baked croissants at the Four Seasons Hotel in Beverly Hills.

You can bury your friends.

Maxwell Bodenheim, Ben Hecht's poet friend, wrote Ben and begged him for some money.

Ben wrote him a letter, saying that he was enclosing two hundred dollars. But he "forgot" to enclose the money.

When Maxwell Bodenheim died broke, Ben said he would pay for his funeral, so that Max wouldn't be buried in a potter's field. Then he put fifty dollars into a fund for his friend's funeral.

Take it from Zsa Zsa

If you make it and get divorced, share custody but keep the help.

"There is nothing harder to find than good servants. I remember when I was sitting in the Plaza Hotel in New York with Porfirio Rubirosa, and George Sanders called from California to say that finally he'd allow me to divorce him, but he also said that Albert, who'd served us for years, was going with him. I started to cry bitterly. Rubirosa said, 'You wanted to divorce him and now that he says "yes," you start to cry.' And I said, 'Don't be silly! I'm not crying for him, I'm crying for the butler.'"

You don't have to be a victim.

Oscar-winning screenwriter William Goldman: "I've never seen a rough cut of a picture I've written. And I rarely get invited to sneaks. *Marathon Man* is a good example, because there were two sneaks, in California. And I live in New York, so it's expensive to bring me out. Except I was in California at the time. Wouldn't have cost a whole lot to have [had] me along."

I've seen the rough cut of almost all of the fifteen films I've written.

I have often been sent by FedEx the tapes of the dailies as they are printed.

I attend all of the research screenings of my films.

I have been to every focus-group preview of my films, flying on the corporate jet along with the director, the producer, studio people, and sometimes even the star to sneaks in Chicago; Paramus, New Jersey; Washington, D.C.; and Kansas City, Missouri.

Why does the studio ask me to participate in these things while shutting out Bill Goldman?

One reason may be that everyone involved with the films knows that I care passionately about them—I am not already thinking about THE NEXT JOB (Bill's caps).

Another reason may be that everyone knows I'm perfectly capable of badmouthing the movie publicly—and getting lots of media attention—if I'm shut out of the process.

Keep on writing and writing.

Screenwriter Dan Harris (*Imaginary Heroes*): "Life is hard, and it often pulls no punches. Sometimes when you think it cannot get any worse, it does. Sometimes the light at the end of the tunnel dies just as you approach it. But sometimes there is healing in catastrophe. Sometimes people are given a second chance."

Don't let the bastards get you down.

Paddy Chayefsky, in a letter to a friend: "I'm out here in California trying to make a movie, which has been a horror show from the beginning. We started shooting the fucker last Friday, and the director not only has turned out to be a monster, but a monster with not enough talent to make it worthwhile. Man, I'm tired of battling. I truly am."

You have to be the toughest person in the world.

Screenwriter/director Ron Shelton: "You have to be the toughest person in the world. If writers take the passive role, they become victims. I tell writer's groups—don't complain. If you're good enough at your work and your craft, get a lot tougher. You have to be ruthless. Writers aren't tough enough."

Don' let anyone walk over you.

Screenwriter/novelist Raymond Chandler: "I have fought many hard battles in my life and I never found that there was any way to fight them except directly, accepting the risks, knowing that all I had to fight with was my brain and my courage, and that I could easily lose against much more powerful people than myself. But I did not become one of the three or four highest-paid writers in Hollywood by letting anyone walk over me."

Write messages from your soul.

Writer/producer William Froug: "In the final analysis of our lives, as well as our writing, what else do we really have to listen to but the messages from our own souls, psyches, guts, instincts, muses, whatever you call it? This is where our personal truth, our themes, our creativity lies. The writers who fearlessly kept writing what they truly believed, in my experience, are the ones who have gone on to the greater glory—not merely money or fame, but something far more basic: inner peace and genuine fulfillment."

Go see your movie in your neighborhood theater.

Columbia Tristar once released a film nationally—*The Bloodhounds of Broadway*—with a whole reel missing from it. No one noticed.

Develop a short memory.

Producer Ben Hecht: "They can screw you, and you can screw them, but if you want to keep on working, both of you need a short memory."

You can make God smile.

Dalton Trumbo: "Once in a while when God smiles and the table is tilted just slightly in our favor, something happens. It comes from inside and reveals what we really are."

Just keep writing.

And writing and writing . . . and if you are good to your fellow humans and if God smiles, the day will come when you are writing something and *you* will stop and smile and jump up and down because it is working, because you know that what you are writing is *good*!

But until that magical sun-kissed moment comes, hang in there and *just keep fucking writing*!

Keep writing even if you're hurling.

For the first couple of years that I wrote screenplays, I was so nervous about what I was doing that I threw up before I began writing each morning.

There's nothing wrong with that. It's much better than reading what you've written at the *end* of the day and throwing up.

Perk of success: fear

My biggest fear . . .

After thirty years of writing scripts, it's a fear that I know you don't have, thank God.

I can't operate a computer. Oh hell, I can't even work an electric typewriter—I hit the keys too damn hard.

I'm a two-finger typist and I slam away at my manual Olivetti with both middle fingers (a lot of critics have made too much about the significance of writing with my two middle fingers, thank you).

The trouble is that one of these days they're going to stop making Olivetti manual typewriters. The only reason they still make them is because there's a big market for them in retirement communities.

Well hell, I don't live in a retirement community. I've got four boys under the age of ten, for Christ's sake. And I've got a lot of script and book ideas for the future.

So what's going to happen to me when Olivetti manuals become obsolete? Well, I have ten brand-new (still in the box) Olivetti manual typewriters in my closet, ready to go. But they're made in all kinds of Third World places (like Hungary) and sometimes I beat these machines to death in a matter of months with my slamming middle fingers.

And, get this: I discovered recently that they have already stopped making Olivetti ribbons for manual typewriters. Naomi has patiently hunted the Internet and we now have sixty-three new Olivetti ribbons in the closet with the ten machines.

> But what happens when I've killed all the machines or used up all the ribbons for the machines? Do I then have to learn how to use a word processor or the dreaded computer?
>
> Or do I hang it up and say God (and all my critics) has silenced me?
>
> I tell you this story to put all your fears into perspective. All you have to do is write your script. All you really have to do is write the first page of your script, because then you'll already be rolling.
>
> I have to figure out my entire future!

No matter what, try to be optimistic.

Screenwriter William Faulkner said, "You have to live so that you can die."

TAKE IT FROM ZSA ZSA

"If you get depressed," said my Hungarian compatriot Zsa Zsa Gabor, "take a bath and wash your hair."

Don't give up.

Paddy Chayefsky's mother said to him, "Listen, you want to be a writer, you've got to write. You submit, and they'll reject. But you've got to keep writing."

Don't ever give up on selling your script.

Warren Beatty said this about trying to bed every woman that he met: "You get slapped a lot, but you get fucked sometimes, too."

You've still gotta believe in happy endings.

When he was an old man, several of producer Sam Spiegel's Oscars were stolen by the prostitute who frequently came to his home.

But it's never too early to consider your epitaph.

This is one Marilyn Monroe wanted: "Here lies Marilyn. No lies. Only lays."

If I made it, you surely can.

Consider the following:

English is my second language. Some critics have said I butcher it.

I stole cars and carried a knife when I was a kid; I almost killed another kid with a baseball bat and almost went to jail.

I flunked both algebra and biology in high school and had to go to summer school two years in a row.

I was a *C* student in high school.

I didn't graduate from college because I was on both academic and disciplinary probation.

I was a *D* student in college, although I won every writing competition I entered.

I started drinking when I was fourteen and was a functional alcoholic by the time I was in college.

I've never believed in chitchatting and networking—I've been a loner all of my life.

Naomi says I'm abrupt, direct, sometimes downright rude, occasionally antisocial.

For much of my life, I've looked and dressed like a Hell's Angel.

I've always preferred reading a book to seeing a movie.

But I've always preferred having sex to reading a book.

For many years, I preferred having a drink to *anything,* but I don't drink anymore.

I've named my company "Barbarian, Ltd."

Hollywood has paid "Barbarian" many, many millions of dollars through the years.

Don't let 'em take your mojo.

They'll try to beat it out of you—depress you, disillusion you, corrupt you.

Keep your mojo hidden deep inside yourself. It's your heart and soul. It's what makes you tick, what makes you write, and what makes you special. It's the source of your work, your worth, and your talent.

Fight the fuckers with every breath of your being. And if, after you've fought the good fight, you lose—if your movie stinks or you're rewritten by five other writers or you feel betrayed by people you thought were friends or thought cared about you—get a good night's rest and sit down at your laptop the next morning and start making up a brand-new story. And fight the fuckers all over again with every breath of your being.

Because *you're* a writer. And *they're* not.

And if you fight hard enough, and write enough stories, one of these days you'll see your work up on-screen just the way you wanted. And you'll change the lives and better the lives and make more enjoyable the lives of the people who see it.

Your film. Your *mojo*. Up there on the big screen.

Epilogue

I had a three-script deal with United Artists. The first script was *Betrayed*, the second was *Music Box,* and the third was going to be *Media Mogul,* a roman a clef about Rupert Murdoch. But as I started writing the third script, it didn't go anywhere for me, and I gave up on it. It had been producer Irwin Winkler's idea anyway to do a filmic assault on Murdoch, not mine.

I started writing another script instead without telling anyone that I was writing it—not even Irwin, who was going to produce all three scripts. The new script's genesis was my unwavering and no doubt naïve belief that someday America would have a president who would tell the American people the truth, no matter how difficult that truth was.

I wrote it as a black but Capraesque comedy. Sam Parr, in his late sixties, the liberal Democrat president of the United States, is running for reelection against a right-wing McCarthyite demagogue. Sam Parr has always screwed around on his long-suffering wife and he's the kind of man who enjoys his Jack Daniel's. One misbegotten day during the campaign when everything goes to shit, he finds himself on the Nebraska farm where he grew up, tilting his Jack Daniel's bottle, and dozes off in the barn. He wakes up more than a little randy and does what he did as a boy. He, um, pops the nearby cow. Yes, *cow*—literally.

A right-wing spy takes a picture of him *in flagrante*. First the right-wingers try to blackmail Sam Parr to drop out of the race and then they release the picture to the tabloids. Sam Parr decides to tell Americans the truth. "Yes, I popped that cow!" he says. And, *mirabile dictu,* every farm boy or suburban ex–farm boy who ever popped a cow or a chicken or a cat in a boot votes for him.

Because he told America the truth, he is reelected to office by a landslide.

I wrote the script in 1989, during the Bush, not the Clinton, presidency; during the era of "Read my lips—no new taxes," before Lewinsky's lips and news of that infamous cigar.

I sent Irwin Winkler the script with a title page that said in big letters, *SACRED COWS.*

He called me when he received it and said, "I thought we were going to call this *Media Mogul.*"

"Well," I said, "um, the piece, um, changed somewhat. You'll see when you read it."

When Irwin called me back, he was laughing. "You son of a gun," he said. But he also said, "No one will ever make it. Even though I think it's one of the funniest and most moving pieces I've every read."

"Maybe somebody will take a chance on it," I said.

"No," Irwin said, "mark my words. A lot of people will read it. A lot of people will love it. A lot of people will say they want to make it. But no one will make it."

"How do you think United Artists will respond?"

Irwin laughed again.

"They think they're getting a piece about Rupert Murdoch called *Media Mogul.* Where's Murdoch in this piece? Maybe he's the cow, I don't know." Then Irwin added, "I'm afraid they'll sue you for nonperformance."

He was serious.

So, in order to avert a lawsuit, I put a new cover sheet on *Sacred Cows.* It was now entitled *Media Mogul,* but it was still about a president who pops a cow and fesses up.

Dick Berger was the head of United Artists.

"I started reading the script," he told me later. "I got to about page twelve—where the president does the cow. I hurled the script across the room. I thought to myself, This son of a bitch Eszterhas! He takes our money to write this *shit?* He writes about fucking a cow and expects us to make the movie? I'm going to sue this son of a bitch!' I seethed for an hour or so. But something made me pick the damn script off the floor. I finished reading it. I sat there crying when I finished it. I *never* cry reading a script. And I thought, It's brilliant, but I still feel like suing the son of a bitch."

United Artists didn't sue me. Nor did they say they were making *Media Mogul,* as the script was officially called.

They left the fate of my script up to me. If my agents (or Irwin) could attract major elements—an actor, a director—United Artists would *consider* making it.

The first person Guy McElwaine, my agent, sent *Sacred Cows* to was Steven Spielberg. Steven read it and called Guy to tell him it was the funniest script he'd ever read.

He said he was directing it. He said it would be his next picture.

Steven called me and told me he was already working on the movie's sound track. He said he thought all the music should be done by the Marine Corps Band.

I called Irwin and told him Steven was directing *Sacred Cows.*

"Never," Irwin said. "Forget it. It'll never happen."

"He's already making plans for the Marine Corps Band," I said.

Irwin laughed again.

Steven called back a week later and said he anticipated "great flak" if he directed *Sacred Cows.* So, to cover himself, he had sent the script to Stanley Kubrick, asking that Kubrick produce it with Irwin.

"I know there's going to be flak," I said to Steven, "but you're the top director in the world. Irwin Winkler is an internationally respected Oscar-winning producer. What do we need Stanley Kubrick for?"

"Oh," Steven said, "having Stanley certainly wouldn't *hurt.*"

Stanley Kubrick wrote Steven a note that said, "This may be the funniest script I've ever read, but I wouldn't want to get within a thousand miles of it."

Steven told me that the Marine Corps Band was still a great idea, but he didn't want to direct *Sacred Cows* anymore. He still wanted to produce it, though. And he had sent it to his friend Bob Zemeckis to direct.

Steven called a month later to say that Bob Zemeckis "loved it" and was considering directing it.

A year passed as Bob Zemeckis kept considering. Then Bob Zemeckis decided he didn't want to direct it.

Since Bob didn't want to direct it, Steven decided he didn't want to produce it, either.

Tony Bill, who had won an Oscar for producing *The Sting* and who had directed *My Bodyguard,* wrote me a note telling me that he had read *Sacred Cows* and thought it one of the funniest scripts he'd ever read.

David Anspach, who had recently directed the hit *Hoosiers* and whom all the studios wanted to work with, read *Sacred Cows* and flew up to Marin County to see me. I liked David, liked his affection for the script, and told him it was fine with me if he directed *Sacred Cows.*

He was so happy, he started to cry.

United Artists turned him down.

David may have been the hottest director in town, but he wasn't hot enough to direct *this* baby.

Michael Lehman had just directed *Heathers,* a big critical hit. *Everybody* wanted to work with him. He read *Sacred Cows,* flew up to Marin to see me, and asked to direct it.

I said great, we celebrated, and he flew back to L.A. to have a meeting with United Artists.

They turned Michael down.

Michael may have been the hottest director in town, but . . . a *cow? The president of the United States and a literal, not metaphorical, cow?*

Edward J. Olmos read it, loved it, wanted to direct it. We met at the Ivy. In the back room of the Ivy, because Eddie had pissed off some Latino gang bangers who were even now, as we spoke, looking for him so they could kill him.

United Artists said, "*Who?* Oh, that guy from *Miami Vice?*"

United Artists said no thank you.

Blake Edwards, in my opinion, was a creative genius who had made some of the funniest movies in Hollywood history. We had lunch at Orso's.

He loved *Sacred Cows.* He was desperate to direct *Sacred Cows.*

"I wish there was some way to avoid the cow fucking," Blake said. "You don't *show* it in your script. We wouldn't show it in the movie, either, of course, but that's not what I'm talking about. I wish we could somehow avoid the fact that the president of the United States actually fucks the cow. I wish we could somehow give people the perception that he'd fucked it but reveal that he really hadn't done it."

"You can't do that," I said, "it would vitiate the power of the piece. The whole point is that he fucks the cow and then tells the truth about fucking it."

"I know," Blake Edwards said. "You're right. I agree with you. But I still wish there was some way we could have it both ways."

Blake went to United Artists and told them he could bring the movie in at a low budget. He mentioned James Garner and Bob Newhart as possible cowpokes.

United Artists said no. Granted, they told me, Blake had once made great movies. But he was too old now. He napped on the set and didn't do enough takes of his scenes—the reason, they said, Blake always came in under budget.

It was the first time I'd heard a director bad-mouthed for coming in under budget.

Irwin got the script to Milos Forman, the Oscar-winning director of *One Flew Over the Cuckoo's Nest.* Milos said he liked the script very much and asked for a meeting at his apartment in New York.

United Artists said up front that if Milos committed to direct the movie, they would finance it.

I liked Milos and thought his ideas about the script were insightful. He wanted to broaden the scope of the piece and include a presidential trip to India, the home of the sacred cows.

I did a serious rewrite incorporating his ideas and thought the script was funnier and more poignant than it had been before. So did Milos. He thought I'd done an "extraordinary job" on the rewrite.

"Are you going to direct it?" I asked him bluntly.

"Give me two weeks to consider it," he said.

"What do you think?" I said to Irwin later. "Will he direct it?"

"No." Irwin smiled. "He won't direct it."

Two weeks later, Milos called and said, "I'll tell you the truth. I love the script and I like you, but as much as I'd like to direct this movie, I can't. My best friend in the world is Václav Havel, who is the president of the Czech Republic. How will it look if Václav Havel's best friend makes such fun of the American presidency? We're both immigrants, you and I—me from Czechoslovakia and you from Hungary. *Two* immigrants joining to make this kind of fun? If your name were Jules Feiffer, then I would direct this movie. But for *both* of us to be foreign-born? No, no, you must find an American director."

Jim Abrahams was an American director of broad farcical comedies like *Airplane* and he wanted to make *Sacred Cows* with Lloyd Bridges as the cowpoke.

I realized I was pretty well charging through a wild gamut of directors with this script: Spielberg, to Kubrick, to Blake Edwards, to Milos Forman, to Jim Abrahams!

Jim Abrahams committed to direct *Sacred Cows* as his next picture and United Artists immediately agreed to make it.

Then Jim Abrahams went off to Hawaii to vacation with his family.

When he got back, he changed his mind. He loved his children, he said, and he didn't want to direct anything his children couldn't see.

Shortly afterward, Lloyd Bridges died.

Paul Michael Glaser, the actor, was on vacation in Hawaii, too, and ran into Jim Abrahams. Jim told him he was thinking about directing this crazy script called *Sacred Cows*.

Paul asked to read it and loved it.

When Jim changed his mind, Paul went to United Artists and asked to direct it.

And United Artists said, "*Starsky and Hutch?*"

The script was being mentioned in the media now as "one of the most famous unproduced scripts in Hollywood history."

Even Michiko Kakutani mentioned it in *The New York Times*.

Somebody at United Artists sent the script to Robert Duvall, thinking of him for the part of Sam Parr. Robert Duvall passed.

Years later, when he met me and realized I had written *Sacred Cows,* Robert Duvall looked at me, shook his head, and kept laughing and laughing.

Betty Thomas was the newest directorial flavor of the month.

She read it, she loved it, and she wanted to direct it.

We had lunch and she asked me to tell United Artists that I wanted her to direct it.

I told Betty I'd tell United Artists that if she agreed not to change anything in the script.

"Anything?" Betty said.

"Anything."

"What if we improvise something great?"

"No improvising," I said. "You shoot the script. You change nothing."

She laughed.

"You're some piece of work, Esty," Betty Thomas said, and agreed not to change anything in the script.

I told United Artists I wanted Betty to direct *Sacred Cows* and United Artists said they'd think about it.

Chevy Chase called and wanted to get together. He'd read *Sacred Cows* and wanted to be the cowpoke.

We had lunch. I liked Chevy a lot and thought he'd make a wonderful cowpoke.

I set up a lunch for Chevy with Betty Thomas, who, I said, I hoped would direct the movie.

Betty and Chevy had lunch and Betty decided that she didn't want to work with Chevy.

United Artists decided that they didn't want to make the movie with Betty or with Chevy.

I was standing outside the front door of the Four Seasons Hotel in Beverly Hills with my wife, Naomi, when a black pickup truck drove toward me and stopped. Steven Spielberg was driving; Kate Capshaw sat next to him.

Steven said, "I was a real chickenshit not to do *Sacred Cows*."

I said, "You sure were."

We all laughed.

Steven waved and drove away.

Steven made an overall production deal with MGM/United Artists a few weeks later and walked into his first meeting with the studio to discuss projects he wanted to produce.

There was only one UA project he wanted to produce: *Sacred Cows*.

His friend Tony Bill, Steven said, who'd loved the script for a long time, would direct it.

A few months later, Steven informed United Artists that he wasn't interested in producing *Sacred Cows*—*again*—anymore.

He and Kate had become good friends with Bill and Hillary Clinton, and while it was true that the script had been written a long time ago, during the Bush era, some people might think—considering Paula and Gennifer and Monica—that the president popping this literal cow might be . . .

So because of his friendship with the president who wouldn't tell Americans the truth, Steven wouldn't produce the script about the president who did.

The producer Rob Fried was playing golf with President Clinton one day at Burning Tree and on the way back to the White House in the limo, Bill Clinton started bitching about Paula Jones's lawsuit.

"Jesus Christ," Bill Clinton said, "one of these days someone's gonna accuse me of fucking a cow."

And Rob Fried said, "Mr. President, Joe Eszterhas has already written a script about that."

He told Bill Clinton about *Sacred Cows* and Bill Clinton asked to read it. Rob Fried sent it to him. He never heard from Bill Clinton again.

Irwin Winkler, all those many years ago, was right. A lot of people have read *Sacred Cows*. A lot of people have loved it. A lot of people have said they want to make it. But no one has made it. And I don't think anyone will.

You can get almost anything that you write made into a movie. Almost anything. But not *everything*.

I think, though, that in Hollywood more people have read *Sacred Cow* than any other of my scripts.

Imagine that! You, too, can be best known in the industry for a movie that was never made.

P.S. In the summer of 2006, producer Craig Baumgarten thought that the time was right—George W. Bush's low poll results may have had something to do with it—to try to launch *Sacred Cows* again. They were going to go to Robin Williams, Will Farrell, and Billy Bob Thornton.

INDEX